Above and Beyond

A History of the Medal of Honor
from the Civil War to Vietnam

Above and Beyond

A History of the Medal of Honor
from the Civil War to Vietnam

by the editors of
Boston Publishing Company

Produced in cooperation with
The Congressional Medal of Honor Society
of the United States of America

Boston Publishing Company
Boston, Massachusetts

Boston Publishing Company
President: Robert J. George
Editor-in-Chief: Robert Manning
Managing Editor: Paul Dreyfus
Marketing Director: Jeanne Gibson
Senior Picture Editor: Julene Fischer
Production Editor: Kerstin Gorham
Editorial Staff: Theresa Slomkowski
Administrative Staff: Amy Pelletier,
Amy Wilson

Staff for *Above and Beyond*
Senior Editor: Gordon Hardy
Assistant Editor: Denis Kennedy
Picture Editor: Peter D. Collins
Contributing Writers: Melanie Billings-
Yun, William C. Davis, Jack Sweetman,
Richard Young
Consultants: Edward F. Murphy
(Historical), Patricia Leal Welch
(Production)
Correspondents: Jerry Adams, Ann
Corson, Cheryl Crooks, Ralph Holmes,
Mary Lind Jorn, Paul Krueger, Marion
Lewenstein, John McManus, Dan Malone,
Jane Pender, Carlton Proctor, Richard
Rose, Helen Ross, David Steinberg
Proofreader: Dalia Lipkin
Indexer: Elizabeth Campbell Peters
Design: Jennie Bush, *Designworks, Inc.*

About the writers
Dr. Melanie Billings-Yun (author of the chapters on World War I and Korea) has a Ph.D. in history from Harvard University and has been a lecturer and director of research in the uses of history in public policy at the John F. Kennedy School of Government at Harvard. *William C. Davis* (Civil War) was for thirteen years editor of the *Civil War Times Illustrated* and is the author or editor of more than a dozen books on the Civil War. *Gordon Hardy* (Medal in Peacetime) is senior editor at Boston Publishing Company and has previously edited a variety of periodical publications. *Denis Kennedy* (Vietnam) is assistant editor at Boston Publishing Company and has been a researcher on Boston Publishing's series *The Vietnam Experience.* *Jack Sweetman* (Wars of Expansion) is a member of the history department at the United States Naval Academy and the author of *The Landing at Veracruz: 1914* and *American Naval History: An Illustrated Chronology.* *Richard Young* (Indian Campaigns and World War II) teaches at Boston University and is working on a book about a Medal of Honor recipient of World War II. *Edward F. Murphy* (Historical consultant) is president of the Medal of Honor Historical Society.

Library of Congress Catalog Card Number: 85-071367

ISBN: 0–939526–19–0

10 9 8 7 6

5 4 3 2 1

Contents

Preface

The making of this book has required a sort of balancing act. Its objective is not to glorify war but to recognize, and demonstrate, that for all its destructiveness and beastliness war often brings out the best in people. Probably if heroes did not happen mankind would have had to invent them because history, made up as it is of so much trumpery, treachery, and tyranny, needs deeds of valor, of sacrifice, and of heroism if it is to be palatable.

America's history is well-stocked with heroes. The most elevated of them are the 3,393 men–and one woman–who have been awarded the Medal of Honor for displaying courage and sacrifice above and beyond the call of duty. Beginning with the Civil War, when it was created to help raise morale in the Union forces, the medal has been the supreme accolade the United States bestows on its citizens. More than one American president has said he would have preferred it to his high office.

The impulse for this book came from our work on *The Vietnam Experience*, a history of America's involvement in war in Vietnam. It was an ugly war, our nation's longest and our first as the defeated participant. But in addition to the ugliness, the frustrations, and the rancor it provoked, the Vietnam War brought forth its own high quota of nobility, of men inspired to brotherhood, to bravery, to the risk–and all too frequently, the giving–of their lives in the service of their country. Of the thousands of soldiers who won medals for valor in that war, 238 Americans received the highest, the Medal of Honor.

It seemed there was a book to be written about those 238. Then we discovered that no history had been written about the Medal of Honor from its inception in 1861. Surely, then, there was a book to be written about all 3,394 of the Americans who have been awarded the medal, and the wartime (and rare peacetime) exploits for which they earned it.

The reader of this volume is requested to think of the award by its correct name. Over the years it has come to be known as "The Congressional Medal of Honor," because the holder of the medal, though chosen for it by his peers and superior officers, is nominally given it by writ of Congress. Its real name, however, is simply the Medal of Honor. This fact is perhaps made more difficult to understand since there is an organization called the *Congressional* Medal of Honor Society (because it is chartered by the U.S. Congress). The society's collaboration with our editors and writers has given this book its extra scope and authenticity.

It is impossible in one volume to tell all the deeds, so considerable selectivity and arbitrary decision making have taken place. Research showed that 254 holders of the medal were still alive, and we proceeded to interview 66 of them, partly to provide the exclusive personal accounts in the latter parts of the volume and partly to flesh out or correct the frequently laconic and sometimes inaccurate official accounts and battle citations.

The accounts are here fitted into the context of the wars in which they happened. In each war, the nature of Medal of Honor deeds or the kinds of incidents that provoked them differed, as the nature of war itself changed with advances in weaponry and the development of increasingly distant capabilities for attacking each other. Through them all, however, from the Civil War to the Vietnam War, there are the constants of singular bravery and sacrifice that proved what General George S. Patton once wrote, "In war nothing is impossible, provided you use audacity."

Robert Manning
Editor-in-Chief
June 1985

1

A Badge for Valor

On the bloodiest single day of the Civil War, a Union color bearer is struck by a Confederate bullet. His regiment's flag falls from his grasp onto the ground between the opposing lines. Rebel riflemen intensify their fire, preparing to seize the enemy's precious standard. Suddenly a lone Yankee soldier dashes out from among the ranks, crouched low to avoid the lead flying all around him. He picks up the flag and rushes back to the Union lines, to the cheers of his comrades.

Thirty-eight years later, outside the massive stone walls of Peking, American infantrymen and marines seek an entrance into the city, where a Chinese faction surrounds hundreds of foreigners. The commanding officer asks for volunteers to scale the sheer side of the fortress under enemy fire. A twenty-one-year-old army trumpeter from Iowa steps forward. "I'll try, sir!" he shouts, and works his way over the top of the fortification.

In World War II, a Japanese gunboat is rammed by an American submarine in the dark, chilly waters of the Pacific. The Japanese fire at the men standing on the bridge of the sub, wounding several, including the commander of the vessel, a Naval Academy graduate and seventeen-year veteran of the sea. The commander quickly realizes that the sub must dive if it is to escape. He sends the rest of the men below, then sees that the enemy guns will find their mark before he will be able to climb down. "Take her down!" he shouts. The men below close the hatch, and the vessel slides under the waves with the wounded commander still on the bridge.

In the humid jungle of South Vietnam, three Americans are left behind during the evacuation of a besieged base. To rescue them, an air force cargo plane lands on a debris-covered runway as guerrilla fire rains down from all around. The pilot, a Georgia farm boy who had first enlisted in the army Air Corps during World War II, slows the aircraft and the three men jump from their hiding place and climb aboard. Suddenly an enemy rocket flies down the runway, straight at the plane. Miraculously, it skids to a halt several yards from the cockpit and fails to explode. The pilot lifts off, and the men on board breathe a sigh of relief.

Stretched over 100 years, these exploits comprise just a few of the millions of stories of Americans at war. But these particular men gained a greater distinction. For their actions in combat, they were singled out for gallantry and intrepidity above and beyond the call of duty. Each was awarded the Medal of Honor, America's highest military decoration.

Since it first was cast in the Civil War, the medal has gone to buck privates and generals, to common seamen and admirals, virtually every rank in the armed forces. Men from all walks of life—midwestern farmers, northeastern factory workers, southern teachers, poor immigrants—have been decorated for actions ranging from charging an enemy bunker or capturing an enemy's flag to saving a fellow sailor from drowning. In war and peace, for over 120 years, almost 3,400 men—and in one case, a woman—have been judged to have performed outstanding individual acts, feats of bravery that have set them apart from their comrades.

The symbol of their distinction is the medal and ribbon bestowed by the president "in the name of Congress." It marks admission into a circle into which few can pass. Many men who have received other accolades have coveted the Medal of Honor. President Theodore Roosevelt wanted it. General George S. Patton once declared, "I'd give my immortal soul for that decoration." And President Harry S Truman often told the men to whom he presented the medal, "I would rather have that medal than be president of the United States."

But the Medal of Honor is earned in action, at the risk of a soldier's life. Once decorated, many Medal of Honor recipients have been singled out for lifetimes of public exposure, even adulation. Alvin York, Eddie Rickenbacker, Audie Murphy, Jimmy Doolittle, and many others have had their stories told in books, articles, and motion pictures. Others have been feted at dedications, testimonials, and patriotic exercises. To their peers, and to millions of Americans, Medal of Honor recipients are the nation's heroes, "the bravest of the brave," as one general called them. The medal, says one who wears it, is "America's form of knighthood."

Many of the "knights" of America have stayed in the service and risen to its upper echelons. Others have left the armed forces and attained success in various occupations:

law, medicine, politics, business, and many others. For many, the medal has afforded greater visibility and helped them advance.

A substantial number of recipients, however, have simply returned to civilian life. Their neighbors and associates may never learn from the recipients themselves that they had been so highly honored.

But usually the Medal of Honor brings with it the prospect of continuous public recognition. It has condemned some recipients to years of unwanted attention and even notoriety. They find themselves exploited by others seeking to turn the medal into profit. The spotlight of the medal can also expose the human shortcomings of ordinary men when they are thrust suddenly into the extraordinary role of war hero and public figure. Some have broken under public pressures, the demands and intrusions that fame can bring. The Medal of Honor can be, in the words of one recipient, "a lot harder to wear than it is to earn."

For all the acclaim accorded it today and the importance attached to it, the Medal of Honor had a rather inauspicious beginning.

W ary of the trappings of European titles and nobility since colonial days, the first Americans were reluctant to bestow titles or lavish honors on their own. The Founding Fathers shared a vehement distaste for royalty and its privilege: The Constitution specifically prohibited the granting of any "title of nobility."

When it comes to military honors, however, the nation has been more indulgent. While dukedoms and earldoms may not fit into the American psyche, the actions of warriors do. A successful soldier was seen as a common man who rose to fame not through birthright but through strength and resourcefulness, and it quickly became the practice to reward such attainment with a medal. Fittingly, the Continental Congress awarded the first American medal to General George Washington for his role in driving British forces from Boston in March 1776. (There was no U.S. Mint at the time, so the medal was crafted in Paris.) Medals also went to several other commanders, most notably General Horatio Gates for his victory at Saratoga in 1777 and Admiral John Paul Jones

for his battle with the *Serapis* in 1779. Yet with only a few exceptions, there was no recognition for individual acts by common soldiers.

On September 23, 1780, three New York militiamen intercepted Major John Andre, a British spy, on his way to meet with a co-conspirator, Benedict Arnold. Andre's capture foiled a British plot to take the American fort at West Point. On November 3 the Continental Congress, declaring that the actions of the three Americans had saved the country from "impending danger," ordered a silver medal struck and awarded to each man. The Andre medals were the first American instance of medals awarded to soldiers for individual actions, although the capture itself was not so much valorous as fortuitous.

Almost two years later, General Washington established the first formal system of rewarding individual gallantry. A directive designed to recognize "instances of unusual gallantry," signed August 7, 1782, read:

The General, ever desirous to cherish a virtuous ambition in his soldiers, as well as to foster and encourage every species of Military merit, directs that whenever any singularly meritorious action is performed, the author of it shall be permitted to wear on his facings, over his left breast, the figure of a heart in purple cloth, or silk, edged with narrow lace or binding.

Washington declared that "the road to glory in a citizen's army is thus open to all"; however, the records show that only three men received the Purple Heart. The award then fell into oblivion until 1932, when it was revived as an honor for those killed or wounded in combat.

The idea of a decoration for individual gallantry remained in the minds of many commanders in the early years of the nation. The outbreak of war with Mexico in 1846 led to the establishment of the first long-standing award for bravery. In March 1847 Congress approved a measure granting to any soldier who distinguished himself in action a "certificate of merit" signed by the president and additional pay of two dollars per month, on the recommendation of his regimental commander.

Five hundred and thirty-nine men received Certificates of Merit during the Mexican War. At the time there was no medal to mark this honor, and thus it received minimal public attention. In the words of one military historian, "New recruits might learn that the old sergeant in the next troop had received a Certificate . . . but there was no way this achievement might be perceived from inspection of his uniform."

The military establishment interpreted the law to mean that the Certificate of Merit was established only for the conflict at hand, so the end of the Mexican War left the country without a standing award for gallantry, or any military award at all. It was not until civil war split the nation in 1861 that the government again considered recognizing notable gallantry. Even then, the medal established was intended not so much to glorify warriors as to boost morale in a demoralized army and navy.

The summer of 1861 was a dark time for Union forces. Chased off the battlefield by the Confederates at Bull Run, northern regiments were drained by wholesale desertions and enlistments of only nine months. The greatest battles, and the ultimate victory, of the Yankee forces were yet to come; for the time being, the likelihood of a long and exhausting conflict sapped Union spirits and resilience. The demands placed on the military necessitated the development of a tangible reward for meritorious action and service in the days ahead.

No one was more cognizant of this need than Lieutenant Colonel Edward D. Townsend, assistant adjutant general of the army. Townsend knew of the abuses and corruption of the system of brevet promotions of officers, which usually had little to do with valor, and that these rewards did not extend to enlisted men. In early 1861 he proposed to his superiors—General-in-Chief of the Army Winfield Scott, Secretary of War Simon Cameron, and the chairman of the Senate Committee on Military Affairs, Henry Wilson of Massachusetts—the creation of a medal for individual valor. But General Scott felt that medals and decorations smacked of European privilege and affectation and quashed any further discussion of the matter at the War Department.

Across the street at the Navy Department, however, the idea of a medal found support. Secretary Gideon Welles was exasperated with what he considered to be the poor quality and spirit of some naval personnel and believed that the conspicuous recognition of courage in the strife to come would infuse the navy with a sense of strength and determination.

At least one powerful man on Capitol Hill shared this sentiment. On December 9, 1861, Senator James W. Grimes of Iowa, chairman of the Committee on Naval Affairs, rose to propose Public Resolution Number 82, "An Act to further promote the efficiency of the Navy." Buried on the second page of the measure, after provisions dealing with retired officers and promotions, was Section 7, which read:

And be it further enacted, that the Secretary of the Navy be, and he is hereby authorized to cause two hundred "medals of honor" to be prepared, with suitable emblematic devices, which shall be bestowed upon such petty officers, seamen, landsmen, and marines as shall most distinguish themselves by their gallantry in action and other seamanlike qualities during the present war, and that the sum of one thousand dollars be, and the same is hereby appropriated out of any money in the treasury, for the purpose of carrying this section into effect.

After approval by Grimes's committee, the measure was approved by the Senate, then by the House of Representatives. On December 21 President Abraham Lincoln signed Public Resolution 82 into law.

The approval of a medal of honor was a first step. Next came the choice of a design, with "suitable emblematic devices." Ten days after President Lincoln signed the navy bill, Gideon Welles contacted James Pollock, then director of the U.S. Mint in Philadelphia, and asked if the mint could prepare "an appropriate design for the medals." Pollock was eager to assume the task and promised to have a possible design ready within a week.

The Navy Department and the mint had no American precedent to guide them on their search for a medal design. Welles proposed a cross, similar to the Victoria Cross, which Great Britain had established seven years earlier during the Crimean War. The American cross would be attached to "three ribbons—the red, white and blue." The mint's experience with making coins suggested the use of a figure of Liberty or some other symbol of the "Indivisible Union." Over the next three months Pollock forwarded at least five different models, but Welles rejected all of them.

Finally, in May 1862, Pollock suggested an inverted five-pointed star, two inches long, suspended from an anchor and attached to a red, white, and blue ribbon. Pollock explained the two figures at the center of the star on the obverse:

The foul spirit of secession and rebellion is represented by a male figure in a crouching attitude holding in his hands serpents, which with forked tongues are striking at a large female figure representing the Union or Genius of our Country, who holds in her right hand a shield and in her left the fasces. Around these figures are thirty-four stars, the number of states in the Union.

The female figure representing America and wearing a helmet bearing an eagle was Minerva, the Roman goddess of wisdom and the arts. In later years, this engraving came to be known as "Minerva Repulsing Discord."

Welles approved the design, and on May 15 the Navy Department ordered 175 medals from the mint. It further directed that the back of each medal be left blank except for the words "Personal Valor," under which the name of each recipient could later be engraved. The medals were made of copper and coated with bronze, which gave them a reddish tint. After preparation of the dies, the initial cost of what became America's premier military decoration was $1.85 apiece.

In the meantime, the army, no doubt prompted at least in part by the passage of the navy legislation, had come to favor the idea of a medal of its own. General Scott had retired, and Simon Cameron's successor as secretary of war, Edwin Stanton, was apparently more amenable to the concept of an award for valor.

On February 17, 1862, Henry Wilson, chairman of the Senate Committee on Military Affairs, introduced a resolution almost identical in language to its navy counterpart of two months earlier. Signed into law July 12, the measure provided for the awarding of a medal of honor "to such noncommissioned officers and privates as shall most distinguish themselves by their gallantry in action, and other soldierlike qualities, during the present insurrec-

tion." As with the navy legislation, commissioned officers were ineligible for the medal, the assumption being that they would be better rewarded or more honored by promotion. (A year later, Congress made army officers eligible for the medal; a similar measure for the navy was not passed until 1915.)

Like Secretary Welles, Edwin Stanton was unimpressed by the mint's early attempts at an army medal. Pollock had suggested a slightly altered version of the navy design, stating that "the devices do not pertain to either arm of the service, but are emblematic of the struggle in which the nation is now engaged." But Stanton wanted a distinctive design for the army.

In October 1862 William Wilson and Son, a Philadelphia silversmith who, with the mint, had been responsible for the navy design, forwarded to Stanton a sketch of another proposed medal. It included the inverse star and "Minerva Repulsing Discord" design of the navy medal, but the anchor had been replaced by the figure of a spread-winged eagle standing on crossed cannons and cannonballs. At each wing the eagle was attached to the ribbon, which like its naval counterpart was comprised of the national colors.

Stanton was finally satisfied. By mid-November the War Department had contracted with Wilson and Son for the preparation of 2,000 medals, to be cast at the mint. The cost of the medals was two dollars each. After months of delay, the army had its own medal of honor.

As the war dragged on and the prestige of its new award grew, the government realized that while it was created for the conflict at hand, the Medal of Honor—and the rewarding of bravery—would be applicable to any future conflicts. In 1863 Congress made the Medal of Honor a permanent decoration.

Over the years the Medal of Honor has grown in stature, as evidenced by the 3,400 men who have received their country's highest award for gallantry. Throughout all of the nation's conflicts they have been cited for singular acts of bravery that have impressed and roused others in the face of danger. The story of the medal is necessarily an assemblage of the tales of those who have earned it and of the inner strength and courage that made them perform, for at least one brief moment, "above and beyond the call of duty."

The Civil War

copyright. Wm T. Trego 18

The War Between the States

All wars are born in failure, the inability of men and nations to resolve their differences short of conflict. Perhaps that in part explains the age-old penchant for honoring the heroics of the individual. Rulers, whether kings or legislatures, in part atone for their own failure to avert war by paying homage to the valorous deeds of those who fight their wars. Certainly it was no different in the 1860s when America went mad and went to war with itself.

"We have pulled a temple down," exulted the men of Charleston, South Carolina, when they seceded from the Union in December 1860. Others spoke less reverently. "We are divorced," wrote diarist Mary Boykin Chesnut, "because we have hated each other so."

No single cause severed the Union in 1860. The split came, rather, from generations of low-grade aggravations and petty resentments, from jealousies personal and national, from fears that were deeply and sincerely felt, however groundless, and from a few elemental issues for which there simply were no universally satisfactory solutions. Typical of the people and the times that brought on that war, the two sides could not agree afterward on what started the conflict, or even on what to call it.

They were regions whose values stood in marked contrast. Americans North and South had followed different paths for two centuries at a separate pace. Divergent political, economic, and social views made the first half of the nineteenth century an era of almost continual crisis. By 1860 the differences between the two sections were being exaggerated aggressively on both sides.

The South had been comfortable in the Union at first, and so long as its interests dominated national affairs, the region and its leaders stood strongly for the nation. But by 1850 things had changed. The North

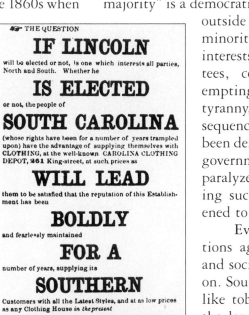

An advertisement in the Charleston Courier *bespeaks southern sentiment.*

The advertisement reads:

THE QUESTION

IF LINCOLN

will be elected or not, is one which interests all parties, North and South. Whether he

IS ELECTED

or not, the people of

SOUTH CAROLINA

(whose rights have been for a number of years trampled upon) have the advantage of supplying themselves with CLOTHING, at the well-known CAROLINA CLOTHING DEPOT, 261 King-street, at such prices as

WILL LEAD

them to be satisfied that the reputation of this Establishment has been

BOLDLY

and fearlessly maintained

FOR A

number of years, supplying its

SOUTHERN

Customers with all the Latest Styles, and at as low prices as any Clothing House *in the present*

CONFEDERACY

of all the States.

Thankful for the liberal patronage extended, the Proprietors desire merely to inform their customers and the public generally, that their present STOCK OF CLOTHING IS COMPLETE in all its departments, and are now prepared to offer Goods on the most reasonable and satisfactory terms. A call is therefore solicited by

OTTOLENGUIS, WILLIS & BARRETT,
November 5   261 King-street.

outstripped the South in population and economic growth. Now its political power was ascendant, and it argued for the national view in public affairs. Southerners argued instead for sectional rights.

"State's rights" and its natural offspring, secession, were not distinctly southern phenomena. The "will of the majority" is a democratic ideal with little appeal to those outside the majority. Finding itself now a minority, the South sensed a threat to its interests and values and sought guarantees, constitutional dispensations exempting it from the will, even the tyranny, of the majority. The consequences of such a course would have been democratic chaos, with the national government in constant danger of being paralyzed by parochial interest. But failing such guarantees, the South threatened to leave the Union.

Everything seemed to set the sections against each other. Economically and socially the land divided them early on. Southern soil was best suited to crops like tobacco and cotton that exhausted the land and required vast acreage and massive cheap labor. The South turned to slavery. The North, with abundant raw materials, turned to manufacturing and commerce. The flood of immigrants from Europe, willing to work cheaply in the Yankee factories, erased any need for slavery and it was gradually abolished.

In time, North and South found convenient justifications for the separate societies and cultures the land produced. Planters who needed slavery to survive economically pointed to the benevolent aspects of an institution that cared for otherwise presumably helpless blacks. The North, not dependent on slavery, called it a disgrace. To the Yankee, the planter was a lazy, conceited, often debauched creature of contempt. To the Southerner, the Northerners were money-grasping, humorless drones. As tempers rose in the decades before 1860, these false stereotypes became increasingly attractive. The stereotypes helped them to hate, and that helped them to war.

Preceding pages. *Sergeant Hiram Purcell saves a Union flag from Rebels at Fair Oaks, Virginia, May 31, 1862.*

Slaves stroll by acres of cotton in the ante-bellum South. Labor-intensive methods and worldwide demand for the crop committed the South to a slave-based economy.

Always the issue came down in the end to slavery. As the nation grew and more states came into the Union, an increasing number of them decided to enter the Union as "free" states, not countenancing bondage within their borders. That threatened the South with the possibility that an antislave majority in Washington might attempt to eradicate slavery where it already existed. An end to slavery would ruin the South economically and create social havoc when several million southern blacks were suddenly freed with no jobs, no homes, and no education.

Compromise had averted crisis in 1820, again in 1850, and yet once more in 1854, as the North gave in to southern fears and offered the demanded guarantees. But then came 1860, an election year with a powerful new antislave Republican party likely to capture the White House. Despite the assurances of its candidate, Abraham Lincoln, that his party would not interfere with slavery where it already existed, the southern leadership foresaw their own doom in his election. By this time the two sides were no longer listening to each other; their differences had become so emotionally fundamental to them that neither North or South could compromise without yielding its basic values.

Lincoln won election in November 1860 in the most purely sectional vote in history. Every southern and slave state went against him; the southern rights candidate, John C. Breckinridge, did not carry a single free state. Even though he got barely 40 percent of the popular vote, Lincoln carried all of the major states with their greater populations and electoral votes and won the presidency.

It was a bitter victory. At once the call went out for a state convention in South Carolina. On December 20 that same convention voted to secede from the Union, and within weeks other states followed. Eventually eleven of them seceded, and in February 1861, in Montgomery, Alabama, the Confederate States of America was born.

Yet no one wanted war. As the newly elected Confederate president, Jefferson Davis, proclaimed, the South wanted merely "to be left alone." Confederates bloodlessly seized Federal military and naval installations and arsenals within their new borders and demanded that the Yankees turn over the rest. After all, places like Fort Sumter in Charleston Harbor were now on Confederate soil, and the Northerners had no business being there. Should they persist in remaining, it would be an act of aggression.

There came the rub. Lincoln saw himself as president of *all* the states, not just the northern ones, and did not recognize the legality of secession. Thus it was his constitutional duty to hold on to all Federal property, wherever located. By seizing some and threatening more, the Confederates were in open insurrection. He would not give up Fort Sumter, and that was all the hot bloods in Charleston needed. After delivering an unsuccessful ultimatum, Confederates stationed at the batteries ringing the harbor

Factories such as this Paterson, New Jersey ironworks spurred the growth of the North before the Civil War.

opened fire on the fort in the predawn hours of April 12, 1861. The next day the garrison surrendered. The Confederacy was jubilant; the Union called for 75,000 volunteers to put down the rebellion. War had come.

No nation is ever "ready" for a civil war, and America in 1860 proved no exception. The United States Army consisted of barely 16,000 men and officers, most of them stationed in the West as a buffer against Indians. The enlisted men remained loyal to the Union almost to a man, but of the 1,080 officers on active duty, 313 abandoned their commissions to join the new Confederacy. Worse, the weapons and equipment of the army were out of date, and only one of its four generals was under seventy. General-in-Chief Winfield Scott was seventy-five, still active in mind, but too infirm to ride a horse. The situation in the U.S. Navy was just as bad.

Since the Confederacy was too new to have raised a substantial standing army of its own, both sides were immediately led to the only expedient capable of quickly building large armies—volunteers. Davis had already been accepting volunteer regiments into the Confederate service for months, and now Lincoln issued the first of what would be many calls for regiments of his own.

North and South, they would be infinite in their variety. The first regiments, enlisted in the expectation of a quick and speedy end to the fighting, were to serve only for ninety days. Later, some of them extended their service

for an additional year. By 1862, when it was evident that this would be no summer's lark, both governments accepted regiments only for three years or the term of the war, whichever lasted longer.

At first, the most readily available units were the various state militia and home-guard units. North and South they rushed to their respective standards, bringing their own arms—anything from antique flintlock muskets to the latest breechloaders—and attired in a dazzling array of uniforms. Ironically, reversing what was to become the standard, many of the southern militia regiments wore blue; scores of Yankee units were dressed in gray.

In time some general standards evolved. The full-strength regiment on both sides numbered roughly 1,000 men, led by officers chosen or elected by the men themselves. The men came to carry deadly powerful muzzle-loading .58-caliber rifles that could be fired several times a minute. The rifles proved accurate at greater ranges than any military weapons before them. The men carrying those rifles were farm boys for the most part, men unaccustomed to drill and regimentation but very familiar indeed with guns. The volunteers were there from deeply felt conviction in their causes, for glory and adventure, for the fun of it, or just to escape the boredom of home. Whatever their motivations, they felt fierce loyalties to their state, their comrades, and their regiments.

The combination of these men, perhaps the finest citizen-soldiers in history, their powerful modern weapons, the natural animosities to be found in any civil conflict, and the dated tactics by which the war was fought

CASH!

All persons that have SLAVES to dispose of, will do well by giving me a call, as I will give the

HIGHEST PRICE FOR

Men, Women, &
CHILDREN.

Any person that wishes to sell, will call at Hill's tavern, or at Shannon Hill for me, and any information they want will be promptly attended to.

Thomas Griggs.
Charlestown, May 7, 1835.

PRINTED AT THE FREE PRESS OFFICE, CHARLESTOWN.

An advertisement offering money for slaves.
At the onset of war a single slave could
fetch as much as $1,800.

was destined to be lethal. The Union officer corps grew rapidly, and newer and younger generals rose to take command. Still, their military schooling at the U.S. Military Academy at West Point and the manuals of warfare that the volunteer officers studied all harked back to the kinds of war fought generations before. These had been wars of limited range, fought with inaccurate muskets. Individual accuracy had mattered far less than massed firepower, and the bayonet at the end of the gun had been regarded as a more deadly instrument than the bullet within it. Battles were still expected to be fought much as in the days of Napoleon, with the regiments standing erect, two or more lines deep, without benefit of earthworks or defenses. They were to be won with a few volleys and then a spirited bayonet charge. And all of it, of course, was expected to be glorious.

Experience after Fort Sumter revealed just how fatally obsolete these old notions were. Instead of running into one, perhaps two, ineffectual volleys from the feeble muskets of their opponents, a regiment in the Civil War that dared to charge would face half a dozen or more powerful and accurate salvos, and anything more than a scratch from a massive .58 bullet was potentially fatal. Most wounds to the legs and arms resulted in amputation, and almost any bullet in the torso would kill a man.

Thanks to the state of the medical arts at the time, those who survived the battle risked equal dangers, even if their wounds were slight.

This was bad enough. Compounding it was the stage on which the Civil War played. It occupied virtually a whole continent in warfare on a scale never before known. Regiments joined together to make brigades, brigades melded to make divisions, divisions gathered into corps, and corps united to become armies. A single division could be greater than the field army that Scott had led into Mexico in 1847, and an army now could number half a dozen such divisions or more. North and South, some 3 million men would take up arms during the four years of the conflict, serving in more than half a dozen major armies that contested possession of a land area of roughly three-quarters of a million square miles. More than 10,000 military actions were recorded, ranging from skirmishes to pitched battles.

The infantry regiments were not the only ones to fight this mammoth war. The Civil War also brought opposing cavalrymen face to face. Their regiments were smaller than the infantry, their role in campaigns primarily reconnaissance, and their participation in major battles relatively rare. Yet when cavalry fought cavalry, the combat was fierce, and the weapons were just as deadly. Worse, and particularly west of the Mississippi, mounted men tended more to the nature of the partisan and guerrilla. Many cavalry and partisan outfits, North and South, were little more than uniformed brigands who would kill cold-bloodedly for the fun of it, whether the enemy was armed or not.

Far more conventional, and just as deadly, was the artillery. The field cannon was perhaps not quite as advanced as the shoulder rifle by 1861, but it was hellishly effective in certain circumstances just the same. Some cannon could fire their exploding projectiles five miles or more. Such firing was generally of little effect since there were few engagements in which an artilleryman could even see five miles in any direction, but at close range the field piece, and particularly the workhorse twelve-pound smoothbore, could visit wholesale slaughter. Loaded with canister—a tin can filled with lead balls—or case shot—an iron shell filled with iron balls—a cannon could become a virtual shotgun. Relatively light and quickly mobile,

Right. *The battlefields of the Civil War ranged from the Atlantic coast to the Midwest. The Union took control of the Mississippi Valley with victories at Forts Donelson and Henry and at Vicksburg. Georgia and the Carolinas were ravaged by Sherman's armies. In the East, early Rebel gains were overshadowed by defeat at Gettysburg and by Grant's sweep through Virginia.*

such guns could move to a threatened point in a defensive line in time to devastate attacking columns. Working in combination with well-disciplined infantrymen, six-gun cannon batteries could produce awful results. At Gettysburg, on July 3, 1863, several batteries supporting the Federal infantry repulsed the famed Pickett's Charge. As many as 15,000 Confederates took part in that frontal assault. Only a handful actually penetrated the Yankee line. More than half were killed or wounded.

It was all insurance that the American Civil War—or War Between the States, call it what you will—would be among the most bloody and fiercely contested in history. The goal of Davis and the Confederacy was simply to hold on to every inch of southern soil possible. Lincoln and the Union had to retake and occupy every one of those inches. So mutually exclusive were those two goals that no strictly military conclusion to the war was possible except absolute victory and absolute defeat.

On land it was three wars, really, and there was much irony in the relative scope of their operations, their overall military importance, and the public's perceptions of them. Then, as now, the greatest attention and effort went into the campaigns in the East, primarily Virginia, and the meager hundred miles or so that separated the two warring capitals, Washington and Richmond.

Here the green volunteers fought the first major land battle of the war on July 21, 1861. Along the banks of Bull Run, in northern Virginia, the hastily raised and trained armies collided in what, by 1864 standards, would be only a small engagement. But then it was a major battle, and the North, already wounded by the loss of Fort Sumter, suffered another defeat. Lincoln's army scampered back to the safety of Washington, leaving the battlefield

Lincoln's election only exacerbated the North-South rift and hastened secession.

to a victor that was almost as badly disorganized as the vanquished.

Lincoln tried to take Richmond in 1862 with a series of campaigns, all of them failures. In the spring an army landed below Richmond and marched on the city, only to be stopped. Another Yankee army in northern Virginia was beaten near Bull Run again, by a Confederate army now led by General Robert E. Lee. On September 17 the northern General George B. McClellan won a battle at Antietam, Maryland, and stopped Lee's invasion of the North but frittered away a chance to destroy Lee in the process. McClellan's replacement, Rhode Island General Ambrose Burnside, did even worse when he almost lost his Army of the Potomac in terribly costly frontal assaults in December at Fredericksburg, Virginia.

The story was the same when next the armies met at Chancellorsville, Virginia, in May 1863. But then came Gettysburg. When Lee advanced once more into the North, Major General George G. Meade, now commander of the Army of the Potomac, stopped him in Pennsylvania in the biggest battle of the war. Yet when it was done, little was changed over the way things had been two years before. Lee still held most of Virginia and Richmond was secure.

Lincoln changed that when he found General Ulysses S. Grant out west and brought him to command all of the Union's armies early in 1864. Grant and Lincoln thought alike. Press the enemy hard, everywhere, and simultaneously. When Grant ordered Meade and his army to start campaigning again in May 1864, they never stopped. The battles fought are legendary—the Wilderness, Spotsylvania, Cold Harbor, the Siege of Petersburg, and finally the pursuit of Lee to Appomattox.

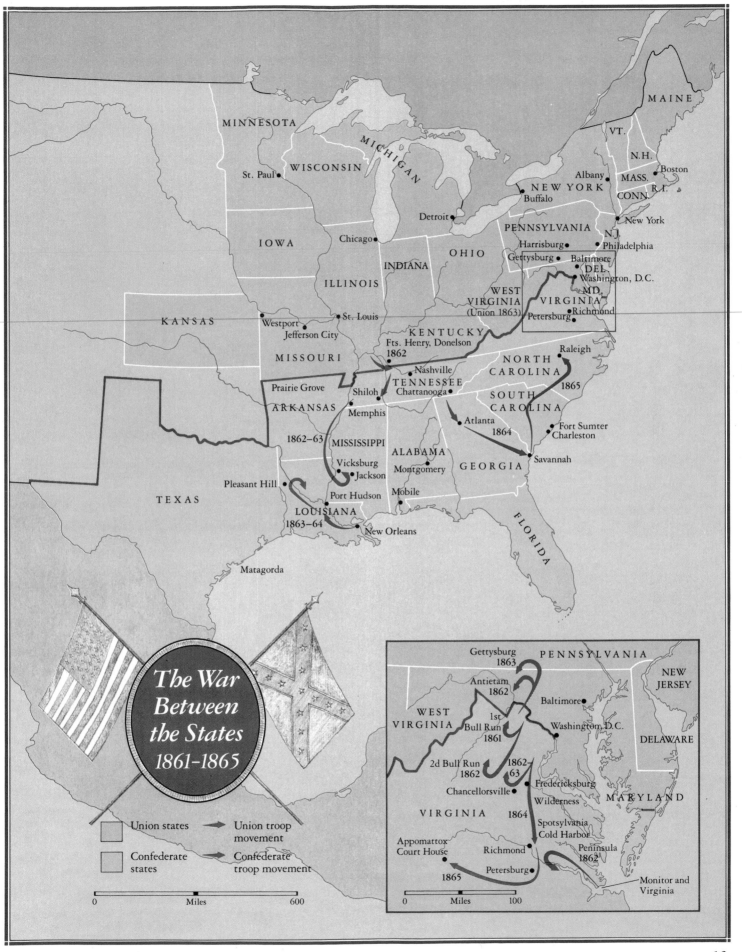

MINNESOTA

MICHIGAN

MAINE

VT.

N.H.

St. Paul

WISCONSIN

Albany

MASS.

Boston

R.I.

NEW YORK

CONN.

Buffalo

New York

Detroit

PENNSYLVANIA

N.J.

IOWA

Chicago

OHIO

Harrisburg

Philadelphia

INDIANA

Gettysburg

Baltimore

DEL.

ILLINOIS

WEST
VIRGINIA
(Union 1863)

VIRGINIA

Washington, D.C.

MD.

KANSAS

St. Louis

Petersburg

Richmond

Westport

KENTUCKY

Raleigh

Jefferson City

Fts. Henry, Donelson
1862

MISSOURI

Nashville

NORTH
CAROLINA

1865

Prairie Grove

Shiloh

Chattanooga

TENNESSEE

SOUTH
CAROLINA

ARKANSAS

Memphis

Atlanta

Fort Sumter

1862–63

1864

Charleston

MISSISSIPPI

Vicksburg

ALABAMA

GEORGIA

Savannah

Jackson

Montgomery

Pleasant Hill

Port Hudson

Mobile

TEXAS

LOUISIANA

FLORIDA

1863–64

New Orleans

Matagorda

The War
Between
the States
1861–1865

☐ Union states

→ Union troop
movement

☐ Confederate
states

→ Confederate
troop movement

0   Miles   600

Inset map

Gettysburg
1863

PENNSYLVANIA

Antietam
1862

Baltimore

NEW
JERSEY

WEST
VIRGINIA

1st
Bull Run
1861

Washington, D.C.

DELAWARE

2d Bull Run
1862

1862–
63

Chancellorsville

Fredericksburg

MARYLAND

Wilderness

VIRGINIA

1864

Spotsylvania
Cold Harbor

Appomattox
Court House

Richmond

Peninsula
1862

Petersburg

1865

Monitor and
Virginia

0   Miles   100

13

Federal troops inside Fort Sumter fire against Confederate forces in Charleston Harbor, April 12-14, 1861. Major Robert Anderson, commanding officer, is at left.

While most of the warring nation—as well as the world—focused its attention on this struggle for Virginia, a huge war was being fought elsewhere. Grant and Lee contested a few hundred square miles of Virginia soil. West of the Mississippi much smaller armies conducted unheralded campaigns and battles that decided the fate of two-thirds of the country, from the great river to the Pacific. A single, small battle like Prairie Grove in December 1862 saved Arkansas for the Union for more than a year. The greatest cavalry operation of the entire war came late in 1864 when an army of Rebel horsemen invaded Missouri, riding all the way to present-day Kansas City before they were stopped at Westport, where the biggest battle west of the Mississippi took place. And even out here Grant made himself felt. When he marched against Lee in the spring of 1864, he ordered his armies in the West to move as well, up the Red River to try to cut in two the so-called Trans-Mississippi of the Confederacy. It was in this forgotten region that the final surrenders took place in 1865, themselves almost as much overlooked as the bitter warfare here that they ended.

The third war was fought between the other two wars, between the Appalachians and the Mississippi, and a different sort of war it was. Here in Tennessee and

Mississippi and Georgia the Union truly won the war. There was seldom a day in which the North did not gain ground. When Grant, then an unknown, took Forts Henry and Donelson, Tennessee, in February 1862, all of Kentucky became untenable for the Confederates. At Shiloh in April, though badly surprised, Grant held out and held on to his gains. Grant's greatest triumph there was at Vicksburg. For more than a year he planned on taking the Mississippi River city. When it and its batteries fell, the Union would be able to navigate freely as far south as Port Hudson, Louisiana. New Orleans had already fallen to the navy in April 1862, thus securing the lower Mississippi. On July 4, 1863, after forty-seven days of siege, Vicksburg fell too. Port Hudson surrendered four days later, leaving the Union in control of the entire river and splitting off the entire Trans-Mississippi from the rest of the Confederacy.

Having cut the South in two, Grant next went to work to cut it into threes. After the Union Army of the Cumberland suffered a disastrous defeat at Chickamauga,

14

A southern flag flies over Fort Sumter, April 15, 1861.

Georgia, in September 1863, Grant took command of its besieged remnant at Chattanooga, broke the siege, and routed the Confederate army facing him. And then in the spring of 1864, as part of his overall strategy of pressing the enemy at all points, he ordered his trusted lieutenant, General William Tecumseh Sherman, to take this army and two others and march into Georgia. Atlanta fell to Sherman that summer, and by Christmas Sherman had marched to the sea, taking Savannah, Georgia, and splitting the Confederacy yet again. Barely more than two weeks after Lee surrendered to Grant on April 9, 1865, the Confederate Army of Tennessee capitulated to Sherman, and the war east of the Mississippi was all but over.

In a war of such mammoth scope, with all the elements in it conspiring to raise the level of combat to heights previously unknown, it is no wonder that the cost proved so terrible. Roughly 623,000 men perished, a third of them killed or mortally wounded in battle. The rest died of disease and other causes, and nearly a half-million more were wounded. One soldier in three was hit by a bullet in this war; one in five died. As a result, soldiers' attitudes toward the nature of war changed dramatically. In 1861 it

was all a lark, a posturing, swaggering exercise in Victorian heroics complete with florid expressions of love of flag and country. But by 1864, the cavalier boys who feared the war would end before they got a taste of it had become sober men who saw war for the grim, deadly business that it is.

Yet, however their attitudes toward war might have changed, the devotion and occasional heroism they showed remained constant. It took brave men to fight a conflict of this kind, to march into the face of enemy guns without flinching, to fight hand-to-hand and spend their lives for their cause, for their comrades, even for their regimental banners.

Both sides tried to honor their heroes. The Confederates created a Roll of Honor and intended to issue medals but never did. With the new Medal of Honor, the Union took a giant stride toward rewarding its heroes. Some 1,500 would be awarded, and the standards for receiving the honor varied from extreme heroism to simple political expedience. Most, however, went to men of a stripe, men who took risks, who rushed faster or farther for their cause, who explored new limits of human daring. So it is today, and so it was at the Medal of Honor's very beginning. ❖

15

Mr. Lincoln's Army

Far from the glory many enlistees anticipated, life in the Union army was a combination of bad food, endless drills, disease, and hardship. Clockwise from above. Soldiers of the 96th Pennsylvania Infantry drill at Camp Northumberland, near Washington; veterans of Grant's 1864-65 campaign through Virginia await the call to battle; the Ringgold Battery practices artillery formation and tactics; General Philip Kearny's wounded troops at a hospital in Fredericksburg, Virginia, May 20, 1864; and three soldiers share hardtack and coffee, an all-too-common army meal.

The Great Locomotive Chase
Andrews Raiders

After the creation of the Medal of Honor, Secretary of War Edwin M. Stanton decided to bestow the first medals upon an intrepid group of behind-the-lines raiders. The recipients were young Northerners who, like thousands of others, had volunteered for dangerous duty to preserve the Union their countrymen were seeking to dissolve.

James J. Andrews, the leader of the "Great Train Raid."

There is a certain perverse irony that dominates the history of the Civil War, and it extends to the Medal of Honor as well. The first soldiers to receive the commendation won their laurels for brave deeds done while they were *out* of uniform. Stranger still, in the aftermath of their heroics they denied responsibility for their acts and actually apologized to the Confederacy for any harm done.

Their story originates with an enigmatic civilian, James J. Andrews, a sometime Union spy who was, ironically, a native of Virginia. The thirty-two-year-old Andrews apparently made several forays into the South posing as a dealer in "contraband," selling medicine and other scarce supplies and gathering some intelligence. Early in 1862 he took an assignment from Major General Don Carlos Buell, entering the enemy-held part of Tennessee with a load of quinine and returning, said Buell, "without information of any value." Nevertheless, Andrews was sent south once more, this time to burn the Western & Atlantic Railroad bridge over the Tennessee River at Bridgeport. This, too, ended in failure.

Buell, meanwhile, had begun to move his army toward what would become the Battle of Shiloh. With the army commander on the move, Andrews reported his failure to Brigadier General Ormsby M. Mitchel in Shelbyville and then, having failed to burn one bridge, proposed now a plan to burn several on the line from Atlanta to Chattanooga. This, he reasoned, would enable Mitchel to advance on the latter point without fear of the enemy sending in heavy reinforcements from Georgia.

Mitchel liked the scheme, and on April 7 he and Andrews went before three Ohio regiments in Shelbyville to ask for volunteers for what they described as "secret and very dangerous

service." They would be operating behind enemy lines, Andrews told them, in civilian dress, and if taken they could well expect to be treated as spies, with hanging almost a certainty. Nevertheless, twenty-four men stepped forward, ready for whatever risks Andrews's scheme offered.

The men about to embark on the daring adventure were a mixed lot, drawn from the 2d, 21st, and 33d Ohio Infantries. All were enlisted men excepting the 200-pound William Campbell, a civilian who just happened to be visiting his friend Private Philip Shadrach. When Shadrach volunteered, so did Campbell. Another volunteer, Corporal William Pittenger, was a bookish fellow with glasses, who had the temperament of a preacher—which he later became—and hardly seemed to be made of the stuff of daring raiders.

Andrews told the men only so much of his plan as was necessary. They were to divide into groups of three and four and make their way separately through enemy lines to join him at Marietta, Georgia, on April 10. After delays caused by heavy rain and the loss of three men along the way, Andrews gathered on April 11 in Marietta with the remaining twenty-one raiders. They were to board a Confederate train, wrest control from its engineer and conductor, and steam northward to Chattanooga, burning bridges behind them. Having seen more soldiers along the line than he expected, and in the face of some suggestions that they should abandon the plan, Andrews gave each of the men a chance to back out. Their decision, to a man, echoed Andrews's own, to "succeed or die."

Singly and in groups they bought tickets for various stations on the Western & Atlantic north of Marietta, and at 5:00 A.M. Andrews and nineteen men boarded the cars. (The other two appar-

The General, *recaptured from Andrews's men, was damaged by an ammunition explosion seventeen months after the raid.*

Kingston he steamed on without interruption, assuming that the damage already done would discourage any train that might try to follow.

He did not account for the persistence of Fuller and Cain. At first they simply ran after their stolen train. A few miles up the track they found a handcar and aboard it muscled their way to the Etowah crossing. And there Fuller reaped enormous profit from Andrews's miscalculation. Steaming over the river, the raiders had passed a siding and saw the old engine, *Yonah,* sitting there with steam up. Instead of stopping to cripple the locomotive, they had continued on their way. Reaching the siding, Fuller found just what he needed. Quickly he abandoned the handcar, boarded the *Yonah,* and raced northward. Already the raiders were becoming the pursued.

The raiders lost a full hour at Kingston, sitting patiently on a siding while southbound trains passed by. Having cut the telegraph, Andrews had little fear of word of his raid getting ahead of him. Then, unwilling to wait longer, the raiders moved back onto the main line and raced north, hoping not to meet further traffic along the way. Their luck stayed with them all the way to Calhoun, nineteen miles north of Kingston. No southbound freights barred the road, and just to discourage any pursuers, Andrews lifted some rails four miles north of Kingston.

Everything seemed to be going well until the *General* stopped two miles above Calhoun to break the track once more. They were at their work, wrote Pittenger, when "not far behind we heard the scream of a locomotive bearing down upon us at lightning speed." It was the dogged Fuller. Forced to abandon the *Yonah* at Kingston because of all the freights in his way, he had commandeered the *William R. Smith* and steamed north, only to be halted by the break in

ently thought better of their brave resolve of the night before.) It was a seven-mile ride to the first stop at Big Shanty, where a twenty-minute breakfast halt was allowed.

Andrews and his men stayed on the train while the engineer, Jeff Cain, conductor William Fuller, and the rest of the passengers alighted for their breakfast. Then Andrews calmly saw to uncoupling the engine, tender, and three boxcars from the rest of the train, told sixteen of the men to get into the rear car, and boarded the engine cab with Wilson Brown and William Knight, both engineers, and another soldier who acted as fireman. It all took place under

the disinterested eyes of soldiers lolling about their tents in Camp McDonald near the tracks. The first idea anyone had of something amiss came when Fuller and Cain heard the sound of their engine, *General,* steaming out of the station without them. In an instant the Andrews raiders had achieved a feat of incredible daring. It was, alas, to be the last success of their bold venture.

The first stop came at Kingston, some twenty miles north of Big Shanty. Concerned about an immediate pursuit, Andrews had lifted rails from the track, dropped crossties on the rails, and cut telegraph lines until he reached the Etowah River, but from that point until

the track. He ran on afoot three miles when luck served him yet again. Andrews had passed the engine *Texas* on a siding at Adairsville on his way to Calhoun, and Fuller encountered the *Texas* coming toward him. At once he commandeered and reversed the train, steamed to Adairsville, where he left its cars on a siding, and, still moving in reverse, raced off after the raiders. Soon he had them in sight.

It was to be known ever after as the Great Locomotive Chase. Their throttles open all the way, the two engines raced northward. The Andrews raiders dropped crossties across the tracks behind them, hoping to stop or derail the *Texas,* but they could do nothing more than briefly delay Fuller. There was not time to halt the *General* to lift a rail or two, which would have stopped pursuit completely.

Through Resaca they steamed, then past Dalton, Georgia. On the way through Tunnel Hill, with wood and water running out, Andrews realized they were not going to make it to Chattanooga as hoped. One by one the raiders began to jump off the train, running into the woods. When finally the *General*

could go no farther, two miles north of Ringgold and barely five miles short of the Tennessee border, Andrews and the remaining raiders abandoned the train that had taken them on their hair-raising eighty-seven-mile ride. Their mission a failure, with not a single bridge burned, they ran for their lives.

Within a week they were all caught and imprisoned. Tried and convicted as a spy, Andrews heard his death sentence and, on June 7, 1862, in Atlanta, the bold raider leader mounted the scaffold and was hanged. Eleven days later another seven of the raiders met their deaths, among them Campbell and Shadrach. Including the two men who never boarded the train in Marietta, but were captured just the same, that left fourteen of the raiders awaiting similar fates.

For a long time that fate looked uncertain. Their captors regarded them as "a desperate, bad set of men," which they proved with a daring October escape, four finding their way into friendly lines in Tennessee, two others journeying clear to Corinth, Mississippi, to safety, and John Wilson and Mark Wood actually reaching the

Yankee fleet blockading the Gulf of Mexico. The other six were recaptured almost immediately, Pittenger among them, and spent another five months in prison. Uncertain what to do with them, and apparently feeling that enough men had been hanged already, the Confederates traded them back to the Federals in exchange for the release of some southern prisoners. In March 1863, nearly a year since they had begun their adventure, the remaining railroad raiders arrived in Washington.

Ironically, in an effort to save their lives while imprisoned, Pittenger and the others had denied any knowledge of the nature of their mission beforehand. They had only followed orders, as soldiers must, they said. In a joint letter addressed to President Jefferson Davis himself, the prisoners asserted that "no real harm was done" as a result of their raid. Asking for mercy from the rope, they went so far as to swear an oath "not to fight or do anything against the Confederacy" for the rest of the war.

While Davis never responded to the appeal, and all of the remaining raiders did return to safety eventually, it might have presented an interesting

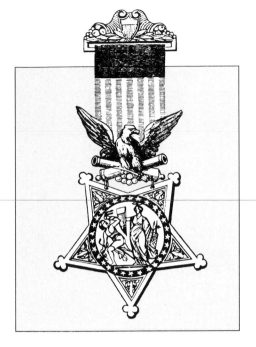

Two of the raiders, Privates Mark Wood (center) and Jacob Parrott, with a facsimile of the original army Medal of Honor awarded them.

Left. *The surviving raiders meet with President Lincoln after receiving their Medals of Honor, March 25, 1863.*

scene indeed if this disavowal of their heroism had come up on March 25 when the six men released from prison met with Secretary of War Edwin M. Stanton. After telling them that "you will find yourselves great heroes when you get home," he emphasized the point by stepping into another room and returning with something in his hand. It was the Medal of Honor. "Congress has by a recent law ordered medals to be prepared on this model," he said, "and your party shall have the first; they will be the first that have been given to private soldiers in this war." He gave it to Private Jacob Parrott, who had just declined an appointment to West Point in favor of going back to fight the enemy.

In time, all of the surviving raiders received their medals as well, and posthumous awards went to the families of those hanged excepting Andrews and Campbell, who were civilians. And poor Private Philip Shadrach never received his, for he had enlisted, served, and been hanged under an assumed name. ❋

Fury at Antietam Creek
First Awards for Battle

Between the time the Andrews railroad raiders performed their deeds and the time they were awarded the Medal of Honor, many other men displayed courage that, in time, would earn them medals as well. With the war going badly for the Union in the first two years, there was an extra need to recognize personal valor. The first cadre of recipients were men who had helped save the soil of the North from an enemy invasion. They were, as well, the first to earn the award for deeds done in actual combat.

What a combat it was! On September 17, 1862, near Sharpsburg, Maryland, along the banks of Antietam Creek, the bloodiest single day of the Civil War ravaged two armies. Robert E. Lee, already the preeminent general of the Confederacy, had led his thus-far invincible Army of Northern Virginia across the Potomac and into Maryland. Invading the North was a bold gamble, but Lee hoped to arouse southern sympathy in Maryland, relieve the pressure on Virginia for a time, and perhaps follow up his August 30 victory at the Second Battle of Bull Run with yet another win on northern soil. Such a victory might attract foreign aid for the Confederacy and force the Union into negotiations for peace.

But on September 17 General George B. McClellan and the Army of the Potomac met and stopped Lee. The cost was horrible: 4,700 men died and over 18,000 on both sides were wounded. The battle began on the Federal right, contesting some woods,

Private William P. Hogarty, an infantry-man who served with the 4th U.S. Artillery at Antietam, later lost an arm at Fredericksburg.

corn fields, and the ground around a Dunker (a German-American sect) church. Soon the fighting spread to the center, where McClellan repeatedly attacked the Confederates posted in a sunken road that became immortalized as Bloody Lane. By the end of the day, when the fighting had ravaged the Yankee left as well, Lee was beaten though still defiant. The Maryland fields were covered with the dead and wounded, and a few special men had covered themselves with glory.

One of them was Private William P. Hogarty of the 23d New York Infantry, although he did not fight with his own outfit this day. A call had gone out from the understrength 4th United States Artillery for volunteers from other units to man its guns, and Hogarty had stepped forward. Thus, trained as an infantryman, the twenty-two-year-old went into the opening of the battle that day manning a twelve-pounder instead.

Their orders sent them toward the Dunker church, where first two guns of the battery and then the remaining four did their part in repulsing withering attacks from Confederates under the command of General Thomas J. "Stonewall" Jackson. For perhaps twenty minutes Hogarty and his battery were in the thick of it, firing cannon that were double- and even triple-loaded with canister at the attacking Rebels, while themselves coming under a devastating fire from the enemy infantry and its supporting artillery.

As the fight raged, Hogarty looked to his right and saw that one of the battery's guns had lost every man killed or wounded. There it sat, abandoned, some distance in front of the battle line, on a small rise of ground. It pointed at the enemy. On his own initiative, Hogarty grabbed a shell and ran through the storm of lead to the silent gun. He trimmed the shell's fuse to time it to

Federal forces advance near the Dunker Church at dawn on September 17, 1862. Beaten back, they nevertheless took a terrible toll of southern lives.

explode just fractions of a second after firing, then single-handedly rammed it home, primed the gun, and fired the deadly missile into the ranks of Jackson's men not far distant.

This act of bravery alone might have earned him a medal, but later that morning Hogarty did more. When the badly mauled battery was withdrawn from active combat and sat resting and awaiting orders, Hogarty saw a dead infantryman's Springfield rifle lying on the ground. Apparently the New Yorker simply could not bear the sight of a gun going unused. Grasping the rifle, he calmly said to a comrade, "Bob, the

supply of ammunition is running mighty low today, I think I will take this gun up to the firing line and help." And so he did.

Four months later, at Fredericksburg, the daring Hogarty would have his own left arm ripped off by an enemy cannon ball, yet he survived and continued his service, rising to the rank of captain. And to help his balance on that lighter left side, he could wear the Medal of Honor, thanks to his valor at Antietam.

When the fighting spread to the center of the line, other men were ready, among them Private Samuel C. Wright of the 29th Massachusetts. The early part of that morning he and his regiment simply lay with their arms behind a wood, awaiting orders and listening to the sound of the battle being fought by

Hogarty and thousands more off to the right. After an eternity of waiting, an officer ordered them forward across Antietam Creek and toward the Sunken Road.

What Wright and the others saw ahead of them was daunting to say the least. Jackson's sharpshooters filled the road itself, firing from the cover of its banks, while the main Rebel line was just behind them. The men of Brigadier General Israel Richardson's Yankee division were ordered to drive the enemy out and take the road, but there was a high rail fence some 200 yards in front of their line. Regiments that attempted to advance to the fence and scale it were almost destroyed by the Confederate fire. Wright could see that "they were actually torn in shreds and wedged into the fence." Those not killed were hugging

23

Samuel Wright with his Medal of Honor (above), earned when he tore down a fence (right) to aid the advance on the Sunken Road on September 17.

the ground unable to retreat, "for to stand was to be instantly killed by the sharpshooters."

The only way for Richardson's attack to proceed was for that fence to come down. Officers called for volunteers to risk almost certain death, and seventy-six men stepped forward. Samuel Wright stood among them.

"We ran straight for the fence amid a hail of iron and lead," he recalled years later, "the dead falling all about us, but to reach the fence was our only thought." Part of the party actually reached the fence and began tearing it down. "As one would grasp a rail it would be sent flying out of his hands by rifle-shots," said Wright. Incredibly, they managed to level the obstruction and then faced the equally hazardous withdrawal under fire.

"Few escaped death or wounds," Wright wrote, and he was no exception. Just before regaining his own lines, he was hit, one of five wounds he would receive in the war, including the loss of an eye. He would wear an eye patch as a badge of honor for the rest of his life, just as he wore the medal he received for his daring at the Sunken Road.

There were more ways than combat to achieve distinction, and one of them was in caring for all the wounded who, like Wright, fell in their acts of daring. Richard Curran was assistant surgeon of the 33d New York, and when his regiment went into the fight, he went with it. Superiors gave him no orders as to where his field hospital should be located, so he simply started treating the wounded immediately behind the battle

line, where he was himself exposed to almost constant fire. Officers told him again and again to get back to safety, "but here were the wounded and suffering of my command," he declared, "and here I believed was my place of duty, even if it cost my life."

Even when he finally was able to remove most of the wounded a few hundred feet back to the vicinity of some haystacks, he continued to work "exposed to the overhead firing of shot and shell." Always there was the danger of the hay catching fire, and even here the wounded were hit again. Curran was tending the leg of one soldier when he turned aside for more dressings. When he turned back, he found the soldier's leg shot away by a cannonball. Yet on he worked, well into the night. "He

24

attended faithfully to his severe duties, and I beg to mention this officer with particular commendation," wrote Colonel W. H. Irwin, who commanded Curran's brigade. "His example is most unfortunately but too rare."

There were many kinds of examples being set at Antietam. One that would be repeated over and over again in this war was the struggle for the colors, either to defend one's own or to capture the enemy's. When General William H. French's division advanced against the Sunken Road and a nearby corn field that day, one of its units, the 1st Delaware Infantry, lost 286 men in the charge and was forced back. One of the fallen was the flag bearer. He and eight others fell while trying to plant it atop the Sunken Road. Second Lieutenant Charles Tanner and those about him looked out with despair at their banner lying barely twenty yards from the line of enemy rifles blazing away from the road.

"We had become desperately enraged," he remembered, "thinking, not of life, but how to regain the broad stripes of bunting under which we had marched." To a Civil War regiment, loss of its colors was a disgrace. Men would vie with each other for the chance to die carrying them in victory or to save them in defeat.

The best the 1st Delaware could do now was to send a withering fire at every Confederate attempt to advance and capture the grounded banner. Other regiments helped them, and then a party of thirty volunteers rushed forward to try and regain the flag. Less than ten returned, and without the prize. "Maddened, and more desperate than ever, I called for the men to make another effort," said Tanner. That, too, failed. Then, when Major Thomas Smyth proposed that twenty-five picked marksmen should lay down a covering fire directly over the colors, Tanner

Deeds of Valor

The highly embellished portraits shown in this account, like others shown in this and the next two chapters, are taken from *Deeds of Valor,* a collection of Medal of Honor stories published in 1906 by the Perrien–Keydel Company. The book contained extensive graphic treatments of Medal of Honor feats, along with accounts drawn from "records in the archives of the United States government" and "personal reminiscences and records of officers and enlisted men who were rewarded by Congress for most conspicuous acts of bravery." Flags, outspread wings, and other devices surrounding the portraits are typical of the romantic illustrations of the time.

Above. *Dr. Richard Curran, who received a Medal of Honor for treating Union wounded at Antietam.* Below. *Sheltered behind a haystack, Curran tends to a soldier.*

Above. *Second Lieutenant Charles Tanner, who charged out to retrieve the fallen colors of the 1st Delaware Infantry at the Sunken Road and was wounded three times.*
Right. *After a furious battle scores of Confederate dead lie in the Sunken Road, known ever after as the Bloody Lane.*

exclaimed, "Do it, and I will get there!" Twenty other men joined him.

"It seemed as if a million bees were singing in the air," Tanner later remembered. Men on both sides were shouting as well as firing. Somehow Tanner got to the banner and had just picked up the tattered flag when a bullet shattered his arm. Refusing to release the colors from his grasp, he found that his legs worked just fine. "I made the best eighty-yard time on record," he joked, and took two more wounds while running.

His pains earned him the regard of his men, a battlefield promotion, and the Medal of Honor. He had much in common with the other medal winners of Antietam. Heroism and devotion tended to be repetitive. A year after Antietam, Tanner was disabled by another wound and discharged. After only three months, however, he enlisted once more and served almost until the end of the war. ✦

colonel of the 6t
to rid Sickles of
asked his regime
willing to drive
place there?"

Six men vol
Sergeants John H
and Corporals L
Furman. They tr
the house by ste
covered. That lef
jump up and rus
a deadly fire fr
Miraculously the
unhurt, battered
rifle butts, and l
for the sharpshoo
no choice but t
Confederates cap
sergeants and tw
the medal for th
did not go to the
though very pro
vive the battle. I
the time to best
posthumously.)

There were
storming buildi
that day. Captai
13th Vermont ha
pany A in a ch
battery the Conf
Sickles. No soo
guns to safety t
fire was hitting h
house in front of
company to the
and strode up to
in. "Surrender!"
here, every dam

*Badly surprised b
1863, Federal tro
south of Gettysbu
furious southern a
dislodge them. Th
3, when Lee sent
Federals in the de*

There
more
days a
Army
anothe
trous
and Ch
rise an
mande
crown
before
anothe
June 1
its tri
Lee cr
more.
even
drivin
to the
fore h
foe.

Above, from top. *John Hart, Levi Roush, George Mears, and Chester Furman, who captured Confederates near the Devil's Den.* Right. *A southern casualty of the fight on July 2 for the Devil's Den.*

At once the Rebels did as ordered, and soon Lonergan had eighty-three prisoners, more men than he had led to capture them. Lonergan's colonel ungenerously failed to mention the captain's heroic deed in his report of the battle, but others had seen what he did, and the Medal of Honor would be his.

An officer whose commander was unsparing in praise of him was Captain J. Parke Postles of the 1st Delaware. This same afternoon General Alexander Hays, commanding a division in the center of the Federal line, was infuriated at the fire hitting his men from a white house on the Bliss farm, several hundred yards in their front. His men did not take the house but did capture the barn about sixty-five yards away. There they sat when Hays ordered that the men in the barn be directed to attack and take the house.

Postles had felt ill all that day. At the moment he sat astride his mount, holding the reins on his arm and his head in his hands, barely able to stay on duty. But when no one else volunteered to take the assault order out to the men in the barn, he raised his head and said, "I will take it, sir."

He set out at once and almost immediately came under fire from the Confederates in the Bliss house. Though the fire grew increasingly hotter, not a bullet touched him, and Postles concluded that the reason was that he was in constant motion. No one could draw a true bead on him. That meant he would

War in the North
The Battle of Gettysburg

There would be more heroes, more medals awarded, in the days after Antietam, but the Army of the Potomac was to wait another ten months, suffer disastrous defeats at Fredericksburg and Chancellorsville, and see the rise and fall of two more commanders before victory again crowned its banners. And, as before, it came at the climax of another Confederate invasion. In June 1863, his army flush from its triumph at Chancellorsville, Lee crossed the Potomac once more. This time he penetrated even deeper into the North, driving into Pennsylvania almost to the capital at Harrisburg before he turned back to meet his foe.

No one had planned to fight a battle at Gettysburg, yet all roads seemed to lead there. Isolated elements of the two armies clashed first, then reinforcements rushed rapidly to the scene until, by July 1, two entire armies were either there or on the way. It was a make-or-break battle for both Lee and his antagonist, General Meade. Lee had to win or else withdraw into Virginia with nothing to show for his invasion; Meade must win, or else risk an attack on Washington or Baltimore. With the stakes so high, both had to fight, and fight hard. So they did. For three days the quiet Pennsylvania community thundered in the greatest and bloodiest battle of the war.

The first day had gone against the Yankees, as they lost the town to the enemy and were forced back onto heights to the south. The next day, with heavy reinforcements arriving, Meade was still on the defensive, but real fighting did not begin until well into the afternoon. The left center of his line was held by General Daniel Sickles's III Corps. Without orders, Sickles moved his corps far in advance of the rest of the line, inviting attack that was not long in coming. The result, in a maelstrom of battle at places ever after called the Peach Orchard, Wheat Field, and Devil's Den, was the near-destruction of the corps.

The 15th New York Light Artillery was ordered into the line to the left of the Peach Orchard as the fighting was about to begin. The captain commanding took direction of the four guns on the left of the battery and told Second Lieutenant Edward M. Knox to command the two cannon on the right. They began firing against a Confederate battery that was supporting Lee's attacks on Sickles.

In fact, in his enthusiasm to rush his section into the fray, Knox led his guns too far forward. "My speed had carried me fully 100 yards ahead of the artillery line on the left." Seeing Knox's

Second Lieutenant Edward M. Knox, 15th New York Light Artillery, rushed his cannon ahead of Union lines, July 2, 1863.

exposed cannon, the enemy rushed forward against him. He had to think fast, with only a handful of men facing hundreds. "I let go both pieces with double canister," he recalled, and then yelled at his men to lie down and feign being killed or wounded. As a result, when the Confederate charge swept over the battery and passed beyond, Knox and his men were left unmolested. Just then a Yankee countercharge struck the Rebels and drove them back through the cannon fire again. Once they were past, Knox and his men arose from the dead and hauled their guns back to safety. Even then he was himself wounded, though that did not prevent him from fighting again the next day and being disabled when a bullet passed through both his hips.

Knox would earn the Medal of Honor for his individual bravery. Others would win it in a group, including four men of the 6th Pennsylvania. Sickles's extreme left was positioned near a rock outcropping called Devil's Den and was taking a beating from enemy sharpshooters inside a nearby log house. The colonel of the 6th Pennsylvania offered to rid Sickles of the nuisance and then asked his regiment, "Are any of you men willing to drive those rebels out of that place there?"

Six men volunteered, among them Sergeants John Hart and George Mears and Corporals Levi Roush and Chester Furman. They tried at first to approach the house by stealth but were soon discovered. That left them no choice but to jump up and rush it, all the while under a deadly fire from the Rebels inside. Miraculously they all reached the house unhurt, battered in the door with their rifle butts, and leaped inside screaming for the sharpshooters to surrender. With no choice but to give up or die, the Confederates capitulated, and the two sergeants and two corporals would win the medal for their valor. (Why medals did not go to the other two is unknown, though very probably they did not survive the battle. It was not the custom at the time to bestow the Medal of Honor posthumously.)

There were other cases of Federals storming buildings full of the enemy that day. Captain John Lonergan of the 13th Vermont had already led his Company A in a charge that recaptured a battery the Confederates had taken from Sickles. No sooner was he moving the guns to safety than he noticed a severe fire was hitting his men from the Codoris house in front of him. At once he led his company to the house, surrounded it, and strode up to the door and knocked it in. "Surrender!" he shouted. "Fall out here, every damned one of you!"

Badly surprised by the enemy on July 1, 1863, Federal troops held the high ground south of Gettysburg for two days while furious southern assaults attempted to dislodge them. The climax came on July 3, when Lee sent 15,000 men against the Federals in the doomed Pickett's Charge.

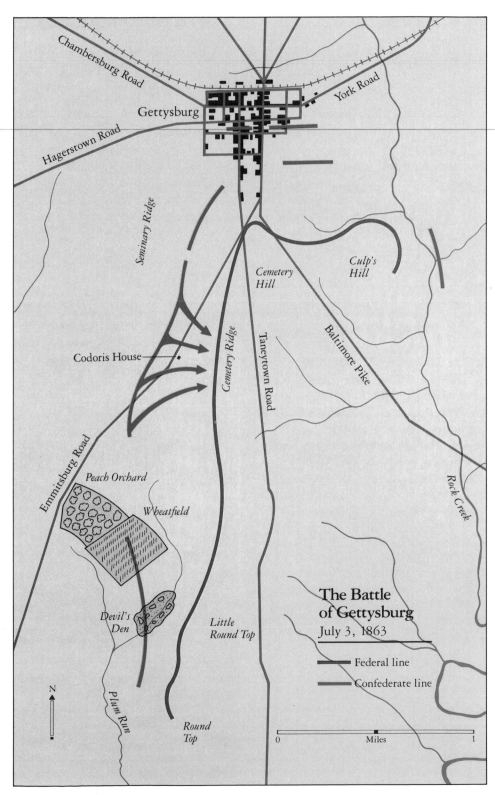

The Battle
of Gettysburg
July 3, 1863

Federal line
Confederate line

0 Miles 1

At once the Rebels did as ordered, and soon Lonergan had eighty-three prisoners, more men than he had led to capture them. Lonergan's colonel ungenerously failed to mention the captain's heroic deed in his report of the battle, but others had seen what he did, and the Medal of Honor would be his.

An officer whose commander was unsparing in praise of him was Captain J. Parke Postles of the 1st Delaware. This same afternoon General Alexander Hays, commanding a division in the center of the Federal line, was infuriated at the fire hitting his men from a white house on the Bliss farm, several hundred yards in their front. His men did not take the house but did capture the barn about sixty-five yards away. There they sat when Hays ordered that the men in the barn be directed to attack and take the house.

Postles had felt ill all that day. At the moment he sat astride his mount, holding the reins on his arm and his head in his hands, barely able to stay on duty. But when no one else volunteered to take the assault order out to the men in the barn, he raised his head and said, "I will take it, sir."

He set out at once and almost immediately came under fire from the Confederates in the Bliss house. Though the fire grew increasingly hotter, not a bullet touched him, and Postles concluded that the reason was that he was in constant motion. No one could draw a true bead on him. That meant he would

Above, from top. *John Hart, Levi Roush, George Mears, and Chester Furman, who captured Confederates near the Devil's Den.* Right. *A southern casualty of the fight on July 2 for the Devil's Den.*

Captain John Lonergan, who earned his medal by capturing Rebels near the Union center on July 2.

be safe enough until he finished his ride, but what about when he had to stop at the barn to deliver his message?

His solution was novel enough, though hard on his horse. When he reached the barn, he did not stop. Instead, he put all his weight into savagely yanking back on the reins, while at the same time sinking his spurs deeply into the animal's flanks. In pain and terror the horse reared and bucked "so that I was as bad a mark as though in full gallop." While thus pitching about he shouted his orders to the men in the barn and then galloped off again in a hail of

Below. *At the foot of Little Round Top, the Union left struggles against James Longstreet's Confederate division.*

Confederate lead. He reached safety untouched and soon saw the Confederates from the Bliss house brought in as prisoners. One of them confessed to having fired three times at him, all misses. "Well sir," said Johnny Reb, "I guess your time hain't come yet."

It was over the same ground where Postles won his medal that the climactic act of the Battle of Gettysburg was fought, the so-called Pickett's Charge on July 3. Fifteen thousand of Lee's best troops marched across open fields in an attempt to destroy the Union center in a single blow. When the 19th Massachusetts was rushed into the Federal line to help defend against the mammoth enemy attack, Corporal Joseph DeCastro went forward with the colors.

Below. *Captain J. Parke Postles shouts orders at the Bliss Farm on July 3.*

Unarmed, he stood with the banner above him as a rallying place for his comrades. The contending lines mixed in a confusion of hand-to-hand fighting. DeCastro got separated from his regiment and came face to face with the color sergeant of the 14th Virginia. "I had the good fortune to get in the first blow," DeCastro recalled. In fact, he struck the Rebel with his own color staff, then grabbed the Confederate's colors from him and ran toward his own lines. Finding his colonel, he handed him the southern banner, said not a word, then ran back to his post. That was the kind of selfless heroism that turned back the attack and won the battle of Gettysburg for the North. ✳

Below. *Peter Rothermel's rendering of the final Rebel assault, Pickett's Charge.*

The Case of the 27th Maine

When the Medal of Honor was America's only military decoration, wholesale distributions to units and groups of men occasionally threatened to demean its value as a combat award. Nothing illustrates this better than the peculiar case of the 27th Maine.

The 27th Maine was a nine months regiment, organized at Portland on September 30, 1862. Thereafter, with only brief exceptions, the regiment spent its entire term of service in the defenses of Washington performing routine garrison duty. The men saw no action and probably never even heard a hostile shot fired. On June 26, 1863, with just four days of their enlistments left, the men in the regiment were ordered to leave their position and prepare to be mustered out.

The timing could not have been worse, for just then Lee and the Army of Northern Virginia were invading the North, and the decisive battle of Gettysburg lay just five days hence. With every veteran regiment that could be spared going to Major General Meade to reinforce the Army of the Potomac, Washington's defenses were fairly stripped, and that left Lincoln and Secretary of War Stanton uneasy. Stanton appealed to the 27th Maine and another Down East regiment, the 25th, to extend their periods of service to see the capital through the emergency. The 25th Maine refused to a man, but when Colonel Mark Wentworth spoke to men of his 27th and explained the situation, about 300 stepped forward and volunteered to remain on duty.

Stanton was overjoyed, and on June 29 he directed the adjutant general to provide a Medal of Honor for every one of the men who volunteered. That was bad enough, since there had been little heroism or self-sacrifice involved in a few hundred men remaining on duty a few extra days. Worse, Stanton's order opened the door to the virtual destruction of any meaning at all for the Medal of Honor,

for he had not specified that only men of the 27th Maine receive it. The wording of his order allowed the presentation of the medal to any troops who volunteered to stay in the capital after their service expired and, furthermore, granted it to volunteers from other states who offered to serve temporarily in Pennsylvania and Maryland during the emergency. One estimate indicates that the total number of such men might have reached 50,000! Additionally, Stanton's order did not specify that these men should receive *the* Medal of Honor, only that "an appropriate Medal of Honor" be given them. Did he mean the Medal of Honor

Colonel Mark Wentworth.

authorized by Congress or some special medallion to be struck for this immediate situation?

In fact, those of the 27th Maine who volunteered were only kept in service an extra four days before mustering out, and they played no role at all in the Gettysburg campaign. But the echoes of Stanton's promise would be heard in Maine and Washington for the next fifty years.

Almost immediately there was a problem in getting an accurate listing of those who had stepped forward. There never would be agreement on the exact number of them. More than a year later bureaucratic mix-ups resulted in an order that medals should be presented to all 864 of the men in the regiment, including those who refused to volunteer. No one in the chain of command caught the oversight.

The medals reached the governor

of Maine in January 1865, and he immediately notified Colonel Wentworth and asked what should be done with them. Wentworth, meanwhile, had served in Grant's overland campaign of 1864 with the 32d Maine. The regiment saw much battle and gave many examples of heroism, yet not a man in the 32d was awarded the Medal of Honor for his deeds. To Wentworth, the idea of giving over 500 of the medals to men who did nothing at all was intolerable.

Wentworth decided to give the medals only to men who had actually volunteered to help defend the capital. The roughly 560 that remained he simply stored in his barn.

But the case of the 27th Maine could not be forgotten. In 1892 the Record and Pension Office of the War Department undertook to compile a list of men in the regiment who had actually stayed in Washington and were thus deserving of a medal. Meanwhile, some of the veterans of the 27th who had not remained found out about the medals with their names on them in Wentworth's barn and broke in and took them. Later that decade, after Wentworth's death, the remaining medals disappeared entirely.

Over the next several years, the army continued to clarify the qualifications for the Medal of Honor and to gather a complete list of all of its recipients. In 1917 the army came to grips with the issue of the 27th Maine. A review board considered all past Medals of Honor. It concluded that the 555 Maine men who had not volunteered (a total drawn from a regimental history published in 1895) were definitely not worthy of the award. Then, looking at the list of 309 who had stepped forward that June day in 1863, the board waffled, but the judge advocate general of the army did not. These men had done nothing in any way heroic. Their medals should be rescinded along with all the others. And so, half a century after the emergency of 1863, the final coda was written to the strangest tale in all the varied history of America's highest military honor—which had very nearly become the cheapest.

Splitting the South
The Siege of Vicksburg

The fortunes of the Union appeared to turn everywhere in that July of 1863. Just the day after Meade's victory at Gettysburg, Grant finally received the surrender of Vicksburg, Mississippi, hundreds of miles to the west. The twin defeats broke the back of the Confederacy, leaving it on the defensive for the rest of the war.

Vicksburg had been a very different sort of operation from Gettysburg. Its fall came after forty-seven days of siege. Yet even then, interspersed among the tedious days of siege, there were fights between blue and gray. On May 19, the day after the siege commenced, Grant launched an unsuccessful attack hoping to penetrate General John C. Pemberton's fortifications. It failed, but three days later Grant tried again, sending almost 45,000 men against the enemy works on a three-mile front. The fighting everywhere was desperate, and here and there the Yankees topped the walls or made a brief breakthrough. But Pemberton held out, inflicting over 3,000 casualties. Repulsed a second time, Grant would not attack again and, instead, slowly starved Vicksburg into submission.

That May 22 produced many heroes, and, as was often the case, their commanders and government seemed more anxious to honor them than when there had been a failed battle. Fre-

quently they were honored for group endeavors, like the exploits of the Chicago Mercantile Battery. Captain Patrick M. White, who was to earn a Medal of Honor that day, was ordered to take two guns into a ravine to help batter down an enemy earthwork. Assisted by some infantrymen, he and his men dragged a cannon up to within a few feet of the Confederate fort, all the while under fire. Others carried ammunition by hand, and once he had the gun in place, White oversaw cutting the fuses so they would explode almost as soon as they left the gun's muzzle.

His first shot struck a Confederate twenty-four-pounder in the fort. After that, White and his men loaded and fired as fast as they could. "I never saw a gun loaded and fired so fast," he declared. "Every man was at his best." So quickly did they work that once or twice someone failed to swab carefully remaining sparks out of the gun tube before the next charge was rammed home, and it discharged prematurely.

The 17th Illinois Infantry forms up near Vicksburg, Mississippi.

Union assaults on Vicksburg fortifications like the one above failed, so Federal forces dug in for a siege of the city.

Soon they completely disabled the Confederate gun, and then their shells set ablaze the cotton bales that formed part of the southern parapet. For twenty minutes the Confederates abandoned the fort, then came back with water to douse the fire only to have White's gun blast the cotton to pieces. That lone gun continued to fire throughout the rest of the attack, and when it was brought back later that day "it was as hot as a live coal." Five other members of the Chicago Mercantile Battery manning the gun would earn the Medal of Honor along with White for their daring exploit.

Even more men earned that distinction elsewhere on the battle line around Vicksburg in what some of them ever after referred to as the "forlorn hope." In front of the XV Corps there stood an enemy fort, behind a ditch twelve feet wide and six feet deep. For Grant's attack to succeed, this fort must fall. Late on May 21 every regimental colonel in the 2d Division of the corps asked for volunteers. Those who stepped forward would lead the attack. Their mission was to build a bridge over the ditch for the attackers to cross and then erect scaling ladders against the side of the fort for them to climb. All of this would be done in plain view of the defenders and under a withering fire. Only unmarried men were to be accepted as volunteers, for it seemed tacitly agreed that few if any would survive.

More than enough answered the call in spite of the dangers, and the next morning they assembled at the staging area for their exploit. They found a pile of logs. Two men each were to run with a log toward the ditch and throw it across. As soon as two or more logs were successfully planted, more men were to rush forward with planks to throw across them to make the roadway for the attackers to follow. Then a final group of volunteers would rush across the bridge and throw up the scaling ladders.

There lay nearly a quarter-mile of open ground for them to cover before they reached that ditch. As soon as the Yankees emerged in the open, their foes opened fire. Perhaps half of them survived to reach the ditch, but so many men had fallen that not enough of the long logs came up for them to start their

A soldier of the "forlorn hope" throws a southern bomb back at Confederate lines on the morning of May 22, 1863.

Survivors of the "forlorn hope": (top to bottom) Matthew Bickford, John W. Conaway, John G. Ayers, Thomas J. Ward.

work. Still under a deadly fire, they could not run back through that gauntlet and had no choice but to jump into the ditch and take what shelter they could find. Private Howell Trogden of the 8th Missouri Infantry had carried a flag along with the party, and here he climbed up part of the Confederate parapet and planted the banner before taking cover. Those Federals with guns kept up a steady fire on any Rebels who tried to reach out to take the colors.

The attackers who came behind the "forlorn hope" fared no better, and barely thirty men of the 11th Missouri reached

Other survivors: (top to bottom) Edward Welsh, William Archinal, John C. Buckley, and Andrew E. Goldsbery.

the ditch to join their comrades. The enemy above could not lean far enough over the parapet to fire on them, nor could they depress their cannon sufficiently to send shot and shell into the ditch. And so, suiting necessity to the task, they took twelve-pounder shells and lit their fuses by hand, then dropped them down into the ditch like grenades. Only the fact that the fuses were cut too long saved the Federals, for while the shells still sputtered, there was time for them to get out of the way. A few even picked up the shells and threw them back up the parapet at the Rebels.

The "forlorn hope" remained in that ditch all day, from ten in the morning until nightfall ended the fighting. When the men finally pulled out in the dark, some 85 percent had been killed or wounded, all for an attack that failed. But fifty-three of the survivors, including Private Trogden, were awarded the Medal of Honor for their unexampled bravery, the largest number of medals given to a single group of men for a single action during the war.

There was heroism everywhere in Grant's attacking line on May 22, and even his foes did not fail to honor it. Private Thomas H. Higgins, a burly Irishman in the 99th Illinois, volunteered to carry the regimental colors when the regular color bearer could not do duty that day. His captain gave him orders for the attack that were simple enough: not to stop until he had that flag planted inside the Confederate works. Higgins obeyed to the letter.

For two hours a cannonade sounded the prelude to attack. Then the advancing column came in sight of the portion of the works held by the 2d Texas Infantry. As soon as the Yankees were within range, the Texans' guns opened a devastating fire. "The blue lines vanished amid fearful slaughter," recalled Confederate Charles Evans of the 2d Texas. The firing stopped.

Nothing seemed to move on the smoke-shrouded field. Then the defenders made out a single Union flag fluttering and moving forward. Thomas Higgins was still obeying his orders. In disbelief, the Confederates saw the lone Yank moving on toward their works. Even when several score rifles began to open fire on him, Higgins did not falter but kept coming on, tripping over the bodies of his dead comrades. "Suddenly," wrote Evans, "as if with one impulse, every Confederate soldier within sight of the Union color bearer

seemed to be seized with the idea that the man ought not to be shot." Cries of "Don't shoot at that man again" ran up and down the line. Seconds later they were actually cheering Higgins on, throwing their hats in the air, and reaching out to pull him over the breastworks when he reached the parapet. Miraculously, he was untouched by the storm of fire through which he had passed.

General Pemberton himself interviewed Higgins before sending him to await prison, but with the fall of Vicksburg the plucky Irishman was freed and returned to his regiment to serve out the war. Years later, at the instigation of the very Confederates who captured him that day, Congress awarded him the medal for his single-minded persistence in carrying out a soldier's orders. ❧

Private Thomas Higgins marches through withering fire toward Confederate breastworks at Vicksburg, Mississippi, on May 22, 1863.

The Only Woman

Mary Walker always stood out in a crowd. When she graduated from Syracuse Medical College in 1855, she became one of the first woman physicians in the country. She preferred pants as more functional than dresses or skirts and even wore a pair at her own wedding. An ardent advocate of women's rights, she often delivered lectures on the subject. Mary Edwards Walker is also the only woman in U.S. history to have received the Medal of Honor.

At the outbreak of war in 1861 Dr. Walker, then twenty-nine, applied for a commission as an army surgeon but was turned down because of her sex. Undaunted, she worked as a volunteer at a Washington hospital for several months. In November 1862 Walker presented herself at the Virginia headquarters of Major General Ambrose Burnside and was taken on as a field surgeon, although still on a volunteer basis.

For much of the next two years, Dr. Walker could be found near the Union front lines, clad in the gold-striped trousers of an army officer and a green surgeon's sash, topped off by an unorthodox straw hat with an ostrich feather. She treated the wounded at Fredericksburg in December 1862; almost a year later she was in Chattanooga tending the casualties of the battle of Chickamauga.

After the battle she again requested a commission as an army doctor. But after an army medical board in Chattanooga pronounced her "utterly unqualified for the position of medical officer," she could only continue as a volunteer. Finally, Major General George H. Thomas appointed her to replace the assistant surgeon of the 52d Ohio Infantry after the previous doctor's death.

Mary Walker tended soldiers and civilians and may also have been a spy for the Union at this time: One army communication mentions her "secret services" for the North, another states that information she gleaned behind enemy lines saved Major General William T. Sherman's forces from "a serious reverse."

Only a month after joining the 52d Ohio, Walker was captured by the rebels and sent to a Richmond prison. After four months she was traded for a Confederate officer; years later she took great pride in this "man for man" exchange.

Civilian doctor Mary Walker treats Union wounded in the field.

Upon her release Walker was granted a contract as an acting assistant surgeon at $100 a month and given back pay for her service with the 52d Ohio (but not her desired commission as an officer). The army denied her request for battlefield duty, and she spent the rest of the war practicing at a Louisville female prison (where she offended both inmates and staff with her abrupt manner) and a Tennessee orphans' asylum.

Though paid in full and released from government contract at the end of the war, Walker lobbied for a brevet promotion to major for her services. Secretary of War Stanton would not grant the request; it was impossible to give Walker a higher rank, the judge advocate general advised, because she was never an officer in the first place. After several angry letters from Walker, President Andrew Johnson asked Stanton if there was some other way to recognize her service. Stanton ordered that a Medal of Honor be prepared for Walker. It was presented to her in January 1866; she would wear it every day for the rest of her life.

After the war Walker devoted herself to many unpopular causes, including women's rights, the wearing of pants, and opposition to smoking. Her taste in clothes caused frequent arrests on such charges as "impersonating a man." At one trial she asserted her right "to dress as I please in free America on whose tented fields I have served for four years in the cause of human freedom." The judge dismissed the case and ordered the police never to arrest Walker on the charge again. She left the courtroom to hearty applause.

Her private practice was never successful, however, and by the mid-1880s Mary Walker, now living on a government pension, was reduced to a side-show existence. Amid various novelty acts, she spoke on women's rights and the advantages of pants, all the while wearing the Medal of Honor on her lapel. Some observers were indignant: In March 1893 an Ohio newspaper huffed, "There was a time when this remarkable woman stood upon the same platform with Presidents and the world's greatest women. There is something grotesque about her appearance on a stage built for freaks."

Age did not diminish her eccentricity. In 1901 Walker outraged her Oswego, New York, neighbors—and nearly lost her pension—by circulating a petition asking for clemency for the anarchist who had assassinated President McKinley.

But Mary Walker's greatest ignominy was yet to come. In 1916 Congress revised the Medal of Honor standards to include only "actual combat with an enemy." Several months later an army board rescinded Walker's medal, citing her ambiguous military status and the fact that her "service does not appear to have been distinguished in action or otherwise." Advised that it was now a crime to wear her medal, she vowed to continue to wear it, every day if she pleased.

Over the next two years Walker appealed to congressmen and War Department officials, but to no avail. On one of these visits she suffered a bad fall on the Capitol steps. She never fully recovered and died on February 21, 1919, at the age of eighty-six.

But like many of the actions of the army review board of 1916-17, the case of Mary Walker was not forgotten. Nearly sixty years after her death, at the urging of a descendant, the army restored Walker's Medal of Honor. Some medal historians and recipients objected, citing her civilian status and allegations of incompetence. Nevertheless, Mary Walker remains on record as the sole female recipient of the Medal of Honor.

Dr. Walker, in men's attire, with the new army Medal of Honor, 1912.

The Union Juggernaut
Grant's Overland Campaign

The ten months that followed the twin victories at Gettysburg and Vicksburg saw even more ground lost to the South out west in Tennessee and in north Georgia. But back in Virginia, where all eyes seemed always to turn, the Yankees stood no closer to Richmond than they had more than a year before. Always Lee stymied their efforts to penetrate his beloved state's interior. The coming of a new Yankee general, however, was to change the fortunes of war in Virginia.

Private John Weeks, who made good use of an unloaded gun at Spotsylvania.

Ulysses S. Grant came from his victories in the West to become general-in-chief of all Union armies in late 1863. He had directed major offensives in every other theater of the war and himself went to Virginia to be with the brave but troubled Army of the Potomac. The capable Meade remained in direct command of the army, but it was Grant who set the strategy, and on May 4, 1864, they all set out across the Rapidan River near Fredericksburg, Virginia—their objective, Lee's army.

Battle was joined the next day in a tangled region known to local Virginians as the Wilderness. For two days they fought, then moved on toward Spotsylvania to renew the battle. The Confederates entrenched and the Yankees attacked again and again, especially at a bulge in the Rebel line called the Mule Shoe and later at a place to be called

Union troops pour into the Mule Shoe at Spotsylvania on May 12, 1864.

Bloody Angle. Lee was the loser in the end, for after several days Grant began to move around his right flank, and Lee had no choice but to pull back.

The hardest fighting came on May 12, 1864. The Yankees awakened early that morning, among them Private John Weeks of the 152d New York. He was barely past his nineteenth birthday, but already a veteran, and when the order came to advance he moved smartly.

"Soon the rebel skirmishers commenced firing," he recalled, "and then for the first time I began to realize that we had work before us." He and his comrades advanced across an open field and into felled trees, strung wire, and other obstructions placed by the enemy. Soon they reached the Rebel works, a ditch several feet deep with an earthen parapet behind it. And all the way in the advance the Federals received a murderous artillery and rifle fire. Still they charged, scaled the parapet, and poured into the Confederate line.

Confusion reigned for a time as the disorganized Yankees tried to consolidate their breakthrough while their foes sought to withdraw. Weeks looked to his right to see another part of the enemy line pull out. He saw a Rebel color company with its flag trying desperately to escape; they fired a volley, then made a run for it. "I made up my mind," wrote Weeks, "that I must have those colors."

Even though his own rifle was unloaded, Weeks ran out in front of the retreating enemy, confronted the Rebel color sergeant, and grabbed the colors from him. Throwing the banner to the ground, Weeks put his foot on it, cocked the hammer of his empty gun, leveled it at the sergeant, and demanded the surrender of the entire company. Bluffed completely, a half-dozen Confederates lay down their guns and became his prisoners. While taking them to the rear, Weeks met General Winfield S. Hancock, his corps commander, who smiled incredulously at the boy's brave deed. But he believed it just the same. Several months later Weeks was in a hospital recovering from a wound when he received a package. "Upon opening it," he said, "I found it to be the Medal of Honor."

Dozens of heroes were born in that hell of fire at the Mule Shoe and the Bloody Angle, often because seeing their comrades fall erased all caution in the urge for revenge. Private William Noyes of the 2d Vermont charged the Angle with his regiment and halted just at the pile of logs the enemy used for defenses.

Ulysses S. Grant at City Point, Virginia, during the fighting at Petersburg.

Left. *Vermonter William Noyes.* Above. *Noyes stands atop the breastworks at the Bloody Angle in Spotsylvania, firing into southern lines.* Right. *Orlando Boss.* Below. *Corporal Boss risks enemy fire to bring water to a wounded officer at Cold Harbor.*

Apparently as a subterfuge, a Rebel raised his rifle with a white rag tied to the barrel, and one Vermont boy took it to mean surrender and raised his head above the parapet. He was shot dead instantly.

"Infuriated beyond control by such treachery," said Noyes, "and determined upon revenge, I called on the men near me to load their pieces as rapidly as possible and hand them up to me." He leaped atop the parapet, fired his rifle into the nearest Confederate, and then proceeded to take rifles from his comrades and fire them one after another into the startled enemy. Fifteen times he aimed and fired before the bullets whizzing past him forced him back to cover. How many Noyes hit is unknown, but the Medal of Honor would be his for this deed.

Concern for the living could be just as powerful a catalyst to bravery as anger over the dead. Six weeks later, at Cold Harbor, Grant again attacked Confederates placed behind well-built defenses. The result was a disastrous and

bloody succession of assaults. In the confusion, the 25th Massachusetts, just 270 strong, advanced unsupported against the enemy breastworks, only to be repulsed with heavy losses. Corporal Orlando Boss and two privates were left on the field, pinned down in a rifle pit midway between the two contending armies. Nearby lay Lieutenant Daly of the same regiment, mortally wounded.

Boss could hear Daly's agonized cries for water and risked his own life by

crawling out of the pit to take his canteen to the officer. When he got back to the rifle pit, Boss found one of the privates wounded and the area too hot with Rebel fire to remain. He put the private on his back and staggered through a virtual gauntlet of Confederate fire to reach the safety of his own breastworks.

That was not enough for the plucky nineteen-year-old. He now asked permission to go back out to bring back Lieutenant Daly. Accompanied by another

Above. *Sergeant Major Christian Fleetwood (center), 4th U.S. Colored Troops, with the Medal of Honor he earned at New Market Heights, also called Chapin's Farm. Below. The 22d Negro Regiment at Petersburg, June 16, 1864. Grant used black troops in some of the worst fighting of his Virginia campaign.*

The Assault Renewed

" *... the firing began somewhere on the regimental line and ripped along in both directions. The level sheets of flame developed great clouds of smoke that tumbled and tossed in the mild wind ... Into the youth's eyes there came a look that one can see in the orbs of a jaded horse. His neck was quivering with nervous weakness and the muscles of his arms felt numb and bloodless. His hands, too, seemed large and awkward as if he was wearing invisible mittens. And there was a great uncertainty about his knee joints ... He began to exaggerate the endurance, the skill, and the valor of those who were coming. Himself reeling from exhaustion, he was astonished beyond measure at such persistency. They must be machines of steel. It was very gloomy struggling against such affairs, wound up perhaps to fight until sundown.* "

Stephen Crane, **The Red Badge of Courage**

man, Boss rushed out to the original rifle pit. From here, using their mess spoons, they scraped their way toward Daly, digging a shallow ditch some fifteen yards long to reach him. Through that ditch they dragged him back to the rifle pit, after four hours of arduous digging under constant fire. More hours of furrowing followed until the two men and their dying officer returned safely to their own lines. It was an incredible feat made no less heroic by Daly's later death and one richly deserving of the Medal of Honor received by Boss.

During Grant's long campaign to conquer Lee there were other heroes who were out of the ordinary. For the medal was not restricted by station, or race. Nearly 179,000 blacks served in the Union forces, and twenty-three of them would win the Medal of Honor. The first had gone to William H. Carney back in 1863 for his part in attacking Battery Wagner outside Charleston, South Carolina (see sidebar, page 44). Another black, Decatur Dorsey, won it for his bravery in the so-called Battle of the

Crater, when Grant had Lee besieged in Petersburg and used several black regiments in an abortive assault made just after tunnelers had exploded a huge mine under the Rebel works.

The largest number of medals awarded to blacks for any single action resulted from fighting at New Market Heights, Virginia, on September 29, 1864. In a bloody charge that failed, the 4th and 6th United States Colored Troops lost perhaps half their numbers. Sergeant-Major Christian Fleetwood was in charge of the left half of the 4th's line, there being no field officers available. He led it forward in the charge, only to see the regiment cut to pieces. Of the color guard of twelve men, just one survived. When a second color bearer fell, Corporal Charles Veal grabbed the regimental flag and Fleetwood himself took the national colors. On they went, struggling through successive lines of enemy defenses and obstructions, all the while under fire. "It was sheer madness," recalled Fleetwood, "and those of us who were able had to get out as best we could."

Once back in their own lines, Fleetwood rallied the remnant of the regiment around his flag. "I have never been able to understand how Veal and I lived under such a hail of bullets," Fleetwood said afterward. He was small, and that helped, but even then his luck was phenomenal. One bullet actually passed inside his running legs, cutting through his boot, trousers, and stocking without giving him a scratch. A grateful government gave him more. Fleetwood, Veal, another wounded color bearer, and a black sergeant from the 6th Colored who also saved his banner would all receive the Medal of Honor for their courage in the service of the Union. ❋

Sergeant Carney's Flag

The call for black Union soldiers in late 1862 convinced William H. Carney to forgo his plans for the ministry. "I felt I could best serve my God by serving my country and my oppressed brothers," he later remembered. Enlisting in the 54th Massachusetts Colored Infantry in February 1863, the twenty-three-year-old former slave was soon in the thick of the fighting.

In the early afternoon of July 18, 1863, Sergeant Carney and the 600 men of the 54th charged along a narrow stretch of sand outside the Confederate stronghold at Fort Wagner, South Carolina. Artillery shells of both sides whistled all around as they pushed forward.

Suddenly, the color bearer was hit by an enemy bullet. Carney threw aside his rifle and seized the flag before it fell. Rebel fire pierced his leg, but Carney made it to the shadow of the fort and planted the colors.

Sergeant William Carney saved this Union flag at Fort Wagner, South Carolina.

After thirty minutes, the Yankees fell back with heavy losses. When Confederate soldiers charged his position, Carney wrapped the flag around the staff and ran back to the Union lines, stumbling through a ditch filled waist-deep with water. Enemy bullets struck his chest, right arm, and right leg, but he kept crawling to the rear. Carney was grazed in the head but refused to let a New York soldier take the flag, saying, "No one but a member of the 54th should carry the colors."

Back at the Union camp, Carney was cheered by the men of his regiment as he proudly proclaimed, "Boys, I only did my duty. The flag never touched the ground."

Several months later, propped on a cane from his injuries, Carney posed with the standard for which he had risked his life (*left*). Though he did not receive his medal until 1900, his was the first Civil War exploit by a black man to merit the Medal of Honor.

The Other War
Battles in the Far West

Least known of all was that war being fought out west. Blood was just as red west of the Mississippi River, in Arkansas, Texas, Missouri, and western Louisiana, heroism just as valuable. But the contending forces were so far from the seats of government, and attention so focused on Virginia, that much less notice went to what happened in the so-called Trans-Mississippi.

At Prairie Grove on December 7, 1862, the fate of northern Arkansas was decided by a Federal victory in a confused and brutal battle. The fight was influenced largely by the grueling thirty-six-hour, sixty-six-mile forced march of northern reinforcements. One of the reinforcing regiments was the 37th Illinois, led by Lieutenant Colonel John C. Black.

After only an hour's rest, he led his regiment against an enemy-held hill that had already repulsed two other units. "I ordered a charge up the hill," Black wrote. "It was executed in fine style." But then the enemy moved out against him in superior numbers, overlapping both flanks. Supporting troops on Black's left crumpled and gave way. Artillery on his right began to open up on his regiment. He was in danger of being overwhelmed. "The only hope from annihilation was the bayonet or retreat."

The trouble was that a rail fence stood directly in Black's front, and his men would never climb it and re-form under fire before the attacking Rebels reached them. Instead, Black and his men stood and simply returned the devastating enemy fire for a few minutes until he could order an organized retreat to safety. Black himself took a bad wound but refused to leave the field until he knew that his regiment had grouped and was ready for more action. He was just twenty-three and now had earned a Medal of Honor.

Another lieutenant colonel won the medal a year later a few hundred miles south on the Texas coast. Frank S. Hesseltine and 100 men of his 13th Maine Infantry were ordered to reconnoiter the Matagorda Peninsula 100 miles southwest of Galveston. On December 28, 1863, he boarded his men on the gunboat *Granite City* and the next morning landed in the surf on the penin-

sula. Rising winds made it impossible for the ship to land any supplies beyond what the men took ashore with them.

There were only a few Confederate skirmishers on the land spit in front of him, and soon Hesseltine was driving them before him when suddenly he heard the steam whistle of the *Granite City.* It warned of danger, and the Yankees discovered two regiments of Rebel cavalry coming toward their rear.

Outnumbered, without supplies, and cut off from the gunboat by winds, Hesseltine was in deep trouble, with the enemy in his front in small numbers and in his rear in much greater force. He had, at least, the support fire from cannon aboard the gunboat, and that helped slow the advancing Confederates. When they were within range, he had his rear line turn about and fire into them. Then the colonel quickly moved his men to a part of the peninsula just 200 yards wide only to see the enemy start riding through the bayou on his flank to reach his rear. Hesseltine rode back to select personally the next place to make a stand.

He led his men to the beach and set them to work erecting a barricade of driftwood and logs, with the surf to their backs. Here they would either defend themselves or be pushed into the sea. The enemy's hesitation, and nightfall, halted any further operations until morning. That night the *Granite City* steamed away for help, while the Yankees burned bonfires to attract the gunboat *Scioto,* known to be steaming along the coast. There was no thought of retreat. But when the Confederates did not renew their attack next morning, and a Rebel gunboat arrived and started shelling the beach, there was nothing to do but leave. They did so by moving slowly along the peninsula all one day and most of the next, amid a terrible storm, marching twenty miles in the sand with-

45

Above. *Lieutenant Colonel John C. Black.*
Right. *On the Matagorda Peninsula of
Texas, men of Colonel Frank Hesseltine's
13th Maine engage superior Rebel forces,
December 29–30, 1863.*

out food or water. The *Scioto* found them
at last and took them aboard. Hesseltine
had not lost a single man.

It was just a few months later that
the only major campaign in the southern
part of the Trans-Mississippi unfolded as
part of Grant's overall strategy. General
Nathaniel Banks led his army up the Red
River, aiming to take Shreveport, Louisiana. But the campaign was ill conceived, and worse, Banks was no
general. It was a failure from start to
finish, the only bright spot coming on
April 9, 1864, when Banks won a battle
at Pleasant Hill. Even this was nearly
lost when the Confederates launched an
afternoon attack and turned back the
Federal left, which had been ill placed.
The 119th Illinois held the position.

"A sickening feeling came over me
as I took in the situation," recalled Sergeant John H. Cook. His lieutenant, in
spite of the horde of Confederates
approaching them, ordered his company
forward, Cook in the lead. Cook looked

back and saw one of his comrades fall
dead. "Then I was mad," he said, "mad
clear through." With his Sharps
breechloading rifle in hand, he ran
toward the enemy, loading and firing as
he went. Confederate marksmen set
their sights on him but missed. "The
bullets whizzed around me thick," he
wrote. "One went through my right coat
sleeve, another through my hat, and one
so close to my cheek that I could feel it
burn; but I cared nothing for life or
death."

His company had to hold their
ground or the flank of the whole army
would be exposed, that was all that ran
through his mind. Feverishly Cook
loaded and fired all forty rounds that he
carried, then raised his smoking gun in
one hand and waved his cap with the
other, cheering on his comrades to follow
him. It worked. The Illinois regiment
rallied, charged, and stopped the threat.
And when reinforcements arrived soon
after, Cook and his mates joined in the

general advance that gave Banks his only
victory of the campaign. As for Cook,
his reward came months later when he
received a bronze medallion, engraved
with the words: "The Congress, to Sergeant John H. Cook, for Conspicuous
Bravery at Battle of Pleasant Hill La.,
April 9th, 1864."

Later that year, in Missouri, the
Federals would be victorious from beginning to end as they met and stopped
Confederate General Sterling Price's
invasion of that state. On October 23,
Price was beaten in the greatest battle
west of the Mississippi, at Westport,
Missouri. He retreated immediately, but
two days later, at Little Osage Crossing,
Kansas, the pursuing Federals caught up
with him.

Confederate General John S. Marmaduke was acting as rear guard to cover
the crossing of Price's supply trains when
the Yankee attacks began and completely disrupted Marmaduke's line. Private James Dunlavy and his 3d Iowa

Above. *Private James Dunlavy, who captured a Confederate general in Kansas on October 25, 1864.* Below. *The battle of Pleasant Hill, Louisiana, April 9, 1864.*

Cavalry were on the right of the attacking line, and he had just seen the Rebels give way when a shell fragment disabled his arm and frightened his horse. It was only after a struggle with the bolting animal that Dunlavy turned its nose toward the front again to find that everything had changed. Marmaduke's line had dissolved and Dunlavy's own outfit was nowhere to be seen.

In the confusion, Dunlavy saw a body of soldiers he took to be Federals and rode toward them. They were Confederates in the act of retreating, and to make the mistaken identity mutual, a general officer among them saw Dunlavy and rode toward him, shouting, "What do you mean, shooting your own men!" The private raised his rifle and fired. Dunlavy's bullet missed, but with his revolver in hand he shouted back at the man, "Surrender or I'll fire."

The officer looked a bit sheepish but finally said, "I surrender; thought I was with my own men." As Dunlavy was taking him to the rear, a fellow Yank ran up on foot and asked for the prisoner's horse. Dunlavy was only too happy to oblige and then set off again with his charge running at a double quick ahead of him. Exhausted, the general asked to slow down, which they did, and then he requested to be taken to the Federal army commander, General Alfred Pleasonton, whom he said he knew personally. Well before they got there another Federal officer approached, and finally the Confederate revealed his identity. "I am General Marmaduke," he said.

No one was more surprised than Dunlavy to discover that he had captured and brought in one of the highest-ranking officers in Price's army. Marmaduke spent the rest of the war in Fort Warren prison, and young Dunlavy recovered from his wound to serve out the war with his regiment and to wear the Medal of Honor on his chest.   ★

Heroism at Sea
The Naval War

Just as unsung as the fighting out west of the Mississippi is the Civil War on the water. Like the army, the Union navy began the conflict woefully unprepared for the mammoth task before it. Only about thirty-five modern service-able warships were available and just 7,600 seamen. The Confederates, of course, had no navy at all in the beginning. Thus both sides were forced to commence a crash program of building ships while at the same time developing their naval strategies.

The U.S.S. Monitor *(left foreground) and the C.S.S.* Virginia *(also called the* Merrimack*) in the world's first clash of ironclads on March 9, 1862.*

The naval strategy of the South in the Civil War was simple enough: to defend its ports and try to keep them open for vital trade in war materiel from abroad; to hold its rivers to prevent the enemy using them as avenues of invasion; and to interrupt Federal shipping on the high seas, thus drawing Yankee warships away from the coast to pursue southern privateers. The Union's goals were directly related. Lincoln's ships must blockade the Confederate coastline, stop traffic into its harbors, control its rivers, and stop its commerce raiders on the ocean.

The building programs of both sides saw many innovations, not the least of them being the advent of practical ironclad warships. Almost simultaneously, the Confederates were converting a captured Yankee warship into the powerful C.S.S. *Virginia*, while in the North a whole new sort of vessel was being created in the U.S.S. *Monitor*. In a case of timing unparalleled, both ships were ready at the same time and place for their first combat.

On March 8, 1862, the *Virginia*—still often called the *Merrimack* because of the ship from which it was made—steamed from its berth at Norfolk, down the Elizabeth River, and into Hampton Roads, Virginia. Its objective was the Yankee blockading fleet, and in a day's action it almost destroyed it, sinking or burning two warships, damaging another, and running others aground. The crew expected to return to the scene the next day to complete its work, but on the morning of March 9 the seamen came upon the unlikely looking *Monitor*. Miraculously, the single-turreted iron-clad had arrived during the night after a harrowing passage from the North.

When the two ships met in battle that day, neither could gain the upper hand. For several hours they hammered at each other indecisively. Only late in the day did a well-aimed shot from the *Virginia* strike the *Monitor*'s pilothouse. It tore away part of the house's iron roof and sent sparks and iron fragments through the viewing slits, temporarily

blinding Lieutenant John Worden, commander of the vessel.

The wheelman standing beside him, Peter Williams, was uninjured and, though dangerously exposed in the damaged pilothouse, remained at his post and skillfully steered the ship away from its antagonist until another officer could take over to renew the fight. Once the battle reached its end—a draw—Williams was rewarded for his coolness and bravery with the only Medal of Honor awarded for the battle.

There were to be more medals associated with the *Monitor*, though not for combat. Seven months later, on December 30, while being towed south along the coast of North Carolina just off Cape Hatteras, she ran into a heavy storm. As the weather worsened, the ironclad began taking in water faster than her pumps could eject it. In time the engines could no longer function, the water level continued to rise, and the order was given to abandon ship.

The U.S.S. *Rhode Island*, the towing ship, sent three boats across the water to rescue the sinking vessel's seamen, and one of them, a ship's cutter, made three perilous passages through the raging seas. Twice she brought back men to the *Rhode Island*, but when she returned a third time for the last of the seamen, they were nowhere to be seen. The *Monitor* had gone to the bottom. The seven men who rowed that cutter back and forth at peril to their own lives all received the medal for their valor.

Indeed, naval actions seemed to earn the medal in numbers. No fewer than twenty seamen earned it for their daring in Admiral David G. Farragut's April 24, 1862, attack on Forts Jackson and St. Philip, both of which guarded New Orleans. When they fell, and the city with them, the lower Mississippi was open to Union navigation, and a wedge was driven into the Confederacy.

The Monitor's *turret house shows the damage incurred during its clash with the* Virginia.

Individual acts of bravery during the attack are too many to enumerate, yet a few stand out. Aboard the U.S.S. *Pensacola*, Seaman Thomas Lyons lashed himself off the port bow with a rope line in hand to take depth soundings as the ship passed the enemy batteries, all the while exposed to everything the Rebels could throw at him. Aboard the U.S.S. *Brooklyn*, Quartermaster James Buck stood at his wheel for seven hours, refusing to go below to safety even though a flying splinter had dangerously wounded him.

Perhaps most daring of all was the quick-thinking action of Gunner's Mate J. B. Frisbee on the U.S.S. *Pinola*. His ship took fire during the battle on April 24, and he watched as the flames advanced dangerously close to the ship's powder magazine. At once he left his post and ran around the flames and into the magazine itself. Then, drawing shut its heavy iron door behind him, he remained inside, ready to catch and extinguish any sparks that might penetrate while other crewmen fought to put out the fire.

Most of the naval combat of the war took place on the Mississippi after Farragut opened it up. More Yankee ships and seamen perished there than anywhere else, frequently not in major battles but during engagements with the enemy on the banks. On May 28, 1863, the thirteen-gun ironclad *Cincinnati* helped silence a Rebel battery that was impeding Grant's encirclement of Vicksburg. Due to confusion in communications, and careful concealment of some of the cannon, the Confederate bat-

tery proved much more powerful than expected.

No sooner did the *Cincinnati* loose her first broadside at the battery on a bluff than it returned fire. Its first shot penetrated the ship's magazine and went on to hole her bottom. Another shot ruined her steering. Under constant fire the vessel tried to escape upstream again, then finally had to run ashore so the crew could abandon ship. But the *Cincinnati* slipped back into the channel and sank in twenty feet of water.

In a circumstance not at all unusual in the navy, many of the seamen could not swim. Fifteen men drowned trying to reach the shore while others were killed by Rebel fire. Those who could swim saved themselves, but four brave seamen, Thomas Corcoran, Henry Dow,

Thomas Jenkins, and Martin McHugh, made repeated trips back and forth to the ship to save those who could not swim. Then they found a small boat that had not been blasted by the enemy fire and loaded it with half a dozen of the wounded from the *Cincinnati*'s upper deck. Among the boat's passengers was Lieutenant George N. Bache, commander of the sunken ship. Corcoran, a twenty-three-year-old Irishman, would win the Medal of Honor for leading the rescue. Dow, Jenkins, and McHugh were similarly awarded.

Actual combat out on the high seas was very rare in this war, but when it happened the world watched. No engagement captured more attention than the duel between the U.S.S. *Kearsarge* and the legendary Confederate

Members of the crew of the U.S.S. Rhode Island *(right) rescue sailors from the sinking* Monitor *off Cape Hatteras, North Carolina on December 30, 1862.*

commerce raider *Alabama*. The scourge of Yankee shipping, the *Alabama* and her commander, Admiral Raphael Semmes, were the object of a massive sea hunt that finally cornered the quarry at Cherbourg, France. On June 19, 1864, Semmes steamed out to meet his foe. Outgunned in a fight of only an hour, the *Alabama* went down to the bottom.

The *Kearsarge* fought like a fine watch, smoothly, efficiently, without missing a tick. She steamed circles around her opponent, thanks to the efficiency of her engine room crew, and her gunnery was markedly superior to Semmes's. Very few of the Confederate

Above. *As the C.S.S.* Alabama *sinks off Cherbourg, France, the victorious U.S.S.* Kearsarge *steams in the background.* Right. *The sailors of the* Kearsarge.

shots even struck the Yankee ship, and only three of its seamen were injured, one mortally. Indeed, it had been a one-sided battle from the start, but so delighted was the Union to be rid of the dreaded *Alabama* that the Congress was more than happy to award seventeen Medals of Honor to crewmen of the *Kearsarge* for their "marked coolness and good conduct." Of heroism there was little, there being little need for it, but then, during the Civil War, the standard for awarding the medal was generally lower than in later years. Yet all of the recipients had done their duty, and their government was grateful. ❖

Fighting for the Colors
Flag Captures

One of the many ironies of the Civil War is the fact that the one deed best calculated to earn any soldier the Medal of Honor was an act that–admittedly very dangerous–possessed almost no military significance whatever: capturing a flag. Men on both sides of the conflict considered their regimental standards worth fighting and dying for. No statute or act of Congress specifically stated that taking an enemy banner was justification for the award, yet more were given for flag captures than for any other kind of heroic endeavor.

One of the very first Medals of Honor to be given for a battle action came as a result of a captured flag. Corporal Jacob Orth of the 28th Pennsylvania fought with his regiment at Antietam early on the morning of September 17 as they attacked Rebels placed in an apple orchard. In the melee Orth took a bullet in his shoulder when he fought hand-to-hand with the color bearer of the 7th South Carolina. "The final result of our short but sharp conflict," said Orth, "was, that the Carolinian was minus his flag, and I had secured the trophy."

A "trophy" is just what it was, but one terribly important to nineteenth-century soldiers, and they would risk their lives for it. At Gettysburg, during the Confederate assault of July 3, Sergeant Major William Hincks of the 14th Connecticut saw an enemy regiment advance to within 150 yards of his line before Yankee fire stopped it. Undaunted, the Rebel color bearer ran forward a few paces and stuck his flagstaff in the ground, then lay down beside it with other members of the color guard to avoid the hot fire.

Thomas Custer, the only soldier to receive two Medals of Honor in the Civil War.

Unaccountably, Hincks jumped over the low stone wall his regiment knelt behind and started running toward the Rebel banner. Two or three others from his outfit had the same idea at the same time, and a virtual footrace ensued to see who, if any of them, would reach the flag first. One fell to a bullet almost immediately. Hincks covered the 100 yards so quickly he beat his comrades to the flag and grabbed it and ran for his own line before the Confederate color guard came to its senses and started to fire at him. Hincks made it back to safety amid a storm of bullets and proudly waved the banner of the 14th Tennessee overhead.

In time the men who took flags in battle would be honored wholesale. At the Battle of Sayler's Creek, on April 6, 1865, as Lee retreated from a fallen Petersburg and Richmond, seeking to escape to North Carolina, one Yankee division alone captured thirty-seven battle flags. It was the cavalry division of General George A. Custer, and all thirty-six of the men who made the captures were sent to Washington to receive the thanks of their government and their Medals of Honor.

They rode down the capital's avenues in a horse-drawn streetcar, their captured banners fluttering from the windows. Secretary of War Edwin M. Stanton received them. Each presented his flag, told his story, and was promised his medal. Most of their tales were of a kind, yet one of these bold cavalrymen stood above the others, not the least because he was General Custer's brother. Second Lieutenant Thomas Custer of the 6th Michigan Cavalry had captured two of those flags personally.

The first one he took in a fight at Namozine Church on April 2, as Grant's cavalry tried to break up Lee's horsemen protecting his flanks. Exhilarated by his capture, Tom Custer apparently decided

The Roll of Honor

Many Americans distinguished themselves in Civil War battles but were not eligible for the Medal of Honor. These men fought for the Confederacy. But while Rebel soldiers could not receive the medal, they were cited for the highest award of the Confederate States of America and listed on its Roll of Honor, the closest the South ever came to its own Medal of Honor.

Like their counterparts in Washington, Confederate representatives and senators in Richmond favored the creation of an award for individual valor. In the fall of 1862 such a measure passed both chambers and was sent to President Jefferson Davis, who signed it into law on October 13. In language similar to the Union resolutions of the past year, the Confederate bill directed

That the President be, and he is hereby authorized to bestow medals, with proper devices, upon such officers of the armies of the Confederate States as shall be conspicuous for courage and good conduct on the field of battle, and also to confer a badge of distinction upon one private or non-commissioned officer of each company after every signal victory it shall have assisted to achieve.

The law made no provision for a medal for the Confederate navy.

In a radical departure from the tradition exemplified by the Union awards, the act mandated that enlisted men would be selected for the medals by majority vote of the men themselves. Such a democratic method of bestowing decorations was virtually unknown. This was more than a typical campaign medal; only a select few from each battle would be recognized by their peers.

Delays in the creation of the medal, however, threatened to dilute the Confederate award's impact on the ranks of southern soldiers. In October 1863, almost one full year after the original act, the Adjutant and Inspector General's Office of the Confederacy published an order acknowledging "difficulties in procuring the medals and badges of distinction" promised earlier. "To avoid postponing the grateful recognition of [the men's] valor until it can be made in the enduring form provided by the act," the order established a "Roll of Honor," with the name of each man cited, to be read before every regiment and published in at least one newspaper in every Confederate state.

Two Rolls of Honor distributed in 1864 listed a man from each company from several battles. In the engagement at Seven Pines, Virginia, in June 1862, for example, nine men from the 8th Infantry Regiment were cited, although no mention was made of their particular actions. The details of elections to the roll are sparse, but the diary of a Confederate captain provides an example of a company election for the roll. Robert Emory Park of the 12th Alabama Regiment wrote the following entry for May 19 and 20, 1863, when his regiment was encamped at Macon, Georgia:

The election held to decide who of the company should wear the "Badge of Honor" for gallantry at Chancellorsville resulted in twelve votes each for Sergeant Wright and Private Chappell. In drawing [as for lots or straws], the latter won, and his name was sent to General Lee.

The Confederate medals were never struck. Nor do any proposed designs survive. In May 1864 a Tennessee representative stood in the Confederate House chamber to ask what progress was being made on the medals and if any further legislation was needed to hasten their creation. There, any mention of the awards in the official records ends. The tide of the conflict had turned against the South, and within a year the Confederacy would be crushed, its medals forgotten, and its heroes never to be recognized by a badge of honor.

to try for another whenever an opportunity might appear. It came four days later at Sayler's Creek, where portions of Grant's army, mainly two infantry corps and General Philip H. Sheridan's cavalry, cut off and captured one-third of Lee's dwindling army. Though the fighting was hot, Sayler's Creek was almost a walkover for many of the Yankees.

The brigade in which Tom Custer served was just charging an enemy battle line when Custer spied a Confederate flag fluttering above its color bearer. He spurred his horse and rode straight toward the prize. The Confederate carrying the flag raised his pistol and fired a shot that hit the advancing Custer in the face, the bullet entering his cheek and exiting behind his ear. The impact knocked him back on his horse, but he stayed in the saddle and kept on coming. Drawing his own revolver, Custer fired it into the Rebel with one hand and grabbed the flagstaff with the other. General Henry Capehart, who would himself be awarded the Medal of Honor thirty years later for his war services, saw 2d Lieutenant Custer's act and later described that "for intrepidity I never saw this incident surpassed."

Men of his brigade saw an elated Tom Custer riding back into their lines, blood running down his face, the captured banner streaming behind him. His first thought was to ride to his brother and proudly show his trophy. General Custer was appalled when he first saw the lieutenant, expecting to see him fall dead from the saddle, though the wound proved to be less fearful than it looked. "The damned rebels have shot me," yelled a jubilant Tom Custer, "but I've got my flag." Only direct orders from the general prevented the boy from riding back into the fight again, perhaps hoping to garner yet another trophy.

Yet for the two flags that he captured Tom Custer had already achieved a measure of extraordinary distinction. The War Department decided to honor him with two Medals of Honor, one for each of his banners. Though he got them for storybook heroics that had little to do with the outcome of the battles he had fought, there is little doubt that Tom Custer was a hero. His considerable courage, though, could not save him eleven years later, when he died beside his brother as they faced the Sioux at the Little Big Horn. ✵

The Union Restored
Final Awards

When the Medal of Honor was created, the only standard for awarding it was the legislative injunction that it be bestowed for "gallantry in action" and other "seamanlike" (or soldierly) qualities. This broad definition caused some actions to be recognized while others, just as gallant, went unrewarded. As the Civil War drew to a close, the whims of commanders who recommended men for medals was often as important as the actions of the men themselves.

Union soldiers at war's end with flags captured from the Army of Northern Virginia.

Examples of varied standards for the Medal of Honor occurred throughout the Civil War. In South Carolina in October 1863, General Quincy Gillmore decreed that Medals of Honor were to be given out to those who distinguished themselves in his attempt to take Charleston, but that no more than 3 percent of the men in each regiment were to receive them. It is perhaps fortunate that Gillmore's plan never went into full effect, for the 3 percent of his command would have accounted for several hundred medals all by themselves.

Elsewhere generals found the medal and the standards for its award so unspecific that they simply failed to recommend worthy soldiers. This accounts for the incredible disparity in the numbers given for different campaigns. In Sherman's campaign through the Carolinas in the early months of 1865, including major battles at Averasboro and Bentonville, North Carolina, only

three Medals of Honor were awarded. In General James H. Wilson's celebrated raid through Alabama, his three divisions of cavalry took five fortified cities, twenty-three colors, 288 cannon, and almost 7,000 prisoners, one of them Confederate President Jefferson Davis. Yet only twelve medals went to Wilson's troopers, all for flag captures.

By contrast, the number of awards that went to men of the Army of the Potomac just for its final week of the war in pursuit of Lee's retreating army to Appomattox was almost embarrassing. On April 1, 1865, when the Battle of Five Forks cut off Lee's right flank and forced him to give up Petersburg and Richmond, sixteen Yankees earned the award. The next day another seventeen were won as Grant and Meade pressed into the Petersburg fortifications. Only one was earned on April 3 and another on April 4, but then on the fifth, eight more medals were bestowed for skirmishes at Paine's Cross Roads and Amelia Springs as Grant pursued Lee.

Then came April 6 and the Battle of Sayler's Creek. Fully fifty Medals of Honor were awarded just for flag captures alone, among them Tom Custer's. In all, 103 medals went to men of this army just for flag captures in those nine days, while other acts of daring and bravery raised the total number awarded to 155. In short, 13 percent of all the Medals of Honor given in the Civil War went to men in just one army, for barely more than a week's campaign against a retreating foe.

This is not to say that the men who won them were not just as entitled as other recipients. It merely reflects the somewhat haphazard way in which the medal was given in its early years, as well as the constant preoccupation of Washington with its army in Virginia. And commanders with Grant, knowing that this must surely be their last campaign, may have been overzealous in trying to garner recognition for their men before they all returned to civilian life.

Indeed, the preoccupation with the Medal of Honor did not end with the war. Already men recognized it as a special badge of gallantry, prized by those who won it, coveted by those who had not. If General Custer's often imaginative widow could be believed, a general officer of their acquaintance, upon seeing Tom Custer's *two* medals, declared that he would rather have won one of those for capturing a flag than all the promotions the War Department had given him.

And so the story of the Medal of Honor for Civil War exploits did not end when the war itself came to a close. For one thing, there were men who had been granted the award who had not yet

received it. Years passed before the government put medals in the hands of all the Andrews raiders or the relatives of those who were hanged. Others never knew they had been honored with the award. Sergeant Llewellyn Norton of the 10th New York Cavalry had jumped his horse over the enemy works at Sayler's Creek and rode straight for the six Confederates manning a field piece. He demanded their surrender, knocked aside the rifles of two with his saber, and finally captured them all with the assistance of another soldier. Both were awarded the medal on July 5, 1865, but Norton's regiment had already mustered out of service, and no one could find him. It was twenty-three years later that Norton, reading through a volume of Appleton's *Cyclopedia,* found his own name in a list of medal recipients and got in touch with the War Department.

In the years that followed the war, there was time to reflect on the way in which the medal had been given and who had received it. More than that, the War Department began looking into the matter of those deserving soldiers who had not received it. No doubt this was spurred in large part by the increasingly powerful veterans' lobby in the 1880s and 1890s, and especially by the enormously influential Grand Army of the Republic (G.A.R.). It may have been no accident that the veterans' organization chose an adaptation of the five-pointed medal as its own emblem.

As a result, in the 1890s especially, scores of medals were sent out to men who were recommended, and others were awarded even into the twentieth century. Beyond this, and often with the backing of the G.A.R. or influential officers or politicians, some men actually took it on themselves to apply to the War Department for the medal, submitting affidavits from wartime comrades as to their heroic service. Of course, there was

always a danger in this, since now and then the affidavits were not all that complimentary. In May 1864 in the Shenandoah, at the Battle of New Market, Lieutenant Charles Hausmann's inefficiency helped lead to the loss of a cannon during that Federal defeat. In 1891 he, nevertheless, applied to the War Department for the medal in recognition of his services in the valley. One of his comrades who had seen Hausmann's folly attested, instead, that the government should give "such a gallant Nature a Medal of good Lasting Shoeleather." Hausmann never got his award.

And in time mature thought led to the conclusion that in some cases the medal had been bestowed too readily, that the acts of some recipients simply did not stand up to the increasingly higher standards being set with the passing years. Consequently, many of the medals awarded during the Civil War came under review, and 911 were actually revoked, most of them from the 27th Maine. It was one of the growing pains of a distinction created in the confusion and pain of war, with too little advance thought given to its intent and requirements. For all that having their medals taken away outraged those few who lost them, it was a step in the direction of making the medal more meaningful for those who would wear it in the future.

Born in chaos, administered haphazardly, sometimes misused for political purposes or military expedient, still the Medal of Honor stood at the pinnacle of soldierly aspirations by 1865. It had honored the bravery of hundreds and inspired the heroism of hundreds more. Most of all, it had begun a tradition of daring, of men reaching beyond themselves, whether to smite their foe or save a comrade or simply to take from the enemy that which he prized most, his battle flags. It captured, in its way, the spirit of the times. ❖

A Soldier's Prize

by DREW MIDDLETON

Not long ago, two couples wandered into a hotel bar on Madison Avenue. They found a group of seven men in dinner jackets having a nightcap after a club dinner.

"Look at that fellow on the right," one woman said, "he's got a sort of collar around his neck and a medal on his chest. What is it? Frank, do you know?" Frank didn't know.

At that moment another man, wearing a row of the small medals called miniatures on his dinner jacket, appeared with a brimming glass in hand.

"Mister," the other woman said. "What's that guy got around his neck?"

"That's the Congressional Medal of Honor."

"Oh! Well, what's that?"

To the majority of Americans and to the majority of service men and women the Medal of Honor, the highest decoration that can be awarded an American, is as distant and mysterious as the Holy Grail. Most haven't heard of it. Those who have don't know what it stands for in this society.

The professional military knows a good deal about lesser decorations. Attitudes range from awe for the winner of the Distinguished Service Cross to disdain for campaign throwaways that, as the saying goes, "come up with the rations."

To some the Medal of Honor seems an anachronism; a decoration conceived for wars far different from future conflicts. Today's soldier, sailor, airman, or marine, and their female counterparts, think that their war will be a business of computers, chemistry, and cavernous underground headquarters. There will be no battle lines, no charges, no aerial dogfights, no fleet actions, no last stands. And, perhaps, no Medals of Honor.

They and their teachers and trainers are likely to be wrong. The individual warrior rather than sophisticated machines will dominate tomorrow's limited wars just as he did those in Korea, Vietnam, and Grenada. Aside from an unwinnable and unlikely nuclear holocaust, when the services next go on operations their actions will not differ much from other wars of this century.

Fewer men will be engaged. They will be more heavily armed. They will strike from a distance. But there will be a need for the sudden flare of valor, the instinctive assertion of leadership in danger. And the voice of the hero shouting "Come on you bastards, let's fix these sons" will be heard.

In the services the Medal of Honor exists in a rarefied atmosphere. At night, in service clubs when jackets and belts are loosened men tell tales of things they have seen. Whenever a story ends with words like, "yeah, a great kid, they gave him the Medal of Honor," there is silence. Those who have been there envisage that short moment of hell; those who have not try but fail to conceive the confusion of battle.

There is an instinctive desire to see the Medal of Honor unblemished. The suspicion that it has been awarded for political reasons brings growls of disapproval. The award of the Medal of Honor to fliers Floyd Bennett, Richard Byrd, and Charles Lindbergh created a resentment that lasted long.

Early in World War II, an artillery colonel pointed to another colonel who wore the Medal of Honor.

"George should have been given two or three medals for what he did in '18," he said. "Now these Congressmen pass it around like crackerjack, to guys who fly airplanes with no one shooting at them."

"No one shooting at them" is the significant phrase. The services believe that the medal must be won in the heat of battle, "the hell where youth and laughter go."

The member of a unit who wins the Medal of Honor automatically casts glory among his fellows. He won it. But they, by staying in the battle, contributed. And to the ends of their lives they will recall that they were there when so-and-so earned the Medal of Honor.

The senior officer who earns the Medal of Honor not only performs a feat of gallantry but by example instructs his peers on leadership. The fundamental of leadership in war is simply that the senior has to show the others that it can be done and how to do it. The "it" may be destroying an enemy machine gun, a desperate dive to take out a SAM site, tirelessly stalking an enemy submarine. Something that has to be done.

That officer is the man who says "come" not "go." In

many wars on three continents I have met only three men, two British, one American, who appeared to enjoy killing. To the others it was something in that situation that had to be done. Those people come in all shapes, sizes, and colors.

Not long ago in Somerset, Kentucky, Sergeant Brent Woods was reburied with full military honors seventy-eight years after his death and more than a century after he had won the Medal of Honor in a half-forgotten war against the Apaches.

Woods and a small party of soldiers and civilians were ambushed in an obscure canyon in New Mexico. His officers were dead or left the field. Woods led a charge against the Apaches as he went. Not until thirteen years later did he receive the Medal of Honor. Perhaps in another America this was because he was a black, a soldier in the 9th Cavalry, the "Buffalo Soldiers."

Unit pride is often cited as a primary motivation of Medal of Honor recipients. In World War II and subsequent wars I sensed another motive. That fellow over there in the coal-scuttle helmet or across the sky in the Me-109 or Zero or sifting through the jungle in a makeshift uniform stood between the citizen-soldier and his hope of reaching home safely.

It didn't matter whether the enemy was fascist or Nazi or Communist. Few understood such matters. He was there and until he was killed the American couldn't go home. So a certain percentage performed incredible deeds of valor because the enemy over there barred a return to the familiarity of home and family or the well-remembered softball field, bar, or church.

Reckless fury is an element but not a predominant one. My observation is that most winners of the Medal of Honor and other decorations calculate their chances, not of surviving, but of success, very closely. They may see in what others consider a lost cause one slim chance of success. In this they may be professionally more accomplished than their peers.

Fury plays its part of course. Men under constant, deadly strain in battle do go berserk. How often have we read of the man, pinned down by enemy fire, seeing his friends killed and wounded, who suddenly springs from cover and charges a tank, a machine gun, a mortar

position? How often have we heard of the fighter-bomber pilot who makes that one last run on the target? Or the bomber pilot with half his crew dead and one engine out who is determined to get back to base and fight again?

The medalist is unlikely to be able to explain his motivation. Often it is simply "Jeez, the lieutenant was dead and I just had to get our guys out of there." You seldom hear much about his country and never ideological reasons. Loyalty runs deep in rifle companies or fighter squadrons, and it is loyalty to others in that unit that inspires many Medal of Honor feats.

World War II demonstrated that as war progressed the award of the highest decoration, indeed all medals, became rarer. One reason may have been that feats of gallantry that appeared extraordinary in the first month of that war became almost commonplace as the fighting spread across continents and oceans.

It is probable, too, that the announcement of awards of the Medal of Honor encouraged a people fed a daily diet of bad news from the Pacific and heartened men who faced inevitable defeat and surrender.

Is the Medal of Honor or any high decoration an incentive? I don't think so. Good officers are good officers whatever the reward. Similarly soldiers are unlikely to calculate that this or that action will win a medal. Emerging from the battle alive is the greatest award the fighting men can imagine. ◈

Drew Middleton, the former military affairs correspondent for the *New York Times,* is a columnist for the New York Times Syndicate.

The Indian Campaigns

Wars for the American Frontier

A Northern Plains Indian chief and two braves gaze out across the landscape of southern Montana.

Brave men who went west with the army after the Civil War discovered that more than bravery was needed to wrest control of the frontier lands from the Indians. The soldiers and officers of the Civil War had known combat on a grand scale: artillery battles and massed troops, cavalry and infantry charges taking their toll by the thousands. On the frontier small groups of soldiers confronted a foe adept in the tactics of guerrilla warfare. The army regulars who fought in the West endured days of frustration and toil on endless marches followed by moments of terror in sudden, running battles against the elusive enemy.

The same brutal strategy that had speeded the capitulation of the South in the Civil War eventually worked with equal success against the Indians. General William Tecumseh Sherman, who had burned a swath of destruction across the green fields of Georgia, fought the Indians with the same sort of ferocity. Sherman and his successor as western commander, General Phil H. Sheridan, were extraordinarily effective. In 1865 over 270,000 Indians roamed free west of the Mississippi. Within thirty years the army had forced this huge population into the reservation system and brought an end to the conflict.

The Indian Wars of the West were but the final battle of a conflict that broke out almost as soon as Europeans arrived to settle in the Western Hemisphere. This conflict involved a clash of two cultures: one an organized and numerous group with modern technology; the other composed of disparate tribes with a Stone Age culture. The outcome was never in doubt.

Land was the critical issue. The Indians had no more concept of individual land ownership than they had of owning the air they breathed. Their cultivation of land had been haphazard and collective. In contrast, the immigrants arriving from Europe brought with them a deeply rooted tradition of land ownership and division of land into plots that were cultivated by the same families year after year. It was natural for them to organize a system of laws to deed the land of the New World and to use its resources. The native inhabitants of the land were reduced to "occupants" whose relationship to the white possessors was to resemble that of a ward to his guardian.

The tribes were hampered by their inability to see themselves as one race. In many Indian languages, a tribe's own name meant "the people," and the word for all other tribes was some variation of "the enemy." Most of these languages did not include a word, such as "Indian" in English, to denote the race as a whole. While whites made little distinction between such disparate and distant tribes as the Cherokees of Georgia and the Iroquois of the Hudson River area, the difference between tribes was crucial to the Indians.

The European whites considered it their "Manifest Destiny" to expand westward. It was their right to use what God had provided for their progress, and it was their prerogative to remove the Indians who stood in the way of this progress. Unwilling to be assimilated into white civilization, the Indians were dealt with by war, treaty, or a combination of the two. Each time the Indians lost in battle, they were forced to sign a treaty that removed them from the land the whites desired and pushed them farther west. The constant flow of white immigrants demanded more space, and the only direction for expansion was into the western land assigned to the Indians by treaty.

White easterners at first believed that the western plains were a wasteland, and while that belief endured, the plains Indians were left undisturbed. In the mid-nineteenth century mighty warrior and hunter tribes ruled the West, often fighting each other and driving

Preceding pages. U.S. scouts under Major George Forsyth (center, with rifle and pistol) hold out against Cheyenne warriors at Beecher's Island, Colorado, in September 1868.

other tribes from their land. In the 1840s the southern plains of Kansas, Oklahoma, and the Texas panhandle were inhabited by the Cheyenne, the Kiowa, and the Comanche. Farther southwest, near the Arizona and New Mexico border with Mexico, the Apaches dominated. In the north the most warlike of tribes, the Sioux, allied with the Northern Cheyennes, routed weaker tribes such as the Crows and Shoshones. The powerful Sioux held sway over land stretching from the Mississippi River in Minnesota to the Big Horn Mountains of Wyoming in the north and as far south as the Platte and Republican rivers of Nebraska and Kansas.

Soon, though, whites learned there was more to the west than sand and scrub brush. The discovery of gold in California and the Rockies brought thousands of whites westward and radically disrupted Indian life. The Homestead Act of 1862 opened vast areas of farmland to any white pioneer brave enough to claim it. The railroads sliced through the Indians' hunting lands and brought more settlements along their routes. During the Civil War state militia and volunteers of the wartime U.S. Army patrolled the frontier. These men had to face an often explosive situation created by the burgeoning movement of the settlers and miners to the west.

A major episode during the Civil War stands out. Elements of the Cheyenne, Kiowa, Comanche, and Arapahoe tribes had left their Colorado territory reservations to raid the surrounding countryside. On November 29, 1864, Colonel John Chivington and his 700 volunteers rode into the camp of Black Kettle, a Cheyenne chief who had actually sought peace, at Sand Creek in Colorado. The volunteers went on a rampage of killing and mutilation, leaving 133 dead, 105 of them women and children. The memory of Sand Creek hardened the Indians' attitude toward all of the soldiers who wore the blue uniform. The soldiers who followed Chivington's volunteers west were to pay for the atrocity.

Sherman's regular army troops replaced the volunteer forces after the Civil War. The men who came west were a varied lot, and they had enlisted for reasons that were as diverse as their backgrounds. George A. Forsyth, a major during the Indian Wars, recalled a wagon escort that included "a bookkeeper, a farm boy, a dentist, and a blacksmith, a young man of position trying to gain a commission and a salesman ruined by drink, an ivory carver and a Bowery tough." Nearly half were recent immigrants, mainly from Ireland, Germany, and England. Many were illiterate, although a few formed library clubs and literary societies.

They went to an unforgiving country, wild and desolate. Their posts were islands in the ocean of plains, sometimes hundreds of miles away from civilization. If a soldier was lucky, he lived in a wooden barracks and slept on a straw-filled mattress on a wooden-slatted bunk. He kept his possessions in a wooden footlocker or on a single wooden shelf that ran along the length of the barracks wall. Heat came from a cast-iron stove, light from kerosene lamps or candles. Most posts were not so sumptuous. One soldier described his accommodations at Fort Selden, New Mexico, as "huts of logs and round stones, with flat dirt roofs that in summer leaked and brought down rivulets of liquid mud . . . in the winter the hiding place of the tarantula and centipede."

In all cases the food was abominable. Regular fare included salt pork, fried corn mush, beans, coffee, and hardtack or bread, with little variation. The salt pork sometimes arrived full of worms or "yellow with age and bitter as quinine" or so rancid that the meat was sloughing off the fat. The flour often was speckled with weevils. The meals were almost always ill-prepared because the men took turns on cooking detail.

Far from the anticipated glory of the call to arms, a trooper found that his every waking moment was monitored, controlled by incessant bugle calls. Bugles called him to a round of unending toil from reveille at 6:00 A.M., through fatigue duty, drills, and guard duty, to taps at 9:30 at night. He was a captive laborer on faraway posts, employed to construct and maintain telegraph lines and roads, to build and add to his fort, to serve as a logger and water carrier, and to work kitchen and stable details. For these duties, in addition to his main job of policing the West, the private was paid sixteen dollars a month until 1870, when Congress lowered his pay to thirteen dollars.

What amusement relieved their dismal lives they often provided themselves in the form of minstrel shows, ball games, and horse races. A less wholesome but more common recreation was alcohol, the "curse of the army."

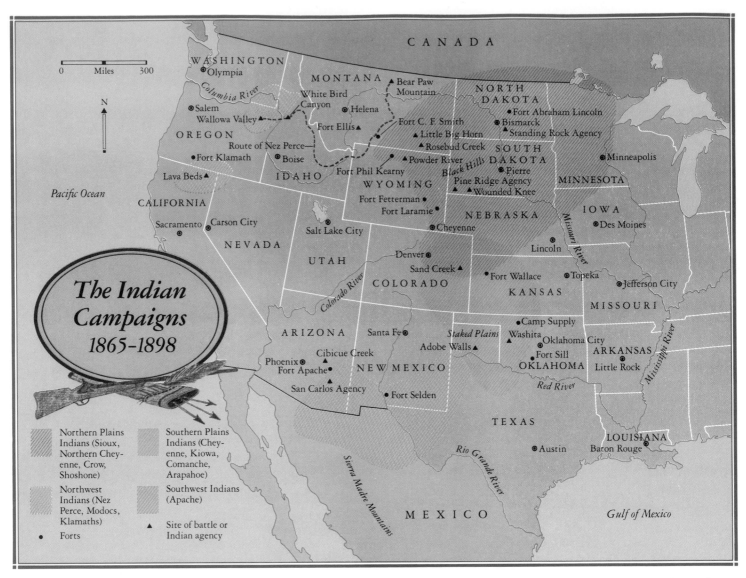

The Indian Campaigns 1865–1898

Northern Plains Indians (Sioux, Northern Cheyenne, Crow, Shoshone)

Northwest Indians (Nez Perce, Modocs, Klamaths)

Southern Plains Indians (Cheyenne, Kiowa, Comanche, Arapahoe)

Southwest Indians (Apache)

● Forts

▲ Site of battle or Indian agency

From remote outposts scattered throughout the region, the U.S. Army set out to conquer the West. Although dozens of Indian tribes lived west of the Mississippi, the army fought its most costly battles against five groups: the Northern and Southern Plains tribes, the Modocs and Nez Perce in the Northwest, and the Apaches along the Mexican border.

Many of the soldiers drank until stuporous at "hog ranches," havens of cheap alcohol and prostitution. An Apache Indian scout and Medal of Honor recipient, whom the records list only by his rank and single name, Sergeant Rowdy, lived up to his name when he pulled out a cocked Winchester during a drunken spree at one of these ranches and was shot to death by the barman. One in twenty-five troopers was hospitalized for alcoholism—which in the army meant the extreme condition of delirium tremens.

If a man extended his drunkenness to his time on duty, he was punished with fines or a reduction in grade. This and other offenses against military discipline were often dealt with severely. Flogging was abolished in 1861 but was occasionally used long after. Until 1870 deserters were branded with the letter D on the thigh. Some officers preferred to mete out their own justice, such as "spread-eagling" a miscreant to four stakes and leaving him to the elements for several hours. Lieutenant Colonel George

Armstrong Custer was known to order offenders to wear heavy vinegar barrels for five to ten days.

Fully one-third of the soldiers in the West deserted the regular army from 1867 to 1891. Eight percent committed suicide. Given the loneliness of their life, their problems with liquor, service under the occasional tyrant NCO or officer, and the low pay, to say nothing of the terrors of warfare against the Indians, it is a wonder so many stayed to do the job.

The job they did was to fight the "hardest kind of war" against a skillful and remorseless opponent. It was fighting marked by long, often fruitless, marches of fifteen miles or more a day through all kinds of terrain and weather. They frequently spent weeks in the field without contact with Indians. When on the march, the regulars modified the issue uniform for pragmatic reasons. In the field, garrison caps were replaced by wide-brimmed hats that blocked the sun. To reduce the discomfort of long hours in the saddle, many cavalry troopers wore buckskin breeches instead of lighter-weight army pants. Moccasins or soft-leather boots replaced the ill-fitting and inflexible boots the army issued. The changes were not a matter of style; they helped to prevent blisters, saddle sores, and sunburn that could take a terrible toll over a long march.

The monotony of life on the trail was unrelieved except by battle. The troopers were not even allowed to break ranks to hunt buffalo, deer, antelope, or any other game. When a fight came, it came quickly and brutally, usually far into the reaches of the frontier wilderness. In such a battle there was no calling for help. The soldiers were cut off, dependent on the reserves they had brought in with them. The Medal of Honor was often earned in such circumstances, especially when small groups fought with little hope of rescue. The bluecoat knew that if he allowed himself to be captured, he would surely face a painful death, often slowly by torture. A maxim of the soldiers was, "Save the last bullet for yourself." They fought hard, and they fought by the rules of the frontier, neither giving quarter nor expecting it.

Culpability for the Indian Wars could often be traced to the actions of the government or of white civilians: Miners moved into Indian territory regardless of treaties forbidding the white man; settlers squatted on their land; white buffalo hunters killed the precious buffalo until there were no more to kill. The agents of the Indian Bureau were often corrupt, cheating the Indian of his rightful due under treaty provisions. The government vacillated, changing policy and abrogating treaties, adapting its actions to political expediency.

It was up to the regular army soldier to clean up the mess. A maximum of 25,000 soldiers fought the wars that others had provoked over 2 million square miles of frontier. The Indian Wars, which included massacres such as Sand Creek and Wounded Knee, represent the darker side of American history, and the soldiers on the western frontier have been stigmatized by the uglier aspects of the job they were sent to do. Brave men often fought in dishonorable circumstances, but that did not diminish the fact of their courage.

By 1890 the Census Bureau declared there was no longer a line of frontier anywhere in the United States. The agent of this change in the West had been the regular U.S. Army. In the quarter-century after the Civil War, the army fought over 1,000 combat actions in twenty-four operations officially designated as wars, campaigns, or expeditions. Nearly all of the Medals of Honor awarded for the Indian Wars were for actions of valor during these western campaigns. ✦

On November 29, 1864, as the American flag and a white flag of truce fly over the Cheyenne and Arapahoe camp at Sand Creek, Colorado, Colonel John Chivington's men swoop in to massacre Black Kettle's peaceful followers.

Winning the West

The army that carried out U.S. policy in the West traveled and fought over great distances. Quartered in Spartan forts and often short of supplies, troopers used horses for transportation to outlying areas. Clockwise, from top left: *The 3d Cavalry pauses during an excursion from Fort Davis, Texas; a unit of pony soldiers leaves Fort Bowie, Arizona, near Apache Pass;* Lieutenant William H. Carter, who earned the Medal of Honor at Cibicue Creek, Arizona, in 1881, poses with natives; a young gallant astride his mount at Camp Cheyenne, circa 1890; near Fort Bayard, New Mexico, men of the 6th U.S. Cavalry train their horses to lie down to provide cover under fire.

Captain Jack's War
Battle in the Lava Beds

In 1872 the army turned its attention to a war in the Pacific Northwest. The Modoc Indians, once powerful hunters, raiders, and slave traders, had been reduced to sharing a reservation in Oregon with the Klamaths, a more numerous enemy tribe who bullied the Modocs and stole their crops. In desperation the Modocs struck out for the freedom of their old hunting grounds.

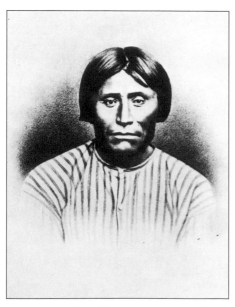

Kientpoos, also called Captain Jack, leader of the Modoc band.

They were known by nicknames like Captain Jack, Hooker Jim, and Scarface Charlie, monikers given them by the white miners who had traveled west in search of gold. They were leaders of a once-noble and plentiful tribe, the Modocs. Now, in late 1872, they led their people back to their ancient homelands near the Lost River, just south of the California-Oregon border. The Indian superintendent there ordered the Modocs back to the reservation in Oregon and called for General Edward R. S. Canby to bring them in. The Modocs fought a small army detachment at Lost River, then killed white settlers as they retreated south to nearby Tule Lake in California.

Thirty-two square miles of volcanic rock formed the lava beds on the south end of the lake. The lava provided a natural fortification of caverns, fissures, passageways, and parapets. The Modocs knew every inch of the labyrinth, which became known as "Captain Jack's Stronghold." Jack boasted that he and

U.S. Army troops prepare to move against Captain Jack's stronghold in the California Lava Beds in early 1873.

his sixty warriors could hold off a thousand soldiers from their fortress.

Colonel Frank Wheaton had gathered a sizable force, though not a thousand. He commanded 225 regulars of the 1st Cavalry and 21st Infantry, together with 100 volunteers from Oregon and California. The men moved to encampments near Tule Lake on the night of January 16, 1873. A dense fog settled in during the night and remained well into the next morning. The soldiers advanced under its cover and walked into an ambush in the nearly impassable maze of jagged rocks and crevices.

Major John Green, a German-born officer known to his men as "Uncle Johnny," commanded a detachment of Wheaton's forces. To cut off the Indians from the water of the lake, Green's men attempted to enter the lava beds in an orderly skirmish line from the west.

Beneath the cover of sagebrush camouflage, however, the Indians moved from position to position in the passages. The soldiers saw the puffs of smoke from rifles, heard the shots and the groans of wounded and dying comrades, but never caught sight of their enemy.

Green's skirmish line rapidly deteriorated as some men moved forward and some took cover, afraid to cross the open ravines. When the fog lifted, several men found themselves in the open with Modocs firing directly above them. Pinned down, they refused to advance.

Green flew into a rage at his own men. As the soldiers hid from the Indians' rifles, Green leaped upon a rock—in clear sight of both his men and the Modocs. The Indians fired at him but he ignored the bullets whizzing past.

Declaring to the men that they had little to fear from the Modoc marksmanship, Green paced back and forth under fire and harangued his soldiers in a profane speech that included references to their character and ancestry. In his anger he slapped his glove into his palm for emphasis. (The Indians later said that they thought Green's glove must have had magical powers to keep him safe from their fire.)

Under Green's inspiration the men finally moved forward but were pinned down again later in the day. They stayed until dark, when they were able to withdraw. Major Green's tirade earned him the Medal of Honor that day. He became the highest-ranking officer to receive the medal during the Indian Wars.

That Battle of the Stronghold was an ignominious defeat for the army, killing eleven of Wheaton's men, and wounding twenty-six. Not a single Modoc was hurt. After the debacle the army replaced Wheaton.

Three months later Captain Jack and the other chiefs asked to negotiate peace with General Canby. During the talks Jack pulled a pistol and shot the general in the face, killing him. After that the Modocs never stood a chance. Reinforcements and cannon were brought in, and the Indians were hunted like animals. Jack and three others were caught and hanged in October of 1873, and the rest of the Modocs were removed to Indian Territory in Oklahoma.   ✴

An Illustrated London News *print shows the harsh terrain of the Lava Beds.*

Clash on the Southern Plains
The Red River

By 1874 the southern Plains Indians—the Kiowas, Cheyenne, and Comanches—had grown increasingly restive on their Oklahoma reservations. Opportunistic traders cheated them. Moreover, white buffalo hunters killed so many animals that the buffalo, mainstay of the Plains Indian's life, began to disappear. Some Indians retaliated by raiding white hunters' settlements, then escaping back to their protected reservations before the hunters could track them down.

On June 27, 1874, a group of Comanche, Kiowa, and Cheyenne raiders led by Lone Wolf attacked a settlement of twenty-eight buffalo hunters at Adobe Walls, Texas. The hunters, with their powerful rifles, beat the Indians badly. In revenge the Indian survivors of the attack went on a rampage of raiding and killing from Texas to Kansas.

When the army moved onto the reservation to separate hostile Indians from peaceful, most of the hostiles left and headed west, to the hunting grounds near the Red River in the Texas panhandle. General Sheridan responded by flooding the area with soldiers. Five columns of soldiers led by five different generals took part in what became known as the Red River War. This huge force surrounded the Indians in an ever-tightening noose.

Colonel Nelson Miles's column of 744 troops fought a decisive battle on August 30 at the Staked Plains deep in the panhandle of Texas. During the course of the fight, Miles chased the Indians over a long stretch of the panhandle and far outstripped his supplies. In the burning heat of a late summer drought, some of the men were so thirsty that they cut themselves to wet their lips with their own blood. Clearly, their lives depended on procuring water and food. Miles ordered Captain Wyllys Lyman to take a detachment of 6th Cavalry and a company of 5th Infantry and ride north to escort a wagon train that was coming from Camp Supply in northern Oklahoma territory.

After several days without word from Lyman, Colonel Miles ordered dispatches carried to Camp Supply, presumably to discover the fate of Lyman and the supply train. He sent six men rather than the usual one or two because of the danger of the mission. In the group were four cavalrymen, Sergeant Zachariah Woodall and Privates John Harrington, George Smith, and Peter Roth. They were accompanied by two civilian scouts, Amos Chapman and Billy Dixon. Each man carried a rifle, a Colt revolver, and 200 rounds of ammunition. They would need it all.

On September 11, the first day of the journey, they traveled nearly fifty miles without incident, but at mid-morning on the twelfth, Chapman caught sight of a large number of horsemen in the distance and assumed that they were a party from Camp Supply. Too late they realized that the riders were Indians. On the treeless, rolling prairie there was no cover so the six men made for a ravine, reaching it just before the Indians could mount a charge. They

Nelson Miles, a Civil War Medal of Honor recipient and army commander in the West.

leaped from their horses to form a skirmish line. Smith took charge of the animals but was shot in the chest almost immediately. The horses stampeded away as he fell. The Indians dismounted and formed a circle around the men. Each time they drew near, the five other men charged madly, firing at the Indians in front of them, while the Indians in the rear held their fire for fear of hitting their own. The men broke through the circle several times, requiring the Indians to re-form. All the while the white men moved toward a nearby hill where there was a shallow buffalo wallow about ten feet across.

The Indians now mounted their horses and attacked with astounding displays of horsemanship. Some rode standing high in the stirrups while firing, then dropped suddenly as if hit and fired again from below their horses' bellies. Others fell to the ground as if they had been shot, then leaped up from behind some tall grass to open fire. Four of the whites were wounded: Woodall was hit in the groin and Harrington in the hip, but both reached the wallow, as did Dixon, who was grazed in the calf, and Roth, who was uninjured. Smith and Chapman lay outside the wallow. The others thought Smith was dead; Chapman's ankle was so badly shot the bone stuck out and his foot dragged uselessly behind him as he crawled toward the others.

Dixon saw Chapman pulling himself inch by inch along the ground. He broke from cover, ran out, and carried him in. The other men dug in with their knives as bullets and arrows tore the dirt around their shallow hole. When their ammunition threatened to run out, they were forced to wait with each shot until

Twenty-Five to One, by Frederic Remington, depicts the ambush of Miles's couriers.

the Indians were almost upon them, to make each bullet count.

In the heat of the afternoon, a thunderstorm arose from the southwest and gathered force, the sky growing blacker every moment. The rain was a blessing, though, for the men were desperately thirsty. From the bottom of the wallow, they drank rainwater mixed with their own blood.

During the storm the Indians withdrew a short distance and tied up their horses. Roth used the respite to retrieve Smith's much-needed ammunition belt and was astounded to see the wounded man twitch. He returned to the wallow, then set out a second time with Dixon to rescue Smith. They carried him back but the valiant effort was in vain. Smith, shot through the lung and begging to be put out of his misery, died during the night. The others propped up his body to make the Indians think that he was still alive.

They decided to divide the ammunition and send the relatively able-bodied Roth and Dixon for help. Roth set out first, in the middle of the night, but was unable to find a trail. When he returned, Dixon waited until dawn and left with only four cartridges in his gun. He had traveled just a mile when he came upon Major Price's 8th Cavalry, who returned with him to rescue his comrades.

The army awarded all six of the men the Medal of Honor but later revoked the awards to the two civilian scouts because by law they were not eligible to receive it. Smith's medal was rare because it was not a common practice to give the medal posthumously during the Indian wars: Only eight such medals were awarded. ✦

Custer's Last Stand
The Little Big Horn

The 1868 Laramie Treaty guaranteed the Black Hills of Dakota Territory to the Sioux as part of their reservation. But when gold was discovered on the land in 1874 white miners entered the reservation illegally. The government attempted to buy the Black Hills, but the Sioux refused to sell land they considered sacred. Many of the Indians left the reservation for Wyoming and Montana, where they joined Indians who had never come into the reservation. In December of 1875 the government delivered an ultimatum to the group's ostensible leader, Sitting Bull: Come into the agency by January 31, 1876, or face war. The Indian ignored the demand and war began.

Lieutenant Colonel George A. Custer, whose impetuosity brought disaster down on him and his men at the Little Big Horn.

The war that was to culminate at a small river called Little Big Horn began when General Sheridan determined to strike quickly and bring the Sioux into the reservation. But a winter campaign in the North proved to be considerably more difficult than one in the South. General George Crook and his men battled snow and cold for three weeks in the field before returning empty-handed and exhausted.

When spring came in 1876, the army pressed on. Three large and mobile columns of troops marched toward eastern Montana to encircle and trap the Indians. In May General Crook pushed north from Fort Fetterman, Wyoming, with more than 1,000 soldiers, and Colonel John Gibbon marched his 5th Infantry east from Fort Ellis, Montana. On May 17 the "Dakota Command" of General Alfred H. Terry left Fort Abraham Lincoln, Dakota Territory, with over 925 men, 700 of whom were troops of the 7th Cavalry under the command of Lieutenant Colonel George Armstrong Custer.

Custer had been the boy wonder of the Civil War. At the age of twenty-five he had been brevetted to Major General. Following the war he took a commission as a lieutenant colonel in the Indian-fighting army and went west, where his long and flowing yellow hair, his buckskin clothing, and his flair for the dramatic caught the attention of the nation's press.

His flamboyance embroiled him in numerous controversies in his ten years in the West, but his penchant for attack and his aggressiveness in seeking battle put him at the heart of the Indian Wars. In the winter campaign of 1868-69 he attacked the village of the unfortunate Black Kettle, victim of the earlier attack at Sand Creek by Colonel Chivington. Custer's rakehell charge left 101 Cheyenne men, women, and children dead

(including Black Kettle and his wife) and was hailed as a victory for Sheridan's policy of a winter war of attrition. Custer thereafter remained one of Sheridan's favorites.

In 1874 Custer led an expedition of 400 civilians and 1,000 soldiers into the Black Hills. Among his reports, Custer sent back word that there was "gold among the roots of the grass." This news brought an influx of miners to the Black Hills, which in turn ignited war.

Crook was the first to encounter the Indians in 1876. On June 17 his column fought a heated battle at Rosebud Creek against a much larger force than he had expected to find. (Later reports of Sioux and Cheyenne strength in the region ranged from 2,500 to 4,500 warriors.) After six hours of heavy fighting, the Indians withdrew. Crook claimed to have won the encounter, but his losses of twenty-eight killed and fifty-six wounded were significant. He was therefore constrained to return to his supply base at Goose Creek, eighty miles to the rear, to await reinforcements.

On the day of Crook's Battle of Rosebud Creek, General Alfred Terry's column was closing in on the Indians from the east. On the twenty-first Terry met with Gibbon and Custer in order to map strategy for the campaign. The focus of attack would be in the area of the Little Big Horn River, where scouts had seen fires from a large Indian village.

The plan called for Gibbon's 5th Infantry and Custer's 7th Cavalry to rendezvous, then attack on June 26. The night of the twenty-fourth Custer led his men to within twenty miles of the Indian encampment and sent out scouts. When they returned to say they had seen dust from the Indian camp, Custer feared the Sioux were escaping. Typically, his reaction was to attack. Rather than wait for the arrival of the slower-moving infantry force, he decided to go ahead

The Indian White Bird painted this view of Custer's defeat. At top left, Custer's unit is trapped north of the Sioux and Cheyenne camp. At right, Reno's and Benteen's columns are besieged by warriors.

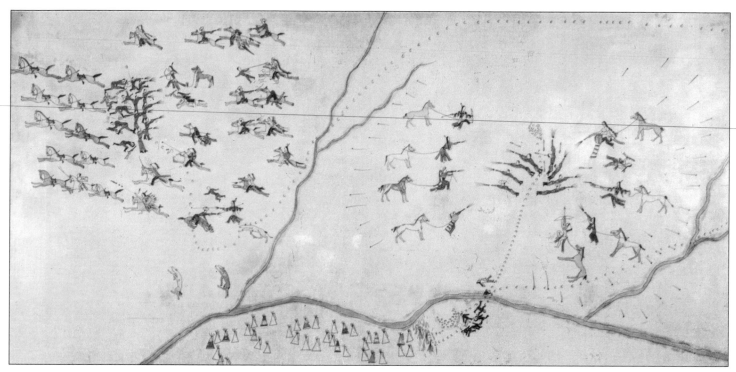

alone on the morning of Sunday, June 25, a day earlier than planned.

He split his forces, sending Major Marcus Reno across the river and into the village from the south with 112 men. Captain Frederick Benteen was to take his 125 men in a wide arc farther west and come in to the village from that direction, while Custer himself would attack from the northeast. It would have taken perfect timing and a great deal of Custer's legendary luck for the plan to succeed, because the 1,200-lodge village contained three times as many Indians as Custer expected to find there.

Reno's attack surprised the Sioux, but they rallied quickly in numbers that threatened to overwhelm his force. Reno ordered his men to dismount and form a skirmish line but resistance proved too fierce. He was slowly forced to withdraw to a cottonwood grove near the banks of the river.

The battle raged through the cottonwood thicket. When the Indians pressed their attack, the major gave the order to remount and cross to the bluffs on the other side of the Little Big Horn. The men crossed the river in a mad, disorganized retreat and struggled up the steep banks. The noise of battle prevented several of the cavalrymen from hearing the order, and they were left stranded on the opposite bank. At the rear of the retreat, several of the officers attempted to mount an orderly defense.

Lieutenant Benjamin Hodgson's leg was broken by a bullet that also brought down his horse, and he cried out for help as he fell. With the Indians firing furiously and closing in on him, Sergeant Benjamin Criswell rode to the rescue. Wheeling his horse around Hodgson, Criswell waited while the wounded man grabbed hold of his stirrup. Criswell then galloped away, dragging the wounded man across the river onto the opposite side. As they reached the bank, though, Hodgson was shot in the head and he fell lifeless. Criswell returned to carry Hodgson's body from the field. He dismounted under fire and threw the lieutenant's body over his horse, then moved among the dead horses on the riverbank, picking up saddlebags full of ammunition before returning to his lines. The Medal of Honor was his reward for performing so coolly under pressure and for the selfless attempt to bring his lieutenant to safety.

After more fighting, Reno's force finally crossed the river and scrambled up a nearby bluff. Of 112 men, three officers and twenty-nine regulars and scouts had been killed, and one officer and 15 men were missing.

Meanwhile, Custer rode parallel to the river until he was opposite the center of the village. According to Indian witnesses of the battle, he was shot in the chest as he led his men across the Little Big Horn. The attack disintegrated, and the troopers retreated to a ridge on the east side of the river, their leader propped up in his saddle for the ride. All

Sergeant Benjamin Criswell, who recovered the body of Lieutenant Hodgson from the banks of the Little Big Horn.

215 of the men were killed in the ensuing battle. It was a bad day for the Custers. Also killed was George's brother Tom, who had received two Medals of Honor for capturing Confederate flags in the Civil War. The Sioux Rain-in-the-Face later claimed that he cut out Tom Custer's heart and bit off a piece of it and spit it in his face to avenge an earlier insult. George's brother Boston, his brother-in-law James Calhoun, and nephew Henry Reed also fell to the Indians in the debacle.

At midafternoon, Benteen's men joined Reno on the bluff. Benteen had failed to reach the Indian encampment because impassable ravines had blocked the westward route. The troopers dug in and dodged sniper fire from the Indians, who shot from higher hills or crawled up the numerous ravines that ran along the hill. It was not until 5:00 P.M. that they attempted to move northward to join Custer's group. By the time the detachment crossed a ridge where they could see the Custer battlefield, the firing they had earlier heard coming from that direction had ceased, and they saw Indians galloping back in their direction.

Reno and his men turned back to the bluff where they had dug in earlier in the afternoon. During the retreat, one of the pack mules, laden with ammunition, became frightened at the firing, broke away from its handler, and started running in the direction of the advancing Indians. Sergeant Richard Hanley jumped up on his horse and rode to head the mule off. It had a good start on him, so it was a long ride, directly into the Indians' line of fire. Even after Hanley had headed it off, the mule continued to elude him by running first one way along the line and then the other. Hanley doggedly pursued the beast, although he was exposed to the Indians' guns like a target in a shooting gallery. His officers shouted for him to give up the effort, but he remained in the open for twenty minutes under a rain of fire until he captured the mule. He brought it and its precious cargo back, to loud cheers from his lines. A Medal of Honor later punctuated those cheers for his gallantry.

After the defeat of Custer, the army pursued relentlessly the Sioux and Northern Cheyenne. The troopers of Colonel Ranald S. Mackenzie and Colonel Nelson Miles campaigned throughout the next winter despite great hardship. By spring nearly all of the fugitives had surrendered. Crazy Horse came in on May 6, 1877. Sitting Bull, however, eluded the soldiers who were hounding him. He took the remnants of his people to Canada, where they lived peacefully but could not find enough to eat. Many of his followers filtered back to the U.S. and to the reservation. Finally, in July of 1881, Sitting Bull followed. When he turned in his rifle to Miles he stated, "I was the last man of my tribe to surrender my rifle." ❖

After years of research, Edgar Paxson
painted this reconstruction of Custer's end.
Custer is at center, in buckskins.

"I Will Fight No More"
The Nez Perce

During the summer and fall of 1877, eastern newspapers were filled with stories about an Indian chief who led his people on a desperate flight from army troops in Oregon, Idaho, and Montana. The chief, named Joseph, was hailed by some as the "Indian Napoleon." In fact, Joseph was a peaceful man who wanted only to return to the land of his birth.

Chief Joseph, leader of the Nez Perce on their doomed 1,700-mile trek to seek safety in Canada.

The Nez Perce were an honorable and respected people who had always lived in peace with the white man. When gold was discovered on their land in the Wallowa Valley of Oregon in 1863, some of the tribe members signed a treaty in which they agreed to leave. Elements of the tribe, however, refused to sign and stayed in their homeland. In May of 1877 the Interior Department requested the army remove the Indians by force if they would not leave peacefully. So began a desperate flight that covered over 1,700 miles.

General Oliver Otis Howard gave Joseph, leader of the Wallowa Valley Nez Perce, an ultimatum: Leave the Wallowa within a month or face war. Chief Joseph left the valley for the assigned reservation, but on June 13 some of his young warriors got drunk, slipped away from camp, returned to the valley, and killed four white settlers. In the next two nights the young warriors killed at least fifteen more whites.

Joseph, knowing that a retaliatory war was now inevitable, gathered his people and pushed east, hoping to escape the army and reach the buffalo hunting grounds on the other side of the Rockies. On the evening of June 16, the Nez Perce camped on the banks of the Salmon River near White Bird Canyon in Idaho. Scouts told Joseph that soldiers were approaching.

In the early morning hours of June 17, Joseph deployed his warriors along the ridges of the hills inside White Bird Canyon. Lieutenant Edward R. Thellar led three groups into the canyon: an advance guard of regulars, a detachment of Oregon volunteers, and a column of ninety soldiers who took up the rear.

They were met by a Nez Perce truce party displaying a white flag. When the volunteers ignored the flag and opened fire, Chief Joseph's warriors returned fire with deadly effect. The volunteers quickly moved to a knoll, but Thellar and his advance guard were trapped under fire in a ravine down below. The column of regulars moved forward into the canyon and set up a skirmish line. Sergeant Michael McCarthy was ordered to take a detail of six men and hold, at all costs, the high, rocky ground to the right.

The Indians pressed forward on foot in a well-organized, relentless attack. The volunteers on the left broke and ran, leaving the left flank of the column exposed. McCarthy, on the right, held his post and continued to fire, but the inexperienced troopers in the column took their cue from the escaping volunteers and turned and ran, leaving Thellar and his advance party cut off at the front. All eighteen of them were soon killed. McCarthy, also abandoned along with his six-man detail, remained in position and beat back an attack.

Meanwhile, Lieutenant William R. Parnell and other officers followed the men who had fled, trying to rally them to counterattack. Parnell led a small detachment to rescue McCarthy and his troops, who were then fighting their way back out of the canyon. By the time the two groups met, two of McCarthy's men had been killed. Parnell organized his and McCarthy's men, a combined force of fourteen, and executed a disciplined retreat toward the mouth of the canyon. During this withdrawal, McCarthy's horse was shot from under him and he became separated from the others. Parnell returned to rescue another man whose horse had been shot, but McCarthy's plight went unnoticed.

McCarthy dashed for a nearby creek where there was a large clump of bushes in which he tried to hide himself. From his cover, he could see the rest of his outfit slowly retreating with Parnell, away from the Indians who were now running past the bushes where he hid.

The contemporary journal Wasp depicted
the Nez Perce as unkempt savages arrayed
against the dashing U.S. cavalry.

McCarthy next saw that a number of Nez
Perce women had moved into the area
and were picking clean the bodies of the
dead soldiers. To his horror, he noticed
that his own boots were sticking out of
the brush and had been seen by one of the
Indian women. He carefully slipped out
of them and crawled farther into the
undergrowth.

Bootless, horseless, and without
ammunition, he waited for nightfall.
When it grew dark, he crawled down the
creek bed and continued into the forest
and mountains. He wandered through
the territory, traveling only at night and
hiding during the day. After three days
of walking, he made contact with the
1st Cavalry at Mount Idaho. His intrepidity was not to go unnoticed. He and
Parnell both received the Medal of
Honor for their bravery at White Bird
Canyon.

Lieutenant Henry Romeyn, who led a
charge against the Nez Perce at Bear Paw
Mountain, Montana, on September 30,
1877.

Amid the bodies of men and horses, Chief Joseph declares an end to his struggle.

For the Nez Perce, the battle represented the beginning of the longest and most desperate odyssey of the Indian Wars. With General Howard in pursuit, the Indians traveled steadily east, winding their way through the Rockies. They fought pitched battles as they crossed Idaho, first at Clearwater, then at the Big Hole River, and finally at Camas Meadows. As expert Nez Perce marksmen covered his withdrawal, Chief Joseph escaped after each of these battles. Often suffering heavy losses, he led the remnants of his people deeper into the Rockies. They crossed the newly opened Yellowstone Park and made their way to Montana, where they fought again at Canyon Creek. General Sherman, alarmed at the Indians' progress, alerted Colonel Nelson Miles to cut off the retreat from the east.

On a cold, clear September 30 Miles's column came upon the trail of the Nez Perce and followed it to Bear Paw Mountain. When the Indian village came into view, Miles ordered the 7th Cavalry, newly replenished after its decimation at the Little Big Horn the year before, to charge directly into the tepees while the 2d Cavalry stampeded the ponies.

The surprise was not total. They had caught the Indians in place, but the Nez Perce were ready to fight. Warriors found cover in deep ravines carved by water into the hillsides and opened fire, concentrating mainly on the officers and NCOs. Within minutes, all of the advancing officers were either dead or wounded. The charge of the 7th faltered as the dead toppled from their horses and the living dismounted to take cover. Seeing that the charge would fail without leadership, Lieutenant Henry Romeyn of the 5th Infantry mounted one of the captured Indian ponies and rode forward into the fray to join the embattled cavalrymen.

Romeyn ordered the troopers to remount and follow him. They tore down a steep hill into the fire of the Indian snipers, and Romeyn led them almost upon the Indians before he was shot. The bullet hit on the right side of his chest, breaking one rib as it entered and another as it exited near his spine. Another shot from the fusillade ricocheted off his shoulder and tore his ear. Sergeant Henry Hogan of the 5th Infantry earned his second Medal of Honor of the Indian Wars by risking his life to rescue Romeyn. He rushed forward, picked up the lieutenant, and carried him from danger. (Hogan's first came for actions in the 1876-77 winter campaign against the Sioux.) Romeyn also received the medal for his courageous charge.

After besieging the camp for five days, Miles negotiated the Indians' surrender. After his three months of keeping the army at bay, Chief Joseph spoke the words that expressed the weariness the Indian felt at trying to defeat an inexorable force: "Hear me, my chiefs! I am tired; my heart is sick and sad. From where the sun now stands I will fight no more forever." ❂

Fighting Apaches
The Pursuit of Geronimo

In 1886 the Apaches were brought permanently within the reservation system—the last Indians to be subdued. They had fought in the Southwest for over three centuries against the white man—first against the Spanish, then the Mexicans and Americans. Under such leaders as Mangas Coloradus, Cochise, Vittorio, and Geronimo, they earned a reputation as feared and cunning guerrilla fighters. More Medals of Honor, nearly half the total for the Indian Wars, were given for actions against the Apaches than against any other tribe.

The Apache leader Geronimo strikes a fierce pose in this 1886 photograph.

The U.S. Army had often forced the Apaches into the reservation at San Carlos, Arizona, between 1871 and 1886, but the Indians had not been easily kept there. Located near Fort Apache in eastern Arizona, San Carlos lay on desert land where farming was difficult at best. The reservation was overcrowded. When rations were short, people went hungry and some starved. For Apaches who left the reservation and became renegades, life offered adventure, riches and livestock from raiding, and a chance to live the old life in hide-outs such as the Sierra Madre Mountains of Mexico. It did not take much coaxing to convince the freedom-loving Apaches to leave San Carlos when they sickened of the rules and regulations of reservation life.

The Chiricahua Apache war chief, Geronimo, was an intermittent resident of San Carlos. Each time he left the reservation, the border towns of Arizona and Mexico trembled. His first major raid occurred when the Chiricahuas were ordered to San Carlos in 1876 and Geronimo refused to comply. He was captured and brought there in shackles. He remained at San Carlos for one year before joining another chief, Juh, in Mexico. After the Mexican army drove them back to the United States, Geronimo and his people lived in relative peace on the reservation—even as the Apaches of Vittorio and Nana rampaged across New Mexico and northern Mexico.

After a fight between renegade Apaches and the army at Cibicue Creek, Arizona, in the summer of 1881, the army increased its presence at San Carlos Reservation. Geronimo, nervous about the number of troops in his midst, left with seventy-four of his followers. He returned to lead a raid that released other Apaches while killing the white police commissioner of the reservation, then headed for the Sierra Madre Mountains.

In September of 1882 General George Crook organized 250 Apache scouts into five companies, put army officers in charge, and sent them into Mexico to find Geronimo. This Indianized U.S. Army was able to enter land in which no American or Mexican white man had previously traveled. The battles fought within their own strongholds induced the Apaches to negotiate. Crook himself went into the mountains and returned the Apaches to the reservation in March of 1884. But, again, the reservation could not hold them.

In May 1885 Geronimo and Nachez, son of the great chief Cochise, and 130 followers again left the reservation for freedom. Crook's border patrols could not prevent the Apaches from raiding back into New Mexico and Arizona, where the citizens were terrified. Meanwhile, the scouts and their officers spent a miserably hot summer and fall giving vain chase through deserts and mountains. Pressure mounted on Crook as the scouts, empty-handed, returned to refit for another attempt.

A new expedition was led by Captain Emmett Crawford in December 1885. This group rode for over a month, subject to the harshest conditions, before a scout found a hostile camp in a Sierra Madre gorge near jagged peaks that formed the so-called Devil's Backbone. At night they struggled down treacherous pathways into the gorge, hoping to surprise the Apaches in their camp. But the braying of Apache mules gave them away. The Apaches scurried into the wilderness before the scouts reached the camp. After burning the empty village and the Apache supplies, they settled down to eat. While they ate, an old woman appeared and told Crawford that Geronimo and Nachez were ready to talk. They arranged a conference for the next day, January 11, 1886.

The meeting was not to take place.

Mexican soldiers who had been trailing the Apaches came upon Crawford's Apache scouts and, believing them to be Geronimo's people, opened fire. Lieutenant Marion Maus of the 1st Cavalry, who spoke Spanish, ran forward with Crawford at his side, shouting for them to stop. The Mexican officers ordered their men to hold their fire, but the Mexican soldiers remained suspicious when they saw the Apaches reloading their rifles. Crawford, Maus, and the Mexican officers proceeded to parlay in the middle of the camp, and it seemed that cooler heads had prevailed. But suddenly a shot rang out, followed by an explosion of fire from both sides. The Mexican officers talking to Maus fell from their horses. Maus scrambled back to the rocks where Crawford had been standing to find that his captain had been wounded in the head. Maus took command, and after a blazing two-hour stand-off, the firing ceased. An uneasy truce gave both sides time to care for their wounded.

Above. *Lieutenant Marion Maus tends the mortally wounded Captain Emmett Crawford.* Left. *A parley between Geronimo (third from left) and General Crook (second from right) in Mexico, March 27, 1886. Lieutenant Maus, with moustache and white hat, is at center.*

The next day the Mexicans summoned Maus for negotiations. He crossed the ridge that separated the two forces only to find the rifles of fifty Mexican soldiers trained on him. They held Maus for six hours until he agreed to let them have some horses to carry their wounded out of the mountains. He was then allowed to return to camp and withdraw with his men.

They started back up the mountain the next morning, carrying on litters Crawford and the other wounded. That first day the climb was so treacherous

Wearing his Medal of Honor, Marion Maus stands for a wedding portrait. The party includes a young officer named John J. Pershing (third row left), later to become the commander of U.S. forces in World War I.

they covered only three miles. After they had stopped for the night, another Apache woman entered the camp to say that Geronimo would negotiate.

As demanded by Geronimo, Maus, scout Tom Horn, and five of the Indian scouts arrived unarmed at the prearranged site. Geronimo and his men, however, were equipped with rifles and bandoliers. When Geronimo asked Maus why he was there, the lieutenant replied, "I came to capture or destroy you and your band." Impressed by his honesty, Geronimo walked over and shook Maus's hand. The two then arranged for a meeting to take place

between General Crook and the Apaches. Maus began a difficult withdrawal north, trying to get the wounded back to the U.S. Crawford died and was buried along the route. After battling a thousand miles of desert terrain, Maus led the remainder of his men into New Mexico. The Medal of Honor would be his for his courage and leadership throughout the bloody attempt to bring in Geronimo.

Crook arranged for the Apaches to return to the San Carlos Reservation at their meeting. But Geronimo, Nachez, and others swilled mescal during the march in and got quite drunk. On the night of March 28, 1886, thirty-five of the Apaches escaped again to Mexico and the Sierra Madre. General Sheridan blamed Crook for the failure to land Geronimo and replaced him with

Nelson Miles, now a brigadier general. Miles then was ordered to capture Geronimo. Doctor Leonard Wood, a Harvard-educated M.D. who had joined the army looking for adventure, told Miles that he believed a hand-picked company of the "right sort of white men" could stay on the trail of the Indians and beat them in their own mountains. Doctor Wood joined Miles's army regulars for the expedition.

Commanded by Captain Henry Lawton, the task force left Fort Huachuca, Arizona, on May 5, 1886, with orders from Miles to "capture or destroy" the Apaches. They crossed over into Mexico and picked up the Apaches' trail, which led toward the mountains. The fleeing Apaches had set fire to everything in their wake, and the smoke and the insects that swarmed away from the blaze added to the misery of the men as they rode through 120-degree temperatures. The Indians used the cover to slip away and split up. Their trail grew increasingly difficult to follow, and the pursuers lost their prey several times. Following one of the larger trails, Lawton's men traveled in a circle taking them back to Arizona, just twenty-five miles from where they had started three weeks earlier.

On May 29, Lawton hoped to send word to Miles of his progress and to request further orders. Twenty-five miles of perilous Apache country lay between Lawton's camp and the telegraph office at Pentano, Arizona. Civilian scouts refused to carry the dispatches unless they were paid an exorbitant fee. Only Dr. Wood was willing to attempt the journey.

Wood had passed the day on a grueling twenty-mile march. That night he rode twenty-five miles to Pentano, losing the trail several times in the darkness. He arrived at Pentano at 10:00 P.M., delivered and received dispatches

Above. *Dr. Wood during the pursuit of Geronimo, 1886.* Right. *Cavalry from Fort Bowie escort Geronimo to exile.*

long enough to lance the festering wound and drain the poison before riding on. Although he eventually collapsed with fever and delirium, he recovered to continue the march.

Just once in two months did they draw close to the Indians. On July 13 they sneaked up on Geronimo's camp, but the Apaches escaped before the army troops could descend upon them. Lawton's men were demoralized by their failure, even though they had captured the camp supplies and many of the Apaches' ponies.

By then, Geronimo and his band were also feeling the effects of the long trek. They were weak and tired, and now they had to face a second group of pursuers, the Mexican army. In late July General Miles sent Lieutenant Charles Gatewood to join Lawton in Arizona. Geronimo trusted Gatewood, and Miles hoped he could convince the renegade Apache to surrender.

Gatewood reached Lawton on August 3, and soon after Geronimo agreed to talk. He apparently hoped for better terms if he were to surrender to the United States rather than Mexico, but Gatewood dashed that hope when he told Geronimo that the Apaches would have to surrender unconditionally and be sent to Florida. Geronimo at first refused but was astounded when he learned that all of his Chiricahua people had already been removed from Arizona to Florida. He now had no choice but to follow them or continue to be hunted. With the Mexicans closing in, he finally agreed to Gatewood's conditions and brought his

while his horse was reshod, then set out for the return journey four hours later at two o'clock in the morning. He arrived in camp at 7:30 A.M., just as the men were deploying to ride out for the day. Wood fell in line and traveled another thirty miles before he was finally able to bed down.

Miles's orders were to travel south in pursuit of Geronimo until the Indian surrendered, so it was back into the scorching heat and choking dust for Lawton's men, many of whom had already endured more than they could take. The march across the rugged Apache territory infested with reptiles and insects began to take its toll. Most of the men who had begun the march had to be replaced during the next two months by troops sent to rendezvous with them along the way.

Wood was bitten on the thigh by a tarantula. He paused occasionally, just

80

The Indian Scouts

Alchesay, one of ten Apache scouts who received the Medal of Honor for the winter campaign of 1872–73.

When Lieutenant Colonel George Crook forwarded twenty-three Medal of Honor recommendations from his campaign against the Apaches in the winter of 1872-73, army officials were incredulous: Included were the names of ten Apache scouts who had served with Crook. The War Department could not believe that all ten Indians had exhibited valor, so it rejected the requests. Crook promptly resubmitted all ten names, stating that the Apaches had in fact merited the medal.

Crook had long been impressed with the tracking and fighting skills of the Apaches; against them, he once said, "regular troops are as helpless as a whale attacked by a school of swordfish." But because the many Apache tribes frequently feuded, Crook was able to recruit men from one tribe to fight against those from another.

While the scouts were not cited for any one particular action, one incident from the Arizona campaign was representative of their contribution that winter. Guided by the scouts, the Americans cornered a group of Yavapai Indians at a cave in the Salt River Canyon. Nantaje, an Apache private who knew the area well, led a group of sharpshooters in a surprise attack at the mouth of the cave. During the battle a Yavapai boy was caught in the crossfire. Nantaje ran from cover and carried the boy to safety. By the end of the day Nantaje and the other scouts had helped rout the Indians in the cave, seventy-six of whom were killed. The place was henceforth known as "Skull Cave."

In March 1875 the War Department reconsidered Crook's request and awarded the Apache scouts Medals of Honor. After that the scouts' paths diverged. One recipient, Alchesay (all the Apache scouts were known by only one name), served with Crook for several more years. In March 1886 he rode with Emmett Crawford and Marion Maus in pursuit of Geronimo (see page 77) and led an advance party to the Apache leader. Two years later he led a group of Apache chiefs to Washington, D.C., where they were received by President Grover Cleveland. Alchesay later returned to Arizona and became a successful cattle rancher.

Other Medal of Honor scouts of Skull Cave faded from the official records. Little or no information exists about such recipients as Chiquito, Blanquet, and Elsatsoosu. The fate of the recipient known only as "Jim" was lost until 1927, when his widow applied for his army pension and reported that he had died almost forty years earlier.

Confusion in the records may also have been responsible for a mix-up in the awarding of a medal. In 1869 the War Department published an order granting the Medal of Honor to Co-Rux-Te-Chod-Ish, also known as Mad Bear, for being wounded by a stray cavalry bullet while chasing an Indian in Kansas. Years later Mad Bear's commanding officer reported that the medal had actually been earned by, and given to, another Indian with a similar name: Co-Rux-a-Kah-Wadde, or Traveling Bear. The error was never corrected.

Apaches near Neuces River, Texas, before embarking for reservations in Florida. Geronimo is seated front row, third from right. At center front is Nachez, Geronimo's cohort.

Apaches near Neuces River, Texas, before embarking for reservations in Florida. Geronimo is seated front row, third from right. At center front is Nachez, Geronimo's cohort.

people, still armed, to Lawton's camp.

The campaign seemed to have drawn to a close, but on August 28 the Mexicans filed out of the mountain wilderness and slowly made their way down to the American camp. The Apaches, alarmed, took up arms and prepared to fight. Some of the regulars began digging in, too, perhaps seeing a chance to avenge Crawford's death at Mexican hands.

Lawton sent Wood and Tom Horn, the scout, to meet the Mexicans. The situation was tense, reminiscent of Crawford's and Maus's predicament seven months before; a single shot could have triggered a bloody incident. The angry Mexicans demanded Geronimo. Wood informed them that the Apache leader would return to the United States. The Mexican leader persisted. He insisted on talking to Geronimo. Wood arranged a meeting. In the tense confrontation that ensued, Geronimo, his pistol drawn, told the Mexican commander that he had surrendered to Lawton and would go north to the U.S. The Mexicans withdrew peacefully.

Dr. Leonard Wood received the Medal of Honor for his role in the capture of Geronimo. It was only the first act of a long and distinguished career. Wood later served as governor-general of the Philippines and as the general of the army on the Joint Chiefs of Staff. In 1920 he nearly became the Republican candidate for the presidency, but lost the nomination to Warren G. Harding.

On September 4, 1886, General Miles met Geronimo at Skeleton Canyon, Arizona, and the Indians returned to the reservation at San Carlos. Again, they were not to stay for long, but this time, the U.S. government held all the cards. When Geronimo and his people boarded a train for Florida, the army band on the platform played "Auld Lang Syne." The regulars who had fought them roared with laughter at the ironic choice of music. They never wanted to see the Apaches again. ❖

Death at Pine Ridge
Wounded Knee

The Ghost Dance religion that sparked the last major conflict of the Indian Wars arose from a mixture of mysticism and hatred for reservation life. The Indian tribes throughout the West believed that a Christlike Indian Messiah had come to teach the Indians a dance that would suspend them in the heavens with their ghost ancestors, where they would be invulnerable as the white man was buried by new earth down below. The Ghost Dance spread like a prairie fire; but to white authorities it posed a threat to the reservation system. By mid-November 1890, anarchy reigned at the Pine Ridge Agency in South Dakota as the Indians defied the agents' orders to stop the dance. The agents called in the army, and over 600 families of the dancers withdrew to far corners of the reservation.

Sitting Bull, whose Sioux people were among the last to resist subjugation by the U.S. Army.

The main act at the Pine Ridge Agency during the winter of 1890-91 was to take place in December by a small stream known as Wounded Knee. Before that, a sideshow played itself out that marked the end of a much longer drama. On December 15, Indian policemen from the Standing Rock Agency, which stood near the border of the two Dakotas, tried to arrest Sitting Bull, mistakenly thought to be a leader of the Ghost Dancers. Sitting Bull, the Sioux medicine man who had led the defeat of Custer fourteen years before, was killed in the melee that followed.

Orders had also been issued for the arrest of Big Foot, chief of the Miniconjous, who decided to join the Oglala Sioux at Pine Ridge with 350 of his people. The 7th Cavalry intercepted them near Wounded Knee Creek in South Dakota. The troops surrounded the Sioux, and the army commander, Colonel James Forsyth, posted small but deadly fifty-rounds-per-minute Hotchkiss cannon on the hills above the camp. At dawn the next morning, Forsyth ordered the Indians to surrender their weapons, and they slowly began to comply. When Forsyth saw the heap of old and broken rifles in the center of the camp he suspected that the Indians were hiding their real weapons. He ordered a thorough search.

While the search proceeded, a medicine man incited the braves to fight, claiming the "powerful medicine" of their ghost shirts would protect them from the soldiers' bullets. A scuffle broke out when a young Indian named Black Coyote protested the seizure of his new Winchester rifle by waving it in the air. There are nearly as many versions of what happened next as there were survivors of the battle that followed. Some of the Indians said that the inexperienced soldiers panicked and fired when Black Coyote waved his weapon. Others

claimed the soldiers fired indiscriminately and without provocation. The officers on the scene, however, reported that the Indians had hidden rifles in the blanket rolls and under women's skirts, and when the soldiers began their search, they pulled the weapons from their hiding places and opened fire.

In the explosive and horrible battle that followed, men clubbed and knifed each other and discharged high-powered weapons at close range. The Indians scattered into surrounding ravines, screaming as they ran. The gunners manning the Hotchkiss guns moved to the attack. Rounds from the rapid-fire cannon cut down men, women, and children as they fled.

A few of the Sioux warriors escaped the first flurry and ran into a ravine that sheltered them from the fire of the cannon. They crawled along in the direction of one of the Hotchkiss guns. When the warriors reached the lip of the ravine they began to pour fire on the crew of the artillery piece. As several of his comrades retreated, Corporal Paul H. Weinert and other soldiers manhandled the gun in the direction of the ravine. Weinert heard his commanding officer, Lieutenant Harry Hawthorne, cry, "Oh, my God." The lieutenant fell wounded and landed on his side. Weinert vowed at that moment, "By God, I'll make them pay for that."

One of Weinert's comrades, Private Joshua Hartzog, rushed to pick up the wounded lieutenant and carry him to safety. Meanwhile, Weinert alone ran the gun farther down the hill to maneuver it into the opening of the ravine. The others in his crew yelled for him to come back, but Weinert paid them no heed. He loaded and fired the single-shot cannon until the gun became too hot to handle. Bullets flew about him. One hit a shell and knocked it from his hand as

Oglala Sioux engage in a Ghost Dance at Pine Ridge. The mystical religion sprang up in the 1890s and spread among many tribes.

he was loading the gun, but fortunately for Weinert the round did not explode. The wheels of his cannon were pocked with bullet holes after the fight but Weinert escaped without a wound. His fire drove the Indians from the ravine.

Weinert, who thought he might be court-martialed for acting independently and ignoring the orders to retreat, was happily surprised when his captain grasped him by the shoulders and said, "That's the kind of men I have in my battery." Weinert not only escaped a court-martial—he was awarded the

highest decoration for a combat action, the Medal of Honor. Hartzog's dash to save the lieutenant merited him a medal as well. And Lieutenant Hawthorne himself was awarded the Medal of Honor for "distinguished conduct" in the battle.

The battle was an ugly affair. The Indians were ragged and hopeless, and many of them were cut down by cannon fire as they fled in panic: 150 of them were killed, including 62 women and children. But some of the warriors fought with an energy only increased by

desperation, and twenty-five soldiers died that day as well. The battle, uneven as it was, brought the same kind of terror to the soldiers as comes to anyone under fire. Some of these men showed great courage in the face of this fear. In all seventeen men were awarded the Medal of Honor for bravery at Wounded Knee and at the fight that followed at Drexel Mission.

When the news of the fight reached the other Indians at Pine Ridge, over 4,000 of them headed for a stronghold fifteen miles to the north of the agency.

The Buffalo Soldiers

The Indians of the West called black troopers "buffalo soldiers" because, it was said, the blacks' hair reminded them of a buffalo's mane. Another possibility for the nickname was the heavy buffalo robes the soldiers wore on winter campaigns. Whatever the origin of the name, black soldiers of the West were regarded by their Indian adversaries as courageous opponents.

Through various campaigns the buffalo soldiers also earned the respect of some of their comrades. Desertion rates were lower and reenlistments higher in the all-black 9th and 10th Cavalry and 24th and 25th Infantry than in white units. Many black soldiers considered the army a chance for economic advancement and respect, so the soldiers were well disciplined and took pride in their profession. Their white officers, who at first had feared that appointments to black regiments might harm their careers, swore by them and considered them excellent soldiers. A few specifically asked to be assigned to black units.

Despite the esteem of their own white commanders, the black soldiers faced racism from others. The army sent them for long stretches to the most remote and least desirable posts. Segregation from white troops was strictly enforced: Many officers ordered the "nigger troops" not to form up close to their white men. Major Eugene Carr took a lower rank with a white unit rather than be assigned to a black regiment. (Ironically, the buffalo soldiers saved Carr's life in a fight at Beaver Creek, Colorado, in 1868.)

Few black soldiers who fought Indians were formally recognized for valor, though they were in the thick of combat and by most accounts conducted themselves admirably. Yet only fourteen black soldiers in all four regiments received the Medal of Honor in over twenty-five years of fighting on the frontier. By contrast, the white soldiers of the 8th Cavalry who saw similar action received eighty-four medals. Men in the white 1st Cavalry received thirty.

The black soldier was never embraced by white society after military service. Sergeant Brent Woods, a former slave who earned the Medal of Honor for actions against the Apaches in New Mexico, is an example. After receiving an honorable discharge in 1902, Woods returned to his native Pulaski County, Kentucky, where he died in 1906. He was buried in an unmarked grave and forgotten for almost eighty years. But through the efforts of Medal of Honor historians, Woods's grave was located, and his remains were moved to a new grave site with a headstone appropriate for a Medal of Honor recipient. In 1984 the army gave Brent Woods a full military funeral, seventy-eight years after his death.

"Buffalo soldiers" of the 10th Cavalry in Montana, 1894. Only one black man from this regiment, Sergeant William McBryar, received the Medal of Honor.

On December 30 they trapped a contingent of the 7th Cavalry at Drexel Mission on the reservation, but the whites were rescued by the "Buffalo Soldiers" of the all-black 9th Infantry, which had marched all night to relieve them. The short-lived rebellion ended on January 15 when General Miles slowly closed a ring of 3,500 soldiers around the Indians' camp at the far reaches of Pine Ridge.

The Ghost Dancers were brought back to the agency, where they lined the ridges in mute witness as the 7th Cavalry and the 9th Infantry, among others, marched in review past General Miles. The winter wind howled and stirred up yellow dust that nearly obscured the view, but the march continued.

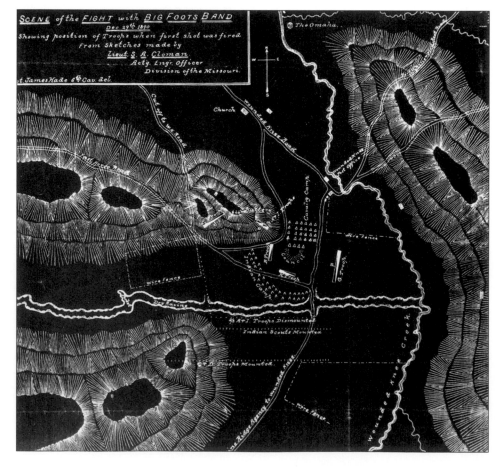

Top. *Army troops exchange fire with Sioux braves during the fight at Wounded Knee on December 29, 1890. Because of the army's superior firepower, Sioux deaths outnumbered the soldiers' six to one. Above. Corporal Paul Weinert (behind gun) and fellow gunners of the 1st Artillery pose with a Hotchkiss gun. Right. An army map shows the scene of the massacre. Devastating cannon fire from the surrounding hills cut down scores of Indians while cavalry troops swept into the Sioux camp.*

Charles G. Seymour, a correspondent for *Harper's Weekly*, wrote of the spectacle:

The column was almost pathetically grand with its bullet-pierced gun-carriages, its tattered guidons, and its long lines of troopers and foot soldiers facing a storm that was almost unbearable. It was the grandest demonstration by the army ever seen in the West; and when the soldiers had gone to their tents, the sullen and suspicious Brules [a Sioux tribe] were still standing like statues on the crests of the hills.

They were witness to the end of an era. The Indians had felt the power that General Miles displayed in this march, a power they no longer had the means to fight. ◈

Below. *The frozen corpse of Big Foot lies in the snow after the Wounded Knee massacre.* Bottom. *Soldiers load Indian bodies onto a wagon in preparation for a mass burial.*

The Wars of American Expansion

America Ascendant

Two towering figures of the era of American expansion: Alfred Thayer Mahan and Theodore Roosevelt.

The U.S. Army's Indian-fighting operations on the western frontier of America reflected one of the nation's main concerns in the latter half of the nineteenth century. For decades after the Civil War, those concerns remained exclusively domestic: the winning of the West, the ever-accelerating industrialization of the North, the Reconstruction of the South. The United States did not possess a single overseas territory, nor did it desire any. American foreign policy sought only two traditional aims, enforcing the Monroe Doctrine forbidding the extension of European power in the Western Hemisphere and defending the right of American citizens to conduct lawful trade throughout the world.

The republic's priorities were reflected in the experience of its navy. During the Civil War the U.S. Navy had become perhaps the most powerful in existence. At the close of the conflict it had 671 vessels in commission, 71 of them ironclads at the forefront of naval technology. Its demobilization was drastic. By 1870 the number of vessels in service had dropped to fifty-two, mostly full-rigged, wooden ships whose steam engines were viewed as auxiliary power. For the next twenty years it would remain at best a third-rate navy, inferior to those of all the great powers and many middling powers as well.

Yet this antiquated little navy was adequate to perform the missions Congress intended it for. Ruling the waves had never been among them. In the event of war, the navy was not to engage the enemy's fleet, but to attack his merchant shipping, as it had in the Revolution and the War of 1812. In time of peace, it was to protect American lives and property in unruly areas of the globe and to promote the growth of American commerce and trade.

The Korean expedition of 1871, which led to the first award of the Medal of Honor for overseas combat operations, was meant to serve both these conventional, peaceful purposes. The "Hermit Kingdom" of Korea was the last Asian land with which the United States had not established diplomatic relations. The desirability of such contacts had been demonstrated several years earlier by the massacre of the crew of an American trading ship. It was thought that diplomatic relations might avoid such incidents in the future. Accordingly, Rear Admiral John Rodgers's Asiatic Squadron was detailed to carry Frederick F. Low, U.S. minister to China, to Seoul to open negotiations. When small boats sent to survey the channel to the city were fired upon by shore fortifications, Rodgers gave the Koreans ten days to apologize. Their refusal to oblige was followed by the landing of a brigade of sailors and marines. In two days' fighting, the offending fortifications were captured and destroyed. The expedition then departed, conscious of the failure of its mission and the rectitude of its actions. A treaty was not negotiated until 1882.

More than a quarter-century would pass before another Medal of Honor was granted for a combat action abroad. By then, America had turned its attention to the outside world. There were many reasons for this. One was the wave of imperialism that arose in Europe in the late 1870s. Colonies, it was claimed, were profitable; colonies were prestigious; colonies were strategic; colonies were romantic; colonies were a Christian duty. By the 1890s large numbers of Americans, many holding influ-

Preceding pages. The U.S. Asiatic Squadron under the command of Commodore George Dewey destroys the Spanish fleet in Manila Bay, the Philippines, May 1, 1898, in the early days of the Spanish-American War.

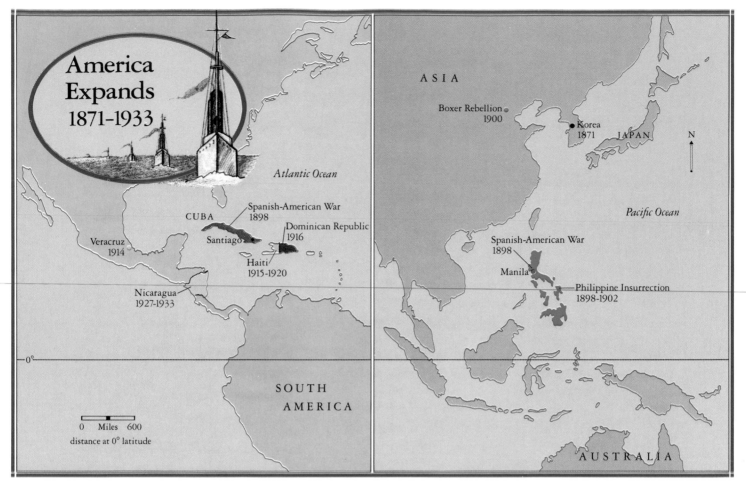

America's international involvements during the expansion era centered on the Caribbean region and the Pacific rim of Asia. In the Caribbean (left), U.S. forces saw action in Cuba, Haiti, the Dominican Republic, Nicaragua, and the Mexican city of Veracruz. Halfway around the world (right), a brief incident in Korea was followed by a war in the Philippines, first against the Spanish, then against native insurgents. American troops in China joined forces with armies of other nations in the relief of the besieged Peking legations during the Boxer Rebellion.

ential positions, had embraced the imperialist argument. Their susceptibility may have been heightened by the closing of the western frontier, which had disappeared by the beginning of the decade. Some historians have concluded that, psychologically attuned to endless expansion, Americans sought a new frontier beyond the seas.

Also important in molding opinion was the unofficial public relations campaign conducted by naval officers to convince their countrymen that a strong navy was necessary to protect the foreign trade that was in turn necessary to the national well-being. By far the most important naval publication was Captain Alfred Thayer Mahan's analysis of *The Influence of Sea Power Upon History, 1660-1783,* which appeared in 1890. Mahan used the long maritime struggle between Britain and France as a test case to develop certain supposedly timeless "principles" of naval warfare. Applied to the United States, his principles clearly called for the renunciation of the strategy of commerce raiding; the construction of a powerful battle fleet capable of defeating an enemy to win "command of the sea"; and the acquisition of colonial naval bases.

The American outlook was also affected by events abroad. Brazil purchased a British-built armored cruiser that was adjudged an even match for the entire U.S. Navy, provoking Congress in 1886 to authorize the first two American battleships. In 1889 a dispute over the right to establish coaling stations in the Samoan Islands led to serious friction with Germany. Then in 1890 the deaths of three bluejackets (as the navy's enlisted men were known) in a brawl in Valparaiso brought the United States close to war with Chile, whose fleet Americans were shocked to learn was superior to their own. Thereafter, the quickening of interest in the overseas world was paralleled by an expansion of the navy. By 1898 the United States had six battleships in commission and five more in the yards.

While these developments set the stage for the nation's entry into the Spanish-American War, they were not directly responsible for it. The two principal causes of the conflict were external. The first was the brutality of the methods by which Spanish colonial authorities sought to suppress the revolution that began in Cuba in 1895, methods that outraged the American sense of humanity. The second was the mysterious explosion of the battleship

$50,000 REWARD.—WHO DESTROYED THE MAINE?—$50,000 REWARD.

EDITION FOR GREATER NEW YORK.

NEW YORK JOURNAL
AND ADVERTISER.

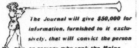

The Journal will give $50,000 for information, furnished to it exclusively, that will convict the person or persons who sank the Maine.

The Journal will give $50,000 for information, furnished to it exclusively, that will convict the person or persons who sank the Maine.

NO. 5,572. — Copyright, 1898, by W. R. Hearst.—NEW YORK, THURSDAY, FEBRUARY 17, 1898.—16 PAGES. — PRICE ONE CENT in Greater New York and Jersey City. Elsewhere Two Cents.

DESTRUCTION OF THE WAR SHIP MAINE WAS THE WORK OF AN ENEMY.

$50,000!
$50,000 REWARD!
For the Detection of the Perpetrator of the Maine Outrage!

The New York Journal hereby offers a reward of $50,000 CASH for information FURNISHED TO IT EXCLUSIVELY, which shall lead to the detection and conviction of the person, persons or government criminally responsible for the explosion which resulted in the destruction, at Havana, of the United States war ship Maine and the loss of 258 lives of American sailors.

The $50,000 CASH offered for the above information is on deposit with Wells, Fargo & Co.

No one is barred, be he the humble but misguided seaman eking out a few miserable dollars by acting as a spy, or the attache of a government secret service, plotting, by any devilish means, to revenge fancied insults or cripple menacing countries.

This offer has been cabled to Europe and will be made public in every capital of the Continent and in London this morning.

The Journal believes that any man who can be bought to commit murder can also be bought to betray his comrades. FOR THE PERPETRATOR OF THIS OUTRAGE HAD ACCOMPLICES.

W. R. HEARST.

Assistant Secretary Roosevelt Convinced the Explosion of the War Ship Was Not an Accident.

The Journal Offers $50,000 Reward for the Conviction of the Criminals Who Sent 258 American Sailors to Their Death. Naval Officers Unanimous That the Ship Was Destroyed on Purpose.

$50,000!
$50,000 REWARD!
For the Detection of the Perpetrator of the Maine Outrage!

The New York Journal hereby offers a reward of $50,000 CASH for information FURNISHED TO IT EXCLUSIVELY, which shall lead to the detection and conviction of the person, persons or government criminally responsible for the explosions which resulted in the destruction, at Havana, of the United States war ship Maine and the loss of 258 lives of American sailors.

The $50,000 CASH offered for the above information is on deposit with Wells, Fargo & Co.

No one is barred, be he the humble but misguided seaman, eking out a few miserable dollars by acting as a spy, or the attache of a government secret service, plotting, by any devilish means, to revenge fancied insults or cripple menacing countries.

This offer has been cabled to Europe and will be made public in every capital of the Continent and in London this morning.

The Journal believes that any man who can be bought to commit murder can also be bought to betray his comrades. FOR THE PERPETRATOR OF THIS OUTRAGE HAD ACCOMPLICES.

W. R. HEARST.

POWDER MAGAZINE

NAVAL OFFICERS THINK THE MAINE WAS DESTROYED BY A SPANISH MINE.

George Eugene Bryson, the Journal's special correspondent at Havana, cables that it is the secret opinion of many Spaniards in the Cuban capital that the Maine was destroyed and 258 of her men killed by means of a submarine mine, or fixed torpedo. This is the opinion of several American naval authorities. The Spaniards, it is believed, arranged to have the Maine anchored over one of the harbor mines. Wires connected the mine with a powder magazine, and it is thought the explosion was caused by sending an electric current through the wire. If this can be proven, the brutal nature of the Spaniards will be shown by the fact that they waited to spring the mine until after all the men had retired for the night. The Maltese cross in the picture shows where the mine may have been fired.

Hidden Mine or a Sunken Torpedo Believed to Have Been the Weapon Used Against the American Man-of-War---Officers and Men Tell Thrilling Stories of Being Blown Into the Air Amid a Mass of Shattered Steel and Exploding Shells---Survivors Brought to Key West Scout the Idea of Accident---Spanish Officials Protest Too Much---Our Cabinet Orders a Searching Inquiry---Journal Sends Divers to Havana to Report Upon the Condition of the Wreck. Was the Vessel Anchored Over a Mine?

BY CAPTAIN E. L. ZALINSKI, U. S. A.

(Captain Zalinski is the inventor of the famous dynamite gun, which would be the principal factor in our coast defence in case of war.)

Assistant Secretary of the Navy Theodore Roosevelt says he is convinced that the destruction of the Maine in Havana Harbor was not an accident.

The Journal offers a reward of $50,000 for exclusive evidence that will convict the person, persons or Government criminally responsible for the destruction of the American battle ship and the death of 258 of its crew.

The suspicion that the Maine was deliberately blown up grows stronger every hour. Not a single fact to the contrary has been produced.

Captain Sigsbee, of the Maine, and Consul-General Lee both urge that public opinion be suspended until they have completed their investigation. They are taking the course of tactful men who are convinced that there has been treachery.

Washington reports very late that Captain Sigsbee had feared some such event as a hidden mine. The English cipher code was used all day yesterday by the naval officers in cabling instead of the usual American code.

92

William Randolph Hearst's newspapers fanned the flames of war after the destruction of the battleship Maine *in Havana Harbor on February 15, 1898. Modern research blames the explosion on a fire in the ship's coal bunker that spread to a weapons magazine.*

U.S.S. *Maine* while it was on a good-will visit to Havana on February 15, 1898. Recent research indicates that the explosion was accidental, but at the time almost everyone assumed that the ship had been destroyed by the dastardly dons. At once the cry went up, "Remember the Maine! To hell with Spain!" William Randolph Hearst, especially, inflamed national opinion in his newspapers. President McKinley attempted to brake the rush to war, instructing Ambassador W. L. Woodford to warn the Spanish government that only its promise to free Cuba could avert hostilities. On April 9, after weeks of negotiation, Woodford extracted the promise. It was too late. Under intense pressure, McKinley submitted a war message to Congress two days later.

The fighting in Cuba lasted slightly more than four months. Everywhere, at El Caney, San Juan Hill, and Santiago, American arms were victorious. In the Pacific, Commodore George Dewey's fleet destroyed the Spanish Philippine squadron in a single engagement. The conduct of operations in many instances was amateurish in the extreme, but this would not become public knowledge until long afterward. In 1898 a jubilant country agreed with Secretary of State John Hay: It had been "a splendid little war."

Victory over Spain laid the foundation of the American empire. Cuba, officially promised independence at the outbreak of war, received it in 1903 but under conditions that made the island an American protectorate. The U.S. also retained all the other Spanish colonies, Puerto Rico, Guam, and, after heated debate, the Philippines. It was in celebration of the annexation of the latter that Kipling wrote "The White Man's Burden," congratulating America on shouldering her imperial responsibility. But the new empire spread beyond the territories won from Spain. It also included Hawaii, annexed during the war; Wake Island, claimed in 1899; and several of the Samoan Islands, divided with Germany in 1900.

Almost at once, Americans were reminded that empires were held together by blood. Insurrections broke out in the Philippines and Samoa in 1899. A year later in China the antiforeign uprising known as the Boxer Rebellion found U.S. troops fighting beside Europeans and Japanese troops in both the defense and the relief of the legations at Peking. The Samoan skirmish lasted only a few weeks and foreign forces made quick work of the Boxers. The suppression of the Filipino *insurrectos,* though, took two years and cost more American lives than the war with Spain. Nor was it the end of the trouble in the Philippines. The assertion of U.S. authority over the fierce Moro tribesmen of the southern islands would require more than a decade of intermittent campaigning.

Grisly reports of the war in the Philippines reinforced the views of a vocal minority of Americans opposed to empire but did nothing to check the nation's rise to world power. In 1901 an assassin's bullet brought an early end to McKinley's second term and Theodore Roosevelt, the hero of San Juan Hill, succeeded to the presidency. The effects of his seven years in office were momentous. A former assistant secretary of the navy and disciple of Mahan, Roosevelt was the first president to believe that the United States should play an active role in international affairs. His policy, he said, was to "walk softly and carry a big stick." The big stick he had in mind was the U.S. Navy, which he set out to make second only to that of Great Britain, traditional mistress of the seas.

Primarily to permit the rapid concentration of the fast-growing fleet in either ocean, Roosevelt resolved to build a canal across Central America. The Colombian province of Panama, where the French had made a start, was chosen as the site. When the Colombian senate rejected Roosevelt's canal treaty, he responded by underwriting a revolution that gave Panama its independence and the United States its canal. Work began in 1904 and was completed ten years later.

The canal increased America's strategic stake in the Caribbean. Indirectly threatening that stake was the propensity of regional governments to default on their debts to European investors, a standing invitation to intervention. Roosevelt took characteristically vigorous preemptive action in 1904 by proclaiming a corollary to the Monroe Doctrine. It stated that the United States had assumed the role of hemispheric policeman. The European powers would have no pretext for intervention; in the case of "chronic wrongdoing" Uncle Sam would take charge.

For the next quarter-century the Roosevelt Corollary provided the basis for repeated interventions in the Caribbean and Central America. Americans called them "banana wars" after the fruit they associated with the region. Roosevelt himself made little use of his corollary. He invoked it only once, in 1905, to accept the debt-ridden Dominican Republic's offer to give American officers control of the collection and disbursement of its customs revenues. (He also reoccupied Cuba from 1906 to 1909 to break what he called "the insurrectionary habit," but that was permitted by the American-authored Cuban constitution.) In 1912 his successor, William Howard Taft, landed marines to put down a revolution in Nicaragua and left a 100-man legation guard in Managua. Two years later Woodrow Wilson, an anti-imperialist whipsawed by his determination "to teach the South American republics to elect good men," began the most extensive interventions of any president by landing troops at Veracruz, Mexico. In 1915 the disintegration of the Haitian government prompted him to send in the marines, initiating an occupation that would last nineteen years. The Dominican Republic was brought into the fold under similar circumstances the following year.

Soon thereafter events in the Caribbean were eclipsed by America's entry into World War I. When in 1919 an uprising in Haiti recalled attention to the region, the mood of the country had changed. Warren Harding's campaign promise to end "bayonet rule" in the Caribbean was applauded. Disillusioned by the outcome of their attempt to make the world safe for democracy, most Americans were ready to leave their neighbors to their own devices. The administration of Haiti was reorganized to speed the black republic's progress toward independence in 1922. The marines were withdrawn from the Dominican Republic in 1924; the Managua legation guard followed in 1925.

Ironically, only two years later civil war in Nicaragua drew the United States into its most controversial banana war. The intervention never became a full-blown occupation, however, and did more to reinforce than retard the trend toward disengagement. In 1933 President Franklin D. Roosevelt inaugurated his "Good Neighbor Policy" toward the Latin American lands. A few months later the United States formally renounced the right to intervene in their affairs, nullifying the earlier Roosevelt's corollary. The last marine units left Nicaragua in 1933 and the occupation of Haiti was terminated in 1934. That same year the Philippines were granted commonwealth status

and promised independence in 1946. The wars of expansion were over.

The motives that gave rise to these conflicts were primarily strategic and ideological rather than economic. McKinley found his answer to the question of whether to annex the Philippines in prayer. In the Caribbean, Roosevelt and Taft acted to promote stability, not to enrich investors. Wilson emphasized an additional purpose, the development of democracy. No doubt all three realized that an orderly, revolution-free Caribbean would be to the advantage of American business, but that realization did not dictate their policies. There was no significant American investment in Haiti, where the marines stayed the longest; and in Mexico, where there was a huge investment, Wilson acted in opposition to the wishes of the investors, helping to overthrow a president they wanted him to support.

In hindsight it is easy to see that the interventions failed to achieve their objective. American hopes centered on the creation of efficient, apolitical armed forces–the *Gendarmerie d'Haiti,* the *Guardia Nacional Dominicana* and, in Nicaragua, the *Guardia Nacional*–trained and during their formative years led by U.S. Marines. These forces were supposed to stabilize the operation of the democratic process in their countries by precluding the losers' customary resort to revolution. It did not work that way. Where the forces provided stability they did so, at the expense of democracy, as the instruments of dictatorship. The Dominican *guardia* produced Rafael Trujillo; the Nicaraguan, Anastasio Somoza.

The failure did not stem from lack of effort. American rule was paternalistic and often patronizing but almost painfully well-intentioned. The marines did more than chase rebels and train troops. They set an example of honest administration, built roads and schools, and undertook extensive programs of public health and sanitation. Materially, the occupied lands benefited from their presence. Weighed against the loss of independence, however, the Caribbean peoples found the improvement insubstantial. Perhaps a Haitian put it best in a conversation with a marine officer who remarked that Haiti would be glad to see the Americans go. The Haitian agreed. "We know that you have helped us in many ways," he added, "and we appreciate that. But, after all, this is our country and we would rather run it ourselves." ◈

Left. *San Juan Hill, east of Santiago, Cuba, scene of the climactic battle of the Spanish-American War on July 1, 1898. Below. Lieutenant Colonel Theodore Roosevelt and his 1st U.S. Volunteer Cavalry, the "Rough Riders," atop San Juan Heights after the battle.*

Building a World Fleet

The projection of American forces overseas was predicated upon the construction of a large ocean-going fleet. During the first years of the twentieth century American naval power expanded dramatically. Right. A hand-colored postcard shows the U.S.S. Indiana in a bird's-eye view of the Brooklyn Navy Yard. Far right, top. President Theodore Roosevelt, standing by a gun turret, exhorts the crew of the U.S.S. Connecticut at Hampton Roads, Virginia, February 22, 1909. Far right, middle. The launching of the U.S.S. South Dakota at Union Iron Works, San Francisco, July 21, 1904. Bottom. The U.S. Atlantic Fleet off Hampton Roads in December 1907; the lead ships are the U.S.S. Kansas and U.S.S. Vermont. Below. A Japanese postcard commemorating the visit of the Great White Fleet to Japan in 1908. The stop was part of the fleet's 46,000-mile round-the-world tour.

B. E. View of Brooklyn Navy Yard. U. S. S.

Dry Dock.

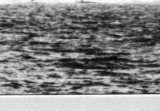

First Stand in Asia
Korea 1871

The first conflict of the wars of expansion took place in the Far East. It resulted from the dispatch of a naval force to convey a diplomatic mission under Frederick F. Low to the "Hermit Kingdom" of Korea. Unfortunately, the Koreans preferred to remain hermits.

On the afternoon of May 30, 1871, five ships of the U.S. Asiatic Squadron, Rear Admiral John Rodgers commanding, entered the Boisee Anchorage on the western coast of Korea. The next day they were fired on by Korean forts. A survey of the Korean positions on June 1 discovered three principal fortifications, some with satellite works, built along the western shore of the river channel on the island of Kanaghwa-do. It also established that the channel was too dangerous for the squadron's three big ships. This eliminated any possibility of shelling the forts into submission. They would have to be stormed.

For this purpose, a naval brigade of sailors and marines was organized under the orders of Commander Lewis A. Kimberly. Commander Silas Casey's bluejacket battalion, 542 strong, was drawn from the vessels that could not enter the channel—Admiral Rodgers's flagship (the screw frigate *Colorado*) and the sloops *Alaska* and *Benicia.* It included an artillery detachment of seven twelve-pound howitzers. The much smaller marine battalion consisted of 100 men led by Captain McLane Tilton. Fire support was to be provided by the gunboats *Monocacy* and *Palos.* Overall command of the operation was entrusted to Commander Homer C. Blake.

Early on the morning of Saturday, June 10, bluejackets and marines began boarding the twenty-two open boats in which the *Palos* was to tow them into action. The expedition left the anchorage around ten o'clock. Admiral Rodgers's orders were precise. The *Monocacy* was to engage the first fort. As soon as the Korean guns had been silenced, the brigade would land abreast of the work, the marines in the lead.

The *Monocacy's* part of the program went without a hitch, but Commander Blake decided to make the landing on a likely looking plain 800 yards downstream from the fort. Greatly to the men's disgust, the plain proved to be a knee-deep mud flat, through which they foundered grimly, leaving shoes and socks behind; the howitzers sank up to their axles. Once ashore, Captain Tilton formed his muddy little battalion into skirmish order and led it toward the fort. The garrison promptly departed and the marines entered unopposed, ending offensive operations for the day. It was four o'clock before the last howitzer had

The gunboat Monocacy *(left) and screw tug* Palos *sail into a channel near present-day Inchon to provide covering fire for sailors and marines attacking Korean forts in June 1871.*

Above. *Sailors atop the first Korean fort on June 10, 1871.* Left. *Korean corpses strew a position near the Citadel.*

while the brigade deployed, marines on the left. Happily, the volume of the Koreans' fire was exceeded only by its inaccuracy. One marine was killed, whereas Captain Tilton estimated that his men dropped at least forty of the fort's defenders. After four minutes, Casey gave the order "Charge!"

The Koreans awaited the assault, singing what seemed to their assailants to be "melancholy songs." When there was no longer time for them to reload their muskets, the Koreans began rolling stones down into the storming party. A company of bluejackets led the rush up the slope. At its head was Lieutenant Hugh W. McKee, whose father, an army colonel, had been killed in the Mexican War. Scrambling over the rampart, McKee dropped into the fort, closely followed by Boatswain's Mate Alexander McKenzie, Quartermaster Samuel F. Rogers, and Ordinary Seaman William Troy. The Koreans swarmed over them in hand-to-hand fighting. McKee was speared; McKenzie went down with a sword cut to the head, and Rogers and Troy were seriously wounded.

been manhandled to firm ground, and Commander Kimberly concluded that the hour was too late to continue.

Sunday morning a marine drummer beat reveille at four o'clock. The *Palos* had struck a rock, so today the brigade would be supported by the *Monocacy* alone. She steamed ahead to shell the second fort as the troops moved out. The approach of the marines again sufficed to put the garrison to flight, and the column pushed on, dragging its guns across broken ground, the contours of which reminded one officer of a choppy sea. Half a mile down the path, white-robed Koreans appeared on the ridges to the left. Commander Kimberly

assigned five guns supported by three companies of bluejackets to guard that flank. The rest of the brigade, some 350 men, continued toward the last and largest of the forts.

This work, christened the Citadel, stood on a conical hill 150 feet high. Above it flew a giant yellow standard inscribed with characters proclaiming the presence of O Chae-yon, governor of Kanaghwa-do. At the crest of a hill 150 yards from the fort, the brigade was greeted by a fusillade that proved these Koreans intended to fight. The two howitzers that had been brought forward slammed into action, and the *Monocacy*'s eight- and nine-inch guns chimed in

Below. *Corporal Charles Brown, Private Hugh Purvis, and Captain McLane Tilton (left to right) aboard the U.S.S.* Colorado *with a flag captured at the Citadel.*

Even as McKee's little band was being overwhelmed, their comrades were clambering into the fort. Ship's Carpenter Cyrus Hayden, the blue-jackets' color bearer, planted his flag on the wall. A Korean leveled a matchlock musket at Private Michael McNamara. McNamara wrenched it out of the man's hands and clubbed him to death with it. Quartermaster Frederick Franklin took command of McKee's company. Private John Coleman tried to reach the wounded McKee, whom the Koreans were dragging into their ranks. They were too many for him, but Coleman did succeed in rescuing McKenzie. By then the superiority of the Americans' weapons had begun to tell and the Koreans were falling back toward the eastern face

Below. *Landsman William Lukes (center) battles Koreans over the fallen Lieutenant Hugh McKee.*

of the fort. Two marines, Corporal Charles Brown and Private Hugh Purvis, darted forward and hauled down the governor's standard. These six men and those in McKee's party were all to be awarded the Medal of Honor for their gallantry at the Citadel.

A member of McKee's company, German-born Landsman William F. Lukes, a twenty-four-year-old cook, saw a group of Koreans carrying his officer down the eastern side of the hill. Cutlass in hand, he ran toward them, shouting for others to follow. Seamen Seth Allen and Patrick Murphy responded to his call. All three were cut down with swords and spears in a short, savage encounter, but the Koreans dropped Lieutenant McKee. Seconds later a party of marines reached the scene to find Allen and Murphy dead and Lukes lying senseless across the lieutenant, bleeding from eighteen spear and sword wounds. It was thirty-nine days before Lukes regained consciousness. The terrible punishment he had taken left him an invalid for life but earned him the medal.

Lukes's action concluded the struggle for the Citadel. Only 3 Americans out of 350 had been killed and 11 had been wounded, Lieutenant McKee mortally. The bodies of 243 Koreans were counted in and around the work; only 20 surrendered. Also captured were fifty flags and, in both days' fighting, 481 cannon of various caliber. The brigade reembarked on the morning of June 12, having demolished the forts, and rolled the cannon into the river.

Altogether, fifteen Medals of Honor were awarded for the expedition: nine to seamen and six to marines. By current standards, this number is clearly excessive, but in 1871 the Medal of Honor remained America's only decoration for valor. As such, it was often used to reward acts that would be recognized by lesser distinctions today. ✧

Conquering Cuba
The Spanish–American War

The Spanish-American War moved America onto the world stage. It also vindicated Alfred T. Mahan's theories of sea power. If the U.S. Navy could win command of the sea, cutting the Spanish colonies off from the homeland, victory was assured. In the Pacific the issue was decided within three weeks of the commencement of hostilities by Commodore Dewey's destruction of the Spanish Philippine squadron at Manila Bay. In the Caribbean, to which Spain sent a cruiser squadron under Rear Admiral Pascual Cervera y Topete, matters were not settled so quickly.

The first Medal of Honor awarded for the "splendid little war" with Spain was earned by Chief Carpenter's Mate Franz Anton Itrich at the Battle of Manila Bay on May 1, 1898. Another fifty-two men received medals for dredging up and cutting the Spanish overseas cables near Cienfuegos, Cuba, under a heavy fire from shore on May 11. Most of the other medals authorized for the conflict were granted for chasing down the Spanish commander Pascual Cervera's cruiser squadron.

Rear Admiral William T. Sampson, commander of the U.S. North Atlantic Squadron, attempted to intercept the squadron off Puerto Rico and Havana. Cervera expected as much and slipped safely into port at Santiago, on the southeastern coast of Cuba, where his ships were discovered on May 28. For Sampson, this was a disappointing development. His squadron was greatly superior to Cervera's, but the only way into Santiago Harbor was through a narrow, mined channel, covered by shore batteries. He dared not risk his battleships. He could, of course, blockade the port, but Cervera might somehow steal out. The solution was to bottle him up by sinking a ship across the channel.

On May 29 Sampson discussed this intention with Assistant Naval Constructor Richmond Pearson Hobson, who immediately volunteered for the mission. A handsome man with strong, symmetrical features and a large handlebar mustache, Hobson was also a peculiar one. Born in Greensboro, Alabama, in 1870, he entered the Naval Academy at the age of fifteen. There his unflinching sense of duty led him to report members of his own class for disciplinary infractions. His diligence violated the midshipmen's unwritten code, in consequence of which his classmates

Lieutenant Richmond P. Hobson (above) guided the Merrimac *into Santiago Harbor under heavy Spanish fire (right).*

Above. *Santiago Harbor after Hobson's attempt. The* Merrimac *was sunk near the point of land at top right. A ruined Spanish vessel lists in the foreground.* Clockwise from top left. *Hobson's volunteer crew: Claus Clausen, George Phillips, Francis Kelly, John Murphy, Osborne Deignan, Daniel Montague, George Charette.*

stopped speaking to him except on official business. During his senior year they decided that they had misjudged him and invited him back into the fold. Hobson responded by declaring that he had grown accustomed to the existing arrangement and would prefer for it to continue. Graduating first in his class, he was chosen for advanced study abroad and earned a degree from the French *Ecole d'Application du Génie Maritime* in 1893. Upon the outbreak of war he was assigned to Sampson's staff.

Sampson had already selected a block ship, the 333-foot collier *Merrimac*. Hobson prepared it for sinking, and around two o'clock on the morning of June 3 he took it out of the blockade line. Accompanying him was a skeleton crew of seven enlisted volunteers: Gunner's Mate First Class George Charette, Coxswain Claus K. Clausen, Coxswain Osborne Deignan, Watertender Francis

Kelly, Chief Master-at-Arms Daniel Montague, Coxswain John E. Murphy, and Machinist First Class George F. Phillips.

In planning the operation, Hobson had concluded that the approach should be made in darkness and at flood tide, just after the moon set. He had strung ten charges at vital locations twelve feet below the water line on the *Merrimac's* port side. The charges would be fired by battery-powered electrical circuits, sinking the ship almost instantaneously. A lifeboat was taken aboard to provide the crew with a chance of escape, and a launch was ordered to stand off the channel to pick them up. For his men, who likely would spend some time in the water, Hobson prescribed a most unconventional uniform consisting of woolen underwear, two pairs of socks, a pistol belt (with pistol), and a life preserver.

Approaching the channel at her full

speed of nine knots, the *Merrimac* managed to come within 500 yards of its mouth before the Spanish opened fire. The ship plunged ahead, shuddering from a succession of hits. The steering gear was soon disabled, but her momentum kept her on course. At the predetermined position, Hobson gave the order to set off the charges. He already knew from tests that three of the circuits were dead. Now he was appalled to find that the Spanish fire had shattered so many batteries that only two of the remaining charges exploded. The damage they did would not be sufficient to sink the ship before the tide swung her out of place. An attempt to hold her by anchoring was frustrated when the chains were shot away. Helplessly, Hobson watched as the ship drifted to the side of the channel.

He and his men now found themselves on a slowly sinking hulk under almost pointblank fire from rifles,

"That Infernal Medal of Honor"

One of the great ironies of the era of American expansion is that its most enduring figure was recommended for a Medal of Honor but was denied the award. Years later the rejection would still rankle Theodore Roosevelt, Rough Rider and president.

After the Rough Riders' legendary charge up San Juan Hill on July 1, 1898, Lieutenant Colonel Roosevelt became a hero back in America. He was praised for his actions and later recommended for the Medal of Honor. The wave of popularity that greeted him on his return to the U.S. led to the governorship of New York, the vice-presidency, and, upon the assassination of William McKinley, the White House.

But while he would gain the presidency, Teddy Roosevelt was denied the other prize he coveted. In the fall of 1898 the War Decorations Board prepared to reject Roosevelt's case due to a lack of eyewitness statements vouching for his actions on the hill.

Roosevelt, elected governor that November, was livid. He quickly asked his friend Senator Henry Cabot Lodge of Massachusetts to look into the matter on his behalf. "The War Department does not intend that I shall have the Medal of Honor," he wrote Lodge in November. "If I didn't earn it, then no commissioned officer can ever earn it." Lodge reported that the War Department offered a retroactive brevet promotion in lieu of the medal, but Roosevelt was adamant. "Don't bother about the brevet," he replied. "It is the medal for which I care."

The governor asked his former comrades to verify his actions, and soon written statements from other Rough Riders arrived in Washington. Major General Leonard Wood, a Medal of Honor recipient from the Indian Wars, stated that Roosevelt was one of the first

up San Juan Hill and that "his services on the day in question were of great value and of a most distinguished character." Captain Robert Howze, another recipient, noted two occasions on which Roosevelt had displayed "the most conspicuous gallantry" on the hill.

But while the Decorations Board may have looked favorably on the evidence, the Secretary of War, Russell A. Alger, was offended by Roosevelt's pressure tactics toward the panel. The former Rough Rider was convinced that Alger was bitter over his complaints that the War Department had mismanaged the American logistical effort in Cuba. The conflict came to a head in early 1899 when Alger announced at a White House dinner that Roosevelt would not receive the medal. Roosevelt and Lodge, in attendance that night, were humiliated.

By the end of January, Roosevelt had given up on his quest. "As for that infernal Medal of Honor," he wrote Lodge, "I really wish and ask that you do nothing more about it at all." Amid mounting charges of mismanagement during the war, Alger was

Roosevelt (right) with Colonel Leonard Wood (to his right) and Major General Joseph Wheeler (with beard).

dismissed in July. Teddy Roosevelt's Medal of Honor was forgotten.

But being denied the honor only increased Roosevelt's respect for the medal. During his presidency the standards were raised for its bestowal, and a new design for the army medal was approved and patented for the first time. Roosevelt also set the tone for future presentations in 1905 when he directed that the medal be awarded "with formal and impressive ceremonial," by the president, if possible.

Though the Rough Rider was denied a medal, the name of Theodore Roosevelt does appear on the Medal of Honor rolls. Forty-six years after his father's Cuban exploits, Brigadier General Theodore Roosevelt, Jr., was awarded a posthumous medal for courage and leadership during the 1944 D-day landing in France. As General Roosevelt's widow accepted the award, President Franklin Roosevelt said, "His father would have been the proudest."

machine guns, shore batteries, and the ships of Cervera's squadron. Afterward Hobson recalled, "The striking of projectiles and flying fragments produced a grinding sound, with a fine ring in it of steel on steel. The deck vibrated heavily, and we felt the full effect, lying, as we were, full-length on our faces. At each instant it seemed that certainly the next would bring a projectile among us. . . . I looked for my own body to be cut in two diagonally, from the left hip upward, and wondered for a moment what the sensation would be."

Incredibly, the entire party survived the sinking of the ship. The Spanish barrage had destroyed their lifeboat, eliminating any possibility of escape, and the next morning they were picked up, clinging to a raft, by a launch containing Admiral Cervera himself. The first word the Spanish officer said as Hobson climbed aboard was "Valiente!" Hobson and his crew were held as prisoners of war in nearby Santiago. Six weeks after the sinking of the *Merrimac,* they were exchanged for a Spanish officer. All seven of his men received the Medal of Honor in 1899. As an officer, Hobson was ineligible under naval regulations of the time.

Richmond P. Hobson came home to find himself a hero. A public peck on the cheek by a cousin at the beginning of a national tour inspired a kissing craze in which he was bussed by an estimated 10,000 women. He retired from the navy in 1903, entered politics in 1906, and served four terms as a Democratic congressman from Alabama. Thereafter he occupied himself promoting such causes as naval expansion, prohibition of alcoholic liquor ("protoplasm poison," he called it), and the suppression of drug dealing. In 1933 a special act of Congress awarded him the Medal of Honor.

After the failure of the attempt to bottle up the Spanish ships in Santiago,

A *fanciful depiction of Lieutenant Hobson's capture by Admiral Cervera, with Hobson's portrait and those of other heroes of the Spanish-American War.*

Admiral Sampson called on the army to flush them out. The 17,000 men of Major General William T. Shafter's V Corps sailed from Tampa, Florida, on June 14 and began landing near Santiago eight days later. On July 1 they stormed the Spanish outposts at El Caney and San Juan Hill. Twenty-five Medals of Honor were granted for these actions. With the

Americans closing on Santiago, the captain-general of Cuba ordered Cervera to try to fight his way out. On Sunday, July 3, the Spanish squadron was annihilated in a one-sided battle in which not a single American vessel was lost. The defenders of Santiago surrendered two weeks later and an armistice with Spain was signed on August 12. ◈

A Restless Colony
The Philippine Insurrection

The victory over Spain was destined to have a bloody aftermath. In the glow of its triumph, the United States decided to annex the conquered Philippines. A violent insurrection ensued, led by a young Filipino named Emilio Aguinaldo. Back home, after the initial outburst of indignation at Filipino ingratitude, few people paid much attention to the struggle, and most of those who did disapproved of American involvement. Major General Adna R. Chaffee, appointed to command in the islands in 1901, told his civilian superior, Governor-General William Howard Taft, that there was no glory in the Philippines.

In contrast to the Spanish-American War, the insurrection in the Philippines was neither splendid nor little. At peak strength U.S. forces in the islands numbered 69,000 men and by July 4, 1902, when Theodore Roosevelt officially declared the conflict at an end, 1,000 Americans had been killed in action and 3,000 wounded. Filipino dead were estimated at 16,000.

For the men in the field, there was little comfort. The climate was hot and humid. During the five months of the rainy season, drenching downpours fell two days out of three. Disease felled as many soldiers as *insurrecto* bullets. Malaria was a fact of life; a man had to have a severe case to be excused from duty. Rations were monotonous: hardtack, canned meats, and black coffee. Any attempt to supplement them with local produce usually led to bouts of dysentery. Even the pleasures available in the bordellos of Manila were questionable. At one time the venereal disease rate of the city's garrison was 25 percent.

The nature of the Philippine campaigns differed sharply from that of the war with Spain. Americans had come to admire the gallantry with which the dons went down to defeat, but few developed any affection for the *insurrectos*. After the first few battles the contest became a guerrilla war, a type of conflict guaranteed to embitter regular troops. In this case, bitterness was compounded by racial prejudice. Most American soldiers referred to their opponents as "googoos" or "niggers." When Taft urged the troops to look on the Filipinos as "little brown brothers," they replied, "He may be a brother o' Big Bill Taft, but he ain't no kin o'mine."

Corporal Frank L. Anders saw action in the opening months of the insurrection. Anders had been an army brat. At the time of his birth, at Fort Abraham Lincoln, Dakota Territory, on November 10, 1875, his father was serving in the 17th Infantry. During his christening he was held by an officer of Custer's cavalry. Anders was only fifteen

Right. *Corporal Frank L. Anders, the sharpshooter from North Dakota.* Far right. *Anders's commander, Arthur W. Young, in Baliuag, the Philippines, 1899.*

when his father died, forcing him to leave school and go to work to augment the family income. In 1894 he joined the 1st Regiment of the North Dakota National Guard, which was assigned to the Philippines in 1898.

Late in April 1899, Brigadier General Henry W. Lawton launched an

Right. *American soldiers in the Philippines await the order to advance.* Below. *Arthur Young (extreme left) and his scouts gather in Baliuag, May 2, 1899.*

offensive on the rebel-held city of San Isidro. During the advance, Lawton authorized Arthur W. Young, a civilian volunteer and former frontiersman, to organize a detachment of scouts. Frank Anders was one of the twenty-five sharpshooters Young picked for his unit. Lawton cautioned Young that his mission was to scout, not to fight. These words apparently made little impression.

Keeping well ahead of the main body, Young set a blistering pace toward San Isidro. On the morning of May 13 all except ten of his men were too fatigued to go on. Young led them forward, accompanied by two officers who had joined the detachment the previous day, Captains William E. Birkhimer and J. F. Case. Around nine o'clock the scouts approached the town of San Miguel de Mayumo only to find 300 Filipinos blocking their path. Their entrenched position was well sited behind the dike of a rice field, with one flank resting on a river and the other on a hill. Captain Birkhimer quickly concluded that a frontal assault would be necessary and sent Case to bring up reinforcements. "We are not waiting for support," Young announced. "We are going forward."

They did just that. Sending five men to try to work around to the left, Young led Anders and four others straight toward the *insurrectos*. Birkhimer went with them. They advanced in short rushes, covering one another. It took them half an hour to cross the 150 yards to the enemy position. During that time they picked off no less than 49 of its defenders. Reaching the entrenchment, they found only the dead.

The other men rejoined them there, and the detachment pushed on another 200 yards toward the bridge crossing to the town. There the *insurrectos* turned and charged. Six were cut down by the scouts' fire and the others fell back, but Young was mortally

wounded. His men carried him across the bridge into San Miguel, where they occupied the church in anticipation of a counterattack. It was not long in coming. For four hours, from 10:00 A.M. to 2:00 P.M., the scouts held the enemy at bay. Shortly thereafter, the approach of American reinforcements caused the Filipinos to retire.

All of the men who had followed Young in his incredible attack on the *insurrecto* entrenchment received the Medal of Honor: Frank Anders, Captain

Birkhimer, and Privates Willis H. Downs, Gotfred Jensen, Edward E. Lyon, and Peter H. Quinn. As a civilian, Young was not eligible for the award. Happily, the passions of the insurrection war soon faded; the Filipino-American friendship that grew up in its aftermath endured. ❖

Philippine insurrectos *man a defensive position. Approximately 16,000 natives died in jungle fighting against the American forces.*

China Stirs
The Boxer Rebellion

In the midst of the war in the Philippines, the United States unexpectedly found itself involved in another imperial conflict, this time on the Asian mainland. The trouble centered in northern China, where a peasant uprising aimed to purify the country of foreign influences by the simple expedient of exterminating the foreigners. The leaders of the movement called themselves the Righteous Society of Heavenly Fists. Westerners called them Boxers.

At the time of the Boxer Rebellion, the United States, Japan, and nine European nations maintained legations in Peking. In May 1900, the members of the diplomatic corps, mildly alarmed by reports of Boxer activities, requested guards from the warships lying off the mouth of the Pei-Ho River, ninety miles to the southeast. The first detachment, 337 American, British, French, Italian, Japanese, and Russian sailors and marines, reached Peking on May 31. In the lead, colors flying, was a contingent of 49 U.S. Marines and 6 sailors under Captain John T. "Handsome Jack" Myers. A detachment of eighty-nine Austrians and Germans followed on June 3.

Thereafter the situation in Peking deteriorated rapidly. On June 9 the British minister, Sir Claude MacDonald, ordered Vice Admiral Sir Edward Seymour, commanding the British China Squadron, to land troops for an immediate advance on the city. Ten days later, an ultimatum arrived from the Chinese government stating that the diplomatic community must leave Peking within twenty-four hours. After heated debate, the ministers replied that, while they were willing to go, they could not do so within the specified time, and they requested an interview with Chinese officials. When no response was received by the following morning, the German ambassador set out for the foreign ministry. En route, he was shot by a Chinese soldier. The news of his murder convinced the other westerners that they must defend themselves; to leave the Legation Quarter would be suicidal. The Boxers launched their first attack that afternoon.

The abandonment of several outlying legations created a reasonably compact perimeter approximately three-

The men of Troop L of the 6th U.S. Cavalry ride along the Great Wall of China just west of the Nan-Kow Pass near Peking, 1898.

First Class Joseph Mitchell, who became one of the celebrities of the siege by virtue of his association with a piece of antique ordnance variously known as the International, Old Betsey, the Empress Dowager, and the Old Crock.

A shortage of artillery was one of the legations' weaknesses, the only gun originally available being the Italians' little one-pounder. (The Russians had left their nine-pounder at the railway station.) Great therefore was the joy when, on July 7, a Christian Chinese discovered an old cannon barrel at an iron foundry inside the quarter. Gunner's Mate Mitchell, at twenty-three a veteran of nearly seven years' service, was put in charge of renovating the piece.

"It was about 100 years old," Mitchell wrote. "To mount it I took a

Left. U.S. artillery fires outside the walls of Peking. *Below.* American forces on top of a gate in Peking fire into an adjacent compound.

quarters of a mile square. Into this area were packed the 400-odd legation guards; approximately 900 civilian men, women, and children, the foreign residents of Peking; a number of missionaries from outside the city; and several thousand Chinese Christians. Sir Claude MacDonald, who had attained the rank of major in the Highland Light Infantry, was chosen commander in chief.

The most vital section of the perimeter was the Tartar Wall that formed its southern face. Part of Peking's great interior wall, forty feet high and sixty feet wide, it was defended by barricades manned by the Americans to the west and the Germans to the east. When the Germans were shelled out of their position on July 1, the Americans erected a new barricade to protect their rear. Among them was Gunner's Mate

piece of timber and lashed the gun to the station water carriage. It had no trunnions or sight, but nevertheless it was of good use. I used Chinese and German powder, Russian shell and Japanese fuses with it, and to work the old cannon I fought under every flag in the legation district, and the breastworks of the enemy were levelled rapidly. Sometimes I was within six feet of the enemy and never more than thirty feet of them. . . . This sort of work I kept up . . . until I was wounded. . . . I had the old gun all by myself, as everyone was afraid it would burst." For his resourceful defense, Mitchell received the medal.

Meanwhile, foreign landing parties had captured the forts guarding the mouth of the Pei-Ho River, and on June 10 Admiral Seymour started for Peking with 2,129 men from ships of eight

Calvin Titus as a West Point cadet.
Below. *Men of Titus's unit with regimental flags after the fighting.*

navies. They included 129 Americans under navy Captain Bowman H. "Billy Hell" McCalla. The column pushed to within twenty-five miles of the city before being forced back.

By then, the Boxers had also besieged the International Settlement at Tientsin, thirty miles up the Pei-Ho.

The first attempt to reach it was made by 440 Russians and 140 U.S. Marines and bluejackets on June 19-21. The attack was beaten off after heavy fighting. The flow of foreign troops into northern China quickly gathered momentum, however, and on June 23 a stronger column broke through to the settlement.

The native portion of Tientsin was captured on July 13-14 by a force of 6,500 men, one-sixth of them American. Nine Medals of Honor were awarded for this engagement.

Finally, on August 3, British Brigadier General Sir Alfred Gaselee marched from Tientsin at the head of an International Relief Expedition of 18,600 men, including 2,500 American soldiers and marines. Eleven days later the expedition arrived at Peking.

When his colonel called for volunteers to scale the city wall, twenty-year-old Trumpeter Calvin P. Titus of the 14th Infantry responded: "I'll try, sir." Without ropes or a ladder, Titus worked his way up the thirty-foot wall by finding hand- and footholds amid the stones. He came under fire at the top but survived the assault. Titus's gallant action inspired his fellow soldiers, who assaulted and penetrated the city wall. The regiment reached the legations that afternoon to find that the British, advancing unopposed, had beaten it by two hours. The defenders had withstood a siege of fifty-five days, although more than 200 had been killed or wounded.

Many years later Calvin Titus recalled that he had been richly rewarded for his actions in Peking. "President McKinley appointed me to West Point and there one morning during the Academy's 100th anniversary celebration the Corps was turned out in full dress and a trembling little plebe was called to the front. President Theodore Roosevelt himself pinned that Medal of Honor on my . . . uniform." Graduating in the upper third of the Class of 1905, Titus went on to become a lieutenant colonel.

The relief of the legations shattered the Boxers' credibility with the Chinese people. Although the allies would conduct a series of punitive expeditions, all of them anticlimactic, for practical purposes the Boxer Rebellion was over. ◈

Incursion in Mexico
Veracruz 1914

In February 1913 General Victoriano Huerta seized the presidency of Mexico in a bloody coup d'état. In Mexico, his initiative provoked a revolution. In Washington, it aroused the indignation of President Woodrow Wilson, who declared, "I will not recognize a government of butchers!" and resolved to force Huerta out, setting the stage for another expansion war, this one in the Caribbean.

President Woodrow Wilson at first believed he could expunge Mexico's new leader through a combination of diplomatic pressure and an arms embargo. But General Huerta was still in power when, on April 9, 1914, the brief detention of nine U.S. sailors at Tampico brought Mexican-American relations to a boil. In the midst of the crisis, it was learned that the German steamer *Ypiranga* was approaching the Mexican city of Veracruz with a huge cargo of munitions for Huerta. Wilson decided that the shipment must not get through. Early on the morning of April 21, 1914, he ordered Rear Admiral Frank F. Fletcher, commanding U.S. naval forces off Veracruz, to intercept the arms as they entered Mexican customs.

The navy had three ships off Veracruz on April 21, 1914: the battleships *Florida* and *Utah* and the transport *Prairie,* which carried a marine battalion. Secretary of the Navy Josephus Daniels's signal to seize the customhouse at Veracruz reached Admiral Fletcher on the *Florida* at 8:00 A.M. Contingency plans for the occupation of the city had already been made.

Hoping to avert bloodshed, Fletcher sent an officer ashore to ask the U.S. consul to urge the Mexican authorities not to resist the landing. The admiral's diplomacy worked too slowly. The Mexican government eventually ordered the military commandant of Veracruz, General Gustavo Maass, to withdraw the garrison, but by the time the message arrived he had freed and armed the convicts in the city jail and sent 100 men toward the waterfront to "repel the invasion." Even had Maass done nothing, however, it is unlikely that the landing could have been made peacefully. Events would reveal that Veracruz was packed with potential defenders. All kinds of people—policemen, the cadets at the Mexican

naval academy, members of the home guard, even ordinary citizens—were ready to go for their guns.

Yet all was quiet when, shortly before noon, steam launches towing long lines of whaleboats filled with troops entered the inner harbor. The American force numbered 787 men: 502 marines from the *Prairie* and 285 bluejackets from the *Florida.* Landing unopposed, the men fanned out toward various objectives, which included the railway yard, the cable office, the post and telegraph office, and the power plant.

The occupation of the customhouse was entrusted to the *Florida*'s 1st Company, led by Ensign George M. Lowry. In the *Lucky Bag,* the Naval Academy annual for 1911, Lowry's classmates had written: "George bobs along with a pleasant smile for everyone and a walk marked by too much stride for a man his size. . . . He commands our admiration that, in this place of unfortunate precedents, he has not been ashamed to do his best." His best would now be tried in combat, for as the *Florida*'s company began to cross Calle Emparan a block from the customhouse, a Mexican policeman two streets ahead opened fire on them. The report of the policeman's revolver was followed by a crackling fusillade from Mexican troops and civilians throughout the area.

Taking cover in doorways and against the sides of buildings, Lowry's men returned the Mexican fire. The heaviest came from two machine guns, one on the curb outside the naval academy and another on an upper floor of the Hotel Oriente. The crew of the first gun was soon forced to withdraw, but heavy fire still swept the block between Calle Emparan and the customhouse. Lowry concluded that an advance down the street would cost too many casualties. Instead, he called for volunteers to follow him into an alley between the

Ensign George M. Lowry, who led a company from the U.S.S. Florida *that seized the customhouse at Veracruz after fierce street fighting.*

Bluejackets of the 2d Company, Utah *battalion, fire down a street in Veracruz, April 1914.*

Paul Foster (seated at desk) later acted as provost marshal of Veracruz, earning the sobriquet "Boy Poo-Bah of Veracruz."

customhouse and the new customs warehouse. Five men responded.

In the alley, the party was exposed to a crossfire from snipers in the customs buildings and the machine gun in the Hotel Oriente. Although Mexican marksmanship was poor, before going far Lowry decided that the machine gun must be silenced and ordered his men to aim at it. There was a sizzling exchange. A bullet knocked one of the buttons off Lowry's cap; another grazed his leg. One of the volunteers was shot through the head and another slightly wounded. Then the body of a Mexican policeman toppled out of a second-story window and the stutter of the machine gun ceased. Dashing through a patter of rifle fire, Lowry led his men to the end of the alley, where they climbed through a window into the customhouse. Inside, the customs clerks were throwing down their arms. Within minutes, a runner was on the way to report that the 1st Company had secured its objective.

When the shooting started, Admiral Fletcher directed the *Utah* to land her battalion. The first company to fall in was commanded by twenty-five-year-old Ensign Paul F. Foster. The leadership

this reflected was typical of Paul Foster, a granite-jawed midwesterner who had received the rare honor of being selected to command the Brigade of Midshipmen both semesters of his senior year at the Naval Academy. According to plan, his company should have been the last to embark, but its readiness resulted in its being put into the lead boats.

Ashore, Foster was told to advance on the double and relieve Ensign Lowry, an Annapolis classmate, at the customhouse. Nearing the scene of the action, Foster's men came under fire from the new customs warehouse, a block-long shed with heavy iron-grille walls. The Mexicans withdrew on their approach and the bluejackets battered down the door with a railroad iron they found nearby. The sight of the bales, sacks, and barrels of cotton, rice, sugar, rum, and molasses filling the warehouse gave Foster an inspiration. Ordering his men to load these stores on the warehouse hand trucks, he created a mobile breastworks. The trucks were then rolled into the street and Foster's company, advancing behind them, spearheaded the attack into the city.

Around three in the afternoon

Admiral Fletcher suspended operations while another attempt was made to contact Mexican authorities. This effort took two hours; when its failure was apparent, he decided to remain on the defensive pending the arrival of reinforcements from the ships now converging on Veracruz. Another 1,500 landed during the night and the advance was resumed the next morning. By noon American forces were in control of the city. In the two days' fighting, they had lost seventeen men killed and sixty-three wounded. Mexican casualties were approximately 800 dead and wounded.

The sailors returned to their ships on April 27, leaving Veracruz to an army brigade that had been rushed from the States. For the next seven months an American military government ruled the city. The German steamer *Ypiranga* finally managed to land her arms at another port, but that made no difference. Before the occupation ended, on November 21, 1914, the object of Wilson's Mexican policy had been attained. Faced with a rising tide of revolution and weakened by the loss of the customs revenues of Veracruz, his government's greatest single source of

Troops raise the U.S. flag over the Hotel Terminal on April 27, 1914, after the fall of Veracruz to American forces.

income, Victoriano Huerta surrendered the presidency of Mexico.

Ensigns Lowry and Foster both received the Medal of Honor for Veracruz, along with fifty-three other men, whose exploits ranged from sending semaphore messages under heavy fire to aiding wounded men in equally dangerous circumstances. Never before or since were so many Medals of Honor awarded for a single engagement. The majority went to navy and marine officers, who were made eligible for the medal by an act of Congress on March 3, 1915.

Even at the time, many persons regarded this number as extravagant. Major Smedley Butler returned his medal to the Navy Department, explaining that he had done nothing to deserve the nation's highest honor. It came back with orders that he would not only retain but wear it. A navy Medal of Honor man attributed the profusion of awards to the fact that President Wilson and Secretary Daniels, both pacifists at heart, were conscience-stricken by the bloodshed at Veracruz and, "in a somewhat maudlin mood," decided to give the maximum possible recognition to the men who fought there.

The inevitable result of the administration's largesse was to diminish the prestige of the Veracruz awards. At least one recipient felt that "the number given was altogether out of proportion to the severity of the fighting and the number of personnel engaged in actual combat." Another veteran of the landing recalled standing for an admiral's inspection in the 1920s. The admiral came to a sailor wearing the ribbon of the Medal of Honor and asked how he had won his decoration. The man replied that it had been during World War I. Turning to the others in the inspecting party, the admiral said, "Holy smoke! Here's a Medal of Honor that's *not* for Veracruz!" ❖

Battles with the *Cacos*
Haiti 1915–1920

Scarcely a year after the landing at Veracruz, the United States intervened in Haiti. American policymakers had long been distressed by affairs in Haiti, where coup seemed to follow coup. To the Wilson administration, the latest of the Haitian revolutions seemed a golden opportunity to set Haiti straight.

Smedley Darlington Butler, a double recipient of the Medal of Honor, saw varied action throughout the Caribbean in his distinguished thirty-three-year military career.

Caco is the Haitian name for a native bird of prey. The *cacos* were earthbound birds of prey, part-time bandits, part-time soldiers of sorts, who lived in the jungled highlands of central Haiti. For generations they had been a crucial force in Haitian politics. As a marine officer explained, whenever anyone felt the presidential urge, he "would go to the North and make an agreement with *caco* leaders; and for a certain sum, to be paid by the Haitian treasury after he was successful, also the privilege of looting some of the towns on the way down, they would descend from the mountains and put the president in power." The *cacos* would then retire to await the coming of the next presidential aspirant. Defending this system to an American, a distinguished Haitian emphasized that its rules were well understood. No one of consequence was ever killed. It was simply a way of changing governments.

Such arguments fell on deaf ears, at least to the Americans. As the Americans saw it, the occupation's first order of business must be to eliminate so unruly an influence from the Haitian political process. An attempt to induce a voluntary disarmament by offering ten dollars for every rifle turned in was largely ignored. On September 18, 1915, a band of *cacos* fired the opening shots of the first Haitian campaign at a marine patrol.

The campaigns against the *cacos* were the most bizarre in the history of the Marine Corps. In Haiti, voodoo was a living faith. Many *caco* commanders were also *bocors*—wizards—who could not be harmed by bullets, or so the *bocors* proclaimed. The unhappy experience of young marine Sergeant Lawrence Muth, who held the rank of lieutenant in the *Gendarmerie d'Haiti,* is instructive. Badly wounded in an ambush, Muth was left for dead by his men. The *caco* chieftain into whose hands he fell had con-

sulted a *papa loa*–voodoo priest–about what to do in such a situation. Adopting the priest's advice, the *caco* cut out and ate Muth's heart and liver, from which he expected to acquire the sergeant's wisdom and courage. He also smeared Muth's brains on the sights of his men's rifles to make them shoot straight.

On October 24-25, 1915, a patrol of forty-four mounted marines was ambushed after sundown by 400 *cacos*. The marines held their perimeter throughout the night and at dawn attacked in three directions, scattering their startled foes. Three men were decorated with the Medal of Honor for this action: Gunnery Sergeant Dan Daly (who already held a Medal of Honor for the Boxer Rebellion), First Lieutenant Edward A. Ostermann, and Captain William P. Upshur.

By mid-November aggressive patrolling had dispersed all but the hard core of *cacos*. These had retired to old Fort Rivière, deep in the hinterland. Taking the fort was the self-imposed task of Major Smedley Darlington Butler, who had tried to return the Medal of Honor he received for Veracruz. A short, slight man with a great beak of a nose and an intimidating stare–his men called him Old Gimlet Eye–Butler was among the most colorful characters ever to wear a broad-brimmed campaign hat. The son of a Quaker congressman, he had obtained a direct commission just shy of age seventeen in 1898 and reached Cuba in time to hear bullets whistle in the Spanish-American War. Three years later, he was wounded and cited for bravery in the Boxer Rebellion. Since then, he had served on almost every coast of Central America and played a leading role in Nicaragua in 1912.

Fort Rivière, a French-built masonry work 200 feet square, capped the peak of Montagne Noire. To the rear and sides of the fort the mountain fell sharply away from its walls. It would have to be attacked head on, up the steep, rocky slope in front. Some officers felt that this was a job for a regiment supported by artillery. Smedley Butler talked his colonel into letting him tackle it with only four companies of twenty-four men each and a detachment of two machine guns.

Arriving outside Fort Rivière around daybreak on November 17, Butler deployed three of his companies to pepper the defenders and started up the slope with the remaining company and the machine guns. A hundred yards from the fort he left one section and the machine guns among the rocks to give covering fire while he led the last nineteen men forward. Sprinting through the *caco* bullets, he reached the dead space beneath the walls to discover that the sally port had been bricked up. The only other entrance to the fort was by means of a drain, four feet high, three feet wide, and fifteen feet long, through which a *caco* was shooting.

For once, Smedley Butler was daunted. Hugging the wall on one side of the drain, he saw Sergeant Ross L. Iams and Private Samuel Gross doing the same thing on the other. They were safe where they were, but they could not remain there indefinitely.

Butler told Lowell Thomas in later years:

I . . . had brought the crowd up there. I . . . had bragged how easy it would be to take the fort. So now it was up to me to lead the procession. A stream of bullets was crashing through the passage. I simply didn't have the courage to poke my head into the drain, although I might have worked myself up to the infernal plunge if I had been given time–a long time.

I had never experienced a keener desire to be some place else. I was writhing . . . with indecision. I glanced across at Iams. My misery and an unconscious, helpless pleading must have been written all over my

face. Iams took one look at me and then said, "Oh, hell, I'm going through."

Iam's initiative broke the impasse. Butler sprang toward the opening, but Gross squeezed in ahead of him. The *caco* at the end of the drain fired in their faces but, to Butler's amazement, missed all three. Before the Haitian could reload, Iams scrambled out the end of the drain and shot him. The marines began to stream into the fort. As they did, a screaming throng of sixty or seventy *cacos* rushed toward them. Iams and Gross picked off the two leaders. A giant Haitian dashed at Butler, brandishing a club. The shot from Butler's .45 went wide, but Gross dropped the *caco* in the nick of time. By then, the other marines were popping out of the drain, and in fifteen minutes the fort was theirs.

Butler, Iams, and Gross each received the Medal of Honor for the storming of Fort Rivière. This time,

Ross L. Iams, who earned the Medal of Honor in action at Fort Rivière.

Butler did not try to send his back. Years later, in 1929, he became the marines' youngest major general at age forty-eight. Upon the death of Major General Wendell C. Neville, commandant of the Marine Corps, in 1930, Butler became the corps's senior officer and could reasonably expect to be its next commandant. Unfortunately, his criticisms of navy brass had made him *persona non grata* with Secretary of the Navy Charles Francis Adams and President Herbert Hoover, and a much junior general received the appointment. A few months later, a speech in which Butler said undiplomatic things about Mussolini brought him the distinction of being the first general officer to be placed under arrest since the Civil War. The vigor with which he defended himself

Herman H. Hanneken, a sergeant when he earned the Medal of Honor, was later awarded a Silver Star for commanding the 7th Marines on Guadalcanal in World War II. He retired a brigadier general in 1948.

reduced a threatened court-martial to a mild reprimand, but it was the last straw. On October 1, 1931, Smedley Butler retired.

He did not mellow with age. Reviewing his career in the November 1935 issue of *Common Sense,* Butler wrote:

I spent thirty-three years and four months as a member of our country's most agile military force—the Marine Corps. . . . And during that period I spent most of my time being a high-class muscle man for Big Business, for Wall Street and for the Bankers. In short, I was a racketeer for capitalism. . . . I helped make Mexico . . . safe for American oil interests in 1914. I helped make Haiti and Cuba a decent place for the National City Bank boys to collect revenues in. . . . I helped purify Nicaraguans for the international banking house of Brown Brothers in 1909-1912. I brought light to the Dominican Republic for American sugar interests in 1916. I helped make Honduras "right" for American fruit companies in 1903. In China in 1927 I helped see to it that Standard Oil went its way unmolested.

Butler was wrong—"Big Business" did

not pull the strings of American policy; but no one could doubt that he was sincere. He died, not yet sixty, in Philadelphia in 1940.

The capture of Fort Rivière crushed the *caco* rebellion. For three years thereafter, something approaching peace prevailed in Haiti. Late in 1918, however, the emergence of a dynamic new leader, Charlemagne Péralte, brought the *cacos* back to life. Lieutenant Colonel Frederic M. Wise, commanding the *gendarmerie,* put out the word: "Get Charlemagne." Wise conceded that this was "a pretty tall order. It meant running down one Haitian out of several million Haitians in a country as big as the state of New York . . . that was almost entirely sympathetic to him."

Twenty-six-year-old Sergeant Herman H. Hanneken, an erstwhile divinity student serving as a *gendarmerie* captain, proposed a solution. Instead of going after Charlemagne, he would lure Charlemagne into coming to him. For a gratuity of $2,000, Jean-Baptiste Conze, a prominent citizen of Grand Rivière du Nord, and two other Haitians agreed to pretend to join the *cacos.* Conze was to raise his own band and gain Charlemagne's confidence—an eventuality Hanneken hoped to encourage by an unsuccessful "attack" on Conze's encampment, after which Hanneken carried a "wounded" arm in a sling stained red with government-issue ink. Once Charlemagne accepted him, Conze was to suggest that they combine forces to capture Grand Rivière. Hanneken would be waiting.

Late in October 1919 one of Conze's confederates brought word that Charlemagne's and Conze's attack on the town was scheduled for the night of October 31. While marine reinforcements slipped into Grand Rivière, Hanneken hand-picked sixteen *gendarmes* and, accompanied by his second-in-com-

mand, marine Corporal William R. Button (who held the rank of first lieutenant in the *gendarmerie*), set up an ambush on the trail Charlemagne was to take. The detachment watched unseen as 700 *cacos* filed past, but Charlemagne was not among them. His absence was explained when a courier arrived from Conze to report that Charlemagne had elected to remain behind.

Hanneken and Button then decided to try to reach Charlemagne's camp. They had already blackened their skin with burnt cork; both spoke the Haitian *patois,* and Conze's man could guide them. With incredible daring, the *gendarmes* bluffed their way through six *caco* checkpoints. As they approached the camp, the courier pointed out Charlemagne standing beside a small fire. Hanneken walked to within fifteen feet of him, drew his .45, and shot him twice. In the ensuing pandemonium, someone smothered the fire, Button opened up with his Browning Automatic Rifle, the *gendarmes* formed a perimeter, and Hanneken flung himself down beside Charlemagne. On the *caco* leader's hip he discovered his own pearl-handled Smith & Wesson, which had disappeared shortly before. He used it to fire two more bullets through Charlemagne's heart.

Hanneken's *gendarmes* held their positions throughout the night, during which the *caco* attack on Grand Rivière was shattered. In the morning they carried Charlemagne down the mountain. Photographs of his corpse were widely distributed to convince his followers that he was indeed dead. No other leader of comparable stature emerged to replace him, and the second *caco* rebellion gradually subsided. For their bravery in removing Charlemagne, Hanneken and Button each received the Medal of Honor, and by the end of 1920 Haiti was again at peace. ◈

Policing the Caribbean
The Dominican Campaign

The politics of the Dominican Republic had long been of official concern to the United States. This concern intensified in April 1916 when General Desiderio Arias, a leader of the anti-American faction, revolted against pro-American President Juan Isidro Jiménez. Rear Admiral William B. Caperton landed troops to maintain order and informed Jiménez that he was ready to help him suppress the rebellion. Jiménez replied that he could not attack his own people and resigned from office. The vacuum thereby created would eventually be filled by an American military government. In the meanwhile, there was the problem of General Arias, who had retired to Santiago, in the northern part of the country. What passed for the Dominican army was in no condition to go after him. The U.S. Marines got the job.

The city of Santiago is located some twenty miles from the sea, behind a range of rugged hills that roughly parallels the shoreline. It was from there that U.S. forces would have to rout the Dominican Republic's rebel leader, General Desiderio Arias, in mid-1916. There were two natural avenues of advance on the rebel stronghold from the coast: one, wheeling southeast around the hills from Monte Cristi; the other, moving south through the hills along the railroad from Puerto Plata. These two ports had already been occupied by the time Colonel Joseph H. "Uncle Joe" Pendleton assumed command of marine forces in the Dominican Republic. Pendleton chose to exploit both possibilities and converge on the city. On June 26, 1916, he led 837 men of the 4th Marines inland from Monte Cristi; a smaller force of bluejackets and marines moved out from Puerto Plata the same day.

The first real engagement occurred on June 27, when Pendleton's column dispersed a body of rebels dug in on two

Marines stand on the line at Guayacanas in the Dominican Republic during the pursuit of Arias's rebels, 1916.

hilltops near Las Trencheras. Two days later, the Puerto Plata column broke through another enemy force outside the railroad tunnel at Alta Mira. The decisive action of the campaign was fought by Pendleton's command at Guayacanas on July 3.

As at Las Trencheras, the rebels had entrenched in heavy underbrush on a ridge across the marines' path. This time, however, the three-inch field guns that had softened up the Dominicans in the previous encounter could not be deployed. To compensate for the absence of artillery support, the marines' machine-gun company was directed to move forward and suppress the enemy fire. As Pendleton's two infantry battalions formed a front along the base of the ridge, the gunners dragged their heavy Colt and Benet-Mercier machine guns through dense scrub to within 200

Medal of Honor recipients for the Dominican campaign: Above. *First Sergeant Roswell Winans.* Right. *First Lieutenant Ernest Williams (with arms crossed).*

yards of the rebel trenches. Corporal Joseph A. Glowin set up his piece behind the trunk of a big tree that had been felled across the trail. As he fired, he was wounded but refused to leave the action until he was hit a second time. Even then his buddies practically had to manhandle him to the rear.

Nearby, First Sergeant Roswell Winans was spraying the trenches when his Colt jammed. Heedless of the rebel fire, Winans strove to get his gun back into service, but it was no use. One of the crew had dropped a needed spare part and the gun could not be cleared. Behind him Winans saw a skirmish line of marines beneath some trees. "Get the hell out of there!" he shouted, gesturing toward the front. The rebels fled as the advance neared their trenches, leaving twenty-seven corpses and five prisoners to the marines. Pendleton lost one man killed and ten wounded. Both Glowin and Winans were awarded the Medal of Honor for their intrepidity. Winans would go on to an illustrious career in the marines. In World War I, he received a Silver Star with Oak Leaf Cluster and a

croix de guerre for gallantry in action.

The closing days of the campaign were uneventful. On July 4 the two marine columns met, as planned, at Navarette, a little town a few miles north of Santiago. The next day General Arias sent an emissary to Pendleton announcing his intention to lay down his arms. Santiago was peacefully occupied on July 6.

In the months after the action at Guayacanas, marine units spread across the Dominican Republic, enforcing the general disarmament decreed by Admiral Caperton. Relatively little opposition was encountered, but there were occasional skirmishes. On November 29, 1916, First Lieutenant Ernest C. Williams gained the third and last Medal of Honor awarded for the Dominican campaign.

Williams earned his medal at San Francisco de Macoris, the capital of a province whose governor, Juan Perez, refused to order his adherents to disarm. Perez held the provincial *fortaleza,* a walled masonry compound that served as both a government house and fort. Williams was given two companies of marines with which to take it. Approaching the *fortaleza* under cover of darkness, he picked twelve men to follow him in a dash for the open gate. A

burst of fire from the forty startled defenders wounded eight of his party, but Williams and the others got through the gate. Their comrades surged forward, and in ten minutes it was all over.

A captain at the time America intervened in the world war, Williams volunteered for the western front and went overseas with the 35th Infantry. In July 1918 he succeeded in transferring to the 6th Marines, in which he took part in the defense of Soissons, the Saint-Mihiel offensive, the capture of Blanc Mont Ridge, and the Meuse-Argonne offensive. For his gallantry in these battles he received the Navy Cross, the Distinguished Service Cross, the Silver Star, and the croix de guerre.

Returning home with the rank of major, Williams was stationed at the Marine Barracks, Quantico, Virginia. An injury sustained while breaking a horse there caused him to be retired for disability in 1921. He was deeply disturbed when in 1927 Congress awarded Charles Lindbergh the Medal of Honor for flying the Atlantic, a deed—performed by a civilian in time of peace—that seemed to him undeserving of the decoration. Williams never wore his medal again. He died of a cerebral embolism at Seneca Falls, New York, on April 11, 1940. ✤

118

Contra Sandino
The Nicaraguan Wars

By the mid-1920s the United States was winding down its Caribbean commitments, symbolizing its new approach by withdrawing the legation guard from Managua, Nicaragua, in 1925. Hardly had the marines departed, however, than the Liberal party leader General José M. Moncada launched a revolt against the Conservative government. Peace-keeping forces of bluejackets and marines landed at coastal cities, and in 1927 former Secretary of War Henry L. Stimson was sent to Nicaragua to negotiate a cease-fire. Stimson promised the warring parties that if they would disarm and surrender their weapons to the marines, the United States would supervise free and fair elections in 1928. The Conservatives agreed. So did General Moncada. A relatively junior Liberal leader named Augusto C. Sandino, however, did not. On July 16, 1927, he began what would be the last of the "banana wars."

Augusto C. Sandino and his followers, the Sandinistas, established the base of their anti-American insurrection in the upland jungles of Nueva Segovina Province, on the Honduran border of northern Nicaragua, where Sandino had once worked for an American mining concern. The illegitimate son of a landowner and a peasant girl, he was thirty-two when he decided to attack the U.S. Marines at the village of Ocotal in the summer of 1927. The first of America's Caribbean adversaries to appreciate the potential of the press, he cultivated it to achieve international renown. Before his death, he had become an inspiration to revolutionary movements throughout Latin America.

In the months following the action at Ocotal, marine patrols fought a series of skirmishes with rebel forces in Nueva Segovina. Finally, in November, aerial reconnaissance located Sandino's headquarters on a mountain called El Chipote, and on December 19 two marine columns with a combined strength of 175 men moved out to attack it. They expected to meet from 200 to 500 Sandinistas. Instead, they were ambushed by 1,000. Badly mauled, with eight men killed and thirty wounded, including both column commanders, the marines fell back to the village of Quilali where they were promptly besieged.

The situation was little short of desperate, especially as the eleven seriously wounded would require litter bearers to be moved, thereby reducing the fighting force available for a breakout. On a flight over Quilali, Major Ross E. Rowell, the commander of Marine

U.S. Marines man a machine gun in the Nicaraguan interior, 1927.

Observation Squadron 7, concluded that if certain shacks were torn down it might be possible for a plane to land on the grass-grown main street. While the marines in the village set about improvising an airstrip, the squadron's mechanics modified one of its 02U-1 Vought Corsair biplanes with landing gear from a DeHavilland DH-4, deemed more suitable for the expected rough landings.

Thirty-two-year-old First Lieutenant Christian F. Schilt, a former enlisted man who had placed second in the Scheider International Seaplane Race in 1926, volunteered to pilot the craft. Between January 6 and 8, 1928, Schilt made ten flights into Quilali, evacuating eighteen of the wounded and bringing in 1,400 pounds of supplies as well as a relief commander, Captain Roger W. Peard. Each landing and takeoff was made under fire from the surrounding Sandinistas. Landing in particular was an adventure. The Corsair lacked brakes, so each time Schilt touched down the men on the ground had to run out and grab the plane's wings before it reached a

ravine at the end of the bumpy, 500-foot runway. After the last flight, Captain Peard conducted a successful withdrawal. Schilt's heroism was rewarded with the Medal of Honor. He went on to enjoy a distinguished career, eventually becoming chief of marine aviation and retiring as a four-star general in 1957.

Four years after the Quilali fight, the American intervention in Nicaragua was drawing to a close. The American-supervised elections Henry Stimson had promised Nicaragua in 1927 were held a year later. General Moncada won by a landslide, but Sandino denounced him as an imperialist lackey and spurned an invitation to lay down his arms. When in 1929 Stimson became secretary of state, there were 5,000 marines in Nicaragua. He reasoned that to eradicate the Sandinistas totally would require a greater military effort than it was sensible to make. He thus instructed the marines to prepare the Nicaraguan *Guardia Nacional* to take over the war. In the course of the year, the number of marines in the country was reduced to 1,800, most of them stationed in urban

areas. The *guardia,* still largely commanded by American officers, assumed all offensive patrolling. In February 1931 Stimson announced that the last marines would withdraw from Nicaragua by the end of 1932.

That year Corporal Donald LeRoy Truesdell, a second lieutenant in the *Guardia Nacional,* was serving his third tour in Nicaragua. Truesdell respected his *guardias.* "They were good men," he recalled, "and they cared a lot about me. They'd kill you if they didn't. I could take my patrol into a town and some officer would tell them to do something, and they'd say No, they'd have to ask me first. They were loyal."

Around nine o'clock on the morning of April 24, 1932, Truesdell was on patrol near the village of Constantzia in Nueva Segovina Province. According to the official citation of his valor:

While the patrol was . . . searching for a bandit group with which contact had just previously been made, a rifle grenade fell from its carrier and struck a rock, igniting the detonator. Several men close to the grenade at the time were in danger. Corporal Truesdell, who was several yards away, could easily have sought cover and safety for himself. Knowing full well the grenade would explode within 2 or 3 seconds, he rushed for the grenade, grasped it in his right hand, and attempted to throw it away from the patrol. The grenade exploded in his hand. . . . In taking the full shock of the explosion himself, [he] saved the members of his patrol from loss of life or serious injury.

Truesdell was knocked unconscious by the blast, which blew off his fingers, mangled his hand, and peppered his legs and chest with fragments. Eleven weeks later he left the Managua hospital, minus his right forearm, which had been

Donald L. Truesdell (left) receives the Medal of Honor. Truesdell later became a marksmanship instructor in World War II.

amputated just below the elbow. The Medal of Honor he received was the first one he had ever seen.

The marines left Nicaragua on January 2, 1933, according to plan. A day earlier, Juan B. Sacasa had assumed office as the country's new president. He appealed to Sandino to enter negotiations, and on February 2 a complicated agreement was reached whereby, in exchange for various concessions, Sandino disbanded his army. Differing interpretations of the agreement soon created friction between the government and the Sandinistas, however, and early in 1934 Sacasa called Sandino to Managua for talks. On the evening of February 21, Sandino and several of his lieutenants dined with Sacasa at the presidential palace. As they were leaving, they were seized by a *guardia* detachment acting under the orders of General Anastasio Somoza and mowed down by machine-gun fire. Three years later, Somoza deposed Sacasa and established an authoritarian regime that would rule Nicaragua until the overthrow of his son, Anastasio Somoza DeBayle, by a new generation of Sandinistas in 1979.

The Medal of Honor Roy Truesdell won in the Nicaraguan jungle was the last to be awarded for heroism in combat before World War II. In Washington, the new Democratic administration of Franklin D. Roosevelt continued the Caribbean disengagement inaugurated by its Republican predecessors. Under the Good Neighbor Policy, proclaimed within a year of Corporal Truesdell's act of valor, there would be no more banana wars. ✷

Augusto Sandino (center) and Anastasio Somoza (right) during peace talks in 1934, shortly before Sandino's assassination.

Changing Standards

The criteria by which the Medal of Honor is awarded have changed greatly over the years. The ambiguity of the original legislation for the army and navy medals gave nineteenth century commanders wide latitude in choosing men "who shall most distinguish themselves by their gallantry in action and other soldierlike [or seamanlike] qualities." In those early years many were undoubtedly given medals for actions that were not extraordinarily valorous but were in some way commendable. Considering a slew of recommendations for the battle of the Little Big Horn in 1877, Brigadier General Alfred H. Terry expressed exasperation with the lack of clear standards for medal-worthy actions. "Medals of Honor are not intended for ordinarily good conduct," he said, "but for conspicuous acts of gallantry." But the years since Appomattox had blurred such a distinction or at least clouded the record.

The 1890s were, in the words of one medal historian, "the Dark Ages in the history of the Medal of Honor. The old veterans of the Civil War were on the march, storming the halls of Congress in their black slouch hats and pestering the overworked clerks at the War Department." In person or by mail, they sought their own Medals of Honor. Since there was no time limit on awards, a constant stream of requests flowed into the capital. "I believe I am entitled to a medal" was a common line, followed by a brief description of an act from years before. There was usually no extensive review or verification of the action; in some cases, the applicant's word was sufficient. The secretary of war would then direct that a medal be engraved and sent to the veteran.

From 1891 to 1897 over 500 Medals of Honor were awarded for Civil War actions. The Medal of Honor Legion, a newly formed organization of medal recipients, expressed concern that the generous bestowal of the award was weakening its intended prestige. By the middle of the decade many army officials agreed.

On June 26, 1897, Secretary of War Russell A. Alger announced a more uniform method of determining Medal of Honor eligibility, stating that a deed must demonstrate "most distinguished gallantry in action" based on "incontestable proof" of the action. Verification, the army announced later, had to come from "official reports of the action, record of events, muster rolls, and returns and descriptive lists." All subsequent recommendations were to be accompanied by the testimony of two or more eyewitnesses. Applications for actions taking place after January 1, 1890, could not be made by the prospective recipient himself but only by another officer or soldier having personal knowledge of the action. A year later the department announced that only officers could submit recommendations.

Alger's order also stipulated that recommendations for actions taking place in the future must be forwarded to the adjutant general within one year of their occurrence. It was the first time that the government placed a time limit on medal applications. The deadline did not apply to past actions, however, so Civil War deeds could still be considered. It was not until 1917 that the last two Union veterans, Henry Lewis and Henry C. Peters, got their Medals of Honor. As a result of these guidelines recommendations for both the army and navy medals decreased, and subsequent citations became longer and more complete.

Though medal policy had been clarified somewhat, the liberality of many past awards still vexed some lawmakers and officers. In April 1916 President Wilson signed a law that not only revised medal standards but also allowed the army to atone for past indiscretions.

The bill provided for the establishment of an "Army and Navy Medal of Honor Roll" and directed that a pension of ten dollars per month starting at age sixty-five be paid to each person who had "been awarded a medal of honor for having distinguished himself conspicuously by gallantry or intrepidity, at the risk of his life, above and beyond the call of duty." This last phrase would set the tone for later Medal of Honor awards for all armed services.

Some veterans were bound to be ineligible for the roll because of the tougher requirements for the medal. The War Department was ready to take a drastic step to correct what some viewed as unwarranted past awards. The opportunity came about in June 1916 when Congress authorized the department to appoint a board of five retired general officers to review every one of the 2,625 army Medals of Honor awarded up to that time.

Chosen to head the panel was Lieutenant General

Nelson A. Miles, a medal recipient from Chancellorsville, a commander during the Indian Wars, and a past commander of the Medal of Honor Legion. Though Miles and his fellow officers later expressed uneasiness at being asked to rescind awards years after they were given, their concern over the dilution of the medal's prestige apparently superseded those feelings.

In a report filed on February 15, 1917, the army board removed from the rolls the names of 911 recipients, more than one-third of the previous total. Included was an entire regiment, the 27th Maine, numbering 864 men (see page 33), and the 29 members of the honor guard that had escorted President Lincoln's body to Illinois in April 1865. All these men were judged not to have merited the medal because they did not distinguish themselves in combat and at the risk of life.

The other eighteen were expunged for either lack of supporting evidence or failure to meet the statutory requirements. Dr. Mary Walker was another casualty of the review (see page 38), as were five men who had been Civil War or Indian campaign scouts, including William F. "Wild Bill" Cody. "These men fully earned their medals," the panel reported, but because they were civilians at the time of their actions they were now officially ineligible.

Some of the canceled recipients were notified that it was now illegal to wear or display their medals. To those who had never received them, such as some from the 27th Maine, such a warning was moot. Others, like Mary Walker, vowed to continue to wear their medals.

With the tightening of standards, however, military officials were left in a bind. Since the Medal of Honor and the Certificate of Merit (revived in 1877 for "distinguished service whether in action or otherwise, of a valuable character to the United States") were the only two awards in existence, how would lesser, but still praiseworthy, deeds be recognized?

The answer was an act that became law on July 9, 1918, creating three additional medals for the army (and later the air force): the Distinguished Service Cross (and later, the Air Force Cross), the Distinguished Service Medal, and the Silver Star. The counterparts for the navy and Marine Corps, established a year later, were the Navy Cross and the Distinguished Service Medal. Each was intended to honor actions that were notable but not "above and beyond the call of duty."

In a subtle yet important shift away from the Civil War legislation, the act authorized the president to award the new medals, "but not in the name of Congress." That imprimatur, and the attendant prestige, were reserved for the nation's highest honor. In later years, with the creation of other military awards, the Medal of Honor retained its place as America's premier military decoration, atop what became known as the "Pyramid of Honor."

Most of the changes concerning the Medal of Honor have dealt with the army version. For almost 100 years the navy regulations were basically unchanged. The phrase "seamanlike qualities" in the original legislation enabled the service to award its medal to sailors for peacetime bravery "in the line of their profession," such as rescues at sea. Finally in 1963 Congress decreed that the navy medal could only be given for combat actions. (The navy has never revoked past awards for statutory ineligibility, but several sailors lost their medals because of subsequent dishonorable conduct, such as desertion.)

Other features of the medal-awarding process have also been refined. The time limit between an action and the awarding of a Medal of Honor for it has occasionally been changed; today it is three years for the army and air force and five years for the navy and marines. Congress can extend the limits by special statute, allowing for reconsideration of a case if new evidence warrants it.

The review process for a Medal of Honor recommendation in modern times is quite strict. A commander's report goes to the awards board of the respective service, then to the service secretary, then to the secretary of defense, and finally to the president. At any point the medal can be denied. But if the recommendation is approved by the president, it has passed the strenuous test of verification and is judged worthy of the nation's highest award. ◈

Medal of Honor Designs

Current navy, air force, and army Medals of Honor

The current navy, air force, and army Medal of Honor designs are the products of almost a century of revision, both to preserve their singularity and to satisfy the changing wishes of military officials.

Cast from the same dies during the Civil War, the original navy and army medals have remained the models for their later incarnations. Both feature "Minerva Repulsing Discord" at the center and different suspension ribbon attachments particular to each service. These two medals, with only a change in the army ribbon in 1896, were presented for the rest of the nineteenth century.

The widespread imitation of the Medal of Honor design by veterans' groups, most notably the Grand Army of the Republic, in the late 1800s caused army officials to consider a new design for their medal. Conceived by Brigadier General George Gillespie, a Civil War recipient, and approved in 1904, the new army design was a five-pointed star, with a profile of Minerva at the center, surrounded by a green enameled laurel wreath. The army eagle now rested on a bar reading "VALOR." Supporting the medal was a blue silk ribbon, spangled with thirteen stars.

Gillespie received a patent for his design, which he turned over to the secretary of war and his successors. After the patent expired in 1918, Congress passed a law forbidding the unauthorized duplication of military medals.

Meanwhile the navy, which had awarded scores of Medals of Honor for peacetime bravery, created a different model for actual combat action in 1919. The Maltese cross designed by Tiffany and Company of New York bore the American eagle surrounded by four anchors. It was attached to a blue, starred ribbon with a bar that inexplicably bore the British spelling of "VALOUR."

Only a handful of men, mostly from World War I, received this type of medal. Noncombat acts of valor continued to be rewarded by the star design of the Medal of Honor, now with a ribbon similar to the army model. In 1942 Congress eliminated the Tiffany cross, and once again all naval personnel were eligible for only one Medal of Honor, the original star. The cross remains the rarest Medal of Honor model and represents the only time that the military deviated from its star design.

The naval star and the 1904 army design were the models awarded during World War II. The medals were attached to a blue ribbon with a clasp, making the Medal of Honor the only American combat award that is draped around the neck. The neck ribbon was the last alteration of the modern army and navy medals.

In both world wars, army Air Corps pilots received the army Medal of Honor. Even in Korea, after the air force had become a separate service, its men continued to receive the army design. In 1963 the air force created its own medal, first presented to Vietnam fliers. The air force Medal of Honor is similar to the army medal, with the head of the Statue of Liberty replacing Minerva and a ribbon attachment more specific to that service.

One need not wear his Medal of Honor to be identified as a recipient. Military men on active duty wear a blue ribbon bearing five stars on the left breast of the uniform, always above all other decorations. A starred rosette is worn in the lapel by civilians.

Original navy 1862

Original army 1862

Army 1896

Army 1904 Gillespie

Navy 1913

Tiffany cross   Navy 1919

Uniform ribbon

Rosette

World War
I

The First World War

It was called the World War, the Great War, the war to end all wars. To this day historians debate its cause: deliberate German aggression, the last gasp of imperialism, an arms race gone wild, an unfortunate chain of events. Its results were more clear cut. The United States entered on the premise that victories for the Allies would usher in an era of world peace. Instead, the defeat of Germany and Austria-Hungary set the victors to squabbling for the spoils. In disgust America retreated into a quarter-century of isolationism.

The First World War erupted with the crack of a Serbian assassin's bullet, killing Archduke Franz Ferdinand of the Austro-Hungarian Empire. In one cataclysmic week, from July 28 to August 5, 1914, Austria-Hungary declared war on Serbia; Russia mobilized in support of its Balkan ally; Germany declared war on Russia and its key ally, France, and marched into strategically vital Belgium; and Great Britain declared war on Germany for violating Belgium's neutrality. In the ensuing weeks and months the powers dragged in their colonies across the globe while the opportunistic joined the side of the alliance they judged most likely to win.

Archduke Franz Ferdinand (far right) and his wife Sophie in Sarajevo, June 28, 1914, moments before they were both assassinated by Serbian terrorist Gavrilo Princip.

The United States proclaimed neutrality at first. Said President Woodrow Wilson, "It is a war with which we have nothing to do, whose causes cannot touch us." But over the next thirty-three months the American president and people slowly changed their minds. The U.S. government came to fear for the future of the United Kingdom and the balance of power it had maintained to America's advantage. More crucial to popular sentiment, the new technology of warfare made the American vision of neutrality obsolete. German submarines, or "U-boats," plied the seas unseen, striking vessels without warning, violating, in Wilson's words, "the sacred immunities of noncombatants."

On May 7, 1915, a German U-boat torpedoed and sank the British passenger liner *Lusitania,* killing over 1,000 people, 128 of them Americans. For a time the United States flamed with war fever. It cooled only when the German government promised to rein in its submarine fleet. But by 1917 Germany felt compelled to break the tight British blockade, which was strangling its imperial war machine. In February Germany resumed unrestricted submarine warfare. In March its submarines, without warning, sank five unarmed American merchant vessels. On April 2 President Wilson called for war. The Senate agreed 82-6; the House followed on April 6 by a 373-50 vote.

So the United States entered a war that had been raging with exhausting brutality for nearly three years. What the German government had initially declared would be a simple, fast-paced affair had instead become a deadly stand-off. Lines of fortified trenches scarred northern France and Belgium. Around them soldiers died by the millions in massed infantry assaults that moved the line only a few feet forward or back. Ten days after the United States declared war, the French launched yet another futile attack near Reims and in ten more days had gained nothing but another 187,000 casualties. Over 13 million soldiers and civilians were to die in the conflict.

The combatants were shackled by their own tech-

Preceding pages. *Men and tanks of the U.S. 1st Infantry Division advance against German machine-gun positions near the Villers-Cotterets Forest, July 1918.*

nology. The widespread expansion of railroad lines across Europe allowed for the mobilization of massive armies, unimaginable before the age of mechanized warfare. More than 6 million troops were transported to the front or support areas in the first month of the war. The old-fashioned military planning staffs throughout Europe could not keep up with the scale of the operations. The massed attacks quickly translated into the terrible toll of casualties. In horror the armies began digging in to protect themselves. By the close of the first year of war the front had become a labyrinth of six-foot-deep trenches, concrete-fortified dug-outs, and barbed wire fences guarded by rows of machine guns.

It was a blueprint for stalemate. Infantry assaults on trench lines resulted in slaughter for the attackers unless they were preceded by an artillery barrage. Heavy artillery was in chronically short supply and, when available, required days to emplace accurately. The delay gave the defenders time to bring in reserve forces. So, even if the assault succeeded, the attackers were so depleted in the fighting they rarely were able to move on to the next trench line—and often retreated at the first counterattack.

German troops marching off to war accept flowers from an admirer. Germany mobilized 11 million men to fight in the World War.

To tip the balance the two sides produced progressively more ruthless weapons of destruction. Machine guns were the biggest killer. At the onset of war France had 2,500 machine guns; by the armistice it had built and deployed 314,000. A single gun could wipe out dozens of charging men in moments. Other relatively new agents of death were hand grenades, trench mortars, and poison gas. In one twenty-minute gas bombardment at Ypres in 1915, 15,000 men died or were left to spend the rest of their lives as gasping invalids. Less destructive in the short run, but of far greater consequence for the future, were developments in aerial warfare and the first use of the mechanized tank in 1916.

The new destructive power had taken an enervating toll on both sides by the time the United States entered the war, but the Allies were in worse shape than their enemies. Low morale following the French failure in the Champagne offensive led to a series of mutinies in the French army. Germany's revival of submarine warfare was having its intended effect on British shipping, the principal Allied resource. And in Russia antiwar rumblings grew louder until in November 1917 they sparked a revolution that resulted in a separate peace. The entry of the fresh, enthusiastic doughboys, backed by the industrial might of the U.S., could not have come at a more opportune time.

In March 1917 the U.S. Army consisted of about 200,000 men. During the war that number leaped to 4 million, over half of them draftees. One and a half million American soldiers ultimately saw combat in France and another half-million supported them. But this was a slow process. Drafting, training, equipping, and moving large numbers of troops across the ocean was a gargantuan task. It took eight months for the Americans to join the fighting. By May 1918 only the first 500,000 troops had arrived in France. And they were still engaged in training or were occupying quiet sectors. Until June the support they gave the Allies was moral.

That all changed, though, once they got engaged. In the last five months of the war, 49,000 doughboys gave their lives in the Allied cause; over 200,000 more were wounded. An additional 63,000 died in the influenza epidemic that lashed the military compounds.

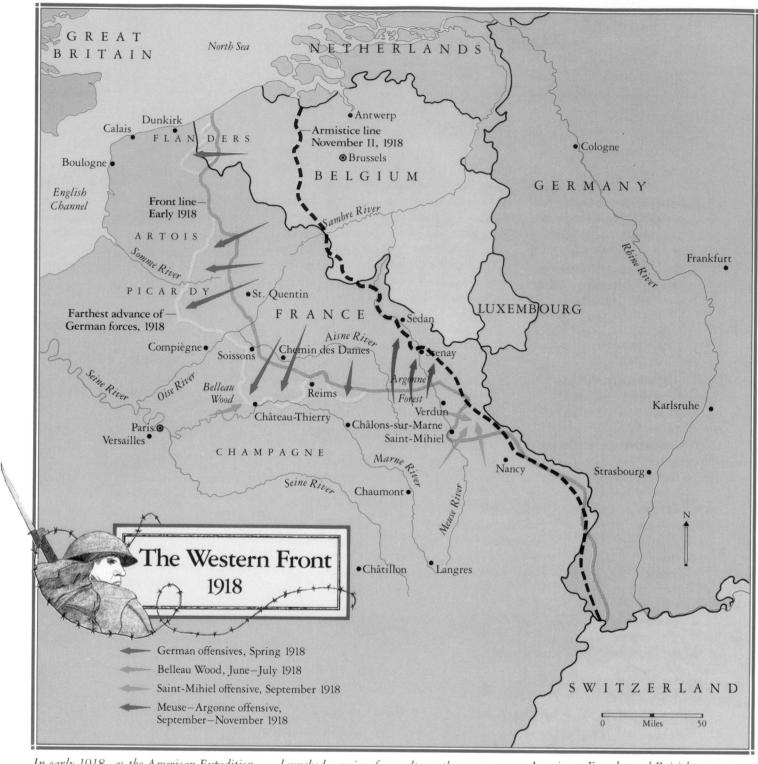

The Western Front 1918

GREAT BRITAIN
North Sea
NETHERLANDS
Dunkirk
Calais
FLANDERS
Boulogne
English Channel
ARTOIS
Somme River
PICARDY
St. Quentin
FRANCE
Compiègne
Soissons
Chemin des Dames
Belleau Wood
Château-Thierry
Paris
Versailles
CHAMPAGNE
Seine River
Seine River
Oise River
Reims
Aisne River
Marne River
Chaumont
Châtillon
Langres
Antwerp
Armistice line November 11, 1918
Brussels
BELGIUM
Sambre River
Sedan
Stenay
Argonne Forest
Verdun
Châlons-sur-Marne
Saint-Mihiel
Meuse River
Nancy
GERMANY
Cologne
Rhine River
Frankfurt
LUXEMBOURG
Karlsruhe
Strasbourg
SWITZERLAND

Front line— Early 1918
Farthest advance of— German forces, 1918

German offensives, Spring 1918
Belleau Wood, June–July 1918
Saint-Mihiel offensive, September 1918
Meuse–Argonne offensive, September–November 1918

N

0   Miles   50

In early 1918, as the American Expeditionary Forces arrived in France to assist their beleaguered Allies, the German Empire launched a series of assaults on the western front. Stopped at the Marne River, German forces fell back in the face of combined American, French, and British counterattacks that swept to the Meuse River and forced the armistice of November 11, 1918.

Commanding the American Expeditionary Forces (AEF) was John J. Pershing. Called "Black Jack" because of his iron will and steely discipline, his powers were sorely tested in creating an army from scratch. He took command of American forces in Europe in 1917, months before there were any such forces. He had orders to cooperate with the Allies but to build the AEF as a distinct and separate unit. This conflicted with the plans of Marshal Ferdinand Foch, commander of French and British operations on the western front, who implored Pershing to turn over his forces to the unified command to be deployed where Foch deemed them most needed. For the most part Pershing held firmly to his orders.

Only during the darkest days of the German offen-

Above. *Unrestricted German submarine warfare took a frightful toll on Allied shipping. Here survivors of a U-boat torpedo attack slide down ropes from their crippled craft to board waiting lifeboats.*

Below. *American doughboys say goodbye to their sweethearts on the first leg of their long journey to the war in Europe.*

sive on the Marne in the spring of 1918 did American troops fight under foreign command. One of the battles of that offensive, at Château-Thierry in June 1918, was the Americans' first significant engagement—and its first victory. In one month of heavy fighting the U.S. 2d Division, fighting under French command, halted a major German advance, then pushed the enemy out of Belleau Wood. Two marines and two navy medics earned Medals of Honor in that action. Germany's defeat in the Aisne-Marne offensive eased the pressure on the Allies considerably. Morale rose, and Pershing reclaimed his troops for the separate U.S. Army.

On September 26, following three months of small engagements, the Allies launched a great counteroffensive along the entire front. The AEF took the eastern sector, centered upon the heavily defended Argonne Forest. Pershing deployed every American division at his disposal—1.2 million U.S. troops. Their goal was to cut off the main German supply line feeding the western front.

The Germans fought desperately, employing their advantages in position, artillery, and experience. But the Americans overpowered them in numbers and audacity. In six weeks of brutal fighting the AEF captured the Argonne, taking 16,000 prisoners in the bargain. Eighty-two men earned the Medal of Honor in the engagements.

On November 11, after a week of strikes, mutiny, and revolution among its allies, Germany surrendered. The peace negotiations at Versailles, France, were a fiasco from the start. Wilson had convinced the German government to sue for peace on the basis of his "Fourteen Points"—including "open covenants of peace, openly arrived at," free trade, mutual armament reduction, and adjustment of colonial claims to give equal weight to the desires of the native populations. Wilson had not bothered to get the Allied governments to agree to these terms—nor would they now. Even the U.S. Congress opposed many of the points. Wilson called for a lenient peace, to bring Germany into the society of democracies, but Britain and especially France insisted on unconditional surrender. With casualties running in the millions and destruction of property in the billions of dollars, the French and British demanded huge reparations, regardless of Germany's ability to pay.

Wilson had envisioned an enlightened treaty that would spell the end of all war. But so different was the document he came back with than his original promise that the nation turned away from it in revulsion. On November 19, 1919, the U.S. Senate rejected the Versailles Treaty and the League of Nations it created. In the economic and social heydays of the 1920s, the United States tried to forget the continent where thousands of its young men lay buried. ❖

Over There

The arrival of American forces in France in 1918 was cheered by the beleaguered Allies, many of whom had been fighting for over three years. The doughboys' high spirits proved the decisive factor in overcoming the same miserable conditions that had bled other nations dry. They tipped the balance of power in favor of the Allies. Clockwise from left. U.S. machine gunners in the devastated Argonne Forest, 1918; a cover for inspirational sheet music likening General Pershing to the father of his country; wearing masks to protect themselves from poisonous gas, soldiers stand guard, March 1, 1918; American tanks in the Argonne, 1918.

Prisoner of the *U–90*
Edouard Izac's Escape

In the months before the dough-boys fought their first battle, the U.S. Navy faced war on the high seas. German U-boats prowled the North Atlantic, sinking Allied ships along the sea routes from America to Europe. One sailor's battle against the Germans began at sea and ended on land. Navy Secretary Josephus Daniels said of him later: "Well, as you know, they only captured one of us. Couldn't keep him."

Navy Lieutenant Edouard Izac, whose unwillingness to accept POW status earned him the Medal of Honor.

Edouard Victor Izac was born December 18, 1891, the last of nine children of a successful, politically inclined family in Cresco, Iowa. His dream for as long as he could remember was to be a naval officer. For a while it looked as if it might not be realized. The local congressman, who chose boys from the district to attend the Naval Academy, was a partisan Republican, but Izac's father was the leading Democrat in the area. Edouard had to move to his brother's home in Chicago and work for three years for the city before he could secure an appointment to Annapolis. When he graduated with ensign's bars he was twenty-three years old.

When America entered the war Izac received a promotion to lieutenant and assignment as the afterdeck gunnery officer on the U.S.S. *President Lincoln,* a confiscated German passenger liner. Refitted as a troopship, the steamer plied the Atlantic carrying 5,000 troops and 7,000 tons of cargo to France each trip. On May 21, 1918, it was returning from its fifth trip in a convoy of four ships making about 12.5 knots. Its usual destroyer escort had peeled off to meet up with a larger troopship heading toward France, so the four vessels were on their own. That night a German submarine, the *U-90,* spotted the convoy of American troopships by the light of the moon.

Izac was finishing breakfast when a double explosion rocked the *President Lincoln.* He rushed to his deck to see what had happened when a third torpedo struck, tossing a lifeboat onto the deck not ten feet in front of him. Izac reached his guns, but there was no hope of fighting it out. The torpedoes had torn giant holes in the ship's holds. By the time Izac had shoved his way through the debris to the afterdeck, the ship was listing sharply to the rear. Izac notified the captain that water was

approaching the main deck. He heard the reply: "Abandon ship."

Twenty minutes later, the survivors watched from their lifeboats as the ship went down. "As the waters closed over," Izac said later, "we rose and gave three cheers for the *President Lincoln,* the best ship that ever carried troops in the cause of freedom." Twenty-six officers and men went down with the ship. For Lieutenant Izac, though, the adventure was just beginning.

As the three remaining ships from the convoy raced from the dangerous waters, the *U-90* slowly rose to the surface and bore down on the flotilla of rafts. The captain was obviously searching for something. He brought his vessel within thirty feet of Izac's lifeboat and stopped. Looking straight at the lieutenant he ordered him to come aboard. "Are you captain of the *President Lincoln?*" the U-boat skipper asked. Izac said no. He lied and said that the captain had gone down with the ship. "When I sink a man o'war I always take the senior officer present prisoner," said the German. "Well, it looks as if I'll have to take you." He ordered Izac below and the submarine sailed away. (The next morning an American destroyer rescued the remaining crew of the *President Lincoln,* including its captain.)

For the next three weeks Izac remained captive on the U-boat as it patrolled the North Atlantic. The voyage was cut short after an extremely close call with some depth charges dropped by a pair of U.S. destroyers ("I don't know which side I was cheering for at that time," said Izac). The submarine survived, but its captain decided it was time to take her home.

The German skipper allowed Izac virtually free movement, since as long as they were out to sea the prisoner had no way of escaping. Izac used his liberty to educate himself. All through the voyage

As survivors crowd lifeboats on the high seas, the U.S.S. President Lincoln *slips down to a watery grave.*

Izac made mental notes of the U-boat's design, habits, and course. Whenever he had the chance he stole a glance at the ship's charts. He tried to catch snippets of conversations and watched for signals to and from other vessels. Soon he had collected a sizable store of intelligence. When the ship neared the Baltic Sea he began making plans for escape.

On June 10, as the U-boat sailed through the narrows between Denmark and Sweden, Izac made his move. In the dark of the night he put on a life jacket and wandered as casually as he could toward the deck railings. Just as he sprang forward, he felt a grip on his arm. It was the captain. Realizing resistance

was useless, Izac accepted the order to return to his hammock.

Two days later the U-boat pulled into dock at Wilhelmshaven, the base of the German fleet. Izac was transferred to a prison ship there. His treatment changed dramatically. He was placed in solitary confinement in a barred room and given no food but a watery soup of inedible leaves and a lump of rock-hard bread (which he later discovered was made of water, potatoes, sawdust, chaff, and sand).

After two or three days of starving him, the lieutenant's captors determined he was ready for interrogation. An English-speaking officer chatted with

him for a while and offered him cigarettes, then began asking questions about the size of the American forces. Izac later recalled, "I rather frightened him with the tales I told of the 2 million men we had in France and 20 million who were on the way, until finally he lost his temper and demanded to know why America had entered the war. . . . 'Why!' he exclaimed, 'we expected you to come in on the side of Germany.'"

Izac could not suppress his hatred for the navy that had sunk so many unarmed vessels. Courting the rage of his interrogators he replied that his country could not have joined Germany as a partner because "we had no reputa-

Inside the cramped quarters of a German U-boat, like the one that carried Lieutenant Izac, crewmen prepare a torpedo.

tion established in the realms of pillage and rapine. We had not murdered any women and children. We were not even Huns!" His interrogation ended abruptly. The next day guards removed Izac to a land-based prison.

More interrogations followed—and more mistreatment. In late June Izac was taken by train to a distribution camp at Karlsruhe. He was the first American to arrive there, causing considerable excitement among the British and French captives. From his first moments in the camp he made plans for escape. Once the other prisoners heard of his desire to get information to the U.S. Navy, they contributed plans, food, money, maps, and a compass. Many of these materials were bought on a lively black market that sprang up between prisoners, who were paid for work, and the prison guards.

His best opportunity for escape came when he was told he was being sent to another camp. He filled a knapsack with the food he had been storing and secreted his compass, map, and money in it. Before he left the camp, guards strip-searched him. Izac broke into a cold sweat as they examined seams of every item of clothing, even slitting open the seams. But they missed his contraband. He walked to the train between his two guards with a feeling of triumph.

The guards sat him down on a bench in a fourth-class compartment of a parked troop train. One guard sat next to him, the other across. Both had loaded guns trained on the prisoner. Fortunately, in the July heat the train became so stifling that someone opened the nearby window. That gave Izac his opportunity. He waited until one of his guards dozed off and the other turned his head to speak to another passenger. They were only about five miles from

their destination; he had to act. Grabbing his knapsack, he leaped out of the window.

The train was going about forty miles an hour when Izac hit the ground. He had planned to land on the running board, which he had noticed lining each of the train cars, then jump off. But the car he had been in had no running board. Instead Izac hit a second train track, cracking his skull and splitting his knees open on the metal rails. He tried to get up and run but his legs would barely move. In moments his guards were closing in on him, shooting. Izac raised his hands and surrendered.

The two Germans beat him mercilessly. They took turns knocking him to the ground with the butts of their rifles, kicking him until he got up, then striking him down again. Finally, on the seventh or eighth blow, one of the guards hit Izac so hard he broke his rifle at the stock. The prisoner's limp body flew back, landing several feet away.

When Izac regained consciousness, his guards wrenched him to his feet and marched him at attention the five miles to Villingen prison camp, kicking him or prodding him with their bayonets whenever he slowed or relaxed his body a bit. The American was a pathetic sight, bleeding from all over his body, his uniform in tatters, unable to move at more than a shuffle. Every few hundred yards his guards would strike him down again in a burst of anger. When he arrived at the camp he was, by his own account, "more dead than alive."

The commandant of Villingen told Izac if he tried to escape again he would be shot. Then he ordered the beaten lieutenant into a vermin-infested solitary cell where he lay for the next two weeks, his wounds festering under paper bandages. As soon as he was released and able to walk, he again searched for a way out of prison.

Izac (right) at Villingen prison with friends. (Note name at top right; Izac and his family occasionally spelled their name Isaacs.)

Word-of-honour.

I declare by my word-of-honour, that I will not make any attempt to escape from the time leaving the camp until returning to it, will make no preparation for a future escape, will not act in any way to the prejudice of the German Empire and that I will submit myself to the order of the escort.

I know that a prisoner of war escaping inspite of the given word-of-honour, according to § 15 of the German army regulation incures the penalty of death.

Signature: E. V. Isaacs.

Izac prepared for another attempt by working himself into top physical shape. Gradually he built up his legs through calisthenics and walking —fifteen miles a day once his strength returned. Next he organized an escape team. He gathered boards and screws to make a ladder, tools, maps, and other materials he might need for the escape. The morning of October 6 Izac gathered the conspirators and announced that they would make their break that night. They would split into four teams, each escaping by a different method. Izac and two aviators, Lieutenants Battle and Tucker, constituted the first team. They were to cut through a window grating with a stolen file, launch Izac's home-made ladder like a bridge to the top of the camp's fence, and crawl out.

The day passed in a flurry of covert activity as Izac and his partners cut away the bottom half of the window grating,

A diagram of Villingen from Izac's 1919 account, Prisoner of the U-90.

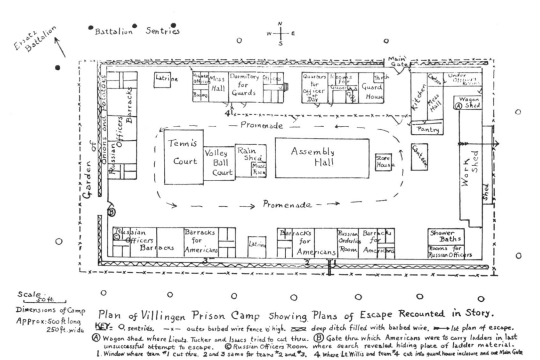

Plan of Villingen Prison Camp Showing Plans of Escape Recounted in Story.
KEY: O, sentries. —x— outer barbed wire fence 6' high. ⊠⊠ deep ditch filled with barbed wire. ▸▸ 1st plan of escape.
Ⓐ Wagon shed where Lieuts. Tucker and Isaacs tried to cut thru. Ⓑ Gate thru which Americans were to carry ladders in last unsuccessful attempt to escape. Ⓒ Russian Officers Room where search revealed hiding place of ladder material.
1. Window where team #1 cut thru. 2 and 3 same for teams #2 and #3. 4. Where Lt Willis and team #4 cut into guard house inclosure and out Main Gate.

Scale: 50 ft.
Dimensions of Camp
Approx: 500 ft. long
250 ft. wide

carefully timing their movements to the pacing of the guard in front of their barracks. After roll call at 7:00 P.M. they finished assembling the ladder and covered it with shoe polish (bought on the camp's black market) so it would blend in with the night. A rainstorm soaked the camp that night, but at 10:30 all was ready to go. At 10:45 a volunteer threw a wire chain against the main electrical grid, shorting out the system and plunging the camp into darkness.

The escapees had to move fast. With the help of "two big, brawny Pennsylvania Guardsmen" Izac, Battle, and Tucker launched the bridge from the window to the fence. The guardsmen leaned on the end of the ladder inside the barracks to act as a counterweight while the three officers crawled across in the pouring rain. The lightest man, Tucker, went first, then Izac, then the 180-pound Battle. The German guards, who

could hear their movement, fired on them at close range, but the shots went wild. The three men jumped over the fence and ran from the camp.

By prearrangement Tucker and Battle split off from Izac and continued on as a pair. Izac ran on alone to a landmark a couple of miles from the camp. There he waited for a fourth escapee, Lieutenant Willis of the Lafayette Escadrille (a corps of American fliers serving with the French before the U.S. entry into the war). Willis had escaped by disguising himself as a German soldier, cutting through a plain wire fence to the guard house, and rushing out with guards in the dark and confusion. Willis and Izac met at the landmark, then took off in the direction of neutral Switzerland. To throw off the bloodhounds they covered their path with pepper.

The pepper worked. Izac and Willis made it through the first night

and kept on going. They traveled at night, avoiding roads and bridges, speaking rarely and then only in whispers, eating raw potatoes and other forage from the fields. After one week they came in sight of the Rhine. Along the shore stood sentries armed with searchlights and rifles. In the black of the night Willis and Izac silently inched out into the river water to find a suitable ford.

"All of a sudden," recalled Izac, "Willis disappeared." He had been caught by the whirling current. Then Izac too was swept up and dragged toward the center of the river. He fought the rapids but it was a losing battle. He was simply too worn out and frozen to go on. "So turning over on my back I commended myself to my God and closed my eyes. Instantly my feet touched ground." He was in Switzerland.

Izac made his way to a nearby house, where the occupants welcomed him warmly. When they heard his story, said Izac, the man of the house, a Swiss customs guard, "was tickled to death. He said, 'Nineteen people have drowned crossing here. . . . You're lucky!'" Izac turned out to have even more reason to cheer: The Swiss found Willis warming up in a tavern about two miles down river. (Only one other American made it out of Villingen to Switzerland that October. Those three, along with a soldier who escaped from another camp at the same time, were the first American servicemen to escape Germany during the war.)

Izac eventually reached the British Admiralty to deliver the information he hoped would allow the Allies to cut off the German submarine route. For three days he and an intelligence officer worked on the plan. "And then," remembered Izac, ". . . we were told that the German submarines were all returning under a white flag." It was November 11, 1918. The war was over. ✤

Advance on the Marne
Belleau Wood

In the late spring of 1918 French morale reached rock bottom. After nearly four years of incessant, grinding war, victory seemed as far out of reach as ever. The U.S. declaration of war was now more than a year old—and still the Americans had made no significant contribution on the battlefield. Then in early June, in an obscure little forest called Belleau Wood, the U.S. Marines stopped, then reversed, a week-long German advance on the Marne River. A French staff officer, seeing the doughboys arrive at the front, declared: "The spectacle of those magnificent youths . . . contrasted strikingly with our regiments in their faded uniforms, wasted by so many years of war. . . . Life was coming in floods to reanimate the dying body of France."

On May 27, 1918, a thunderous barrage of gas and high-explosive shells signaled the start of Germany's major offensive in the Marne region. Thirty German divisions punched through the French lines at the *Chemin des Dames* and began to push toward Paris. By June 1 they had less than forty miles to go. The French were in disarray; the enemy had scored tremendous victories, including the capture of over 65,000 prisoners. In a tense meeting of the Allied Supreme War Council, French Premier Georges Clemenceau blamed the massive defeat on General Pershing's unwillingness to throw his troops into the fight. Pershing thought otherwise; he laid the blame on the Allies' stubborn commitment to trench warfare. As much as his French counterparts, however, he feared the loss of Paris—and with it the loss of the war. On May 30 Pershing dropped his insistence on a separate U.S. Army and temporarily turned over his first five divisions to fight under French command. Hours later the U.S. 2d Division

Marine Sergeant Ernest A. Janson, who received two Medals of Honor under two different names.

was ordered to head for the very center of the German advance at Château-Thierry.

The 2d Division of U.S. regulars was a "bastard" division, half marine, half army. Though they were called regulars, not even a quarter of its men had been in the service for more than a year. Most, army and marine alike, had enlisted in the flush of patriotism that followed the U.S. declaration of war. But they were more than ready to take on the Germans, having spent the last four and a half months in France training and patrolling away from the front.

Two days and several changes of orders later, the division stood on the battle line. On June 4 the marine brigade halted the Germans at Belleau Wood. So far, however, action had been light. By June 6 they were ready to go on the offensive. They eagerly accepted orders to flush the Germans out.

The 49th and 67th Rifle Companies of the 5th Marines led the attack. Their objective was Hill 142, a commanding position overlooking the wood. To secure it they would have to defeat two German battalions backed up by three machine-gun companies hidden in the trees. At 3:45 A.M. the marines headed up. For the first fifty yards they advanced easily, protected by the morning fog. Then, as the sun cut through, the machine guns from the hill opened up. A number of Americans fell; many more hit the ground in fear. For several minutes the marines halted. Then, the initial shock over, they rushed the wooded ridge.

Gunnery Sergeant Ernest Janson, a thirty-nine-year-old career man, urged his platoon into the forest. Janson was a man as mysterious as he was brave. In 1910, after eleven years in the army, he left the service and enlisted with the marines as a buck private under the name of Charles Hoffman. He never explained why.

No explanations about names were required in Belleau Wood on June 6, 1918, however. Janson's job was to take the hill. He and his comrades in 49th Company ran from clearing to forest to ravine, taking machine-gun fire and giving more than their share of casualties in return. In just over two hours they not only reached their objective, but, because of a map-reading error, they overran it by 600 yards. By midmorning they had begun consolidating their position on the hill.

Janson was in the midst of organizing a strong point on the north side of the hill when the enemy counterattacked. Experts at infiltration, the Germans penetrated within twenty feet of the marines unobserved. Then Janson spotted a dozen Germans armed with five machine guns crawling through the thick underbrush. The sergeant shouted a warning to his company, then rushed their position before the enemy could recover their momentum. Singling out the two leaders, Janson bayoneted both. The others dropped their machine guns and ran. Company commander Captain George Hamilton, who had witnessed the incident, credited Janson's quick action with saving 49th Company and keeping American possession of the hill. The sergeant had also earned a Medal of Honor, with two citations, and the confusion about Janson/Hoffman's name went down in history. Under the dual arrangement for members of the marine brigade serving in the First World War under army command, Medal of Honor recipients received two awards—one from the army, one from the navy. Janson's two citations carry separate names. The army medal went to Ernest Janson, the navy medal to Charles F. Hoffman.

With Hill 142 securely in American hands by midafternoon June 6, the marines struck into Belleau Wood itself. The 3d Battalion of the 6th Marines attacked from the south. They moved into the wood, slowly pushing the Germans back, but they could not break through to their objective, the village of Bouresches on the forest's southwest corner. So the job fell to 96th Company.

To reach Bouresches the company had to cross an open wheat field directly in front of a line of German trenches, machine-gun emplacements, and sharpshooter pits nestled just inside the wood.

In fierce fighting at battle-scarred Belleau Wood, a doughboy dispatches a German soldier.

Below. *A victim of poison gas is led to a field hospital in Froissy, France, May 1918.*

needed relief. For four days the company stayed in support, the closest thing to a rest the Germans and the thin Allied line would give them On June 13, somewhat revived and reinforced by their treated wounded, they were ordered back to the mile-square wood, two-thirds of which now lay under marine command. But the battle was not over.

At midnight, just as the 96th was arriving on line, the Germans launched a powerful counterattack. The Germans directed a five-hour barrage of high explosives, artillery shells, and mustard gas into the thinning, gouged-out forest. The 96th, caught in the blast before it could properly entrench and prepare

Below. *German prisoners taken during the fight in Belleau Wood are escorted to the rear.*

Storming the Germans seemed the only way to make it through without getting everyone killed. Company commander Captain Donald Duncan put his men in line and ordered the charge. Less than 200 yards out, Duncan fell, a machine-gun bullet in his stomach.

Casualty figures mounted steadily. By the time the 96th had crossed the 700-yard field, only thirty remained in good enough shape to fight. One was Gunnery Sergeant Fred Stockham. A ten-year veteran of the Marine Corps who had seen combat in Nicaragua, Stockham urged on the green recruits under him. Fighting in the streets of Bouresches, nine more marines fell. But Stockham and the others under the command of Lieutenant Clifton B. Cates pressed forward. With only twenty-one men left on their feet, they took the village. For that day's action Stockham won a division citation and the croix de guerre with gilt star.

The 96th held on to Bouresches for three days until it received desperately

The village of Vaux, near Belleau Wood, after a savage artillery barrage.

itself, lost half its men, most to gas. Many gas masks proved defective, others were rendered useless by shrapnel. Sergeant Stockham was evacuating wounded and gassed marines through the barrage to the dressing station when shrapnel from a high explosive shell ripped through the mask of the man he carried. He pulled off his own mask and placed it on the wounded man while taking him to the aid station. He then returned to the front, maskless, to pull out more wounded. Choking and gasping from lack of air, he made several more trips. Then he collapsed, to die the horrible death of the gas victim nine days later.

Twenty-one years went by before Stockham was awarded a Medal of Honor for his sacrifice. Lieutenant Cates had submitted a formal recommendation the night of the incident, but like all the citations that chaotic night, it was lost before reaching division headquarters. Stockham's comrades would not let the matter drop. At a company reunion in the 1930s they voted to press the claim, even though the final extension for granting medals for World War I had lapsed. Cates, who was soon to become commandant of the Marine Corps, prevailed upon some acquaintances in Congress to make a special case of Sergeant Stockham, whom Cates called "the bravest man I ever knew." On July 15, 1939, President Franklin D. Roosevelt signed into law a special resolution passed by both houses awarding the medal to Gunnery Sergeant Fred Stockham. By then, no one remained alive in his family to receive it.

As Stockham was carried from Belleau Wood, the marines threw back the German counterattack. On June 25 the Americans staged their final assault and took the wood completely. The marine brigade had defeated four enemy divisions in their three-week battle. Second Division casualties neared 10,000–1,811 dead–but the Americans had proved they could fight and win. Allied morale soared. On order of the French army, the Bois de Belleau was renamed Bois de la Brigade de Marine. ◈

Survival in the Argonne
The Lost Battalion

After the Allies beat back the German assault on the Marne, attention turned to eastern France. First the Allies reduced the Saint-Mihiel salient in September 1918. Then the Americans, fighting under General Pershing, launched an attack against enemy positions in the Argonne Forest. German resistance was fierce at first, then crumbled as the Allies attacked along the entire western front.

The most legendary American unit to emerge from the Meuse-Argonne campaign was the so-called "Lost Battalion." Like all legends, however, the story of the stranded outpost that held out for a week against concerted German attack has been mixed heavily with myth. The very name "Lost Battalion" is a misnomer. The unit, which was made up of parts of three battalions plus support personnel, knew precisely where it was, and so did its superiors. The name was coined by a wire-service editor in the United States. Reading a dispatch on the plight of the besieged task force, he penciled in the term "lost"—not, he later explained, meaning confused, but rather "being done for, of being in a hopeless situation." In that sense, he came very close to being right.

The 1st Army began its drive on the forbidding Argonne Forest on September 26 but bogged down after only a few miles. The forest itself was the principal enemy. A nearly impenetrable tangle of trees and underbrush, strewn with ravines and rock-covered hills, the wood gave cover to dozens of German machine gunners and snipers, while it fiercely resisted penetration by the Allies' heavy weapons. As Pershing threw his troops into the forest in waves, the well-hidden and entrenched Germans picked them off with devastating ease. By October the Argonne Forest had become the black spot on the Allied line.

On the evening of October 1, General Robert Alexander, commander of the 77th "Statue of Liberty" Division, drew up yet another plan to crack the Argonne from the south. His sector was holding up the American advance line. More critically, his troops were growing weaker with each rebuffed assault. He needed to break the German defense soon. All attempts to flank the wood having failed, Alexander ordered a three-pronged drive right through the middle. The center of the attack would be the 308th Infantry. The advance bat-

Lost Battalion officers read a German demand for surrender delivered by the blindfolded soldier.

talion would be the 1st, under Major Charles Whittlesey.

A quiet, serious Yankee, Whittlesey considered his orders with growing gloom. They read that he should proceed with three of his companies north to the German line, breach it, then advance up a hill to a road, there to wait for the rest of the regiment and further orders. Whittlesey protested that his battalion had fallen to half-strength over the past grueling week of failed offensives. The men were tired—certainly in no shape to hit the Germans head-on where the thick woods prevented close artillery support. Moreover, to move as swiftly and lightly as possible the battalion would have to leave behind reserve rations, blankets, and overcoats, even though the weather was cold and often damp. The plan allowed for resupply and victualling only after the whole regiment attained the objective. "What if the flanks did not keep pace?" Whittlesey asked. Alexander issued a curt reply: Proceed as directed.

At 8:10 A.M. on October 2, the 77th headed into a driving rain. Between the weather and the woods, the men could barely see where they were going. From their hiding spots in the forest, however, German machine guns and artillery could get an easy fix on the stumbling and crashing Americans. Whittlesey's battalion trudged forward slowly but steadily, casualties mounting at a frightening pace as it advanced farther and farther ahead of its flanks. At 10:00 A.M. the major phoned headquarters to protest his orders. The battalion would be cut off if it continued, he warned. He urged a halt until the flanks caught up. Alexander was even more clear this time: The objective must be attained that day.

In the early afternoon three companies of the 2d Battalion under Captain

Sergeant George Norman of the 308th Infantry (left front) is led to an ambulance on October 2, 1918. His injury saved him from being trapped that day with the rest of the Lost Battalion.

George G. McMurtry were ordered to aid Whittlesey. This time the going was much easier, the Germans having turned their full attention to the flanks. The first sunshine in a week gave the assault force an added boost. Making rapid progress up the ravine, the two battalions reached the German line near dusk. There they had a considerable surprise: The trench was empty. Congratulating themselves on their good fortune, the Americans crossed the line and made for their objective, 500 yards up the hill.

In an elongated pocket on the hillside, just beneath the road, Whittlesey called a halt. The position was a fairly secure one, protected by thick forest and the slope of the hill, with a creek providing fresh water only fifty yards below. It seemed the safest place to set up camp until the flanking forces joined them.

Whittlesey set up a "runner chain," a relay team of soldiers who would carry messages to headquarters. Then he positioned the companies and ordered them to dig in. A quick head count showed that of about 700 men from the 308th that began the assault, fewer than 600 were now present for duty. The rest were casualties or stretcher-bearers who had brought the casualties to the rear.

While the outpost settled in for the night, back at headquarters concern grew. Neither flank had gained any ground; indeed, in some areas they had lost territory. Whittlesey's task force was all alone. Alexander decided to send it more help. He ordered another battalion to the position. Moving across the wretched terrain in total darkness, however, all but one company got lost, and that one lost two of its squads. Only seventy-nine men from Company K, under Captain Nelson Holderman, reached the outpost. They were the last Americans to make it in or out for the next five days. That night the Germans, too, discovered the hole in their lines and immediately filled it. As Whittlesey had feared, by sunrise he was surrounded.

October 3 opened with an artillery barrage from a German regiment holding the crest of the hill above the Americans. Whittlesey had chosen a good position. The angle of the pocket tilted against the guns' trajectory. Shells fell all around, but few made it into the perimeter. Trench mortars and potato masher grenades followed with greater accuracy but little effect since they were most lethal in an enclosed space. The deadliest enemies were machine guns—and time. The men had rations and medical supplies for only one day, ammunition for not much more. Their water supply depended on free access to the brook below them—which a German machine gun now monitored closely. Without relief the task force would become ever more vulnerable to infantry charge.

To build their manpower, Whittlesey sent Company E back down the hill to find and bring back two companies headquarters had held for reserve. A little more than an hour later eighteen of Company E's fifty men staggered back to the outpost. Most were wounded. They had been ambushed by English-speaking Germans. The runner chain had likewise been annihilated. Now the only means of communication with division command was the battalion's six carrier pigeons. Whittlesey dispatched one reporting his position and requesting immediate aid.

Dawn, October 4, 1st and 2d Battalions reported 82 killed and 140 wounded since arriving in the pocket. An American machine-gun emplacement had been wiped out by a trench mine, lowering to five the number of machine guns, and those operated on only half crews. There were only three enlisted medics to minister to the wounded, and they had already run out of bandages and most other supplies. The seriously wounded were lying in foxholes and behind fallen trees—anywhere that might afford them a bit of protection and keep their moans at some distance from the already skittish defenders. Whittlesey and McMurtry walked among the men, trying to give them some assurance that they had a reason to hang on, but it was not easy.

The major had sent off three pigeons, without any indication that the messages had been received. Patrols dispatched to the right and left found no sign of allies on either flank. Those sent down the hill never got more than halfway. With relief no closer, at 5:30 A.M. the second day's assault began.

At headquarters, Alexander was doing everything he could to send help to the besieged unit. After receiving Whittlesey's carrier-pigeon message calling for reinforcements, the general ordered the two reserve companies to join their battalions in the pocket. The

Second Sight

" At the sound of the first droning of the shells we rush back, in one part of our being, a thousand years. By the animal instinct that is awakened in us we are led and protected. It is not conscious; it is far quicker, much more sure, less fallible, than consciousness. One cannot explain it. A man is walking along without thought or heed;—suddenly he throws himself down on the ground and a storm of fragments flies harmlessly over him;—yet he cannot remember either to have heard the shell coming or to have thought of flinging himself down. But had he not abandoned himself to the impulse he would now be a heap of mangled flesh. It is this other, this second sight in us, that has thrown us to the ground and saved us, without our knowing how. If it were not so, there would not be one man alive from Flanders to the Vosges.

We march up, moody or good—tempered soldiers—we reach the zone where the front begins and become on the instant human animals. "

Erich Maria Remarque, **All Quiet on the Western Front**

Below. *Captain Nelson Holderman, 307th Infantry, one of the last Americans to reach the Lost Battalion before the siege began.*

companies headed up the hillside with 100 men, ran into a barbed wire trap, and returned with 50. Alexander ordered them to try again. Again they failed, their strength by now reduced to platoon size.

More bad news reached the command post at midmorning. A message from Whittlesey reported that after beating off a concerted attack earlier in the day, his effective strength was down to 235, and those were suffering from hunger and exposure. The wounded, without tents, blankets, or even coats to ward off the cold were in especially bad shape. "Cannot support be sent at once?" he implored. Alexander phoned the division's artillery commander and told him to train his guns on the Germans on the hill above the pocket. At 1:15 the American guns let fire.

The next four hours were by all accounts the worst of the entire siege. Somehow the artillery commander got

the wrong coordinates. Believing they were pinpointed on the Germans, the gunners sent a massive barrage directly onto the Americans. Men, at first elated to hear guns barking from the south, scrambled in a panicked race to escape the fusillade. Many were not quick or lucky enough. Nearly all of what was left of Company E was captured when its lieutenant tried to lead it to a safer position. Eighty others were killed or wounded.

The normally calm Whittlesey rushed to his command post and dashed off a message to headquarters: "Our own artillery is dropping a barrage directly on us. For heaven's sake stop it." The frightened bird keeper released the first pigeon before he had attached the message. That left only one bird. He clipped on Whittlesey's note, tossed the pigeon into the air, and watched with breath held as the confused bird flew to the nearest tree and perched. Only by throw-

Above. *The scene of the Lost Battalion's agony. In foreground is the water hole covered by German machine guns. At top left is the cleft in the hillside where the unit held out for six days. Below. Cher Ami, the carrier pigeon that brought a critical message to the rear and lost a leg in the process.*

Second Lieutenant Eugene Bleckley sketched a map of German positions near the Lost Battalion. Note the half wings of an aerial observer on his blouse.

First Lieutenant Harold Goettler, Bleckley's pilot, was able to land his plane behind Allied lines before succumbing to his wounds.

Captain George G. McMurtry, a former "Rough Rider," led three companies of the 2d Battalion, 308th Infantry, in support of Major Whittlesey's men.

ing stones at it could Whittlesey persuade the pigeon to fly through the artillery barrage. Once the message was airborne, he could only pray that it would make it to the base.

The major gathered a party to evacuate the wounded to a place that afforded some modicum of cover from the falling shells. After that, he resumed his tour of the defense. The men took heart from the sight of Whittlesey and McMurtry walking steadily among them, issuing reassuring words, promising the attack would soon end. The leaders' fortitude was all the more impressive since both were wounded. McMurtry, whose kneecap had been blown away, moved with considerable pain.

At 4:00 P.M. the last pigeon, by then badly injured, reached division headquarters, and the aghast commanders called an immediate halt to the shelling. It was too late to spare the outpost, though. In addition to killing and

wounding dozens of Americans, the four-hour barrage had wiped out their cover. The halt in the artillery assault was thus followed immediately by the most accurate German machine-gun and grenade attack so far. Behind it came the enemy's first concerted infantry rush. Twice the Germans made it across the road to the very edge of the perimeter before the Americans knocked them back. Heavy fighting continued for the rest of the day. At nightfall the battalions still remained in command of the position, but they held it by their fingernails.

After a night of renewed rainfall, the morning of October 5 finally brought some relief. A thick ground fog blanketed the pocket, preventing the Germans from launching their usual dawn artillery and machine-gun attack. Hunger, cold, and diminishing morale were now the principal enemies. Men licked up coffee grounds, seeds, any-

thing edible they could find. They rummaged through the pockets of their dead comrades in a mostly futile search for food. Others, too weak even to forage, huddled shivering in foxholes. Perhaps most damaging to the morale of the men, many of whom were desperate for water, was the constant rush of the brook below. Whenever the Germans heard the clank of a bucket or helmet against the streambed, they sprayed the area with machine-gun fire. So many men died making unauthorized water runs that Whittlesey had to post riflemen along the path leading to the creek with orders to shoot anyone seen going that way.

Overhead the Lost Battalion could hear airplanes searching for its position. Now and then the defenders noted the thump of falling parcels. But none fell within retrievable distance. The starving Americans did not have to guess the contents of the airdrops; the enemy let them know in sickening detail. "Ham!"

The survivors of the Lost Battalion in October 1918, shortly after their rescue.

they called out in English. "Chocolate, biscuits, butter!" The Germans surrounding them were eating better than they had in years. Messages of encouragement sent from headquarters by plane fell even farther afield—one was picked up by a reserve unit some seven miles to the rear.

The pilots did their best. Two, Lieutenants Harold Goettler and Erwin Bleckley, flying a two-seater observation plane, made a number of extremely low passes over the area trying to pinpoint the battalion despite crippling anti-aircraft fire by the Germans on top of the hill. These pilots had no more luck than any of the others in getting supplies to the outpost, but Bleckley was able to map out the enemy gun positions before he passed out from wounds. After taking a number of direct hits, Goettler somehow coaxed the biplane to a rough landing inside French lines. When the Allies reached the cockpit, however, they

found the pilot dead. Bleckley died a few minutes later. (Both men were to be awarded the medal posthumously.)

With the help of Bleckley's map, 77th Divisional Artillery readjusted its sights. Once the mist cleared, the Germans were the ones to feel the power of the American guns. The barrage hit them just as they were massing for an attack. It probably saved the task force from being overrun. When the Germans were finally able to regroup and launch their attack late that afternoon, they were a greatly weakened force. Once again the defenders beat them back.

But they could not keep it up much longer, even with artillery support. The wounded were piling up. The only bandages for them were those taken from dead men, a sure route to gangrene. Captain Holderman had a mortified leg wound. McMurtry walked around with the stick of a potato masher lodged in his back until the attack ended and he could take a few minutes to have it removed. Whittlesey reluctantly ordered that the dead henceforth were merely to be cov-

ered with fallen leaves; he could not afford to lose any more burial parties to exhaustion and sniper fire.

Meanwhile, beneath them the 308th's commander asked to be relieved rather than send his decimated forces on another suicidal attempt to break through to the stranded 1st and 2d Battalions. Alexander relieved him and ordered the 3d Battalion up again.

Day four of the siege was an even crueler version of those that had preceded it. The enemy brought in flame throwers in a desperate move to finish off the Americans. The liquid fire actually did little real damage in the defoliated pocket, but it was nearly the last straw for the terrified defenders. Whittlesey had to spend every waking moment now encouraging his men to hold on. The sounds of a major battle were getting closer, he told them; they would soon be free. Few any longer believed him. They fought on, but for the first time they lost ground. That night Whittlesey's greatest fear began to materialize. Nine men snuck out from the perimeter to get some airdropped parcels and were captured. His command was coming apart.

October 7, as men down at headquarters discussed the meaning of the news they had just received of Germany's preliminary bid for peace talks, the soldiers in the pocket wrote farewell notes to their families. There were no writing supplies, so they scrawled their letters on shirttails and old bandages, using mud or even blood for ink. They had been without food or water for three days of nearly constant warfare. Around them the bodies of their dead comrades had begun to putrefy. They had no idea that on the crest of the hill the Germans, too, were ready to quit. The 77th Division's persistent assault on the Argonne was draining the enemy badly. The German division commander ordered the regiment besieging Whittlesey's outpost to prepare to move out that night—with or without a victory.

At the German regiment's command post the officers discussed how they could avoid the blotch of a defeat on their records. They tried a bold gambit. Picking out one of the prisoners captured the night before, they sent him back to the pocket with a message calling for the task force's surrender. "The suffering of your wounded men can be heard over here in the German lines," it read, "and we are appealing to your human sentiments. A white flag shown by one of your men will tell us that you agree. . . ." Whittlesey, McMurtry, and Holderman read the message a couple of times. Then, for the first time in days, they broke into genuine smiles. "We've got them licked or they wouldn't have sent this," McMurtry grinned. Whittlesey crumpled up the message.

Word of the German demand spread rapidly through the pocket. The appeal to humanitarianism infuriated men who had watched their buddies die and their unburied bodies rot. Men who had not spoken for days joined in a chorus of abuse aimed at the German line. The enemy answered with their most determined assault yet. The Americans, revived by their anger, fought back.

Wounded men limped out of their foxholes to the front line and fired guns that had long been silent. Those who could not get to their feet loaded ammunition. Holderman went nearly wild with rage, standing in the open and blasting away at the enemy, whooping whenever he scored a hit. He and his sergeant, acting on their own, broke up a concerted charge against their flank, saving it from envelopment. Then, though Holderman was bleeding heavily from several wounds, they staged a two-man counterattack that pushed the Germans off the road and actually regained lost territory. After an hour of this unex-

Charles Whittlesey receives the Medal of Honor on Boston Common, December 24, 1918.

pected punishment, the enemy called retreat and ran back up the hill.

That afternoon the 77th Division finally crossed the German line. At 6:00 P.M. a patrol from the 307th Infantry made it into the wretched perimeter. A messenger reported to Whittlesey that there was a captain on the road who wanted to see him. With effort the major rose from the ground, telling McMurtry he need not bother getting up. An enlisted man asked, "Is it safe now on the road?" Whittlesey muttered, "I guess so" and slowly walked out. A few minutes passed before McMurtry realized what that meant—the road had not been safe since they got there. They were relieved.

The resistance of the Lost Battalion carried a tremendous cost. Of the more than 600 men who entered the pocket, only 194 marched out October 8. One hundred seventy were dead; the rest were carried out on stretchers, many to die of their wounds in army hospitals. Holderman's medical report revealed ten separate wounds—two listed as severe—in

both legs, his right arm, left hand, right foot, pelvis, and face. McMurtry had a shattered knee and a number of surface lesions. Both, however, along with a number of their men, volunteered to go back on the line just as soon as they had downed a good meal. And both men would later receive the Medal of Honor for their courage during the long siege.

Whittlesey, too, had wounds on his body; but none were as severe as the mental anguish he felt from the many orders he had given and patrols he had sent off to their doom. In later years that anguish grew amid misguided accusations that he had brought on the siege by pursuing the Germans overzealously, overstepping his orders. The memory of the week in which he earned the Medal of Honor would not let him go. In 1921 Charles Whittlesey boarded a vacation liner to Cuba and jumped over the side. His body was never found. His friends pronounced him "a war casualty." ✦

The Last Days
Lieutenant Furlong's War

Just as the machine gun was the most significant weapon of the war, more Americans received the Medal of Honor for charging machine-gun nests than for any other kind of action. To many, such an act might seem the height of courage—or madness. For one American soldier fighting late in the war, it was just part of the job.

When Dr. Harold D. Furlong was asked why, as a young lieutenant, he took on an enemy emplacement of four machine guns and more than twenty soldiers, he seemed surprised that it even merited a question. "There was no choice to do anything different," he said. "The machine gunners had to be stopped. . . . I had no idea that it was a heroic deed. . . . The machine guns were silenced. I was grateful and so were my compatriots."

Lieutenant Furlong was at the front line on November 1, 1918, the first day of the final stage of the Meuse-Argonne offensive. He had trained for that moment for four years: first, in the required military science course at Michigan Agricultural College; then, after the U.S. declared war, at the First Officers' Training Camp; and, once he enlisted, another eighteen months at army camps. Not until June 16, 1918, did he debark in Europe, ready for war.

After a few weeks on the battlefield in the Saint-Mihiel offensive, Furlong received orders to report to the AEF school at Gondrecourt for more training. There Furlong took a class on the fine points of attacking machine guns. That course "probably saved my life," Furlong said later. When Furlong returned to his unit at the end of October, he learned he had been promoted to first lieutenant. He was ordered to ready his platoon for an assault on November 1 on the German line at the Bois de Bantheville.

Furlong recalled vividly the events of the next few days: "The Bois de Bantheville was a heavily wooded area repeatedly under attack with artillery and gas. It had been 'cleared' by the 1st and 2nd battalions of the 353rd Infantry when the 3rd battalion was ordered forward to its northern edge. My platoon of Company M advanced to the very edge of the forest and remained far enough from the edge so that we were not visible to the enemy. The men dug foxholes and prepared to spend the night. The jump-off time was set at 5:30 A.M., November 1. There was a light rain throughout the night and we were very uncomfortable. We received a ration of salmon and bread (colder than ice), since our kitchen equipment was back in the forest so that smoke from the cooking fires would not attract artillery fire."

Several hours before the assault the 3d Battalion got orders to move up to the jump-off point. "From the edge of our position, there was a clear space in front. Crossing that open space caused many casualties. The German front was just beyond the open area and their guns had clear shooting on the advancing men. We finally reached a position only a few yards from tremendous bombardment. The noise was deafening. We followed our barrage dangerously close. I left First Lieutenant Jared Jackson to look over my platoon and learned later that he was killed by a sniper moments later. I was appalled to see how many of our men had been killed."

Furlong checked his platoon for casualties, regrouped his men, then led them against the fiercely resisting enemy line. "On my reconnaissance, I could see a country road that crossed out front and, on the side toward the enemy, there was a small elevation. I ran, zig-zagging to the protection of the slight rise and crawled along until I reached four of my men. There was a deep shell hole about twenty-five feet in front of us and I said that we must get to the hole. No one moved. I bounded up, ran to the protection of the hole and, from there, into the edge of the woods. Corporal John W. McKay followed me. . . . The Germans had sighted our location and turned a machine gun in that direction, which kept the other men from following.

"When I entered the woods, I saw a machine gun emplacement that had

First Lieutenant Harold D. Furlong.

German machine gunners in the Argonne Forest, 1918.

"Our barrage was advancing and I knew we had to follow as closely as we could. . . . [Our colonel] told me that Jared Jackson was dead and he put me in command of the company. With what men I could gather around me, we started through the thick woods. I had not been wounded but, in making my way through the thorns, I was soon covered with blood and felt like I had been attacked by a thousand cats. We reached our objective and stopped. Our part was temporarily over but other units of the 353rd passed us and went on to our second objective. . . . When we laid down on the ground to rest, I found that I was shaking like an aspen leaf. But, not from fear, just from nervous exhaustion and fatigue."

Furlong remained adamant that what he did that November day years ago was part duty, part training, part luck, and in no way the result of any special quality he possessed. The army command did not see it that way. Three months later, he was on occupation duty in Germany when a courier approached him and told him to report at once to regiment headquarters. "I made my way to headquarters and stood before Colonel James Reeves, the commanding officer of the regiment, wondering what I had done or what he wanted me to do. He glowered at me and my heart sank. He handed me an order sheet and commanded me to read it. It was an official order from General Pershing, commander of the AEF, to report to his headquarters in Chaumont to be decorated with the Congressional Medal of Honor. I felt odd and a little lightheaded and then an entire barrage of emotions intermingled with a feeling of unreality. Then the colonel, who had enjoyed pulling my leg, said that it was a great honor for our regiment. His praise filled me with pride and was, at the time, far more real than any medal." ⬦

The graves of Jared Jackson and other casualties in the Bois de Bantheville.

been wiped out by our artillery. There was a path, apparently made by the Germans who had been servicing the gun. Down the path, we could see the heads and shoulders of Germans who were firing another machine gun at our men. I lifted my rifle, cursed at McKay to jolt him back to reality, and started to shoot. We both fired at all the Boche that we could see firing the machine gun. Our firing was accurate and we saw the Germans slumping down and [all four of] the machine guns stopped firing. . . . I did not know how many men I (we) killed or wounded. . . . I started forward; McKay signaled to our men to advance. There were probably 10-15 Germans milling around when McKay and I walked into their midst. I had my pistol in my hand and the Germans seemed so surprised that they made no move to shoot me or McKay. My men stormed into the emplacement and took over the captured German prisoners. . . . The entire incident with the machine guns lasted less than 10 minutes."

Including the wounded, Furlong sent twenty prisoners back to the compound. Then, without so much as a breathing spell, he resumed the assault.

Sergeant York

The American guards were astonished as the tall red-haired corporal marched his prisoners into camp. They had seen large groups of captured Germans before, but nothing like this. The date was October 8, 1918, in the first month of the Meuse-Argonne offensive. Alvin Cullum York, a sharp-shooting blacksmith from the Tennessee hamlet of Pall Mall, was about to become Sergeant York, the greatest hero of the Great War.

York's colonel visited the site where York had fought, counted the German bodies and abandoned guns, and talked to other Americans who were on the scene. They explained that after capturing several Germans they had been pinned down by machine-gun fire from the top of a ridge. York had pressed forward alone, shooting enemy soldiers whenever they appeared over the trenches. At last a German major promised to order his men to surrender if York would stop picking them off. In less than three hours Corporal York had single-handedly killed twenty-five Germans, silenced thirty-five machine guns, and taken 132 prisoners.

York was quickly promoted to sergeant and awarded the Medal of Honor. He became the toast of Europe, lauded by President Wilson in Paris and by people all across the continent. Marshal Ferdinand Foch told him, "What you did was the greatest thing accomplished by any private soldier of all the armies of Europe."

York was an unlikely war hero. He had registered for the draft as a conscientious objector, explaining that the Bible forbade killing. At boot camp, his captain quoted various Scripture passages concerning righteous war which, he argued, were applicable to the conflict at hand. After much deliberation, York pronounced himself satisfied and went off to France.

America was waiting for Alvin York when his troopship pulled up to a Hoboken dock on May 22, 1919. Rushed by photographers, digni-

Alvin York's mother welcomes him home to Pall Mall, Tennessee, May 30, 1919.

taries, and spectators, he was whisked to the Waldorf-Astoria Hotel and given a suite adjacent to the one reserved for the president. Then came a staggering line-up of public appearances. At the stock exchange, trading was suspended and members paraded York around the floor on their shoulders. Earlier he had expressed a desire to see the city's famous subway system; transit officials obliged with a tour in a private car. York admitted that "New York is certainly a great city, but it do tire a fellow out some." He and his congressman traveled to Washington, where he was applauded on the floor of the House of Representatives. After making the rounds of the capital, York said that he had "seen it all."

York was deluged with offers for lectures, tours, and books but wanted none of it. "This uniform ain't for sale," he said, and boarded a train back to Pall Mall. There he was paraded through town in a caravan of automobiles and mules. To his beloved mother and neighbors, the national hero was still "the same old Al."

But the rest of the nation had followed York to Tennessee. The state presented him with a fully stocked 400-acre farm. When his long-time girlfriend agreed to marry him, the news made front pages across the country. Though they had planned to have the ceremony in the simple chapel where York had converted to the Church of Christ in Christian Union, Alvin and Gracie York were married on their new farm, in a rite performed by the governor of Tennessee before 3,000 people. The couple turned down a complimentary honeymoon to Salt Lake City, calling the journey "merely a vainglorious call of the world and of the devil."

Instead the Yorks stayed in Pall Mall, where Alvin continued farming and blacksmithing, the trades of his late father, and teaching Bible school. He was frequently sought out in the fields by dignitaries and curious visitors; according to one later account, "It became obligatory for Tennessee politicians running for office to pose for campaign pictures with him." But York shunned politics, declining the vice-presidential nomination of the Prohibition party in 1936.

It took another world war to draw Sergeant York back onto the public stage. At age fifty-four he registered for the draft at the same country store where twenty-five years earlier he had signed up as a conscientious objector. "If they want me for active duty, I'm ready to go," York declared. "I'm in a mighty different mood now from that other time." Though he was never called, York served as head of the local draft board and sent two of his sons off to war.

A series of strokes in the fifties confined him to a wheelchair, and on September 2, 1964, Alvin York died in a Nashville veterans' hospital. To millions of Americans, he was Sergeant York, an American hero; to his neighbors in Pall Mall, Tennessee, he was just "the same old Al."

Warriors Aloft
The Air Aces

The air aces of World War I displayed a special kind of courage. Attacking alone, with no place to take cover, in a machine that was often as deadly as enemy bullets, the aviator had to possess the fearlessness of a lone wolf. The best, like Eddie Rickenbacker, combined daring with prudence. Others, like Frank Luke, were determined to engage the enemy no matter what the cost.

Captain Eddie Rickenbacker in his Spad fighter, October 1918.

The airplane had been in existence barely more than a decade when the world went to war, but development of air power surged after that. In the first year of the war, the role of the aviator was limited to observation. He was seen as "a useful extension of the traditional cavalry scout." Any "dogfights" were semicomical affairs, with pilots hanging out of their planes trying to shoot one another with their revolvers or just shaking their fists angrily. In 1915, however, a Dutch inventor named Anthony Fokker, working for the Germans, invented a gear to synchronize machine-gun fire with the turning of the propeller blades. After that, guns could be mounted in front of a pilot's seat. The era of aerial combat had begun.

When the United States entered the war, it was woefully behind the European powers in aviation technology. There were less than 250 American planes. But there were a number of combat-trained U.S. pilots: the 180 fliers of the Lafayette Escadrille. These men eventually formed the core of the army Air Service that flew into action in February 1918. Filling out its ranks were the hundreds of young men who responded to posters calling on them to "Be an American Eagle!" The total Air Service was small and played only a marginal role in the war, but it captured the nation's imagination.

The man who became best known in the households of America was "ace of aces" Captain Eddie Rickenbacker. To become an ace a pilot had to shoot down five enemy planes. Rickenbacker downed twenty-eight (two unconfirmed) in only five months of combat. Twice his plane was crippled, forcing him to crashland; he also needed an operation for an ear infection caused by flying at high altitudes. But Rickenbacker never received a scratch in combat.

Rickenbacker (top foreground) leads his squadron against German planes attacking an American patrol.

Rickenbacker came into aviation from auto racing, a sport that encouraged boldness and remarkable reflexes. Fatherless at twelve, he had to quit school to help support his family and soon became an auto mechanic—it paid better than his $3.50-a-week factory job. He was hooked by the machine. At night, after putting in twelve hours on the job, he studied for a correspondence degree in engineering. In 1908, at the age of seventeen, he became a test driver. By 1910 he was making $40,000 a year as America's top racer.

When Congress declared war, Rickenbacker immediately wrote the army to propose the development of a flying squadron made up of race-car drivers. Their knowledge of combustion engines combined with their quick reflexes and speed-driving skill made them perfect candidates for mastering the new air technology, he said. The army rejected the idea but made a counterproposal. Would Rickenbacker go to Europe to be a driver for Pershing? Rickenbacker said yes, but he still intended to become a flier.

Once overseas, Rickenbacker thought he could switch easily to the Air Service. Pershing thought otherwise. He was quite happy with his new driver and consistently rejected Rickenbacker's requests for transfer. "War flying is for youngsters just out of school. It's not for mature men," the ace, then twenty-seven, recalled Pershing telling him.

Quite by accident, Rickenbacker found a powerful advocate. Driving along the front, he came upon a broken-down car and stopped to fix it. Its grateful passenger, Colonel Billy Mitchell, a top commander of the American Air Service, asked Rickenbacker what he could do in exchange. In January 1918 Rickenbacker received his commission as an Air Service lieutenant.

Because of his knowledge of mechanics, he was first made chief engineer at the main training base at Issoudon. This did not slacken his desire to fly. On his hours off, Rickenbacker logged in flight time and requested advanced combat training. Ultimately his pertinacity won out. He joined the 94th Aero Squadron—the "Hat-in-the-Ring Squadron"—on March 4. Ten days later he flew his first mission. On March 29 he scored his first victory, the fourth by an American serving for the United States. And on May 30 he shot down his fifth enemy plane, becoming the second American ace.

The qualities that marked Ricken-backer as a star among aviators were at odds with the popular image of the impetuous fighter-pilot. He was cautious, deliberate, even scientific in his approach to combat flying. He would avoid a fight when the odds were greater than two-to-one on the side of the enemy but stay awake nights thinking of ways to improve the odds. He had no blood lust for the Germans, once saying "the pleasure of shooting down another man was no more attractive to me than the chance of being shot down myself." But he showed no fear or reluctance to kill when he encountered the enemy. Most of all, he was a perfectionist. He never left the testing of his plane or machine gun to his mechanic. When he discovered serious design flaws in the Nieuport airplane the French had given the Americans, he badgered the Allied command until they turned over a fleet of the more advanced Spads. If he had had the time, he told his flight mates, he would have designed his own machine.

On September 24 Rickenbacker received his captain's bars and command of the Hat-in-the-Ring Squadron. He celebrated the next day by scoring his first of six double victories.

Midmorning on September 25, the day before the scheduled start of the Meuse-Argonne offensive, Capt. Rickenbacker flew out alone across German lines near Verdun. Below him he sighted a pair of German LVG two-seater photographer aircraft heading in the opposite direction. They were guarded by five Fokkers, fast, high-flying fighter planes. Rickenbacker slipped by above them without being noticed. Then he turned his aircraft around, switched off his engine, and glided silently down toward the rear Fokker. Drawing near, he fired a long burst. The German machine plummeted to the ground.

Surprised by the sudden attack, the four remaining Fokkers panicked and broke formation. Rickenbacker had intended to make a quick escape after the first strike, but he changed his mind as he watched the Fokkers diving wildly right and left, leaving the LVGs unprotected. He changed course again and headed for the nearest two-seater.

The observer in the rear seat of the plane opened up on Rickenbacker with his machine gun, but its fire fell short. To escape the enemy gun as he closed in, Rickenbacker went into a dive until he fell below the LVG, then circled up on the enemy. But the LVG pilot was ready for him. He pulled around, putting Rickenbacker right back in the gunner's

path. Rickenbacker had to pull up sharply. In the meantime, the second LVG got on his rear and opened fire. "I saw tracer bullets go whizzing and streaking past my face," the ace recalled. Again he had to zoom out of range and try again.

Several times the scenario repeated itself. Fortunately for Rickenbacker, the Fokkers continued to struggle ineffectually to resume formation. But the battle pulled him ever farther into enemy territory. He eventually decided to give it one more try. Waiting until the LVGs were parallel to each other, Rickenbacker burst up from the side and began firing.

The nearest Boche passed directly through my line of fire and just as I ceased firing I had the satisfaction of seeing him burst into flames. Turning over and over as he fell the LVG started a blazing path to earth just as the Fokker escort came tearing up to the rescue. I put on the gas and headed for home.

A dozen years later the army rewarded him for this day's work by presenting him with a Medal of Honor. That honor crowned a stack of medals that included the Distinguished Service Cross with nine oak leaf clusters, the French Legion of Honor, and the croix de guerre with four palms.

The reason for Rickenbacker's zeal September 25 was his grim discovery the night before that the 94th Squadron had been overtaken in official victories. That had never before happened to the Hat-in-the-Ring. The challenger was the upstart 27th Squadron, which had joined the flight group only three months before. It had jumped into the lead because of the extraordinary record of its top ace, Second Lieutenant Frank Luke. Between September 12 and 18, Luke shot down thirteen enemy aircraft. In less than a week he had scored his first kill, become an ace, and surpassed

Rickenbacker to become for a few weeks the American ace of aces.

Luke and Rickenbacker were like night and day. Brash, boastful, and audacious, Luke had few friends and considerable trouble adapting to military life. Impatience and showing off marred his performance in training, resulting in barely passing marks. Had Air Service casualties not run so high in June and July, it is likely the army would have kept him behind the lines ferrying planes to combat squadrons, his assignment for his first month. But once Luke began knocking observation balloons out of the sky, it became apparent to all that he was, in Rickenbacker's words, "the most intrepid fighter that ever sat in an airplane."

Recognition came to Luke only after weeks of humiliation. He arrived at the front in late August, full of talk of the havoc he was going to wreak on the enemy. At first the veteran pilots just ignored him. When he returned from an early mission claiming he had attacked a German formation and shot down one of its planes but was unable to produce any witnesses, his comrades took to laughing at him openly as a "boastful four-flusher." Said his commanding officer, Lieutenant Colonel Harold Hartney, also a skeptic, "Frank Luke was a lonesome and despised man from that day until he brought down his first balloon."

The *drachen* balloons that reversed Luke's reputation were 200-foot cigar-shaped bags of hydrogen, attached to the ground by a 2,000-foot cable running from a truck-borne winch. Placed at strategic intervals a couple of miles behind the front, they gave the enemy a complete view of Allied positions and movements. Their crews then called down the exact coordinates for artillery fire. Because of this deadly power, the Air Service made destroying *drachen* its top priority.

Second Lieutenant Frank Luke pulls away in his Spad as an enemy balloon bursts into flames on September 29, 1918. Three German Fokkers close in on him from behind.

Attacking huge, flammable targets would seem an easy job, but it was more difficult and dangerous than taking on a warplane. The *drachen* were surrounded by antiaircraft batteries and a half-dozen or more machine guns. Above, Fokkers patrolled the balloon line. The attacker had to come in perilously low, hit the bag at the top where the hydrogen concentrated, and position the bullet holes in a tight enough mass to open a large enough leak to set off a hydrogen-oxygen explosion. During the onslaught, the balloon crew would lower the bag rapidly to the ground, exposing the attacker to progressively closer fire and greater risk. The terrors were so considerable, Rickenbacker testified, that only those pilots who were blind to danger sought out balloon combat.

On September 12, in the Saint-Mihiel region, Luke knocked down his first balloon. This time he would not be denied his victory. He landed at a nearby airfield and handed to a lieutenant who had watched a confirmation form he had typed up in advance. Two days later he brought down another pair in two flights, disabling both of his planes in the process. When he limped back to base and demanded a third plane so he could go after yet another balloon, his superior, Captain Alfred Grant, put his foot down. "Balloons or no balloons, we must have discipline," he said.

Grant, however, confronted an irresistible force. Once Luke had tasted victory he was insatiable. He would sneak out, attack a few balloons, spend the night away from base, then go after some more on his way back. "Luke was simply not susceptible to ordinary army discipline," said Hartney.

Luke burst three more balloons on September 15. By this time he had perfected his technique. He made his assault at dusk, when the *drachen* made a huge silhouette in the sky but his small

Spad could barely be seen. The dangers were great since planes then had no night-flying equipment and the only airfield lights were flares that burned only for a short time. But Luke's flying skill was so finely tuned these hazards were of little concern to him.

The day after his triple victory he gave a demonstration of his new technique to his now-impressed comrades. As he walked toward his plane, he pointed to two *drachen* in the distance, about four miles apart. "Keep your eyes on those two balloons," he said. "You will see that first one there go up in flames exactly at 7:15 and the other will do likewise at 7:19." Observers, including Rickenbacker, saw two tremendous flames in the sky at precisely those times.

While Luke concentrated on wiping out the German army's balloon fleet, he was being protected from enemy

attack planes by his wingman and only close friend, Lieutenant Joseph Wehner. Three times Wehner saved Luke's life by drawing the fire of the oncoming Fokkers. While Luke pressed the attack, seeing nothing but the target in front of him, Wehner shot down or destroyed enemy planes zooming in on the "balloon buster."

September 18 was Luke's most spectacular day in the air. In less than ten minutes he destroyed five enemy aircraft to take over as America's top ace. But for Luke it was a hollow victory. As he pulled away from a burning balloon, he realized that Wehner had disappeared. He knew his friend would not have abandoned the fight. He shot down three enemy airplanes in revenge.

The first thing Luke asked when he returned to the base was whether his friend had made it back. When his fears were confirmed, he tried to take a car to

Frank Luke on September 19, 1918, with the Spad he had used to destroy his first German plane the day before. Luke was shot down and killed ten days later.

the front to search for him. The new ace of aces showed no interest in his title or the praise heaped upon him. The next evening, to cheer him up, the flight group gave him a victory dinner. They called on Luke to make a speech. The normally loquacious flier, who had so often irritated those around him by recounting his exploits at tedious length, stood up, said he was having "a bully time," and sat down.

Seeing the obvious strain of his friend's death on Luke, Hartney ordered the ace to take a ten-day leave. A week later Hartney was shocked to discover on his desk a combat report describing the shooting down of a Fokker, signed by Luke. No one had even seen him come back.

After the death of Wehner, Luke flew alone. He was less in control than ever. He defied orders, took greater chances, and remained away from the base for long unauthorized periods. Despite Luke's continued victories, Captain Grant grounded him. "Luke is going hog-wild," he told Hartney. "He thinks he is the whole Air Service." Hartney, however, decided that Luke deserved the chance he had been demanding to fly as a "lone wolf" from an advance field near Verdun. The commander gave him approval and on September 29 Luke flew off.

After flying over an American balloon company to drop a note that read "watch for burning balloons," Luke flew into German territory. The American ballooners cast their eyes skyward. One by one, three *drachen* exploded. That was the last his countrymen saw of Frank Luke.

Hoping his star pilot was simply up to his old tricks, Grant told Rickenbacker that if Luke ever did show up he would "court-martial him first and then

recommend him for the Medal of Honor." In November he gave up the wait and put Luke in for the medal. In only eighteen days the twenty-one-year-old pilot had scored eighteen confirmed victories. Hartney credited him with at least another ten for which there had been no witnesses. In Rickenbacker's estimation, Luke was "the greatest fighting pilot in the war."

No word of Luke was heard until after the armistice. Then a graves registration officer discovered, in the village of Murvaux, the grave of an American aviator: early twenties, blond hair, heavy build, medium height. The villagers reported he had been shot down September 29 after destroying three balloons and two Fokkers. His Spad was hopelessly crippled from counterfire, but the American maneuvered his falling plane over a German trench and opened fire with his machine gun, killing eleven soldiers and wounding numerous others. Even after he had crash-landed, he fought on. With German riflemen drawing near he pulled out his pistol and held them off until he died of his wounds.

At the eleventh hour of the eleventh day of the eleventh month, the World War ended. Unlike Frank Luke, Captain Eddie Rickenbacker was there to see it. In a rare defiance of orders, Rickenbacker snuck up to the front in his Spad to get a bird's-eye view of the cease-fire. "There were some shots fired at me," he said,

but at the appointed hour all shooting ceased, and then slowly and cautiously, soldiers came out of the German and American trenches, throwing their rifles and helmets high into the air. They met in no-man's land and began fraternizing just as a group of school kids would after a football game—happy in the realization that they would not be killed in this terrible conflict. It was fantastic to them, and to me, to know that the war was over. ◈

The Medal
in
Peacetime

Between the Wars

Since its creation in the 1860s, the Medal of Honor has usually been considered a wartime decoration—a symbol of the highest achievement of men in the terrible field of arms. Yet the long history of the medal includes almost 200 awards for gallantry performed when the nation was at peace. The peacetime awards have been bestowed for various reasons, some formulaic, some as individual as the recipient himself. Most are founded in the emergencies that arise in a peacetime navy, as the inevitable consequence of life at sea. Others are "special legislation" awards bestowed by Congress for courageous, nonbelligerent actions of military men. Still others, while called "medals of honor," are not the award as it is generally understood.

The first set of these, and the ones most clearly defined as military Medals of Honor, are those bestowed by the navy. The purpose for awarding them was set forth in the original medal legislation of December 1861. The navy bill called for Medals of Honor to be awarded for gallantry in action "and other seamanlike qualities." Later this was clarified to include "deeds of gallantry and heroism in times of War and of Peace." The Senate register of medal citations records that these awards "recognized bravery in saving life, and deeds of valor performed in submarine rescues, boiler explosions, turret fires, and other types of disaster unique to the naval profession."

Approximately 180 naval peacetime Medals of Honor were awarded from 1866 to 1940. In almost all cases, these medals involved gallantry by seamen at the risk of their lives. The recipients include such men as Henry Williams, who in 1879 went over the stern of the U.S.S. *Constitution* to perform "important carpenter's work upon her rudder" in a heavy gale. They also include others: John F. Auer and Matthew Gillick, who "rescued from drowning a French lad who had fallen into the sea from a stone pier" near the U.S.S. *Lancaster* as that ship rode in Marseilles Harbor on November 20, 1883; Watertender John King, who earned the Medal of Honor twice for heroism during boiler explosions aboard the U.S.S. *Vicksburg* in 1901 and the U.S.S. *Salem* in 1909; the divers who rescued the crew of the submarine *Squalus* in 1939;

and Ensign Thomas J. Ryan, who pulled a woman from the wreckage of the Grand Hotel in Yokohama, Japan, when an earthquake struck that city in September 1923.

During the early twentieth century, the navy sought to distinguish its peacetime and wartime recipients by awarding medals of two different designs. In 1919, Congress approved the "Tiffany cross" Medal of Honor for naval combat awards, retaining the old medal design for noncombat awards. In 1942, however, another act of Congress restored the dual status of the old design. Since then, no naval peacetime Medals of Honor have been bestowed, nor are any likely to be in the future: An act of Congress adopted on July 25, 1963, specified that the naval Medal of Honor was to be awarded only for combat actions. Different naval awards are now bestowed for gallantry outside of combat.

The "special legislation" awards were Medals of Honor bestowed by special acts of Congress. The nature of these awards has been complicated by the fact that throughout American history, the Congress has awarded "Congressional gold medals" or "Congressional medals of honor" to many citizens for special acts or contributions to American life. These gold medals are not the military Medal of Honor, but the similarity of nomenclature has been a source of confusion. Often the difference can be understood only by the use of two words: "a" medal of honor as opposed to "the" Medal of Honor. Sometimes, the only decisive piece of evidence as to whether an award is *the* Medal of Honor is the thing itself—the design of the medal bestowed.

"Special legislation" awards of *the* Medal of Honor have been made to military men turned explorers: Commander Richard Byrd, Machinist Floyd Bennett, and Reserve Colonel Charles Lindbergh. Another is a "lifetime of service" award to a man who contributed mightily to the service, yet whose name is almost forgotten to modern Americans: Major General Adolphus W. Greely. Another medal, created by special legislation, was probably not intended to be "the" Medal of Honor: the award to Colonel Billy Mitchell, the prophet of American military aviation. The inclusion of his name in the official Congressional compilations of the Medal of Honor, however, has stirred controversy since the award was bestowed in 1946.

Other Congressional gold medals are less controversial. Most of the earlier gold medals went to military

Preceding pages. The Point of No Return, by William J. Reynolds, depicts the midway mark in Charles Lindbergh's solo flight across the Atlantic Ocean, May 1927.

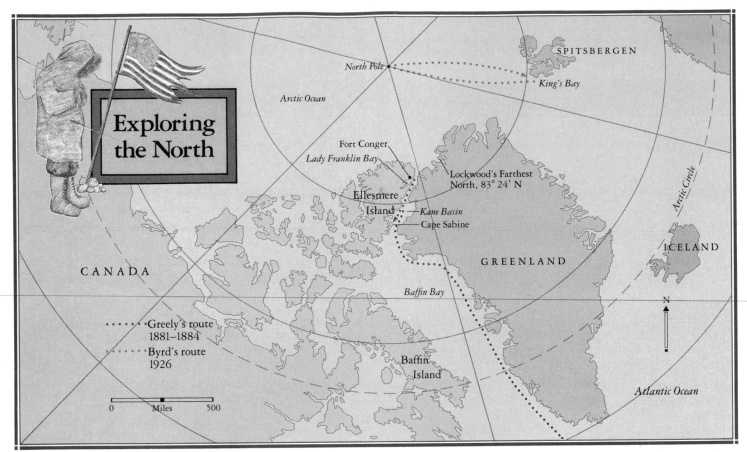

Exploring the North

North Pole

Arctic Ocean

SPITSBERGEN

King's Bay

Fort Conger
Lady Franklin Bay

Lockwood's Farthest
North, 83° 24′ N

Ellesmere
Island

Kane Basin
Cape Sabine

GREENLAND

ICELAND

CANADA

Baffin Bay

Arctic Circle

•••••• Greely's route
1881–1884

•••••• Byrd's route
1926

Baffin
Island

N

Atlantic Ocean

0   Miles   500

For a time the Medal of Honor was given for peaceful pursuits. This map shows two of these: Greely's northern expedition in 1881–84 and Byrd's flight to the North Pole in 1926.

heroes. The first recipient was George Washington, for his "wise and spirited conduct" in the siege of Boston; his medal was approved on March 25, 1776, even before independence from Great Britain was declared. The practice of giving gold medals to military figures became less frequent with the establishment of the Medal of Honor during the Civil War, but in the twentieth century, Congressional gold medals have been awarded to other military men: Generals John J. Pershing, Douglas MacArthur, Jr., George C. Marshall, and Admiral Ernest J. King, to name a few. More frequently, gold medals have recognized the special contribution of citizens from all walks of American life. Medals went to George M. Cohan for his patriotic songs ("Over There," "A Grand Old Flag"); to Robert Frost for his poetry; to John Wayne for his acting and "service to the Nation"; and to Bob Hope, Walt Disney, Marian Anderson, Roberto Clemente, and other notables. In addition, foreigners such as Winston Churchill, Simon Wiesenthal (for his "contribution to international justice through the documentation and location of war criminals from World War II"), and Canadian Ambassador Kenneth Taylor (who aided the safe return of six American embassy officials during the Iranian hostage crisis of 1979-1981) have been awarded Congressional gold medals.

There is one more set of actual Medals of Honor that, while bestowed in peacetime, are inseparably linked to war: the medals to the Unknown Soldiers. Since World War I, the United States has interred an Unknown Soldier from each of its wars at Arlington National Cemetery. After each conflict, the body of an American soldier whose identity could not be determined has been selected for this purpose. The soldier, "known but to God," represents the supreme sacrifice of all Americans who died in that war. On Armistice Day 1921, President Warren G. Harding affixed a Medal of Honor to the flag-draped casket of the American Unknown Soldier from World War I. Further special legislation awarded the medal to the World War I unknowns of Belgium, Great Britain, France, Italy, and Rumania—the only foreigners not serving in U.S. forces ever to receive the award. The Medal of Honor was also bestowed upon the American Unknown Soldiers of World War II and the Korean War. And on May 28, 1984, after more than a decade of official peacetime, President Ronald W. Reagan bestowed the Medal of Honor upon the Unknown Soldier of the Vietnam War.

The peacetime Medals of Honor were awarded for gallantry and intrepidity in special circumstances. Some were for specific actions; some were symbolic. Taken together, they represent only a small fraction of the total number of Medals of Honor America has awarded. All of them, however, hold true to the most fundamental principle of the Medal of Honor: They recognize actions by military men above and beyond the call of duty.

161

The Unknown Soldiers

Four times in the twentieth century, the United States has honored one of its own who gave his life for his country but whose name is a mystery to all. For this sacrifice, and to represent the gallantry of all American soldiers, the country has presented him with the Medal of Honor. After a selection process steeped in ritual, each soldier has been interred in a white marble tomb at Arlington National Cemetery that bears the words, "Here rests in honored glory an American soldier known but to God."

On November 11, 1921, the Unknown Soldier of World War I was borne on a caisson through the streets of Washington, escorted by a contingent of pallbearers that included Samuel Woodfill and Ernest Janson, two Medal of Honor recipients from the conflict. At Arlington, President Warren G. Harding said of the soldier: "We know not whence he came, but only that his death marks him with the everlasting glory of an American dying for his country." Then on the casket he placed the Medal of Honor and the Distinguished Service Cross, while representatives of Great Britain, France, Belgium, Italy, Rumania, Czechoslovakia, and Poland presented the highest honors of their countries.

The interment of the Unknown Soldier from World War II was delayed by the outbreak of hostilities in Korea; it was not until 1958 that the men from both conflicts made the trip across the Potomac to Arlington. On a sweltering Memorial Day, over 200 Medal of Honor recipients looked on

Presidents Harding in 1921 (above) and Reagan in 1984 (right) at exercises for Unknown Soldiers of World War I and Vietnam.

as President Dwight D. Eisenhower presented the medal to each unknown "on behalf of a grateful people."

On May 28, 1984, over nine years after the last American soldier died in Vietnam, President Ronald Reagan placed the Medal of Honor by the casket of the Unknown Soldier from that conflict. "Let us, if we must, debate the lessons learned at some other time," the president said. "Today we simply say with pride: Thank you, dear son, and may God cradle you in His loving arms."

Left. *The tomb at Arlington.* Below. *Korean War Medal of Honor recipient William Charette places a wreath by the remains he has chosen to be the Unknown Soldier of World War II, aboard the* U.S.S. Canberra, *May 23, 1958.*

The Frozen North
Greely's Arctic Expedition

The "special legislation" Medals of Honor were bestowed largely in the 1920s and 1930s, when Congress chose to honor certain men for unique reasons. One of these is a Medal of Honor designated to recognize the entire military career of a general officer. His life in the army began even before the medal existed and continued through the early twentieth century. His contributions were manifold, but one event is particularly noteworthy: an early attempt to explore the farthest northern reaches of the world.

Adolphus Washington Greely as a young soldier, from a New Orleans carte de visite *of the 1860s.*

Of all the Medals of Honor awarded by Congress for actions outside of combat, few carry citations less specific, and more intriguing, than that of Major General Adolphus W. Greely. The general, who received his award on March 21, 1935, had retired from active service twenty-nine years before. He had fought in the Civil War and had served with distinction throughout the latter half of the nineteenth century. Yet no specifics of his career were mentioned in his citation. The most important passage of that document stated only that Greely had been recognized "for his life of splendid public service."

Missing entirely was the incident for which Greely was best known to America. Fifty-four years before, his name made headlines as commander of a disastrous army expedition to the Arctic. The story of the Lady Franklin Bay Expedition was one that the military might well have wished to ignore, for besides showing the endurance of Greely and his men, it exposed the bungling and incompetence of the War Department and the carelessness of the government's early polar explorations.

Greely was born in Newburyport, Massachusetts, on March 27, 1844. He first saw war at seventeen as a member of the 19th Massachusetts Volunteers, fighting at Balls Bluff and the Peninsula before being wounded at Antietam. After seeing more action at Fredericksburg, he transferred to the 54th Massachusetts Infantry (Colonel Robert Shaw's "colored" regiment) as a white officer and earned a reputation as a good administrator in the sensitive task of occupying New Orleans with black troops. After the war he joined the regular army and spent years stringing telegraph wire throughout the frontier West as a lieutenant of the Signal Corps. The Signal Corps was charged also with predicting weather, and along the way

Greely developed an interest in meteorology and polar science.

Greely found himself in Washington, D.C., just as America and Europe declared an International Polar Year for 1882-83. The far north had fascinated Western explorers for 300 years as they searched for a "northwest passage" from the Atlantic to Asia. Interest intensified in the 1840s when Sir John Franklin's expedition disappeared and his wife, Lady Franklin, threw her considerable resources behind numerous searches for her husband. In 1881 Congress voted money for an expedition to Lady Franklin Bay, an inlet of Ellesmere Island near the northern tip of Greenland. Because of his experience, Greely was chosen to command the effort.

His party of about twenty men left Newfoundland on July 8, 1881, aboard the ice-going ship *Proteus,* commanded by Captain Richard Pike. After stopping in Greenland to pick up two Eskimo hunters and a French doctor named Octave Pavy, the expedition landed at Lady Franklin Bay with three years' supply of food and provisions. Immediately they set about building a large house they called Fort Conger and settled in for the months-long arctic night.

But events at home took a fateful turn. First, Greely's chief sponsor, a Signal Corps officer named Howgate, was arrested for embezzling government funds. An investigation revealed widespread corruption throughout the Signal Corps, and this created a residue of ill will for all Signal Corps projects in the mind of the new secretary of war, Abraham Lincoln's son Robert. Moreover, the government was in an uproar over the assassination of President Garfield, which occurred only days before the expedition left for the north.

But Greely and his men were ignorant of the scandal. They whiled away the days in meteorological experiments

and in learning how to hunt and use dog sleds. To relieve the boredom of arctic life, they published a post newspaper and devoured the library that Greely had brought with him to the Arctic. One of the men trained the puppies of the sled dogs, while others caught owls and made pets of them. Almost everyone kept diaries, played cards (for tobacco stakes–Greely forbade gambling for money), and engaged in marksmanship contests. Monotony prevailed, however, and the men looked forward to the arrival of a resupply ship in 1882.

That ship never came. After getting approval from a balky War Department and a Congress wary of the Signal Corps, William Beebe, secretary to the chief of the Signal Corps, sailed in *Neptune* to reach Greely. Beebe expected the same easy passage to Fort Conger that Greely had experienced the year before. Instead, the *Neptune* ran into foul weather and drifting ice before July was

out. In early August, the ship was trapped in pack ice for three days; when it broke free, Beebe gave up his attempt and headed south, leaving a supply cache at Cape Sabine more than 200 miles south of Lady Franklin Bay. Greely's party would have to wait another year for respite.

In the meantime, three of Greely's men achieved the most notable success of the mission: Lieutenant James Lockwood, Sergeant David Brainard, and Eskimo Fred Christiansen, traveling by sledge, surpassed the British record of farthest north by following the coast of Greenland past Royal Navy Lieutenant Albert Markham's record of 83 degrees, 20 minutes 26 seconds. Further, Greely and Lockwood led expeditions into the interior of Ellesmere Island, mapping geographic features, making natural observations, and investigating the remains of Eskimo camps. So far, their journey was a success.

Once it was evident that relief would not arrive in 1882, however, discipline began to break down. Greely's second-in-command, Lieutenant Kislingsbury, had been insubordinate, querulous, and a general nuisance from the earliest days of the journey, to the point where Greely relieved him of his post in favor of Lockwood. Kislingsbury ingratiated himself with the men and spent hours conspiring with Dr. Pavy (by now Greely was calling the shady doctor "an arrant mischief-maker," which he was). Others started making trouble too. Sergeant William Cross turned out to be a dipsomaniac with a taste for spirit-lamp fuel; some other men became insubordinate. Greely juggled ranks and gave responsibility to levelheaded men,

165

Above. *Greely (second from left) and three of his party with sled and dogs at Fort Conger, March 1882.*

a dubious choice, but he enjoyed the confidence of the Signal Corps's chief.

Aboard the *Proteus,* Garlington proved his worth by urging Captain Pike, against his own better judgment, to sail on through ice-choked waters north of Cape Sabine. Soon the relief ship was beset by, then crushed in, the huge ice floes of Kane Basin. As the *Proteus* sank, the crew threw what supplies they could overboard, then made their own treacherous journey south in small boats to join the *Yantic.* Along the way the miserable Garlington left some meager stores for Greely near the agreed upon rendezvous point.

By early August 1883 Greely was deeply concerned. He decided to pack

Below. *The* Lady Greely, *used by the expedition to escape south, sits at anchor in Discovery Harbor, August 1882.*

but their isolation required more diplomacy from him than most officers would require to keep men in line. By the second winter at Fort Conger, nerves were badly frayed. Sergeant Brainard's diary for December 5 read: "Everything annoys and aggravates us. We give way readily in any situation with a burst of unreasonableness." And he was among the most reasonable of the lot.

Still, Greely was satisfied with the expedition's progress and felt confident of relief by the second summer. Unbeknown to him, though, a second mission was ending in failure. Secretary Lincoln, embarrassed by the *Neptune* fiasco, had sent two ships north in 1883, the *Proteus* and the *Yantic,* under the authority of a Signal Corps lieutenant named Ernest A. Garlington. As a pony soldier with no seagoing experience, Garlington was

166

up and make a dash south with all his men, before another boreal winter trapped them at Lady Franklin Bay. This was a mistake, for there were sufficient supplies at Fort Conger to support the expedition for another year. Yet Greely was determined to make the rendezvous that had been scheduled for August if no relief had come before then. The rendezvous was to take place on an island southeast of Cape Sabine. Traveling by sea between Greenland and Ellesmere, the party picked its way through the growing ice floes of Kane Basin. The leader insisted on making straight for Cape Sabine through the middle of the basin, while others favored sticking close to shore. Mutinous murmurings arose. Some men wanted to return to Fort Conger, but Greely demanded they continue south.

On August 26, less than fifty miles from Cape Sabine, Greely's small boats were beset by ice. Days passed as the men waited to break free. Finally they loaded two boats and their supplies onto three sledges and began to haul them over the ice. For nineteen days they battled the unpredictable floes of ice that pushed them toward shore, then away. At last, on September 29, they made land twenty miles from Cape Sabine.

They learned of Garlington's failure when one soldier found a note left by the relief mission. Greely's exhausted crew then moved to Cape Sabine, collecting Garlington's caches and some old rations left by previous explorers. They built shelter from stones and a whaleboat, measured their stores against the closing winter, and hunted with little success for the dwindling game around the basin.

With little food and no hope of relief until summer, Greely and his men began to starve. One soldier, Sergeant Joseph Ellison, lost both hands and feet to frostbite; others showed signs of scurvy, long the bane of arctic explorers.

As rations were cut, then cut again, the weakest men faded. On January 18 the alcoholic Cross, eldest of the crew, died in his sleeping bag. Dr. Pavy told the others that Cross's drinking had weakened him but privately told Greely the real cause of death was starvation.

In Washington, meanwhile, word of Garlington's failure had arrived, and debate was raging over what to do about Greely. Senator Eugene Hale of Maine took up Greely's cause, but others had had their fill of arctic disasters. Senator Ingalls of Kansas declared that such expeditions should be entirely private and implied that any rescuers might one day need rescuing themselves. President Arthur ducked the issue. Yet in mid-April an agreement was achieved. With little hope held out, preparations for a third relief party began. It set out for the north on April 24, 1884.

But things were falling apart at Cape Sabine. More of Greely's men died, although they killed a polar bear in March and added some food to the stores. Some men gathered "shrimps," actually water fleas, with a sieve, but these had little nutritional value. Others stole from the food supply, and in his weakened condition, Greely was unable to watch the cache constantly. Most men stuck to their sleeping bags, fading in strength until they died.

By May men were expiring at a faster rate, yet Greely tried to keep everyone alive. Sergeant Brainard, who had earned Greely's respect as one of the most stalwart of the party, wrote: "Everything looks dark for us. If the

Its hull crushed by ice, the Proteus *sinks twenty miles north of Cape Sabine on July 23, 1883.*

Greely (seated right) with other survivors of his expedition. Clockwise from lower left. *Sergeant David Brainard, Privates Francis Long, Julius Frederick, Maurice Connell, and Henry Beiderbick.*

An unsent letter from Greely to his wife describes his party's dire straits in May 1883. Entry for the thirtieth includes the request, "Do not wear mourning for me I beg."

C.O. does not pull through the expedition will have lost its best friend. . . . He has indeed proved himself a man under the most trying circumstances." On May 10 Greely penned a last letter to his wife, adding an informal will a few days later. He began to lose his senses.

Strangely, some men did not show the effects of starvation as markedly as others. Private Charles Henry and Dr. Pavy, in particular, were stronger than the others. Greely threatened Pavy with arrest and punishment from time to time, and eventually Henry was discovered stealing food. As more men died and were buried in shallow graves, these two proved less and less reliable. Loyal Brainard watched them as best he could, since Greely was now confined to his sleeping bag.

On June 5 Greely issued a warning to Henry, then gave a note to Brainard ordering Henry to be executed if he stole more provisions. The next day Henry stole from the breakfast pot, then admitted boldly that he had other caches of food outside the tent that was now their shelter. Greely wrote another note to Brainard and the remaining two sergeants. They caught up with Henry outside the tent and, after a struggle, shot him to death. Doctor Pavy died of starvation the same day.

Major General Adolphus Greely in later years. His lifetime of service to the army was rewarded with the Medal of Honor seven months before his death on October 20, 1935.

After the execution, Greely attempted to keep order among his dwindling band. When Private Maurice Connell suggested that it was now "every man for himself," Greely replied: "We have come this far by working together. We must continue to do so in the last days. If we must die, let's do it helping each other to keep alive."

By June 22 only seven men were alive. That day Sergeant Francis Long climbed a nearby hill to replace a fallen signal flag. As he looked out over the sea, a small cutter rounded the edge of Cape Sabine. It was the *Cub*, attached to the rescue ships *Thetis* and *Bear*. At last, the navy had gotten through to the stranded men. Long waved the flag, then started down toward shore, directing the rescue team to the small tent where Greely and the others lay. Inside the tent they found a ghastly sight: six men, nearly skeletons, some unable to walk, one without hands and feet, all nearly incoherent. Greely was still in his bag, dazed, and seemed to believe that his rescuers were British. The newcomers fed him and his men bits of food, then carried them and the bodies of the dead to the rescue ships.

Greely enjoyed a tumultuous reception on his return to the United States. Soon, though, the events were overshadowed by reports of cannibalism at Cape Sabine. Some men's bodies were found to have been cut in neat slices, including Henry's, implying that a survivor may have been one of the culprits. Other reports implicated Kislingsbury and Dr. Pavy. Greely attempted to ignore the reports but admitted in private he was sure only that he and Brainard were innocent of such charges.

The scandal eventually died down, however, and Greely came to be honored by the government that had served him so poorly. In 1887 he was named chief signal officer, with general rank. He held

the post for nineteen years, leaving in 1906 to command the San Francisco Presidio just as the great earthquake there destroyed the city. His fame spread as he kept order in the city during the disaster. He never forgave Garlington and Lincoln but kept in touch with the men of his mission, even those who had behaved badly in the last days.

As Greely prepared to retire, he befriended a young officer, urging the man to take up the new phenomenon of flying. In 1935 this officer, realizing that Greely's feats had not been well recognized, went to Capitol Hill and saw through the passage of a special Medal of Honor for the general who had given "a life of splendid service" to his country. By then the young officer was famous himself and would one day also be presented a special medal of honor. His name was Billy Mitchell. ❖

The Medal That Wasn't
General Billy Mitchell

Unlike his friend Greely, William Mitchell was not a by-the-book military man. By the end of his career, Mitchell was more notorious than famous. Yet his prophetic stance on American military aviation constituted a crucial contribution to the nation's military life. His "medal of honor," while controversial, is a tribute to a man who sacrificed his commission for the sake of principle. It was, for him, a duty.

General Billy Mitchell's abundance of decorations included awards from Italy, France, and the United States—but not the Medal of Honor.

From the time he joined the U.S. Army, Billy Mitchell seemed destined for a brilliant career. Son of a U.S. senator from Wisconsin, he entered service at age eighteen, during the Spanish-American War. Within a week he was a second lieutenant, the youngest officer in the army. Cuba was conquered before he got the chance to see action there, but his father saw to it that he was transferred to the Philippines in time to play a role in suppressing rebels there. He rose rapidly in the military hierarchy, took on diverse assignments (including laying telegraph wire in Alaska and spying on Japanese installations in China) before he went to Washington in early 1913 to join the general staff. He was then only thirty-two years old.

From associations with General Adolphus Greely and other Signal Corps officers, he developed an early interest in aviation as a military tool (for its role as an observer craft, the airplane fell under Signal Corps jurisdiction at the time). When World War I broke out in Europe in 1914, Mitchell was already lecturing on military aviation. Familiar with Washington from his days as a senator's son, he became a skilled politician in his own right, briefing Congress daily on the progress of the war and using his social contacts to promote aviation and military reform. Conservative, old-line generals and admirals had little use for the young officer's brash style and advanced notions such as a unified military department and compulsory service. Many were also skeptical about his zealous arguments in favor of the military use of air power, despite the fact that reports from Europe indicated the growing importance of aerial observation and military uses of the airplane and airship.

Mitchell, however, had a skill for being in the right place at the right time to advance his career and ideas. In March 1917 he obtained a position as an observer of French air power developments, and when the United States entered the war one month later, Mitchell wrangled a high post in the new American Air Service. He studied tactics with French and British air warfare strategists and sought aggressively to put American forces in the air as soon as possible. He took command of front-line air forces, and in mid-September 1918 one of his ideas—a coordinated assault by air and land forces—was used to blast the Germans out of their long-held salient at Saint-Mihiel. Mitchell commanded 1,500 French and American airplanes in that battle, the largest concentration of air power to that time. The destruction visited on enemy forces from the air at Saint-Mihiel was to Mitchell proof that the future of warfare lay in the air. His propensity for strongly held opinions built his belief in air power into an obsession.

After occupation duty in 1919, Mitchell used his considerable energies to lobby Congress for a build-up of America's air forces. He began to focus on one particular theory: that airborne bombs could destroy naval fleets. This did not endear him to the navy: Franklin Roosevelt, then assistant secretary of the navy, labeled his ideas "pernicious." But Mitchell was indefatigable. Through a round of Washington social engagements and growing public activity, he pursued his vision constantly.

In February 1920 Col. Mitchell sketched out an attempted naval invasion of the United States, with air power turning back the supposed enemy fleet. Again, the navy was not impressed, although it viewed his forceful arguments with growing alarm. Mitchell requested the means to prove his theories but was ordered to be silent about naval affairs. He responded by attempting to obtain a battleship for a demonstration bombing. The navy tried to thwart him by conducting its own blatantly rigged test: It dropped dummy bombs on an old ship, then exploded charges that had been lashed to its decks to simulate a real bombing. The tests, the navy said, showed the "improbability" of a successful aerial attack. Secretary of the Navy Josephus Daniels wrote confidently that Mitchell "will soon discover, if he ever tries laying bombs on the deck of a naval vessel, that he will be blown to atoms long before he is near enough to drop salt on the tail of the Navy."

Yet Mitchell's skills as a politician, and his public reputation (which he had carefully nourished through newspaper and magazine articles) created enough pressure to give him his chance. For months he trained crews in the tactics of aerial bombardment. He conducted tests against a light cruiser and sank it, which caused some stir. Then, in July 1921, he gathered a large group of politicians, reporters, and high military figures to watch his attempt on the *Ostfriesland,* an "unsinkable" battleship

obtained from Germany after the world war. The navy's confidence was shattered when the heavily armored ship, bombarded by Mitchell's planes, heeled over and sank in the waters off Chesapeake Bay. A few months later he repeated the feat, this time sinking an American battleship, the *Alabama.* Mitchell had made his point.

A more tactful man might have let things proceed naturally from that emphatic demonstration, but Mitchell continued to press for his belief in a unified air service (by this time the army and navy were pursuing separate paths to air power). This made him more enemies within the military hierarchy. He curried favor on Capitol Hill and in the press but alienated anyone whose ideas or strategy were different from his own. He muttered about "conspiracies" against him and charged privately that the navy had tried to prevent the sinking of the *Ostfriesland.* It was obvious from his behavior that he wished to go over the heads of his superiors to the public at large, to educate them about his views

on air power. But his loose charges and harsh style were such that some felt his real love was not aviation: Jerome Hunsaker, a designer of dirigibles, described him as a "politician in uniform. We . . . thought the cause was Billy Mitchell himself, and not air power."

A break was inevitable, and one came in the late summer of 1925. First, a navy plane was lost at sea during a poorly planned flight from California to Hawaii. Then, in September, Hunsaker's airship *Shenandoah,* the pride of the American fleet, was torn to pieces in a violent thunderstorm over Ohio. Fourteen men, including the captain, Mitchell's friend Zachary Landsdowne, were killed. The press asked for Mitchell's opinion, and he delivered a bombshell: "These accidents are the result of the incompetency, the criminal

Mitchell flies his De Havilland DH4B, the Osprey, *off the Virginia coast in 1921. Pennant attached to the tail identifies him to other fliers.*

negligence, and the almost treasonable administration of the national defense by the Navy and War Departments . . . ," he wrote. "The bodies of my former companions of the air molder under the soil in America and Asia, Europe and Africa, many, yes, a great many, sent there directly by official stupidity."

By any measure, Mitchell had now passed the boundaries of military decorum. The army decided to court-martial him. President Coolidge, who had taken a hostile interest in Mitchell by then, convened the court himself on October 20, 1925. Even then Mitchell was defiant: He complained about the make-up of the court, demanding trial by "flying officers" rather than the high-ranking landsmen who had been named. The request was denied.

The irony was that by 1925 many general officers agreed that the air services were deficient, including General Pershing and a Medal of Honor recipient from the Indian Wars, retired General Leonard Wood. (Wood wrote that "Mitchell has been a gallant, hard-fighting officer but with always a turn for overstating things.") As if to agree that something was wrong, Coolidge set up a board of investigation along with the court-martial, headed by his old friend Dwight Morrow (soon to be Charles Lindbergh's father-in-law). The board produced a report during Mitchell's trial that called for numerous reforms in the air services, yet confirmed the army's and navy's separate control over their own programs. Morrow's shrewd work helped to isolate the strident and impolitic Mitchell by agreeing with many of his points but making them diplomatically and with presidential support.

The trial itself strayed from the question of insubordination to a recitation of Mitchell's familiar charges against the government and military. The foregone conclusion was announced

December 18, 1925: guilty of insubordination. Mitchell was sentenced to five years' suspension without rank, command, or pay. His offer to resign instead was accepted with alacrity.

Now free of martial constraints, Mitchell set out on the lecture circuit to promote his views on air power. He enjoyed some success, yet interest faded in a short time. Rather than enhancing his prestige, as he had hoped, his court-martial tainted him somewhat in the eyes of his countrymen. When the Great Depression came three years later, Mitchell and the debate over air power faded from public view. He died in 1936, still insisting on the righteousness of his views.

The world war that burst forth in 1939 provided a graphic exoneration of

Right. *Major Mitchell stands in a trench on the western front during World War I.* Below. *The* Ostfriesland *is hit during aerial bombing tests on July 21, 1921.*

Confusion about whether Mitchell's medal of honor is *the* Medal of Honor stems from the fact that it is included in the accounting and numerical totals of the U.S. Senate's Committee on Veterans' Affairs publication, *Medal of Honor Recipients, 1863-1978.* Mitchell's award is one of the "special legislation" awards that include those of Charles Lindbergh, Richard Byrd, Floyd Bennett, and others. Most of these medals are indeed the Medal of Honor.

Yet a careful reading of Mitchell's citation, and a look at the object itself, confirm that his award is not the Medal of Honor as it is normally construed. The citation calls upon the president of the United States "to cause a gold medal to be struck, with suitable emblems, devices and inscriptions, to be presented

Left. A phosphorous bomb scores a direct hit on the Alabama, *September 1921. Below. The wreck of the dirigible* Shenandoah, *destroyed in Ohio on September 23, 1925.*

Mitchell's opinions. The Luftwaffe's mastery of continental European skies, the carrier battles of the Pacific, and the Allied bombings of Germany and Japan proved the importance of air forces to modern warfare. In a later review of the court-martial sentence a decade after the war, Secretary of the Air Force James H. Douglas called Mitchell's vision "amazingly accurate." Yet Mitchell's actions and rhetoric while in uniform were clearly unsuitable for a high-ranking officer of the army. In the review, his conviction was upheld. Nevertheless, Congress had already eased the sting of the court-martial somewhat by voting a medal of honor for Billy Mitchell on August 8, 1946, "in recognition of his outstanding pioneer service and foresight in the field of American military aviation."

Right. *Obverse of Mitchell's "medal of honor." Below. An excerpt from a diagram of aerial tactics devised by Mitchell. Bottom. Mitchell stands as the charges are read at his court-martial. His wife is seated next to him.*

to the late William Mitchell." The medal itself is a medallion, the obverse of which shows Mitchell in a flying helmet and scarf and the reverse a flying eagle with the words "Award of Congress" above and "for outstanding pioneer service and foresight in the field of American military aviation" below. The actual intent of Congress in awarding "a" medal of honor to Mitchell is still debated among Medal of Honor authorities. Yet one fact seems clear: Billy Mitchell's vision of the importance of military aviation was essentially correct. Flaws in the man may have made him impolitic to the point of insubordination, but his willingness to risk his career for correct principles may be viewed in the light of history as above and beyond the call of duty. ◈

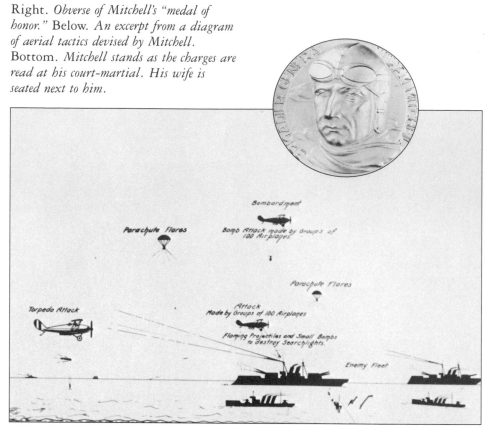

The Lone Eagle
Charles A. Lindbergh

In addition to Greely, other men who made their fame as explorers were honored in the early decades of the twentieth century. These were men who pioneered the use of aircraft to explore the far reaches of the planet and to connect the continents with air travel routes. All were careful professionals who, despite the thoroughness of their preparations, earned the Medal of Honor in perilous circumstances. Their gallantry was not found in the courage of a single moment's action, but in calculated leaps into the unknown. Charles Lindbergh was one such man.

On May 21, 1927, a fisherman's midday duties were disrupted by the sound of a motor overhead. Peering out a porthole, the astonished boatman watched as a small monoplane circled above him and a young man stuck his head out the side window crying, "Which way is Ireland?" It was Charles Lindbergh, piloting the *Spirit of St. Louis* in the most stupendous feat of a roaring decade: the first nonstop journey from New York City to Paris, France.

Word of Lindbergh's progress over Ireland and Great Britain had already reached the capital of France that evening, and as he touched down at Le Bourget Airport, a delirious crowd swarmed about his plane. The weary pilot, who had not slept in over fifty hours, was seized by the crowd as he opened his cockpit door and passed hand over hand into the throng. He broke free with the help of two French aviators, escaped to a hangar, and drove to the American embassy in town. There he met briefly with the press, borrowed a pair of pajamas, took a long nap, and awoke to find himself the hero of the age.

Not even the most avid publicist could have imagined the wellspring of adulation that greeted Lindbergh in the next few months. In Paris, in Brussels, and in London the hysteria mounted. Despite Lindbergh's wish to return to the United States in the *Spirit of St. Louis* (flying eastward around the world), he was informed that President Calvin Coolidge had dispatched a ship to return both him and his plane to America as soon as possible. His entry to the United States could hardly have been grander: In Washington the president stood under the Washington Monument and pinned the nation's first Distinguished Flying Cross to his chest. In New York City, over 4 million people cheered him along Broadway, dumping some 1,800 tons of confetti on his motorcade. *Time*

magazine declared him its first Man of the Year. Some expected the frenzy to die down after a few weeks, but it did not. Every politician, booster group, and organization wanted to share in his unprecedented fame; in December of 1927, both houses of Congress passed resolutions awarding Colonel Lindbergh (Army Reserve) the Medal of Honor.

The twenty-five-year-old Minnesotan's easy grin and unassuming manner masked a dual character that was both careful and adventurous. His path to the famous flight started at the Nebraska Aircraft Company, a ragtag flying school like many that had grown up after the world war. Using shaky war surplus models, Lindbergh learned to fly, then found work as a barnstormer and daredevil—walking airplane wings, parachuting, and performing stunts at county fairs. He joined the army long enough to gain some experience in its relatively powerful planes, then moved to the reserves and sought out other opportunities. He conceived his Atlantic flight while flying the mails between St. Louis and Chicago. Air mail transport was a risky business in those days; often a flight would end with a bumpy landing in a cow pasture along the route. But taking chances—flying at night and through all kinds of weather—was an excellent training ground for Lindbergh. Years after the transatlantic flight, he would characterize it as no more dangerous than a winter of flying the mails through the Midwest.

The flight of the *Spirit of St. Louis* was itself fairly uneventful. Lindbergh chose the shortest path possible, a great-circle route that took him far north of normal shipping lanes. Starting amid intense press coverage from New York early on the morning of May 20, he flew over New England, Nova Scotia, and Newfoundland, diverting from his circle route just enough to be noticed over the

Charles Lindbergh at Curtiss Field, Long Island, after his flight from San Diego.

town of St. John's. As he turned toward the sea, his greatest enemy was sleep. He had left New York suddenly, when skies were clearing over his route, and had not slept the night before. His flight became a test of his ability to stay awake during the monotonous hours over the ocean. Once he noticed ice forming on his wings and had to fly through a thunderhead until clear of its icing clouds. Another time he dropped to within ten feet of the Atlantic, then pulled up to avoid inadvertently ditching the plane into a large swell. All in all, the flight was a matter of endurance. His plane performed flawlessly, leaving the human element of Lindbergh's skill and perseverance as the greatest test of the flight.

The reasons for Lindbergh's singular fame were more complicated than the fact that he had fulfilled a goal of early aviation. Before his flight, more experienced pilots had tried and failed to win the $25,000 prize established by Raymond Orteig for the first nonstop flight from New York to Paris. All previous attempts had been expensive projects involving well-known aircraft designers, teams of aviators flying multi-engined planes, and sometimes years of preparation before any actual flight. Lindbergh flew solo, using a single-engined monoplane designed by an unknown company, with financing from small-city St. Louis businessmen. As opposed to the well-publicized attempts of large consortiums, Lindbergh's flight seemed to many the stuff of courage and American can-do individualism.

In fact, Lindbergh was courageous, occasionally to the point of recklessness. His feats as a motorcyclist and aerial acrobat were sometimes foolhardy. Yet there was nothing uncalculated in his

transatlantic flight. His physical courage was coupled with a native sense for mechanical things and an awesome determination for thorough preparation once he decided upon a project. During the construction of the *Spirit of St. Louis,* he oversaw every detail, going so far as to insist on replacing the engine when it sustained a tiny chip during installation. The mathematics of fuel and flight path had also been carefully worked out in advance, and he trained for his flight with a one-stop journey from his plane's San Diego factory to New York City—a flight that, because of its great length, established a more respectable record for himself before his transatlantic sojourn. He made lists for everything, figuring all aspects of the project even before he

had financial backing. One list, labeled "Action," included not only items such as "backers" and "equipment," but also "propaganda," "accessory information," and "advertising."

Part of his success also lay in the fact that, despite his compulsively organizational bent, he thought creatively about the project from the start. A loner most of his young life, he determined against the conventional wisdom to fly alone. He reasoned that this would not only save him precious weight (a 160-pound navigator translated into twenty-five extra gallons of fuel), but would also give him more freedom of action, since he would be responsible for only one life—his own. His specifications for his plane were also unusual but again

176

Below. *The Spirit of St. Louis is ringed by police at Le Bourget Airport in Paris. Moments later the throng of well-wishers broke through, rushing the plane and its weary pilot.*

Right. *Lindbergh and Ambassador Myron Herrick on a balcony of the American embassy in Paris, May 22, 1927. Lindbergh wears the Legion of Honor just presented to him by the president of France.*

creative. He insisted, for example, that the cockpit be located behind the oversized fuel tanks. This meant that he had no forward vision, which he considered unnecessary, since air traffic would be nonexistent and he could stick his head out a side window when landing. It also assured that in case of a crash, he would not be crushed between the engine and fuel tanks. His boldness lay not only in his adventure, then, but also in his imaginative approach to the problem of long-range flight.

The glory that was showered upon him for years after his flight was also a function of the America of his day. Just before he took off, government officials had been quoted as saying that his attempt was "suicide." And yet he succeeded. The sense that a brave young American with brains and determination could triumph where internationally famous aviators had failed

electrified an America jaded by the experience of an unhappy, wasteful European world war, a flawed peace, and a decade of rampant hedonism and moral decline. To an America weary of itself, Lindbergh represented the best in the American character. Just after his arrival in Paris, the American ambassador cabled Wash-

ington with words that summed up the general impression of Lindbergh that was to persist for years to come: "If we had deliberately sought a type to represent the youth, the intrepid adventure of America . . . we could not have fared as well as in this boy of divine genius and simple courage." ❖

177

Below. *Four million spectators regale Charles Lindbergh in a ticker-tape parade up New York's Broadway, June 13, 1927. Insets. Time magazine's first Man of the Year cover (top) and a lapel pin celebrating America's new hero (bottom).*

To the Pole
Byrd and Bennett

In the 1920s, a military man from an old Virginia family caught the imagination of the world with bold flights into the polar regions. Born to privilege, Richard Byrd overcame personal handicaps and professional frustrations to contribute to the fields of polar science and air exploration.

One of Charles Lindbergh's closest rivals for the New York to Paris title was Commander Richard Evelyn Byrd of the U.S. Navy. An explorer, navigator, and naval lobbyist whose fame had grown in government and political circles during the twenties, Byrd had chased the dream of a transatlantic flight for a decade before Lindbergh's flight. Indeed, he almost beat the younger man to Paris, but a bad crash on a test flight the month before had damaged his plane and seriously injured his flying partner, navy Machinist Floyd Bennett. While he awaited repairs Byrd offered the use of his flying field to Lindbergh—a gracious offer characteristic of the man.

Also characteristic, for good and ill, was a strange run of good and bad luck that marked his early career. A sports injury had washed him out of the navy soon after his graduation from Annapolis. He was restored to the service despite his game leg only when World War I intervened—a time when, in his words, "a willing cripple suddenly became to a mad world as valuable as a whole man who might be unwilling." He convinced doctors to let him enter the naval air service, where he fulfilled his childhood ambition of learning to fly, then proposed a bold scheme to get himself over to France: He would fly a huge new seaplane of the NC series across the

Richard E. Byrd in polar garb, holding the business end of a ski pole. His flights to the poles thrilled an adventure-hungry public.

Atlantic, by way of Newfoundland and the Azores, and put it at the disposal of General Pershing. This plan was tentatively approved, then fate again stepped in: He was ordered to Canada to establish a naval aerial observation station in Nova Scotia.

The war ended, but Byrd persisted in his proposal to fly across the sea. At last approval was given, and in 1919 three NCs took off from New York for Newfoundland, with Byrd aboard one as navigator. In Newfoundland, however, bad luck struck again: He was transferred to a balloon airship. Byrd watched helplessly as the planes took off from Newfoundland for the Azores without him (one plane, piloted by Lieutenant Commander A. C. Read, made the islands, then Lisbon, for the first actual transatlantic flight).

Yet his reputation as a project organizer and navigator had grown with the success of the NC flights. Along the way he had developed two important aerial navigation tools, the drift indicator and bubble sextant, and had made friends in high places in the Navy Department. He spent time in Washington, lobbying for naval air power in opposition to General Billy Mitchell's proposal for a separate air service. Here he impressed other men in government, among them assistant navy secretaries Franklin Roosevelt and Theodore Roosevelt, Jr. By 1924, he was ready for

another great adventure, one he had dreamed of as a child: a flight over the North Pole.

The first polar attempt the navy proposed was to be a flight by the doomed dirigible *Shenandoah* (the airship was to be destroyed in a storm on September 3, 1925). When this was suddenly canceled by President Coolidge, Byrd pressed for a private expedition. He organized support, put together a crew, and found financial backing from industrialists Edsel Ford and John D. Rockefeller.

In June 1925 he set sail for the

Above. *Navy Machinist Floyd Bennett was Byrd's companion and pilot on the flight to the North Pole.* Right. *Banking into a turn upon takeoff, Byrd and Bennett leave Spitsbergen in their Fokker trimotor, the* Josephine Ford, *on their way to the pole, May 9, 1926.*

President Coolidge presents Medals of Honor to Byrd (center) and Bennett (right), February 1927. At left is Secretary of the Navy Curtis Wilbur.

calculations showed them to be over the North Pole. The two men circled around the point they thought was the pole to cover any reasonable margin of error, taking photos and movies of the battered ice cap below them. Then they turned the only direction possible from that point—south—and dashed back to Spitsbergen, arriving there about fifteen hours after their departure.

Upon their return to the United States, Byrd and Bennett were lauded as heroes of air exploration. Not only had they shown the worthiness of the airplane as an instrument of exploration, but their necessary dependence upon advanced navigational techniques had proven that air travel was possible over an area with no landmarks and no reliable compass readings. President Coolidge presented each of them with the rare Hubbard Medal of the National Geographic Society. Congress later awarded Byrd and Bennett each the Medal of Honor.

Byrd had secured his title as America's premier explorer. He set about immediately to achieve his dream of a transatlantic crossing. Unlike Lindbergh, he hewed to the navy line that a multiengined plane was the only proper vehicle for overseas travel of such vast distance. Yet his strange luck thwarted him again when his new Fokker trimotor, the *America,* crashed on a trial flight. True to form, though, he welcomed Lindbergh's success, writing later that he "realized what it meant to aviation and to international good-fellowship." A final accident of fate gave the commander a chance to show his sportsmanship: The same day Lindbergh landed, Byrd had scheduled a christening of his newly repaired *America.* With the French and American flags flying, he lauded his young rival and turned the occasion into a celebration of his countryman's triumph ⊛

north, landing at Etah in Greenland. Over the arctic summer he flew Loening Amphibians, seaplanes with wheels, over Cape Sabine, where General Greely and his men had starved over the long arctic winter some forty years earlier. Before returning to the United States in the fall, Byrd developed a fast friendship with and high respect for Machinist Floyd Bennett, a heretofore unknown navy mechanic with an uncanny sense for the workings of airplane engines. Byrd and Bennett's partnership was to last past this journey to the next step in Byrd's plans: the flight to the North Pole.

On April 5, 1926, Byrd, Bennett, and fifty chosen men sailed from the Brooklyn Navy Yard, bound for Spitsbergen, a rocky Norwegian-owned island some 600 miles from the pole. They set up camp at King's Bay, where a Norwegian expedition commanded by explorer Roald Amundsen was already preparing for a dirigible flight over the pole and on to Alaska. Both groups later claimed that there was no real competition between them to be first to the pole, but Byrd and his men set about with all deliberate speed to prepare his airplane, the *Josephine Ford,* for a flight north.

The first trials of Byrd's plane ended in crackups, but each time damage was minor and the crew was able to patch up the Fokker trimotor for another attempt. Byrd determined that the plane was overweight, so everything not crucial to the flight was removed from the *Josephine Ford* (while stripping the plane down, Byrd found numerous souvenirs stashed by his men who hoped they would later become mementos. One souvenir, however, escaped his detection—a ukelele). Final preparations were completed on May 8, 1926.

At 1:22 A.M. Greenwich time on May 9, the trimotor took off with Bennett at the stick and Byrd in the navigator's chair. After taking some bearings, the pair headed due north. Byrd was constantly employed at taking wind-drift measurements and shooting the sun for bearings. His nonstop figuring was crucial to the flight's success, for at that far northern latitude, both the compass and gyroscopes of the day were unreliable.

One hour from the pole, Byrd noticed oil leaking from the starboard motor. Over the engines' roar, Bennett passed him a note: *That motor will stop.* Byrd decided to press on, figuring that a forced landing near the pole was better than one farther away. The leak was temporary, though, and at 9:02 A.M., Byrd's

Rescue off the Isles of Shoals
The *Squalus* Affair

No controversy exists as to the Medals of Honor awarded to sailors during peacetime: These are actual Medals of Honor, bestowed under the regulations stipulating medals for distinguished conduct at sea, in war or in peace. The last set of these was awarded just before America entered World War II. The men who earned them risked their lives to save fellow sailors trapped beneath the waves.

Torpedoman First Class John Mihalowski of the salvage ship Falcon *was the first to reach the trapped crew of the* Squalus.

On the morning of May 23, 1939, Torpedoman First Class John Mihalowski stood on the dock of a New London, Connecticut, naval yard, tending to his chores as a sailor aboard the U.S.S. *Falcon.* The *Falcon,* a salvage ship, was the navy's premier rescue vessel and the mother ship for a new type of underwater diving bell, the McCann rescue chamber. In 1927, the *Falcon* had participated in the effort to save the men of the submarine *S-4* when the ship went down off Cape Cod. Now, as Mihalowski ran cable onto the reel of the McCann chamber, a new alarm sounded: The U.S.S. *Squalus,* America's newest submarine, had sunk off the coast of New Hampshire with all hands on board.

The men of the *Falcon* jumped to their stations, preparing the ship for a race to the disaster site. A sister sub to the *Squalus,* the U.S.S. *Sculpin,* had spotted distress signals and a marker buoy off the Isles of Shoals when the *Squalus* failed to report on time. Now it held position over the sunken sub as the *Falcon* passed through the Cape Cod Canal and steamed up the coast toward the Portsmouth, New Hampshire, Navy Yard, home of the *Squalus.*

Using an underwater oscillator, the *Sculpin* established communication with the stricken sub, whose crew pounded out messages in Morse code with hammers against the hull. The *Squalus,* it seemed, had proceeded with a normal test dive that morning, and everything had gone smoothly, as it had in eighteen prior test dives. A few seconds into the dive, however, disaster struck. The radioman in the control room heard an anguished report from the engine room: "Take her up! The inductions are open!" The huge valve that transported air to the engines when the sub was running on the surface had somehow failed to seal when the *Squalus* slipped under the waves. Now the sea was pouring into the

engines and the aft sections of the ship. Horrified sailors in the control room glanced toward the control board of the sub, still indicating the "valves closed" green light for diving.

Lieutenant Oliver F. Naquin, commander of the *Squalus,* and his crew reacted instinctively at the first sign of trouble. Men dogged the hatches between compartments, sealing them off; one quick-thinking sailor, realizing the risk of short circuit and explosion if the ship's electrical system came into contact with water, shut down the lights and power. At 70 feet, the *Squalus* leveled off, paused, then lunged stern down toward the ocean floor. Within four minutes of the dive order, the *Squalus* was settled on the bottom of the sea, immobile and dark under 240 feet of ocean.

Lieutenant Naquin, sealed in the control room with twenty-two others, assessed his situation. Ten men reported by intercom from the forward torpedo room, still dry and shut tight. From the aft compartments, where the trouble had started, no sound emerged. Twenty-six men were back there, unaccounted for. Naquin feared the worst.

As the *Falcon* steamed toward the Isles of Shoals, John Mihalowski noticed how cold the day was and realized the extent of the job ahead. Rescuing the men of the *Squalus* would require a massive effort of divers and rescue-bell operators, in waters deeper than any rescue previously attempted by the U.S. Navy. Mihalowski himself was a crack deep-sea diver who had spent years at the navy's Experimental Diving Unit, testing the limits of human endurance underseas. His own story was a classic among divers: Visiting the *Falcon* as a child, he had determined to join the navy as a diver. At fourteen, fifteen, and sixteen, he had tried to join up, until an exasperated recruiter told him to come back with a birth certificate stating he was

A diver prepares to go over the side of the Falcon *on the 240-foot descent to the* Squalus. *At left is the diving bell that will follow him down.*

seventeen. This he did, with the help of a friend adept at altering documents. After eleven years in the navy, he was now an operator of the McCann chamber, a bell-shaped vessel designed with just such an emergency in mind. "I considered that *my* bell," he said, "I took care of it. I babied it." This was the purpose for which he had trained.

As the *Falcon* neared the Isles of Shoals, other divers and salvage specialists arrived from the Experimental Diving Unit. Among them was Chief Machinist's Mate William Badders, coholder of the world diving record of 500 feet; Commander Allen R. McCann, codesigner of the diving chamber that bore his name; and Chief Metalsmith James H. McDonald, a master diver. They, along with Mihalowski and his buddy Orson L. Crandall of the *Falcon,* were among the chief figures of the rescue effort.

Once the *Falcon* moored over the sunken sub, a diver was sent down to attach a "downhaul" cable to the forward escape hatch of the *Squalus,* located atop the torpedo room. In the diving equipment of the time—the venerable "dry suit" with fishbowl helmet and lead shoes—a diver descended by cables, slowly increasing the pressure inside the suit and his body to equalize the tremendous force of the water around him. At deep levels this pressure caused physical and mental slowdown, so that a diver had to be reminded constantly by surface-to-diver telephone of where he was and what he was doing. The risks were manifold, but a good team was capable of performing operations at depths even greater than the 240 feet of water under which the *Squalus* was trapped.

With the downhaul cable attached to the hatch of the *Squalus,* Mihalowski and another operator, Gunner's Mate

First Class Walter E. Harman, prepared for their descent in the McCann chamber. The chamber looked something like an inverted egg, with a rounded top chamber eight feet across and a cylindrical lower chamber five feet in diameter. The downhaul cable was attached to a reel in the lower chamber. The reel pulled the bell downward toward the sub by winding up the cable; once the job was finished, the reel would unwind the cable, allowing the bell to rise to the surface. In addition, a "preventer" cable ran from a winch on the *Falcon* to the top of the bell to help guide the chamber on its path. Operating the bell was a balancing act, for its ballast and buoyancy had to be carefully adjusted to the tolerances of both cables.

Mihalowski and his partner first sealed themselves into the bell's top

Chief Machinist's Mate William Badders accompanied Mihalowski on the fifth and most treacherous descent.

Chief Boatswain's Mate Orson L. Crandall received a Medal of Honor for "important and difficult dives" to the crippled Squalus.

chamber, then flooded the lower chamber and blew out the water in the ballast tanks for proper buoyancy. Keeping an eye on the downhaul cable through a glass portal set in the hatch between chambers, they used a motor to tug the 18,000-pound chamber toward the sunken *Squalus*. Soon the two men saw the outline of the sub. They settled the rescue chamber over the sub's escape hatch, then flooded the ballast tanks so the chamber rested heavily on the *Squalus's* topside deck. There they blew pressurized air into the bell's lower chamber, forcing all but a few inches of water out of it. A rubber gasket around the bottom rim of the lower chamber, pressed flat against the sub by the great pressure of the ocean at 240 feet, held water out as the rescuers equalized pressure between the chambers of the bell.

Mihalowski then opened the hatch between the chambers and dropped down to the topside deck of the *Squalus*. After further securing the diving bell to the sub with steel bolts, he loosened the sub's escape hatch and pulled it open. The icy, ankle-deep water remaining in the lower chamber of the bell splashed down to a second hatch at the bottom of the sub's escape port. Both men yelled a greeting, but there was no reply from below.

The rescuers realized the trapped men did not respond because they had heard the excess water splash down to the inner hatch. Mihalowski dropped down, banged on the hatch with a wrench, then opened it up. Down the cold water splashed again, this time all over the men inside the sub. It did not matter. Mihalowski looked down at the beaming faces of the *Squalus's* crew. For the first time in history, men whose submarine had gone down were about to be saved by a rescue bell. "Hello, fellows," Mihalowski grinned, "here we are!"

The bell could accommodate seven to nine survivors. While Lt. Naquin determined who was to go on the first trip up, Mihalowski passed a pot of steaming coffee down to the crew. Helping seven men into the chamber, the rescuers sealed off the bell, blew enough ballast to achieve buoyancy, and slowly rose, playing out the downhaul wire to regulate their ascent. Just after 1:30 P.M. on the twenty-fourth, twenty-nine hours after the start of their ordeal, the first survivors stood on the deck of the rescue ship *Falcon*.

Two more trips to the sub went off without a hitch. On the fourth trip, however, the downhaul cable jammed on the way back up. It was cut by a diver, but then the preventer cable showed signs of fraying. If it gave, the bell would tear off its air line, drowning the men inside.

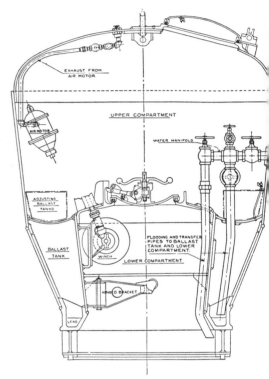

The McCann diving chamber included upper and lower compartments separated by a hatch. Manifolds regulated water in the lower compartment and ballast tanks. A winch coiled or let out the downhaul cable to move the bell up or down, and an air motor provided fresh air from a hose leading to the surface.

It looked tight, but in the midst of the situation, Mihalowski and the others kept up a cheering banter. "We were talking about women," he said later with a laugh, "about steaks, drinks, parties." Word came from the ship for the rescuers to adjust the bell's buoyancy just enough for it to be coaxed to the surface. Slowly it rose until, after four hours underwater, it broke the surface with the last of the survivors inside.

One trip remained, though, before the rescue mission could be called off. Since the first moments of the disaster, no sign of life had come from the aft portion of the *Squalus*. Despite the dim

The bow of the Squalus *bursts through the ocean surface during salvage operations. Although the sub sank immediately after this photo was taken, a later attempt was successful in raising it.*

Chief Metalsmith James H. McDonald, the fourth recipient of the Medal of Honor for the Squalus *rescue, was cited for directing and performing hazardous dives.*

odds of any survivors, that part of the ship had to be checked through the escape hatch of the aft torpedo room. This job was far more hazardous than the other missions: If the compartment was flooded at bottom pressure, the water would smash into the diving bell the instant the hatch was opened, unless the bell itself were pressurized to equal the force of the water. Further, the bell's crew could not vent carbon dioxide from the bell during the operation. William Badders and John Mihalowski were chosen for the risky job.

A diver preceded them to the bottom, shackling the downhaul line to the aft escape hatch. Then Badders and Mihalowski descended. Atop the sub, they built the bell's air pressure to 109 psi, where it equaled the pressure of the surrounding sea. Here another hazard presented itself: With equal pressure, there could be no suction seal between the bell and the sub. Carefully balancing the pressure, the rescuers used the pull of

the downhaul cable to hold them in place until Badders dropped down to the lower chamber and bolted the bell in place. Both men were now feeling the same effects of pressure experienced by divers at that depth; combined with the growing levels of carbon dioxide, they suffered the syndrome Mihalowski described simply: "You get drunk."

As Mihalowski maintained air pressure, Badders bent over the sub's escape hatch and slowly turned the release wheel. Suddenly, air and seawater rushed past the hatch's seal and began to fill the lower chamber. Mihalowski added more air pressure, forcing the sea back into the sub. It was clear that no survivors remained, but Badders opened the hatch a crack nonetheless. All he saw was dark water. Now barely conscious from the effects of high air pressure, he sealed the hatch, allowing Mihalowski to ventilate the carbon dioxide-fouled air from the bell. The fresh air cleared their heads as the divers sealed their bell and

reported their findings to the surface. They ascended slowly, adjusting to decompression, whiling away the hours planning what everyone on the surface already had in mind: raising the *Squalus* from the ocean floor.

Several weeks later, after one spectacular failed raising, the *Squalus* was raised to the surface with the aid of huge, air-filled pontoons. Throughout the salvage operation, Badders and Mihalowski, as well as James McDonald and Orson Crandall, made dangerous dives to the sunken sub. When World War II struck American shores, the *Squalus* had already been refitted and renamed the *Sailfish* (wags in the service called it the "Squailfish"). By that time, too, the four divers had been awarded Medals of Honor—the last time sailors earned it in a time of peace. ❖

World War II

The World at War

Young German troops in 1932. Hitler's accession to the chancellorship of Germany the next year caused a large build-up of German forces.

The war that was to thrust America to the forefront of world affairs began when the country was preoccupied with troubles of its own.

In the dark years of the Great Depression of the 1930s, the United States was engulfed in joblessness, poverty, and civil disturbances. Even then, Americans could not ignore the waves of violent change that were washing over Europe and Asia. One by one throughout the decade, democracies succumbed to the rule of dictators. Free people bowed to servitude; oppression and silence became the fate of those who had once spoken openly; death awaited millions opposed to the new order. To Americans who listened to the voices from abroad, the hysterical chants signified a world gone mad.

The seeds of the great war were sown at the moment that marked the end of the First World War. An American observer of the negotiations at Versailles said the scene reminded him of ancient times "when the conqueror dragged the conquered at his chariot wheels." After the German delegation signed the treaty on June 28, 1919, they walked from the hall and broke the pen they had used for the document. The treaty saddled Germany and its allies with all responsibility for the war and became a hated symbol of the humiliation Germans felt in defeat, a defeat made especially bitter because many felt they had not been conquered in over four years of fighting on the battlefield.

The Allies saw the peace process as a chance to make certain their enemy would not rise again, but the harsh demands the treaty made on Germany and its allies would soon lead the world toward a new and more dreadful conflict. The treaty divested Germany of large sections of territory. The new states created from German and Austro-Hungarian lands provided Germany a rationale for war. Even David Lloyd George, British prime minister and an architect of the treaty, foresaw the potential for calamity created by the new countries: "I cannot conceive any greater cause of a future war than that the German people should be surrounded by a mob of small states, many of them consisting of peoples who have never previously set up stable governments by themselves, but each of them containing large masses of Germans." His prophecy would be fulfilled.

For the Germans the most galling provision of the pact left them liable for crushing reparations payments. The first reparations installment left the country prostrate. By 1923 inflation was so severe that a U.S. quarter was valued at 1 billion marks. People burned mark notes for fuel and pushed wheelbarrows full of marks to the store. Inflation wiped out the middle class and left older people and veterans on fixed pensions rooting in the garbage for food. Though international aid helped restore the German economy, it did not reverse an enduring psychological effect: the German tendency thereafter to trace every economic ill directly to the Versailles treaty. The intellectual climate favored popular leaders who told the German people what they wanted to hear and who offered simple solutions to complex problems.

Germany and other countries in Europe became fertile soil for dictators to plow. Demagogues attracted people who had been uprooted and alienated from their past by the World War. In Italy Mussolini seized power, leading his Fascists on an audacious march on Rome in October of 1922. Afraid to send the Italian army against him and risk civil war, King Victor Emmanuel III asked Mussolini to form a cabinet.

Preceding pages. Robert Capa recorded this image of an American soldier struggling through the surf to reach the French shore at Normandy on D-day, June 6, 1944.

Russia, too, succumbed to a new autocratic rule. Between 1917 and 1921, the Russians' state had been convulsed by a civil war. Thirteen million Russians had died from war, famine, and disease during the fighting between the Communist Red Army and the counterrevolutionary White Army. The Reds prevailed and the Soviet Union soon became an antagonistic, insular nation that, under Joseph Stalin, turned

Hitler salutes the crowd at a rally in Nuremberg, the center of Nazi culture, in 1938. At far left is Deputy Führer Rudolph Hess.

increasingly inward in an effort to develop its industrial might. The rest of the world learned that Stalin was purging all potential opponents to his plans, killing them or sending them to die in labor camps. Eight million were expunged in a graphic exhibition of totalitarian power.

In Germany in 1919, thirty-year-old Adolph Hitler became one of the first members of the newly formed German Worker's party, later known as the Nationalsozialistische Deutsche Arbeiterpartei. The world would come to know them as the Nazis. The group's first attempt to seize control of the state by violence ended in failure and imprisonment in 1923. While in jail Hitler wrote a book that would give form to his vision of the future–*Mein Kampf.* After his release he altered his tactics, turning to elective politics. The German people responded by voting for Hitler's Nazi party in steadily increasing numbers. By the elections of 1932 it was Germany's largest party, capturing 37 percent of the vote. Hitler demanded and received the title of chancellor, then consolidated his power through a series of legal and extralegal moves, emerging as the unchallenged *führer* of Germany.

Hitler's first priority was to build the "mighty sword" of the military. His second was to seize *lebensraum,* living space, which he took in installments, at first by bombast, bluff, and threat, and later by military force. On

March 7, 1936, Hitler moved his army into the demilitarized Rhineland. The world did nothing, even though Hitler later admitted that if the French army had challenged them the Germans would have been forced to retreat. Feeling himself free of constraints, Hitler accelerated the build-up of his military machine. He annexed Austria in March 1938. In September of that year British Prime Minister Neville Chamberlain, who had consistently appeased the Germans, betrayed Britain's commitments to Czechoslovakia when he signed a document at Munich allowing the Germans to enter the Sudetenland in exchange for Hitler's promise of peace. Chamberlain returned to London and proclaimed that he had made "Peace with honor. Peace for our time." Hitler ignored the accord and occupied the rest of Czechoslovakia in March of the following year.

The final obstacle to Hitler's plans for European conquest was removed when the Germans and the Russians signed a nonaggression pact in the summer of 1939. The two countries proceeded to attack and dismember Poland on September 1, 1939. Unwilling to surrender yet another country to the policy of appeasement, Britain and France declared war on Germany on September 3.

After nine months of winter quietude, the German *blitzkrieg* knifed to a series of stunning victories in Norway, Denmark, Holland, and Belgium. The German tanks then skirted the "impregnable" Maginot line of France and took Paris in thirty days. In May 1940 the British just barely succeeded in evacuating their army from the beaches of Dunkirk as France fell. Now only the valiant fighter-pilots of the Royal Air Force stood between Great Britain and German occupation. The RAF turned back the German air assault in the Battle of Britain, providing the free world its first bit of good news, but the British fought alone in defense of their small island.

The Allied struggle against the Axis required total war on both sides of the globe. In Europe (top), German conquests reached from the Atlantic Ocean to Stalingrad. Gradually, however, Hitler's armies were reduced by Soviet counterattacks all along the huge eastern front, while the British, Americans, and other Allies liberated North Africa, Sicily, and southern Italy. The Normandy invasion of 1944 was the beginning of the end for the Reich in western Europe. In the Pacific (bottom), American amphibious forces hopped from island to island, pushing the Japanese back to the gates of their homeland. The war ended after atomic bombs were dropped on Hiroshima and Nagasaki in August 1945.

In the Pacific the Japanese had outlined their own version of *lebensraum* with the Tanaka Memorial, a plan for expansion devised in 1927. Their burgeoning industrial complex and growing military machine demanded raw materials that the home islands and their minor Pacific colonies could not supply. World War I left the traditional colonial powers enervated and preoccupied with their own problems in Europe, and the Japanese seized the opportunity to fill the vacuum with their own brand of imperialism.

In September 1931 the Japanese used the pretext of a dynamite explosion in a Japanese railroad yard in Manchuria to invade the region. Then they pushed farther into China, destroying property and raping and murdering as they went. In Nanking alone, Japanese military forces slaughtered over 40,000 unarmed people. By October of 1938, Japan had a strangle hold on nearly half of China, including most of the major cities.

They set up a "New Order" for an Asian "Co-Prosperity Sphere," the blueprint for a Japanese-controlled empire that called for conquest from Manchuria to New Guinea. Only one obstacle remained to the Japanese drive to secure hegemony over the entire Pacific: the United States and its powerful navy of 171 warships.

The United States spent the years between the wars gripped by a profound desire to avoid future military involvement in Europe. President Woodrow Wilson went to the peace talks in 1919 because of his fervent belief that the world must join together in a League of Nations to preserve the peace. He returned home to a country that repudiated his vision. The U.S. was the only one of the "Big Four" Allies (France, Great Britain, and Italy were the other three) that did not ratify the treaty or join Wilson's league.

America turned away from Europe and its problems in the 1920s, then became preoccupied with the depression of the 1930s. Isolationism became an explicit policy with the Neutrality Act of 1935, which prohibited loans to belligerent countries, proclaimed an arms embargo on all nations at war, and banned travel by U.S. citizens to warring countries. After Germany attacked Poland in 1939, President Roosevelt attempted to lift the provision of the act forbidding the sale of arms. In the three days following Roosevelt's appeal, the isolationists held mass rallies featuring speakers as diverse as Charles Lindbergh, socialist Norman Thomas, and former president Herbert Hoover. They deluged Congress with over 1 million pieces of mail. But it was the interventionists who prevailed, and the Neutrality Act of 1939 allowed belligerent nations to buy weapons on a cash-and-carry basis. Since Britain controlled the Atlantic Ocean, this effectively excluded the Germans and Italians from American help.

The lifting of the arms embargo ignited the American war machine, which started slowly, then gathered steam. In January 1930 Roosevelt asked for a $2 billion defense package, but by December the figure ballooned to $10.5 billion. In September of the same year Congress authorized the resumption of the draft, albeit with heavy restrictions on the number of men who could be called up, where they could serve, and for how long.

The next spring, the U.S. responded to Japanese aggression in China by moving the Pacific fleet from San Francisco to Pearl Harbor, Hawaii, and shutting off shipping to Japan military goods such as aviation gasoline and high-grade scrap iron. The Japanese perceived the U.S. moves as a threat to the New Order in Asia and signed a tripartite alliance with Germany and Italy in September. In spring 1941 the Japanese invaded Indochina. The U.S. froze all Japanese assets and extended embargoes to all trade, including the export of oil.

The Japanese, with less than a year's supply of oil to feed their military machine, were faced with a stark choice: give up dreams of empire or go to war with America. The militarist Hideiki Tojo, who had been named prime minister in October of 1941, later explained their decision by saying, "Rather than await extinction it were [sic] better to face death by breaking through the encircling ring and find a way for existence." The Japanese negotiated with the U.S. until the day before attacking Pearl Harbor, all the while planning the operation in minute detail.

George Street, who received his Medal of Honor four long years later, recalled a tendency among Americans at that time to underestimate the Japanese. "We thought we were invincible. The navy as an organization had a big head in terms of: 'Hell, we can beat the little Nips.' "

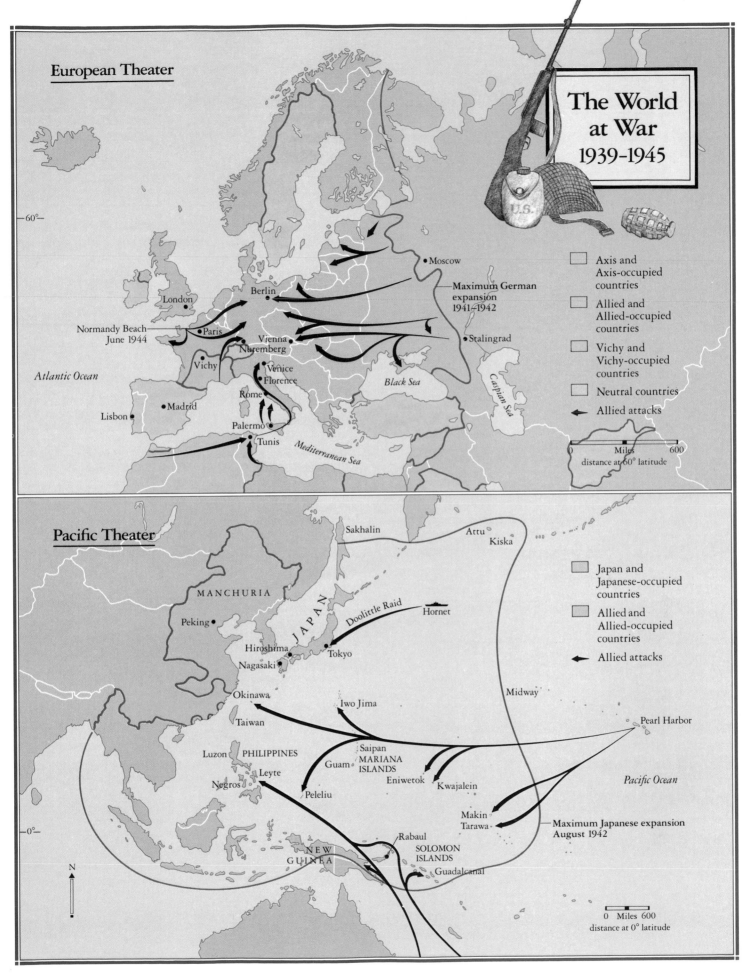

European Theater

The World
at War
1939–1945

60°

Moscow

Berlin

Maximum German
expansion
1941–1942

London

Normandy Beach
June 1944

Paris

Vienna
Nuremberg

Stalingrad

Atlantic Ocean

Vichy

Venice
Florence

Black Sea

Rome

Madrid

Palermo

Lisbon

Tunis

Mediterranean Sea

Caspian Sea

☐ Axis and
Axis-occupied
countries

☐ Allied and
Allied-occupied
countries

☐ Vichy and
Vichy-occupied
countries

☐ Neutral countries

← Allied attacks

0   Miles   600
distance at 60° latitude

Pacific Theater

Sakhalin

Attu
Kiska

MANCHURIA

JAPAN

Doolittle Raid

Hornet

Peking

Hiroshima
Nagasaki

Tokyo

☐ Japan and
Japanese-occupied
countries

☐ Allied and
Allied-occupied
countries

← Allied attacks

Okinawa

Iwo Jima

Midway

Taiwan

Pearl Harbor

Luzon   PHILIPPINES

Saipan
MARIANA
ISLANDS

Guam

Leyte

Eniwetok   Kwajalein

Pacific Ocean

Negros

Peleliu

Makin
Tarawa

Maximum Japanese expansion
August 1942

N

Rabaul

NEW
GUINEA

SOLOMON
ISLANDS

Guadalcanal

0   Miles   600
distance at 0° latitude

Perhaps as a result, the Japanese attack caught America unprepared, despite the fact that Japanese diplomatic codes had been broken and U.S. leaders knew war was imminent. The first strike came on December 7, 1941, a day President Roosevelt said would "live in infamy." Japanese torpedo bombers swooped in on Pearl Harbor at altitudes as low as forty feet and launched torpedoes. Dive bombers swarmed down and dropped armor-piercing and high-explosive bombs before the ships' gunnery crews could react. High-level bombers, deployed in a line above the battleships, delivered their payloads.

That first blow left America stunned and reeling. Six battleships, three cruisers, and numerous small vessels were either sunk or crippled in less than two hours. The U.S. lost 265 airplanes; some 2,403 men were killed and 1,178 wounded. Time was needed to recover but time was not available. Guam and Wake Island fell almost immediately and the Philippines followed in May 1942. The Germans and the Italians declared war on December 11, forcing America to fight on two fronts over two oceans.

Pearl Harbor induced the once-isolationist United States to make a total commitment to fight and win a global war. In conferences in early 1941, America had agreed with Britain to defeat Hitler first, but the Japanese could not be ignored. Roosevelt promised that "American armed forces must be used at any place in all the world." At the beginning of 1942 that seemed to be little more than false bravado. Gerry Kisters, an early draftee and a later Medal of Honor recipient, recalled being issued a World War I bolt-action rifle and a pie-plate helmet when he arrived at his mechanized unit in Fort Bliss, Texas, where "the men who were supposed to train us had been taken off horses. They didn't know any more about what they were doing than the fellows that had just come in." Matt Urban, fresh from ROTC and destined for the Medal of Honor for actions in France, recalls training

President Franklin D. Roosevelt, whose confidence and vision helped his nation through depression and world war.

with dummy wooden guns right up to the time his 9th Division shipped out for North Africa.

But the war machine that started so slowly was transformed into a juggernaut in extremely short time. U.S. industry matched and exceeded heretofore unimaginable goals of production. The costs were enormous, but the country absorbed a bill of $288 billion and actually prospered. By 1945 U.S. industry had supplied nearly 300,000 aircraft, over 70,000 ships, nearly 100,000 tanks, and the ultimate weapon, the atomic bomb.

The enemy Axis powers had been the first to understand the nature of modern warfare. The machine would rule triumphant. While the French waited in their defensive position on the Maginot line, the Germans sliced around them with armored cars and tanks. The Japanese built a huge carrier force and sailed it so close to Pearl Harbor that they made the old rules of naval warfare obsolete in one devastating strike. The swift new machines meant offensive mobility, and the commander who did not properly understand that was condemned to failure. The Americans adapted quickly to the lessons of modern warfare.

The war produced an unprecedented degree of cooperation among the branches of the American armed forces. The army Air Corps battered the enemy into submission as the navy carried supplies and men to the beaches. If a new kind of craft were needed to get the troops ashore, it was invented and rushed into production. Seemingly overnight, the Seabees built new airstrips in the Pacific, and the combat engineers built bridges and whole ports in Europe.

America clearly possessed the industrial might to create a giant arsenal, but putting it to use required that enormous logistical problems be solved. It was a formidable task to supply the armies on several different fronts across both oceans, but the American machine hummed efficiently in both theaters. The army and marine infantrymen who waded ashore went into battle as the best-supplied fighting men in the world. For each man in the field, there were three in the rear echelon seeing to his needs. The U.S. shipped more of everything to its men: more weapons, more medicine, more filing cabinets, more cigarettes—a total of 450 tons of supplies per day for every division in the field. Soldiers were deposited on European shores by the largest armadas in history. War correspondent Ernie Pyle wrote that the strength of America was "appalling even to those who [made] up the individual cells of that strength." In both Europe and in Asia that muscle would be used to defeat powers that had rolled, seemingly at will, to victories, and it would defeat them both at once.

A wartime poster reminds American home-front workers of the high stakes involved in the conflict.

World War II changed the world irrevocably. Over 30 million died, with the worst of the brutality unleashed not against soldiers, but civilians. Total war brought estimated death tolls of over a million in the siege of Leningrad; 135,000 in the bombing of Dresden; 83,000 in one fire-bombing of Tokyo. As the Allies rolled into Germany they found the Nazi death camps. The worst nightmare could not match the reality of the Holocaust, which in George Steiner's words, "altered our sense of the limits of human behavior." Six million Jews were systematically exterminated.

The nuclear age arrived precisely at 8:15 A.M. on August 6, 1945, in Hiroshima, when 78,000 were killed in one stroke. The impact of the bomb forever changed war and politics. Two giants stood astride the world after the war: the Soviet Union, which despite the loss of 20 million people to the Nazi onslaught had emerged stronger than before, and the United States, which had begun the war in profound isolation and had emerged an international power that could not again turn its back on the rest of the world.

Yet, at the beginning, during those darkest hours when the Japanese were knifing through the Pacific, there was doubt. Wrote James Jones, the "Japanese, with their warrior code of the *bushi,* had been in active combat warfare for ten years; the Germans almost as long." He wondered if the U.S. could "evolve a soldier, a *civilian* soldier who could meet them man to man in the field. . . . Not everyone was sure we [could]." All of the technology and production the U.S. might muster would mean nothing if the country could not produce men with the will to prevail. The U.S. found them in the ranks of the career officers and also in the ranks of the draftees—farm boys, students, and city kids. More than 16 million served in uniform; 405,399 died; 433 received the Medal of Honor.

They were ordinary Americans. Most of the young men who fought were born during World War I and shortly after. In childhood they had known want during the depression. When they reached adolescence they were met with uncertainty and rumors of war. And when they came of age they were plunged into the worst conflict in history. It must have seemed to them that they were not born for happiness. Yet they endured.

The Medal of Honor recipients among them symbolized the strength and adaptability of the American civilian soldiers. They listened for every bump in the night on the steaming jungle islands, and they dug into the iron-hard ground of the Ardennes in winter. They sweated out depth charges deep under the sea and peered anxiously for *kamikaze* suicide planes from the bridges of destroyers. They bounced on a carpet of flak at 20,000 feet in heavy bombers and outmaneuvered Japanese "Zero" fighter planes from the cockpit of their own swift fighter planes. Some died so that others could live. Others lived against all odds. These were the everyday Americans who served, in George Street's words, "on the cutting edge." ◈

Fighting on Two Fronts

American soldiers in World War II battled across the globe, on land, sea, and in the air. Above. A navy Dauntless dive-bomber prepares to attack Wake Island in the central Pacific, 1943. Right. U.S. Marines raise the flag over Mount Suribachi, Iwo Jima, on February 23, 1945.

Left. *A Japanese suicide plane plunges toward the U.S.S.* Missouri *on May 8, 1945.* Below. *Troops rush ashore from a landing craft at Normandy during the invasion of France on June 6, 1944.* Bottom. *A German surrenders to an American soldier in Illy, France, in 1944.*

195

Day of Infamy
Pearl Harbor

The dive bombers that shattered the peace of a beautiful Sunday morning at Pearl Harbor plunged the United States into global war. The attack was a complete surprise; in a few moments, the seven battleships lined up in a neat row off Ford Island in the harbor were ablaze, their crews desperately battling to keep them afloat as more bombers and torpedo planes swarmed to the attack. Only the quick action of a few men saved the U.S. Navy from more complete destruction.

Captain Samuel Fuqua, a sailor who had grown up in Laddonia, Missouri, had just finished Sunday breakfast in the wardroom of the battleship U.S.S. *Arizona* when the air-raid sirens sounded. He turned to the man who had just been relieved as officer of the deck and inquired if the sirens signaled a drill. The officer was unsure. Fuqua called the bridge to find out what was happening. When no one answered he went topside to see for himself. He heard planes overhead as he emerged from a hatch and walked around a rear turret.

The next thing Fuqua remembered was picking himself up from the deck. He had been felled by the blast of torpedoes blowing holes in the hull of the *Arizona*. When Fuqua regained consciousness, he found himself lying next to a gaping shell hole in the deck. He staggered to his feet and saw high-level bombers dropping their bombs, which "looked like bowling balls as they came down." They struck everywhere along the ship, piercing the steel deck and exploding below. The engine room, the boilers, and the oil tanks exploded. The wounded struggling up from the lower decks added to the chaos. Some of them were on fire and some had been blinded. A few of the wounded, driven by pain, attempted to leap overboard, but Fuqua and uninjured members of the crew knocked them unconscious to keep them from jumping and surely drowning.

Fuqua saw that oil on the surface of the water had ignited. Battleship Row was an inferno. He organized firefighters to keep the flames away from the wounded lying on the quarter-deck—the open stern of the ship's main deck.

Above. *Captain Samuel Fuqua, whose cool and courage saved many sailors aboard the U.S.S.* Arizona *(right) as it burned and sank in Pearl Harbor.*

A view from a Japanese plane shows aircraft attacking American vessels at Ford Island on the morning of December 7.

Then a bomb struck the *Arizona* next to the bridge. It penetrated the forward magazine of ammunition and the ship "erupted like a volcano." Debris and bodies flew in all directions. Rear Admiral Isaac Kidd and the ship's captain, Franklin Van Valkenburgh, were among the estimated 1,000 killed in that one terrible explosion. From the shore, observers could see the ship lifted up and broken by the force of the blast before settling back deep in the water.

Fuqua rushed forward to battle the fires near the captain's bridge, but a tower of smoke already rising from the ship signaled that the *Arizona* was past saving. As more wounded poured back to the quarter-deck, Fuqua attempted to protect them by keeping the fire from spreading farther aft. Despite the desperate situation, he worked calmly, put-

ting the wounded aboard undamaged lifeboats to be transported to the relative safety of Ford Island.

The blast in the *Arizona*'s magazines was so powerful that it hurled nearly 100 men overboard from the *Vestal,* an ammunition tender that was moored alongside the battleship. One of those thrown into the water was the ship's captain, Cassin Young. Tons of debris from the *Arizona* covered the *Vestal*'s deck, and the ship was on fire from numerous bomb blasts. The *Vestal,* listing precariously, was still tied to the blazing *Arizona,* and the oil-covered water between the ships was blazing as well. Sailors remaining aboard the *Vestal* began to abandon ship.

Commander Young swam to the gangway and emerged from the water just as some of his crew had started to clamber down. Covered with oil from the slick, he blocked their path and shouted, "Where in the hell do you think you're going?" When they said that they were abandon-

ing ship, Young ordered them back to their stations, bellowing, "You don't abandon ship on me!" The *Vestal* was cut free from the wreckage of the *Arizona* later in the morning. The steering gear had been blown away, but with the help of a tugboat and the *Vestal*'s own engines, Young got under way. The *Vestal* cleared the *Arizona* but soon began to sink. Young ordered the tug to pull the *Vestal* into shore, where he beached the still-salvageable ship on a coral reef.

Almost all the other ships in the harbor near the *Arizona* and *Vestal* were also in danger of sinking. The *West Virginia* had been damaged by three torpedo blasts and took on so much water that it was listing dangerously. On the bridge, Captain Mervyn Bennion quickly ordered counterflooding on the side opposite the list and righted the ship, but more torpedo planes struck.

Captain Bennion had just moved to the starboard side of the bridge when Japanese high-level bombers made a

Below. *The* Vestal *lies beached on a coral reef after the Japanese attack.* Bottom. *Captain Cassin Young chats with Admiral Chester Nimitz after being presented with the Medal of Honor aboard the* Vestal, *April 18, 1942.*

direct hit on his ship and on the nearby *Tennessee.* Shrapnel from the blast struck Bennion in the abdomen; but he refused evacuation from the bridge as his crew fought the flames that engulfed the deck. As the fire spread, he ordered his men to leave him, but they refused. Bennion continued to think of the welfare of his ship, receiving reports and issuing commands until he finally lost consciousness. He died shortly after.

Back on the *Arizona,* Samuel Fuqua realized that Captain Van Valkenburgh and Admiral Kidd had been killed. He took command, but the ship's back was broken and the guns were no longer firing. Less than 200 of the 1,400 men aboard had survived those first few moments. Fuqua gave the order to abandon ship three hours after the beginning of the attack. The *Arizona* settled into the water, its burning hull now a tomb for over 1,000 men whose bodies were never removed.

Fuqua, who had shown cool and effective leadership in the midst of the blazing chaos, was the only man aboard the *Arizona* who lived to receive the Medal of Honor. Admiral Kidd and Captain Van Valkenburgh were awarded the medal posthumously, each for "devotion to duty, extraordinary courage, and complete disregard of his own life." Another posthumous medal went to Mervyn Bennion, whose only concern was for his ship and his men as he lay dying on the bridge. Eight others at Pearl Harbor were awarded the Medal of Honor posthumously. Cassin Young, who received his Medal of Honor for saving the *Vestal,* lived through the action only to die aboard the *San Francisco* on November 13, 1942, during the Naval Battle of Guadalcanal. In all, fifteen men were awarded the Medal of Honor for acts of valor at Pearl Harbor, the fiery beginning of World War II for the United States. ◈

Defending the Philippines
Bataan and Corregidor

For the Japanese, control of the Philippine Islands was crucial. Wresting the archipelago from its American and Filipino defenders would give the empire clear passage to the raw materials of the southwest Pacific. The Americans, who had held the islands in protectorate since the Spanish-American War, fought a desperate holding action under the command of General Douglas MacArthur. His gallant soldiers, furnished with outdated equipment and cut off from resupply, bore the full weight of Japanese carrier attacks and amphibious landings as they waited for help that would never come.

When Japanese high-level bombers caught the planes of the U.S. Army Air Corps on the ground at Clark Field in the Philippines a full ten hours after Pearl Harbor, they effectively sealed the fate of the Philippine Islands. The Japanese destroyed eighteen of thirty-five B-17 bombers and fifty-six fighters in that first strike. The U.S. Navy pulled its Asiatic Fleet out of the Philippines the next day, and the remainder of the B-17s flew south to Australia on December 15.

General Douglas MacArthur and his army remained to oppose the Japanese invasion. Small landing parties of Japanese came ashore at six different beaches on Luzon as a preliminary to the main invasion, which came December 22 and 23 at Lingayen Gulf on the west of the island.

In order to buy time, MacArthur declared open the capital city of Manila and abandoned it to the Japanese. The Allies staged a fighting retreat to the Peninsula of Bataan, across Manila Bay from the city.

The retreat called for army units to leapfrog past each other as one unit protected the retreat of others by fighting the Japanese at the rear. It was brilliantly executed despite the inexperience of the troops. Eighty thousand men and their artillery gained the peninsula by January 6, 1942.

MacArthur set up headquarters on Corregidor, a fortress island at the tip of Bataan. His soldiers, who called themselves "The Battlin' Bastards of Bataan," gave ground over the next three months, but they made the Japanese pay in blood.

General Douglas MacArthur (left) sits glumly in a tunnel on Corregidor Island with his chief of staff, Major General Richard K. Sutherland, during the Japanese conquest of the Philippines.

Mess Sergeant José Calugas, whose artillery skill held off advancing Japanese on the Layac Road, near Bataan.

Second Lieutenant Alexander Nininger, shown in his West Point uniform, fought on despite grievous wounds.

By the time of the surrender of Corregidor on May 6, MacArthur and his family had escaped to Australia under direct orders from President Roosevelt. (They left Corregidor in the PT boat of Lieutenant John Bulkeley, who received the Medal of Honor for his many daring missions in the Philippines in the months from December 8, 1941, to April 10, 1942.) In ordering MacArthur to leave his command, President Roosevelt and General George C. Marshall, his army chief of staff, made a political calculation. They reasoned that an inspirational figure planning a return to his command from Australia was a much more potent force than a dead hero in the Philippines. In Australia General MacArthur was presented with the Medal of Honor. MacArthur had been personally courageous in the face of bombing attacks on Corregidor, but he did not get the medal for any single specified act of bravery. His award is one of the few of the war that could be described as "symbolic," in large part because MacArthur's Philippine army was an inspiration to the American people during those dark days.

MacArthur himself acknowledged this when he accepted the medal, saying that he felt it was "intended not so much for me personally as it is a recognition of the indomitable courage of the gallant army which it has been my honor to command." (MacArthur's medal came seventy–eight years after his father, Arthur, earned a Medal of Honor for rallying Northern troops on November 25, 1863, at Missionary Ridge, Tennessee, during the Civil War. Together the MacArthurs are the only father and son both to receive the Medal of Honor.)

The Philippine Scouts comprised a large part of MacArthur's gallant army. They were Filipino soldiers who had been trained under American supervision, equipped with American weapons, and commanded by American army officers. Mess Sergeant José Calugas served in Battery B, 88th Field Artillery, Philippine Scouts, one of the units assigned to cover the retreat of Americans and Filipinos down the Layac Road to Bataan.

On January 6 Sergeant Calugas had set up his field kitchen under some trees near the settlement of Culis. He finished serving breakfast and was leading a detail of KPs to fetch water for the cleanup. Suddenly, Japanese artillery rounds landed all around the men. Japanese fighter planes followed, bombing the guns of the 88th, which were deployed in the woods and hills about 900 yards north of the mess area. Calugas and the other men dove for the safety of some nearby caves and stayed hidden there throughout the morning-long barrage.

At 2:00 P.M., the Japanese were still firing but the American guns had fallen silent. Calugas walked to a clearing and surveyed the scene as Japanese airplanes dove and the hillsides erupted in orange flashes and black smoke. When he heard that one of the 88th's batteries had been knocked out and the crew killed, Calugas rounded up volunteers to go with him to investigate. With carbines and .45-caliber pistols in hand, sixteen men followed Calugas toward the batteries. Calugas never knew what became of his tiny force. Some of the men were killed or wounded and some of them may have run away, but by the time the sergeant reached the gun emplacement, he was alone.

The gun had been hit and had toppled into a bomb crater. All of its crew were killed or wounded. Although Calugas was a mess sergeant, he had been trained in combat arms and was a typically versatile and resourceful Philippine Scout. He could not right the cannon himself, so he found one of the wounded gunners and rounded up other men from a nearby emplacement to help. Together the men lugged the gun back into place and put it in firing order. Another man climbed a tamarind tree to act as spotter. From his perch, he could see the Japanese attack force moving forward less than a mile away. As the spotter directed his fire, Calugas aimed, loaded, and discharged the gun. In Calugas's

American prisoners Samuel Stenzler, Frank Spear, and James Gallagher (left to right) rest during the infamous "Death March."

American prisoners Samuel Stenzler, Frank Spear, and James Gallagher (left to right) rest during the infamous "Death March."

words, "We kept this up about two hours. Then, they must have called for more planes to try and spot our gun. The enemy was not making any progress at that time because our shooting was very good." Each time the Japanese planes appeared, Calugas and his makeshift crew stopped firing and dived for cover in the jungle, hoping that the plane would not be able to locate the gun. This cat-and-mouse game continued until Calugas ran out of shells.

The mess sergeant's deadly accuracy stopped the enemy advance until the next day, when Japanese reserves arrived. Calugas's barrage had given the 88th valuable time to regroup and fight on.

After the battle, Calugas returned to his duties as a mess sergeant. Shortly after the action, he heard himself praised on "Voice of Freedom" radio for his valor at Culis. Three years were to pass, however, before he would receive the symbol of that valor. He was taken prisoner in the general surrender of Bataan on April 9. The 75,000 survivors were forced to march from Mariveles in the south to a railroad siding at San

Fernando, some forty-five miles away. Exhausted and hungry after four months of hard fighting on half-rations, many of the men also came down with dysentery and malaria. Under a blinding tropical sun, their Japanese captors denied them food and water during the ordeal that became known as the Bataan Death March. Those who fell from the ranks were shot and left on the road by Japanese death squads. An estimated 7-10,000 died, 2,300 of them Americans. The captives were sent by boxcar to Camp O'Donnell, northwest of Clark Field, where they were interned. Calugas survived two savage beatings during the Bataan Death March and spent three years in a Japanese prison camp before General George C. Marshall draped the blue ribbon of the Medal of Honor around his neck on April 30, 1945.

One of the scouts' American officers was Second Lieutenant Alexander Nininger, a Georgia native who had graduated from West Point in 1941. Nininger was on his first assignment after being commissioned. He and his unit raced to build a line of defense as the Allied forces tried to seal off the Bataan

Peninsula from Japanese attack. Nininger's men cut trees and constructed fortifications in the swamps near the town of Abucay, on the eastern coast of Bataan.

The Japanese attack, however, came to the west of Nininger's position, near the spine of low mountains that ran down the center of the peninsula. The Americans and Filipinos pushed back the first onslaught, but over 1,000 Japanese snipers infiltrated the Allied defense line during the struggle.

Nininger volunteered to leave his company and join the reserve units that had moved up to reinforce the Allied line at the point of the Japanese assault. When Nininger arrived at the front line on January 12, he found that the Japanese had overrun the Allies' foxholes and were now occupying them, firing at the Allies from the Allies' former positions. Nininger loaded himself with grenades and led a counterattack through a hail of fire. Shrapnel from Japanese artillery raked the dirt around him. The rest of the soldiers following the young lieutenant faltered in their attack and sought cover, but Nininger sprinted on. Hit by a bullet, he fell to the ground but then crawled forward and threw his grenades. When a medic caught up with him and tried to administer aid, Nininger broke away to renew his one-man assault.

In sight of his comrades, Nininger attacked another Japanese foxhole. He was again hit by rifle fire but even that did not halt his advance. When three Japanese soldiers charged with bayonets, Nininger killed them with his .45. Then at last, he succumbed to his wounds.

Nininger was the first of 37 men of his 424-man West Point class to die in World War II. The first to die was also the only one to be awarded the Medal of Honor. ❖

Turning the Tide
The Tokyo Raid and Midway

The first five months of the Pacific war were unremittingly bleak. But that was to change in April 1942 when Lieutenant Colonel Jimmy Doolittle led a carrier-based force of B-25 bombers on a daring raid over Japan. The damage to the Japanese was slight, but the mission provided an enormous morale boost for America. Two months later, the Japanese launched a carrier strike force for an invasion of the U.S. base on Midway Island at the far western end of the Hawaiian chain. Navy planes from American carriers and marine planes based on Midway were launched to meet the threat.

Jimmy Doolittle and his crew. From left: Lieutenant Henry Potter, Doolittle, Staff Sergeant Fred Beamer, Lieutenant Richard Cole, Staff Sergeant Paul Leonard.

When the long-awaited moment finally arrived, Lieutenant Colonel Jimmy Doolittle revved his airplane's engines to top rpm's and waited for the signal to take off from the deck of the aircraft carrier *Hornet*. The signal came when the bow of the ship was on its upward rise. He began his slow taxi to the end of the short runway, only 467 feet away. Once his wheels left the deck, the crews in fifteen B-25s still on the aircraft carrier could see the entire top of his bomber as it strained upward in a steep climb. Gaining altitude and speed, Doolittle set course for Japan.

Jimmy Doolittle, a forty-five-year-old former stunt flier and racer, had helped Colonel Billy Mitchell in the bombing demonstration that brought attention to the offensive potential of aircraft. Because of his age and his position on the staff of army Air Corps Chief Hap Arnold, Doolittle was not supposed to fly to Tokyo. It was his job to organize the mission, train the pilots, and modify the aircraft so that they could take off from the short distance of an aircraft carrier's runway. His request for permission to lead the raid was at first refused flatly. He continued to plead his case, pointing out that he knew more than anyone else about the planes, the crews, and the mission. He finally won Arnold's grudging assent.

The *Hornet* took the flight of bombers as close to Japan as its safety would allow. The original plan had called for takeoff 400 miles from Japan, but that strategy was scuttled when the carrier was spotted by a Japanese patrol boat. The planes left on their historic mission a day earlier than had been planned and a full 668 miles from Tokyo.

Each of the B-25s carried a five-man crew, four 500-pound bombs, and extra gasoline tanks for the long one-way journey, a total of 31,000 pounds. For three weeks, Doolittle and his pilots had practiced taking off within the limited number of feet required on an aircraft carrier, but that was on the ground and under ideal conditions at Eglin Field, Florida. A fully loaded B-25 had never before taken off from the pitching and rolling deck of a carrier, which was designed for much smaller fighter planes and torpedo and dive bombers.

After Doolittle's plane left the deck, there came fifteen takeoffs, each as heart-stopping as his. Once airborne, each plane sped toward the target on its own; to wait for a formation would waste fuel. They stayed low over the water, flying straight for Japan. Success demanded nearly perfect timing and better luck. As Doolittle said, it was "in the laps of the gods."

Flying at 200 feet, Doolittle reached the coast five hours after takeoff. As he neared Tokyo, Japanese "Zero" fighter planes spotted him, but he plunged even closer to the earth, escaping the enemy fighters by allowing his plane's camouflage to blend into the ter-

rain. He came in "hugging the deck" over Tokyo, found the target, then popped up to 1,200 feet to drop his bombs. (A book and movie about the raid were entitled *Thirty Seconds Over Tokyo*. Doolittle later said that they were over the city longer than thirty seconds, "but it brings up the point that we did not tarry.")

Although he was exposed to anti-aircraft guns, no more fighters found him as he set course for China. The plan had called for the bombers to fly to the mainland, where they were to land at an airfield called Chuchow. However, fierce headwinds encountered on the flight into Japan had caused the planes to use more fuel than anticipated. As the B-25s approached the coast of China, they met dense clouds and rainstorms. The fuel gauges soon neared empty, and the pilots all arrived at the same hard realization: They would have to choose between ditching, or, if they could reach land, either bailing out or crash-landing.

Doolittle's fuel lasted until he was over the mainland. He and the other four men of his crew all managed to parachute safely into Chinese territory and return home. Others were not so fortunate. Two planes crash-landed in Japanese-occupied territory, and three of the eight surviving crew members were summarily executed. Another man starved to death while in Japanese custody. The four survivors remained prisoners until the end of the war. Of the eighty men who began the mission, six died, either in captivity or in crash-landing. One plane landed at Vladivostok in the Soviet Union. Its five crew members were interned together at various places inside Russia until May 29, 1943, when they escaped over the Persian border. Their B-25 was kept by the Soviets.

When Doolittle discovered that all of his planes were lost and that two of his crews had been captured by the Japanese, he thought the mission had been a costly failure. Later, realizing the raid had struck a great psychological blow at the enemy and raised the spirit of America, he revised his estimate, saying, "The mission gave the American people the first piece of good news they had had. It caused the Japanese to question their warlords, who had said that Japan would never be attacked."

After he returned to Washington, Doolittle discovered while riding in a staff car with General Arnold and General George C. Marshall that he was to receive the Medal of Honor. When he protested that he did not deserve it, General Marshall turned to him and said gravely and quietly, "I think you do."

Less than two months after the Doolittle raid, a Japanese four-carrier strike force bore down on Midway Island. On June 4, 1942, it launched 108 dive-bombers and Zero fighters to destroy the American forces at the island's airfield. Awaiting them were two squadrons of mostly inexperienced

A B–25 bomber of Doolittle's command clears the bow of the U.S.S. Hornet *on its way to Japan, April 18, 1942.*

Below. *Marine Captain Richard Fleming followed his bombs into the Japanese cruiser* Mikuma. *Bottom.* The wreckage of Fleming's plane is strewn over an aft gun turret of the ship.

marine pilots flying mostly obsolescent planes. Major Lofton Henderson's dive-bomber squadron consisted of just twenty-seven serviceable planes: sixteen modern SBD Dauntless bombers and eleven outdated SB2U Vindicators. One of the pilots of Major Floyd B. Parks's fighter squadron said that anyone flying their old F2A Brewster fighters into combat against Japanese Zeros was "lost before leaving the ground." The pilots called the planes the "Flying Coffins."

On June 4, twenty-five marine fighter-pilots in Brewsters rose up to meet the Japanese aerial armada. Fifteen of the Americans were shot down in the dogfight without registering a single kill as the Japanese pummeled the airfield. Henderson's two-man dive-bombers, meanwhile, flew out to attack the Japanese fleet. When the slow-moving planes tipped into their dives, they were easy targets for the Zeros and for Japanese antiaircraft gunners who waited on the carriers.

Henderson's squadron included an untested young pilot from Minnesota named Richard Fleming. In the first few moments of the bombing run, he saw Henderson's lead plane burst into flames after taking several hits from the carrier *Akagi*'s guns. Fleming and the rest of the squadron took over for the commander and dove toward the targets, straight into heavy clouds of antiaircraft fire. Fleming's gunner said the shrapnel hitting the dive-bomber sounded like "buckets of bolts" being thrown into the propeller.

The standard operating procedure for a dive-bomber called for releasing bombs at 1,500 feet, but with his plane bouncing from antiaircraft bursts, Fleming plunged to within 400 feet of the carrier. He dropped his bombs, narrowly missing the deck, and somehow managed to pull out of the dizzying dive. Both he and his gunner were wounded

by the firing but they survived the daredevil attack. His ground crew on Midway counted 179 holes in the plane after his return.

The dive-bombers recorded several near misses but did not hit any of the carriers. Their mission was not in vain, however. The arrival of these land-based dive-bombers convinced the leader of the carrier strike force, Admiral Chuichi Nagumo, to send his planes again against the landing strip at Midway Island. The Japanese planes were loaded with high-explosive bombs for the airfield rather than the armor-piercing variety designed to destroy ships. Before the planes took off, Nagumo received word from one of his surveillance planes that American carriers were within striking range. He hastily ordered the bombs changed. Just as the Japanese were re-arming their planes, torpedo bombers from the U.S. carriers *Hornet*, *Yorktown*, and *Enterprise* attacked.

These brave carrier pilots had flown beyond the fuel capacities of their fighter escorts, and thus came in without protection. The Japanese Zeros and anti-aircraft fire tore them apart. Of the forty-

one planes of the three torpedo squadrons, thirty-five were shot down.

Again, the price was high but brought a valuable return. The Zeros stayed near the water for the fight with the torpedo planes, leaving their carriers exposed to U.S. Navy dive-bombers, which attacked from 14,000 feet. The dive-bombers ripped great holes in the carriers *Akagi*, *Soryu*, and *Kaga*. Gasoline explosions erupted and all three Japanese carriers were destroyed. The fourth Japanese carrier, *Hiryu*, was attacked and sunk later but not before its dive-bombers were unleashed against the U.S.S. *Yorktown*, badly damaging it. A submarine sank the crippled *Yorktown* the next day.

On June 5 Fleming led the remaining planes of the squadron (now reduced to only twelve of the original thirty-six) in an attack against the heavy cruisers *Mogami* and *Mikuma*. He repeated his bold strategy of the day before, piloting his bomber into a screaming dive. Another pilot saw Fleming's plane spit out black smoke after being hit by anti-aircraft fire early in the dive. At 350 feet Fleming released his bombs, then fol-

Dive bombers attack the Japanese fleet at Midway. Four enemy carriers and one cruiser were destroyed on June 4–5, 1942.

lowed them down. No one knows if his action was intentional, but the plane crashed directly into the *Mikuma*. The resulting flames were sucked into the air intake of the ship and ignited gas fumes in the starboard engine room, killing the Japanese crew.

The captain of the *Mogami*, A. Soji, observed Fleming's dive against the *Mikuma*. He later remarked, "I saw a dive-bomber dive into the last turret and start fires. He was very brave."

All of the pilots who fought the decisive battle of Midway were "very brave." The battle turned the tide of war in the Pacific, halting Japanese expansion. Yet of all the courageous pilots who sacrificed their lives during the battle, only Captain Richard Fleming was awarded the Medal of Honor. He stands as a symbol of all those who faced death squarely and did their duty "with dauntless perseverance and unyielding devotion." The stage was set for America to go on the offensive. ✷

South Pacific
The Naval Battle of Guadalcanal

Japanese bombers stationed on Guadalcanal in the Solomon Island chain put Allied New Caledonia and Australia in jeopardy. The Americans took the offensive for the first time in the war when the marines landed on Guadalcanal and took the airfield on August 7, 1942. The U.S. Navy lost so many ships trying to defend and supply the marines that the narrow strip of water between Guadalcanal and Savo Island became known as "Iron-bottom Sound." Resupply became difficult and the marines were isolated. The Japanese took position to press their advantage.

The Japanese wanted desperately to land a killing blow against the Americans who hung on to their sliver of Guadalcanal. On the night of November 12 a major Japanese force sailed to the "Slot" (the U.S. sailors' nickname for the passage of water in the midst of the Solomon Island chain), intent on shelling the marines. The Japanese fleet was composed of two columns, each headed by a battleship protected by a screen of light cruisers and destroyers, twenty ships in all. The only American ships in the area ready to meet them were two heavy cruisers, three light cruisers, and eight destroyers, all under the command of Rear Admiral Daniel Callaghan.

Setting out from Guadalcanal at dusk on the twelfth, Callaghan's ships sailed in single column through Ironbottom Sound in the early morning hours of Friday the thirteenth. Callaghan, aboard the flagship cruiser U.S.S. *San Francisco,* reasoned that his only hope of defeating the superior force lay in executing some bold and unlooked-for strategem. Dis-

carding orthodox battle strategy, he ran the gauntlet between the two Japanese battleships and their cover of smaller ships, exposing his column to fire from both sides. The opposing forces sailed into chaos. U.S. ships zigged and zagged to within yards of the enemy, sometimes nearly colliding with each other or with enemy ships as they took evasive maneuvers. Ships from both sides occasionally fired on their own during the melee. The noise of the guns and the explosions of the hits at such close range were deafening. Searchlights flashed about wildly and gunfire lit the night sky.

The *San Francisco* was in mortal danger from the first exchange of fire. The Japanese battleships found the range immediately, and shells simultaneously struck each side of the ship. Explosions

The U.S.S. San Francisco *(background) spews smoke after a Japanese plane crashed into it on November 12, 1942. At left is the U.S.S.* President Jackson.

Left. *The* San Francisco *enters San Francisco Bay after the long return voyage from Guadalcanal.*

Rear Admiral Daniel Callaghan (above) and Boatswain's Mate Reinhardt Keppler (below) both died aboard the San Francisco.

rocked the superstructure, killing Admiral Callaghan and his staff on one bridge. At the same time, the ship's captain, Cassin Young (who earlier had received the Medal of Honor at Pearl Harbor), was killed when the Japanese scored a direct hit on his bridge.

Three decks down on the ship, below the water line, Lieutenant Commander Herbert Schonland, the damage control officer, had his hands full. Since all lights were extinguished at the first salvo, Schonland and his crews had to rely on hand-carried lanterns. Japanese shells had torn open holes all along both sides of the ship; fires were breaking out everywhere. One fire raged in the Group 2 magazine below one of the forward turrets and threatened to blow the ship to bits. Schonland directed a party for-

ward to open sea valves and flood the fire. When a direct hit killed twenty men in the repair party, Schonland sent another group of men, which succeeded in putting out the fire. In the midst of fire, shelling, darkness, and confusion Schonland toiled calmly on.

Boatswain's Mate First Class Reinhardt Keppler, a son of German immigrants from Washington State, was one of those battling the fires. Leaving one of the crews, he attempted single-handedly to extinguish a large fire in the ship's hangar. Keppler walked steadily into the blaze, cutting his way through the flames with the jet of a fire hose. Oblivious to the constant rain of enemy shellfire, he advanced into the heart of the fire. Although critically wounded by shrapnel from one of these shell bursts, he refused to leave his duties. He extinguished the fire in the hangar and went on to fight new fires until he collapsed from loss of blood.

The ship was by now listing at a thirty-five-degree angle. Lt. Commander Schonland realized that until he stopped the flow of water, he would be unable to counterflood the ship to correct the list. He assembled a party and led it up to the second deck and water line. The three-foot-high circular walls around the hatches had dammed the water and kept it at waist-deep level. Seawater poured in through holes in the ship's hull that, Schonland remembered, "you could have walked through." Lantern light revealed the gruesome sight of dead bodies and torn limbs floating on the surface of the oily water. Schonland and his men waded to the hull of the ship and stuffed mattresses into the holes, effectively slowing the rush of water. Schonland then ordered the crew to evacuate the ship's sick bay. Opening the sea valves to flood that section of the ship, he countered the weight of the water on the other side of the ship. When the ship righted, he and his repair party groped underwater to open flush valves manually, first on one side and then the other.

During this desperate balancing act Schonland heard from the officer of the deck, Commander Bruce McCandless, that both the admiral's flag bridge and the captain's navigational bridge had been destroyed. Both officers and their staffs were presumed dead, making Schonland the ship's commanding officer. Instructing McCandless to follow the admiral's plan of battle, Schonland remained below and attended to the urgent task of fighting the flooding and fires threatening his ship. At one point he was directing the efforts to extinguish twenty-five simultaneous fires while bringing the ship to an even keel.

After one-half hour of desperate

Lieutenant Commander Herbert E. Schonland (second from left) describes damage to the bridge of the San Francisco to Admiral Chester Nimitz (left) several days after the battle at Guadalcanal. Schonland later received the Medal of Honor for his efforts to control damage during the engagement.

battle, the *San Francisco* sailed beyond the range of Japanese guns. The Naval Battle of Guadalcanal cost the navy eight ships, including the cruisers *Juneau,* which was sunk later that day by a submarine, and *Atlanta,* which had to be beached. The Americans destroyed one Japanese battleship and two destroyers, but more important, they prevented the Japanese ships from bombarding the hard-pressed marines on Guadalcanal.

The badly damaged *San Francisco* limped back to port carrying four men who would be awarded America's highest medal for bravery in action, more than on any ship for a single action in World War II. Reinhardt Keppler, who died a few days after the battle, was awarded the Medal of Honor posthumously for his selfless battle to save the ship from fire. Commander Herbert Schonland, who had kept the *San Francisco* afloat, and Commander Bruce McCandless, who had guided her to safety, both received the medal. Admiral Callaghan, architect of the bold stroke of strategy that had halted the Japanese advance and saved the marines on Guadalcanal, was awarded the medal posthumously ◈

Bombers Over Europe
The Mighty 8th

Despite the stunning Japanese attack on Pearl Harbor, America and its allies weighted their attention toward the defeat of Germany, the most powerful of the Axis nations. U.S. ground forces were woefully unprepared to take the offensive, so the first U.S. contribution in Europe would have to be in the air. The 8th Air Force arrived in England in the spring of 1942 to begin daylight strategic bombing raids against Germany. The men of the 8th suffered terrible losses in these early missions. When a man climbed aboard a B-17 bound for Germany, he knew that he might well never return. His chances of surviving all twenty-five of the combat missions he was expected to fly were slim indeed.

Technical Sergeant Forrest Vosler of the 8th Air Force, a native of upstate New York, said that it took him just one flight over Germany to be "absolutely sure [he] was doomed" and that he should "sit down and write [his] folks a last letter." His fourth mission as a radioman/gunner for the 358th Bomber Squadron of the 303d Bomber Group nearly proved him correct.

As Vosler's B-17 neared Bremen on December 22, 1943, flak destroyed one of its four engines. After unloading bombs, the plane wheeled 180 degrees to begin the return trip to England. Then flak hit a second engine, forcing the craft to drop out of formation and fly at the mercy of the German fighters below, who awaited crippled B-17s like sharks in a feeding frenzy.

Just after Vosler saw two other bombers explode and disintegrate, a 20MM shell from a German Messerschmidt fighter exploded into his compartment. Hot metal burned into his legs, arms, and chest. Vosler remembered: "I couldn't control my hands. I was so nervous I couldn't have held the gun. Then things happened. My whole life . . . went past me in seconds. . . . I'm not talking about skimming. Getting up in the morning, doing the whole routine." The fear of death left him, though, to be replaced by a feeling that he "might as well die standing up." He climbed back into his turret and fired his machine gun until another 20MM shell exploded near him; this time particles sliced into his chest and eyes. Fortunately, the German fighters had to turn back before they could finish off the crippled plane. Although seriously wounded, Vosler helped the badly wounded tail gunner before receiving aid himself.

The pilot struggled to keep the plane airborne until it reached the English Channel while Vosler repaired the radio, which had been knocked out during the attack. He transmitted a distress signal to a British base as the plane ditched into the channel. While the plane began to sink, the crew scrambled out onto a wing and the unwounded readied a raft. In doing so they left the tail gunner standing unattended for a few seconds. Vosler saw the gunner pitching forward into the water. Despite the great pain from his own wounds, he grabbed the falling man and held him up with one hand while holding the plane's wire radio antenna with the other. The others scrambled to Vosler's aid and helped both wounded men aboard the raft. Vosler's radio transmission had alerted boats in the channel, and the men were rescued by a Norwegian fishing boat two hours later.

At first, Vosler thought that the blood he saw flowed from an external wound, but the blood was on the retinas of his eyes. For eight months he was totally blind. One eye was removed in an operation, but doctors held out hope that he might regain sight in his other eye. President Roosevelt delayed the ceremony in which Vosler was to receive his medal, waiting for the heroic airman to regain his sight. Eight months later, Vosler was indeed able to see the president as he spoke to him in the Oval Office.

A few months before Vosler's heroism, the 8th Air Force was called upon to perform an unusual mission over Rumania; General Louis H. Brereton, the commander of the 9th Air Force, called the raid on Ploesti of August 1, 1943, "the most difficult assignment ever given an air force." The plan called for 178 B-24 Liberator bombers to fly 1,400 miles from Benghazi in Libya to the Ploesti oil fields in Rumania, attack at treetop level, and return on a carefully synchronized schedule, all without fighter support. For the raid, Brereton

Technical Sergeant Forrest Vosler (fourth from left) and his crewmates with their B-17 bomber during training in Pyote, Texas, summer 1943.

combined two bombing groups from his own North Africa-based 9th Air Force with three groups on temporary duty from the 8th Air Force in England.

The mission went wrong from the beginning. Without apparent cause, one plane crashed on takeoff. Shortly after the planes were airborne, the lead plane of the 376th Bombing Group, the first group of the five-group formation, burst into flames. The pilot pulled out to try to make the airstrip near Benghazi. As he attempted to crash-land, the plane skidded, hit a telephone pole, and exploded. Another plane moved up to take the lead of the formation, but it also crashed. Everyone had been ordered to keep radios off, so all watched in silence

Below. A B-17 of the 96th Bomber Group unloads over Bremen, Germany, as contrails from the other planes streak the sky.

A B-24 Liberator flies above smoke and flames in this painting of the attack on Ploesti, Rumania, on August 1, 1943.

Major John Jerstad volunteered for the Ploesti raid event though he had flown enough missions to go home.

as the bomber carrying the lead navigator spiraled down into the Mediterranean. The reasons for the crashes were never discovered. The 376th's group leader, Colonel Jack Compton, who was carrying mission leader Brigadier General Uzal Ent, moved up to take the first position. Compton's navigator was inexperienced, and this would prove crucial later in the mission.

As the bombers approached the Alps, they ran into heavy clouds. The 376th and the second bombing group, the 93d under Lieutenant Colonel Addison Baker, climbed over the cover while Colonel John Kane took his 98th under the clouds.

Colonel Leon Johnson, the commander of the 44th Bombing Group that was next in line, could see that Kane had lost track of the movements of the two lead groups and was circling over the Danube. Because Johnson's 44th was supposed to follow Kane's group into Ploesti, Johnson circled behind Kane until the latter regained his bearings. The planes maintained radio silence to avoid alerting the defenses. Johnson waited until Kane waggled his wings to indicate he was back on course. The two groups were now twenty minutes behind schedule, while the first two groups, unaware of the delay behind them, had flown ahead and arrived at their checkpoints on time.

The first two groups descended to fifty feet for their approach on the target. Compton's lead plane came to a landmark, a railroad crossing, which Compton and Ent mistook for the crossing that led to Ploesti. The young navigator was convinced that the crossing was the wrong one, but Ent overruled him. The bombers of the first two groups sped on—but toward Bucharest instead of Ploesti. By the time the commanders discovered the error, it was too late for the two groups to return to their course for their bombing run. General Ent broke radio silence to give the order for them to approach the target from the more heavily defended south. All of the planes of the two groups were also compelled to abandon their assigned targets and bomb any "target of opportunity."

Approaching Ploesti, the bomber groups flew into a wall of fire and split into squadrons. Most of the 376th swung east in a wide end run to come at Ploesti from the northeast, while the 93d continued straight through the defenses. Three miles from the 93d's selected target, antiaircraft fire hit the lead plane flown by Lieutenant Colonel Addison Baker and his copilot, Major John Jerstad. Flames licked down the sides of the fuselage and onto the wings. Even as their aircraft turned to a ball of flame, Baker and Jerstad continued to the target, jettisoning their bombs to stay airborne. They passed up an open field where they might have crash-landed, hoping to lead the squadron to the target. Moments later the bomber exploded and plummeted to the ground near the refinery. The rest of the squadron had already begun its successful bombing raids.

Meanwhile, the 389th, the last group in the formation, flew toward a separate target, another refinery in Campina, eighteen miles from Ploesti. On the low-flying approach through a valley, the B-24 of Second Lieutenant Lloyd Hughes was hit by ground fire, and its gas tanks began spraying fuel. Hughes continued the attack and released his bombs on target. The leaking gasoline caught fire, and Hughes prepared to crash-land in a dry creek bed. At the last moment he tried to pull up to avoid hitting a bridge, but a wing caught and sent the plane cartwheeling in a fiery crash, killing Hughes and six of his crewmen. (Two men were thrown free when the plane flipped, and they miraculously survived the crash.)

By the time Kane's and Johnson's bomber groups, the 98th and the 44th, arrived at Ploesti, their assigned targets were already engulfed in flames caused by the first two groups. Johnson later remarked, "It was more like an artist's conception of an air battle than anything I had ever experienced. We flew through sheets of flames, and airplanes were everywhere, some of them on fire and others exploding." Kane and Johnson realized that the billowing smoke and fire were no guarantee that the all-important plants containing refining machinery had actually been destroyed. The 98th and 44th, therefore, stayed on course to confront the alerted defenses. As their aircraft neared the target area, sudden explosions from delayed-action bombs rose 300 feet into the air. A carpet

Three leaders of the Ploesti raid: Colonel Leon Johnson, Brigadier General Uzal Ent, and Colonel John Kane (left to right), back at their North African base, 1943.

of antiaircraft fire exploded below and around them, and German fighters waited above, biding their time until the American bombers climbed from the blazing target area. The turbulence from the heat of the fires rocked the planes so violently that in each of the bombers pilot and copilot strained together to keep the plane on course. Yet Johnson's 44th, the last group to enter the inferno, scored direct hits on the refinery plants.

The trip back to North Africa was a race for survival. The battered aircraft had to fend off fighter attacks all the way out of Rumania and over the Mediterranean. Some of the planes that had survived the bombing run were shot down on the return trip to Benghazi, while others in distress were forced to make for Turkey, Cyprus, Malta, or Sicily. Only

92 of the 178 planes completed the 1,400-mile return leg to Benghazi. Others were forced to land in Sicily, Cyprus, and Turkey. The mission cost the Air Corps 54 planes lost and 532 airmen killed, taken prisoner, or missing. The daring raid destroyed 42 percent of the refining capacity at Ploesti, but the long-range effects were questionable because the Germans repaired the plants immediately.

Of the five men awarded the Medal of Honor for that mission, only Kane of the 9th Air Force and Johnson of the 8th lived to receive it. Baker, Jerstad, and Hughes of the 8th never wavered from their missions while knowing that it meant almost certain death. Before the war ended, thirteen other men of the 8th received the Medal of Honor. ◈

War of Attrition
Sicily and Italy

The American infantryman met his German counterpart face to face for the first time with the Operation Torch invasion of North Africa on November 8, 1942. The green GIs were defeated soundly at the Kasserine Pass in Tunisia but regrouped and helped drive the Germans from Africa. The victory in Africa was viewed as a prelude to a great confrontation in Europe—the second front that would relieve pressure on the Soviet Union and begin to drive toward Germany. Allied dreams of a quick campaign through the "soft underbelly" of the south, however, turned into the nightmare of an offensive bogged down in the mud and mountains of Italy. Salerno and Cassino, Anzio and the Gustav line—these names became synonymous with grinding frustration as the Allies had to slug it out with the Germans for every foot of Italy.

Gerry Kisters was, by his own admission, a terrible garrison soldier. He was too independent and sure of himself for an inexperienced draftee, and he spoke his mind, even if it meant telling an NCO what he thought of him. Because of these tendencies, the Indiana resident remained a buck private for eighteen months, the maximum amount of time a man could be forced to stay at that lowest rank.

Yet these were the very qualities that made Kisters an exceptional combat soldier as an advance scout for the 91st Reconnaissance Squadron. The advance men, in their armored cars and jeeps, were the first to move ahead after an air or artillery bombardment. They scouted, cleared roads of obstructions, and defused mines and booby traps. It was a dangerous job, and the reconnaissance men were granted more autonomy than the average GI because they had to think quickly. Kisters excelled in this role. In seven months of combat in North Africa and in Sicily, he was promoted to staff sergeant for his reconnaissance work.

In Tunisia near the end of the North Africa campaign, Kisters was the point man for an armored column moving from Mateus to Ferryville. The fields on both sides of the road were heavily mined, so the vehicles were forced to lumber straight down the road. Kisters scouted ahead. Near a small creek he found the road blocked by captured British vehicles parked just past a small culvert bridge. Spotting two German soldiers hiding in the culvert, he threw grenades in their direction. Then he spotted a German 88MM artillery piece hidden on a hill just behind the creek, the muzzle trained on the road where the American armor would be coming. Kisters followed the creek bed toward the hill, then crawled around the slope to the rear of the artillery emplacement. He threw three grenades and wiped out the unsuspecting artillery crew, allowing the armor column to continue unmolested. That day Kisters earned the Distinguished Service Cross.

Kisters described his actions in combat as "battle fever." "There is such a thing," he explained. "You get so caught up in an action that the danger you're in doesn't really penetrate. You want to do the job . . . and you're going to do it, come hell or high water. You've stuck your neck out so far it's as dangerous to go back as to go forward . . . maybe more so."

That was the case on July 31, 1943, when Kisters and his unit were assigned to take out a roadblock on a winding mountain road near Gagliano, Sicily. Kisters and a newly arrived second lieutenant rode in the lead jeep at the head of a column of the 91st's vehicles. At each turn in the road, they halted the column,

Recruit Gerry Kisters stands in front of a barracks at Fort Benjamin Harrison, Indiana, in January 1941.

Second Lieutenant Gerry Kisters receives the Medal of Honor from President Franklin D. Roosevelt at the White House, February 9, 1944.

edged around the bend, and nervously surveyed the terrain ahead for any sign of Germans. At one of these bends, machine-gun fire surprised them but fell short. They had found a roadblock: To their left, the mountain rose precipitously; to the right, the terrain dropped more gently toward ditches and a ravine. It was up to Kisters and the lieutenant to eliminate the German machine guns.

The two crept through the cover of ditches and moved behind the closer of the two machine-gun nests. They lobbed their grenades at the German gun, and the crewmen surrendered and were taken prisoner. The second machine gun opened up from its position on a higher ridge, raking them with fire. Kisters left the lieutenant guarding the prisoners and advanced alone.

Now out of grenades and armed with only a carbine rifle, he crept close to the gun as German snipers, hidden in the mountains, found his range. He was hit by a ricocheting bullet that "damn near tore my leg off," but he went on, dragging his useless leg while firing steadily at the machine-gun crew. Snipers grazed him twice more in the legs but he continued to crawl forward painfully. As he closed in on the emplacement, he saw the crew above him scrambling to remove sandbags in order to lower their gun and aim it at him. That was all the opening Kisters needed. He fired through the gap in the sandbags and killed the crew.

Just then, another sniper's bullet ripped into his arm "like a sledgehammer" and knocked him out. When he came to, his own men had advanced and routed the snipers. Kisters was carried from the mountain by the Germans he had captured in the first machine-gun nest. He had suffered seven bullet wounds, but his feat brought him a Medal of Honor.

He was shipped home on the *Queen Elizabeth,* pressed into service as a transport for the wounded. The ship also carried German prisoners to prison camps in the United States. One of the Germans aboard the huge liner escaped, and the heavily bandaged Kisters, who was born of German immigrants, awoke from a nap with an American M.P.'s pistol pointed at his head. The man who had just earned the DSC and the Medal of Honor had been mistaken for a German soldier.

Charles Kelly was another soldier who did not shine until he shipped overseas. His first months in the army were even more inauspicious than Kisters's. Numerous minor scrapes with the discipline code kept him on KP and latrine details through much of basic training. Much more serious was an AWOL trip home to Pittsburgh from airborne train-

ing at Fort Benning. No longer eligible for the paratroopers, he was shipped to Camp Edwards, Massachusetts, where he hooked up with the North Africa-bound 36th Division. As Kelly put it, "The only way I could get overseas was to screw up."

The 36th spent some time in North Africa, but Kelly's first real combat came during the invasion of Salerno in Italy, where he found himself and his unit pinned down under heavy fire. Kelly advanced, reasoning, "I had enough ammunition so I said, 'The hell with it. I'm going forward.' "

Kelly fulfilled a commander's dream. When someone was needed to lead patrols, Kelly always volunteered. That attitude led him to join a patrol near Altavilla, Italy, on the morning of September 13, 1943. Kelly's company was drawing fire from a nearby hill that

Corporal Charles "Commando" Kelly holds a carbine in Italy. Beside him are (left to right) two captured German rifles, a submachine gun, and a Garand M1 rifle.

was supposed to be in American hands. He reported that Germans held the position, then led an attack on it. He fought until he ran out of ammunition for his Browning Automatic Rifle (BAR) and was forced to return to Altavilla for more. The mayor's house there was being used by the Americans as an arsenal, and it was under heavy German attack when Kelly arrived, GIs firing from every window.

He entered the house and in the next twenty-four hours became a one-man army and a legend. He fired his BAR until the barrel grew red-hot and the gun useless. He threw it on a bed in the house, where it started a small fire in the bedclothes. Kelly then looked around for another weapon. He used a Tommy gun until he could find no more ammunition for it, then fired another BAR until it, too, overheated. Climbing to the third floor, he found an astounding array of weapons at his disposal. Other Americans fell around him during the heated battle, but Kelly seemed to be invulnerable as he moved from window to window. He fired four rounds from a bazooka, then discarded it when he could find no more ammunition. He tossed an incendiary grenade on the roof of a nearby house the Germans were using for cover, then looked down to see some German troops advancing on the mayor's house from an adjoining alley. He pulled the firing pins from several 60MM mortar shells and dropped the live rounds on the men below; the explosions rocked the foundation of the house.

Next, Kelly spotted a 37MM anti-tank gun in the courtyard and went downstairs to give it a try. He had never fired one before, but he loaded it from a nearby pile of shells, aimed it at a church steeple across the way where he had seen some snipers, and pulled the lanyard. The round hit the top of the garden wall

just beyond the muzzle of the gun, and the impact threw Kelly against the wall of the house. Luckily, he had loaded it with an armor-piercing shell and not a high-explosive round or the blast would have killed him. He raised the muzzle to clear the wall and blasted the church steeple, then continued firing until he was out of shells.

After disposing of much of the arsenal, Kelly volunteered to cover the withdrawal of the other American troops. He stayed behind, still firing as they left. When he later joined the unit, one of his buddies told him that they had already made plans to go back and "try and find your body."

"Commando" Kelly was harder to kill than that. He survived seven more months in combat, including some vicious fighting at the Rapido River in January of 1944. The only thing that

stopped Kelly was his own government, which brought him back to the U.S. for a war bonds tour. The one-time AWOL returned to Pittsburgh in May 1944 for a parade and a tumultuous ovation. This time he wore the Medal of Honor.

Kelly had grown up in a large family in a tough part of Pittsburgh. He and his nine brothers had slept in shifts in a house without electricity or plumbing, so he knew something about hardships when he joined the army. He also knew about the protection and love a tightly knit group of brothers provided for each other. Kelly received the Medal of Honor, in part, because he extended that fraternal feeling to his buddies in the 36th Infantry: "You live with me and you become a family . . . just like brothers. If one of them gets hurt, you're mad. That's it. We were a family. [If] they hurt them, they hurt me." ❖

Liberation
The Battle for France

On D-day, June 6, 1944, the greatest armada in history sailed across the English Channel to the shores of Normandy. The Allied invasion of Europe marked the beginning of the end for the German war machine. Between D-day and the end of June nearly a million men landed in France, but the Germans kept them bottled up within a 100-mile front in northern France for more than a month. The fate of the entire invasion rested on the shoulders of the soldiers who were asked to break out from the narrow front and to push through the Germans at the village of St. Lô.

Captain Matt Urban (right) with a fellow soldier, Lieutenant William Voller, in France. After being wounded in France, Urban spent weeks in a hospital in England but returned to lead men into combat—and earn the Medal of Honor.

One of the key players in the successful fighting that pushed the Germans back from St. Lô was Captain Matt Urban. Urban, a native of New York, was already highly decorated for his actions with the 60th Infantry, 9th Division in Tunisia and Sicily. He spent the six-month period before D-day training in England. On D-day plus four the 9th waded ashore. Urban led his company in fighting through French hedgerows, tree- and vine-covered banks of dirt that for centuries bounded the open fields of the northern French farming country. Each field had to be taken separately by the Americans, who battled to root out German machine guns and tanks dug in behind the natural walls of the hedgerows. Each hedgerow taken meant another hedgerow to attack at the end of the next field.

On June 14, in one such field near Renouf, France, heavy fire from two tanks pinned down Urban's company. When his bazooka man was wounded, Urban picked up the weapon. One of his men carried ammunition for him. Under withering fire the two worked their way up to and around the hedgerow. They crawled to within fifteen feet of the tanks and destroyed them. Later in the same day, a 37MM tank shell narrowly missed Urban and hit the hedgerow just behind him. "It splattered . . . [and I] took it in the left leg." Badly wounded, he refused evacuation until the next day because he knew he and his men had only another quarter of a mile to go to secure the area.

Three weeks later, while recovering in a hospital in England, Urban heard that the 9th was suffering very heavy casualties and that many of its officers and sergeants had been killed. He left the hospital, crossed the English Channel on a troopship, and hitched rides to the front. He arrived leaning on a homemade cane, just as the U.S. bombers were striking targets for the beginning

of Operation Cobra—the planned breakout at St. Lô, less than twenty-five miles inland from Utah and Omaha beaches where the U.S. Army had stormed into France nearly a month and a half before.

He found some of the 9th Division troops in disarray, huddled in shell holes with their tanks in flames just 100 yards in front of them. Although the men were not Urban's own, he ordered them to follow him, leading them forward until they came to two tanks, one smoking and in ruins, the second usable with the driver still inside but with no gunner atop it. The entire area was under intense fire from the Germans who, after the bombing, had reorganized in a dominant position on a long, sloping hill. With no radio or mortars and no time to get them, Urban knew that he had to make do with what he had—the disabled but still usable tank. After a lieutenant and a sergeant were killed trying to man the turret gun, Urban decided, "I'm not going to send any more of these guys . . . to certain death," so he "crawled like a snake" up the tank and dropped in as machine-gun bullets ricocheted off the steel plate.

Barely able to believe he was still alive, he realized he had to stick his head up to fire the machine gun. Later recalling that he was certain he was going to die, Urban remembered a sensation of living "years of life in five to ten seconds." He said a quick prayer, then came up firing the .50-caliber machine gun. The Germans were stupefied when Urban opened fire, some of them "actually standing up." The driver began to move the tank forward and the men, "yelling like Geronimo," advanced with it. "We had them," said Urban. The German line of defense cracked.

Back with his own unit, Urban was made battalion commander when the commanding officer of 2d Battalion was killed by artillery. Urban was wounded again on August 15, when he was hit by shrapnel in the lower back and chest. Again he refused evacuation.

On September 3 Urban led the battalion's attack to establish the crossing point over the Meuse River. A battalion leader normally commands from the rear echelon, but Urban personally led the attack because of his belief that a good leader stayed in the thick of the action—in front of his men.

Machine-gun fire smashed into the center of his throat as he scrambled across open terrain to relieve three trapped men. Braving heavy fire, his men brought him out on a litter. As he drifted in and out of consciousness from loss of blood and the shock of his terrible wound, Urban saw his battalion chaplain administer last rites and saw a surgeon shake his head bleakly when asked whether Urban would survive.

Urban fought off death and spent seven months in hospitals in England. The neck wound, his seventh of the war, kept him out of further combat. Urban fought a different kind of battle to learn to speak again. A series of operations restored somewhat his mangled larynx. With speech therapy and the same grit and determination he had evidenced at St. Lô and the Meuse, he slowly recovered his power of speech.

Matt Urban had to wait nearly forty years to receive the recognition due him. Letters pertaining to the recommendations for his award were lost because his unit was overrun shortly after Urban was wounded at the Meuse, the witnesses to Urban's actions captured. Thirty-five years later, Urban mentioned in a casual conversation with a Veterans' Administration representative that he thought he had once been recommended for the Medal of Honor. The man made an inquiry, and Warrant Officer Carl Hansen of the Pentagon's Awards Office took up the case.

In 1979 Urban picked up the phone and heard Warrant Officer Hansen say, "Colonel Urban . . . I have some great news for you." Hansen had found a long-lost letter recommending Urban for the Medal of Honor. The Medal of Honor was his. The next year Urban received the award from President Jimmy Carter at an emotional ceremony in Washington. Urban's medal is unusual not only because he had to wait so long but also because it was awarded for actions and leadership over a period of nearly two months of his combat odyssey through northern France.

Besides the Medal of Honor, Urban also received his seventh Purple Heart, the French croix de guerre for valor, and the Legion of Merit in the 1980 ceremony. The Medal of Honor was his twenty-ninth combat decoration, and with it Matt Urban joined the ranks of America's most highly decorated World War II soldiers.

Audie Murphy is perhaps the most well known of this elite group. Murphy was born in Hunt County, Texas, to a family of sharecroppers. His youth in the depression was hard: "Poverty dogged our every step," he later wrote. His father deserted the family when Murphy was still quite young, and his mother died when he was sixteen. He took odd jobs until the war came, then tried to enlist in the marines. The recruiter looked over the skinny, small youth and told him he did not measure up to corps standards. Murphy then tried the paratroops, who also rejected him, before

A GI tries to draw sniper fire in France on June 27, 1944. When the sniper shoots at his helmet, the other soldiers can locate and fire on his position.

Actress Wanda Hendrix feeds wedding cake to her new husband, Audie Murphy, on January 8, 1949.

settling for a place in the "unglamorous" infantry.

At first, the army found him a dubious soldier. His commanding officer in boot camp tried to make him a cook. Murphy swore he would go to the guardhouse first. Another officer wanted him to work in a post exchange. Again he resisted and finally was allowed to ship overseas as a combat infantryman.

He began the war in North Africa as a private and proved to be an adept and resourceful fighter. He advanced through the ranks, saw action in Sicily and Italy, and was a much-decorated second lieutenant by the time he went into action on January 26, 1945. Murphy and the men of his casualty-depleted Company B, 15th Infantry, 3d Division, were in the forefront of an American attack on a German position in the village of Holtzwihr, France. Told to wait for support, they tried to dig into the snow-covered frozen ground at the edge of a forest about a mile away from Holtzwihr. With them were two armored tank destroyers, each with a turret cannon and a .50-caliber machine gun.

At two in the afternoon, six German tanks rumbled out of Holtzwihr, fanned out in the open field that lay in front of Murphy's position, and ground their way toward Company B. Enemy infantrymen, wearing white camouflage cover, followed the tanks. As the Germans advanced, one of the American tank destroyers slid into a ditch while maneuvering for firing position, its cannon now pointed at the ground uselessly.

The German tanks opened fire on Murphy and his men. A round burst in the trees above his machine-gun squad, killing the men and disabling the gun. Another round blasted into the second tank destroyer and set it afire. Survivors from the crew poured out the hatch and ran to the rear.

By radio Murphy called for artillery fire. When the rounds fell behind the advancing tanks, he designated coordinates closer to his own position. American artillery rounds began to find the ranks of German infantry, but the tanks pressed on, spraying the Americans with machine-gun fire. Murphy ordered his men to fall back.

He now faced the advancing Germans alone. He fired his carbine at the infantrymen until he ran out of ammunition, then jumped up on the burning tank destroyer and blasted away with its machine gun. When the Germans were virtually on top of him, Murphy called in artillery fire on his own position. The barrage turned back the attack. Miraculously, Murphy survived heavy pounding by his own artillery, crawling down from the tank destroyer with only a slight shrapnel wound in the left leg. The tank destroyer exploded shortly after Murphy limped away toward the rear. There he rejoined his men and organized them for a successful counterattack against the Germans.

Murphy fought for three more months, until the Germans surrendered. On June 2, 1945, he received the Medal of Honor, the most prized of his World War II decorations.

When he returned to America, Murphy was hailed as the country's "most decorated soldier." His fame led him to Hollywood, where movie contracts and marriage to starlet Wanda Hendrix in 1949 kept him in the public eye. Yet he always seemed ambivalent about his life after the war. "I'm not an actor at heart," he said, and most critics seemed to agree. One of his best performances, in the autobiographical *To Hell and Back,* only underscored the nation's identification of him as a combat soldier. In later years brushes with the law and bankruptcy dogged him until, on May 28, 1971, he died in a plane crash, just before his forty-seventh birthday. ◈

Nightmare in the Ardennes
The Bulge

In the summer and fall of 1944, British and Americans fought their way across France and Belgium. By late autumn they had dug a toehold in Germany's Huertgen Forest, and Soviet troops were closing in on the Germans from the east. In a final desperate attempt to stave off defeat, Hitler ordered his Panzers to break through the American lines in the Ardennes Forest of Belgium and Luxembourg, then push to the Belgian port of Antwerp and seize vitally needed fuel supplies. The Germans successfully concealed their build-up, and when they hurled twenty divisions into combat, on December 16, an American force of only five divisions stood against them. German tanks roared through the American lines on a fifty-mile front, bulging sixty miles into Allied territory. The Americans scrambled to regroup and stem the onrushing tide.

On the snowy afternoon of December 14, 1944, two days before the German assault in the Ardennes, Sergeant Ralph Neppel and the rest of his machine-gun squad set up a defensive position at the end of the main street of Birgel, Germany, a hamlet on the edge of the Huertgen Forest. Before that time, Neppel's company had advanced steadily from the day it landed at Normandy on D-day plus thirteen. The combat through the hedgerows and into Germany had been fierce, but nothing had prepared Neppel for what he was to endure that evening in Birgel. Near dusk, the machine-gun crew was astonished to hear the rumble of tanks entering the town. (Neppel later reasoned that he and his men had not seen them earlier because the tanks were well camouflaged for winter.) The sound of the grinding machinery came closer until a number of tanks emerged from the narrow side streets and turned toward the squad's position. German infantry followed the lead tank, using it as a shield.

Neppel held his fire until the Germans had advanced to within 100 yards, then released a burst that killed several of the foot soldiers. The tank lumbered forward to within 30 yards, then fired one cannon shot that blasted the Americans and sent the machine gun flying. Neppel was thrown ten yards from the gun, his legs wounded terribly. In shock, he looked down to see that his foot had been blown off. He realized the other men were either dead or dying, so he crawled on his elbows back to the gun and tried to set it up himself. When he found the tripod had been knocked loose, he cradled the gun in the crook of his arm and fired until he was too weak to lift it anymore. He killed the remaining infantrymen around the lead tank.

Without infantry cover the Panzer was left vulnerable to attack from bazookas or foot soldiers with phosphorous grenades, so it stopped. Neppel remembered the furious commander emerging from his tank and, like a vision from a nightmare, advancing on him with Luger pistol in hand. The officer fired, hitting Neppel in the helmet, and left him for dead. The helmet apparently diverted the course of the bullet; Neppel's skull was creased but he was alive and conscious.

When he again heard the rumbling of the tanks he was gripped by the awful thought they were moving forward and would soon crush him under their tracks. Instead, they withdrew. Neppel was rescued by American troops as they took Birgel. He was to spend six months regaining his strength at a hospital.

He had single-handedly turned back a Nazi armor attack but had lost both of his legs in the effort. When he heard that he was to receive the Medal of Honor his reaction was "to feel humble. You see so many die . . . then in the hospital you see triple amputees, guys who lost their eyesight . . . you feel there are so many more deserving that you shouldn't be taking the glory as an individual."

Private First Class Melvin "Bud" Biddle and the rest of his unit were in Reims, France, waiting to go home when the Germans launched their attack. Veterans of campaigns in Italy and in southern France, they had turned in their equipment and were passing the time listening to "Axis Sally," an English-speaking Nazi propagandist who played the latest hits from America while spouting misinformation in an attempt to demoralize the Allies. The troops were more amused than influenced by her show. That night, she announced, "The men of the 517th Parachute Infantry Regiment think you're going home . . . but you're not." This time, her information was correct.

The men of the 517th were issued new equipment, so new, in fact, that their rifles were still packed in Cosmoline grease, which the men had to clean off before they were boarded into trucks and driven to a crossroads in the area near the most advanced point of the German thrust into Belgium. The men were to face again the elite troops of the German army: Panzer divisions, paratroops, and SS soldiers. The mission of the 517th was to clear the Germans out of three miles of territory between the towns of Soy and Hotton.

Biddle was the lead scout for the 517th, a job he had inherited when other scouts were wounded or killed during the Italian campaign. One of his qualifications was his superb vision. "I saw every German out in front before they saw me, which was a large part of keeping me alive." He was keenly aware of the responsibility he held as the lead scout and said later it helped him forget his fear. "I think I got so I would rather die than be a coward . . . I was terrified most of the time but there were two or three times when I had no fear, and it's remarkable . . . it makes it so you can operate [in the lead]."

One of those times came on the twenty-third of December. Biddle was ahead of his company as it crawled through thick underbrush toward railroad tracks leading out of Hotton. Unseen by the Germans, he crawled to within ten feet of three sentries. Firing with his M1 rifle, he wounded one man in the shoulder and killed a second with two shots near the heart. The third sentry fled, but not before Biddle shot him twice in the back. "I should have got him. He kept running and got to their machine guns and all hell broke loose."

Under heavy fire from several machine guns, Biddle stayed on point as his unit crawled to within range, lobbed grenades, and destroyed all but one of the guns. With his last grenade, Biddle blew up the remaining machine gun. Then he charged the surviving gunners, killing them all.

That night, the Americans heard a large number of vehicles, which Biddle figured had to be American: "I'd never heard so many Germans. They didn't have equipment like we had, not in numbers." Biddle volunteered to lead two others in a scouting foray to make contact with these "Americans." In the darkness the three men came upon a German officer who fired at them. Separated from the others, Biddle crawled toward the German lines by mistake. Realizing his error, he continued to reconnoiter alone and carried back valuable information to use in the next day's attack.

The next morning Biddle spotted a group of Germans dug in along a ridge. He ducked behind a small bank for cover but found that he could not properly maneuver in order to shoot. In basic training Biddle had learned to shoot from a sitting position, but at the time he had thought that there would be no way to use it in combat. Now, moving to a sitting stance, he shot fourteen men. He hit each one in the head, imagining that the helmets were the same as the targets he had aimed at in training. Although others in his unit later went to view the bodies, Biddle could not bring himself to look on the carnage he had wrought. His sharpshooting, however, had made it possible for his unit to secure the village.

Biddle was wounded a few days later when a German 88MM artillery shell exploded against a building behind him. As he was returning to his unit from a hospital in London, another soldier asked him if he had heard about "that guy in the Bulge that shot all those people. My God, between Soy and Hotton it was littered with Germans. I think they're going to put that guy in for the Medal of Honor."

Biddle's outfit was one of many units to be rushed to the Ardennes to relieve the embattled 1st Army there. When General George S. Patton's 3d Army rolled out of Lorraine, it left the Allied units in its wake vulnerable to attack. The Germans moved the 17th SS Panzer to the attack near Bitche, France, in an area where the 44th Division struggled to hang on.

Sergeant Charles MacGillivary was a Canadian national who joined the U.S. Army in Boston, Massachusetts. He and the rest of Company I, 71st Regiment, had been taken off the line for Christmas dinner after they had held a key position during the initial German attacks of December 14-19. It was only their third respite from front-line combat in seven months of tough fighting across France. MacGillivary was cheered that Christmas by the knowledge that he had accumulated enough points to return stateside. But his company was summoned back to the front.

In the enemy attack, MacGil-

The Battle of the Bulge

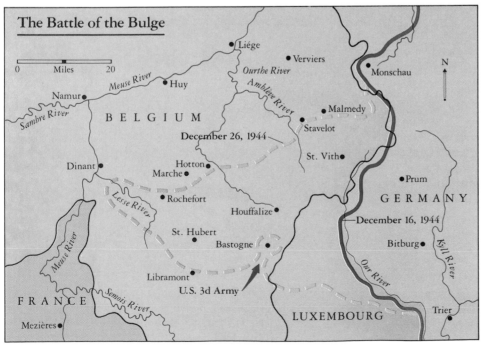

Top left. *A German "Panther 6" tank in the Ardennes, December 1944.* Above. *Sergeant Ralph Neppel poses with a French rifle prior to his battle with a German tank.* Map. *The bulge in Allied lines reached almost the Meuse River before stiffened resistance halted its progress. The relief of Bastogne by Patton's 3d Army on December 26, 1944, turned the battle in the Allies' favor.*

livary's squad was cut off from the others. On New Year's Day, 1945, the men found themselves trapped in a heavily wooded gully, surrounded by Germans, separated from their unit, and running out of food and ammunition. Four protected German machine guns held positions above them. Some of the men wanted to surrender but MacGillivary pointed out that there was no one to surrender to other than the SS, and "we

Above. American soldiers hunker down in the snow-covered Ardennes during the Battle of the Bulge in the winter of 1944-45. Left. Men of the 83d Infantry race through a German-held town in the Ardennes on January 15, 1945. Below. President Harry Truman presents the Medal of Honor to Sergeant Charles MacGillivary for bravery near Bitche, France, in a ceremony at the White House on August 23, 1945.

saw them leading prisoners in front of tanks . . . with their hands on their heads . . . and then we saw the prisoners fall. The SS troops were up on the machine guns shooting them."

For the moment, the squad was protected by the rise of the gully, but MacGillivary knew that gaps between the trees allowed enough space for Panzer tanks to roll through. Something had to be done quickly. MacGillivary took what grenades remained from his troops and then ordered the men to cover him

with the few rounds of ammunition they had left. He inched close to the side of the bank, waited for his men to fire, then scrambled out of the gully.

The machine guns, protected by infantrymen to their rear, faced the gully. MacGillivary's mission was twofold: to knock out the guns and to eliminate the protective fire of the infantry. He crawled forward to the first machine gun and lobbed his grenade, keeping an eye out for any sign of the infantrymen to the rear.

His aim was perfect. After the grenade detonated, he followed it in and shot down the gunners with his .45-caliber Tommy gun. He then attacked the infantrymen, killing them with more grenades.

By now his submachine gun was out of ammunition, so he retraced his steps to an area where he had seen some abandoned haversacks and another submachine gun with ammunition clips. Under heavy fire, he returned to the machine-gun nests, remembering something he had learned in the hedgerows: "With automatic weapons you keep moving. You move towards them and the guy gets excited."

MacGillivary destroyed the remaining three nests in much the same manner as the first, using his last grenade on the fourth gun. He was just lifting his numbed hands out of the snow after the blast when he saw one of the wounded gunners crawl to the gun. MacGillivary emptied his submachine gun into the gunner, but the man brought the gun down on its swivel as he fell, and the fire scraped across MacGillivary's chest and carved a line down his left arm, cutting it off. "When you're hit by bullets it's like a burn . . . as if you've been hit with a poker. To cool it off . . . I kept jabbing it in the snow." MacGillivary's efforts froze his wound. "When they picked me up they picked up a red cake of ice [frozen to his severed arm]. I would have bled to death in the summer or in the South Pacific."

By January 29, 1945, the Germans had been pushed back to the line they had held before the Battle of the Bulge, but pockets of resistance still had to be eliminated. First Sergeant Leonard Funk and the men of his Company C, 508th Parachute Infantry, 82d Airborne Division, discovered that the Germans, even in retreat, fought with ferocity. Company C had been decimated by the fighting in the preceding weeks. The executive officer of the company had been killed, so Funk, a veteran of the jumps on Normandy and Arnhem, had become acting executive officer as well as first sergeant.

That day it was snowing hard and was so cold that Funk had difficulty getting his Thompson submachine gun to work. "Everybody in my company had frostbitten feet . . . but there were no replacements, so we had to stick it out." Under heavy artillery fire, Funk led two columns into Holzheim, Belgium, taking prisoners along the way in furious house-to-house fighting.

Because Company C was understrength, Funk could spare only four men to stay behind and guard eighty German prisoners. When the four guards saw shadowy figures moving toward them through the snowstorm, they assumed that a patrol from nearby Company B was coming in for a prearranged meeting. The soldiers were indeed from Company B, but they had been captured and were followed by Germans. Since all of the men on both sides were wearing white camouflage cover, the four Company C guards were unable to distinguish the Germans, who captured them and freed their German prisoners.

Sergeant Funk's men at the front had encountered an unexpected number of enemy soldiers, so Funk and his company clerk backtracked to alert the guards to be ready to move. He was so confident of the rear that he had shouldered his Tommy gun. His confidence soon dissipated. He later recounted that as he approached his guards, "a guy I'd never seen before in my life comes up to me speaking German." The officer pushed a submachine gun into Funk's stomach and demanded his surrender.

Funk realized that if he did not do something his command would be hit from the rear. In a lightning move, Funk sidestepped and got his own gun down. He still remembers the look of surprise on the man's face as he emptied his clip into the German officer. "It seemed like I had hollow bullets. . . . I've never seen a man take so many in my life." Other Germans fired, and the company clerk, who was standing beside Funk, was killed. The sergeant reloaded and continued firing as men hit the ground and others sprinted toward nearby houses. During the chaos, the American prisoners seized weapons and began to fire as well. At the center of a firefight that killed twenty-one Germans and wounded many others stood Leonard Funk, unscratched and firing to the end. His Medal of Honor was presented to him on August 23, 1945, at the same ceremony honoring Ralph Neppel and Charles MacGillivary. ✦

First Sergeant Leonard Funk, whose speed with a submachine gun freed his unit from capture in Holzheim, Belgium, on January 29, 1945.

The End in Germany
Siegfried Line and Nuremberg

The desperate, failed gamble in the Ardennes cost Germany her lifeblood in men and materiel: more than 100,000 soldiers, as well as 1,600 airplanes, 700 tanks, and countless other vehicles. In January 1945 the Allies pushed the Germans back to the "Siegfried line" in western Germany, near the Rhine River. The offensive culminated in a lightning strike when Americans seized an intact railway bridge over the Rhine at Remagen on March 7. Allied forces poured over the bridge into Germany from the west while the Russians advanced from the east to within thirty miles of Berlin. The end of the Third Reich was at hand.

Many a front-line infantryman who lived through the European winter of 1944-45 must remember feeling the way Master Sergeant Nick Oresko felt: "You're dirty and hungry and cold . . . you get so miserable and you feel so terrible you say, well, if I give my life and it helps win the war, so be it." Oresko, of Company C, 302d Infantry, 94th Infantry Division, had been in what he later called "good combat," mostly patrolling and some minor firefights—until the Battle of the Bulge. His unit went on the offensive at the beginning of the year against both the Germans and the winter weather. On the evening of January 22 Oresko fell through the ice of a twelve-foot-deep water-filled tank trap during a battle. He was able to survive by holding his rifle like a chinning bar across the hole in the ice, until his men arrived and pulled him out. He was soaked to the skin and slept on the ground that night in a uniform frozen down to the underwear.

Late the next afternoon, the flush of anticipated danger replaced the cold. Oresko's platoon was ordered to take and hold a German position near the Siegfried line without benefit of covering artillery. Oresko had a terrible moment when he gave the order to "move out" and nobody stirred. A sergeant, Oresko said, has "to be ready to put [his] life on the line" so he stood up and started forward. The others followed. The Germans began dropping mortar shells behind Oresko but in front of his men. Cut off from the others, Oresko slowly groped forward while searching for cover. He moved close

Soldiers of the 39th Infantry, 9th Division, accompany a tank through the tank traps and fortifications of the Siegfried line near Roetgen, Germany.

enough to the first of two machine guns to dismantle it with a well-aimed grenade, then charged forward and shot the gunners. "What do you do?" he said later. "I knew I was alone. . . . [I] looked for a place to hide."

Then the second machine gun opened up; a bullet tore a hole in Oresko's hip. "As I lay there, I could see . . . just over my head . . . the machine gun was spitting fire at my troops." Again he crawled forward, toward the second gun. When he realized he had lost his grenades, he crawled back again, retrieved them, and advanced once more. Alone in a no man's land, he tripped a booby trap; instead of injuring him the explosion went over him.

Right. *Americans crawl past a fallen comrade near Statusforst, Germany.* Below. *Nick Oresko at his homecoming parade in Bayonne, New Jersey, Nov. 17, 1945.*

The Medal in the Movies

When he reached the machine-gun bunker he pulled the pin from a grenade, waited three seconds, threw it in the opening, and jumped in after the explosion. Oresko found three of the six men dead from the blast; he killed the others with his rifle, then lay bleeding among the bodies until his men came to carry him out.

While recovering from his wound, Oresko worked on limited duty in Le Havre, where he heard that he would be getting the Distinguished Service Cross for his action near the Siegfried line. He assumed that he would soon be returning to combat. One day the officer in charge asked him, "How do you want to go home, by boat or by plane?" Oresko responded that he had not collected enough combat points to be rotated back to the States and the man replied, "You don't need them." Oresko knew at that moment that the DSC had been upgraded to the Medal of Honor.

During Hitler's rise to power, Nuremberg had been the scene of spectacular Nazi party rallies, a showcase for the Reich. By the time the U.S. 3d Infantry Division bludgeoned its way into the city, the showcase had been reduced to rubble. Private First Class Joseph Merrell of Company I, 15th Infantry, 3d Division, helped open the way into Nuremberg on April 18, 1945. Reaching a hill on the outskirts of the city, his company met a determined enemy force. Alone, Merrell attacked two machine guns that were dug into the hill. He ran 100 yards through a storm of fire and killed four Germans. A sniper's bullet smashed into his rifle and destroyed it, but Merrell continued his attack with hand grenades. He zigzagged another 200 yards and tossed two grenades into a machine-gun nest, then followed the explosions, prepared to fight with his bare hands. Spotting a Luger, he picked it up and killed the

surviving Germans. He charged toward a second machine gun, but a rifle shot to his abdomen felled him 30 yards in front of the emplacement. Despite his wound, he struggled forward as bullets ripped through his clothing and ricocheted off his helmet. He tossed his last grenade just before a German killed him.

Merrell's Medal of Honor was one of the last two awarded for deeds during the ground war in Europe. The other was earned the same day by another soldier of the 15th Infantry, 3d Division, Lieutenant Michael Daly of Company A. Daly, a twenty-year-old from Southport, Connecticut, had fought in every major battle from his days as private first class with the 18th Infantry on Omaha Beach to Nuremberg, where he fought with the 3d Division. Already holding the Silver Star, the Purple Heart, and a battlefield commission, Daly "felt an obligation to protect [the surviving members of the company]. You do all the time. Maybe, in a way, more than normal, knowing the war was nearly over."

Daly acted as the lead man for his troops as they fought toward the center of war-destroyed Nuremberg, although as commander of Company A, he could have relegated this task to others. The city was contested from one pile of rubble to another, each pile a small fortress for hardened SS troops who ferociously resisted every inch of the American advance. For four days the Americans went about the bloody task of rooting them out.

April 18 was the second day of the attack. Daly was scouting a rail bridge that led into the city when a German machine gun on the other side of the bridge caught him and his men in the open. He charged forward, running to within fifty yards of the Germans before he opened fire with his carbine and killed the three gunners.

He again pushed ahead of his com-

Many war films have featured Medal of Honor exploits, both real and fictional. Some medal recipients have allowed their names and stories to be featured in films ranging from newsreels to complete biographies. In addition, some fictionalized accounts of combat have included characters who earned the medal.

The largest crop of Medal of Honor movies was created during World War II, when Hollywood and Washington collaborated to produce films that featured fast-paced action and a clear struggle of good versus evil, to arouse patriotic fervor and to support the war effort. Drawing from both contemporary and past Medal of Honor anecdotes, producers brought many of the most exciting tales of Americans in combat overseas to theaters across the country.

Spencer Tracy starred as Jimmy Doolittle in Thirty Seconds Over Tokyo, *released in 1944. The Tokyo raid was also featured in two other movies of that year,* Destination Tokyo *and* Purple Heart.

GARY COOPER IN "SERGEANT YORK"

Presented by WARNER BROS. PICTURES, Inc.

Above. *Gary Cooper won an Academy Award for his portrayal of Alvin York, the conscientious objector turned World War I hero, in 1941's* Sergeant York, *produced with York's assistance.*

Below. *In* They Were Expendable (1945), *navy veteran Robert Montgomery played Lieutenant "John Brickley," a character based on PT boat commander and Medal of Honor recipient John D. Bulkeley.*

Above. *Audie Murphy recreated his wartime exploits, including the one that earned him the Medal of Honor, in 1955's* To Hell and Back. *Murphy made over forty films, most of them westerns.*

Top. *American tanks in the shattered city of Nuremberg.* Above. *Michael Daly, who led troops into the heart of the city.*

pany, advancing on a house that contained a German antitank gun. In the words of one of his men, he was "taking his life in his hands and we all knew it." As he worked his way to the house, rifle fire kicked up the dust around him. With only his carbine, Daly killed all six Germans manning the antitank equipment.

Then, when he saw a long-time friend fall in the assault, Daly, in "hot blood," twice more led attacks on German machine-gun positions, each time moving to within pointblank range while directing the fire of his troops on the Germans. At one critical point, he seized a discarded M1, crawled forward to within ten yards of a German machine-gun nest, and killed the gunners, securing the position.

Daly was wounded badly in the face the following day. Once he recovered he was shipped home. Like so many medal recipients, Daly refused to see his award as a testament to individual heroism. "The medal is very important to me. . . ." he later said, "to insure the memory of those who died." ⬦

The Silent Service
Submarines in the Pacific

While U.S. ground forces concentrated on defeating the Axis in Europe, the war half a world away also raged. In the Pacific, the U.S. submarine service spent the war years choking off resources vital to Japan's survival. Yet at the outset of World War II, problems plagued the submarine force—outmoded equipment, defective torpedoes, and excessively cautious commanders. During the war new submarines were produced with the latest refinements in radar, data computers, and reliable torpedoes. Most important, though, the ineffective commanders were replaced by bold young men who dared to take their boats deep into harm's way.

Commander Richard H. O'Kane of the U.S.S. Tang, *with some of the fliers he rescued in the Pacific in April 1944.*

The submarines of the Pacific war were manned by a tightly knit band of volunteers who called themselves the "silent service" because their operations were cloaked in utmost secrecy. When sub commanders returned from a patrol, they gathered at the Royal Hawaiian Hotel in Honolulu, not only for rest and relaxation but to swap information and to catch up on the news of the other boats. They remembered those who had been lost and spoke of men whose heroic feats had made them legends.

One such man of legend was Commander Howard Gilmore of the *Growler*. During a patrol in the South Pacific near Rabaul in February of 1943, Gilmore's sub closed on a small ship that he had been stalking on the surface, when the ship changed course and steamed toward the *Growler*.

The two collided and the submarine sliced a hole amidships in the enemy vessel. Japanese machine gunners raked the bridge of the submarine, killing two men and wounding Gilmore and two others. Gilmore ordered the survivors to clear the bridge but could not get to the hatch himself. Still topside, he shouted to his executive officer "Take her down!" The exec obeyed, and Gilmore was last seen clutching to the bridge as the Japanese continued to sweep the submarine with fire. The badly damaged *Growler* escaped and eventually struggled to Australia. Gilmore's Medal of Honor was the first ever awarded to a submariner.

The fate of Captain John Cromwell of the *Sculpin* was only revealed at the war's end by men returning from Japanese prison camps. Cromwell was in command of a submarine attack group off Truk Island in the central Pacific. He was the only man on patrol in possession of intelligence concerning top-secret, detailed plans for submarine warfare and fleet movements in the Pacific. The

Sculpin was discovered by Japanese destroyers escorting a convoy between Truk and the Marshall Islands. The destroyers rocked the submarine with a savagely effective depth charge attack. When the badly damaged boat sank deep below the surface and seemed in danger of sinking farther, the captain ordered the *Sculpin* to the surface and commanded the crew to abandon ship. Cromwell stayed aboard the crippled submarine as the crew escaped. Rather than face the possibility of revealing his secret information under torture or drugs, Cromwell chose to go down with his ship. His Medal of Honor citation reads, "His great moral courage in the face of certain death adds new luster to the traditions of the U.S. Navy."

In order to protect their merchant convoys and military task forces from submarines, the Japanese employed destroyers equipped with depth charges. In the early parts of the war American sub commanders dove or took evasive action to avoid the dangerous escort ships. In the spring of 1944, however, the submarine command decided that going after destroyers would be worth the risk. They reasoned that every enemy destroyer sunk exposed more enemy convoy ships to attack. In addition, by 1944 the Japanese were not able to replace shipping quickly enough to replace the destroyers that went down.

The Japanese escorts were still as dangerous as ever, but one intrepid commander, Samuel Dealey of the *Harder*, sought out the predators with a special avidity. On one patrol in the Sibutu Passage near Borneo in the South Pacific, Dealey had already sunk three destroyers and damaged two. On the night of June 6, 1944, Dealey was on another patrol. A bright moon that night exposed the *Harder* to two Japanese destroyer escorts as Dealey closed on a convoy. Dealey kept his boat on the surface, as if taunting the escorts, and submerged only at the last moment. Then he veered hard to port, fired stern torpedoes into one destroyer, but missed the second. The *Harder* escaped after enduring a severe attack by depth charges.

The next day, while at periscope depth, he invited the charge of two oncoming destroyers, holding fire until the ships had closed to within 650 yards.

Dealey stuck his torpedoes directly into the bow of the onrushing lead ship, an extremely difficult and dangerous maneuver called "down-the-throat" firing. A fourth *Harder* torpedo hit the second destroyer. The subsequent explosions rocked the submarine and practically heeled it over. Not content with his success, Dealey used the same maneuver and method of firing on June

10, this time passing the *Harder* directly under a destroyer as it erupted in a thunderous explosion. He came to be known as "Down-the-Throat" Dealey.

On the *Harder*'s next patrol, Dealey hunted as one of a three-boat wolf pack near Luzon. Frank Haylor, skipper of the *Hake,* one of the other boats in the pack, saw the *Harder* on August 23, when Dealey told him he was going after a particularly troublesome mine sweeper. A few hours later Haylor heard on sonar the concussions from at least fifteen depth charges. Dealey and the *Harder* were never heard from again. His Medal of Honor was presented to his widow.

Commander Richard H. O'Kane was a skipper cut from the same cloth as Gilmore, Cromwell, and Dealey. Fellow Medal of Honor recipient and submariner George Street called O'Kane "absolutely fearless." O'Kane explained himself differently, saying that it was the duty of any commanding officer "to overtake and destroy an enemy ship." Commanding the *Tang,* O'Kane never shirked that duty and became the most successful submariner in the U.S. Navy, sinking twenty-four ships in just nine months.

On the night of October 23, 1944, the *Tang* was patrolling the waters of the narrow, dangerous Formosa Strait. The radar operator reported what seemed to be an island where no island should be. The "island" proved to be a convoy including a transport, four enemy freighters, and numerous escorts. As the submarine maneuvered on the surface toward the Japanese ships, the radar screen showed a blip breaking away and moving in their direction. O'Kane made

Mortally wounded Commander Howard Gilmore orders his sub, the Growler, *to dive, leaving him and the bodies of two sailors topside. At top left is the sub's damaged nose.*

Below. *The U.S.S.* Harder *helps a seaplane rescue a downed flier under fire from Japanese hidden in the trees of a Pacific island.* Bottom. *Commander Samuel Dealey, skipper of the* Harder.

a wide arc and positioned the *Tang* in the spot the Japanese escort had vacated and began to "zig when they zigged." As soon as he was certain that he was dead ahead of the convoy, he stopped and waited on the surface for it to come to him.

In the darkness O'Kane turned his submarine so that it was pointing in the same direction as the convoy and allowed the Japanese ships to overtake him. Once he was between the two lines of ships, he fired from his bow on three of the leading ships.

A lookout warned O'Kane that a transport had veered from its line and was bearing down on the *Tang.* The ship barreled in so quickly that O'Kane had no time to dive. He ordered full speed in a frantic attempt to get across the bow of the giant ship. Gunners poured fire on

the *Tang* from above. With less than 100 yards between ships, O'Kane ordered "left full rudder," and the *Tang* pivoted into a turn and steamed straight down the side of the big ship, so nearly under it that the machine gunners could not lower the guns enough to score a hit.

O'Kane ordered his men to clear the bridge in preparation for diving but then saw that the transport was about to collide with a Japanese freighter that had also steamed forward to ram the sub. The two ships collided, and O'Kane stayed topside and called for fire from the stern tubes, hitting the freighter with a parting shot. The night sky was ablaze and the *Tang* was boxed in, but O'Kane broke through the convoy by heading directly for an escort, which gave way before him.

The next night, finding the seam

The battle flag of the U.S.S. Barb *records its awesome toll on the enemy. Rising sun flags mark Japanese merchantmen sunk; suns with rays indicate warships sunk; hollowed-out suns of both kinds indicate* ships damaged. The swastika represents a German cruiser sunk in the Atlantic in 1943. At top are citation ribbons, including the Medal of Honor (top center) earned by Commander Eugene B. Fluckey.

between escorts and merchant vessels, O'Kane slipped into the front of another convoy. The *Tang* was sighted by destroyers, but O'Kane stayed on the surface long enough to hit a tanker and two transports. He had two torpedoes left, but the destroyers were closing so fast that he had to make his escape before using them.

O'Kane waited an hour until he thought it would be safe to return in order to finish off the transport he had crippled. He fired his twenty-third Mark-18 torpedo of the mission at the crippled ship, then the twenty-fourth. The twenty-third hit the mark, but the twenty-fourth took a sharp turn, and, as the men on the bridge watched in horror, began to circle back toward the *Tang*. O'Kane called for emergency speed as the berserk torpedo porpoised in and out of the water on a direct line for the center of the boat. It hit the *Tang* with a "devastating detonation" that blew O'Kane and the eight other men topside into the water. The sub immediately started to go down, and O'Kane watched helplessly as it sank—"like a pendulum might sink in a viscous fluid."

Thirteen men escaped through air locks and fought their way to the surface. Of the twenty-two men in the water, only O'Kane and eight others lived through the night. They were picked up by a Japanese patrol boat the next morning. O'Kane endured the remainder of the war in a secret POW camp at Ofuna, during which time the Japanese never released word of his capture to the Red Cross. His wife spent nearly a year without word of his fate. Because of fear of retaliation against O'Kane if he were alive, his Medal of Honor was not announced until his release.

Three more submarine commanders received the Medal of Honor during the war. Commander Eugene B. Fluckey

of the *Barb* stalked a convoy until he found it anchored in fogged-in Namkwan Harbor, China. He sailed right into the center of it on the surface and fired torpedoes in all directions, sinking several ships. Commander Lawson Ramage of the *Parche* received his medal for an attack similar to O'Kane's night attack off Formosa. On a patrol in Luzon Strait on July 31, 1944, Ramage located an enemy convoy. He kept his boat on the surface, attacking ships as the night exploded around him.

Lieutenant Commander George Street's Medal of Honor was the last given to a submariner in World War II. By the time of his action on April 14, 1945, the submarine service had been so effective that few of the remaining Japanese ships dared venture into the East China Sea. They preferred to dart in close to land from safe harbor to safe harbor. Street, of the *Tirante,* crept in close to shore in waters too shallow for a dive and slipped into a mined harbor on Quelpart Island off the coast of Korea. He avoided patrol boats and torpedoed an ammunition ship and two escorts as they lay at anchor.

Street and other daring skippers like him applied the final turns to the vise that crushed Japanese shipping. At the end of the war, the U.S. submarine force hunted at will near the home islands of Japan. After Japan's surrender, Prime Minister Tojo said that the U.S. submarines had played a key role in defeating the Japanese. ◈

Island Fighting
Iwo Jima

By November of 1944, marine island-hopping invasions had made possible an American air base on Saipan, an island 1,300 miles from Tokyo. From there new B-29 Superfortresses could pound the Japanese in ever-increasing and more effective bombing raids. However, the B-29s needed shorter-range fighter escorts and an emergency landing area between Saipan and Japan. For that purpose, the island of Iwo Jima would have to be taken, but entrenched on Iwo were 22,000 Japanese prepared to die in defense of the island. The job of taking the island was delegated to marine combat infantrymen, who fought yard by bloody yard over thirty-six days.

Bedlam awaited the marines who struggled ashore at Iwo Jima on D-day, February 19, 1945. In the smoke and the noise of battle, those fortunate enough to live through the first few moments thought only of digging for cover into the shifting black volcanic sand. Equipment and men in subsequent waves piled up behind the logjam on the beach.

One of the early casualties on Iwo was Sergeant John Basilone, killed by a mortar blast while he urged his crew to get off the killing ground of the beach. Iwo thus claimed the man who had received one of the Marine Corps's first Medals of Honor of World War II. Basilone led the defense that held off a night-long *banzai* charge on Guadalcanal in 1942. After a much-publicized return to the U.S., the veteran volunteered to return to combat—just in time for Iwo Jima.

Fire was so intense that first day that the 1st Battalion, 26th Marines, lost many of its sergeants and all its officers, except two second lieutenants and Captain Robert Dunlap. Dunlap commanded Company C, 1st Battalion, 26th Marines, 5th Marine Division, part of a force ordered to storm across the narrow neck of land that connects Mount Suribachi at the western end of the island with the large expanse of flatter land to the east. He led his men out of the carnage on the beach and forward to the attack. Dunlap later said, "If I'm going to get men killed, I want them accomplishing something."

After advancing quickly up the neck of land, Dunlap and his men turned east, destroying Japanese fortifications as they went. Then they moved in the direction of a large airfield on the eastern side of the island. Now far in advance of the rest of the American attack forces, they paused to wait for support. With an open area of about 400 yards of rolling hills in front of him, Dunlap could see

Waves of U.S. Marines in landing craft approach Iwo Jima on February 19, 1945. The American flag was planted on Mount Suribachi (background) four days later, but fighting lasted over a month.

Above. *Captain Robert Dunlap, who led his men off the beach at Iwo Jima.* Above right. *Marines of the 4th Division crowd the black-sand beaches under heavy Japanese fire, February 19, 1945.*

that they had pierced the middle of a heavily defended area. Beyond the hills, he could make out a cliff face dotted with fortifications.

As Japanese artillery from the cliff began to pinpoint Company C's position, Dunlap watched a Japanese soldier stand up and walk calmly back toward the rear. This gave him an idea. Instructing his men not to shoot at the Japanese soldier, he rose and walked toward the enemy lines in just the same manner, hoping the Japanese would mistake him for one of their own. "My medal [citation] says I crawled. . . . There's no way to crawl [that distance] without getting killed, so I walked just like the Japanese." The ruse worked. He mounted the top of a ridge nearly 400 yards in front of his lines and looked out at the large guns hidden on the other side of

the rise and in front of the cliff.

"All of a sudden the Japs realized who I was. . . . I got back running and diving. I'd dive into a bomb crater . . . and then look for my next hole, [then] I'd zigzag, dive. The Japs were on me all the time." His own men covered his retreat with a storm of fire. He rejoined them on the low sand hill from which he had started out. By now, the American advance had ground to a halt in the face of the enemy's intense artillery and mortar fire. Company C's flanks were unprotected, and the battalion commander ordered the men to fall back 200 yards, flush with the line that marked the rest of the advance.

Dunlap, however, remained at the front to act as a forward observer as his men fell back. Out front in a foxhole on the exposed hillside, he presented an inviting target to the Japanese. Runners from his company brought several field telephones to him, and Dunlap used them to call in coordinates for artillery fire. The Japanese hammered the hillside with mortar and artillery rounds but

Dunlap would not move. For forty-eight hours he directed both the marine artillery and naval fire at the caves in the cliff face. By staying at his front-line vantage point, exposed to enemy gunfire, Dunlap made it possible for the bombardment to pinpoint and destroy Japanese resistance in his sector of the attack. Astoundingly, he walked down the hillside unwounded after two days of braving steady fire (although he was seriously wounded later in the battle). The reward for his vigil was the Medal of Honor.

As casualties mounted on Iwo, it was natural that medical corpsmen found themselves in the hottest parts of the action. Pharmacist's Mate First Class Francis Pierce was already a veteran of the landings on Roi-Namur, Saipan, and Tinian. When he landed on Iwo, he knew what to expect but found the beach on Iwo was "hotter than hell."

The Pacific campaign was not fought according to any rules of war. The Japanese refused to honor the Geneva Convention code, which forbade firing on medics. "We didn't wear the Red

Cross because those were just good targets," said Pierce. Pierce received the same training a marine infantryman received in rifle, machine-gun, bayonet, and other combat skills; he had to apply it all to tend the wounded.

Pierce approached his patients with Tommy gun in hand to fend off the enemy. It required "a firefight to get up to them and get them out," and Pierce reasoned that if he came at the Japanese shooting they "would have to do some ducking too." He combined this aggressive approach with a seasoned veteran's knowledge of how to do his job. Pierce memorized every detail of the terrain in his three-company area of responsibility and marked an "X" on his map at every place where he had received fire. Using the map, he then plotted routes that would be relatively safe. Depending on luck and planning, he had avoided being wounded, even while operating in front of the lines for twenty-five days during one of the worst battles of the war.

On March 15 he could find no safe route to the wounded. Pierce and a group of corpsmen and stretcher-bearers were caught in a vicious crossfire while attempting to evacuate some wounded men. Two of his party were hit, but Pierce was able to lead the others back to an aid station while firing his Tommy gun to cover the litter bearers as they carried the wounded to safety. He then returned for the two wounded stretcher-bearers, who had remained under fire.

As Pierce worked on one of the wounded, a Japanese sniper fired from close range and hit the wounded man again. Pierce stood up to draw fire away from his patient, explaining later: "If I stood up, he'd be bound to make a motion. . . . I was a good shot." Pierce used the last of his ammunition to kill the sniper, then hoisted the wounded man on his shoulders and carried him 200 feet back to his line. Ignoring his

"What Should Be Done"

The night before the marine invasion of the Marshall Islands in February 1944, nineteen-year-old Private Richard Sorenson and the rest of his machine-gun crew talked about what their first combat might be like. One soldier asked what they should do if a grenade landed on their position. Sorenson replied matter-of-factly, "Someone should smother it."

On February 2 that "someone" was Sorenson himself. When a Japanese grenade landed near his comrades, he jumped on the charge and took the full force of the explosion in his abdomen and chest. Luckily for the young marine, the shrapnel did not penetrate any vital organs, and he recovered from his wounds. Years later Sorenson said that though his act meant almost certain death, "I didn't have time to think it out. Maybe it was the subconscious telling me what should be done."

Twenty-six marines in the Pacific received the Medal of Honor for jumping on grenades to protect their comrades. Only Sorenson and two others lived to tell about it. On Iwo Jima, Private First Class Jacklyn Lucas pulled not one but two grenades under his body and survived both blasts. Corporal Richard Bush was being treated by a corpsman for leg wounds on Okinawa when a grenade landed between the two men. Bush rolled over onto the charge and absorbed the explosion, suffering terrible wounds to his chest, legs, and hands, as well as fragments in his eyes. But he saved the corpsman, who survived with minor wounds. Bush lost one eye and underwent several operations on the other after the war. He marveled at the fact that he kept his sight. "I think about it every day," he said later, "how lucky I am."

These men who were prepared to sacrifice their lives were not easily forgotten. One day Richard Sorenson received a letter from a college student he did not know. Enclosed was an essay she had written about "the most important thing in my life." The last line read, "Richard Sorenson is a man I held in awe even before I learned his name, because one of the men he saved is my dad."

President Truman presents the Medal of Honor to Jacklyn Lucas on October 5, 1945.

commander, who told him not to go back out, Pierce returned unarmed for the second wounded man and carried him to safety as Japanese fire swept the earth around him. Pierce said later that a bullet "sounds like a bullwhip . . . [if it is] real close. I heard a few that day."

By marking his map assiduously, Pierce identified an area where a particularly troublesome group of Japanese snipers was hiding. The next day, he led a patrol there. A furious firefight cleared the snipers out, but Pierce was shot in the left shoulder and wounded in the back and legs by shrapnel.

Pierce claimed that in all his actions he was just playing carefully calculated percentages, but he was never, as his Medal of Honor citation states, "completely fearless." He said that if he ever met a man who was completely fearless, "I want that man as far away as

he can get because he's going to get me killed. One of the most exhilarating feelings is to know fear and be able to conquer it . . . to be scared to death yet be able to function."

The conquest of Iwo Jima meant that 2,251 crippled B-29s were able to use its airfields for emergency landings before the war's end. One flier who was saved by the conquest of Iwo Jima was U.S. Army Air Corps Staff Sergeant Henry "Red" Erwin of Alabama. Erwin was flying his seventeenth bombing mission to Japan as a radioman of the B-29 *City of Los Angeles* when his ordeal began.

On April 12, 1945, *City of Los Angeles* was the pathfinder, the lead plane

that marked the way for the rest of the bombers on the mission. It was the plane's task to circle about fifty miles from the coast and release phosphorous smoke bombs to guide the bombers that followed. They were dropped down a chute designed for the purpose. Approaching the coast on this mission, Erwin's plane was attacked unexpectedly by Japanese fighters. While eluding the fighters, it continued to circle, waiting for the mission's other planes.

Perhaps what followed was the result of the bomber's efforts to evade the fighters. Or the B-29 might have flown into an air pocket. Or perhaps one of the phosphorous devices was faulty. No one

Above. *Pharmacist's Mate First Class Francis Pierce charted Japanese positions while tending wounded on Iwo Jima.*
Above right. *Corpsmen patch up wounded marines on Iwo Jima.*

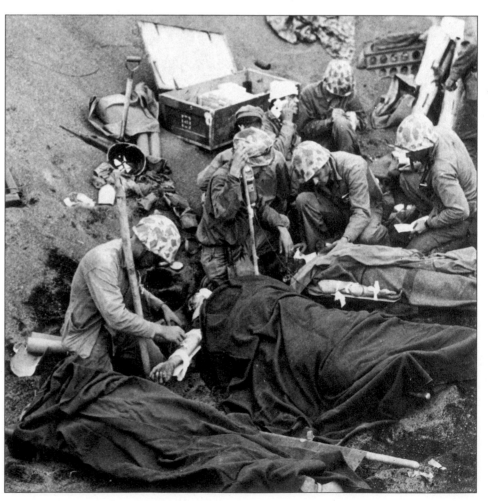

knew why, but just after Erwin dropped one of the bombs, it shot back up the chute and hit him in the face. The device, spewing chemical flame, bounced at his feet. Temporarily blinded by the chemicals and "literally burning alive," Erwin groped for the white-hot bomb, cradled it between his forearm and his body, and began to make his way toward the pilot's window at the front of the aircraft.

The thirty-foot journey "seemed like an eternity" of unspeakable agony. His flight suit had burned off and his upper body was completely in flames by the time he felt his way past the navigator's table. The cockpit was now filled with noxious smoke and flaming phosphorus and the pilot could not see to control the plane, which was headed into a sickening dive. Erwin screamed for the copilot to open the window, then pitched his awful cargo into the sea. He fell to the floor as others extinguished the flames. Although burned in the face beyond recognition and charred over the upper half of his body, Erwin remained conscious. The pilot pulled the plane out of its dive and Erwin heard him turn to the navigator and ask, "How far to Iwo Jima? How fast can we get to Iwo?"

General Curtis LeMay hurried Erwin's Medal of Honor through channels and it was presented to him at bedside on April 19, 1945. Erwin thought that they sped the presentation because they assumed he was dying. But Erwin would not give up on life. "I never thought I would die. I said, 'Lord, you showed me how to get that bomb out, you're surely not going to let me die now.'"

Erwin had to fight another battle with the same courage that had saved his plane from immolation: He endured the agony of forty-one major plastic surgery operations. Later, when he went to work for the U.S. Veterans' Administration, he had to fight down nausea each time he smelled ether when he walked into a VA hospital. He continued to make the visits, however, because he felt a kinship with vets in the burn wards: "I knew the agony and pain they went through. . . . It's indescribable. If I live to be a hundred, I'll never forget it. The pain." ❖

Above. *Henry "Red" Erwin.* Left. *On April 19, 1945, only one week after he was injured, Erwin is given the Medal of Honor by Major General Willis Hale (right) as the crewmen he saved look on.*

Endgame in the Pacific
The Philippines Restored

When he left the Philippines in 1942, General Douglas MacArthur had vowed, "I shall return." There was some question whether the Allied stepping-stone to Japan would be Formosa or the Philippines, but when the Philippines was chosen, MacArthur returned in glory. The U.S. Navy won the last decisive sea battle of the war while providing cover for the October 1944 invasion of Leyte Island. The Japanese military empire was in its death throes, but it would take ten more months and cost countless lives before it would finally die.

John C. Sjogren, the former 4-F who led a battalion-sized attack on the Philippine island of Negros on May 23, 1945.

Curvature of the spine prevented John Sjogren from being accepted for service by his draft board in Rockford, Michigan. Sjogren always wanted to be in the infantry, so he kept trying. Friends from his hometown were fighting in the Pacific with Michigan's 32d Infantry Division. Sjogren desperately wanted to join them and play "an actual part in winning this war."

He never did fight alongside his friends in the 32d, but he persevered and was finally accepted for limited service in 1943. First assigned to serve as an M.P. in Camp McCoy, Wisconsin, he continually volunteered for infantry assignments and was finally sent to the 87th Division. While he was with the 87th in Mississippi, a call went out for volunteers for the Pacific-bound 40th Infantry. Sjogren volunteered once more. He was assigned to Company I, 160th Infantry, 40th Infantry Division.

Sjogren was wounded on Luzon as his unit fought to retake Clark Field. By the time he rejoined his company, it was on the island of Negros. The Americans pushed steadily inland until the Japanese halted the advance before a heavily fortified hill commanding a broad plain. The hill presented the Americans on Negros with the same problem Monte Cassino had presented their comrades in Italy: The enemy held the high ground in a nearly unassailable observation post. Two days of artillery and bombing from the air had done little to break down the Japanese resistance. The men of Company I were told that the hill was jeopardizing the success of the entire Negros operation and that it "had to be taken regardless of cost of life."

Sjogren's squad tackled the hill first. On the morning of May 23, 1945, Sjogren walked point for an entire battalion operation, leading an attack against what appeared to be an insurmountable obstacle. Sjogren knew "we

were in for a rough day. No one was naive enough to believe there wasn't going to be considerable loss of life."

The squad struggled forward, pulling themselves up the nearly vertical slope by grasping tree trunks split by artillery fire. The Japanese pinned them down with fire from machine guns, mortars, and even from antiaircraft guns pointed downward. Sjogren saw his second-in-command take a machine-gun burst in the head. He realized they would all be dead if they stayed there. He ordered his men to pour fire on the fortifications as he went forward, loaded with grenades. "If they had hit me [it would have been] just like hitting a barrel of gasoline. I had grenades in every pocket."

Using the shattered trees, he made his way slowly, painfully up the slope. Somehow he dodged the automatic-weapons fire and reached the first level of fortifications. The men crawling behind him covered him by firing at the gun slits of the enemy fortifications, allowing Sjogren to crawl close enough to leap forward and drop grenades into the first bunkers. The machine-gun fire from them ceased, and the squad started firing on the next fortification. Again, Sjogren rushed up and dropped a grenade.

The attackers leapfrogged their way up the hill, but Sjogren had several close calls. At one of the bunkers the Japanese dropped grenades back out near Sjogren's feet, but he turned and flattened himself against the wall of the bunker and sustained only minor shrapnel wounds. Farther on, a Japanese rifleman froze inexplicably after he had drawn a bead on Sjogren, allowing the sergeant to flip a grenade in his direction. Sjogren later burned his hand when he yanked a machine gun out of a bunker by its barrel, but he escaped without serious injury as the squad took the hill.

Years later, he still could not

The hill attacked by Sjogren and his men near San Jose Hacienda shows damage from several hours of shelling.

The 40th Division had been training for the impending invasion of the Japanese home islands, and Sjogren later discovered that the 40th was slated to go ashore a small island just off Honshu three days before D-day. On his birthday, August 19, Sjogren was just leaving chapel services when he received a telegram saying that he would receive the Medal of Honor. With that he held a distinction that may be unparalleled in U.S. history. He was a 4-F with a Medal of Honor.

The same day Lieutenant General Jonathan Wainwright heard from his Japanese captors the news that the war was over. Wainwright was the man who had taken over the defense of the Philippines in March 1942 when President Roosevelt ordered General MacArthur to Australia. He spent three years and three months in Japanese custody after his defense and surrender of Bataan and Corregidor. Wainwright wrote that on August 19 a Japanese officer in the prison camp began an announcement this way:

believe he survived: "We were taking fire from all directions . . . it just doesn't make any sense that we weren't all killed."

Sjogren's 40th Division was in the field on the Philippine island of Panay on August 6 when the B-29 *Enola Gay* dropped an atomic bomb on Hiroshima. Sixty percent of the city was destroyed in a single blast. Seventy-eight thousand people were killed. Three days later another bomb was dropped on Nagasaki. The atomic bombs destroyed the Japanese will to resist. The next day, August 10, they declared their intention to surrender. The formal signing came on September 2, 1945.

Abstract Words

❝ I was always embarrassed by the words sacred, glorious, and sacrifice and the expression in vain. We had heard them, sometimes standing in the rain almost out of earshot, so that only the shouted words came through, and had read them, on proclamations that were slapped up by billposters over other proclamations, now for a long time, and I had seen nothing sacred, and the things that were glorious had no glory and the sacrifices were like the stockyards at Chicago if nothing was done with the meat except to bury it. . . . Abstract words such as glory, honor, courage, or hallow were obscene... ❞

Ernest Hemingway, **A Farewell to Arms**

239

Aces Over the Pacific

The usual measure of a fighter-pilot's skill and daring is the number of enemy aircraft he shoots down. Many World War II fliers dreamed of breaking Captain Eddie Rickenbacker's World War I record of twenty-six planes. A handful in the Pacific earned the Medal of Honor for their high tallies. Probably many died trying to equal or exceed those totals.

Many pilots, and the press, kept a running total of kills, and this put pressure on strong performers. Gregory "Pappy" Boyington, a marine ace, recalled being hounded as he approached Rickenbacker's mark: "Everywhere I turned there was a correspondent waiting for me and asking the same old question, and it began to get on my nerves something terrific." Going into a dry spell after number twenty-five, and with only a few days left on his tour of duty, Boyington began to push himself for the record. He flew extra missions and took chances that he otherwise might not have taken. "I knew I couldn't stop," he wrote later. "Whether I died in the attempt made no difference." Boyington bagged number twenty-six on January 3, 1944, but was himself shot down and spent the rest of the war in a Japanese prison camp.

One unit especially known for competition was Marine Fighting Squadron 223, also known as the "Flying Fools." Two of its members, Majors Robert Galer and John L. Smith, received Medals of Honor for their dogfights with the enemy. A third 223d pilot, Captain Marion E. Carl, was shot down, then drifted on a raft for several days until he was picked up by friendly island natives. Upon his return to the 223d, the first thing Carl wanted to know was Smith's score. He then asked that Smith be grounded for five days, the time he had been lost at sea, to give Carl a chance to catch up. Carl eventually received the Navy Cross but not the Medal of Honor. He never did catch up to Smith's total of nineteen.

The flamboyant marine pilots overshadowed their counterparts in the navy. Of all the navy fighter pilots who flew off carriers, only two were singled out for the Medal of Honor.

The first was Lieutenant Edward H. "Butch" O'Hare, who received his medal for a single action in February 1942. During an attack on the carrier *Lexington* in the southwest Pacific, the twenty-seven-year-old pilot shot down five bombers, thus becoming the navy's first ace. O'Hare was shot down and killed during a night battle off the Gilbert Islands on November 26, 1943; today the international airport in Chicago bears his name.

The other carrier pilot to receive the medal was Commander David McCampbell of the U.S.S. *Essex*, who in the course of the war downed thirty-four planes, a navy record. McCampbell's highest totals were rung up during the "Marianas Turkey Shoot" of June 1944, when he shot down seven Japanese "Zero" fighters, and the Battle of the Philippines that October, when he scored nine in ninety minutes of fierce action. In all, McCampbell and his air group accounted for over 600 enemy aircraft shot down and numerous ships damaged or sunk. Twenty-six of McCampbell's men qualified as aces.

The competition among some army Air Corps pilots was also fierce. When Lieutenant Colonel Neel E. Kearby arrived at the air base at New Guinea in June 1943, one of the first questions he asked his new commander was who had shot down the most planes and what was his total. The answer was Captain Richard I. Bong, with eleven. Kearby spent the rest of his life trying to catch up to Bong. On March 4, 1944, the day he tied Bong at twenty-five, he was shot down and killed by three enemy fighters that had snuck up on him.

On April 12, 1944, Bong became the first American to shoot down twenty-seven planes. Rickenbacker had promised a case of Scotch to the first army pilot to break his record; he was deluged with offers to pay his end of the bargain. But Bong did not drink, so he gave the liquor to his wing mates and took the two cases of

Left. *Commander David McCampbell's plane notes 34 enemy planes downed, an all-time navy high.* Above. *Marine pilot Major Robert Galer shot down a total of 27 Japanese aircraft during the war.*

Above. *Top ace Richard Bong stands by his fighter, named after his girlfriend and future wife.* Below. *Navy Lieutenant Edward "Butch" O'Hare received the Medal of Honor for single-handedly attacking a group of nine enemy bombers.*

Above. *Colonel Neel Kearby, whose race with fellow ace Richard Bong cost him his life.* Right. *Captain Gregory "Pappy" Boyington was later shot down and imprisoned by the Japanese.*

Coca-Cola sent by his commander, General George C. Kenney. In December General Douglas MacArthur presented Bong with the Medal of Honor as the men of his squadron looked on. Setting aside his prepared speech, MacArthur grasped the young flier by the shoulders and said, "Major Richard Ira Bong, who has ruled the air from New Guinea to the Philippines, I now induct you into the society of the bravest of the brave, the wearers of the Congressional Medal of Honor of the United States."

After Bong's fortieth kill, General Kenney began to fear for the safety of his top ace and ordered him grounded. Bong wanted to keep flying and aim for the fifty mark. One incident changed his outlook, though. As he and Kenney watched from the ground, a Japanese pilot bailed out without a parachute and plummeted some 15,000 feet, landing only about 100 feet from the pair.

It was then that Bong, in Kenney's words, "found out that he was not shooting clay pigeons" and fully realized the stakes in the race of the aces. He was violently ill after the incident and became more amenable to being grounded. Dick Bong returned to the United States and was toasted as America's "Ace of Aces." Less than nine months later, on August 6, 1945, he was killed in a test plane crash. His total of forty kills became the record for World War II.

Lieutenant General Jonathan Wainwright (foreground, second from left) salutes General Douglas MacArthur during surrender ceremonies on September 2, 1945.

Signing for the defeated Japanese are Foreign Minister Mamoru Shigemitsu (background, with cane) and General Yoshijiro Umezu (beside Shigemitsu).

General MacArthur welcomes an emaciated General Wainwright to freedom at Yokohama, August 31, 1945. Wainwright had spent over three years as a POW after his capture on Corregidor in 1942.

"By the order of the Emperor the war has now been amicably terminated."

Wainwright was flown to Yokohama to take part in "one of the great days of history"—September 2, 1945, the day of the surrender of Japan aboard the *Missouri*. An emaciated Wainwright was called forward by General MacArthur to accept the first of the fountain pens he used for the signing. For Wainwright the pen was a "wholly unexpected and very great gift." He also received another unexpected gift from President Truman: a promotion to four-star general along with an invitation to visit the White House.

On September 19, 1945, Wainwright and Truman talked briefly in the president's office. The president then suggested a stroll in the garden because "some photographers want to get a picture of us together." Once in the Rose Garden, Truman led Wainwright to a battery of microphones. Wainwright wrote of the event that when the president stepped up and read a citation that included the words "above and beyond the call of duty," he "suddenly realized when I heard these magic words that this was the citation for the . . . Medal of Honor. . . . Nothing can supplant in my mind that afternoon in the garden of the White House."

On another kind of day in Washington, a gray and rainy August 23, 1945, the weather forced officials to move a Medal of Honor ceremony into the East Room. It was extremely crowded, even in that grand room, in large part because of the number of participants in the ceremony, the largest of its kind ever. President Truman presented twenty-eight Medals of Honor that day. Many of the awards had been delayed because the recipients, including Michael Daly, Ralph Neppel, and Charles MacGillivary, had been badly wounded.

The president stood rigidly at attention as the citations were read, then stepped forward to place a medal around the neck of each recipient in turn. Lieutenant Donald Rudolph, who had earned his medal in the Philippines, remembered, "My knees were knocking. [I was] just out of combat in the Pacific and all of a sudden [I was] in Washington." The president told Rudolph what he said to most of the men he honored: "I would rather have this medal than be President of the United States." In a short speech, Truman declared the men to be a "great cross-section of the United States. . . . These men love peace, but are able to adjust themselves to the necessity of war." As such, they were the living representatives of the kind of fighting man America had produced: the civilian soldier who defeated the warriors of the Axis. These men lived, but many others who earned the Medal of Honor in World War II died in action. In Ernie Pyle's words, "They died and thereby the rest of us can go on and on . . . there is nothing we can do for the ones beneath the wooden crosses, except perhaps to pause and murmur, 'Thanks, pal.'" ❖

The Korean War

Korea Divided

North Korean troops on the march. The Communists spent five years preparing for their June 1950 invasion of the South.

Just before dawn on June 25, 1950, the small Asian peninsula of Korea erupted into war as 90,000 soldiers of the Communist *Inmin Gun,* the North Korean People's Army, swept across the border into South Korea. They met little organized resistance. The South Korean army, already badly outmanned, was caught by surprise; only one-sixth of its forces were on the border that morning. The rest raced north when they got word, but their defense was more suicide than battle as they confronted the heavily equipped *Inmin Gun's* seven divisions one regiment at a time. Three days later, when the capital of Seoul was overrun, the South Korean army had lost three-fourths of its original men.

For centuries Korea had been a single nation. Only after the defeat of Japan in World War II and the occupation of Asia by the Soviet Union and the United States was it split into a Communist north and a Western-aligned south. The division was supposed to be temporary. In 1948, under United Nations auspices, the U.S. zone of southern Korea became the Republic of Korea (ROK). Three weeks later the Soviets announced the creation in the North of the Democratic People's Republic of Korea. Each side of the peninsula vowed it would someday reunite the country under its own form of government. Now, in June 1950, North Korean Premier Kim Il Sung announced confidently that all of Korea would be in Communist hands by the end of the summer.

In Washington, President Harry S Truman faced what he would call "my most important decision as President." Months earlier, his government had determined that Korea was outside America's "defensive perimeter."

But, in the plummeting cold war atmosphere, Truman felt he could not ignore the aggression of a Soviet bloc state against even a remote, dispensable ally of the United States. "If the Communists were permitted to force their way into the Republic of Korea without opposition from the free world, no small nation would have the courage to resist threats and aggression by stronger Communist neighbors," he explained years later. "If this was allowed to go unchallenged it would mean a third world war, just as similar incidents had brought on the second world war." He decided to act.

Within a day of the invasion Truman ordered General Douglas MacArthur, commander of U.S. forces in the western Pacific, to ship South Korea whatever material aid it needed. To emphasize his commitment, he dispatched the 7th Fleet to the area to join MacArthur's command. Washington, as well as MacArthur's Far East Command (FECOM) in Tokyo, was still confident that the North Koreans could be pushed back. "I can handle it with one arm tied behind my back," the general told a State Department delegation. But it was not long before the *Inmin Gun's* lightning march convinced the world otherwise. On June 26 (the twenty-seventh in Korea) Truman dispatched the U.S. Navy and Air Force to the ROK's aid. The next night, one hour after the fall of Seoul, the United Nations Security Council passed a resolution, drafted by the U.S. State Department and approved in advance by the president, calling on all members to help South Korea repel the attack. (The Soviet delegate boycotted the Security Council over a separate dispute so he did not exercise his veto.)

On June 30 Truman granted MacArthur's request for U.S. ground forces to stop the Communist tide. The first men were rushed in from occupation duty in Japan and

Preceding pages. U.S. Marines trudge along a snowy mountain pass during the bitter evacuation from the Chosin Reservoir to Hungnam in North Korea, November-December 1950.

were followed in swift succession by elements of the small post-World War II regular army, the reserves, and, in late autumn, the first draftees. Before the war was over, 5.5 million Americans would serve in Korea. More than 100,000 would return as casualties; 35,000 would never return. Ultimately, twenty-one nations contributed troops or other direct assistance to the Republic of Korea. The United States took command under General Mac-Arthur, providing over 90 percent of the foreign commitment, material and human.

At first the Americans found themselves as helpless as their ROK allies before the North Korean tide. From their opening engagement a few kilometers south of Seoul, the U.S. forces fell back steadily until they clung to a county-sized perimeter around the southeastern port city of Pusan. But Pusan was not Dunkirk. Along the 80-by-160-kilometer front the Americans were able to fight the kind of war they had planned and trained for since World War I. With a clear and continuous battle line, connected by good roads, they could bring their superior firepower and mechanization to bear to halt the *Inmin Gun*'s "human wave" assaults. All August the stretched and weakened North Koreans slammed futilely against the perimeter in a losing battle with time, while behind its lines the U.N. prepared a counterblow.

The landing of the marines on September 15 at Inchon, twenty-nine kilometers west of Seoul, proved to be one of the brilliant moments in American military history. MacArthur boldly struck the North Koreans hundreds of kilometers to their rear, trapping them inside South Korea, then crushed them in a giant pincer between the U.N. X Corps (marines and infantry) moving south from Inchon and the rest of the 8th Army heading north from Pusan. The navy and Joint Chiefs of Staff had predicted failure, but the move was an almost unqualified success. On September 29, in front of hundreds of thousands of wildly cheering Koreans, MacArthur formally announced the restoration to the ROK of the seat of its government.

There the fighting might have ended. The aggressors had been turned back to their own borders. The U.N. had proved its mettle, and the status quo was preserved. But

some 25,000 North Korean soldiers had managed to escape north. In the exhilaration of near-triumph, the nature of the action changed dramatically. "Your military objective is the destruction of the North Korean Armed Forces," Truman cabled MacArthur. On October 1 the first South Korean troops crossed the thirty-eighth parallel into North Korea. The GIs were close behind. The U.N. General Assembly approved of Truman's order at the end of the week.

As the U.N. force swept north, meeting little resistance, civilians and soldiers alike talked confidently of reuniting Korea by Christmas. The 8th Army command ignored increasingly audible rumblings from China that it would tolerate no American presence on its border with Korea. Even reports of a Chinese build-up along the Yalu River were discounted by MacArthur. In case the Chinese did move against his forces, the general confidently told the president in mid-October, "there would be the greatest slaughter." MacArthur's prediction materialized, though in a way he had not envisioned.

The day after Thanksgiving 180,000 Chinese troops attacked the 8th Army on the northwest coast of Korea at the Chongchon River, wiping it out. Three days later, X Corps received similar treatment. At the Chosin Reservoir in northeastern Korea, 120,000 Chinese hit the marines. There followed the longest retreat in U.S. history. By early January the Chinese had recaptured all of Korea to the thirty-seventh parallel, including Seoul. Then, tired and short on supplies, they stopped.

The scene was set for stalemate. On February 5 the U.N. launched a second counteroffensive and again pushed the Communists back. On March 18 Seoul changed hands for the fourth time in less than a year. By now, however, the leaders of the Western world had lost their enthusiasm for reunification. The U.N. General Assembly, reversing its October position, called for a peaceful settlement between North and South Korea. On March 20 Truman notified MacArthur that he was preparing to announce his willingness to negotiate peace and that U.N. forces were not to advance beyond the thirty-eighth parallel. MacArthur replied by openly requesting freedom to strike at China. Each man sought to end the war, but their prescriptions offered no room for compromise. Moreover, the public argument had U.S. allies, as

President Truman decorates General MacArthur with his fifth Distinguished Service Medal on Wake Island, October 1950. Six months later he fired the general for insubordination.

well as its own citizens, growing jittery. Truman ordered MacArthur to be silent. MacArthur defied him by sending a letter, read on the floor of Congress, charging that "There is no substitute for victory." Faced with this repeated insubordination, on April 11 the president relieved MacArthur of his command. Though he arguably had little choice, Truman's action sapped much of the remaining public support for the already unpopular war.

During the war, Truman sought neither a declaration of war nor even the informal approval of Congress, avoiding that arm of government by refusing to classify the conflict as a war. "Police action" was the term the White House preferred. Nevertheless, it was a war—and one for which Americans were called upon to sacrifice their lives and dollars without really understanding why. The cause was not the easily grasped self-defense against attack, nor even the maintenance of American rights abroad. Rather, it was an issue of principle—the maintenance of the United Nations and the balance of power—and of ideology. As similar issues had been in World War I, those concepts could have been sold to the public. But the Truman administration was too caught up in reacting to events on the battlefield and at the U.N. to perform the necessary educating and persuading.

The result was one of the least popular wars in American history. When the U.N. forces were driving the *Inmin Gun* northward, the public was enthusiastic. Two-thirds of those polled in October 1950 favored conquering North Korea. Once the victories ceased, however, so did

domestic support. Six months after Truman committed American troops the numbers reversed: Sixty-six percent of Americans polled called for withdrawal from Korea. The president's own approval rating dropped to 23 percent, the lowest of his presidency.

The Americans thought the war would be over in a few weeks. Instead, it lasted another two years, to be concluded only by an armistice. During the negotiations the fighting continued, but no longer was its goal a victory on the field. Strong points and perimeters were assaulted to remind the enemy of the U.N.'s seriousness and to keep the troops in fighting trim. Both sides knew, however, that the final settlement would be at the thirty-eighth parallel. It was a disconcerting style of warfare for the GIs, who were used to a war of movement with conquest the ultimate aim.

The Korean conflict was fought more like wars of the nineteenth and early twentieth centuries than the modern technical war the Americans had trained for. In the first months, when U.N. forces faced a highly mobile, unmechanized enemy in isolated actions over unimproved, mountainous terrain, it resembled the Indian Wars of the American West. Later, when the war became a stalemate, it turned into the grinding trench warfare of World War I. Weapons also harkened to the past. Although air power and modern artillery played an impor-

248

The Korean War began with a Communist invasion of the South (left inset) that drove U.N. forces to a perimeter around Pusan. The September 1950 Inchon landing and breakout from Pusan swept the Communists almost to the Chinese border (center inset) *before Chinese intervention pushed the U.N. back into South Korea (right inset). After more months of fighting, the front stabilized near the 38th parallel, where a bloody stalemate prevailed until the July 1953 armistice.*

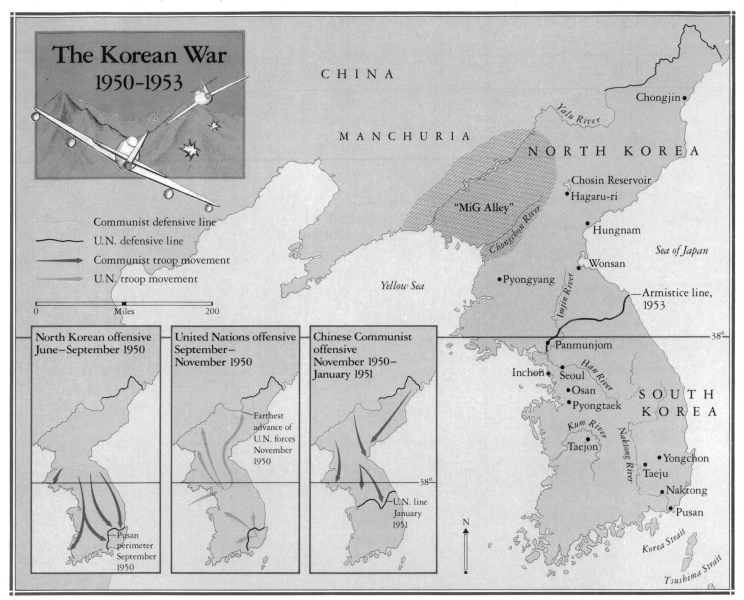

The Korean War
1950–1953

Communist defensive line
U.N. defensive line
Communist troop movement
U.N. troop movement

0   Miles   200

CHINA

MANCHURIA

Yalu River

Chongjin•

NORTH KOREA

Chosin Reservoir
•Hagaru-ri

"MiG Alley"

Chongchon River

•Hungnam

Sea of Japan

•Wonsan

•Pyongyang

Imjin River

Armistice line, 1953

Yellow Sea

38°

Panmunjom

North Korean offensive June–September 1950

United Nations offensive September–November 1950

Farthest advance of U.N. forces November 1950

Chinese Communist offensive November 1950–January 1951

38°

U.N. line January 1951

Inchon• Seoul• Han River
•Osan
•Pyongtaek

SOUTH KOREA

Kum River

Naktong River

•Taejon

•Yongchon
Taeju•
•Naktong
•Pusan

Korea Strait

Pusan perimeter September 1950

N

Tsushima Strait

tant role, the brunt of the fighting was born by the rifle-wielding foot soldier. In the constricted valleys and hill masses that blanket Korea, bayonets and even trench knives achieved a renewed importance. The Communists' communication lines consisted of bugles, whistles, and drums, and their transportation system relied on the feet and backs of their soldiers. The U.S. Army could never quite adapt itself to this guerrilla style of warfare.

Equally disconcerting to the GIs was that they had to face the enemy from the very first days of the war. This contrasted sharply with the U.S. experience in the two world wars. In those cases Americans entered war only after a long psychological, physical, and material build-up—and after its allies had taken much of the fight out of the enemy. In Korea, though, a shrunken peacetime military found itself pitted against a foe at the peak of its power and motivation. That fact alone would take a shocking toll in American lives in the first weeks of war. The centuries-old belief that the United States could not lose a war was to face in Korea its severest test. ◈

"Police Action" in Asia

The undeclared war in Korea pitted U.S. and other United Nations forces against a determined Communist foe. Clockwise from above. Three GIs of the 160th Infantry warm themselves by a homemade stove, February 1952; U.S. Marines in Seoul stand ready as a North Korean, his clothes on fire, crawls out of a dugout; an M26 tank fires at enemy positions in South Korea, August 3, 1950; a soldier of the 24th Infantry, 25th Division, fires into a Communist bunker on the west-central front, May 4, 1951.

Above. A medic of the 3d Battalion, 23d Infantry, 2d Division, tends a wounded soldier as other U.N. troops scramble up the side of a hill, February 14, 1952. Left. Marines in eastern Korea duck in their bunker as an enemy 82MM mortar shell explodes nearby. To a nation that had just endured a world war, the Korean conflict was expected to be brief and decisive; instead American soldiers faced seasoned North Korean and Chinese regulars in bloody battles reminiscent of previous all-out wars.

Fighting for Time
General William F. Dean

The first commander of U.S. ground forces in Korea was Major General William F. Dean. For twenty days Dean and his 24th Infantry Division fought a holding action against the North Koreans while other United Nations forces created a defensive perimeter around the southern port of Pusan. His commander, Lieutenant General Walton Walker, credited Dean with saving South Korea. Dean countered: "Very few of the things I did could not have been done by any competent sergeant–and such a sergeant would have done some of them better."

A Communist tank destroyed by General William Dean on a Taejon street.

On the evening of June 30, 1950, Major General William F. Dean jumped into his sedan and told the driver to rush him to the Itazuki airfield in Japan. Minutes before, the commander of the Japan-based 24th Infantry Division had received orders to fly at once to Tokyo for an important conference. The summons came as no surprise. Since he first heard of the Korean invasion, Dean had been expecting something big–despite FECOM assurances that the ROK army would soon quell this "border incident." He had made a different prediction: It was the beginning of World War III.

Before Dean had traveled more than a few miles, he got orders to return to his headquarters. At midnight the teletype began to clatter. Lieutenant General Walton Walker, 8th Army commander, was ordering Dean's division to Korea to act as a delaying force while the U.N. organized its counterattack. The urgency of the situation, combined with mobilization and transportation problems, meant that the commitment would be made piecemeal. An initial

unit of two reinforced rifle companies, under Lieutenant Colonel Charles B. Smith, would fly at once to Pusan. From there its men were to advance north until they contacted the enemy. Dean, given temporary command of U.S. forces in

Scenes from "That War in Korea," an NBC News film. Above. *General Dean (right) confers with General Walton Walker at the front in the first days of the war.*

Korea, was to follow closely behind, accompanied only by his headquarters and one infantry battalion. The rest of the division, spread out all over southern Japan, would have to make it across the Korea and Tsushima Straits to Korea as best it could.

Dean read the orders grimly. He knew the usual fate of regiments committed in bits and pieces against an advancing army. He also knew how very unprepared the division was. Long years had passed since the 24th had earned the name "the Victory Division" for its defeat of the Japanese Imperial Army. Since then, the division had fallen to two-thirds strength, and what remained had grown fat on occupation duty. Only 15 percent of its officers and men had seen battle. Dean was not optimistic about how long he could delay the North Koreans. But he was a tough commander and intended to give them a fight.

Piercing through the dense fog, an air force C-45 carried General Dean and his staff into Taejon, a key air and rail center in the middle of South Korea ninety-six kilometers south of the advancing North Korean army. Chaos confronted the Americans there. Tens of thousands of fleeing Koreans—civilians, national police, even soldiers—jammed the rain-drenched streets in a continuous southward wave. The scene at the U.S. advance command post was only slightly less disordered. Communication lines were spotty or nonexistent. ROK army liaison officers assured Dean that their men were fighting well against the North Koreans in the mountains to the east, but there was no way to confirm this. And the U.S. force was still scattered between Taejon, Pusan, and Japan.

On July 4 Dean ordered Task Force Smith to hold at Osan. He sent the 34th Infantry to back it up at the strategically crucial Pyongtaek-Ansong line, a narrow neck between the Yellow Sea and the rugged central mountain range. If they could stop the enemy anywhere north of Pusan, this seemed the likeliest spot.

A wounded GI grimaces in pain during evacuation from a threatened area.

With so small and green a force, Dean knew it was a long shot, but if the Americans could put some life back into the ROK resistance, it just might work.

Early the next day thirty-three Russian-built T34 tanks, followed by two North Korean regiments, bore down

on the 540 officers and men of Task Force Smith. The cool assuredness of the GIs—who had marched into this "police action" believing that the very sight of U.S. soldiers would send the North Koreans scurrying back behind the border—melted away. In its place grew panic, as Americans fell to the fire of enemy rifles, grenades, and mortar shells. The six available rounds of outdated U.S. artillery were ineffectual against the overwhelming tank force. Air support could not find its way through the low clouds. Communications broke down. There was not even enough small-arms ammunition.

An American soldier carries a wounded comrade down a war-torn street during heavy fighting in South Korea.

Realizing there was no hope of hanging on, Colonel Smith called retreat. Within minutes it became an uncontrollable rout. In the driving rain men poured down the hills in ones and twos. They abandoned their headgear, weapons, the dead, even the dozens of wounded who could not walk.

The rout did not stop at Osan. On July 6, after learning the fate of the task force, the commander of the 34th pulled his regiment back twenty-four kilometers without engaging the enemy. Dean was furious at this news. He jumped into his jeep, raced to the 34th's command post, ordered the regiment

back to Pyongtaek, and relieved the commander. But he knew this would not be enough.

Two days later, when General Walker flew into Taejon to find out how Dean's delaying action was faring, the two generals decided to drive up to the front to have a look. What they saw sickened them. The 34th had been told to hold at Chonan, but the officers were having a difficult time keeping their troops on the line. Twice the new commander, Colonel Robert Martin, had to go to the front to settle things down and induce the men to fight. The second time he was cut down while leading a bazooka assault against a group of tanks. Martin's death completely broke the regiment's spirit. As Dean and Walker watched from a nearby hill, the Americans once more fled the front line.

Now the job would be doubly hard, for there was no good defensive line before Taejon. On July 16 two North Korean divisions, supported by some fifty tanks, broke through the main U.S. line at the Kum River. Taejon was now less than 24 kilometers away, defended only by the U.S. 34th.

On July 19 the enemy reached the U.S. line, thinly spread out five kilometers north of Taejon. The defenders were hopelessly outmatched. Against the Americans' assortment of leftover

A tank shifts into battle position, its motion blurring the picture.

weaponry, the North Koreans delivered as heavy an artillery barrage as Dean had ever seen. It took extraordinary effort by the officers to keep the men from bolting, but they held. When the enemy threatened to break through, the division commander stood at the front with his men, directing tank fire. At day's end, the U.S. still held its position.

Artillery fires against North Korean positions on the front lines.

When gunfire dwindled to sporadic sniping, Dean returned to his command post for a few hours' rest. Before dawn, though, the din of a major assault wrenched him awake. The *Inmin Gun* had broken through the line. At 6:30 A.M. the general heard that North Korean tanks had entered Taejon. For now, there were no decisions to make. The 34th's new commander was leading a fighting withdrawal. When the regiment reached Taejon, Dean would lead the retreat himself. But he had grown tired of sitting and waiting—especially when the enemy was at the gate. So, coining a term that would become famous among the men of the 8th Army, he went "tank hunting."

Dean, his aide Lieutenant Arthur Clarke, and his Korean interpreter headed out into the streets of Taejon. Spotting a stalled T34 in the center of a once-busy intersection, the general commandeered the first artillery truck he

could find and guided it into position. But the nervous gunner missed the tank with all five of his rounds. Cursing, Dean resumed the hunt. Not too far from two more idle tanks he found a soldier carrying a new-model 3.5-inch bazooka and a single round of ammunition. Dean grabbed the man, and the small party crept toward their prey. Suddenly, machine-gun fire from one of the turrets scattered over their heads. The bazooka party ran for cover. Again Dean led them on the attack. Maneuvering to within five meters of the street, he ordered the gunner to fire when they drew within range of the tank. But the bazooka man was too jittery and wasted his one round while the tanks were still well over ninety meters away. Dean had

An American soldier fires an M1 rifle at the approaching enemy.

to stand there helplessly as the giants trundled past. Overcome with rage, he emptied his pistol into the last one.

Now he was really angry. After calling in air strikes against the enemy tank force, Dean continued his hunt. This time he got lucky. A lone North Korean tank passed right by the regimental command post. Rounding up another bazooka man and an ammunition carrier, Dean's little army set out in hot pursuit, dodging and returning sniper fire all the way. They found the T34 parked on a bombed-out business street lined with

Two GIs narrowly escape the blast of an exploding round.

crumbling two-story buildings. The first time they approached it they were knocked back by a small-arms barrage. They tried another direction but again received fire. The third time Dean decided to stage the attack from inside one of the buildings, where they could strike at the tank from above.

Silently the Americans entered the rear of the building closest to the tank and climbed to the second floor. Dean and the gunner crawled to the window. The tank stood less than three and one-half meters away. Without speaking, Dean pointed where to aim. The bazooka fired—and this time scored a direct hit. The general had his tank.

It was now nearing dusk. At least fifteen enemy tanks lay dead in the streets. Dean's division had held back the North Koreans for the time Walker needed to deploy fresh troops. Dean gave the order to withdraw.

Shortly after 6:00 P.M., the convoy of Americans began to move out. Enemy fire grew heavier from all sides. It knocked out several of the lead trucks, blocking the division's planned exit route. Then North Korean rifle and machine-gun snipers lined up along the approach, blazing away at the stalled vehicles. Dean urgently looked for an alternate route, but word came that a large force of North Korean infantry was

General William Dean at a North Korean prison compound. This picture was released shortly before Dean's own release at Panmunjom on September 4, 1953.

rapidly advancing on the city center. The convoy had no choice but to move.

The rest of the evening was a story of increasingly worse fortune for General Dean: ambushes, roadblocks, broken-down vehicles, lost weapons. By nightfall he found himself on foot, leading seventeen stray soldiers on a cross-country trek through North Korean lines. After guiding them across a river, up a ridge, and around a machine-gun nest, Dean relinquished the lead to help carry a badly wounded man. In the darkness and under order of silence, few noticed the general falling farther and farther back. Fewer still saw when he left to get the now-delirious man some water from a nearby stream. Nobody knew when he plunged down an embankment, cracked his head, and passed out.

Dean spent the next thirty-six days in the Korean hills trying to reach U.S. lines. For most of the time he had no food and very little water. The fall had broken his shoulder and given him a concussion and severe stomach injuries. During his trek he would lose 80 pounds, dropping to an emaciated 130 on his six-foot frame. Still, Dean eluded capture a half-dozen times and managed to travel fifty-six kilometers south before being sold out by some Korean civilians on August 25. His ordeal was only beginning; for the next three years he would hold the bitter rank of POW.

Dean's treatment at the hands of his captors was atypical. They kept him in total seclusion; he never saw another American nor even a Chinese. The first weeks were brutal. His guards stripped him and forced him to sit on the floor of an unheated room in freezing weather. His captors interrogated and propagandized him for days, allowing him no sleep and little food. Even though his wounds abscessed, he was refused treatment. Finally, unable to break his spirit, his chief interrogator threatened torture.

Dean was already concerned that his captivity gave the Communists a propaganda tool. Now he grew fearful that in his weakened condition he might reveal something under torture. He determined that his only way out was to kill himself, and he almost succeeded. Only a faulty bolt in the gun he stole from a sleeping guard prevented his death.

After that, his treatment improved. The North Koreans did not want to lose so valuable a prize. They still kept him isolated and, for most of his captivity, refused even to let him stand up. But they made sure he was cared for adequately to keep him alive. The months stretched to three years. Finally, on September 4, 1953, a gaunt William Dean ended his tour of duty in Korea at Freedom Village. He came home to receive the Medal of Honor for his intrepid stand at Taejon. ✶

Holding the Line
The Naktong Bulge

While General Dean's 24th Division retreated down the Korean peninsula, thousands of American troops poured into a perimeter surrounding the port of Pusan. By August 31, 1950, United Nations troops outnumbered North Korean forces by almost two to one. The North Koreans, however, believed they could win the war if they struck the Pusan perimeter with all their remaining strength.

Less than sixty-four kilometers west of Pusan, a ridge-backed pocket of land juts into a bend of the Naktong River. This six-by-eight-kilometer stretch, the so-called "Naktong Bulge," saw the heaviest fighting on the Pusan perimeter during the late summer of 1950. On August 5 the enemy broke through the bulge, to be driven back only after two weeks of intense warfare costing several thousand lives. The worst was yet to come. Realizing that time, casualties, and the huge U.S. build-up were daily sapping the *Inmin Gun* of its material and moral advantage, the leaders of the North Korean army planned an offensive they hoped would end the war. It was to begin on August 31. The attack would strike the entire perimeter, but the heaviest blow would land on the Naktong Bulge. The next fifteen days were to be the bloodiest of the Korean War.

Strung out along the river's edge, the "Manchu Raiders"—the U.S. 9th Infantry, 2d Division—watched and waited. The Manchus had been guarding the bulge since early August, a few days after their arrival in Korea from Fort Lewis, Washington. Less than three weeks later, they had become combat veterans. They understood that surviving a "human wave" assault meant keeping all sides of a defensive perimeter covered and being ready to fight at close range with grenades, small arms, even bayonets. They no longer underestimated—or overestimated—their opponents. On the sweltering night of August 31, their mission was to hold the perimeter at all costs—in General Walker's words, to "stand or die." The Manchus watched for the green flares, crashing cymbals, and cries of "Manzai!" that signaled a North Korean attack.

At the midpoint of the bulge, one group of soldiers did not wait. Several days before, a reconnaissance patrol had discovered a North Korean command post near the Paekchin Ferry dock across the Naktong. Division headquarters ordered a combat team, Task Force Manchu, to destroy the post, capture its occupants, and learn what it could of enemy plans. The team consisted of a regimental reserve unit of 250 men reinforced by men drawn from two heavy weapons companies—a total of about 700 men. The date of the operation was set, coincidentally, for August 31.

As darkness settled on the Naktong, the weapons companies moved to the base of a hill overlooking the Paekchin Ferry. The reserve force was still preparing itself some eight kilometers to the east. Leaving the main force below, First Lieutenant Edward Schmitt guided about fifty men of the heavy weapons units up the hill to cover the river crossing. It was a tortuous climb in the still-brutal heat of evening, made worse because the troops also hauled mortars and heavy machine guns up the rocky incline. At 10:00 P.M. Schmitt and his men were only halfway up the hill setting up weapons when they heard cries and shooting below.

The North Koreans had just launched their Great Naktong Offensive. Wading quietly over bridges they had concealed carefully under the water, an entire enemy division crossed unseen into the 9th Infantry's sector. Thick fog aided their deception. In half an hour North Korean soldiers ambushed and massacred the main body of the heavy weapons companies waiting at the foot of the hill. The surprised Americans could not organize a defense, and the reserve force never reached the area. Only the men on the hillside escaped the slaughter. Under Schmitt's command, they scurried to the top of the nearest knob and dug into a tight perimeter. The enemy force moved past them on its march east. "Operation Manchu" was now a desperate defensive action.

A marine squad patrols the hills near the Naktong River in search of North Korean snipers on August 19, 1950, two weeks before the Great Naktong Offensive.

In the first night of the Great Naktong Offensive the North Koreans scored impressive victories. By the morning of September 1 they held positions thirteen kilometers inland and had almost reached 2d Division headquarters in the town of Yongsan. They had cut the division in two, dividing the 9th Infantry from its sister regiments, and split the Manchu Raiders themselves into numerous isolated pockets.

Daylight brought a vision of horror to Schmitt's tiny outpost. From their hilltop perimeter they could see the hills around them alive with enemy soldiers. Where a U.S. infantry company had stood one kilometer up the ridge above them, North Koreans now looked down. Below, hundreds more of the enemy crossed over the river, bringing truckloads of supplies and ammunition. Lieutenant Schmitt surveyed his position

quickly. He counted five officers and about sixty-five men. To defend themselves they had one Browning Automatic Rifle, two heavy machine guns, twenty M1 rifles, and approximately forty carbines and pistols. Their food and water consisted only of what the men had brought up the hill. For medical supplies they had the pack of a single medic. And they had a radio. With the radio Schmitt called headquarters for help but could get little encouragement. There simply was no force available to come to their aid.

In the light of day the Schmitt group could no longer elude the enemy, and that afternoon the North Koreans struck. They were soon repulsed, so they tried again at night, increasing their force to company size. Three times they charged the tight perimeter. Three times the Americans beat them back. But the odds remained with the enemy. As September 2 dawned, the Schmitt group remained intact, although it was desperately low on ammunition, food, and water.

Firepower was the first priority if the defenders were to have any chance of survival. Master Sergeant Travis Watkins, an eleven-year army veteran from a family of military men, knew that the only sure source of supply sat right in front of them—the enemy's own weapons. The problem was reaching them. All night long Watkins had dodged the bullets of North Korean snipers as he moved back and forth over the perimeter, directing defense and encouraging his platoon. Now, spotting a pair of enemy soldiers about forty-five meters out, he aimed his rifle and fired. As they fell, he leaped from his hole and dashed over to collect their weapons. He had gone only thirty meters when three North Koreans emerged from hiding and opened fire. Watkins killed them, too, then grabbed up the weapons and ammunition of the five dead men and raced back to the perimeter.

An hour later Watkins again rose from his protected position. One of his platoon's machine guns had come under grenade barrage. He spied the source of the attack, stood up for better aim, and fired at the attackers. Enemy machine-gun fire caught him in the midsection, breaking his back, but through sheer strength of will Watkins kept pulling the trigger until he had killed all six

A machine-gun squad of the 1st Cavalry Division fires .50-caliber rounds at North Korean troops patrolling the far side of the Naktong River on September 4, 1950, on the fifth day of the offensive.

grenade throwers. Then he fell into his hole, paralyzed from the waist down.

The broiling sun was rising high on the second day of the Schmitt group's ordeal. Again Schmitt called for help. This time some arrived–an airdrop of supplies. But the plane had trouble targeting the tiny perimeter, and most of the supplies rolled down the slopes into enemy hands. Like his paralyzed sergeant, Private First Class Joseph R. Ouellette was not the type to sit pinned down. He scrambled down the hill to retrieve the airdropped water cans, only to find they had all broken on impact. Ouellette returned empty-handed.

As evening approached, Ouellette slipped out once more to gather

ammunition from the enemy dead strewn over the hillside. Grabbing all he could, Ouellette headed back to the perimeter, only to come face to face with a North Korean. Dropping an arm load of grenades, Ouellette leaped on the soldier and killed him in hand-to-hand combat. Then he picked up his ammunition and brought it to his unit.

The next forty-eight hours were a perpetual torment for the shrinking band of survivors. The enemy kept up the pressure night and day, alternating artillery barrages with infantry attacks. On September 3 alone, the North Koreans charged the perimeter some twenty separate times. During one of those onslaughts, Ouellette's quick re-

flexes finally failed him. Six times he had escaped exploding grenades by leaping from his foxhole into the rain of enemy small-arms fire. The sixth time he did not make it back.

By September 4 it was clear that the Schmitt group could not survive another day of assault. Half the men and all but two of the officers were dead. Schmitt himself had been killed by a mortar blast. (He was to be awarded the Distinguished Service Cross posthumously.) The rest had gone without sleep for over 100 hours. They were completely out of food; the only water they had to drink in two days was what they had wrung from their clothes following a rainstorm the night before. Ammunition was down to a single clip per man. The only hope of survival for any of them was to break into groups of four and five and sneak out separately under cover of darkness. At 10:00 P.M. the thirty remaining men divided up. One, however, refused to go.

Since being wounded, MSgt. Watkins had refused all food and water, insisting it should go to those who were fighting. Now he told the others to leave him behind. Any attempt to save him would imperil the lives of others, he said. He asked only that someone load his carbine and hand it to him. He placed the rifle on his chest, muzzle under his chin. Then he smiled. Just as he had spent his last immobile days encouraging his men to hold on, he now wished them luck.

Twenty-two men eventually made it back to friendly lines. Two who did not, MSgt Travis Watkins and PFC Joseph Ouellette, were posthumously awarded the Medal of Honor.

Meanwhile, other Americans were turning the tide along the Pusan perimeter. On September 2 the 2d Division cleared Yongsan of enemy forces. With the help of marines and the U.S. Air Force, the division pushed to restore the river line. In small units, Americans stood and fought, using bayonets, knives, even their bare hands. To the North Koreans, these must have seemed very different men from those they so easily humbled north of Taejon. Fighting sputtered along the perimeter but was soon to be overshadowed by events farther north: the landing at Inchon and the allied march through North Korea to the Chinese frontier. ✦

Right. *Private First Class Joseph R. Ouellette, who braved enemy fire to retrieve ammunition.* Below. *GIs hold a ridge on the Naktong perimeter on September 23, 1950.*

Valor in a Mountain Pass
The Chosin Reservoir

On September 15, 1950, General Douglas MacArthur's X Corps struck the enemy rear at Inchon Harbor, near the South Korean capital of Seoul. The brilliant maneuver shattered the North Korean offensive. Soon Seoul was liberated and X Corps and the 8th Army headed north to end Communist rule over all Korea. The 8th drove up the west coast to the Manchurian border, and X Corps approached from the east. Despite thinning supply lines and increasing evidence of impending Chinese intervention, however, MacArthur believed the war would soon be over. His error presaged one of the greatest defeats in U.S. military history. The 8th Army was nearly destroyed. Only the tremendous fighting spirit and personal sacrifice of individual marines saved X Corps from a similar fate.

The U.N. advance to the north ended the day after Thanksgiving, when 300,000 Chinese Communist troops poured south from the Yalu River. Half of them defeated the 8th Army forces on the western side of Korea. Three days later, at the Chosin Reservoir in eastern Korea, the rest of the Chinese hit the marines and infantrymen of X Corps. They too retreated but fought all the way out, bringing their dead, wounded, and all their equipment with them.

The 5th and 7th Marine Regiments were caught halfway up the finger-shaped reservoir at Yudam-ni. The only route through the mountain range was along the forbidding Toktong Pass to Hagaru-ri and from there to Koto-ri and finally the port of Hungnam. Eight thousand marines battled their way out of Yudam-ni. It was bitter cold on the mile-high pass, but the climate was less a concern than the terrain: Mountains closed in on either side of the dirt road, turning the marines' escape route into a shooting gallery for the Chinese.

On November 28 Captain William Barber, Company F, 2d Battalion, 7th Marines, received orders to hold the Toktong Pass until the American marines could escape from Yudam-ni. He positioned his 240-man company on a hill overlooking the highway and established a small but strong perimeter. It took the marines hours of hacking away at the frozen earth to dig even shallow foxholes, but Barber made his men keep digging. His precautions were justified. That night a regiment of Chinese attacked. The company held but took twenty-two casualties.

The next day Barber radioed regiment headquarters, telling of the attack and the approximate size of the opposing force. His colonel advised him to withdraw. But Barber contested the order. There were two reasons for his decision: his own wounded and the thousands of marines still trapped in Yudam-ni.

The perimeter held through five days of grinding day-and-night fighting. When Company F marched off the hill and joined the tail end of the marine retreat line, only seventy-two of its men were still on their feet. One of the casualties was Captain Barber himself, a bullet lodged in his groin. But they had left behind them over 1,000 dead Chinese. More important, they had kept the pass clear for their comrades.

While the 5th and 7th Marines battled down the narrow mountain passage to Hagaru-ri, Captain Carl Sitter's Company G, 3d Battalion, 1st Marines, fought its way up from Koto-ri. Sitter was guarding X Corps's command post on November 28 when he heard that the Chinese had captured the only road out of Hagaru-ri. The next morning he was ordered to add his company to a task force under the command of Lieutenant Colonel Douglas Drysdale of the British Royal Marine Corps. They were to reopen the highway and deliver needed supplies to Hagaru-ri.

At 9:00 A.M. Sitter's marines, Drysdale's 41st Commandos, a U.S. Army company, eight tanks, and 100 supply trucks began the eighteen-kilometer clearing operation. They faced fierce opposition. Every few hundred meters enemy machine-gun and small-arms fire forced the column to halt until the U.N. troops could clear the nearby hill. At sunset the convoy got started again through the hail of enemy bullets and mortar shells. One shell landed in the path of Sitter's jeep, sparing him but incinerating a box of cigars he had just received from home. That made him angrier than the loss of the jeep. When he saw his first sergeant drive by in a truck, Sitter jumped onto the running board and continued.

Again the lurching convoy came to

Chosin-Hungnam Evacuation Route
November–December 1950

Chosin Reservoir

Yudam-ni

East Hill

Toktong Pass

Hagaru-ri

Kŏto-ri

Hamhung

Hungnam

Sea of Japan

N

0   Kilometers   40

Map. *The 130-kilometer retreat from the Chosin Reservoir to the North Korean port of Hungnam pitted U.S. forces against tremendous odds of freezing weather, hostile terrain, and constant attacks by Communist troops. Starting at Yudam-ni, the 5th and 7th Marine Regiments battled their way through the Toktong Pass while other Americans held Hagaru-ri and the strategic high point of East Hill. Assembling at Hagaru-ri, X Corps then followed a mountainous road to the sea.* **Below.** *Elements of the convoy round a corner along the frozen escape route.*

Christmastime in Korea. A soldier eats frozen beans one at a time on the road from Chosin. When photographer David Douglas Duncan asked this young man what he wanted for Christmas, he replied, "Give me tomorrow."

a dead stop. Sitter ran forward to see what the trouble was and found that the front of the column had been halted by machine-gun fire. Drysdale was wounded. He told Sitter to take charge of getting the supplies to Hagaru-ri. The captain ordered the task force into a circle facing out ("like in the Western movies," he later said). When the Chinese charged they fought them off in a pitched battle, then headed down the road once more.

The task force groped its way through the black night, unsure of how far it had come and how many more kilometers it had yet to go to reach Hagaru-ri. Finally, the lead truck turned a corner and caught the welcome sight of lights a few thousand meters ahead. "We've made it home," thought Sitter. No sooner had the men begun to breathe easier, however, than dozens of Chinese emerged near the road and opened fire. Five more trucks were lost before the U.N. force reached the perimeter. But the supplies that they brought—ammunition, blankets, food, and medicine—saved the lives of hundreds of hurt and exhausted marines.

The men of Sitter's company were given only one night to rest on rock-hard ground in a snow-covered field, then went back to fighting. The new objective was East Hill, a point dominating the withdrawal route from Hagaru-ri. The Chinese had wrested the hill from a motley assortment of army headquarters personnel the night of November 28. A few hours later, however, another hodgepodge of U.S. servicemen had retaken part of it and were now barely holding on. Their commander was Major Reginald Myers, executive officer of the 3d Battalion, 1st Marines.

When the army force lost East Hill, the commander of the 3d Battalion, Lieutenant Colonel Thomas Ridge, had ordered Myers to grab all the men he could find to seize and hold the hill. This was not the usual line of work for a staff officer, nor for the twenty-five or so marines he gathered up. They were, Myers said, "the cooks and the candlestick makers and the bakers and whatnot," adding, "I'm sure that everybody was just absolutely frightened to death about the whole thing." Nevertheless, Myers put rifles in their hands and marched them to East Hill, adding anyone else he found along the way who seemed to have nothing better to do. By the time he reached the hill, he had between fifty and seventy-five marines. To that force he added approximately 200 stray army personnel (more cooks and bakers) whom he found milling around the base of the hill after being thrown off by the Chinese.

Myers asked if there were any noncoms or officers present. He designated those who raised their hands to lead ad hoc squads. Myers knew his greatest problem was morale. "I didn't know what to say to the men who had just been decisively beaten off the hill. I didn't know them—we were like foreigners. . . . I was their commanding officer and they didn't even know my name." Swallowing hard, he ordered them to advance.

As the men climbed, they were shot at by hundreds of Chinese above

Above. *President Truman congratulates Majors Reginald R. Myers (left) and Carl L. Sitter during Medal of Honor ceremonies on October 29, 1951.* Below. *Marines escort the bodies of their fallen comrades to Hungnam. Determination to evacuate their dead characterized the spirit of the marines during the march.*

them. Said Myers, "As you went up the hill the bitter cold made every bullet sound like it was going through your eardrums. It would just be a *whack!* you know, and it made you feel like they were shooting at you instead of somebody else. So as we went up the hill, all of a sudden everybody fell on their faces and we couldn't get them up. They just lay on the snow and didn't want to move." Only by running up and down the line, talking to the men, threatening them, kicking them, grabbing them by the collars, and hoisting them to their feet, could Myers keep the advance going.

Fortunately, the Chinese pulled back, thinking they were facing a powerful force. That allowed Myers's men to take the crest of the hill. They held it all the next day, despite heavy fire from a higher position. They also suffered heavy losses, although many of those lost in the fight were not casualties. "For every man that you had wounded, two or three people would jump up and grab that guy and take him down to the bottom of the hill and you wouldn't see those two or three people again." Myers called for a marine guard to be posted at the bottom of the hill to send the strays back up, and even then most stopped before they got halfway up the hill. By 6:00 P.M. Myers had only seventy-five troops. Ridge ordered him to pull back to a reverse-slope defense. From there those "ragtags" held off the enemy for another night, until Sitter's reinforced rifle company took over the position.

Sitter and his men, though exhausted from their trek from Koto-ri, attacked the hill with spirit and held it for four days. In hand-to-hand combat, the men of Sitter's staff were all so badly wounded they had to be evacuated, but Sitter, himself wounded, stayed on his feet.

On December 3 Capt. Sitter and ninety-six men walked off East Hill. The next day the marines from Yudam-ni reached Hagaru-ri. Without the efforts of Capt. Barber, many of them would not have made it; without those of Sitter and Myers, many would have gone no farther. For their role in the Chosin escape, the three marine officers would receive Medals of Honor. But on December 4, 1950, none was thinking of his own heroism. Their thoughts were on the courage of their comrades. Myers recalled:

In the distance you could see the men wearily placing one foot in front of the other as they staggered down the road. . . . As they started to move within the perimeter, their heads came up, they straightened their shoulders, the wounded sat up in their stretchers. Uncontrolled cheers from the Hagaru-ri defenders spontaneously arose. . . . Tears uncontrolled were running down my cheek. I blew my nose and wiped my face. I wasn't alone. ❖

Stalemate
Heartbreak Ridge

By January 1951 the Communist counteroffensive in Korea had driven U.N. forces out of the North and deep into southern territory. MacArthur's forces fought their way back to the thirty-eighth parallel over the spring months, and in July peace talks began. The conflict changed from a war of movement to a stagnant trench war. "Each day was like the last," a 2d Division lieutenant wrote, "fight, suffer, meet or escape death, sweat out the nights only to move out each new day to climb and battle up the endless hills."

Private First Class Herbert K. Pililaau covered the withdrawal of his unit from Heartbreak Ridge on September 17, 1951.

It was the second year of the war, the fourth month of truce talks. No longer was there talk of victory. There were no more full-scale offensives. But the fighting—and dying—continued. General James Van Fleet, commander of the 8th Army, called them "tidying up" operations, limited attacks designed to keep the U.N. line, and the men on it, taut. The first such limited engagement was the three-week battle for Bloody Ridge in central Korea. Even though U.N. forces prevailed, that fight produced over 2,700 U.N. casualties, most to the already brutalized 2d Division. Only eight days after taking Bloody Ridge, the 2d Division marched northward to more battle. Again the objective was an uninhabitable rock- and scrub-covered hill mass. It did not have a name, except for a series of army numbers (Hills 894, 931, 605), until the men came to know it by a more meaningful label: Heartbreak Ridge.

Van Fleet planned the attack on Heartbreak Ridge to straighten the U.N. line and to keep the *Inmin Gun* off balance after its defeat at Bloody Ridge. Neither 8th Army nor 2d Division command thought it would be a very difficult mission. Heartbreak was occupied by a sizable force of North Koreans, but most were the soldiers whom the 2d Division and attached units had just defeated. So confident was the division commander that he decided to commit only one regiment to the main assault force. What he did not know was that beneath the scrub trees covering the ridge, the enemy had built an elaborate system of connected bunkers, impervious to air strikes and most artillery fire. Within those fortified chambers they had rebuilt and reinforced their units. The 2d Division was about to face the North Korean army's main line of resistance.

On September 13 the 23d Infantry Regiment and its attached French battalion approached the steep slope of Heartbreak's central peak. Before they had scaled even the foothills, they were knocked back by a flurry of mortar, machine-gun, and rifle fire from concealed bunkers above. Next day they tried again. The hostile terrain prevented tanks from assisting the GIs, so the men moved up the ridge on their own. Slowly they fought through the avalanche of bullets, taking out enemy bunkers one by one. By nightfall they gained the crest. But the cruel, inching struggle up the hill had worn out the men. When the North Koreans attacked a few hours later, the Americans fell back. The next day they tried—and failed—again. And the next day.

So it continued. By September 16 Heartbreak Ridge was a pockmarked mass of loose rocks and metal. Where once there grew thick underbrush, barely a bush survived. The North Koreans remained in control. All the U.N. could claim for its efforts was a piece of ridge line connecting two main hills. There, in a trio of perimeters, the 1st Battalion, 23d Infantry, settled in for the night.

Private First Class Herbert K. Pililaau, Charlie Company, 1st Battalion, 23d Infantry, was not the type of man people would have taken for a hero. Except for his tremendous strength and stamina—he was the top physically of his company in basic training—and his six-foot height, the native Hawaiian did not stand out in a crowd. He spoke little, did not smoke or drink, rarely socialized with the other men, spent most of his spare time reading the Bible or writing his family. It surprised his platoon mates when he volunteered for the high-risk job of BAR gunner shortly after joining the 23d in Korea that summer. Pililaau's explanation was characteristic: Someone had to do it. On September 17, 1951,

Pililaau gave his comrades in Company C an even bigger surprise.

At 3:00 A.M. a battalion of North Koreans struck the company from a hill adjoining its ridge position. Charlie Company fought hard to hold on, but lack of ammunition finally forced its withdrawal to the back of the hill. Joined now by Company A, the men of Charlie prepared a countercharge, this time fixing bayonets and preparing for hand-to-hand fighting. Unfortunately, the enemy had plenty of ammunition.

The first American charge broke under the weight of heavy North Korean fire. The commander reorganized his men and sent them up again. Private Pililaau took the lead. In the dim light of early morning the Americans forced the North Koreans back, regaining their perimeter and reaching the crest. But they had little time to rest. At midday the enemy battalion burst up the hill and the men of Company C once more

found themselves fighting for their lives. The American resistance still suffered from lack of ammunition. Finally, the commander called retreat. Pililaau, behind his BAR, said he would cover. As his unit scrambled down the hill, Pililaau remained on top, firing his automatic at the onrushing enemy until he had exhausted his ammunition. Then he hit them with grenades. When those, too, were used up, he pulled out his trench knife and fought on.

From 180 meters down the ridge, Pililaau's company watched in awe. His squad leader recalls the last long minutes of the one-man battle:

There was Herb standing up fighting a lot of the enemy. It was hand-to-hand and just Herb against all of them. We all wanted to go back up to help him but the captain said "No." We tried to help Herb by firing a few shots, but they didn't do any good. All of a sudden, they shot him and when he went down they bayoneted him. That was it.

Heartbreak Ridge lies shattered after a fierce battle. U.N. assaults on such ridges were common, even though the actual strategic significance of many of them was slight.

Pililaau's courageous example put heart back into his tired unit. A half-hour after he fell, the Americans retook the ridge. There they found the body of the quiet private. Around it lay more than forty dead North Korean soldiers. For his valiant stand, Pililaau was awarded a posthumous Medal of Honor.

The battle for Heartbreak Ridge raged for several more weeks after the death of Private Pililaau. Eventually, though, the 8th Army straightened the sag in its lines. While the peace talks dragged on for two more years, men like Pililaau were to fight and die for other uninhabitable ridges and nameless valleys. Victory or defeat, however, was out of their hands. ◈

Jets Go to War
MiG Alley and Sniper Ridge

War in the skies over Korea saw the first use of American jet-powered fighter aircraft in combat. Aerial dogfights were sharp and swift, most of them taking place in a thin strip of territory close to the Chinese border. Although the technology of aerial warfare had advanced rapidly in the years since World War II, the United States Air Force, and the air wings of the U.S. Navy and Marines, still relied on the courage and initiative of their combat pilots.

Although the Korean conflict was for the most part an old-style infantry war, the air force and navy played an early and crucial role. In its first war as an independent service, the air force monopolized the skies. Within a month it had wiped out the 150-plane North Korean air force. From then until the Chinese entered, it operated over Korea virtually undisturbed, supporting directly U.N. troops and wreaking havoc on *Inmin Gun* supply lines. General William F. Dean credited the air force with providing the

Two American pilots head for their F-86 Sabres at Kimpo airfield, near Seoul, on their way to combat over the North.

edge that allowed his soldiers to hold back the enemy at Taejon.

The Chinese entry dramatically altered the air war. A few days before the Chosin Reservoir attack, a U.S. F-80 Shooting Star, piloted by Lieutenant Russell Brown, encountered a Soviet-built MiG-15 over North Korea. The result was history's first jet dogfight. The

American won. Allied pilots went on to win ten out of every eleven encounters. But the air over Korea was no longer a U.N. preserve. More than 1,000 U.S. planes were downed before the war was over, and the air force suffered 1,700 casualties. In exchange, the airmen put out of service nearly 100,000 enemy vehicles, well over 1,000 tanks, and almost 18,000 bunkers and gun positions. Aerial support of the infantry forced the enemy to limit its assaults to nighttime. Jets and bombers may not have been able to stop the attackers, but they made their lives more difficult.

Because U.N. policy forbade combat over Chinese territory, jet pilots assigned to interdict enemy MiGs could attack only in Korean airspace. Usually that meant "MiG Alley," a strip of sky just south of the Yalu River, which separates North Korea from China. From there they could look across the river to Chinese airfields and see rows of jet fighters and bombers—see them, but not touch them. Instead, with the fifteen to thirty minutes of fighting fuel they had left after their long journeys from Seoul or Pusan, they had to lure the MiGs over the border and engage them. If a pilot took longer or his plane was disabled, he had to try to ditch in the freezing waters of the Yellow Sea and hope for a quick rescue before the enemy or the elements got him first. If he was shot down over land and survived, he found himself alone several hundred kilometers within enemy territory.

One of the air force's best fliers was George Davis. Major Davis, with a Distinguished Flying Cross from the Pacific campaigns of World War II, arrived in Korea in late October 1951. On November 10 he took command of a squadron of F-86 Sabrejets. Less than three weeks later he had become the Korean War's fifth jet ace by downing three MiGs and three Chinese bombers.

In December he shot down six more enemy jets. The four he destroyed on December 13 alone set a Korean record. Air force Chief of Staff Hoyt Vandenburg cabled his personal congratulations.

Davis's appearance belied his reputation. The men of the 334th Fighter Squadron who flew beside him described the premier ace as looking "about as aggressive as Bugs Bunny." But Davis was a relentless attacker. In the Second World War he flew 266 combat missions, destroying seven enemy aircraft in one-on-one combat. It took him little

Major George A. Davis, Jr., sits in the cockpit of his F-86 as a ground crewman prepares the jet for battle.

time in Korea to earn a second Distinguished Flying Cross. Before his career ended, only three months after becoming an F-86 squadron leader, Davis downed fourteen enemy jets over North Korea. "When it came to flying there was no one like him," said Davis's wingman. "George Davis had 'the touch.'"

On February 10, 1952, Major Davis set off from Seoul at the head of a

A sequence from a camera mounted on an American jet fighter records the death of an enemy MiG airplane in the skies over North Korea.

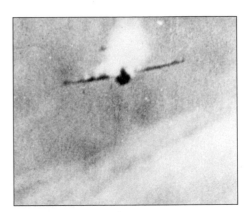
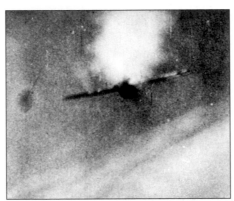

flight of eighteen Sabres. Their mission—Davis's sixteenth in Korea—was to shield low-flying U.S. fighter-bombers attacking rail lines near the Chinese border. On the flight Davis spotted the white contrails of a dozen MiGs coming from the northwest. He and his wingman peeled off to meet them. Speeding into MiG Alley, they took the Chinese by surprise. Within seconds Davis reduced their number by two. But the ten enemy pilots left quickly, regrouped, and bore down on the Sabres from the rear. Davis could have taken advantage of his plane's superior speed and escaped. Instead, he slowed down to take on a third MiG.

At 32,000 feet he pulled behind an enemy jet and took aim. A burst of cannon split the air. This time, though, the target was Davis. A MiG had swooped in on the Sabre from seven o'clock and scored a direct hit. Davis's jet exploded into a ball of flames as it careened into an icy mountainside.

Doris Davis, the pilot's widow, expressed the angry confusion of many Americans when she accepted his posthumous Medal of Honor and promotion to lieutenant colonel after the armistice. "If I could feel that he lost his life for some good reason, I could feel better about it," she said. Perhaps her husband, had he lived, could have given her some hint of that reason. Davis had declined the air force's offer to return him to noncombat duty after he achieved ace status by shooting down his fifth enemy plane. A desk job or training post held no allure for him. Jet fighter flying, he told his squadron, was simply "the best profession in the world."

Three months after George Davis

downed his last MiG, Major Charles Loring arrived in Korea. Not much had changed. Across central Korea isolated battles raged for a few days at a time, then broke off as if by some tacit agreement. No territory of consequence was won or lost. Still, casualties mounted steadily. At "Sniper Ridge," in the U.N. X Corps zone, the fighting maintained a particular intensity. Loring's wing of F-80 Shooting Star jets received orders to support the U.N. outpost by knocking out enemy artillery concentrations.

That was just the job for Charles Loring. He had been trying to get back into action since the Korean conflict began. Instead he had spent two frustrating years in the U.S. as instructor at the Army Information School. Over beers with his fellow instructors he frequently talked of valor in combat. It was a quality he knew firsthand.

As a fighter-pilot in World War II, Loring flew fifty-five strafing and dive-bombing missions over the hottest battle areas in Europe, earning the Distinguished Flying Cross. Twice he was hit. The first time he managed to bring his crippled plane and wounded body back to base. The second time—Christmas Eve 1944 at the Battle of the Bulge—he had to bail out behind enemy lines. Loring spent the next few months in a German POW camp.

In 1952 Major Loring was thirty-four, older than the average pilot but no less a fighter. As a squadron operations officer in the 8th Fighter-Bomber Wing, he led fifty-one artillery-strafing missions between June and November. From October on he concentrated on the area around Sniper Ridge, where X Corps battled a renewed and effective Communist offensive.

An F-80 Shooting Star releases napalm over a North Korean supply depot as antiaircraft fire (bright spot under jet) searches for its target.

On November 22 Loring led a flight of four Shooting Stars to the ridge on an artillery dive-bombing mission. After positioning the jets he swooped on the enemy. Intense antiaircraft fire greeted the flight leader, but he pressed on. Then a burst of ground fire hit his plane. Although Loring himself seemed to be all right, his jet was badly crippled. His flight team deployed around him to cover his withdrawal. But Loring made no attempt to retreat. The other airmen watched for the billow of a parachute, ready to radio in the location to a rescue unit. Instead, they were amazed to see Loring force his smoking plane back around and deliberately aim the plummeting aircraft at the heart of the harassing artillery position. Moments later, the bomb-laden Shooting Star crashed to earth directly on target. Loring, going down fighting, lost his life, but he silenced the enemy guns. He also received the Medal of Honor posthumously.

Heroism has many origins. For Major Charles Loring, an ex-bantamweight boxer, it sprang from an indomitable fighting spirit. Years after his bailout and capture in World War II he had remained angry that he had let off those who shot him down. A fellow instructor at the Army Information School, then-Captain John Paul Heffernan, recalled a conversation he had with Loring about his capture.

Loring had mused whether he would "go that same route again. . . . Your airplane is beat up, you're beat up, you don't know if you'll make it and you wonder if there's anything you can do before you go down." At Sniper Ridge Loring had decided to do something. ◈

269

To Save a Life
Rescuers and Medics

Seven navy men earned the Medal of Honor in the Korean War. None was at sea during his medal-earning actions. The U.S. Navy took control of the seas so early the enemy never could launch a challenge. The navy men singled out for their gallantry served on the land or in the skies. Five were medics attached to marine units, one piloted a rescue helicopter, and the seventh flew a carrier fighter aircraft in support of both army and marine troops. Though all were armed for battle all seven received the medal for their efforts to save lives.

Lieutenant (j.g.) Thomas Hudner receives the Medal of Honor from President Truman as the widow of Jesse Brown, Daisy (left), looks on, April 13, 1951.

On December 4, 1950, Lieutenant (j.g.) Thomas J. Hudner and three other F4U Corsair pilots from the carrier U.S.S. *Leyte* were flying an armed reconnaissance mission about twenty-four kilometers north of the Chosin Reservoir. The Chinese had ambushed the marines at Chosin nine days earlier. Hudner's flight group was covering the marines' escape, looking for more Communist forces advancing from the north. Flying 150 meters above the snow-covered mountains, they saw no sign of enemy troops. Perhaps they were down there; dressed in white for winter, Chinese soldiers could be hard to detect in the snow. But all seemed clear until Ensign Jesse Brown reported that he was losing power. "I think I may have been hit," he radioed. "I've lost my oil pressure and I'm going to have to go in."

Brown crash-landed in a clearing on a heavily wooded mountainside. The force of the impact mangled his plane. The engine broke off, and the fuselage twisted at a forty-five-degree angle near the cockpit. Tensely, Brown's flight mates circled overhead looking for a signal that he was alive. On the second pass they saw Brown open his canopy and wave. But Hudner, Brown's wingman, sensed something was wrong. Why, he wondered, did not Brown get out of the cockpit? His concern heightened when he saw a line of smoke wafting from the nose back toward the cockpit. Any moment that smoke could turn to flame. Since Brown's plane faced into the wind, a fire in the front would rapidly engulf the trapped pilot. The flight leader called for a rescue copter, but Hudner, knowing it could be a half-hour before help arrived, informed his flight mates that he was going down.

Hudner, a graduate of Annapolis in 1946, had been with Fighter Squadron 32 since receiving his wings. One of the old hands he met when he joined the squadron was Jesse Brown, the navy's first black pilot. Hudner believed that Brown was special, an inspiration to all blacks. More than that, the two pilots were friends. But, said Hudner later, he did not follow Brown into the Korean mountains for either of those reasons. He acted on the unspoken rule that a squadron looks out for its own: "If something happened to one of us it wasn't 'OK, buddy. Somebody's got to go and you've gone.' You had that feeling of camaraderie and a team spirit that, by God, if there's anything that could be done, somebody was going to try to do it."

Hudner dropped his rockets and extra fuel tanks, put down his flaps, aimed his plane at the clearing next to Brown, "and made believe I was just making a carrier approach." His plane hit the mountainside hard and skidded across the snow, but it was a clean landing. Hudner's Corsair stopped only a couple of hundred meters from Brown's.

He leaped out of his plane and ran to the crash site. As he had feared, Brown was trapped. The fuselage had broken at the cockpit, pinning the pilot's leg at the knee. Brown was by now suffering badly from the subfreezing cold. He had removed his helmet, then taken off his gloves to unbuckle his parachute. In the numbing cold he had dropped his gloves beyond reach. Now his hands were frozen solid. Hudner dashed back to his plane and grabbed a wool hat and scarf he kept for emergencies. He pulled the hat down over Brown's head and wrapped the scarf around his stiff hands. Then he wrestled hopelessly to pull him free.

The Corsair's cockpit was too high off the ground for Hudner to reach. He tried clambering up the plane's inverted gull wing, but his snow-covered soles slid off the icy metal. Finally, grasping the handholds in the fuselage side, he pulled himself to the top. Straddling the

Below. *A navy Corsair fighter like the one flown by Hudner comes in for a landing on the U.S.S.* Leyte, *off the Korean coast.* Bottom. *An aerial photograph shows the plane Hudner crash-landed (top left) in an effort to assist Jesse Brown out of his downed plane (right).*

mountains at night could be fatal. "You can stay here if you want," he told Hudner, "but I can't see that either of us can do any good."

Hudner understood the sense of Ward's words. To remain would only doom all three men. The only way they could extricate Brown would be to cut off his pinned leg with an ax. Neither man was willing to do that, because they thought in Brown's present condition it would kill him. The single dim hope was to return to the base camp and round up some better metal-cutting equipment. Privately, though, they knew the injured man could not survive the wait.

Hudner told Brown he was going back for more help. Brown mumbled a last message for his wife. "He must have realized by that time that that was about it," Hudner later said sadly. "He couldn't move at all. And there were the two of us jumping in and out and not accomplishing a damn thing. . . . One

cockpit, he tried to reach down to grasp Brown but could not get a hold on him. Hudner ran back to his own plane and radioed for the helicopter to bring an ax and a fire extinguisher. Desperate to help his friend, Hudner piled handfuls of snow into the still-smoking nose.

Through all of this Brown remained calm and alert. While waiting for rescue they talked a bit, but there was not a lot either could say. Hudner suspected that Brown had internal injuries from the crash, but the injured man gave no indication. "Never once did he say 'I hurt,' " Hudner recalled. "Just sort of a plea to get him out of there. But there was no panic in his voice."

After about another half-hour, marine rescue helicopter pilot Lieutenant Charles Ward arrived and set his craft down on the slope. He brought out an ax and fire extinguisher and joined Hudner at Brown's plane. The situation looked

ever more hopeless. The ax bounced like a toy hammer off the thick metal plate pressing against Brown's knee. The small fire extinguisher had no effect on the smoldering fire. And Brown was beginning to fade. His words became fewer, fainter. As the daylight began to dim, Ward reluctantly called Hudner aside. They had to get out before dusk, he said. His helicopter had no night-flying instruments, so to fly among the

of the worst things when something has happened to you is the feeling that you're all alone. Just being with him to give him as much comfort as we could was worth the effort."

When Hudner returned to Brown for the last time, to say good-bye, he found him unconscious. If he felt any satisfaction, it was that they had stayed with his fellow pilot until the end.

Hudner and Ward climbed into the

A Code of Conduct

As the U.S.S. *Leyte* prepared to pull out of Tokyo in January 1951, Lieutenant (j.g.) Tom Hudner was surprised to see among the crew of another carrier an old friend from his first days as a fighter pilot, Lieutenant (j.g.) John K. Koelsch. In a short conversation, Koelsch mentioned that he had become a helicopter rescue pilot. Then the two parted. Hudner embarked for the United States, where he would receive the Medal of Honor, Koelsch for a stint in Korea.

Rescue flying was much more than a job to Koelsch. He refused rotation to the United States at the end of his tour of duty; his conscience would not permit him to leave, he told a fellow officer, when others needed his help. In his off-duty hours he tinkered with inventions that would make rescues safer and more successful. In the icy Korean winter Koelsch came up with several devices to improve the operation of helicopters in cold weather. He also developed a widely used floating sling for pulling downed airmen from the sea.

But Koelsch's greatest distinction would develop from his greatest trial. On July 3, 1951, he and a machinist's mate were shot down while trying to rescue a marine pilot in the mountains. The three hid from enemy troops for three days, subsisting on one candy bar, two half-canteens of water, and a flask of brandy. Rescue aircraft combed the area, but no one spotted the downed Americans. On July 6 the three headed east to the sea, twenty-four kilometers away, but were captured by a North Korean patrol in a fishing village on the coast. Wounded and sick from hunger and exposure, the Americans were paraded past villagers who showered them with taunts and abuse.

Lieutenant (j.g.) John K. Koelsch, whose actions as a prisoner of war set the standard for future American POWs.

Koelsch's first concern was for his comrades. He demanded medical attention for the badly wounded pilot and better treatment for all three. When the guards ignored him, his protests grew louder. Finally the airman was evacuated to a medical facility.

Later Koelsch and the other American were taken to a prison camp. Though malnourished himself, Koelsch shared his meager rations with sick and injured prisoners. At the same time he defied his captors by demanding proper treatment under the Geneva Convention guidelines for POWs. He refused to give any information beyond his name, rank, and serial number and resisted the daily brainwashing sessions.

John Koelsch's resolve survived isolation and other mental abuse. His body was not so strong. On October 16, 1951, Lieutenant Koelsch died of malnutrition in prison. His perseverance inspired those imprisoned with him and earned him a posthumous navy Medal of Honor. In addition, his actions were the basis for the Code of Conduct, the set of standards adopted in 1955 to guide all American prisoners of war.

helicopter and took off, leaving Hudner's plane behind. At nightfall, they reached the marine base where troops were straggling in from the tortuous trek down from the Chosin River valley. Hudner remained snowed in at the marine base for three days. When he returned to the *Leyte* the captain, Thomas Sisson, called him immediately to the bridge. He asked Hudner what had happened. Instead of reprimanding him for acting without orders, Sisson nominated Hudner for the Medal of Honor.

Five other Medals of Honor in Korea went to navy medics, all but one posthumously. By all odds, the man who lived to accept the honor from President Eisenhower, Hospital Corpsman Third Class William Charette, should not have made it either. In one day the platoons he served lost three-quarters of their men. Though Charette remained out in the open the entire time tending the wounded in the hottest of battle, he somehow escaped with only surface wounds. His story is one of the most miraculous of the Korean War.

When Charette joined the navy in 1951 he never expected to go to Korea. Only after he put in for hospital corpsman did he find out that medics served with the marines. But after eighteen months of stateside duty, Charette requested assignment to the war zone. In January 1953 he joined the 2d Battalion, 7th Marines, at the so-called Nevada complex north of Seoul. There the marines fought the fiercest battles of the stalemated days of war. On March 26 the Chinese overran the marine outposts on Reno, Vegas, and Carson hills. On night maneuvers, Charette saw the flashes of artillery fire in the distance. The next day he got word that his battalion was moving up to retake Vegas. The day broke sunny but cold as Charette's outfit headed out to Vegas Outpost. As they neared the bat-

Hospital Corpsman Third Class William Charette (right) with President Dwight D. Eisenhower during Medal of Honor ceremonies on January 12, 1954. Other men who received the medal are First Lieutenant Edward Schowalter, Jr. (left), and Private First Class Ernest West.

tleground the soldiers' attention fixed on the horrors remaining from the previous night. The marines, for all their reputation for getting out their wounded and dead, had been overwhelmed so quickly they left the field strewn with men, dead and living. Corpses of Americans hung from the barbed wire surrounding the outpost. Men wounded hours earlier groaned for help. Charette broke from his platoon to treat the survivors, working his way slowly up the hillside of shattered men.

Throughout the day moderate rifle and mortar fire peppered Vegas. The Chinese pulled back some, but they retained the crest of the hill. The marines knew that after dark the Chinese would counterattack with everything they had. It would be another long, bloody night. At dusk the 1st Platoon, 2d Battalion, assaulted the hill. Charette, now back with his own platoon, was waiting in reserve when an emergency call came in for a medic. Two of 1st Platoon's point men had been hit and needed attention badly. Their own corpsman was out of commission. Charette worked his way past the front lines to where the wounded men lay. By the time he reached them it was dark.

Charette had just started treating the two marines when the hill exploded in mortar and rifle fire. Worse for Charette and the five point men, the Chinese began rolling hand grenades down on them. In the dark, the guns and artillery shot wildly, but the grenades rolled right into the Americans' position. One burst near Charette, wounding him in the face and temporarily blinding and deafening him. Fortunately, his medical kit, blown completely off him, took the brunt of the blast. When his sight returned, Charette saw that he was the least injured of the group. Though now without medical supplies and hampered by darkness, he

rushed to do what he could for the others. He had already given away his overcoat to a wounded man. Now, in the freezing night, he ripped up his clothes to make bandages and tourniquets.

As he bound the wounds of the marine most badly mauled by shrapnel, Charette heard the man on the other side of him shout "grenade." The navy corpsman threw himself over his patient to protect him from the blast. "I admire a man who can throw himself on a grenade," he said later. "I couldn't personally do that, because with grenades your chances of survival are fairly good if you can get some distance away. But this guy I was treating, I knew if he got hit any worse . . . and of course I did have a flak jacket on. So I just covered him." When the dust cleared, Charette resumed bandaging.

After Charette had treated the point men, help arrived. First Platoon's leader, Sergeant Stagwell, led a small party up to the forward position to evacuate the wounded. They had taken the first injured man only a short distance, though, when they hit a snag. A mortar shell had caved in a portion of the trench they were using as cover. The only way to get the casualties past the logjam would be to bring them overland, directly through the enemy's line of fire. Charette leaped from the trench, lifted a man out, and carried him to a safe spot. Then he returned, straddled the trench, and

picked up a second. He ran back and forth, lifting and carrying casualties through a cascade of bullets, until he had brought all the point men to safety. Then he sought more wounded.

Before the night was over, Charette had become the medic for all three platoons. The pace he kept was grueling, the conditions horrible. At one point he was working on injuries to his assistant platoon leader in darkness so complete he could barely see the wounds. A few moments later he stopped. Rigor mortis was setting in. The man was dead. But Charette saved many other lives that night. His actions inspired many men; when Sergeant Stagwell recommended him for the Medal of Honor, all three platoons in his battalion contributed testimony to support the recommendation.

Nine months later, after the armistice, Charette was still in Korea, working in a postwar MASH unit, when the chief surgeon brought him the news that he had been awarded the Medal of Honor. "I would have rather heard I was going home," he remembered of the moment, with a laugh. Still, he was clearly proud to receive another honor: In 1958 he was chosen to select the remains that would become the Unknown Soldier of World War II.

Many years later, when questioned about his actions on that hill in Korea, William Charette gave a prosaic reply: "What'd I do it for? The guys." ◈

273

The Psychology of Heroism

by ROBERT COLES

To talk with men who have fought bravely in war is to be reminded, yet again, that our psychological lives are thoroughly complex—and often capable of offering the world a surprise or two. Few of the military men I have known, as an air force medical officer and in the course of my conversations with American veterans (some of them much decorated during our various wars), would ever claim for themselves the title of "hero," or acknowledge a specific ambition to conduct themselves heroically. Quite the contrary. As a West Virginia veteran of the Vietnam War made quite clear to me one day:

I look at myself in the mirror and I say I'm not the one who everyone thinks was such a hotshot hero. I was scared, rotten scared in Nam; so scared I thought I'd end up with my mind broken in a hundred pieces. When I first got there, I was ready to fight; but it didn't take long for lots of us to figure out that we were in one hell of a mess there, and we were going nowhere real fast! A lot of us tried to do the best we could, but we weren't fired up the way I'm sure soldiers were in some other wars. . . . When I got into battle I said to myself: Try to get out of this alive, but give it what you have, because you want to remember yourself as being as good as the next fellow. . . . So I did. And the next thing you know, you're hurt, real bad hurt, and everyone's messing with you and telling you how "great" you are!

In various ways, in various accounts, I have heard similar remarks from other Americans—heard them express their surprise that they acted with courage and bravery in the face of extreme danger. As one talks with veterans about their bravery under the duress of the battlefield, one begins to realize how detached they felt *then,* never mind months and years later—how removed they felt from what they had always considered to be their essential selves in those minutes and hours and days of combat.

"I'm a guy who's cautious, and I've always wanted to live to be a hundred," one man told me in Albuquerque as he puzzled over his almost unbelievable performance in far-distant Asia a few years before. He talked about himself as if he were a stranger:

There was this guy, and he went out there to save his buddies, and he was headed straight for the bullets, and they were

coming at him, hundreds of bullets, and he came back, with one guy, and then went to get another one, and it wasn't real, it was just a few minutes. I blacked out at the end. I think I left my body! I didn't know what to make of the guy—me, it was!

When he had finished his story, he insisted that he never in his life prior to military service would ever have pictured himself capable of such behavior. Indeed, he would have expected "just the opposite" of himself. "That guy," he kept calling himself. "That guy, I mean, well, me." He was not displaying modesty, or psychopathology, or sly, seductively rendered boasting. His sense of detachment reflected instead the mind's mechanism for coping with certain utterly desperate circumstances—when the choice is between a dramatic psychological effort to protect one's available energy and competence, or complete emotional deterioration and collapse.

Soldiers fighting on the battlefield must quickly manage to be far less preoccupied with their own immediate survival than they would usually find it possible or desirable to be. Psychiatrists call this "denial" or "reaction formation." It is the way we drive fear and trembling out of our conscious minds, and even work ourselves into an energetically confident or assertive state, in order to subdue the sense of danger. Another soldier described it this way:

I was over there, in Asia, and I'd never been out of New England, and I suddenly realized I just might never get back to New England and my whole body was shaking. But there were my friends, my buddies, and they were probably shaking inside, like I was, but they didn't show any sign of it, and I guess I didn't . . . and the next thing I knew I was out there on the battlefield, and I tell you, there wasn't a bone in my body that was scared, not then. Hell, now I sit here and talk with you, and I know I must have been scared somewhere inside. But it was well hidden for me, and for my buddies, though as I look back I realize some probably weren't as good as I was at hiding!

His remarks reflect another phenomenon of men in battle: the effects of so-called "group psychology." When an individual's conscience is threatened by a military danger, the company of others becomes a big boost. This man and his buddies not only helped one another with talk and kidding and all sorts of friendliness, but in effect became together much more than any of them were separately. Such solidarity can be utterly transformational, enabling men who otherwise would cower or hesitate or only tentatively do their sworn duty to become vigorous and able combatants. "We were together," the man just quoted explained to me, "and I can still hear myself saying: 'Hell, we'll get through this!'" Then he added tersely, "*I* couldn't, but *we* did!"

Other factors help support a man in battle, including his moral and religious beliefs, and his nationalistic loyalties. These urge the soldier to think of others, *their* situation, and to think of his civic obligations. Many veterans vividly recount those fleeting but important emotional moments before battle, when a whole lifetime (in images) parades speedily before them: memories of parental injunctions, of principles and values learned at home or church or school, the patriotic music and lyrics of their nation, not to mention scenes of anticipation, wherein one has survived the fear, the danger, and is now home with loved ones, and (very significant) at home with one's self-respect intact. One former soldier put it for me in a way I'll never forget: "I think I was more afraid of going home and living the rest of my life remembering that I'd been a coward than I was afraid of being killed over there—though for awhile, to be honest, it might have been fifty-fifty."

There are especially brilliant, agile, determined, and apparently fearless men whose military courage is stunning—and who, in their earlier lives, seem to have been headed for the exemplary moments the rest of us come to know about when our presidents or cabinet officers or generals hand out medals. There are others who are a touch mad or wild or vicious—and have found in war the "right" occasion for behavior that in other circumstances might be described as "sociopathic" or just plain criminal. Veterans have often with puzzlement described that latter kind of person to me, a person who seems to have been reckless and truculent well before

his military life, who seems "itching to have a fight, any fight," as one man described a buddy of his. But most brave warriors, I suspect, have seemingly stumbled into their heroism—found in their lives a haunting moment of transcendence, when moral energy is released in response to the terrible exigence of a particular battlefield situation. As an Alabama veteran remarked several years ago: "I was there, and I thought I'd die, the Cong would get me, I was scared out of my mind. Then I looked at my buddies, and they looked at me, and we all looked at each other, and we said, what the hell, we've got no choice, and we might as well die thinking good of ourselves, and so we went right to it; and to tell you the truth, I don't remember too much after that, because I was sort of sprung from myself, you could say." He could say—and so saying, tell us a lot. ❖

Dr. Robert Coles is professor of psychiatry and medical humanities at Harvard Medical School and the author of the five-volume series *Children of Crisis*.

The Vietnam War

A Different Kind of War

It was a war that few understood and many opposed. Born of cold war power politics and a missionary zeal for democracy, the American effort in Vietnam ended in ambiguity and division. In 1965, after over ten years of indirect opposition to the Communist forces of Ho Chi Minh, the United States stepped up its commitment of men and firepower to counter the threat to South Vietnam. With the American military deploying a vast amount of its nonnuclear resources against a smaller, scattered fighting force, it seemed the conflict would soon be over, the Communists quickly pounded into surrender. Eight years later, the United States had withdrawn; ten years later, North Vietnamese troops had captured Saigon, and North and South were reunited. In the eyes of many, Vietnam was the first war America lost.

American involvement in Indochina grew steadily from 1954, when France relinquished control of the region after more than eighty years of colonial rule. The French defeat by Ho's Vietminh guerrillas at Dien Bien Phu that year led to the Geneva accord that partitioned North from South Vietnam, leaving Ho and his followers to establish a Communist government in the northern capital of Hanoi. For the Vietminh who remained in the South, however, the struggle was not over, and the fight began for a reunified Vietnam. In the Mekong Delta and central highlands, clashes between the Army of the Republic of Vietnam (ARVN) and the Vietcong, as the Communist guerrillas came to be known, became bloodier.

In the United States, the growing Soviet influence in Europe after World War II and the fall of China to the forces of Mao Tse-tung lent urgency to the fight against communism. Given Ho Chi Minh's association with Mao and Stalin, the U.S. foreign policy establishment considered him more a Communist than a nationalist and therefore a danger to freedom and democracy in Asia. During Dien Bien Phu, President Eisenhower had warned that "the loss of Indochina will cause the fall of Southeast Asia like a set of dominoes." The "domino theory," and the consequent commitment to the preservation of an anti-Communist government in South Vietnam, would haunt American foreign policy for the next twenty years.

Despite American aid, the South Vietnamese could not maintain a stable government, and ARVN forces could not get the upper hand against the Vietcong, whose ranks had been bolstered by ever-larger numbers of North Vietnamese regulars since 1959. By the summer of 1964, ten years after Dien Bien Phu, Communist forces were firmly entrenched in the countryside, and government control of some areas was in name only. Ho's forces threatened to destroy the southern government and reunify Vietnam—unless the United States stepped up aid. President Johnson, who had inherited from Presidents Eisenhower and Kennedy the presence of U.S. military advisers in South Vietnam, was pressed by various aides and military commanders to broaden the American military role in Southeast Asia.

The Gulf of Tonkin incident of August 1964 brought the country closer to such a commitment. On August 2, a U.S. Navy electronic surveillance ship, the U.S.S. *Maddox,* was fired upon by North Vietnamese gunboats twelve miles off the coast of North Vietnam. Two days later, the *Maddox* was back in the Gulf of Tonkin, escorted by a destroyer, the U.S.S. *C. Turner Joy.* "The United States was not seeking to provoke another attack," wrote one historian, "but did not go out of its way to avoid one either."

What happened in the Gulf of Tonkin on the night of August 4 remains unclear to this day. While the two American vessels reported that they were under attack, no enemy ships were sighted, and radar readings that stormy night were unreliable. Regardless, the White House insisted that a second attack had taken place, and the president ordered retaliatory air strikes against North Vietnamese naval bases and fuel depots. On August 7 both houses of Congress passed a resolution that allowed "the president, as commander-in-chief, to take all necessary measures to repel any armed attack against the forces of the United States and to prevent further aggression."

But Johnson did not take further action, at least not immediately. "We seek no wider war," he told crowds along the 1964 campaign trail. On the other hand, he

---

Preceding pages. *Troop-laden helicopters of the 25th Infantry Division return to their base at Tay Ninh, South Vietnam, after an incursion into Cambodia, May 1970.*

Vo Nguyen Giap (left), commander of Vietminh and North Vietnamese troops, and Ho Chi Minh in 1945. Over the next thirty years their guerrilla war would engage and frustrate two larger powers.

realized a greater commitment might be necessary to shore up the weak ARVN defenses—and save lives.

After a Vietcong attack on an American base in Pleiku in February 1965 left eight dead, the president was ready to act. "We have kept our gun over the mantel and our shells in the cupboard for a long time now," he said to a wary Senator Mike Mansfield, "and what was the result? They are killing our men while they sleep in the night. I can't ask our American soldiers to fight with one hand tied behind their backs." Johnson ordered reprisal strikes against North Vietnam and a few days later approved Operation Rolling Thunder, the sustained bombing of the North. The bombing was to become one of the most

pervasive, and controversial, American tactics in Southeast Asia.

Johnson's commander in Vietnam was still pessimistic about the success of a limited American effort. Predicting "a VC takeover of the country" if the president did not act further, General William Westmoreland, backed by the Joint Chiefs of Staff, urged escalated bombing of North Vietnam and supply routes along the "Ho Chi Minh Trail" through Laos and Cambodia, as well as increased security for in-country air bases. To accomplish the latter, he requested two battalions of U.S. Marines to defend the American base at Da Nang.

Despite misgivings among Johnson's staff, the president assented to the request. At dawn on March 8, 1965, two battalions of marines splashed ashore at Da Nang and were met by smiling Vietnamese girls who draped garlands of flowers around their necks. It was an ironically tranquil beginning to a bitter and bloody eight-year task. By the end of 1965, there were over 184,000 U.S. military personnel in Vietnam—eight times the number there in 1964. LBJ was firm: "We will stand in Vietnam."

The aim of American involvement in Southeast Asia seemed clear from the beginning: to assist the South Vietnamese in their struggle to defend themselves against Communist aggression, ensuring a stable, independent nation in the South. Support for the endeavor was widespread. A majority of Americans approved of the original deployment of troops in 1965, and thousands of men enlisted for their nation's latest war. One veteran remembered the prevailing sense of obligation: "Everybody told you that that was the thing to do." A marine who was part of the original landing party recalled the optimistic mood of many of his countrymen: "America seemed omnipotent then: the country could still claim that it had never lost a war, and we believed that we were ordained to play cop to the Communists' robber and spread our own political faith throughout the world."

But playing cops and robbers with the Communists involved a fair amount of chasing. American forces soon expanded beyond their defensive posture and moved inland to engage the enemy in the jungles and paddies of the South. Traditional American infantry tactics called for the application of superior manpower and firepower, so American generals hoped to engineer clashes with large

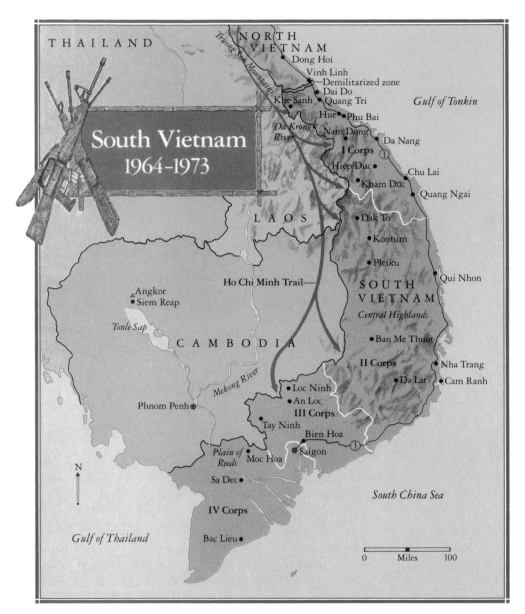

Above. *President Lyndon B. Johnson prepares the March 31, 1968, address in which he announced he would not accept renomination.* Map. *After the marine landing at Da Nang in 1965, the American presence in South Vietnam expanded to remote areas in hopes of eliminating the Communist guerrillas, who were aided by supply lines along the Ho Chi Minh Trail. Large battles in I Corps and the central highlands were followed by the enemy's 1968 Tet offensive, which caused the U.S. to reconsider its commitment to the war. After gradual American disengagement, the weak South Vietnamese army could not hold back advancing Communist forces. Saigon fell in April 1975.*

units of the North Vietnamese Army (NVA).

Large-scale battles were, however, rare in Vietnam. The Communists realized quickly that they could never match the mammoth U.S. war machine. Instead, guerrillas operated in small cadres, relying on stealth and mobility to fight. In order to survive against a stronger foe, they struck selectively, ambushing and harassing the enemy. Ho Chi Minh's analogy for the struggle against the French rang true for the Communist fight against the Americans a decade later. Comparing the guerrilla to a tiger and the stronger enemy to an elephant, Ho said, "If the tiger ever pauses, the elephant will impale him on his mighty tusks. But the tiger will not pause, and the elephant will die of exhaustion and loss of blood."

The guerrillas' elusiveness eventually forced American tactics to include counterinsurgency and guerrilla fighting, although large "search and destroy" sweeps remained common. Vietnam was a war without fronts; the enemy was not across the trenches, he was usually under-foot, or hiding in the countryside. The average infan-tryman in Vietnam spent much of his time sloshing through swamps and jungles or trudging through ele-phant grass on patrols in search of the enemy. When American forces encountered VC or NVA troops, they often called in air or artillery strikes to flush them out of the dense undergrowth. One officer explained the stan-dard operating procedure for many commanders when engaging the enemy: "Blow the hell out of him and police up." While this tactic often saved American lives, it usually drove the Communists from the battlefield, either into vast tunnel complexes in nearby villages or to sanctu-aries in Laos and Cambodia. U.S. forces rarely occupied remote areas for any length of time; after the enemy had been forced out, the Americans usually moved on to the next area, often allowing the Communists to reoccupy their old territory until the next U.S. patrol.

A more subtle battle with the Communists took place in Vietnamese villages, where both sides vied for control of the "hearts and minds" of the peasants. Sub-scribing to Mao's aphorism that "the people are the ocean in which the guerrilla swims," the VC elicited the support and material assistance of the people, often with notable success. As a result, many populated areas were Commu-nist-controlled, despite American and ARVN pacification programs. Describing one region particularly sympa-thetic to the VC, one soldier said, "We owned them in the daytime and the VC owned them at night. . . . We stayed the hell out of the villages at night." The question-able loyalty of the population led American soldiers to wonder sometimes just who the enemy was. The same villager who welcomed them by day may have ambushed them by night. Homemade booby traps were common: Americans entering a village would frequently trip a rudimentary grenade or step onto "punji" stakes.

Complicating the American task was the inexorable intertwining of military strategy and political goals that frustrated many military men. Commanders were exas-perated by the limits imposed on them by their govern-ment. Washington occasionally halted the bombing of North Vietnam and the Ho Chi Minh Trail as a peace gesture, despite requests that it be continued in order to wear down the enemy and to protect American troops.

Although the Communists used Laos and Cambodia as sanctuaries, American units were forbidden to go in and rout them. General Westmoreland continually expressed frustration at not being allowed to take the war to the enemy wherever he was, but President Johnson, fearful of provoking China into entering the conflict, as had hap-pened in Korea, was determined to have Vietnam remain a "limited war." American forces would respect interna-tional boundaries, even though their enemy did not. Incursions into Laos and Cambodia later in the war had little effect on enemy activity; for the American com-mand, they were too little, too late.

As the war wore on, the elephant showed signs of exhaustion. While U.S. forces had the upper hand in the vast majority of actions against the enemy, the Com-munist Tet offensive in 1968 shattered the illusion that an American victory was in sight. The generation that had been told that fighting the war was "the thing to do" questioned the conflict in much greater numbers. Popular opposition continued to climb: By March 1968 polls showed a majority of Americans had come to believe that U.S. involvement in Vietnam was a mistake. Later that month President Johnson opened the door for a negotiated settlement, denying Westmoreland's request for more than 200,000 additional troops and announcing that he would not seek reelection.

Johnson's successor, Richard Nixon, began to reduce American participation in the fighting. He pushed "Vietnamization," an ultimately futile process that was supposed to shore up ARVN forces to continue the fight alone. To Nixon, however, withdrawal did not necessarily mean weakness: The fury of the Christmas 1972 bombing of North Vietnam indicated that "Peace with Honor" included a clear exhibition of American might.

The Paris accords signed in January 1973 and the North Vietnamese conquest of the South two years later made many Americans wonder what the country had been doing in Vietnam in the first place. But after 58,000 American deaths, billions of dollars, and twenty years, the answer to such a question was still not evident. The war had split America in two. It took nearly a decade before the wounds would start to heal. ❖

America in Vietnam

In order to deny control of the jungles and highlands of South Vietnam to the Communists, American forces employed a combination of modern technology and traditional tactics against an elusive enemy force. Clockwise from right. U.S. Marines carry the body of a comrade killed in an ambush near the DMZ, September 1966; soldiers of the 1st Cavalry Division (Airmobile) leap from a helicopter during a 1967 operation against the enemy near Chu

Lai; American B-52s such as this one dropped tons of bombs on North Vietnam and the Ho Chi Minh Trail in an effort to halt infiltration into the South; Firebase Fuller, the northernmost U.S. outpost in South Vietnam, provided fire support for American troops operating near the DMZ; (inset) an American AE-1 Skyraider drops a phosphorous bomb on a village in the highlands in 1966.

The Outposts
Fighting in the Highlands

The remote jungles and high-lands of Vietnam were the battle-field of the Vietcong. To monitor enemy presence in these areas, the American military command established Special Forces camps, manned by "Green Berets" trained in counterinsurgency guerrilla fighting and in working with local militia. When these camps came under attack, as they often did, commanders faced a tough choice: Either defend the outpost against a frequently stronger force or evacuate, temporarily conceding the area to the enemy.

On July 5, 1964, many of the twelve Green Berets manning the camp at Nam Dong were convinced that their post was about to be attacked. Nam Dong's location in the central highlands of South Vietnam, only twenty-four kilometers from Laos, invited constant probing by VC and NVA troops infiltrating over the border. In the past two days, patrols had encountered evidence of a greater enemy presence, including the bodies of two murdered village chiefs. Also, a recent scuffle between the South Vietnamese troops and the montagnard natives of the highlands had fragmented the force, and this infighting had probably come to the attention of the enemy. By the night of the fifth, the mood was one of jittery anticipation: One American wrote his wife, "All hell is going to break loose here before the night is over."

Early the next morning Captain Roger H. C. Donlon was finishing his patrol of the American sector of the camp. A native of New York State, Donlon had enlisted in the army in 1958 after two years in the air force and one year at West Point. Now, after training at the army's Special Forces school at Fort Bragg, he was commander of Detachment A-726 at Nam Dong, numbering over 300 men, mostly South Vietnamese and montagnards. Donlon also expected an attack that night, but as he walked around the camp at 2:25 A.M., all was quiet, leading him to think that perhaps he had been wrong.

Moments later Captain Donlon's worst fears were confirmed. An enemy mortar round whistled into the camp, destroying the mess hall Donlon was about to enter. Another shell hit the command post, setting it on fire. Small-arms fire and explosions erupted in the darkness around the camp.

A nearby mortar explosion knocked Donlon to the ground. Pulling himself up, he scrambled to a mortar pit, grabbed a flare gun, and fired, only to hear the shell fizzle out in the darkness. He moved to the next emplacement for more rounds.

In the light of another flare, Donlon saw three VC sappers—guerrillas wired with explosives—lurking near the gate. He set his AR15 rifle on semi-automatic and squeezed off six rounds, then threw a hand grenade, killing all three of the raiders.

As Donlon ran for the next pit a grenade exploded near him, driving shrapnel into his left arm and stomach. Despite his wounds, he visited three

Captain Roger Donlon stands in the pit where he was wounded by a mortar blast during a Vietcong attack on the Special Forces camp at Nam Dong on July 6, 1964.

Roger Donlon receives the first Medal of Honor for the Vietnam War from President Johnson on December 5, 1964.

additional emplacements, helping his men direct fire at guerrillas trying to scale or blast through the fence. He was hit again by fragments from at least three mortar blasts, which wounded his leg and side. Bleeding heavily now, Donlon made for another pit, where he and three other Americans continued firing. The pit was, in Donlon's words, "a hellhole." The VC had overrun part of the outer sector of the camp and threatened to breach the inner American perimeter. Grenades were now coming over the fence five or six at a time.

As the onslaught continued, the four men prepared to evacuate the bunker. Donlon fired cover as two men fled, but the third, Master Sergeant

Below. *The bodies of Vietcong sappers killed by Donlon lie near the gate of the camp at Nam Dong after the battle.*

Gabriel Alamo, was too badly wounded to move. Donlon started to pull Alamo up the steps of the pit just as a mortar round landed at the top of the stairs in front of the captain's face. Donlon remembered screaming as he took the brunt of the explosion. "*I am going to die*, I thought. The screaming . . . was the wail of death."

Donlon did not die, but he was badly hurt, bleeding from wounds to the left shoulder, head, and stomach. He checked Alamo, but the sergeant had been killed by the blast. Donlon ran over to some montagnards and tended their wounds, tearing his T-shirt for bandages and using one of his socks as a tourniquet. Ordering the men to cover him, he scuttled over to another bunker, bent over by the pain of his stomach wounds. After getting a report on the defense of the camp, he was hit again by shrapnel but did not stop for treatment, instead directing his men in the darkness.

An American flareship arrived at 4:00 A.M. but the enemy persisted. From the dark jungle a voice called in Vietnamese and then in English. "Lay down your weapons!" the voice said. "We are going to annihilate your camp! You will all be killed!" But Captain Donlon and the defenders of Nam Dong held out. By daylight what was left of the enemy force, later estimated at over 800, had retreated, leaving over 50 dead. Captain Donlon was directing the treatment and evacuation of the wounded, including, finally, himself. By the end of the year Donlon had recovered from his wounds and was called to the White House to receive the first Medal of Honor for the Vietnam War.

The Special Forces camp at Kham Duc, like its counterpart at Nam Dong, was tucked away in the central highlands, sixteen kilometers from the Laotian border. After the fall of Camp Lang Vei during the Tet offensive in February

1968, Kham Duc was the only observation camp remaining in I Corps, the northernmost military district in South Vietnam and the scene of some of the heaviest fighting. In the spring of 1968, intelligence reports indicated an enemy build-up in the area, and a nearby forward operating post was overrun on May 10. When Kham Duc came under heavy mortar attack on the tenth and eleventh, General Westmoreland ordered it evacuated the next day.

As the sun came up on the twelfth, Mother's Day, a heavy fog hung over the camp, obscuring enemy movements in the surrounding hills. An army CH-47 helicopter and two air force C-130 Hercules cargo ships tried to land and take off with personnel, but all were disabled by enemy fire. One C-130 burst into flames at the end of the runway, killing the crew and over 150 Vietnamese civilians. Finally a C-130 was able to land and take off with passengers, but as it left its pilot warned other aircraft: "For God's sake stay out of Kham Duc. It belongs to Charlie."

At three that afternoon, an air force C-123 Provider cargo plane took off from Da Nang, bound for Kham Duc. At the controls was Lieutenant Colonel Joe M. Jackson, a twenty-seven-year veteran who had flown 107 combat missions in Korea. In 1967 Jackson received orders to go to Vietnam to fly transport planes, although, in his words, "my bag was really fighter planes." The C-123 was a "pretty big clumsy old airplane," Jackson remembered, "very slow, but very strong."

Jackson and his three-man crew reached the Kham Duc area at about three-thirty, just as a plane was about to take off with the last of the men on the ground aboard. By now flames engulfed the camp, and enemy shells still rained down from the hills. As the last C-130 pilot to leave the ground announced that

Lieutenant Colonel Joe M. Jackson, a Korean War veteran and former U-2 pilot, earned the Medal of Honor piloting a cargo plane in Vietnam.

he had picked up the remaining personnel, the airborne commander ordered the fighters circling overhead to descend and destroy the camp.

Just then the C-130 broke in. "Negative! Negative! Three men are still on the ground!" The combat control team, in charge of directing the evacuation, was still at the base, unaware that the evacuation was complete. As they searched the camp for anyone who had been left behind, they realized that they were the only ones left.

Meanwhile, above the camp, the airborne commander asked the next aircraft in line to try to land on the airstrip to pick up the men. Lieutenant Colonel Alfred Jeanotte guided his C-123 down over the hills and onto the debris-covered runway, cutting his speed as he and his crew looked for the three men. Enemy fire intensified, however, so Jeanotte accelerated for takeoff—too late to see the men jump from a ditch and try to signal him. As Jeanotte took off, sev-

In the only known photograph of a Medal of Honor action, Jackson turns his C-123 on the runway of the Kham Duc base under heavy fire as three men left on the ground run to the plane. This photo was taken by another American pilot circling overhead.

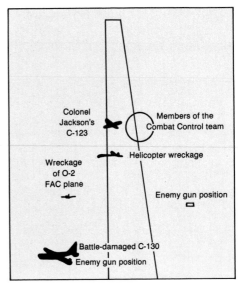

This diagram of the photograph at left indicates the positions of the wreckage on the runway that prevented a full landing and the two enemy guns.

eral pilots overhead spotted the team. When the commander asked for a volunteer to go in for another try, Jackson and his copilot, Major Jesse Campbell, realized that they were in the best position to land. While Campbell radioed, "Roger, going in," Jackson started the descent from 9,000 feet.

The approach was more like that of a jet fighter than a "big clumsy old airplane"; the C-123 dove at a rate of almost 4,000 feet per minute—nearly eight times the standard drop for a normal cargo plane's landing. At 4,000 feet the C-123 came under heavy fire that followed it down onto the runway.

Jackson realized that if he reversed his propellers to stop the aircraft, he would shut off the two auxiliary engines he needed for a quick escape. Instead, he simply jammed on the brakes, and the C-123 skidded halfway down the 6,000-foot runway. Campbell spotted the three men in a ditch beside the runway, but debris prevented Jackson from taxiing any closer to them. As the C-123 turned to take off the way it came in, the three men jumped from the culvert and ran for the plane, under fire from enemy gun positions farther down the runway. They jumped into the open cargo door at the rear, the loadmaster shouted, "All on board!" and Jackson prepared to take off down the runway.

Just then Campbell shouted, "Look out!" From the edge of the runway came

a 122mm rocket, fired from just outside the perimeter. The two watched as the shell skidded along the asphalt, broke in half, and stopped only ten meters from the plane. It did not explode. Jackson taxied around the shell and applied full power, taking off under heavy fire from the hills on either side. The plane had been on the ground at Kham Duc for less than a minute. Upon landing at Da Nang, Jackson and Campbell inspected the plane and were amazed to discover that it had not been hit by enemy bullets. "I will never understand that," said Jackson.

Later that day, Joe Jackson wrote a Mother's Day letter to his wife. "I had an extremely exciting mission today," he said. "I can't describe it to you in a letter but one of these days I'll tell you all about it." Eight months later, on January 16, 1969, Rosie Jackson heard the rest of the story as President Johnson hung the air force Medal of Honor around her husband's neck. ❖

Jungle War
No Permission to Die

Combat can be a solitary action. The soldier fighting in the field is concerned not so much with the movement of divisions and regiments as with a more immediate, personal goal: staying alive. While thousands of men may march in a single battle, each fights not for the glory of nations but for his own world—his personal survival and that of those closest to him.

Many of the acts of valor in Vietnam reflected this individual aspect of war. While these incidents may not have been part of some grand offensive or victory, they typify a more personal triumph of men in the isolated forests and jungles of Southeast Asia.

Jay Vargas had never seen a Medal of Honor recipient in person until he was a twenty-five-year-old second lieutenant with the 3d Marine Division in Okinawa in 1964. Absent-mindedly walking into the office of Brigadier General Raymond G. Davis, a Korea Medal of Honor recipient, Vargas was flabbergasted to see Davis talking to four other men—Reginald Myers, Carl Sitter, William Barber, and Louis Wilson—all wearing the distinctive blue ribbon of the medal. He sheepishly excused himself, but Davis asked him to stay, and the young officer spent some time with the group. Reporting back to his commander, Vargas almost forgot the message he was to deliver; all he could say was that he had just met five Medal of Honor men.

Four years later, on the morning of May 1, 1968, Captain Jay Vargas and his unit, Company G of the 2d Battalion,

Jay Vargas led a company of marines in a two-day battle with enemy soldiers in the village of Dai Do. Though he was wounded three times, he carried several other injured men to safety.

4th Marines, floated down the Cua Viet River in tank-bearing boats. The objective was the village of Dai Do, fifteen kilometers south of the demilitarized zone (DMZ), the border between North and South Vietnam, where two marine companies had been battered by a North Vietnamese regiment. Pulling ashore one kilometer southeast of the village, Vargas and his men, with Bravo Company on the left flank, set out across 700 meters of rice fields toward Dai Do. For the next two days, they would be involved in a bloody seesaw battle for control of the village.

Company G came under heavy fire almost as soon as it hit the shore. As the Americans swept across the open fields, NVA soldiers popped up from hidden "spider holes" and poured AK47 fire on them. Nearby, Bravo Company lost most of its officers in the fire. An inexperienced second lieutenant assumed command, then got on the radio and started babbling hysterically, talking of pulling his men back.

Vargas realized that Bravo's withdrawal could decimate his own company, so he got on the radio and calmed the lieutenant down. Then he continued the attack by bringing up his reserve platoon to help. Soon the marines had taken Dai Do and had pushed the NVA into another village a few kilometers away, where they were battered by American gunships.

Eventually, however, the enemy counterattacked and pushed the marines to the other side of Dai Do. Vargas and sixty men took cover in a graveyard, pulling bodies from freshly dug graves to improvise foxholes. The enemy threatened from all sides as the marines drew a perimeter. When night fell Vargas ordered his men to stay down and shoot at anything that moved above them.

AC-130 gunships circled overhead, and American artillery shells, some fired

U.S. Marines in the decimated village of Dai Do after heavy fighting between North Vietnamese and American troops, May 1968.

from navy ships offshore, landed within fifty meters of the men of Company G. Through the night several American commanders, even General Westmoreland, spoke to Vargas on the radio, offering encouragement. "It was almost as if the World Series had started and they didn't have a ticket," Vargas recalled. "And all they could do was listen on the radio." Years later Vargas met one of the admirals who had spoken to him on that occasion; the admiral told him that he and his fellow officers had doubted that any of the marines would last the night.

At sunrise on May 2 the men were still in the graveyard, and Vargas, as he recounted later, "decided that I'd had enough." Hooking up with Echo Company, commanded by Captain James E. Livingston, Vargas launched a counterattack through Dai Do and once more cleared out the enemy. In the aftermath of ground fighting and air strikes, recalled Vargas, the village "almost looked like the moon," with bomb craters, denuded trees, and leveled shacks. Scores of North Vietnamese bodies lay in the streets.

No sooner had the marines relaxed than the enemy reversed and counterattacked yet again. Vargas and his men were low on ammunition, so they grabbed anything that could be used as a weapon and fought the enemy hand-to-hand. Vargas was wounded by shrapnel for the third time in as many days: One piece lodged between his skull and scalp; another split his lip, making it difficult for him to speak.

The 2d Battalion commander joined Vargas and his men in a trench in the village. As artillery fire edged closer, an NVA soldier fired into the ditch, killing three men and wounding the commander. Vargas hoisted the colonel onto his back and, armed with only a .45-caliber pistol, made his way through a nearby paddy. On the way an enemy soldier raised his rifle to fire at the two men. Vargas stumbled and his pistol discharged; the bullet ricocheted off a wall and struck the enemy soldier in the stomach. "He was more surprised than I was," Vargas remembered.

That afternoon Captain Vargas brought at least six men back for medical attention, fighting his way to his men each time and killing eight enemy soldiers at close range. By the night of the second, reinforcements had arrived and the enemy was routed, with over 800 dead. Seventy-two marines were killed, hundreds wounded. Said Vargas, "I don't know why I didn't get killed."

Both Jay Vargas and James Livingston (who led Company E against

James E. Livingston also received the Medal of Honor for bravery at Dai Do. Even after his wounds made it impossible for him to walk, Livingston continued to lead his company in the battle.

289

enemy emplacements despite shrapnel wounds) were awarded the Medal of Honor for this battle. The men were told to bring their families to Washington for the presentation at the White House on May 14, 1970.

A few months before the ceremony Vargas's mother, an Italian immigrant widely respected in her Arizona community, died suddenly. Grieved by the loss, Vargas had a unique request: He asked that the name of his mother, Maria Teresa Sandini Vargas, be engraved on the back of his medal instead of his own. President Nixon was touched by the sentiment and granted the request. So the name on the medal, and the name entered onto the Medal of Honor rolls, is "M. Sando Vargas," a tribute not only to a marine's valor in Vietnam, but also a son's love for his mother.

"Get us out of here! For God's sake, get us out!" The voice coming over the radio was frantic. A twelve-man Special Forces reconnaissance team had been inserted forty-eight kilometers inside Cambodia on a top-secret intelligence-gathering mission but had come under fire from a much larger North Vietnamese force. Now the team leader was calling the base at Loc Ninh urgently to request helicopter extraction.

Special Forces Staff Sergeant Roy P. Benavidez, standing inside the radio shack at Loc Ninh that day, May 2, 1968, was amazed at the sound of gunfire coming over the radio. "There was so much shooting," he remembered, "it sounded like a popcorn machine." Benavidez rushed to the helicopter pad as the first chopper returned from Cambodia. The wounded door gunner spilled out of the aircraft and died in Benavidez's arms. A few minutes later Benavidez jumped into a UH-1 "Huey" helicopter as it readied for takeoff. "Where are you going?" asked the surprised pilot. "I'm going with you," Benavidez said.

Over the border, enemy fire around the men on the ground was too heavy to allow the Huey to land near them. The pilot reached another clearing seventy-five yards away, where Benavidez told him to drop him off and wait for his call on the radio after he had reached the besieged men. Benavidez crossed himself, jumped ten feet to the ground, and started running toward the American position.

Enemy fire poured at him from trees and bushes all around. Benavidez felt the bullets cut into his legs and face. The fire knocked him down several times, but he kept on going. "When you're shot, you feel a burning pain, like you've been touched with hot metal," Benavidez explained later. "But the fear that you experience is worse—and that's what keeps you going."

Reaching the team, Benavidez found four men already dead, and the other eight lying wounded in the grass. He set off a smoke grenade to mark the spot for the helicopter and ordered the men to provide covering fire for the landing. When the helicopter touched down, a few Americans climbed aboard while Benavidez ran to the body of the team leader to retrieve classified documents and a camera. While returning, Benavidez was shot in the back and knocked down; looking up, he saw the helicopter crash and burn after being hit by sniper fire. He ran to the aircraft and pulled out two crewmen, then led them and the remaining six men to the edge of the pickup zone, where they drew a small defensive perimeter.

Benavidez called for additional air support on the radio and distributed water and ammunition to the men. He gave the wounded shots of morphine, injecting two doses into his own veins. Then he was hit in the thigh by another bullet. By now he was bleeding heavily from bullet wounds all over his body,

and the blood from his head wounds made it practically impossible for him to see. He could hear the moans of the men above the gunfire. One man whose leg had been blown off begged Benavidez to kill him. The sergeant tried to silence them. "Shut up!" he said. "We don't have permission to die!"

Benavidez and the others were on the ground almost eight hours. Several helicopters were shot down trying to evacuate the men, but finally one got close enough to land. After taking some men to the aircraft, Benavidez was about to pick up another when he was struck on the back of the head by a rifle butt. Wheeling around he saw a North Vietnamese soldier thrusting a bayonet toward his midsection. Benavidez grabbed the blade, cutting open his own hand, pulled the man to him, and stabbed him with his knife.

Stumbling back to the helicopter, Benavidez helped load the wounded onto the aircraft, pulling in anyone he could make out through the blood dripping into his eyes. He picked up a rifle and killed two enemy soldiers as they charged the ship. Finally he was pulled aboard and collapsed near the pile of bodies in the back, holding his intestines in with his hands. As the Huey rose, blood trickled out its side doors.

The helicopter made it back to Loc Ninh with seventeen men, both dead and alive. As the bodies were unloaded, a doctor thought that Benavidez was dead, and a body bag was prepared for him. Unable to move or speak, Benavidez spit into the startled doctor's face. The doctor ordered him flown to Saigon for treatment.

The men at Loc Ninh assumed that Roy Benavidez would die. His commanding officer, Lieutenant Colonel Ralph Drake, awarded him the Distinguished Service Cross so that he would receive some recognition before

Retired Master Sergeant Roy Benavidez (right foreground) walks with President Ronald Reagan before his Medal of Honor presentation ceremony in the Pentagon court-yard, February 24, 1981.

he died. But Benavidez slowly recovered from his wounds and was discharged from the army in 1976 with 80 percent medical disability classification. Meanwhile, Lieutenant Colonel Drake learned that his former sergeant was alive and petitioned the army to elevate his award to the Medal of Honor.

The web of regulations that govern Medal of Honor reviews slowed Drake's recommendation. In order for Benavidez's case to be reopened, at least two eyewitness statements were needed: one to verify that he had jumped on the helicopter at Loc Ninh and another to account for his actions on the ground. There was verification of the former action, but as far as Benavidez knew, all of the eight men whose lives he had been credited with saving had since died.

But one had survived. In 1980,

after publication of a national newspaper story concerning Benavidez's campaign for the medal, the sole surviving member of the team that he had saved was located on the Fiji Islands. Like the others, he had thought that Benavidez had died from his wounds. Finally, on February 24, 1981, almost thirteen years after the episode in the Cambodian jungle, President Ronald Reagan awarded Roy Benavidez the Medal of Honor. Benavidez was the last living man to receive the medal for the Vietnam War. ◈

Hill 875
The Battle for Dak To

In November 1967, one of the few large battles of the war pitted American troops against a well-entrenched North Vietnamese force near Dak To in the central highlands beside the Laotian and Cambodian borders. After two weeks of fighting, American and ARVN troops got the upper hand, and the NVA began to retreat to its sanctuaries across the border, leapfrogging over its fortifications to slow down its pursuers. But the Communists were determined to make one last stand inside the border and on November 19 began a furious battle just six kilometers from Cambodia. Like many others in the war, it was a battle for a remote hill known to most only by its height in meters: 875.

On the morning of November 19, 1967, U.S. Army paratroopers poised to push the North Vietnamese over the border into Cambodia. The NVA was still dug in on the summit of Hill 875, despite American bombs and artillery that had reduced much of the heavy foliage to twigs and branches. At 9:45, after American planes peppered the hill with fire, Companies C and D of the 2d Battalion, 503d Infantry, 173d Airborne Brigade, started up the steep north side of 875. Taking up the rear was Alpha Company, on the lookout for NVA attacks from the forest below. Despite the bare trees and scattered bamboo, the Americans knew that the enemy still had plenty of places to hide.

Contact was not long in coming. Within forty-five minutes the two lead companies came under rifle and grenade fire from above. Alpha Company, 100 meters downhill, braced for an assault from below.

Taking up the rear of Company A was a four-man squad led by Specialist Fourth Class James Kelley. Just after two o'clock the four heard rustling in the brush below. Holding his fire until the enemy got close, Private First Class Carlos Lozada, a twenty-one-year-old native of Puerto Rico, gripped his M60 machine gun and waited.

Suddenly enemy fire broke out on the left. Lozada yelled "Here they come, Kelley!" and started firing down the hill at a group of about fifteen regulars advancing toward him. Several fell, but others continued to press up the slope. Kelley ordered the other three to fall back, and Lozada carried his machine gun to a log and continued firing in long sweeps. Kelley shot an enemy soldier at close range, but then his M16 jammed. To cover him, Lozada jumped up from his cover and into the trail, holding the twenty-four-pound M60 at his hip as he fired at the advancing enemy.

Men of the 4th Battalion, 503d Infantry, search the scarred landscape of Hill 875 for signs of the enemy, November 1967.

292

Above. *Private First Class Carlos Lozada.* Right. *A wounded paratrooper is given plasma in the heat of battle on Hill 875.*

Kelley cleared his rifle and started firing downhill. Lozada ran out of ammunition, so he retreated up the trail behind another member of the squad. An instant later an enemy bullet struck him in the head, knocking him into his comrade. Lozada was mortally wounded, but Kelley and the others carried him uphill as they fired at the enemy and dropped grenades on the trail. By the time they had rejoined the rest of the men farther up the hill, the NVA were swarming up the side of 875. The three companies were surrounded by close to 300 North Vietnamese, firing from bunkers and tunnels amid the bamboo.

As the afternoon wore on, the three companies consolidated their perimeters. Enemy rifle and rocket fire fell all around them. American fighters dropped bombs and strafed NVA positions just outside the 2d Battalion lines. At the center of the perimeter a combined command post was established where the scores of wounded were brought for treatment.

One of those assisting was Major Charles J. Watters, a Roman Catholic priest from New Jersey, one of the 173d's chaplains. In the months before Dak To, Father Watters had been a comfort for many of the weary men of the 173d. One soldier had told Watters of his brother, who had just been drafted. He spoke of his fear that his brother might be killed. "I said, 'If it's got to happen, let it happen to me.'" Watters replied, "Let it happen to me, then, son."

On the morning of the nineteenth, Charlie Watters had celebrated mass with the men of the 2d Battalion before they started up Hill 875. Several hours later, he was braving enemy fire to care for the wounded and dying. When a wounded soldier had frozen in shock before the NVA, Father Watters ran out to pull him to safety. Six times he went beyond the perimeter to retrieve wounded men, braving heavy enemy fire. In the late afternoon, with so many men lying wounded in the hot sun, Father Watters continued to perform his duties, assisting the medics and administering last rites while fighters pounded enemy positions on the hill.

Just before 7:00 P.M. dusk fell over the area. From out of the west flew an American fighter, about to strike an enemy position. One of its 750-pound bombs fell short of its target, however, and landed directly on the center of the Charlie Company command post. At least forty-two men were killed, including the entire company command group. Also killed instantly was Father Watters, a victim of "friendly fire."

Below. Wearing vestments made from parachute silk, Father Charles Watters says mass in the field in the summer of 1967.

Watters was one of two chaplains who was awarded a posthumous Medal of Honor during the Vietnam War.

Ninety-eight pairs of boots signify the dead of the 2d Battalion, 503d Infantry, in a memorial service for the men of the unit killed during the battle for Hill 875. Included is a pair of boots for Private First Class Carlos Lozada.

Four days later, Hill 875 fell to the 173d paratroopers. It was Thanksgiving Day; in the afternoon helicopters flew in turkey dinners, which the men ate amid the ruins of a costly battle. The two battalions that had fought for Hill 875 had lost 158 men, with another 402 wounded. North Vietnamese dead from the fighting around Dak To exceeded 1,600. General Westmoreland, stating the Communists were seeking a headline victory, called Dak To "the beginning of a great defeat for the enemy."

Private First Class Carlos Lozada and Major Charles J. Watters were later awarded the Medal of Honor posthumously for their actions on Hill 875. Father Watters was one of seven chaplains who have received the medal, three of whom were decorated for service in Vietnam. His uncle, John J. Doran, received the medal sixty-eight years earlier during the Spanish-American War for helping cut the enemy cables in Cienfuegos Harbor, Cuba. ◈

The *Liberty*

While Americans were fighting thousands of miles away in Vietnam, one navy vessel ran afoul of another conflict. Its commander's leadership under fire earned him the only Vietnam-era Medal of Honor given for action outside of Southeast Asia.

On June 8, 1967, the U.S.S. *Liberty* cruised quietly in the eastern Mediterranean Sea near Egypt's Sinai Peninsula. The *Liberty,* a "spook ship," or spy vessel, had sailed to the area under the direction of the National Security Agency. Loaded with electronic intelligence-gathering equipment, its mission was to monitor the communications of both sides during the Six Day War between Israel and the Arab states.

Twenty-two kilometers off the Sinai Peninsula, the *Liberty* began to attract attention. After Israeli aircraft flew overhead several times to reconnoiter the vessel, its supervisors in the Pentagon decided to pull back the ship to avoid danger. But inexplicably, the order to withdraw never reached the *Liberty.* The ship sailed on to its doom.

On the deck of the *Liberty,* Commander William L. McGonagle addressed his crew on the intercom after the third general quarters drill in four days. Pointing out the black smoke rising from the city of El Arish to the south, McGonagle reminded the 286 men on board that the ship was near a war zone and that all hands had to be "heads-up ballplayers."

Just a few minutes after 2:00 P.M. the war descended on the American ship. From the north came an Israeli Mirage fighter. McGonagle ordered the men at the two forward guns to be ready. Two more Mirages swept down from astern. Then, remembered one officer, "searing heat and terrible noise suddenly came from everywhere." The *Liberty* was under attack.

A terrific explosion rocked the bridge. Rockets and bullets pounded the vessel, punching holes in the bulkheads and scattering the confused men. For the next seven minutes the jets battered the *Liberty.* At each of the ship's four .50-caliber machine guns, sailors were struck down by the fire from overhead. French-built Mystère jets appeared and started dropping napalm. The deadly gelatin splattered on the deck, burning both steel and flesh.

Eight minutes later the attack ended. The jets disappeared, leaving eight men dead. McGonagle was bleeding from a shrapnel wound in the right leg; he left a trail of blood as he checked on casualties and directed damage-control teams. An ensign applied a tourniquet to the commander's leg, but McGonagle remained in command. He would not leave the bridge for seventeen hours.

At 2:24 three motor torpedo boats were sighted off the starboard quarter. Minutes later they moved in and opened fire. One torpedo missed the stern by seventy-five feet, but another struck the Number 3 hold and ripped into the communications center, killing twenty-five, including the civilian NSA supervisor.

The second attack left the *Liberty* almost completely powerless, its radio disabled. Thirty-four men were dead or dying. Over 800 holes had been shot in the ship, and the torpedo had left a gaping hole at the water line. When one of the boats neared and signaled, "Do you need help?" McGonagle leaned over the wing of the bridge and shouted, "Go to hell!"

Minutes later two helicopters full of Israeli troops appeared and hovered overhead. The men of the *Liberty* watched tensely, expecting an armed boarding. But the helicopters departed, followed soon by the boats.

The *Liberty* regained power and limped north at eight knots. McGonagle lay down and propped his wounded leg on a chair to stop the bleeding. After dusk, he guided the ship by watching its wake and the stars and directing the manipulation of the rudder.

Throughout the night McGonagle remained on the bridge. Weak from loss of blood, he occasionally lapsed into incoherence, slurring his commands. To the men of the *Liberty,* dazed by the attack, the commander's determination was an inspiration. "To know that he was on the bridge grievously wounded," the ship's medical officer testified later, "was the thing that told [the wounded] 'we're going to live.'"

At seven the next morning the *Liberty* rendezvoused with the destroyer U.S.S. *Jefferson Davis.* As the dead and wounded were transferred, William McGonagle gave up command. After medical treatment he went below to his cabin, where fire had scorched the furniture and a rocket had exploded in his pillow. McGonagle ordered an unexploded shell removed from his shower, then retired and slept almost twenty-four hours.

Though the attack was over, the repercussions from it were just beginning. Israel apologized immediately, claiming that the vessel had not been flying its flag and that Israeli planes mistook it for an Egyptian freighter. Anxious to avoid embarrassing an ally, the U.S. finally accepted the Israeli apology (and later monetary compensation) but rejected the explanation.

The navy was willing to recognize courage, regardless of the political situation. On June 11, 1968, in what one navy account called "a muted ceremony" at the Washington Navy Yard, Captain William McGonagle received the Medal of Honor for his "superb professionalism, courageous fighting spirit, and valiant leadership." McGonagle's citation, however, makes no mention of the nationality of his ship's attackers.

Three Weeks at Hue
The Tet Offensive

Dak To and the other "border battles" of 1967 were only a dress rehearsal for things to come. Despite optimistic public pronouncements, General Westmoreland and other American commanders expected a bold Communist offensive sometime in early 1968, probably after Tet, the Vietnamese New Year, at the end of January. Instead the enemy attacked in the middle of Tet, catching many American and ARVN troops off guard. Over 80,000 Vietcong and North Vietnamese troops emerged from the countryside to attack more than 100 South Vietnamese cities, towns, and military installations. Although the Communists were not able to hold any towns and suffered tremendous casualties, the Tet offensive struck a fatal blow to American resolve to continue the war.

At 3:40 on the morning of January 31, 1968, a savage rain of mortar shells and rockets began to pour down out of the early morning fog over Hue, eighty kilometers south of the DMZ. Like scores of other cities and towns all across South Vietnam, the ancient imperial capital was under Communist attack. The Tet offensive, the enemy's attempt to take the war to the streets of the South, had begun.

Over the next several hours five battalions of North Vietnamese regulars swarmed into the city, meeting little resistance as they swept along both banks of the Perfume River. Outnumbered ARVN troops quickly called for help. Two companies of U.S. Marines moved from Phu Bai, thirteen kilometers to the south, but were unsuccessful in their first attempts to breach the Citadel, the sacred palace of mandarin rulers of traditional Vietnam. By late morning the gold, blue, and red flag of the National Liberation Front, the formal Vietcong organization, flew over Hue.

To the south of the Citadel, across the Perfume, the enemy seized houses and controlled entire streets, threatening the U.S. advisory compound. At 10:00 A.M. an American Huey helicopter was shot down near the base, but the crew escaped to the compound under heavy fire. Five choppers tried to touch down to retrieve the men, some of whom were wounded, but were driven off by withering enemy fire. By noon all South Vietnamese and American aircraft were advised to stay clear of Hue.

At a base near Phu Bai at least one Huey pilot was preparing to ignore that advice. Chief Warrant Officer Fred Ferguson, whose flight service with the 227th Aviation Battalion ran the gamut from carrying troops to jungle landing zones to shipping supplies to isolated outposts, had been following the plight of the downed crew on his radio. He

Chief Warrant Officer Fred Ferguson in a UH-1 Iroquois "Huey" helicopter. On the first day of the Tet offensive Ferguson flew into Hue to rescue five men.

Sergeant Alfredo Gonzalez, Company A, 1st Battalion, 1st Marines, was killed in the fight to retake Hue.

decided to try to get into the compound. "If I was there, I'd want someone to get me out," Ferguson said later. "It was my duty, my job, to get them out."

After takeoff, Ferguson radioed the besieged crew that he was going to attempt a rescue. Flying parallel to the Perfume River and covered by volunteers in three other gunships, he made his approach through enemy mortar rounds and bullets. The chopper took several hits, scattering shrapnel in the cabin.

The only area in the compound where Ferguson had any chance of landing was a small space between one of the buildings and a flagpole. With only a few meters of clearance on either side for the overhead rotor, Ferguson touched down. The downed crew jumped on board as mortar shells slammed into the ground around them. The last of the five men climbed safely aboard, but just then a mortar round exploded near the tail, wounding the crew chief and causing the craft to shudder violently. When Ferguson saw that all were aboard, he applied full power, and the Huey rose slowly.

Just as the chopper got off the ground a mortar shell landed on the

patch of ground where the ship had been. The explosion spun the aircraft around, but Ferguson regained control and continued his ascent, passing within fifty meters of the enemy. The three ships covering for him were shot down and his own gunners ran out of ammunition, but the chopper limped back to Phu Bai. "The helicopter was coming apart," Ferguson remembered. "It was shaking so bad, I couldn't read the instruments." But the Huey made it back with the five men Ferguson had rescued.

In the first week of February, it became apparent that the enemy intended to hold Hue as long as they could. Eight to ten NVA battalions controlled the city, and efforts to dislodge them met with little success. By February 3, four days into the fight, 1,000 U.S. Marines had arrived in Hue, but they had seized only three blocks. They took on the enemy house by house, combat the likes of which had not been seen by Americans since the battle for Seoul in Korea seventeen years earlier.

Sergeant Alfredo Gonzalez was a platoon leader in Alpha Company of the 1st Battalion, 1st Marines, 1st Marine Division, the first unit deployed to Hue on the morning of January 31. After a battle with snipers along Highway 1 south of the city, Gonzalez and the rest of the company climbed aboard five tanks and slowly crossed the Perfume to the Citadel, where they came under immediate attack. A rocket-propelled grenade knocked the marines off the lead vehicle. Sergeant Gonzalez leaped from his tank, ran down the fire-swept street, and carried one of the men to safety, but was wounded by a fragmentation grenade.

Moving down the street, the men came under attack from a machine gun fired by a guerrilla hidden in a house. Gonzalez led his men to a low wall, then ran up to the window of the house and lobbed in a few grenades, silencing the gun. During the fighting, the Alpha

Amid rubble and smoke from a napalm strike, U.S. Marines take cover during heavy fighting in the Citadel at Hue.

Sergeant Joe R. Hooper of the 101st Airborne Division was one of the most decorated soldiers of the Vietnam War.

commander was wounded and evacuated, making Gonzalez commander.

The marines of Company A remained in the thick of the fighting over the next few days. On February 3, Gonzalez was wounded again in street fighting but refused evacuation. The next day, the men were again pinned down by rocket and small-arms fire. Gonzalez picked up single-shot M72 light antitank weapons from the dead and wounded as he moved down the street, firing at enemy positions in the houses and on the rooftops. During this exchange he was cut down by a burst of enemy machine-gun fire. Sergeant Gonzalez died after five days of fighting in the streets of Hue.

As the marines continued their push through Hue, the army moved to cut the supply lines that had allowed the enemy to hold the city. Elements of the 1st Cavalry Division (Airmobile) and the 101st Airborne Division took up positions west of the city and pushed through villages and rice fields toward

the Citadel. By February 21, the combined force was about to break through.

In the early afternoon of the twenty-first, Delta Company of the 2d Battalion, 501st Infantry, 101st Airborne Division, was approaching a river west of the city when Communist troops fired upon the men from the opposite shore. One squad leader, Sergeant Joe R. Hooper, led eight men across the river. After killing several enemy soldiers, they set up a machine-gun position in the nearby woods. Two grenades exploded nearby, wounding Hooper in the leg and groin, but he went back and led more men into the woods.

There the fighting intensified. Hooper destroyed five enemy positions and wrestled with several enemy troops, killing one officer with his bayonet. Although bleeding badly, he continued to lead the assault into the woods.

Inside the small forest, another squad leader, Staff Sergeant Clifford C. Sims, led his unit against an enemy force that had pinned down another platoon. Moving forward to hook up with another group, the men came upon a burning enemy ammunition shack. Exploding ordnance injured two men almost immediately; Sims moved the rest of his men back, knowing that the rest of the ammunition could blow any time.

On the move again, Sims and his men were advancing through the woods when they suddenly heard a distinctive click: the sound of a trip wire activating a booby trap. Within seconds the charge would explode, killing or wounding many of Sims's men. Shouting a warning to his men, Sims threw himself on the charge and was killed instantly by the blast. Saved by their squad leader, the men pressed on through the woods.

When the battle was over, all but 8 of the 190 Americans in Delta Company had been killed or wounded. Nonetheless, the Americans had overrun a North

Staff Sergeant Clifford Sims gave his life to save his comrades battling in the fields west of Hue.

Vietnamese radio complex that had been relaying messages to Hue. Isolated from their supply and communication lines, the NVA lost control of the Citadel two days later, and the South Vietnamese flag once again went up over the city.

For their actions during the battle at Hue, Fred Ferguson, Alfredo Gonzalez, Joe Hooper, and Clifford Sims later received the Medal of Honor. Despite an unwritten rule prohibiting Medal of Honor recipients from serving again in combat, Joe Hooper returned to Vietnam to serve once more with the 101st Airborne.

The Tet offensive began the period of the heaviest fighting of the war. After the setbacks suffered during the offensive, North Vietnamese regulars beefed up the depleted ranks of Vietcong battalions. In subsequent engagements American forces faced a better-equipped, more professional enemy force. With the escalation of the fighting also came a rise in the number of incidents for which the Medal of Honor was later awarded. Fifty-eight medals were awarded for actions during 1968, more than in any other year of the war. ◈

Dustoff
Rescue from Above

Helicopter evacuation of wounded was first practiced in Korea, but it came of age in Vietnam. Flying the UH-1 Iroquois, better known as the Huey, American pilots went unarmed into combat areas, loaded on casualties, and took off for field hospitals, often under heavy enemy fire. Such an operation carried the code name "dustoff," after the call sign of an early medevac pilot. To the wounded man in the field, the call sign meant rescue.

Michael Novosel straps into his Huey before a rescue mission in Vietnam. In two tours of duty Novosel evacuated more than 5,500 wounded men.

Michael J. Novosel was a twenty-two-year-old bomber pilot at the end of World War II. Joining the Army Air Corps ten months before Pearl Harbor, he was eager to see action overseas but spent most of the war as a flight instructor in Texas. In mid-1945, Novosel at last flew a few bombing missions over Japan. In the last days of the war, he also dropped supplies to American POWs in Japanese camps. When General Douglas MacArthur accepted the Japanese surrender on the deck of the U.S.S. *Missouri* on September 2, Lieutenant Novosel piloted one of the B-29s that passed overhead.

Nineteen years later, Novosel, by then a lieutenant colonel in the air force reserve, took a leave of absence from his job as a commercial airline pilot and asked to be returned to active duty and assigned to Vietnam. "I had skills my country needed," he later explained. After being told that the air force already had enough officers and that he was too old at forty-two, Novosel enlisted in the army as a warrant officer, a substantial reduction in rank. Because he did not require extensive training, Novosel recalled, "I came to the army quite cheap." Neither age nor size (he barely met the 5 feet 4 inch minimum height for pilots) deterred him: "Given enough cushions," he joked, "I could fly anything."

In a year of duty in Vietnam, Novosel flew medical evacuation helicopters, ferrying over 2,000 soldiers and civilians from the battlefield to local hospitals. It was a gratifying experience: He remembered thinking, "For the first time, I'm involved in a war and I'm not hurting anybody." After his tour, he was set to go back to his airline, but his discharge physical found that he had glaucoma, disqualifying him from further commercial flying. So Novosel reenlisted in the army, where he was able

to fly after agreeing to take medication four times a day. By the beginning of October 1969, he was flying Hueys again, this time near the Cambodian border west of Saigon.

At 4:00 P.M. on October 2, Novosel and his three-man crew had been on various dustoff missions for about seven hours when an urgent, highest-priority call came over the radio. A South Vietnamese strike force had been pinned down by the enemy on the border since early morning and now needed immediate medical evacuation. Novosel's Huey, given the call sign "Dustoff 88," headed for the battle area, flying through heavy thunderstorms before coming upon the thick elephant grass of the Plain of Reeds.

A command and control pilot flying overhead told Novosel that three ARVN companies now lay scattered and demoralized below. Hovering over the high grass, Novosel and his crew searched for any wounded men hiding in the growth, but the "friendlies" were unwilling to signal the chopper, fearing exposure to enemy fire. When small-arms fire intensified, Novosel backed off, radioing to the command and control helicopter, "They're most unfriendly down there."

Knowing that there might be men in the high grass, Novosel circled the area, a standard signal to the men below to prepare for evacuation. As he flew clockwise, enemy automatic weapons spit fire from every direction. "I never heard so much enemy fire before," Novosel's veteran crew chief said later, remembering enemy gun flashes "all around us."

One man stood up in the waist-high grass and started running toward the chopper. Novosel dropped to about one meter off the ground, still moving forward to evade fire. The ARVN soldier reached the ship and was pulled aboard by the crew chief and medic. "All of a sudden," Novosel recalled, "we started seeing others all over," waving to the helicopter or running after it as enemy bullets flew around them. Each was pulled in by the crewmen and shoved to the floor. After nine or ten men had been loaded, Novosel headed for his base at Moc Hoa. There he refueled and headed back for more pickups. He rescued a second load, refueled, then headed back a third time as dusk began to fall. While air force jets strafed the area, Novosel flew over a group of soldiers, leading them away from deep irrigation ditches to shallower water.

He was about to head back with his third load when he saw a wounded soldier lying in front of an enemy bunker. Novosel turned his craft around, warned his men to stay down, and gingerly backed toward the bunker. This tactic would allow for a quick getaway and also put the tail between the passengers and enemy bullets. The chopper reached the

man, and the crew chief grabbed him to pull him aboard.

At that moment an enemy soldier jumped up from the grass in front of the Huey and fired directly at Novosel. An AK47 round shattered the Plexiglas windshield, sending fragments into his leg and hand. Novosel momentarily lost control of the aircraft, then regained it. The wounded soldier slipped from the crew chief's grasp but held onto the skid of the aircraft as it gained altitude. He was pulled into the helicopter sixty feet off the ground. With another load of wounded, Dustoff 88 headed back to Moc Hoa. In all, Novosel had carried twenty-nine men out of the Plain of Reeds.

Novosel knew that the events of those three hours went "beyond a regular mission. You know when you go a little bit further than you're supposed to." Discounting his own actions, he recommended his three crew members for the Silver Star. But as he found out later, his

men recommended him for a higher award. On June 15, 1971, President Nixon presented the Medal of Honor to CWO Michael Novosel as his son, Michael Junior, who served with his father as a dustoff pilot, looked on. (The two Novosels were the only father-son flying team of the war, evacuating more than 8,000 wounded men.) On March 1, 1985, Mike Novosel, Sr., the last World War II army aviator on active duty, retired after forty-four years of military service.

When Novosel was awarded his army "Master Aviator" badge, it was pinned on by Major Patrick Henry Brady, who had been a dustoff pilot since 1964. Brady acquired a reputation as an especially good foul weather flier, able to operate in even "zero-zero" conditions, when rain or fog allowed only minimum visibility in both distance and altitude.

Such were the conditions in the mountains near Chu Lai on the morning of January 6, 1968. After a firefight in the area known as "Death Valley," two ARVN soldiers lay badly wounded on the valley floor. A thick ground fog made it seem unlikely they would be evacuated. Early that morning Major Brady, the most experienced pilot in the 54th Medical Detachment and the one who flew most of the "weather missions," took off to try to reach the wounded men.

The fog was several hundred feet deep, so Brady used a technique he had perfected on previous missions in fog. Tilting his UH-1H sideways, he used the chopper's rotor to blow away some of the mist. He found a trail on the valley floor and followed it, staying at an angle to cut through the stubborn murkiness and also to avoid presenting a clear target for

Patrick Henry Brady acquired a reputation as an excellent foul-weather dustoff pilot in South Vietnam.

the enemy. "The VC couldn't see me, so I was pretty secure," Brady remembered. "The trick was just flying sideways in that ground fog." Hugging the treetops, Brady came upon a small clearing near the ARVN troops and touched down. His crew helped the wounded aboard and "Dustoff 55" took off through the mist and headed for the hospital at Chu Lai.

On the way to the base, Brady received another call to fly to the Hiep Duc Valley to the north after dropping off his patients. A hilltop firebase had come under attack overnight, and now at least sixty men of the 198th Light Infantry Brigade lay wounded on the hillside and in the valley below the firebase. Two other aircraft had been shot down trying to reach the men in the fog,

and enemy troops were within fifty meters of the Americans.

Descending through the fog from the firebase, the helicopter passed over the heads of a group of North Vietnamese regulars but disappeared too fast to draw any fire. On the valley floor, recalled Brady, "there was a hell of a fight going on." Flying through occasional enemy fire, he landed at the pickup site, where his crewmen took on twelve wounded. The Huey rose straight up through the fog and returned to the firebase to the cheers of the waiting men. After explaining the rescue procedure to the other pilots, Brady led four ships down into the mist, but the pilots all panicked and turned back. So Dustoff 55 went down alone three more times, carrying out thirty-nine men.

In Vietnam scenes like this were common: almost 900,000 wounded soldiers and civilians were evacuated by helicopter to field hospitals.

In subsequent missions that day, Pat Brady rescued soldiers from two more locations, including a minefield. It was well after dark when he ended his day's work. He had evacuated fifty-one men, using three helicopters, but he considered January 6, 1968, "a series of rather routine missions. I had a lot worse days." Still, Major Brady's actions on that particular day impressed more than one eyewitness, and he was recommended for the Medal of Honor, which he received at the White House on October 9, 1969. Brady remained in the army after the war to become a brigadier general in 1985. ❖

Airborne Valor
The War in the Skies

Some Americans in Vietnam only saw the jungle from the air. In fast–moving aircraft they took to the skies, operating hundreds, even thousands of feet above the humid plains and jungles of Vietnam, striking military and industrial targets in North Vietnam and supporting American and ARVN ground troops in the South. Many fliers were career military men, experienced veterans of Korea and World War II. Some were recruits fresh out of flight school. All fought a war of modern machines, flying faster and controlling weapons more lethal and accurate than ever before.

The largest concentration of anti-aircraft guns ever assembled guarded the area around Hanoi. The defensive arsenal ranged from small hand–sighted machine guns to radar–guided surface–to–air missiles. Every day, American pilots dodged heavy fire in raids against North Vietnam. Every flier faced being shot down and killed or taken prisoner. Many never came back.

Part of the American air arsenal was the F–105 Thunderchief fighter–bomber, or "Thud." Although primarily used as a conventional bomber, it could be equipped with radar detection and jamming equipment for use as a "Wild Weasel" to attack missions against SAM (surface–to–air missile) sites and protect strike-force bombers. For air force Major Leo K. Thorsness, one Wild Weasel mission turned into a hair–raising dogfight and rescue attempt.

Flying an F-105F Thunderchief (top), Major Leo Thorsness engages enemy MiGs over North Vietnam on April 19, 1967.

On April 19, 1967, Thorsness and his backseater, Captain Harry Johnson, who tended to the navigation and target equipment, were part of a four–aircraft team attacking the defenses at the Xuan Mai army base, sixty kilometers southwest of Hanoi. A few miles southeast of the base, the Wild Weasel's radar picked up a SAM site ahead. Maneuvering into position, Thorsness launched a Shrike missile with a device that homed in on the SAM's radar. Seconds later the blip disappeared from the screen, indicating the SAM site had been destroyed.

Turning north, Thorsness headed for another SAM site with his wingman, Captain Tom Madison. Thorsness dove toward the emplacement, releasing a

Above. *Leo Thorsness is released by the North Vietnamese in Hanoi, March 4, 1973. Thorsness had learned from a fellow prisoner that he was to be awarded the Medal of Honor.* Right. *Thorsness's F-105 refuels over Laos in early 1967.*

cluster bomb at 8,000 feet, then dropped another 3,000 feet in time to see the site explode. Unsure of the location of additional SAM sites, Thorsness and Madison stayed close to the ground, on the lookout for more.

But with increased visibility came greater danger. Ground fire erupted around the two Wild Weasels, and soon Madison radioed that he had been hit. Thorsness ordered him to head for the nearby hills and ditch the craft if necessary, then listened for a radio signal in case Madison and his backseater, Captain Tom Sterling, ejected. Seconds later a

high-pitched beep told him that the two men had bailed out.

Thorsness, now the only Wild Weasel pilot in the area, headed for the descending parachutes of his fellow fliers. Suddenly an enemy MiG-17 appeared at nine o'clock. "I wasn't sure whether he was going to attack the parachutes," Thorsness recalled later, "so I said, 'Why not?' and took off after him." No sooner

had he pulled up for a shot at the enemy plane when Johnson's voice crackled in his headphones: "Leo, we've got MiGs on our ass!" Thorsness hit the front MiG with his second 20mm cannon burst, then switched on his afterburner to outrun the pursuers. After he had lost them, he rendezvoused with an airborne tanker over Laos and refueled while a convoy of choppers and small planes was dis-

303

patched to pick up Madison and Sterling. Thorsness and Johnson headed back to Xuan Mai as darkness fell to provide cover for the rescue team, even though they were low on ammunition.

As Thorsness briefed the pilots from the rescue team by radio, he spotted three MiGs ahead. Johnson warned him of four more closing on the rear. He turned the aircraft toward the mountains, twisting through valleys and around peaks; at least one MiG crashed in the hills as Thorsness outran his pur-

American gunships, like this AC-47, were armed with machine guns, tracer bullets, and flares for nighttime operations. They provided spectacular displays of concentrated firepower in the skies over South Vietnam.

suers. Again low on fuel and now out of ammunition, Thorsness headed for the remaining MiGs to divert them from the rescue craft. At last more F–105s arrived on the scene, and Thorsness and Johnson headed back to their base in Thailand. (Despite the efforts of Thorsness and the other pilots, the MiGs made the rescue of Sterling and Madison impossible. The two men spent the next six years in a North Vietnamese prison.)

Nearing a tanker on the way back, Thorsness received an urgent call from another pilot who was also low on fuel. He directed the tanker to the other plane and headed for base, hoping that his fuel would hold out. "With just seventy miles to go, I pulled the power back to idle and we just glided in," he said. "We were indicating 'empty' when the run-

way came up in front of us, and we landed a little long."

Eleven days later, on another Wild Weasel mission, Thorsness and Johnson were shot down and taken prisoner by North Vietnam. Not until after his release in 1973 was Lieutenant Colonel Thorsness presented with the air force Medal of Honor by President Richard Nixon for his actions on that April day six years earlier.

Airborne acts of valor were not limited to pilots and officers. Although air force Medals of Honor were usually given for actions carried out while flying a plane or helicopter, one medal was awarded for quick thinking and courage on the part of a gunship crewman that saved the lives of his fellow fliers.

At 8:00 P.M. on February 24, 1969, an air force AC–47 gunship took off from Bien Hoa airfield near Saigon on a scheduled patrol around the capital. Nicknamed "Puff the Magic Dragon," AC–47s were equipped with three rapid–firing 7.62MM miniguns and magnesium illumination flares to provide light for ground troops below or to highlight a target. Because of its use in nighttime actions, the AC–47 had acquired the call sign "Spooky."

One of "Spooky 71's" eight–man crew that night was twenty–three–year–old Airman First Class John L. Levitow, who had been transferred to Vietnam the previous July. Levitow was filling in for a sick friend that night. As gunship load master, his job was to set the timing and ignition controls on each flare before it was dropped underneath a parachute. Levitow would adjust the three–foot–long, twenty–seven–pound cylinder, then pass it to Sergeant Ellis Owen, the gunner, who would pull the lanyard, which triggered the flare's time–delay firing mechanism, and drop the flare out the open cargo door at the command of the pilot.

In this air force painting, Airman First Class John Levitow drags the live flare toward an open cargo door as the gunship pilot tries to regain control of the aircraft and other crewmen attend to the wounded.

Four hours after takeoff, Spooky 71 had just finished firing on enemy positions outside of Bien Hoa when it received a request for illumination near Long Binh, the large military complex just north of Saigon. Pilot Major Ken Carpenter turned toward Long Binh and the flashes of enemy mortars. Amid enemy shelling, Owen began dropping illumination rounds.

Suddenly the gunship was jarred by a tremendous blast. An enemy 82MM shell had struck the right wing and exploded inside the frame, rocking the entire plane. A three-foot hole was blown in the side of the aircraft, sending shrapnel flying across the cabin.

Four crewmen, including Levitow, were knocked off their feet. As Owen fell to the floor, he inadvertently pulled the lanyard from one flare. The cylinder rolled across the cabin, fully charged. In ten seconds the parachute canister would explode, and another ten seconds later the magnesium would ignite, causing a blast of heat reaching 4,000 degrees Fahrenheit.

John Levitow had taken over forty shrapnel wounds in his right leg and hip, a sensation that he later recalled "felt like a two-by-four had been struck against my side." He pulled himself up and helped one of the more severely wounded men to the front of the plane. Then he turned around and saw the live flare lying between the number one gun and some ammunition cans.

"From that point," Levitow said later, "I don't remember anything. My mind went blank." As the wounded men watched, Levitow moved to the back of the plane and fell on the flare. He slowly and painfully dragged himself toward the open cargo door, his wounds leaving a trail of blood. Though he almost lost consciousness, Levitow finally reached the door and shoved out the armed flare. Moments later it exploded with a brilliant white flash.

Levitow remembered being conscious as the plane landed at Bien Hoa and being loaded onto a medical chopper still wearing his radio headset. Major Carpenter pieced together what had happened by studying the trail of blood on the cabin floor and recommended Levitow for the nation's highest decoration, saying that he had "never seen such a courageous act performed under such adverse circumstances."

When John Levitow received the Medal of Honor on May 14, 1970, he became the only enlisted man and the youngest to receive the air force award during the war. Asked what made him risk his life to get rid of that flare, Levitow chuckled and said, "temporary insanity." ❖

Bending the Border
Operation Dewey Canyon

Even though the first American units were to withdraw from Vietnam in 1969, that year brought a period of intense fighting throughout South Vietnam. Early in the year, U.S. forces mounted sustained operations against enemy base camps to help buy time for "Vietnamization" to be implemented. One such operation, Dewey Canyon, deployed the 9th Marines, 3d Marine Division, against enemy border positions in I Corps. To one marine, the prospect of going into "Charlie's backyard made the trip worthwhile."

On the morning of February 11, 1969, the 3d Battalion of the 9th Marines, or 3/9, crossed the Da Krong River, thirteen kilometers from the Laotian border, on a sweep through southern Quang Tri Province. The next morning the 1/9 and the 2/9 struck out from their fire support bases, also heading south. Phase III of Operation Dewey Canyon had begun.

After almost three weeks of preparation during Phases I and II, the marines now advanced toward North Vietnamese Base Area 611, astride the border. Constant fog and rain made helicopter transport almost impossible, so the men swept across the countryside on

First Lieutenant Wesley Fox of the 1st Battalion, 9th Marines, in the A Shau Valley, Quang Tri Province, during Operation Dewey Canyon, February 1969.

the ground in a regiment-in-attack formation reminiscent of World War II and Korea tactics.

For the next two weeks, the three battalions pushed toward the border, occasionally encountering enemy resistance in the hilly forests. On February 20 the marines reached the Laotian border, a line the American command forbade them to cross.

To 9th Marines commander Colonel Robert Barrow, however, "the political implications of going into Laos were pretty unimportant to me at that point." The understanding among the American commanders had always been that their units were allowed to enter Laos and Cambodia if American lives were endangered by an enemy force just over the border. Though he risked a rebuke—or worse—from his superiors, Colonel Barrow ordered Hotel Company of the 2d Battalion to cross the border and establish ambush positions along Route 922, the highway leading into South Vietnam. For the next week the 2/9 operated inside Laos, while the other two battalions stayed within range of Laos. (Approval for the cross-border operation came from General Creighton Abrams, then commander of U.S. forces in Vietnam, only after the marines had entered Laos.)

On the morning of February 22 the men of the 1/9, encamped on a ridge overlooking Laos, were low on water, so a detail was dispatched to a nearby stream. Moving ahead of the unit was Alpha Company, commanded by First Lieutenant Wesley L. Fox. Fox, a Korean War veteran, had recently extended his tour in Vietnam another six months, hoping to see action with the "Walking Dead," as the 9th Marines were called. Now he lead a rifle company in the 1st Battalion, 9th Marines.

Trudging through the thick morning fog, Alpha Company reached the

Marine Corporal William D. Morgan, a native of Pittsburgh, was killed coming to the aid of wounded comrades during an ambush across the border in Laos.

Minutes later, the company executive officer was killed and another lieutenant wounded, leaving Fox the only officer in the field. When the fog abated temporarily, he made radio contact with a gunship overhead and directed an attack on a heavily defended enemy bunker. Later he led an attack on another gun position, suffering another shrapnel wound.

Despite Fox's injuries, his corpsman reported later, "he did not call me to him . . . but instead he continued to shout into the radio. He was in command, and I could tell he had complete control of the situation by the way the men advanced at his command." By late afternoon, the enemy position had fallen, and up the ridge came a relief column from Delta Company.

Alpha Company lost 10 men that day. Of the 153 that had started out that morning, only 66 were able to continue the next day. One of them was Wesley Fox, who had refused evacuation. For his actions in that battle, Lieutenant Fox was later awarded the Medal of Honor.

As Alpha Company closed its fateful battle, Hotel Company of the 2d Battalion operated only a few miles away, but inside Laos. On the afternoon of February 25, a Company H patrol was ambushed along the road by ten to fifteen North Vietnamese regulars. The NVA, firing from fortified bunkers, poured automatic-weapons fire and rocket-propelled grenades on the Americans. The patrol radioed for reinforcements.

Numerous caches of enemy weapons, such as these 12.7MM antiaircraft guns, were uncovered by U.S. Marines during Operation Dewey Canyon.

stream. Fox called the water detail forward. Soon after mortar, machine-gun, and small-arms fire burst forth from the surrounding mist. NVA soldiers jumped from "spider holes" to fire on the marines. All around men fell wounded and dying.

Fox moved ahead through the thick undergrowth and bamboo palms. He fired his M16 at a sniper in a tree, killing him, then directed his platoons to move forward through the heavy foliage. As the platoon leaders departed, two enemy mortar rounds landed in the command position, killing Fox's two radiomen and the air and artillery observers. Fox took shrapnel in the shoulder but grabbed both radios and continued maneuvering his platoons. He ordered his executive officer to move forward and take command of the 2d Platoon, whose lieutenant had been seriously wounded. Hearing that the 3d Platoon leader had been killed, Fox moved to that unit's position and took over.

Men of the 1st Battalion, 9th Marines, take cover from enemy fire in Quang Tri Province during Dewey Canyon fighting.

Two marines fell wounded near an enemy bunker, and each time the others tried to pull them away they were repulsed by heavy fire. Finally one of the marines, twenty-one-year-old Corporal William D. Morgan, crawled through the undergrowth to an open road in front of the bunker, then leaped from the brush and ran toward the bunker, shouting to the wounded as he ran.

With the enemy diverted by Morgan, the other marines pulled the two men away from the bunker. But Morgan paid a heavy price for his actions. Hit almost immediately by automatic fire, he fell mortally wounded. The rest of the platoon rushed forward and eventually overran the position, uncovering a large cache of weapons and supplies.

By the time Operation Dewey Canyon ended on March 18, American forces had struck at the heart of the enemy logistical system, capturing over 500 tons of enemy armament, including twelve 122MM guns, and over 100 tons of rice. It was the first—and last—time that a large American unit would strike at an enemy sanctuary in Laos, although the next year American forces assaulted enemy camps in Cambodia.

On August 6, 1970, President Nixon presented the Medal of Honor to Mrs. Helen Morgan on behalf of her son, William. Because the marines had entered Laos on the condition that there be "no public discussion" of their unprecedented foray, Corporal Morgan's citation lists the place of action as "Quang Tri Province, Republic of Vietnam." Although declassified documents now indicate the real location, Morgan and seven other marines who also perished in Laos are still listed as having been killed in action in South Vietnam. ❖

Hell Hole
Prisoners of War

For most American soldiers, one of the greatest fears was being captured by the enemy. One put it simply: "I'd rather die." Seven hundred and sixty-six men were taken prisoner by the North Vietnamese and Vietcong, most of them air force and navy airmen shot down over the North. Because the United States never declared war on North Vietnam, the Communists refused to honor the Geneva guidelines regarding POWs. Instead, they withheld mail, tortured prisoners to the brink of death, and constantly tried to force them to confess to being war criminals against the people of Vietnam. Throughout this ordeal most of the men resisted, surreptitiously organizing and communicating to bond together to follow the Prisoners' Code of Conduct.

The stars were shining brightly overhead as U.S. Air Force Major George "Bud" Day crawled out of his tiny underground cell, unseen by his North Vietnamese guard. It was Friday night, September 1, 1967. Shot down near Vinh Linh just five days before, Day, a forty-two-year-old veteran of both World War II and Korea, had been beaten several times, then placed in an underground bunker, stripped to his shorts with hands and feet bound. He had worked his way out of his knots and escaped from his cell. Now he prepared to navigate by the stars to reach South Vietnam, some fifty kilometers away.

Day was barely fit to travel. His arm had been broken in three places during the ejection from his F-100 Supersabre fighter, and his sprained left knee was now swollen from his having been hung upside down for several hours by his captors. Limping through the mud, his right arm totally encased in a crude cast, Day set out for freedom.

Slogging through the paddies, feeling with every step the terrible pain of his injuries, Day could see the moving lights of his pursuers behind him. When he reached solid ground, he cut his feet running on sharp rocks strewn over land that had been devastated by American bombs and artillery. During the next few days he survived on berries, one balefruit, and two frogs, swallowed live.

Day had stopped to rest when an American rocket or shell landed right near him, tossing him up in the air, wounding him in the right leg, and rupturing his sinuses and eardrums. With virtually no equilibrium and vomiting profusely, Day lay in the brush "like a sick animal" for several days. When he was able to rise he limped south and came upon a sight over which he had flown many times. It was the Ben Hai River, the boundary between North and South Vietnam in the DMZ.

Sleeping near the edge of the river, trying to muster the strength to cross, Day once again came under a barrage of American artillery. His ears and nose started bleeding and he lost his sense of direction. At last he got his bearings and floated across the Ben Hai, clinging to a bamboo log.

Although he was now in South Vietnam, Day knew that there was still a very good chance that he would run into North Vietnamese, so he carefully concealed his movements. He came upon enemy units but was able to evade them.

Finally, over one week after his escape, Day thought that salvation had come when an American scout plane passed overhead. He tried to signal the aircraft, but the pilot did not see him. Later Day tried to flag down two marine helicopters, but once again he was not seen. After these two missed chances, Day said later, "I could have cried."

Freedom continued to tantalize him. Hearing more helicopters and artillery guns, Day knew that he was near a marine camp but wondered if he had the strength to go farther. Down to almost 100 pounds, his arm mangled under the wet, broken cast, his legs throbbing, Day was "almost at the end of my tether. If I was going to make it, it was going to have to be today or tomorrow."

As he headed toward the American base, Day was startled to hear excited shouting and turned to see two teen-age Vietnamese boys running toward him. Realizing from their AK47s that they were the enemy, he jumped into the bushes just as two rounds cut into his hand and thigh. Soon the youths were upon him. One of them cocked his rifle and kicked Day as he lay on the ground. His twelve-day bid for freedom was over.

Carried back to the same camp from which he had escaped, Day was devastated. He had come so close to freedom, but now, given his injuries and

Life With the Medal

Medal of Honor recipients are introduced by actor James Stewart (left) at Madison Square Garden, New York, in 1948. Left to right. *John Kane; William Shomo; John Morgan; Jay Zeamer, Jr.; Pierpont Hamilton; William Lawley, Jr.; Forrest Vosler; Maynard Smith.*

The Medal of Honor changes profoundly the lives of the men who earn it. One day they are ordinary soldiers, anonymous as any in the American armed forces. Then for some reason—courage, training, luck, or a combination of the three—they perform acts that set them apart from their peers. If they live, they may be whisked away from the field of war, dressed in fresh uniforms, and escorted to a ceremony that declares they are the bravest of the brave. From that moment on, they are no longer simple soldiers but public heroes, keepers of a great trust and tradition. And their lives are never the same.

A man who receives the Medal of Honor will find that much is still expected of him. First there is the award ceremony. Perhaps the soldier has an interview with the president or a high official before the blue ribbon is placed around his neck. A man who may have never seen a general finds himself saluted by men of high rank. Photographers snap his picture, reporters ask him questions. His family is subject to publicity. Then come the

hometown parades, the public speeches, the talks to veterans, the autographs, the affections and gifts of strangers. The rush of recognition continues day and night, and the soldier finds that his life is not entirely his own. It can be a bewildering experience.

Even years after the war has ended, the medal is a powerful force in his life. Ronald Ray, a Vietnam recipient, described it this way: "The medal is one of those things that calls attention to you. If you're good at what you're doing, it's going to be a big help to you." Vietnam veteran Jay Vargas also noted that the medal "opened some doors" for him. But it is uncommon for a recipient to use the medal for personal gain. Most modern recipients speak modestly of it and are reluctant to make a special case of themselves because they have earned the Medal of Honor. Instead, most men who hold the medal strive to uphold its dignity. They realize that everything they do may reflect upon the honor, and so most try to avoid behavior that would sully its reputa-

tion. It is, in Ray's words, an "awesome responsibility."

Yet receiving the medal does not usually change the character of a man. A good man will likely remain good after he has received the award. Likewise, a ne'er-do-well is not apt to change simply because he has earned the medal. Of course, most men need a period of adjustment. This can cause a sober young man to let others buy him drinks into the night or make a vice-ridden man temporarily clean up his behavior. But once that adjustment is over, a man is left pretty much the same as before the special honor became his. As Jay Vargas said: "It sure as hell didn't make me any smarter."

The never-ending stream of public recognition can be trying for even the most well-adjusted recipient. After his return from a Vietnamese prison camp, James Bond Stockdale found that he was sometimes "embarrassed by people's reactions to the medal. To be pawed is not enjoyable." Stockdale's solution was one that many recipients discover: "You learn after a while to pick your audiences–those who are sophisticated enough not to expose you to these fawning experiences."

There are other facts of life with the medal that are not entirely pleasant. Recipients may be subject to the jealousy of others. Because the medal goes only to a select few, other soldiers may resent the comparative lack of attention to their own deeds. Vietnam recipient Michael Novosel recalled another aviator who said, "I know damn well I did as much as you did, and they didn't give me anything." Another fact of life is more personal, more darkly connected to the might-have-beens of war and courage. Again, Novosel: "[The] Medal of Honor recipient carries within himself a fear, the possibility that . . . [he] did not deserve the medal." This is similar to the uncertainty other veterans experience years after the war is over. A recipient might wonder why he lived while so many others–ordinary soldiers as well as other Medal of Honor men – died. But the bearer of the Medal of Honor knows that in some way his medal represents the courage of all good soldiers. This can ease the uncertainty that comes with being singled out as one of the bravest.

Another fact of life is also the longest. For the rest of his life, a recipient may be honored for a few moments of action performed when he was a very young man. Everything he accomplishes afterward may seem less glorious, at least in the public's estimation, than those moments. Thus the Medal of Honor recipient rarely escapes his war years, even if he dearly wants to, for they are the cornerstone of his public image.

The pressure to be a public figure rarely subsides. William Shomo, a Pacific veteran of World War II, was recruited to make public appearances until he was spending more time than he could afford. Finally he said, "'That's it. No more. Period.' I ran into quite a bit of castigation." It is sometimes unfair to ask a man who has already given much to his country to give even more, but that can be the fate of a Medal of Honor man.

Some recipients feel acutely the dissonance between their own lives and the public perception of them. Being thrust suddenly onto the public stage is not always easy, or appropriate. The slightest failings of their lives are carefully documented. "Medal of Honor Winner Jailed" may be an irresistible headline, but it is also cruel to a man whose habits and weaknesses cannot withstand public scrutiny.

In the end, how a recipient lives with the medal is a personal matter. For all the help friends, family, and other recipients can give him, a Medal of Honor man must come to terms with the award by himself. Michael Daly, a World War II veteran, put it this way: The Medal of Honor is "a very personal thing . . . you always have to treat it that way." Joe Foss of World War II was more blunt: "I don't sit and listen to the grass grow because I have the medal." To know you are an American hero, yet not lose yourself in that knowledge, is the great challenge of life with the medal. As Daly said: "Life is a dynamic thing. . . . For your own peace of mind, you've got to move on."

emaciated condition, he was certain that he would not survive the journey to a North Vietnamese prison.

After a number of severe beatings at the camp, Day was taken farther north, to Vinh. There the punishment was public and even more sadistic. In a common North Vietnamese torture, Day's upper arms were bound behind his back, then a stick was inserted into the ropes. By twisting the stick, the torturer could nearly pull the prisoner's arms out of their sockets. Shortly thereafter, another rope was tied to the first rope, and Day was hoisted up by his arms as civilians and soldiers watched. Despite attempts to block it out, Day felt "a slow, insidious horrible pain, as your body tries to tear itself apart." Through all the pain, "I really had hopes that they would kill me. But torture's not like that. You're never lucky enough to die."

Several days later, Day and another prisoner were brought north to Hanoi. There they joined the other American prisoners at prisons such as Son Tay, "The Zoo," "Alcatraz," and Hoa Lo, the central jail for prisoners of war.

Built by the French at the end of the nineteenth century, Hoa Lo (Vietnamese for "hot furnace," also known as "Hell Hole") stood in downtown Hanoi, a few kilometers from the residence of Ho Chi Minh. Surrounded by five-meter walls topped with broken glass and barbed wire, the camp held approximately 150 men in three sectors given names by the Americans: "New Guy Village," "Heartbreak Hotel," and "Las Vegas." Although many prisoners were moved to various prisons around Hanoi, a substantial number spent some time at "The Hanoi Hilton."

As in past wars, American prisoners were obligated to follow the orders of senior commanders in the camp, just as they would in normal military situations. The senior officer at Hoa Lo was

Commander James Bond Stockdale, a navy pilot shot down in September 1965 (and the cousin of Robert Dunlap, a World War II Medal of Honor recipient). By means of the "tap code," which allowed Americans to communicate from cell to cell, Stockdale established a command chain, issuing orders to resist North Vietnamese efforts to extract "confessions" or use the prisoners for other propaganda purposes.

Stockdale had a special reason to be concerned about being used for propaganda statements. On August 4, 1964, Stockdale had flown one of three jets supporting the *Maddox* and the *C. Turner Joy* in the Gulf of Tonkin. The vessels radioed that they were coming under attack from North Vietnamese boats that night, but after searching the stormy waters and not seeing any enemy ships, Stockdale became convinced that the "Gulf of Tonkin Incident," the "enemy attack" that caused Congress and many Americans to support President Johnson's handling of the war, was nothing but "a Chinese fire drill."

After being shot down, Jim Stockdale lived in fear that the North Vietnamese would somehow discover that he possessed "the most damaging information a North Vietnamese torturer could possibly extract from an American prisoner." Every torture session, every statement he was asked to sign, brought new anxieties: "When was the Tonkin Gulf shoe to fall? How in God's name was I going to handle it?"

At the beginning of September 1969, a torture session pushed Stockdale to the limits of his resistance. Caught writing a message to another prisoner, he was forced to kneel (although he could barely bend his left leg because of an earlier injury) and slapped repeatedly across the face with a strip of rubber from a truck tire. Although by dusk his face was bleeding, Stockdale did not divulge the names of any other prisoners with whom he had communicated. Finally he was put in leg irons and ropes. His torturer promised even harsher punishment in the morning. "You have seen nothing yet," he snarled. "Tomorrow you will give me details. . . . Tomorrow is when we start; you will be brought down!"

After his guard had left, Stockdale, as he later recounted, thought quickly. "I've got to go on the offensive. . . . I

Below. *Americans were given cellmates later in the war, when their captors allowed photographers into the camps.*

Above. *American POWs Robinson Risner (left) and James Stockdale (second from left) at Hoa Lo Prison, February 1973.*

have to stop that interrogation. I have to stop the *flow*. If it costs, it costs."

Moving to a window, he broke the glass with the heel of his hand, grabbed one of the large pieces, and sat down in the center of the room. He quickly chopped at his wrists with the shard, causing blood to ooze all over his arms and onto the floor. Wringing his hand to increase the flow of blood, Stockdale collapsed on the floor as his jailers returned.

Stockdale's wounds were bandaged, and he was not tortured the next day. When one of his jailers told him that he would be moved out of the torture room, Stockdale realized that his bold action had worked. The North Vietnamese never asked Stockdale about the Gulf of Tonkin incident.

As Stockdale, Day, and the other Americans continued to follow the code of conduct for prisoners, conditions improved slightly at the camps. In the early seventies, the North Vietnamese realized that the Americans might soon be released; as a result, beatings occurred less often, and many prisoners who had been in solitary confinement were allowed roommates. In turn the prisoners became more daring in their expressions of solidarity. In February 1971 some inmates of Hoa Lo gathered quietly for a religious service, forbidden by camp rules. After the guards burst in and broke up the gathering, Day started singing "The Star Spangled Banner," and Stockdale and the other Americans quickly joined in. One by one, the other prison buildings broke out in song. Stockdale wrote later that although he

Rear Admiral James Stockdale (center) and Colonel George Day receive the Medal of Honor from President Ford.

was punished for the episode, it was exhilarating: "Our minds were now free, and we knew it."

On January 27, 1973, the Paris accords were signed, and the American combat role in the Vietnam War came to an end. Over the next two months, 473 Americans walked across the tarmac of Hanoi's Gia Lam Airport to waiting air force C-141s—and freedom. As they took off, they left behind a nightmare that for some had dragged on for eight years.

Day, Stockdale, and Captain Lance P. Sijan, an air force pilot who died in captivity, were recommended by their

fellow prisoners for the Medal of Honor for their conduct as POWs. On March 4, 1976, Day, Stockdale, and Sijan's family were presented medals by President Gerald Ford.

Compared to earlier ceremonies, public notice of the presentation was scant, typical of the attitude of the times. For several years Americans tried to put Vietnam out of the national mind. It was not until almost a decade after the last American soldier had left Vietnam that the country appeared ready to come to grips with one of its most divisive wars, and the men who fought it. ◈

Epilogue

The stated purpose for creating the Medal of Honor was prosaic as could be: "to improve the efficiency" of the northern troops in the Civil War. In the dark days of 1861, no one knew what meaning to attach to the medal or indeed if the Union would last long enough for it to take on any important meaning.

Soon that small object of bronze and silken ribbon was inspiring both an army and a people. The honoring of courage and sacrifice in the ranks gave heart first to the men who fought and then to citizens being called upon to sacrifice their sons or brothers, husbands or lovers for the cause. The medal came to signify something noble, something worth honoring in the dirty, bloody business of a war of Americans against Americans, brothers against brothers.

What it honored then it has honored since—a vital truth that war is waged and won or lost by individual men. Great armies, clever strategies, industrial might all contribute to the success of a nation in war. On the battlefield, though, the ordinary soldiers more often than not turn the odds to victory. The Medal of Honor is bestowed on a man for his personal valor; it symbolizes the gratitude America feels when that soldier finds it within himself to perform with extraordinary courage.

Beyond its personal meaning, the medal over the years has acquired another import: By recognizing the few it also recognizes the courage and sacrifice of all good American soldiers. This representative nature of the award by implication attributes gallantry to men other than those who receive it, men whose names are not found in books and are not portrayed in motion pictures but who have also put their lives on the line for their country.

This is especially brought home by the custom of choosing for a Medal of Honor one of the unknown soldiers of each American conflict. The Unknown Soldier's sacrifice stands for that of many. In honoring the courage of one who lies nameless, the nation honors the courage of all who have served above and beyond the call of duty.

Register of Recipients

Register of Recipients

Total medals awarded:
	AIR FORCE	16
	ARMY	2,342
	COAST GUARD	1
	MARINES	300
	NAVY	744
	UNKNOWN SOLDIERS	9
		3,412

Total number of recipients
(Total medals minus double awards) 3,394

Glossary

Adj.	Adjutant	Gen.	General	QG	Quarter Gunner
Adm.	Admiral	Gy. Sgt.	Gunnery Sergeant	Reg'tal	Regimental
BM	Boatswain's Mate	LCpl.	Lance Corporal	QM	Quartermaster
Brig. Gen.	Brigadier General	Lman	Landsman	SQM	Signal Quartermaster
CB	Chief Boatswain's Mate	Lt.	Lieutenant	SSgt.	Staff Sergeant
CWO	Chief Warrant Officer	Lt. (j.g.)	Lieutenant (junior grade)	Sfc.	Sergeant First Class
Capt.	Captain	Maj.	Major	Sgt.	Sergeant
Cmdr.	Commander	MSgt.	Master Sergeant	Sman	Seaman
Col.	Colonel	NOR	Place of action not on record	Sp4c/5c	Specialist Fourth Class/Fifth Class
Comm.	Commissary	Ord. Sman	Ordinary Seaman		
Cpl.	Corporal	Pfc.	Private First Class	*posthumous award
GM	Gunner's Mate	Pvt.	Private	+ second award (first award earned in earlier conflict)

The Civil War   1861–1865

Number of medals: 1,520

ARMY:	1,196
MARINES:	17
NAVY:	307

ARMY

Adams, Pvt. James F. (Nineveh, Va)
Adams, 2d Lt. John G. B. (Fredericksburg, Va)
Alber, Pvt. Frederick (Spotsylvania, Va)
Albert, Pvt. Christian (Vicksburg, Miss)
Allen, Cpl. Abner P. (Petersburg, Va)
Allen, Pvt. James (South Mountain, Md)
Allen, Cpl. Nathaniel M. (Gettysburg, Pa)
Ames, 1st Lt. Adelbert (Bull Run, Va)
Ammerman, Pvt. Robert W. (Spotsylvania, Va)
Anderson, Pvt. Bruce (Fort Fisher, NC)
Anderson, Pvt. Charles W. (Waynesboro, Va)
Anderson, Sgt. Everett W. (Crosby's Creek, Tenn)
Anderson, Pvt. Frederick C. (Weldon Railroad, Va)
Anderson, Capt. Marion T. (Nashville, Tenn)
Anderson, Pvt. Peter (Bentonville, NC)
Anderson, Cpl. Thomas (Appomattox Station, Va)
Apple, Cpl. Andrew O. (Petersburg, Va)
Appleton, 1st Lt. William H. (Petersburg & New Market Heights, Va)
Archer, 1st Lt. & Adj. James W. (Corinth, Miss)
*Archer, Sgt. Lester (Fort Harrison, Va)
Archinal, Cpl. William (Vicksburg, Miss)
Armstrong, Pvt. Clinton L. (Vicksburg, Miss)
Arnold, Capt. Abraham K. (Davenport Bridge, Va)
Avery, Lt. William B. (Tranter's Creek, NC)
Ayers, Sgt. David (Vicksburg, Miss)
Ayers, Pvt. John G. K. (Vicksburg, Miss)
Babcock, Sgt. William J. (Petersburg, Va)

*Bacon, Pvt. Elijah W. (Gettysburg, Pa)
Baird, Brig. Gen. Absalom (Jonesboro, Ga)
Baldwin, Capt. Frank D. (Peach Tree Creek, Ga)
Ballen, Pvt. Frederick (Vicksburg, Miss)
Banks, Sgt. George L. (Missionary Ridge, Tenn)
Barber, Cpl. James A. (Petersburg, Va)
Barker, Sgt. Nathaniel C. (Spotsylvania, Va)
Barnes, Pvt. William H. (Chapin's Farm, Va)
Barnum, Col. Henry A. (Chattanooga, Tenn)
Barrell, 1st Lt. Charles L. (Camden, SC)
Barrick, Cpl. Jesse T. (Duck River, Tenn)
Barringer, Pvt. William H. (Vicksburg, Miss)
Barry, Sgt. Maj. Augustus (NOR)
Batchelder, Lt. Col. & Chief QM Richard N. (Catlett-Fairfax Stations, Va)
Bates, Col. Delavan (Cemetery Hill, Va)
Bates, Sgt. Norman F. (Columbus, Ga)
Baybutt, Pvt. Philip (Luray, Va)
Beatty, Capt. Alexander M. (Cold Harbor, Va)
Beaty, 1st Sgt. Powhatan (Chapin's Farm, Va)
Beaufort, Cpl. Jean J. (Port Hudson, La)
Beaumont, Maj. & Asst. Adj. Gen. Eugene B. (Harpeth River, Tenn & Selma, Ala)
Bebb, Pvt. Edward J. (Columbus, Ga)
Beckwith, Pvt. Wallace A. (Fredericksburg, Va)
Beddows, Pvt. Richard (Spotsylvania, Va)
Beebe, 1st Lt. William S. (Cane River Crossing, La)
Beech, Sgt. John P. (Spotsylvania Courthouse, Va)
*Begley, Sgt. Terrence (Cold Harbor, Va)
Belcher, Pvt. Thomas (Chapin's Farm, Va)

Bell, Sgt. James B. (Missionary Ridge, Tenn)
Benedict, 2d Lt. George G. (Gettysburg, Pa)
Benjamin, Cpl. John F. (Sayler's Creek, Va)
Benjamin, 1st Lt. Samuel N. (Bull Run-Spotsylvania, Va)
Bennett, Pvt. Orren (Sayler's Creek, Va)
Bennett, 1st Lt. Orson W. (Honey Hill, SC)
Bensinger, Pvt. William (Georgia)
Benyaurd, 1st Lt. William H. H. (Five Forks, Va)
Betts, Lt. Col. Charles M. (Greensboro, NC)
Beyer, 2d Lt. Hillary (Antietam, Md)
Bickford, Cpl. Henry H. (Waynesboro, Va)
Bickford, Cpl. Matthew (Vicksburg, Miss)
Bieger, Pvt. Charles (Ivy Farm, Miss)
Bingham, Capt. Henry H. (Wilderness, Va)
Birdsall, Sgt. Horatio L. (Columbus, Ga)
Bishop, Pvt. Francis A. (Spotsylvania, Va)
Black, Lt. Col. John C. (Prairie Grove, Ark)
Black, Capt. William P. (Pea Ridge, Ark)
Blackmar, Lt. Wilmon W. (Five Forks, Va)
Blackwood, Surgeon William R. D. (Petersburg, Va)
Blasdel, Pvt. Thomas A. (Vicksburg, Miss)
Blickensderfer, Cpl. Milton (Petersburg, Va)
Bliss, Capt. George N. (Waynesboro, Va)
Bliss, Col. Zenas R. (Fredericksburg, Va)
Blodgett, 1st Lt. Wells H. (Newtonia, Mo)
Blucher, Cpl. Charles (Fort Harrison, Va)
Blunt, 1st Lt. John W. (Cedar Creek, Va)
Boehm, 2d Lt. Peter M. (Dinwiddie Courthouse, Va)

Bonebrake, Lt. Henry G. (Five Forks, Va)
Bonnaffon, 1st Lt. Sylvester, Jr. (Boydton Plank Road, Va)
Boody, Cpl. Robert (Williamsburg & Chancellorsville, Va)
Boon, Capt. Hugh P. (Sayler's Creek, Va)
Boquet, Pvt. Nicholas (Wilson's Creek, Mo)
Boss, Cpl. Orlando (Cold Harbor, Va)
Bourke, Pvt. John G. (Stone River, Tenn)
Boury, Sgt. Richard (Charlottesville, Va)
Boutwell, Pvt. John W. (Petersburg, Va)
Bowen, Cpl. Chester B. (Winchester, Va)
Bowen, Pvt. Emmer (Vicksburg, Miss)
Box, Capt. Thomas J. (Resaca, Ga)
Boynton, Lt. Col. Henry V. (Missionary Ridge, Tenn)
Bradley, Sgt. Thomas W. (Chancellorsville, Va)
Brady, Pvt. James (Chapin's Farm, Va)
Brandle, Pvt. Joseph E. (Lenoire, Tenn)
Brannigan, Pvt. Felix (Chancellorsville, Va)
Brant, Lt. William (Petersburg, Va)
Bras, Sgt. Edgar A. (Spanish Fort, Ala)
Brest, Pvt. Lewis F. (Sayler's Creek, Va)
Brewer, Pvt. William J. (Appomattox, Va)
Breyer, Sgt. Charles (Rappahannock Station, Va)
Briggs, Cpl. Elijah A. (Petersburg, Va)
Bringle, Cpl. Andrew (Sayler's Creek, Va)
Bronner, Pvt. August F. (White Oak Swamp, Va)
Bronson, 1st Sgt. James H. (Chapin's Farm, Va)
Brosnan, Sgt. John (Petersburg, Va)
Brouse, Capt. Charles W. (Missionary Ridge, Tenn)
Brown, Sgt. Charles (Weldon Railroad, Va)
Brown, Cpl. Edward, Jr. (Fredericksburg & Salem Heights, Va)
Brown, Sgt. Henri L. (Wilderness, Va)
Brown, Capt. Jeremiah Z. (Petersburg, Va)
Brown, 1st Sgt. John H. (Vicksburg, Miss)
Brown, Capt. John H. (Franklin, Tenn)
*Brown, Capt. Morris, Jr. (Gettysburg, Pa)
Brown, Pvt. Robert B. (Missionary Ridge, Tenn)
Brown, Pvt. Uriah (Vicksburg, Miss)
Brown, Pvt. Wilson W. (Georgia)
Brownell, Pvt. Francis E. (Alexandria, Va)
Bruner, Pvt. Louis J. (Walker's Ford, Tenn)
Brush, Lt. George W. (Ashepoo River, SC)
Bruton, Capt. Christopher C. (Waynesboro, Va)
Bryant, Sgt. Andrew S. (New Bern, NC)
*Buchanan, Pvt. George A. (Chapin's Farm, Va)
Buck, Cpl. F. Clarence (Chapin's Farm, Va)
Buckingham, 1st Lt. David E. (Rowanty Creek, Va)
Buckles, Sgt. Abram J. (Wilderness, Va)
Buckley, Pvt. Denis (Peach Tree Creek, Ga)
Buckley, Sgt. John C. (Vicksburg, Miss)
Bucklyn, 1st Lt. John K. (Chancellorsville, Va)
Buffington, Sgt. John E. (Petersburg, Va)
Buffum, Pvt. Robert (Georgia)
Buhrman, Pvt. Henry G. (Vicksburg, Miss)
Bumgarner, Sgt. William (Vicksburg, Miss)
Burbank, Sgt. James H. (Blackwater, Va)
Burger, Pvt. Joseph (Nolensville, Tenn)
Burk, Pvt. E. Michael (Spotsylvania, Va)
Burk, Sgt. Thomas (Wilderness, Va)
Burke, 1st Sgt. Daniel W. (Shepherdstown Ford, Va)
Burke, Pvt. Thomas M. (Hanover Courthouse, Va)
Burns, Sgt. James M. (New Market, Va)
Burritt, Pvt. William W. (Vicksburg, Miss)

Butterfield, Brig. Gen. Daniel (Gaines's Mill, Va)
Butterfield, 1st Lt. Frank G. (Salem Heights, Va)
Cadwallader, Cpl. Abel G. (Hatcher's Run & Dabney's Mills, Va)
Cadwell, Sgt. Luman L. (Alabama Bayou, La)
Caldwell, Sgt. Daniel (Hatcher's Run, Va)
Calkin, 1st Sgt. Ivers S. (Sayler's Creek, Va)
Callahan, Pvt. John H. (Fort Blakely, Ala)
Camp, Pvt. Carlton N. (Petersburg, Va)
Campbell, Pvt. James A. (Woodstock & Amelia Courthouse, Va)
Campbell, Pvt. William (Vicksburg, Miss)
Capehart, Maj. Charles E. (Monterey Mountain, Pa)
Capehart, Col. Henry (Greenbrier River, W Va)
*Capron, Sgt. Horace, Jr. (Chickahominy & Ashland, Va)
Carey, Sgt. Hugh (Gettysburg, Pa)
Carey, Sgt. James L. (Appomattox Courthouse, Va)
Carlisle, Pvt. Casper R. (Gettysburg, Pa)
Carman, Pvt. Warren (Waynesboro, Va)
Carmin, Cpl. Isaac H. (Vicksburg, Miss)
Carney, Sgt. William H. (Fort Wagner, SC)
Carr, Col. Eugene A. (Pea Ridge, Ark)
Carr, Cpl. Franklin (Nashville, Tenn)
Carson, Musician William J. (Chickamauga, Ga)
Cart, Pvt. Jacob (Fredericksburg, Va)
Carter, 2d Lt. John J. (Antietam, Md)
Carter, Capt. Joseph F. (Fort Stedman, Va)
Caruana, Pvt. Orlando E. (New Bern, NC & S. Mountain, Md)
Casey, Pvt. David (Cold Harbor, Va)
Casey, Pvt. Henry (Vicksburg, Miss)
Catlin, Col. Isaac S. (Petersburg, Va)
Cayer, Sgt. Ovila (Weldon Railroad, Va)
Chamberlain, Col. Joshua L. (Gettysburg, Pa)
Chamberlain, 2d Lt. Orville T. (Chickamauga, Ga)
Chambers, Pvt. Joseph B. (Petersburg, Va)
Chandler, Sgt. Henry F. (Petersburg, Va)
Chandler, QM Sgt. Stephen E. (Amelia Springs, Va)
Chapin, Pvt. Alaric B. (Fort Fisher, NC)
Chapman, Pvt. John (Sayler's Creek, Va)
Chase, Pvt. John F. (Chancellorsville, Va)
Child, Cpl. Benjamin H. (Antietam, Md)
Chisman, Pvt. William W. (Vicksburg, Miss)
Christiancy, 1st Lt. James I. (Hawes's Shops, Va)
Churchill, Cpl. Samuel J. (Nashville, Tenn)
Cilley, Capt. Clinton A. (Chickamauga, Ga)
Clancy, Sgt. James T. (Vaughn Road, Va)
Clapp, 1st Sgt. Albert A. (Sayler's Creek, Va)
Clark, Lt. & Adj. Charles A. (Brook's Ford, Va)
Clark, Cpl. Harrison (Gettysburg, Pa)
Clark, Pvt. James G. (Petersburg, Va)
Clark, 1st Lt. & Reg'tal QM John W. (Warrenton, Va)
Clark, Cpl. William A. (Nolensville, Tenn)
Clarke, Capt. Dayton P. (Spotsylvania, Va)
Clausen, 1st Lt. Charles H. (Spotsylvania, Va)
Clay, Capt. Cecil (Fort Harrison, Va)
Cleveland, Pvt. Charles F. (Antietam, Md)
Clopp, Pvt. John E. (Gettysburg, Pa)
Clute, Cpl. George W. (Bentonville, NC)
Coates, Sgt. Jefferson (Gettysburg, Pa)
Cockley, 1st Lt. David L. (Waynesboro, Va)
Coey, Maj. James (Hatcher's Run, Va)
Coffey, Sgt. Robert J. (Bank's Ford, Va)
Cohn, Sgt. Maj. Abraham (Wilderness, Va)

Colby, Sgt. Carlos W. (Vicksburg, Miss)
Cole, Cpl. Gabriel (Winchester, Va)
Collins, Cpl. Harrison (Richland Creek, Tenn)
Collins, Sgt. Thomas D. (Resaca, Ga)
Collis, Col. Charles H. T. (Fredericksburg, Va)
Colwell, 1st Lt. Oliver (Nashville, Tenn)
Compson, Maj. Hartwell B. (Waynesboro, Va)
Conaway, Pvt. John W. (Vicksburg, Miss)
Conboy, Sgt. Martin (Williamsburg, Va)
Connell, Cpl. Trustrim (Sayler's Creek, Va)
Conner, Pvt. Richard (Bull Run, Va)
Connors, Pvt. James (Fisher's Hill, Va)
Cook, Bugler John (Antietam, Md)
Cook, Sgt. John H. (Pleasant Hill, La)
Cooke, Capt. Walter H. (Bull Run, Va)
Copp, 2d Lt. Charles D. (Fredericksburg, Va)
Corcoran, Pvt. John (Petersburg, Va)
Corliss, Capt. George W. (Cedar Mountain, Va)
Corliss, 1st Lt. Stephen P. (South Side Railroad, Va)
Corson, Asst. Surgeon Joseph K. (Bristoe Station, Va)
Cosgriff, Pvt. Richard H. (Columbus, Ga)
Cosgrove, Pvt. Thomas (Drewry's Bluff, Va)
Coughlin, Lt. Col. John (Swift's Creek, Va)
Cox, Cpl. Robert M. (Vicksburg, Miss)
Coyne, Sgt. John H. (Williamsburg, Va)
Cranston, Pvt. William W. (Chancellorsville, Va)
Creed, Pvt. John (Fisher's Hill, Va)
Crocker, Capt. Henry H. (Cedar Creek, Va)
Crocker, Pvt. Ulric L. (Cedar Creek, Va)
Croft, Pvt. James E. (Allatoona, Ga)
Crosier, Sgt. William H. H. (Peach Tree Creek, Ga)
Cross, Cpl. James E. (Blackburn's Ford, Va)
Crowley, Pvt. Michael (Waynesboro, Va)
Cullen, Cpl. Thomas (Bristoe Station, Va)
Cummings, Sgt. Maj. Amos J. (Salem Heights, Va)
Cumpston, Pvt. James M. (Shenandoah Valley, Va)
Cunningham, 1st Sgt. Francis M. (Sayler's Creek, Va)
Cunningham, Pvt. James S. (Vicksburg, Miss)
Curran, Asst. Surgeon Richard (Antietam, Md)
Curtis, Sgt. Maj. John C. (Baton Rouge, La)
Curtis, 2d Lt. Josiah M. (Petersburg, Va)
Curtis, Brig. Gen. Newton M. (Fort Fisher, NC)
Custer, 2d Lt. Thomas W. (Namozine Church, Va)
Second award (Sayler's Creek, Va)
Cutcheon, Maj. Byron M. (Horseshoe Bend, Ky)
Cutts, Capt. James M. (Wilderness, Spotsylvania, & Petersburg, Va)
Darrough, Sgt. John S. (Eastport, Miss)
Davidsizer, Sgt. John A. (Paine's Crossroads, Va)
Davidson, Asst. Surgeon Andrew (Vicksburg, Miss)
Davidson, 1st Lt. Andrew (Petersburg, Va)
Davis, Maj. Charles C. (Shelbyville, Tenn)
Davis, Sgt. Freeman (Missionary Ridge, Tenn)
Davis, 1st Lt. George E. (Monocacy, Md)
Davis, Pvt. Harry (Atlanta, Ga)
Davis, Pvt. John (Culloden, Va)
Davis, Cpl. Joseph (Franklin, Tenn)
Davis, Sgt. Martin K. (Vicksburg, Miss)
Davis, Pvt. Thomas (Sayler's Creek, Va)
Day, Pvt. Charles (Hatcher's Run, Va)
Day, Pvt. David F. (Vicksburg, Miss)
De Castro, Cpl. Joseph H. (Gettysburg, Pa)
De Lacey, 1st Sgt. Patrick (Wilderness, Va)
De Lavie, Sgt. Hiram H. (Five Forks, Va)
De Puy, 1st Sgt. Charles H. (Petersburg, Va)

De Witt, Cpl. Richard W. (Vicksburg, Miss)
Deane, Maj. John M. (Fort Stedman, Va)
Deland, Pvt. Frederick N. (Port Hudson, La)
Delaney, Sgt. John C. (Dabney's Mills, Va)
Di Cesnola, Col. Louis P. (Aldie, Va)
Dickey, Capt. William D. (Petersburg, Va)
Dickie, Sgt. David (Vicksburg, Miss)
Dilger, Capt. Hubert (Chancellorsville, Va)
Dillon, Pvt. Michael A. (Williamsburg, Va)
Dockum, Pvt. Warren C. (Sayler's Creek, Va)
Dodd, Pvt. Robert F. (Petersburg, Va)
Dodds, Sgt. Edward E. (Ashby's Gap, Va)
Dolloff, Cpl. Charles W. (Petersburg, Va)
Donaldson, Sgt. John (Appomattox Courthouse, Va)
Donoghue, Pvt. Timothy (Fredericksburg, Va)
Doody, Cpl. Patrick (Cold Harbor, Va)
Dore, Sgt. George H. (Gettysburg, Pa)
Dorley, Pvt. August (Mount Pleasant, Ala)
Dorsey, Cpl. Daniel A. (Georgia)
Dorsey, Sgt. Decatur (Petersburg, Va)
Dougall, 1st Lt. & Adj. Allan H. (Bentonville, NC)
Dougherty, Pvt. Michael (Jefferson, Va)
Dow, Sgt. George P. (Richmond, Va)
Downey, Pvt. William (Ashepoo River, SC)
Downs, Sgt. Henry W. (Winchester, Va)
Drake, 2d Lt. James M. (Bermuda Hundred, Va)
Drury, Sgt. James (Weldon Railroad, Va)
Du Pont, Capt. Henry A. (Cedar Creek, Va)
Duffey, Pvt. John (Ashepoo River, SC)
Dunlavy, Pvt. James (Osage, Kans)
Dunne, Cpl. James (Vicksburg, Miss)
Durham, 2d Lt. James R. (Winchester, Va)
Durham, Sgt. John S. (Perryville, Ky)
Eckes, Pvt. John N. (Vicksburg, Miss)
Eddy, Pvt. Samuel E. (Sayler's Creek, Va)
Edgerton, Lt. & Adj. Nathan H. (Chapin's Farm, Va)
Edwards, Pvt. David (Five Forks, Va)
Elliott, Sgt. Alexander (Paine's Crossroads, Va)
Elliott, Sgt. Russell C. (Natchitoches, La)
Ellis, Pvt. Horace (Weldon Railroad, Va)
Ellis, 1st Sgt. William (Dardanelles, Ark)
Ellsworth, Capt. Thomas F. (Honey Hill, SC)
Elson, Sgt. James M. (Vicksburg, Miss)
Embler, Capt. Andrew H. (Boydton Plank Road, Va)
Enderlin, Musician Richard (Gettysburg, Pa)
Engle, Sgt. James E. (Bermuda Hundred, Va)
English, 1st Sgt. Edmund (Wilderness, Va)
Ennis, Pvt. Charles D. (Petersburg, Va)
Estes, Capt. & Asst. Adj. Gen. Lewellyn G. (Flint River, Ga)
Evans, Pvt. Coron D. (Sayler's Creek, Va)
Evans, Capt. Ira H. (Hatcher's Run, Va)
Evans, Pvt. James R. (Wilderness, Va)
Evans, Pvt. Thomas (Piedmont, Va)
Everson, Pvt. Adelbert (Five Forks, Va)
Ewing, Pvt. John C. (Petersburg, Va)
Falconer, Cpl. John A. (Fort Sanders, Tenn)
Fall, Sgt. Charles S. (Spotsylvania Courthouse, Va)
Fallon, Pvt. Thomas T. (Williamsburg, Va)
*Falls, Color Sgt. Benjamin F. (Gettysburg, Pa)
Fanning, Pvt. Nicholas (Selma, Ala)
Farnsworth, Sgt. Maj. Herbert E. (Trevilian Station, Va)
Farquhar, Sgt. Maj. John M. (Stone River, Tenn)
Fasnacht, Sgt. Charles H. (Spotsylvania, Va)

Fassett, Capt. John B. (Gettysburg, Pa)
Fernald, 1st Lt. Albert E. (Five Forks, Va)
Ferrier, Sgt. Daniel T. (Varnell's Station, Ga)
Ferris, 1st Lt. & Adj. Eugene W. (Berryville, Va)
Fesq, Pvt. Frank (Petersburg, Va)
Finkenbiner, Pvt. Henry S. (Dingle's Mill, SC)
Fisher, 1st Lt. John H. (Vicksburg, Miss)
Fisher, Cpl. Joseph (Petersburg, Va)
Flanagan, Sgt. Augustin (Chapin's Farm, Va)
Flannigan, Pvt. James (Nolensville, Tenn)
Fleetwood, Sgt. Maj. Christian A. (Chapin's Farm, Va)
Flynn, Cpl. Christopher (Gettysburg, Pa)
Flynn, Sgt. James E. (Vicksburg, Miss)
Follett, Sgt. Joseph L. (New Madrid, Mo & Stone River, Tenn)
Force, Brig. Gen. Manning F. (Atlanta, Ga)
Ford, 1st Lt. George W. (Sayler's Creek, Va)
Forman, Cpl. Alexander A. (Fair Oaks, Va)
Fout, 2d Lt. Frederick W. (Harper's Ferry, W Va)
Fox, Sgt. Henry (Jackson, Tenn)
Fox, Sgt. Henry M. (Winchester, Va)
Fox, Pvt. Nicholas (Port Hudson, La)
Fox, Pvt. William R. (Petersburg, Va)
Frantz, Pvt. Joseph (Vicksburg, Miss)
Fraser, Pvt. William W. (Vicksburg, Miss)
Freeman, Pvt. Archibald (Spotsylvania, Va)
Freeman, 1st Lt. Henry B. (Stone River, Tenn)
Freeman, Pvt. William H. (Fort Fisher, NC)
French, Pvt. Samuel S. (Fair Oaks, Va)
Frey, Cpl. Franz (Vicksburg, Miss)
Frick, Col. Jacob G. (Fredericksburg, Va)
Frizzell, Pvt. Henry F. (Vicksburg, Miss)
Fuger, Sgt. Frederick (Gettysburg, Pa)
Funk, Maj. West (Appomattox Courthouse, Va)
Furman, Cpl. Chester S. (Gettysburg, Pa)
Furness, Capt. Frank (Trevilian Station, Va)
Gage, Pvt. Richard J. (Elk River, Tenn)
Galloway, Pvt. George N. (Alsop's Farm, Va)
Galloway, Commissary Sgt. John (Farmville, Va)
Gardiner, Pvt. James (Chapin's Farm, Va)
Gardner, Pvt. Charles N. (Five Forks, Va)
Gardner, Sgt. Robert J. (Petersburg, Va)
Garrett, Sgt. William (Nashville, Tenn)
*Gasson, Sgt. Richard (Chapin's Farm, Va)
Gaunt, Pvt. John C. (Franklin, Tenn)
Gause, Cpl. Isaac (Berryville, Va)
Gaylord, Sgt. Levi B. (Fort Stedman, Va)
Gere, 1st Lt. & Adj. Thomas P. (Nashville, Tenn)
Geschwind, Capt. Nicholas (Vicksburg, Miss)
Gibbs, Sgt. Wesley (Petersburg, Va)
Gifford, Pvt. Benjamin (Sayler's Creek, Va)
Gifford, Pvt. David L. (Ashepoo River, SC)
Gillespie, 1st Lt. George L. (Bethesda Church, Va)
Gilligan, 1st Sgt. Edward L. (Gettysburg, Pa)
Gilmore, Maj. John C. (Salem Heights, Va)
Ginley, Pvt. Patrick J. (Reams's Station, Va)
Gion, Pvt. Joseph (Chancellorsville, Va)
Godley, 1st Sgt. Leonidas M. (Vicksburg, Miss)
Goettel, Pvt. Philip (Ringgold, Ga)
Goheen, 1st Sgt. Charles A. (Waynesboro, Va)
Goldsbery, Pvt. Andrew E. (Vicksburg, Miss)
Goodall, 1st Sgt. Francis H. (Fredericksburg, Va)
Goodman, 1st Lt. William E. (Chancellorsville, Va)
Goodrich, 1st Lt. Edwin (Cedar Creek, Va)

Gould, Capt. Charles G. (Petersburg, Va)
Gould, Pvt. Newton T. (Vicksburg, Miss)
Gouraud, Capt. & Aide-de-Camp George E. (Honey Hill, SC)
Grace, Sgt. Peter (Wilderness, Va)
Graham, 2d Lt. Thomas N. (Missionary Ridge, Tenn)
Grant, Surgeon Gabriel (Fair Oaks, Va)
Grant, Col. Lewis A. (Salem Heights, Va)
Graul, Cpl. William (Fort Harrison, Va)
Gray, Pvt. John (Port Republic, Va)
Gray, Sgt. Robert A. (Drewry's Bluff, Va)
Grebe, Capt. M. R. William (Jonesboro, Ga)
Green, Cpl. George (Missionary Ridge, Tenn)
Greenawalt, Pvt. Abraham (Franklin, Tenn)
Greene, Maj. & Asst. Adj. Gen. Oliver D. (Antietam, Md)
Gregg, Pvt. Joseph O. (Richmond & Petersburg Railway, Va)
Greig, 2d Lt. Theodore W. (Antietam, Md)
Gresser, Cpl. Ignatz (Antietam, Md)
Gribben, Lt. James H. (Sayler's Creek, Va)
Grimshaw, Pvt. Samuel (Atlanta, Ga)
Grindlay, Col. James G. (Five Forks, Va)
Grueb, Pvt. George (Chapin's Farm, Va)
Guerin, Pvt. Fitz W. (Grand Gulf, Miss)
Guinn, Pvt. Thomas (Vicksburg, Miss)
Gwynne, Pvt. Nathaniel (Petersburg, Va)
Hack, Pvt. John (Vicksburg, Miss)
Hack, Sgt. Lester G. (Petersburg, Va)
Hadley, Sgt. Cornelius M. (Knoxville, Tenn)
Hadley, Cpl. Osgood T. (Pegram House, Va)
Hagerty, Pvt. Asel (Sayler's Creek, Va)
Haight, Sgt. John H. (Williamsburg, Bristol Station & Manassas, Va)
Haight, Cpl. Sidney (Petersburg, Va)
Hall, Chaplain Francis B. (Salem Heights, Va)
Hall, 2d Lt. & Capt. Henry S. (Gaines's Mill & Rappahannock Station, Va)
Hall, Cpl. Newton H. (Franklin, Tenn)
Hallock, Pvt. Nathan M. (Bristoe Station, Va)
Hammel, Sgt. Henry A. (Grand Gulf, Miss)
Haney, Chaplain Milton L. (Atlanta, Ga)
Hanford, Pvt. Edward R. (Woodstock, Va)
Hanks, Pvt. Joseph (Vicksburg, Miss)
Hanna, Sgt. Marcus A. (Port Hudson, La)
Hanna, Cpl. Milton (Nolensville, Tenn)
Hanscom, Cpl. Moses C. (Bristoe Station, Va)
Hapeman, Lt. Col. Douglas (Peach Tree Creek, Ga)
Harbourne, Pvt. John H. (Petersburg, Va)
*Hardenbergh, Pvt. Henry M. (Deep Run, Va)
Haring, 1st Lt. Abram P. (Bachelor's Creek, NC)
Harmon, Cpl. Amzi D. (Petersburg, Va)
Harrington, Sgt. Ephraim W. (Fredericksburg, Va)
Harris, Pvt. George W. (Spotsylvania, Va)
Harris, Sgt. James H. (New Market Heights, Va)
Harris, 1st Lt. Moses (Smithfield, Va)
Harris, Pvt. Sampson (Vicksburg, Miss)
Hart, Sgt. John W. (Gettysburg, Pa)
Hart, Pvt. William E. (Shenandoah Valley, Va)
Hartranft, Col. John F. (Bull Run, Va)
Harvey, Cpl. Harry (Waynesboro, Va)
Haskell, Sgt. Maj. Frank W. (Fair Oaks, Va)
Haskell, Sgt. Marcus M. (Antietam, Md)
Hastings, Capt. Smith H. (Newby's Crossroads, Va)
Hatch, Brig. Gen. John P. (South Mountain, Md)

Havron, Sgt. John H. (Petersburg, Va)
Hawkins, 1st Lt. Gardner C. (Petersburg, Va)
Hawkins, Cpl. Martin J. (Georgia)
Hawkins, Sgt. Maj. Thomas R. (Chapin's Farm, Va)
Hawthorne, Cpl. Harris S. (Sayler's Creek, Va)
Haynes, Cpl. Asbury F. (Sayler's Creek, Va)
Hays, Pvt. John H. (Columbus, Ga)
Healey, Pvt. George W. (Newnan, Ga)
Hedges, 1st Lt. Joseph (Harpeth River, Tenn)
Heermance, Capt. William L. (Chancellorsville, Va)
Heller, Sgt. Henry (Chancellorsville, Va)
Helms, Pvt. David H. (Vicksburg, Miss)
Henry, Col. Guy V. (Cold Harbor, Va)
Henry, Sgt. James (Vicksburg, Miss)
Henry, Col. William W. (Cedar Creek, Va)
Herington, Pvt. Pitt B. (Kenesaw Mountain, Ga)
Herron, Lt. Col. Francis J. (Pea Ridge, Ark)
Hesseltine, Col. Francis S. (Matagorda Bay, Tex)
Hibson, Pvt. Joseph C. (Fort Wagner, SC)
Hickey, Sgt. Dennis W. (Stony Creek Bridge, Va)
Hickok, Cpl. Nathan E. (Chapin's Farm, Va)
Higby, Pvt. Charles (Appomattox, Va)
Higgins, Pvt. Thomas J. (Vicksburg, Miss)
Highland, Cpl. Patrick (Petersburg, Va)
Hill, Capt. Edward (Cold Harbor, Va)
Hill, Cpl. Henry (Wilderness, Va)
Hill, 1st Lt. James (Champion Hill, Miss)
*Hill, Sgt. James (Petersburg, Va)
Hilliker, Musician Benjamin F. (Mechanicsburg, Miss)
Hills, Pvt. William G. (North Fork, Va)
*Hilton, Sgt. Alfred B. (Chapin's Farm, Va)
Hincks, Sgt. Maj. William B. (Gettysburg, Pa)
Hodges, Pvt. Addison J. (Vicksburg, Miss)
Hoffman, Cpl. Henry (Sayler's Creek, Va)
Hoffman, Capt. Thomas W. (Petersburg, Va)
Hogan, Cpl. Franklin (Petersburg, Va)
Hogarty, Pvt. William P. (Antietam, Md)
Holcomb, Pvt. Daniel I. (Brentwood Hills, Tenn)
Holehouse, Pvt. James (Marye's Heights, Va)
Holland, Cpl. Lemuel F. (Elk River, Tenn)
Holland, Sgt. Maj. Milton M. (Chapin's Farm, Va)
Holmes, 1st Sgt. Lovilo N. (Nolensville, Tenn)
Holmes, Pvt. William T. (Sayler's Creek, Va)
Holton, 1st Sgt. Charles M. (Falling Waters, Va)
Holton, 1st Sgt. Edward A. (Lee's Mills, Va)
Homan, Color Sgt. Conrad (Petersburg, Va)
Hooker, 1st Sgt. George W. (South Mountain, Md)
Hooper, Cpl. William B. (Chamberlain's Creek, Va)
Hopkins, Cpl. Charles F. (Gaines's Mill, Va)
Horan, Sgt. Thomas (Gettysburg, Pa)
Horne, Capt. Samuel B. (Fort Harrison, Va)
Horsfall, Drummer William H. (Corinth, Miss)
Hottenstine, Pvt. Solomon J. (Petersburg & Norfolk Railroad, Va)
Hough, Pvt. Ira (Cedar Creek, Va)
Houghton, Capt. Charles H. (Petersburg, Va)
Houghton, Pvt. George L. (Elk River, Tenn)
Houlton, Comm. Sgt. William (Sayler's Creek, Va)
Howard, Cpl. Henderson C. (Glendale, Va)
Howard, Pvt. Hiram R. (Missionary Ridge, Tenn)
Howard, Sgt. James (Battery Gregg, Va)
Howard, Brig. Gen. Oliver O. (Fair Oaks, Va)
Howard, 1st Sgt. Squire E. (Bayou Teche, La)
Howe, Musician Orion P. (Vicksburg, Miss)

Howe, Sgt. William H. (Fort Stedman, Va)
Hubbell, Capt. William S. (Fort Harrison, Va)
Hudson, Pvt. Aaron R. (Culloden, Ga)
Hughes, Cpl. Oliver (Weldon Railroad, Va)
Hughey, Cpl. John (Sayler's Creek, Va)
Huidekoper, Lt. Col. Henry S. (Gettysburg, Pa)
Hunt, Pvt. Louis T. (Vicksburg, Miss)
Hunter, Sgt. Charles A. (Petersburg, Va)
Hunterson, Pvt. John C. (Peninsula, Va)
Hyatt, 1st Sgt. Theodore (Vicksburg, Miss)
Hyde, Maj. Thomas W. (Antietam, Md)
Hymer, Capt. Samuel (Buzzard's Roost Gap, Ga)
Ilgenfritz, Sgt. Charles H. (Fort Sedgwick, Va)
Immell, Cpl. Lorenzo D. (Wilson's Creek, Mo)
Ingalls, Pvt. Lewis J. (Boutte Station, La)
Inscho, Cpl. Leonidas H. (South Mountain, Md)
Irsch, Capt. Francis (Gettysburg, Pa)
Irwin, 1st Sgt. Patrick (Jonesboro, Ga)
Jackson, 1st Sgt. Frederick R. (James Island, SC)
Jacobson, Sgt. Maj. Eugene P. (Chancellorsville, Va)
James, Pvt. Isaac (Petersburg, Va)
James, Cpl. Miles (Chapin's Farm, Va)
Jamieson, 1st Sgt. Walter (Petersburg, Va)
Jardine, Sgt. James (Vicksburg, Miss)
Jellison, Sgt. Benjamin H. (Gettysburg, Pa)
Jennings, Pvt. James T. (Weldon Railroad, Va)
Jewett, 1st Lt. Erastus W. (Newport Barracks, NC)
John, Pvt. William (Vicksburg, Miss)
Johndro, Pvt. Franklin (Chapin's Farm, Va)
Johns, Cpl. Elisha (Vicksburg, Miss)
Johns, Pvt. Henry T. (Port Hudson, La)
Johnson, Pvt. Andrew (Vicksburg, Miss)
Johnson, Cpl. Follett (New Hope Church, Ga)
Johnson, Pvt. John (Fredericksburg, Va)
Johnson, 1st Lt. Joseph E. (Fort Harrison, Va)
Johnson, Maj. Ruel M. (Chattanooga, Tenn)
Johnson, Pvt. Samuel (Antietam, Md)
Johnson, Sgt. Wallace W. (Gettysburg, Pa)
Johnston, Pvt. David (Vicksburg, Miss)
Johnston, Musician Willie (NOR)
Jones, Pvt. David (Vicksburg, Miss)
Jones, 1st Sgt. William (Spotsylvania, Va)
Jordan, Cpl. Absalom (Sayler's Creek, Va)
Josselyn, 1st Lt. Simeon T. (Missionary Ridge, Tenn)
Judge, 1st Sgt. Francis W. (Fort Sanders, Tenn)
Kaiser, Sgt. John (Richmond, Va)
Kaltenbach, Cpl. Luther (Nashville, Tenn)
Kane, Cpl. John (Petersburg, Va)
Kappesser, Pvt. Peter (Lookout Mountain, Tenn)
Karpeles, Sgt. Leopold (Wilderness, Va)
Kauss, Cpl. August (Five Forks, Va)
Keele, Sgt. Maj. Joseph (North Anna River, Va)
Keen, Sgt. Joseph S. (Chattahoochee River, Ga)
Keene, Pvt. Joseph (Fredericksburg, Va)
Kelley, Pvt. Andrew J. (Knoxville, Tenn)
Kelley, Capt. George V. (Franklin, Tenn)
Kelley, Sgt. Leverett M. (Missionary Ridge, Tenn)
Kelly, 1st Sgt. Alexander (Chapin's Farm, Va)
Kelly, Sgt. Daniel A. (Waynesboro, Va)
Kelly, Pvt. Thomas (Front Royal, Va)
Kemp, 1st Sgt. Joseph (Wilderness, Va)
Kendall, 1st Sgt. William W. (Black River Bridge, Miss)
Kennedy, Pvt. John (Trevilian Station, Va)
Kenyon, Sgt. John S. (Trenton, NC)

Kenyon, Pvt. Samuel P. (Sayler's Creek, Va)
Keough, Cpl. John (Sayler's Creek, Va)
Kephart, Pvt. James (Vicksburg, Miss)
Kerr, Capt. Thomas R. (Moorfield, W Va)
Kiggins, Sgt. John (Lookout Mountain, Tenn)
Kimball, Pvt. Joseph (Sayler's Creek, Va)
Kindig, Cpl. John M. (Spotsylvania, Va)
King, Maj. & QM Horatio C. (Dinwiddie Courthouse, Va)
King, 1st Lt. Rufus, Jr. (White Oak Swamp Bridge, Va)
Kinsey, Cpl. John (Spotsylvania, Va)
Kirby, Maj. Dennis T. (Vicksburg, Miss)
Kirk, Capt. Jonathan C. (North Anna River, Va)
Kline, Pvt. Harry (Sayler's Creek, Va)
Kloth, Pvt. Charles H. (Vicksburg, Miss)
Knight, Cpl. Charles H. (Petersburg, Va)
Knight, Pvt. William J. (Georgia)
Knowles, Pvt. Abiather J. (Bull Run, Va)
Knox, 2d Lt. Edward M. (Gettysburg, Pa)
Koogle, 1st Lt. Jacob (Five Forks, Va)
Kountz, Musician John S. (Missionary Ridge, Tenn)
Kramer, Pvt. Theodore L. (Chapin's Farm, Va)
Kretsinger, Pvt. George (Vicksburg, Miss)
Kuder, 2d Lt. Andrew (Waynesboro, Va)
Kuder, Lt. Jeremiah (Jonesboro, Ga)
Labille, Pvt. Joseph S. (Vicksburg, Miss)
Ladd, Pvt. George (Waynesboro, Va)
*Laing, Sgt. William (Chapin's Farm, Va)
Landis, Chief Bugler James P. (Paine's Crossroads, Va)
Lane, Pvt. Morgan D. (Jetersville, Va)
Lanfare, 1st Lt. Aaron S. (Sayler's Creek, Va)
Langbein, Musician J. C. Julius (Camden, NC)
Larimer, Cpl. Smith (Sayler's Creek, Va)
Larrabee, Cpl. James W. (Vicksburg, Miss)
Lawson, 1st Sgt. Gaines (Minville, Tenn)
Lawton, Capt. Henry W. (Atlanta, Ga)
Leonard, Sgt. Edwin (Petersburg, Va)
Leonard, Pvt. William E. (Deep Bottom, Va)
Leslie, Pvt. Frank (Front Royal, Va)
Levy, Pvt. Benjamin (Glendale, Va)
Lewis, Capt. DeWitt C. (Secessionville, SC)
Lewis, Cpl. Henry (Vicksburg, Miss)
Lewis, Cpl. Samuel E. (Petersburg, Va)
Libaire, Capt. Adolphe (Antietam, Md)
Lilley, Pvt. John (Petersburg, Va)
Little, Sgt. Henry F. W. (Richmond, Va)
Littlefield, Cpl. George H. (Fort Fisher, NC)
Livingston, 1st Lt. & Adj. Josiah O. (Newport Barracks, NC)
Locke, Pvt. Lewis (Paine's Crossroads, Va)
Lonergan, Capt. John (Gettysburg, Pa)
Longshore, Pvt. William H. (Vicksburg, Miss)
Lonsway, Pvt. Joseph (Murfree's Station, Va)
Lord, Musician William (Drewry's Bluff, Va)
Lorish, Comm. Sgt. Andrew J. (Winchester, Va)
Love, Col. George M. (Cedar Creek, Va)
Lovering, 1st Sgt. George M. (Port Hudson, La)
Lower, Pvt. Cyrus B. (Wilderness, Va)
Lower, Pvt. Robert A. (Vicksburg, Miss)
Loyd, Pvt. George (Petersburg, Va)
Lucas, Pvt. George W. (Benton, Ark)
Luce, Sgt. Moses A. (Laurel Hill, Va)
Ludgate, Capt. William (Farmville, Va)
Ludwig, Pvt. Carl (Petersburg, Va)

Lunt, Sgt. Alphonso M. (Opequan Creek, Va)
Lutes, Cpl. Franklin W. (Petersburg, Va)
Luther, Pvt. James H. (Fredericksburg, Va)
Luty, Cpl. Gotlieb (Chancellorsville, Va)
Lyman, QM Sgt. Joel H. (Winchester, Va)
Lyon, Cpl. Frederick A. (Cedar Creek, Va)
McAdams, Cpl. Peter (Salem Heights, Va)
McAlwee, Sgt. Benjamin F. (Petersburg, Va)
McAnally, Lt. Charles (Spotsylvania, Va)
MacArthur, 1st Lt. & Adj. Arthur, Jr. (Missionary Ridge, Tenn)
McCammon, 1st Lt. William W. (Corinth, Miss)
McCarren, Pvt. Bernard (Gettysburg, Pa)
McCauslin, Pvt. Joseph (Petersburg, Va)
McCleary, 1st Lt. Charles H. (Nashville, Tenn)
McClelland, Pvt. James M. (Vicksburg, Miss)
McConnell, Capt. Samuel (Fort Blakely, Ala)
McCornack, Pvt. Andrew (Vicksburg, Miss)
McDonald, Pvt. George E. (Fort Stedman, Va)
McDonald, Pvt. John W. (Pittsburg Landing, Tenn)
McElhinny, Pvt. Samuel O. (Sayler's Creek, Va)
McEnroe, Sgt. Patrick H. (Winchester, Va)
McFall, Sgt. Daniel (Spotsylvania, Va)
McGinn, Pvt. Edward (Vicksburg, Miss)
McGonagle, Pvt. Wilson (Vicksburg, Miss)
McGonnigle, Capt. & Asst. QM Andrew J. (Cedar Creek, Va)
McGough, Cpl. Owen (Bull Run, Va)
McGraw, Sgt. Thomas (Petersburg, Va)
McGuire, Pvt. Patrick (Vicksburg, Miss)
McHale, Cpl. Alexander U. (Spotsylvania Courthouse, Va)
McKay, Sgt. Charles W. (Dug Gap, Ga)
McKee, Color Sgt. George (Petersburg, Va)
McKeen, 1st Lt. Nineveh S. (Stone River & Liberty Gap, Tenn)
McKeever, Pvt. Michael (Burnt Ordinary, Va)
McKown, Sgt. Nathaniel A. (Chapin's Farm, Va)
McMahon, Capt. & Aide-de-Camp Martin T. (White Oak Swamp, Va)
McMillen, Sgt. Francis M. (Petersburg, Va)
*McVeane, Cpl. John P. (Fredericksburg Heights, Va)
McWhorter, Comm. Sgt. Walter F. (Sayler's Creek, Va)
Madden, Pvt. Michael (Mason's Island, Md)
Madison, Sgt. James (Waynesboro, Va)
Magee, Drummer William (Murfreesboro, Tenn)
Mahoney, Sgt. Jeremiah (Fort Sanders, Tenn)
Mandy, 1st Sgt. Harry J. (Front Royal, Va)
Mangam, Pvt. Richard C. (Hatcher's Run, Va)
Manning, Pvt. Joseph S. (Fort Sanders, Tenn)
Marland, 1st Lt. William (Grand Coteau, La)
Marquette, Sgt. Charles (Petersburg, Va)
Marsh, Sgt. Albert (Spotsylvania, Va)
Marsh, Pvt. Charles H. (Back Creek Valley, Va)
Marsh, Sgt. George (Elk River, Tenn)
Martin, Lt. Sylvester H. (Weldon Railroad, Va)
Mason, Sgt. Elihu H. (Georgia)
Mathews, 1st Sgt. William H. (Petersburg, Va)
Matthews, Cpl. John C. (Petersburg, Va)
Matthews, Pvt. Milton (Petersburg, Va)
Mattingly, Pvt. Henry B. (Jonesboro, Ga)
Mattocks, Maj. Charles P. (Sayler's Creek, Va)
Maxham, Cpl. Lowell M. (Fredericksburg, Va)
May, Pvt. William (Nashville, Tenn)

Mayberry, Pvt. John B. (Gettysburg, Pa)
Mayes, Pvt. William B. (Kenesaw Mountain, Ga)
Maynard, Pvt. George H. (Fredericksburg, Va)
Meach, Farrier George E. (Winchester, Va)
Meagher, 1st Sgt. Thomas (Chapin's Farm, Va)
Mears, Sgt. George W. (Gettysburg, Pa)
Menter, Sgt. John W. (Sayler's Creek, Va)
Merriam, Lt. Col. Henry C. (Fort Blakely, Ala)
Merrifield, Cpl. James K. (Franklin, Tenn)
Merrill, Capt. Augustus (Petersburg, Va)
Merrill, Pvt. George (Fort Fisher, NC)
Merritt, Sgt. John G. (Bull Run, Va)
Meyer, Capt. Henry C. (Petersburg, Va)
Miles, Col. Nelson A. (Chancellorsville, Va)
Miller, Pvt. Frank (Sayler's Creek, Va)
Miller, Capt. Henry A. (Fort Blakely, Ala)
Miller, Pvt. Jacob C. (Vicksburg, Miss)
Miller, Pvt. James P. (Selma, Ala)
Miller, Cpl. John (Gettysburg, Pa)
Miller, Pvt. John (Waynesboro, Va)
Miller, Capt. William E. (Gettysburg, Pa)
Mills, Sgt. Frank W. (Sandy Cross Roads, NC)
Mindil, Capt. George W. (Williamsburg, Va)
Mitchell, 1st Lt. Alexander H. (Spotsylvania, Va)
Mitchell, Pvt. Theodore (Petersburg, Va)
Moffitt, Cpl. John H. (Gaines's Mill, Va)
Molbone, Sgt. Archibald (Petersburg, Va)
Monaghan, Cpl. Patrick (Petersburg, Va)
Moore, Cpl. Daniel B. (Fort Blakely, Ala)
Moore, Pvt. George G. (Fisher's Hill, Va)
Moore, Pvt. Wilbur F. (Nashville, Tenn)
Morey, Pvt. Delano (McDowell, Va)
Morford, Pvt. Jerome (Vicksburg, Miss)
*Morgan, Pvt. Lewis (Spotsylvania, Va)
Morgan, Cpl. Richard H. (Columbus, Ga)
Morrill, Capt. Walter G. (Rappahannock Station, Va)
Morris, Sgt. William (Sayler's Creek, Va)
Morrison, Pvt. Francis (Bermuda Hundred, Va)
Morse, Pvt. Benjamin (Spotsylvania, Va)
Morse, Sgt. Charles E. (Wilderness, Va)
Mostoller, Pvt. John W. (Lynchburg, Va)
Mulholland, Maj. St. Clair A. (Chancellorsville, Va)
Mundell, Cpl. Walter L. (Sayler's Creek, Va)
Munsell, Sgt. Harvey M. (Gettysburg, Pa)
Murphy, 1st Lt. & QM Charles J. (Bull Run, Va)
Murphy, Sgt. Daniel J. (Hatcher's Run, Va)
Murphy, Sgt. Dennis J. F. (Corinth, Miss)
Murphy, Pvt. James T. (Petersburg, Va)
Murphy, Pvt. John P. (Antietam, Md)
Murphy, Lt. Col. Michael C. (North Anna River, Va)
Murphy, Musician Robinson B. (Atlanta, Ga)
Murphy, Cpl. Thomas (Chapin's Farm, Va)
Murphy, Cpl. Thomas (Vicksburg, Miss)
Murphy, 1st Sgt. Thomas J. (Five Forks, Va)
Myers, Pvt. George S. (Chickamauga, Ga)
Myers, Pvt. William H. (Appomattox Courthouse, Va)
Nash, Cpl. Henry H. (Vicksburg, Miss)
Neahr, Pvt. Zachariah C. (Fort Fisher, NC)
Neville, Capt. Edwin M. (Sayler's Creek, Va)
Newman, Pvt. Marcellus J. (Resaca, Ga)
Newman, Lt. William H. (Amelia Springs, Va)
Nichols, Capt. Henry C. (Fort Blakely, Ala)
Niven, 2d Lt. Robert (Waynesboro, Va)
Nolan, Sgt. John J. (Georgia Landing, La)

Noll, Sgt. Conrad (Spotsylvania, Va)
North, Pvt. Jasper N. (Vicksburg, Miss)
Norton, 2d Lt. Elliott M. (Sayler's Creek, Va)
Norton, Lt. John R. (Sayler's Creek, Va)
Norton, Sgt. Llewellyn P. (Sayler's Creek, Va)
Noyes, Pvt. William W. (Spotsylvania, Va)
Nutting, Capt. Lee (Todd's Tavern, Va)
O'Beirne, Capt. James R. (Fair Oaks, Va)
O'Brien, Cpl. Henry D. (Gettysburg, Pa)
O'Brien, Pvt. Peter (Waynesboro, Va)
O'Connor, Sgt. Albert (Gravelly Run, Va)
O'Connor, Pvt. Timothy (NOR)
O'Dea, Pvt. John (Vicksburg, Miss)
O'Donnell, 1st Lt. Menomen (Vicksburg, Miss)
Oliver, Sgt. Charles (Petersburg, Va)
Oliver, Capt. Paul A. (Resaca, Ga)
O'Neill, Cpl. Stephen (Chancellorsville, Va)
Opel, Pvt. John N. (Wilderness, Va)
Orbansky, Pvt. David (Shiloh, Tenn, & Vicksburg, Miss, etc.)
Orr, Pvt. Charles A. (Hatcher's Run, Va)
Orr, Maj. Robert L. (Petersburg, Va)
Orth, Cpl. Jacob G. (Antietam, Md)
Osborne, Pvt. William H. (Malvern Hill, Va)
Oss, Pvt. Albert (Chancellorsville, Va)
Overturf, Pvt. Jacob H. (Vicksburg, Miss)
Packard, Pvt. Loron F. (Raccoon Ford, Va)
Palmer, Musician George H. (Lexington, Mo)
Palmer, Cpl. John G. (Fredericksburg, Va)
Palmer, Col. William J. (Red Hill, Ala)
Parker, Cpl. Thomas (Petersburg & Sayler's Creek, Va)
Parks, Pvt. Henry J. (Cedar Creek, Va)
Parks, Cpl. James W. (Nashville, Tenn)
Parrott, Pvt. Jacob (Georgia)
Parsons, Pvt. Joel (Vicksburg, Miss)
Patterson, 1st Lt. John H. (Wilderness, Va)
Patterson, Principal Musician John T. (Winchester, Va)
Paul, Pvt. William H. (Antietam, Md)
Pay, Pvt. Byron E. (Nolensville, Tenn)
Payne, Cpl. Irvin C. (Sayler's Creek, Va)
Payne, 1st Lt. Thomas H. L. (Fort Blakely, Ala)
Pearsall, Cpl. Platt (Vicksburg, Miss)
Pearson, Col. Alfred L. (Lewis's Farm, Va)
Peck, Pvt. Cassius (Blackburn's Ford, Va)
Peck, 1st Lt. Theodore S. (Newport Barracks, NC)
Peirsol, Sgt. James K. (Paine's Crossroads, Va)
Pennypacker, Col. Galusha (Fort Fisher, NC)
Pentzer, Capt. Patrick H. (Blakely, Ala)
Pesch, Pvt. Joseph (Grand Gulf, Miss)
Peters, Pvt. Henry C. (Vicksburg, Miss)
Petty, Sgt. Philip (Fredericksburg, Va)
Phelps, Col. Charles E. (Laurel Hill, Va)
Phillips, Pvt. Josiah (Sutherland Station, Va)
Phisterer, 1st Lt. Frederick (Stone River, Tenn)
Pickle, Sgt. Alonzo H. (Deep Bottom, Va)
Pike, 1st Sgt. Edward M. (Cache River, Ark)
Pingree, Capt. Samuel E. (Lee's Mills, Va)
Pinkham, Sgt. Maj. Charles H. (Fort Stedman, Va)
Pinn, 1st Sgt. Robert (Chapin's Farm, Va)
Pipes, Capt. James (Gettysburg, Pa)
Pitman, Sgt. George J. (Sayler's Creek, Va)
Pittinger, Sgt. William (Georgia)
Plant, Cpl. Henry E. (Bentonville, NC)
Platt, Pvt. George C. (Fairfield, Pa)

Plimley, 1st Lt. William (Hatcher's Run, Va)
Plowman, Sgt. Maj. George H. (Petersburg, Va)
Plunkett, Sgt. Thomas (Fredericksburg, Va)
Pond, Pvt. George F. (Drywood, Kans)
Pond, 1st Lt. James B. (Baxter Springs, Kans)
Porter, Comm. Sgt. Ambrose (Tallahatchie River, Miss)
Porter, Capt. Horace (Chickamauga, Ga)
Porter, Pvt. John R. (Georgia)
Porter, Sgt. William (Sayler's Creek, Va)
Post, Col. Philip S. (Nashville, Tenn)
Postles, Capt. James P. (Gettysburg, Pa)
Potter, Pvt. George W. (Petersburg, Va)
Potter, 1st Sgt. Norman F. (Lookout Mountain, Tenn)
Powell, Maj. William H. (Sinking Creek Valley, Va)
Power, Pvt. Albert (Pea Ridge, Ark)
Powers, Cpl. Wesley J. (Oostanaula, Ga)
Prentice, Pvt. Joseph R. (Stone River, Tenn)
Preston, 1st Lt. & Comm. Noble D. (Trevilian Station, Va)
Purcell, Sgt. Hiram W. (Fair Oaks, Va)
Purman, Lt. James J. (Gettysburg, Pa)
Putnam, Sgt. Edgar P. (Crump's Creek, Va)
Putnam, Cpl. Winthrop D. (Vicksburg, Miss)
Quay, Col. Matthew S. (Fredericksburg, Va)
Quinlan, Maj. James (Savage Station, Va)
Rafferty, Pvt. Peter (Malvern Hill, Va)
Ramsbottom, 1st Sgt. Alfred (Franklin, Tenn)
Rand, Pvt. Charles F. (Blackburn's Ford, Va)
Ranney, Asst. Surgeon George E. (Resaca, Ga)
Ranney, Pvt. Myron H. (Bull Run, Va)
Ratcliff, 1st Sgt. Edward (Chapin's Farm, Va)
Raub, Asst. Surgeon Jacob F. (Hatcher's Run, Va)
Raymond, Cpl. William H. (Gettysburg, Pa)
Read, Lt. Morton A. (Appomattox Station, Va)
Rebmann, Sgt. George F. (Fort Blakely, Ala)
Reddick, Cpl. William H. (Georgia)
Reed, Sgt. Axel H. (Chickamauga, Ga & Missionary Ridge, Tenn)
Reed, Bugler Charles W. (Gettysburg, Pa)
Reed, Pvt. George W. (Weldon Railroad, Va)
Reed, Pvt. William (Vicksburg, Miss)
Reeder, Pvt. Charles A. (Battery Gregg, Va)
Reid, Pvt. Robert A. (Petersburg, Va)
Reigle, Cpl. Daniel P. (Cedar Creek, Va)
Reisinger, Cpl. J. Monroe (Gettysburg, Pa)
Renninger, Cpl. Louis (Vicksburg, Miss)
Reynolds, Pvt. George (Winchester, Va)
Rhodes, Pvt. Julius D. (Thoroughfare Gap & Bull Run, Va)
Rhodes, Sgt. Sylvester D. (Fisher's Hill, Va)
Rice, Maj. Edmund (Gettysburg, Pa)
Rich, 1st Sgt. Carlos H. (Wilderness, Va)
Richardson, Pvt. William R. (Sayler's Creek, Va)
Richey, Cpl. William E. (Chickamauga, Va)
*Richmond, Pvt. James (Gettysburg, Pa)
Ricksecker, Pvt. John H. (Franklin, Tenn)
Riddell, Lt. Rudolph (Sayler's Creek, Va)
Riley, Pvt. Thomas (Fort Blakely, Ala)
Ripley, Lt. Col. William Y. W. (Malvern Hill, Va)
Robbins, 2d Lt. Augustus J. (Spotsylvania, Va)
Roberts, Sgt. Otis O. (Rappahannock Station, Va)
Robertson, 1st Lt. Robert S. (Corbin's Bridge, Va)
*Robertson, Pvt. Samuel (Georgia)
Robie, Sgt. George F. (Richmond, Va)

Robinson, Pvt. Elbridge (Winchester, Va)
*Robinson, Pvt. James H. (Brownsville, Ark)
Robinson, Brig. Gen. John C. (Laurel Hill, Va)
Robinson, Pvt. John H. (Gettysburg, Pa)
Robinson, Pvt. Thomas (Spotsylvania, Va)
Rock, Pvt. Frederick (Vicksburg, Miss)
Rockefeller, Lt. Charles M. (Fort Blakely, Ala)
Rodenbough, Capt. Theophilus F. (Trevilian Station, Va)
Rohm, Chief Bugler Ferdinand F. (Reams's Station, Va)
Rood, Pvt. Oliver P. (Gettysburg, Pa)
Roosevelt, 1st Sgt. George W. (Bull Run, Va & Gettysburg, Pa)
*Ross, Sgt. Maj. Marion A. (Georgia)
Rossbach, Sgt. Valentine (Spotsylvania, Va)
Rought, Sgt. Stephen (Wilderness, Va)
Rounds, Pvt. Lewis A. (Spotsylvania, Va)
Roush, Cpl. J. Levi (Gettysburg, Pa)
Rowand, Pvt. Archibald H., Jr. (Virginia)
Rowe, Pvt. Henry W. (Petersburg, Va)
Rundle, Pvt. Charles W. (Vicksburg, Miss)
Russell, Cpl. Charles L. (Spotsylvania, Va)
Russell, Capt. Milton (Stone River, Tenn)
Rutherford, 1st Lt. John T. (Yellow Tavern & Hanovertown, Va)
Rutter, Sgt. James M. (Gettysburg, Pa)
Ryan, Pvt. Peter J. (Winchester, Va)
Sacriste, 1st Lt. Louis J. (Chancellorsville & Auburn, Va)
Sagelhurst, Sgt. John C. (Hatcher's Run, Va)
Sancrainte, Pvt. Charles F. (Atlanta, Ga)
Sands, 1st Sgt. William (Dabney's Mills, Va)
Sanford, Pvt. Jacob (Vicksburg, Miss)
Sargent, Sgt. Jackson (Petersburg, Va)
Sartwell, Sgt. Henry (Chancellorsville, Va)
*Savacool, Capt. Edwin F. (Sayler's Creek, Va)
Saxton, Brig. Gen. Rufus (Harper's Ferry, W Va)
Scanlan, Pvt. Patrick (Ashepoo River, SC)
Scheibner, Pvt. Martin E. (Mine Run, Va)
Schenck, Pvt. Benjamin W. (Vicksburg, Miss)
Schiller, Pvt. John (Chapin's Farm, Va)
Schlachter, Pvt. Philipp (Spotsylvania, Va)
Schmal, Blacksmith George W. (Paine's Crossroads, Va)
Schmauch, Pvt. Andrew (Vicksburg, Miss)
Schmidt, 1st Sgt. Conrad (Winchester, Va)
Schmidt, Pvt. William (Missionary Ridge, Tenn)
Schneider, Sgt. George (Petersburg, Va)
Schnell, Cpl. Christian (Vicksburg, Miss)
Schofield, Maj. John M. (Wilson's Creek, Mo)
Schoonmaker, Col. James M. (Winchester, Va)
Schorn, Chief Bugler Charles (Appomattox, Va)
Schubert, Pvt. Martin (Fredericksburg, Va)
Schwan, 1st Lt. Theodore (Peebles's Farm, Va)
Schwenk, Sgt. Martin (Millerstown, Pa)
Scofield, QM Sgt. David H. (Cedar Creek, Va)
Scott, Cpl. Alexander (Monocacy, Md)
*Scott, Sgt. John M. (Georgia)
Scott, Capt. John W. (Five Forks, Va)
Scott, Drummer Julian A. (Lee's Mills, Va)
Seaman, Pvt. Elisha B. (Chancellorsville, Va)
Sears, 1st Lt. Cyrus (Iuka, Miss)
Seaver, Col. Thomas O. (Spotsylvania Courthouse, Va)
Seitzinger, Pvt. James M. (Cold Harbor, Va)

Sellers, Maj. Alfred J. (Gettysburg, Pa)
*Seston, Sgt. Charles H. (Winchester, Va)
Sewell, Col. William J. (Chancellorsville, Va)
Shafter, 1st Lt. William R. (Fair Oaks, Va)
Shahan, Cpl. Emisire (Sayler's Creek, Va)
Shaler, Col. Alexander (Marye's Heights, Va)
Shambaugh, Cpl. Charles (Charles City Crossroads, Va)
Shanes, Pvt. John (Carter's Farm, Va)
Shapland, Pvt. John (Elk River, Tenn)
Shea, Pvt. Joseph H. (Chapin's Farm, Va)
Shellenberger, Cpl. John S. (Deep Run, Va)
Shepard, Cpl. Irwin (Knoxville, Tenn)
Shepherd, Pvt. William (Sayler's Creek, Va)
Sherman, Pvt. Marshall (Gettysburg, Pa)
Shiel, Cpl. John (Fredericksburg, Va)
Shields, Pvt. Bernard (Appomattox, Va)
Shilling, 1st Sgt. John (Weldon Railroad, Va)
Shipley, Sgt. Robert F. (Five Forks, Va)
Shoemaker, Sgt. Levi (Nineveh, Va)
Shopp, Pvt. George J. (Five Forks, Va)
Shubert, Sgt. Frank (Petersburg, Va)
Sickles, Maj. Gen. Daniel E. (Gettysburg, Pa)
Sickles, Sgt. William H. (Gravelly Run, Va)
Sidman, Pvt. George E. (Gaines's Mill, Va)
Simmons, Pvt. John (Sayler's Creek, Va)
Simmons, Lt. William T. (Nashville, Tenn)
Simonds, Sgt. Maj. William E. (Irish Bend, La)
Simons, Sgt. Charles J. (Petersburg, Va)
Skellie, Cpl. Ebenezer (Chapin's Farm, Va)
Sladen, Pvt. Joseph A. (Resaca, Ga)
*Slavens, Pvt. Samuel (Georgia)
Sloan, Pvt. Andrew J. (Nashville, Tenn)
Slusher, Pvt. Henry C. (Moorefield, W Va)
Smalley, Pvt. Reuben (Vicksburg, Miss)
Smalley, Pvt. Reuben S. (Elk River, Tenn)
Smith, Sgt. Alonzo (Hatcher's Run, Va)
Smith, Col. Charles H. (St. Mary's Church, Va)
Smith, Sgt. David L. (Warwick Courthouse, Va)
Smith, 1st Lt. & Adj. Francis M. (Dabney Mills, Va)
Smith, 1st Lt. Henry I. (Black River, NC)
Smith, Pvt. James (Georgia)
Smith, Lt. Col. Joseph S. (Hatcher's Run, Va)
Smith, Pvt. Otis W. (Nashville, Tenn)
Smith, Pvt. Richard (Weldon Railroad, Va)
Smith, Capt. S. Rodmond (Rowanty Creek, Va)
Smith, Cpl. Thaddeus S. (Gettysburg, Pa)
Smith, Cpl. Wilson (Washington, NC)
Snedden, Musician James (Piedmont, Va)
Southard, Sgt. David (Sayler's Creek, Va)
Sova, Saddler Joseph E. (Appomattox, Va)
Sowers, Pvt. Michael (Stony Creek Station, Va)
Spalding, Sgt. Edward B. (Pittsburg Landing, Tenn)
Sperry, Maj. William J. (Petersburg, Va)
Spillane, Pvt. Timothy (Hatcher's Run, Va)
Sprague, Cpl. Benona (Vicksburg, Miss)
Sprague, Col. John W. (Decatur, Ga)
Spurling, Lt. Col. Andrew B. (Evergreen, Ala)
Stacey, Pvt. Charles (Gettysburg, Pa)
Stahel, Maj. Gen. Julius (Piedmont, Va)
Stanley, Maj. Gen. David S. (Franklin, Tenn)
Starkins, Sgt. John H. (Campbell Station, Tenn)
Steele, Maj. & Aide-de-Camp John W. (Spring Hill, Tenn)

Above and Beyond

Steinmetz, Pvt. William (Vicksburg, Miss)
Stephens, Pvt. William G. (Vicksburg, Miss)
Sterling, Pvt. John T. (Winchester, Va)
Stevens, Capt. & Asst. Adj. Gen. Hazard (Fort Huger, Va)
Stewart, 1st Sgt. George W. (Paine's Crossroads, Va)
Stewart, Pvt. Joseph (Five Forks, Va)
Stickels, Sgt. Joseph (Fort Blakely, Ala)
Stockman, 1st Lt. George H. (Vicksburg, Miss)
Stokes, Pvt. George (Nashville, Tenn)
Stolz, Pvt. Frank (Vicksburg, Miss)
Storey, Sgt. John H. R. (Dallas, Ga)
*Strausbaugh, 1st Sgt. Bernard A. (Petersburg, Va)
Streile, Pvt. Christian (Paine's Crossroads, Va)
Strong, Sgt. James N. (Port Hudson, La)
Sturgeon, Pvt. James K. (Kenesaw Mountain, Ga)
Summers, Pvt. James C. (Vicksburg, Miss)
Surles, Pvt. William H. (Perryville, Ky)
Swan, Pvt. Charles A. (Selma, Ala)
Swap, Pvt. Jacob E. (Wilderness, Va)
Swayne, Lt. Col. Wager (Corinth, Miss)
Sweatt, Pvt. Joseph S. G. (Carrsville, Va)
Sweeney, Pvt. James (Cedar Creek, Va)
Swegheimer, Pvt. Jacob (Vicksburg, Miss)
Swift, Lt. Col. Frederic W. (Lenoire Station, Tenn)
Swift, 2d Lt. Harlan J. (Petersburg, Va)
Sype, Pvt. Peter (Vicksburg, Miss)
Tabor, Pvt. William L. S. (Port Hudson, La)
Taggart, Pvt. Charles A. (Sayler's Creek, Va)
Tanner, 2d Lt. Charles B. (Antietam, Md)
Taylor, 1st Lt. Anthony (Chickamauga, Ga)
Taylor, Capt. Forrester L. (Chancellorsville, Va)
Taylor, Sgt. Henry H. (Vicksburg, Miss)
Taylor, Pvt. Joseph (Weldon Railroad, Va)
Taylor, Pvt. Richard (Cedar Creek, Va)
Taylor, Sgt. William (Front Royal & Weldon Railroad, Va)
Terry, Sgt. John D. (New Bern, NC)
Thackrah, Pvt. Benjamin (Fort Gates, Fla)
Thatcher, Pvt. Charles M. (Petersburg, Va)
Thaxter, Maj. Sidney W. (Hatcher's Run, Va)
Thomas, Maj. Hampton S. (Amelia Springs, Va)
Thomas, Col. Stephen (Cedar Creek, Va)
Thompkins, Cpl. George W. (Petersburg, Va)
Thompson, Pvt. Allen (White Oak Road, Va)
Thompson, Sgt. Charles A. (Spotsylvania, Va)
Thompson, Cpl. Freeman C. (Petersburg, Va)
Thompson, Pvt. James (White Oak Road, Va)
Thompson, Surgeon J. Harry (New Bern, NC)
Thompson, Sgt. James B. (Gettysburg, Pa)
Thompson, Cpl. John (Hatcher's Run, Va)
Thompson, Sgt. Thomas (Chancellorsville, Va)
*Thompson, Sgt. William P. (Wilderness, Va)
Thomson, 1st Lt. Clifford (Chancellorsville, Va)
Thorn, 2d Lt. Walter (Dutch Gap Canal, Va)
Tibbets, Pvt. Andrew W. (Columbus, Ga)
Tilton, Sgt. William (Richmond, Va)
Tinkham, Cpl. Eugene M. (Cold Harbor, Va)
Titus, Sgt. Charles (Sayler's Creek, Va)
Toban, Sgt. James W. (Aiken, SC)
Tobie, Sgt. Maj. Edward P. (Appomattox, Va)
Tobin, 1st Lt. & Adj. John M. (Malvern Hill, Va)
Toffey, 1st Lt. John J. (Chattanooga, Tenn)
Tompkins, Sgt. Aaron B. (Sayler's Creek, Va)

Tompkins, 1st Lt. Charles H. (Fairfax, Va)
Toohey, Sgt. Thomas (Franklin, Tenn)
Toomer, Sgt. William (Vicksburg, Miss)
Torgler, Sgt. Ernst (Ezra Chapel, Ga)
Tozier, Sgt. Andrew J. (Gettysburg, Pa)
Tracy, Lt. Col. Amasa A. (Cedar Creek, Va)
Tracy, Col. Benjamin F. (Wilderness, Va)
Tracy, Sgt. Charles H. (Spotsylvania & Petersburg, Va)
Tracy, 2d Lt. William G. (Chancellorsville, Va)
Traynor, Cpl. Andrew (Mason's Hill, Va)
Treat, Sgt. Howell B. (Buzzard's Roost, Ga)
Tremain, Maj. & Aide-de-Camp Henry E. (Resaca, Ga)
Tribe, Pvt. John (Waterloo Bridge, Va)
Trogden, Pvt. Howell G. (Vicksburg, Miss)
Truell, Pvt. Edwin M. (Atlanta, Ga)
Tucker, Sgt. Allen (Petersburg, Va)
Tucker, Cpl. Jacob R. (Petersburg, Va)
Tweedale, Pvt. John (Stone River, Tenn)
Twombly, Cpl. Voltaire P. (Fort Donelson, Tenn)
Tyrrell, Cpl. George W. (Resaca, Ga)
Uhrl, Sgt. George (White Oak Swamp Bridge, Va)
Urell, Pvt. M. Emmet (Bristoe Station, Va)
Vale, Pvt. John (Nolensville, Tenn)
Vance, Pvt. Wilson (Stone River, Tenn)
Vanderslice, Pvt. John M. (Hatcher's Run, Va)
Van Matre, Pvt. Joseph (Petersburg, Va)
Van Winkle, Cpl. Edward (Chapin's Farm, Va)
Veal, Pvt. Charles (Chapin's Farm, Va)
Veale, Capt. Moses (Wauhatchie, Tenn)
Veazey, Col. Wheelock G. (Gettysburg, Pa)
Vernay, 2d Lt. James D. (Vicksburg, Miss)
Vifquain, Lt. Col. Victor (Fort Blakely, Ala)
Von Vegesack, Maj. & Aide-de-Camp Ernest (Gaines's Mill, Va)
Wageman, Pvt. John H. (Petersburg, Va)
Wagner, Cpl. John W. (Vicksburg, Miss)
Wainwright, 1st Lt. John (Fort Fisher, NC)
Walker, Pvt. James C. (Missionary Ridge, Tenn)
Walker, Contract Surgeon (Civilian) Mary (Bull Run, Va & Chattanooga, Tenn, etc.)
Wall, Pvt. Jerry (Gettysburg, Pa)
Waller, Cpl. Francis A. (Gettysburg, Pa)
Walling, Capt. William H. (Fort Fisher, NC)
Walsh, Cpl. John (Cedar Creek, Va)
Walton, Pvt. George W. (Petersburg, Va)
Wambsgan, Pvt. Martin (Cedar Creek, Va)
Ward, Pvt. Nelson W. (Staunton River Bridge, Va)
Ward, Pvt. Thomas J. (Vicksburg, Miss)
Ward, Capt. William H. (Vicksburg, Miss)
Warden, Cpl. John (Vicksburg, Miss)
Warfel, Pvt. Henry C. (Paine's Crossroads, Va)
Warren, Cpl. Francis E. (Port Hudson, La)
Webb, Brig. Gen. Alexander S. (Gettysburg, Pa)
Webb, Pvt. James (Bull Run, Va)
Webber, Musician Alason P. (Kenesaw Mountain, Ga)
Weeks, Pvt. John H. (Spotsylvania, Va)
Weir, Capt. & Asst. Adj. Gen. Henry C. (St. Mary's Church, Va)
Welch, Pvt. George W. (Nashville, Tenn)
Welch, Cpl. Richard (Petersburg, Va)
Welch, Sgt. Stephen (Dug Gap, Ga)
*Wells, Pvt. Henry S. (Chapin's Farm, Va)

Wells, Chief Bugler Thomas M. (Cedar Creek, Va)
Wells, Maj. William (Gettysburg, Pa)
Welsh, Pvt. Edward (Vicksburg, Miss)
Welsh, Pvt. James (Petersburg, Va)
Westerhold, Sgt. William (Spotsylvania, Va)
Weston, Maj. John F. (Wetumpka, Ala)
Wheaton, Lt. Col. Loyd (Fort Blakely, Ala)
Wheeler, 1st Lt. Daniel D. (Salem Heights, Va)
Wheeler, Pvt. Henry W. (Bull Run, Va)
Wherry, 1st Lt. William M. (Wilson's Creek, Mo)
Whitaker, Capt. Edward W. (Reams's Station, Va)
White, Cpl. Adam (Hatcher's Run, Va)
White, Pvt. J. Henry (Rappahannock Station, Va)
White, Capt. Patrick H. (Vicksburg, Miss)
Whitehead, Chaplain John M. (Stone River, Tenn)
Whitman, Pvt. Frank M. (Antietam, Md & Spotsylvania, Va)
Whitmore, Pvt. John (Fort Blakely, Ala)
Whitney, Sgt. William G. (Chickamauga, Ga)
Whittier, 1st Lt. Edward N. (Fisher's Hill, Va)
Widick, Pvt. Andrew J. (Vicksburg, Miss)
Wilcox, Sgt. William H. (Spotsylvania, Va)
Wiley, Sgt. James (Gettysburg, Pa)
Wilhelm, Capt. George (Champion Hill, Miss)
Wilkins, Sgt. Leander A. (Petersburg, Va)
Willcox, Col. Orlando B. (Bull Run, Va)
Williams, Pvt. Elwood N. (Shiloh, Tenn)
Williams, QM Sgt. George C. (Gaines's Mill, Va)
Williams, Sgt. Le Roy (Cold Harbor, Va)
Williams, Pvt. William H. (Peach Tree Creek, Ga)
Williamson, Col. James A. (Chickasaw Bayou, Miss)
Williston, 1st Lt. Edward B. (Trevilian Station, Va)
Wilson, Sgt. Charles E. (Sayler's Creek, Va)
Wilson, Pvt. Christopher W. (Spotsylvania, Va)
Wilson, Cpl. Francis A. (Petersburg, Va)
Wilson, Sgt. John (Chamberlain's Creek, Va)
Wilson, Pvt. John A. (Georgia)
Wilson, 1st Lt. John M. (Malvern Hill, Va)
Winegar, Lt. William W. (Five Forks, Va)
Wisner, 1st Lt. Lewis S. (Spotsylvania, Va)
Withington, Capt. William H. (Bull Run, Va)
Wollam, Pvt. John (Georgia)
Wood, 1st Lt. H. Clay (Wilson's Creek, Mo)
Wood, Pvt. Mark (Georgia)
Wood, Capt. Richard H. (Vicksburg, Miss)
Woodbury, Sgt. Eri D. (Cedar Creek, Va)
Woodruff, Sgt. Alonzo (Hatcher's Run, Va)
Woodruff, 1st Lt. Carle A. (Newby's Crossroads, Va)
Woods, Pvt. Daniel A. (Sayler's Creek, Va)
Woodward, 1st Lt. & Adj. Evan M. (Fredericksburg, Va)
Wortick, Pvt. Joseph (Vicksburg, Miss)
Wray, Sgt. William J. (Fort Stevens, DC)
Wright, Capt. Albert D. (Petersburg, Va)
Wright, Pvt. Robert (Chapel House Farm, Va)
Wright, Cpl. Samuel (Nolensville, Tenn)
Wright, Pvt. Samuel C. (Antietam, Md)
Yeager, Pvt. Jacob F. (Buzzard's Roost, Ga)
Young, Sgt. Andrew J. (Paine's Crossroads, Va)
Young, Cpl. Benjamin F. (Petersburg, Va)
Young, Sgt. Calvary M. (Osage, Kans)
Young, Pvt. James M. (Wilderness, Va)
Younker, Pvt. John L. (Cedar Mountain, Va)

MARINES

Binder, Sgt. Richard (Fort Fisher, NC)
Denig, Sgt. J. Henry (Mobile Bay, Ala)
Fry, Orderly Sgt. Isaac N. (Fort Fisher, NC)
Hudson, Sgt. Michael (Mobile Bay, Ala)
Mackie, Cpl. John F. (Drewry's Bluff, Va)
Martin, Sgt. James (Mobile Bay, Ala)
Miller, Sgt. Andrew (Mobile Bay, Ala)
Nugent, Orderly Sgt. Christopher (Crystal River, Fla)
Oviatt, Cpl. Miles M. (Mobile Bay, Ala)
Rannahan, Cpl. John (Fort Fisher, NC)
Roantree, Sgt. James S. (Mobile Bay, Ala)
Shivers, Pvt. John (Fort Fisher, NC)
Smith, Cpl. Willard M. (Mobile Bay, Ala)
Sprowle, Orderly Sgt. David (Mobile Bay, Ala)
Thompson, Pvt. Henry A. (Fort Fisher, NC)
Tomlin, Cpl. Andrew J. (Fort Fisher, NC)
Vaughn, Sgt. Pinkerton R. (Port Hudson, La)

NAVY

Aheam, Paymaster's Steward Michael (Cherbourg, France)
Anderson, QM Robert (Various)
Angling, Cabin Boy John (Fort Fisher, NC)
Arther, SQM Matthew (Forts Henry & Donelson, Tenn.)
Asten, QG Charles (Red River, Va)
Atkinson, Yeoman Thomas E. (Mobile Bay, Ala)
Avery, Sman James (Mobile Bay, Ala)
Baker, QG Charles (Mobile Bay, Ala)
Baldwin, Coal Heaver Charles (Roanoke River, NC)
Barnum, BM James (Fort Fisher, NC)
Barter, Lman Gurdon H. (Fort Fisher, NC)
Barton, Sman Thomas (Franklin, Va)
Bass, Sman David L. (Fort Fisher, NC)
Bazaar, Ord. Sman Philip (Fort Fisher, NC)
Bell, Capt. of the Afterguard George (Galveston Bay, Tex)
Betham, Coxswain Asa (Fort Fisher, NC)
Bibber, GM Charles J. (Fort Fisher, NC)
Bickford, Capt. of the Top John F. (Cherbourg, France)
Blagheen, Ship's Cook William (Mobile Bay, Ala)
Blair, BM Robert M. (Fort Fisher, NC)
Blake, Robert (Legareville, SC)
Bois, QM Frank (Vicksburg, Miss)
Bond, BM William (Cherbourg, France)
Bourne, Sman & Gun Capt. Thomas (Forts Jackson & St. Philip, La)
Bowman, QM Edward R. (Fort Fisher, NC)
Bradley, Lman Amos (Forts Jackson & St. Philip, La)
Bradley, BM Charles (NOR)
Brazell, QM John (Mobile Bay, Ala)
Breen, BM John (Franklin, Va)
Brennan, Sman Christopher (Forts Jackson & St. Philip, La)
Brinn, Sman Andrew (Port Hudson, La)
Brown, QM James (Red River, Tex)
Brown, Capt. of the Forecastle John (Mobile Bay, Ala)
Brown, Capt. of the Top Robert (Mobile Bay, Ala)
Brown, Lman William H. (Mobile Bay, Ala)

Brown, Lman Wilson (Mobile Bay, Ala)
Brownell, Coxswain William P. (Great Gulf Bay & Vicksburg, Miss)
Brutsche, Lman Henry (Plymouth, NC)
Buck, QM James (Forts Jackson & St. Philip, La)
Burns, Sman John M. (Mobile Bay, Ala)
Burton, Sman Albert (Fort Fisher, NC)
Butts, GM George (Red River, Tex)
Byrnes, BM James (NOR)
Campbell, BM William (Fort Fisher, NC)
Carr, Master-at-Arms William M. (Mobile Bay, Ala)
Cassidy, Lman Michael (Mobile Bay, Ala)
Chandler, Coxswain James B. (Mobile Bay, Ala)
Chaput, Lman Louis G. (Mobile Bay, Ala)
Clifford, Master-at-Arms Robert T. (Wilmington, NC)
Colbert, Coxswain Patrick (Plymouth, NC)
Conlan, Sman Dennis (Fort Fisher, NC)
Connor, Ord. Sman Thomas (Fort Fisher, NC)
Connor, BM William C. (Wilmington, NC)
Cooper, Coxswain John (Mobile Bay, Ala)
Corcoran, Lman Thomas E. (Vicksburg, Miss)
Cotton, Ord. Sman Peter (Yazoo River, Miss)
Crawford, Fireman Alexander (Roanoke River, NC)
Cripps, QM Thomas (Mobile Bay, Ala)
Cronin, Chief QM Cornelius (Mobile Bay, Ala)
Davis, QG John (Elizabeth City, NC)
Davis, Ord. Sman Samuel W. (Mobile Bay, Ala)
Deakin, BM Charles (Mobile Bay, Ala)
Dempster, Coxswain John (Fort Fisher, NC)
Denning, Lman Lorenzo (NOR)
Dennis, BM Richard (Mobile Bay, Ala)
Densmore, Chief BM William (Mobile Bay, Ala)
Diggins, Ord. Sman Bartholomew (Mobile Bay, Ala)
Ditzenback, QM John (Bell's Mills, Tenn)
Donnelly, Ord. Sman John (Mobile Bay, Ala)
Doolen, Coal Heaver William (Mobile Bay, Ala)
Dorman, Sman John (Various)
Dougherty, Lman Patrick (NOR)
Dow, BM Henry (Vicksburg, Miss)
Duncan, BM Adam (Mobile Bay, Ala)
Duncan, Ord. Sman James K. L. (Harrisonburg, La)
Dunn, QM William (Fort Fisher, NC)
Dunphy, Coal Heaver Richard D. (Mobile Bay, Ala)
Edwards, Capt. of the Top John (Mobile Bay, Ala)
English, Signal QM Thomas (Fort Fisher, NC)
Erickson, Capt. of the Forecastle John P. (Fort Fisher, NC)
Farley, BM William (Stono River, SC)
Farrell, QM Edward (Forts Jackson & St. Philip, La)
Ferrell, Pilot John H. (Bell's Mills, Tenn)
Fitzpatrick, Coxswain Thomas (Mobile Bay, Ala)
Flood, Boy Thomas (Forts Jackson & St. Philip, La)
Foy, Signal QM Charles H. (Fort Fisher, NC)
Franks, Sman William J. (Yazoo City, Miss)
Freeman, Pilot Martin (Mobile Bay, Ala)
Frisbee, GM John B. (Forts Jackson & St. Philip, La)
Gardner, Sman William (Mobile Bay, Ala)
Garrison, Coal Heaver James R. (Mobile Bay, Ala)
Garvin, Capt. of the Forecastle William (Fort Fisher, NC)
George, Ord. Sman Daniel G. (NOR)
Gile, Lman Frank S. (Charleston Harbor, SC)
Graham, Lman Robert (Plymouth, NC)

Greene, Capt. of the Forecastle John (Forts Jackson & St. Philip, La)
Griffiths, Capt. of the Forecastle John (Fort Fisher, NC)
Griswold, Ord. Sman Luke M. (Cape Hatteras, NC)
Haffee, QG Edmund (Fort Fisher, NC)
Haley, Capt. of the Forecastle James (Cherbourg, France)
Halstead, Coxswain William (Mobile Bay, Ala)
Ham, Carpenter's Mate Mark G. (Cherbourg, France)
Hamilton, Coxswain Hugh (Mobile Bay, Ala)
Hamilton, Coal Heaver Richard (NOR)
Hamilton, QM Thomas W. (Vicksburg, Miss)
Hand, QM Allexander (Roanoke River, NC)
Harcourt, Ord. Sman Thomas (Fort Fisher, NC)
Harding, Capt. of the Forecastle Thomas (Beauford, NC)
Harley, Ord. Sman Bernard (NOR)
Harrington, Lman Daniel (NOR)
Harris, Capt. of the Forecastle John (Mobile Bay, Ala)
Harrison, Sman George H. (Cherbourg, France)
Hathaway, Sman Edward W. (Vicksburg, Miss)
Hawkins, Sman Charles (Fort Fisher, NC)
Hayden, QM Joseph B. (Fort Fisher, NC)
Hayes, Coxswain John (Cherbourg, France)
Hayes, Coxswain Thomas (Mobile Bay, Ala)
Hickman, 2d Class Fireman John (Port Hudson, La)
Hinnegan, 2d Class Fireman William (Fort Fisher, NC)
Hollat, 3d Class Boy George (Forts Jackson & St. Philip, La)
Horton, GM James (NOR)
Horton, Sman Lewis A. (Cape Hatteras, NC)
Houghton, Ord. Sman Edward J. (NOR)
Howard, Lman Martin (Plymouth, NC)
Howard, BM Peter (Port Hudson, La)
Huskey, Fireman Michael (Deer Creek, Miss)
Hyland, Sman John (Red River, Tex)
Irlam, Sman Joseph (Mobile Bay, Ala)
Irving, Coxswain John (Mobile Bay, Ala)
Irving, Coxswain Thomas (Charleston Harbor, SC)
Irwin, Sman Nicholas (Mobile Bay, Ala)
James, Capt. of the Top John H. (Mobile Bay, Ala)
Jenkins, Sman Thomas (Vicksburg, Miss)
Johnson, Sman Henry (Mobile Bay, Ala)
Johnston, Lman William P. (Harrisonburg, La)
Jones, Chief BM Andrew (Mobile Bay, Ala)
Jones, Lman John (Cape Hatteras, NC)
Jones, QM John E. (Mobile Bay, Ala)
Jones, Coxswain Thomas (Fort Fisher, NC)
Jones, Capt. of the Top William (Mobile Bay, Ala)
Jordan, Coxswain Robert (Nansemond River, Va)
Jordan, QM Thomas (Mobile Bay, Ala)
Kane, Capt. of the Hold Thomas (Fort Fisher, NC)
Kelley, 2d Class Fireman John (Roanoke River, NC)
Kendrick, Coxswain Thomas (Mobile Bay, Ala)
Kenna, QM Barnett (Mobile Bay, Ala)
Kenyon, Fireman Charles (Drewry's Bluff, Va)
King, Lman Robert H. (NOR)
Kinnaird, Lman Samuel W. (Mobile Bay, Ala)
Lafferty, Fireman John (Roanoke River, NC)
Laffey, Sman Bartlett (Yazoo City, Miss)
Lakin, Sman Daniel (Franklin, Va)
Lann, Lman John S. (St. Marks, Fla)

Above and Beyond

Lawson, Lman John (Mobile Bay, Ala)
Lear, QM Nicholas (Fort Fisher, NC)
Lee, Sman James H. (Cherbourg, France)
Leland, GM George W. (Charleston Harbor, SC)
Leon, Capt. of the Forecastle Pierre (Yazoo River, Miss)
Lloyd, Coal Heaver Benjamin (Roanoke River, NC)
Lloyd, Coxswain John W. (Roanoke River, NC)
*Logan, Capt. of the Afterguard Hugh (Cape Hatteras, NC)
Lyons, Sman Thomas (Forts Jackson & St. Philip, La)
McClelland, 1st Class Fireman Matthew (Port Hudson, La)
McCormick, BM Michael (Red River, Tex)
McCullock, Sman Adam (Mobile Bay, Ala)
McDonald, BM John (Yazoo River, Miss)
McFarland, Capt. of the Forecastle John (Mobile Bay, Ala)
McGowan, QM John (Forts Jackson & St. Philip, La)
Machon, Boy James (Mobile Bay, Ala)
McHugh, Sman Martin (Vicksburg, Miss)
McIntosh, Capt. of the Top James (Mobile Bay, Ala)
Mack, Capt. of the Top Alexander (Mobile Bay, Ala)
Mack, Sman John (St. Marks, Fla)
McKnight, Coxswain William (Forts Jackson & St. Philip, La)
McLeod, Capt. of the Foretop James (Forts Jackson & St. Philip, La)
McWilliams, Lman George W. (Fort Fisher, NC)
Madden, Coal Heaver William (Mobile Bay, Ala)
Martin, QM Edward S. (Mobile Bay, Ala)
Martin, BM William (Yazoo River, Miss)
Martin, Sman William (Forts Jackson & St. Philip, La)
Melville, Ord. Sman Charles (Mobile Bay, Ala)
Mifflin, Engineer's Cook James (Mobile Bay, Ala)
Miller, QM James (Legareville, SC)
Milliken, QG Daniel (Fort Fisher, NC)
Mills, Sman Charles (Fort Fisher, NC)
Molloy, Ord. Sman Hugh (Harrisonburg, La)
Montgomery, Capt. of the Afterguard Robert (Fort Fisher, NC)
Moore, Lman Charles (Legareville, SC)
Moore, Sman Charles (Cherbourg, France)
Moore, Sman George (Cape Hatteras, NC)
Moore, BM William (Haines's Bluff, Miss)
Morgan, Capt. of the Top James H. (Mobile Bay, Ala)
Morrison, Coxswain John G. (Yazoo River, Miss)
Morton, BM Charles W. (Yazoo River, Miss)
Mullen, BM Patrick (Mattox Creek, Va)
Murphy, BM Patrick (Mobile Bay, Ala)
Naylor, Lman David (Mobile Bay, Ala)
Neil, QG John (Fort Fisher, NC)
Newland, Ord. Sman William (Mobile Bay, Ala)
Nibbe, QM John H. (Yazoo River, Miss)
Nichols, QM William (Mobile Bay, Ala)
Noble, Lman Daniel (Mobile Bay, Ala)
O'Brien, Coxswain Oliver (Sullivan's Island Channel, SC)
O'Connell, Coal Heaver Thomas (Mobile Bay, Ala)
O'Donoghue, Sman Timothy (Red River, Tex)
Ortega, Sman John (NOR)
Parker, Capt. of the Afterguard William (Forts Jackson & St. Philip, La)

Parks, Capt. of the Forecastle George (Mobile Bay, Ala)
Pease, Sman Joachim (Cherbourg, France)
Peck, 2d Class Boy Oscar E. (Forts Jackson & St. Philip, La)
Pelham, Lman William (Mobile Bay, Ala)
Perry, BM Thomas (Cherbourg, France)
Peterson, Sman Alfred (Franklin, Va)
Phinney, BM William (Mobile Bay, Ala)
Poole, QM William B. (Cherbourg, France)
Prance, Capt. of the Main Top George (Fort Fisher, NC)
Preston, Lman John (Mobile Bay, Ala)
Price, Coxswain Edward (Mobile Bay, Ala)
Province, Ord. Sman George (Fort Fisher, NC)
Pyne, Sman George (St. Marks, Fla)
Read, Ord. Sman Charles (St. Marks, Fla)
Read, Coxswain Charles A. (Cherbourg, France)
Read, Sman George E. (Cherbourg, France)
Regan, QM Jeremiah (Drewry's Bluff, Va)
Rice, Coal Heaver Charles (Fort Fisher, NC)
Richards, QM Louis (Forts Jackson & St. Philip, La)
Ringold, Coxswain Edward (Pocataligo, SC)
Roberts, Sman James (Fort Fisher, NC)
Robinson, BM Alexander (Wilmington, NC)
Robinson, BM Charles (Yazoo River, Miss)
Rountry, 1st Class Fireman John (NOR)
Rush, 1st Class Fireman John (Port Hudson, La)
Sanderson, Lman Aaron (Mattox Creek, Va)
Saunders, QM James (Cherbourg, France)
Savage, Ord. Sman Auzella (Fort Fisher, NC)
Schutt, Coxswain George (St. Marks, Fla)
Seanor, Master-at-Arms James (Mobile Bay, Ala)
Seward, Paymaster's Steward Richard E. (Ship Island Sound, La)
Sharp, Sman Hendrick (Mobile Bay, Ala)
Shepard, Ord. Sman Louis C. (Fort Fisher, NC)
Sheridan, QM James (Mobile Bay, Ala)
Shipman, Coxswain William (Fort Fisher, NC)
Shutes, Capt. of the Forecastle Henry (New Orleans, La, & Fort McAllister, Ga)
Simkins, Coxswain Lebbeus (Mobile Bay, Ala)
*Smith, Coxswain Charles H. (Mobile Bay, Ala)
Smith, Ord. Sman Edwin (Franklin, Va)
Smith, Capt. of the Forecastle James (Mobile Bay, Ala)
Smith, 2d Capt. of the Top John (Mobile Bay, Ala)
Smith, Capt. of the Forecastle John (Mobile Bay, Ala)
Smith, Coxswain Oloff (Mobile Bay, Ala)
Smith, Sman Thomas (St. Marks, Fla)
Smith, Ord. Sman Walter B. (Mobile Bay, Ala)
Smith, QM William (Cherbourg, France)
Stanley, Shell Man William A. (Mobile Bay, Ala)
Sterling, Coal Heaver James E. (Mobile Bay, Ala)
Stevens, QM Daniel D. (Fort Fisher, NC)
Stoddard, Sman James (Yazoo City, Miss)
Stout, Lman Richard (Stono River, SC)
Strahan, Capt. of the Top Robert (Cherbourg, France)
Sullivan, Ord. Sman James (Fort Fisher, NC)
Sullivan, Sman John (Wilmington, NC)
Sullivan, Coxswain Timothy (NOR)
Summers, Chief QM Robert (Fort Fisher, NC)
Swanson, Sman John (Fort Fisher, NC)
Swatton, Sman Edward (Fort Fisher, NC)

Swearer, Sman Benjamin (Fort Clark, Md)
Talbott, Capt. of the Forecastle William (Arkansas)
*Tallentine, QG James (Plymouth, NC)
Taylor, Armorer George (Mobile Bay, Ala)
Taylor, Coxswain Thomas (Mobile Bay, Ala)
Taylor, Capt. of the Forecastle William G. (Fort Fisher, NC)
Thielberg, Sman Henry (Nansemond River, Va)
Thompson, Signal QM William (Hilton Head, NC)
Todd, QM Samuel (Mobile Bay, Ala)
Tripp, Chief BM Othniel (Fort Fisher, NC)
Truett, Coxswain Alexander H. (Mobile Bay, Ala)
Vantine, 1st Class Fireman Joseph E. (Port Hudson, La)
Verney, Chief QM James W. (Fort Fisher, NC)
Wagg, Coxswain Maurice (Cape Hatteras, NC)
Ward, QG James (Mobile Bay, Ala)
Warren, Coxswain David (Wilmington, NC)
Webster, Lman Henry S. (Fort Fisher, NC)
Weeks, Capt. of the Foretop Charles H. (NOR)
Wells, QM William (Mobile Bay, Ala)
White, Capt. of the Gun Joseph (Fort Fisher, NC)
Whitfield, QM Daniel (Mobile Bay, Ala)
Wilcox, Ord. Sman Franklin L. (Fort Fisher, NC)
Wilkes, Lman Henry (NOR)
Wilkes, Pilot Perry (Red River, Tex)
Williams, Sailmaker's Mate Anthony (Fort Fisher, NC)
Williams, Sman Augustus (Fort Fisher, NC)
Williams, BM John (Hilton Head, NC)
Williams, Capt. of the Maintop John (Mathias Point, Va)
Williams, Sman John (Franklin, Va)
Williams, Sman Peter (Hampton Roads, Va)
Williams, Signal QM Robert (Yazoo River, Miss)
Williams, Lman William (Charleston Harbor, SC)
Willis, Coxswain Richard (Fort Fisher, NC)
Wood, Coxswain Robert B. (Nansemond River, Va)
Woods, Sman Samuel (Nansemond River, Va)
Woon, BM John (Grand Gulf, Miss River)
Woram, Sman Charles B. (Mobile Bay, Ala)
Wright, QM Edward (Forts Jackson & St. Philip, La)
Wright, Yeoman William (Wilmington, NC)
Young, Coxswain Edward B. (Mobile Bay, Ala)
Young, Sman Horatio N. (Charleston Harbor, SC)
Young, BM William (Forts Jackson & St. Philip, La)

The Indian Campaigns   1861–1898

Number of medals: 423

ARMY: 423

Albee, 1st Lt. George E. (Brazos River, Tex)
Alchesay, Sgt. (Arizona)
Allen, 1st Sgt. William (Turret Mountain, Ariz)
Anderson, Pvt. James (Wichita River, Tex)
Aston, Pvt. Edgar R. (San Carlos, Ariz)
Austin, Sgt. William G. (Wounded Knee Creek, S Dak)
Ayers, Pvt. James F. (Sappa Creek, Kans)
Babcock, 1st Lt. John B. (Spring Creek, Neb)
Bailey, Sgt. James E. (Arizona)
Baird, 1st Lt. & Adj. George W. (Bear Paw Mountain, Mont)
Baker, Musician John (Cedar Creek, Mont)
+ Baldwin, 1st Lt. Frank D. (McClellan's Creek, Tex)
Bancroft, Pvt. Neil (Little Big Horn, Mont)
Barnes, Pfc. Will C. (Fort Apache, Ariz)
Barrett, 1st Sgt. Richard (Sycamore Canyon, Ariz)
Beauford, 1st Sgt. Clay (Arizona)
Bell, Pvt. James (Big Horn, Mont)
Bergerndahl, Pvt. Frederick (Staked Plains, Tex)
Bertram, Cpl. Heinrich (Arizona)
Bessey, Cpl. Charles A. (Elkhorn Creek, Wyo)
Bishop, Sgt. Daniel (Turret Mountain, Ariz)
Blair, 1st Sgt. James (Arizona)
Blanquet (Arizona)
Bowden, Cpl. Samuel (Wichita River, Tex)
Bowman, Sgt. Alonzo (Cibicue Creek, Ariz)
Boyne, Sgt. Thomas (Mimbres Mountains & Ojo Caliente, N Mex)
Bradbury, 1st Sgt. Sanford (Hell Canyon, Ariz)
Branagan, Pvt. Edward (Red River, Tex)
Brant, Pvt. Abram B. (Little Big Horn, Mont)
*Bratling, Cpl. Frank (Fort Selden, N Mex)
Brett, 2d Lt. Lloyd M. (O'Fallon's Creek, Mont)
Brogan, Sgt. James (Simon Valley, Ariz)
Brophy, Pvt. James (Arizona)
Brown, Sgt. Benjamin (Arizona)
Brown, Sgt. James (Davidson Canyon, Ariz)
Brown, Pvt. Lorenzo D. (Big Hole, Mont)
Bryan, Hospital Steward William C. (Powder River, Wyo)
Burkard, Pvt. Oscar (Leech Lake, Minn)
Burke, Farrier Patrick J. (Arizona)
Burke, Pvt. Richard (Cedar Creek, Mont)
Burnett, 2d Lt. George R. (Cuchillo Negro Mountains, N Mex)
Butler, Capt. Edmond (Wolf Mountain, Mont)
Byrne, Sgt. Denis (Cedar Creek, Mont)
Cable, Pvt. Joseph A. (Cedar Creek, Mont)
Callen, Pvt. Thomas J. (Little Big Horn, Mont)
Calvert, Pvt. James S. (Cedar Creek, Mont)
Canfield, Pvt. Heth (Little Blue, Neb)
Carpenter, Capt. Louis H. (Kansas & Colorado)
Carr, Pvt. John (Chiricahua Mountains, Ariz)
Carroll, Pvt. Thomas (Arizona)
Carter, Sgt. George (Arizona)
Carter, 1st Lt. Mason (Bear Paw Mountain, Mont)
Carter, 2d Lt. Robert G. (Brazos River, Tex)
Carter, 1st Lt. William H. (Cibicue, Ariz)
Casey, Capt. James S. (Wolf Mountain, Mont)
Cheever, 1st Lt. Benjamin H., Jr. (White River, S Dak)
Chiquito (Arizona)

Clancy, Musician John E. (Wounded Knee Creek, S Dak)
Clark, Pvt. Wilfred (Big Hole, Mont, & Camas Meadows, Idaho)
Clarke, 2d Lt. Powhatan H. (Sonora, Mex)
Comfort, Cpl. John W. (Staked Plains, Tex)
Connor, Cpl. John (Wichita River, Tex)
Coonrod, Sgt. Aquilla (Cedar Creek, Mont)
Corcoran, Cpl. Michael (Agua Fria River, Ariz)
Co-Rux-Te-Chod-Ish (Mad Bear), Sgt. (Republican River, Kans)
Craig, Sgt. Samuel H. (Santa Cruz Mountains, Mex)
Crandall, Pvt. Charles (Arizona)
Crist, Sgt. John (Arizona)
Criswell, Sgt. Banjamin C. (Little Big Horn River, Mont)
Cruse, 2d Lt. Thomas (Big Dry Fork, Ariz)
Cubberly, Pvt. William G. (San Carlos, Ariz)
Cunningham, Cpl. Charles (Little Big Horn River, Mont)
Daily, Pvt. Charles (Arizona)
Daniels, Sgt. James T. (Arizona)
Dawson, Trumpeter Michael (Sappa Creek, Kans)
Day, 2d Lt. Matthias W. (Las Animas Canyon, N Mex)
Day, 1st Sgt. William L. (Arizona)
*De Armond, Sgt. William (Upper Washita, Tex)
Deary, Sgt. George (Apache Creek, Ariz)
Deetline, Pvt. Frederick (Little Big Horn, Mont)
Denny, Sgt. John (Las Animas Canyon, N Mex)
Dickens, Cpl. Charles H. (Chiricahua Mountains, Ariz)
Dodge, Capt. Francis S. (White River Agency, Colo)
Donahue, Pvt. John L. (Chiricahua Mountains, Ariz)
Donavan, Sgt. Cornelius (Agua Fria River, Ariz)
Donelly, Pvt. John S. (Cedar Creek, Mont)
Dougherty, Blacksmith William (Arizona)
Dowling, Cpl. James (Arizona)
Edwards, 1st Sgt. William D. (Big Hole, Mont)
Eldrige, Sgt. George H. (Wichita River, Tex)
Elsatsoosu, Cpl. (Arizona)
Elwood, Pvt. Edwin L. (Chiricahua Mountains, Ariz)
Emmet, 2d Lt. Robert T. (Las Animas Canyon, N Mex)
Evans, Pvt. William (Big Horn, Mont)
Factor, Pvt. Pompey (Pecos River, Tex)
Falcott, Sgt. Henry (Arizona)
Farren, Pvt. Daniel (Arizona)
Feaster, Pvt. Mosheim (Wounded Knee Creek, S Dak)
Fegan, Sgt. James (Plum Creek, Kans)
Ferrari, Cpl. George (Red Creek, Ariz)
Fichter, Pvt. Hermann (Whetstone Mountains, Ariz)
Foley, Sgt. John H. (Platte River, Neb)
Folly, Pvt. William H. (Arizona)
Foran, Pvt. Nicholas (Arizona)
Forsyth, 1st Sgt. Thomas H. (Powder River, Wyo)
Foster, Sgt. William (Red River, Tex)
Freemeyer, Pvt. Christopher (Cedar Creek, Mont)
Gardiner, Pvt. Peter W. (Sappa Creek, Kans)
Gardner, Pvt. Charles (Arizona)
Garland, Cpl. Harry (Little Muddy Creek, Mont & Camas Meadows, Idaho)
Garlington, 1st Lt. Ernest A. (Wounded Knee Creek, S Dak)

Gates, Bugler George (Picacho Mountain, Ariz)
Gay, Pvt. Thomas H. (Arizona)
Geiger, Sgt. George (Little Big Horn River, Mont)
Georgian, Pvt. John (Chiricahua Mountains, Ariz)
Gerber, Sgt. Maj. Frederick W. (Various)
*Given, Cpl. John J. (Wichita River, Tex)
Glavinski, Blacksmith Albert (Powder River, Mont)
Glover, Sgt. T. B. (Mizpah Creek & Pumpkin Creek, Mont)
Glynn, Pvt. Michael (Whetstone Mountains, Ariz)
Godfrey, Capt. Edward S. (Bear Paw Mountain, Mont)
Golden, Sgt. Patrick (Arizona)
Goldin, Pvt. Theodore W. (Little Big Horn, Mont)
Goodman, Pvt. David (Lyry Creek, Ariz)
Grant, Sgt. George (Fort Phil Kearny-Fort C. F. Smith, Dak Terr)
Greaves, Cpl. Clinton (Florida Mountains, N Mex)
Green, Sgt. Francis C. (Arizona)
Green, Maj. John (Lava Beds, Calif)
Gresham, 1st Lt. John C. (Wounded Knee Creek, S Dak)
Grimes, Sgt. Edward P. (Milk River, Colo)
Gunther, Cpl. Jacob (Arizona)
Haddoo, Cpl. John (Cedar Creek, Mont)
Hall, Pvt. John (Arizona)
Hall, 1st Lt. William P. (White River, Colo)
Hamilton, Pvt. Frank (Agua Fria River, Ariz)
Hamilton, Pvt. Mathew H. (Wounded Knee Creek, S Dak)
Hanley, Sgt. Richard P. (Little Big Horn River, Mont)
Harding, Blacksmith Mosher A. (Chiricahua Mountains, Ariz)
Harrington, Pvt. John (Wichita River, Tex)
Harris, Sgt. Charles D. (Red Creek, Ariz)
Harris, Pvt. David W. (Little Big Horn River, Mont)
Harris, Pvt. William M. (Little Big Horn River, Mont)
Hartzog, Pvt. Joshua B. (Wounded Knee Creek, S Dak)
Haupt, Cpl. Paul (Hell Canyon, Ariz)
Hawthorne, 2d Lt. Harry L. (Wounded Knee Creek, S Dak)
Hay, Sgt. Fred S. (Upper Wichita, Tex)
Heartery, Pvt. Richard (Cibicue, Ariz)
Heise, Pvt. Clamor (Arizona)
Herron, Cpl. Leander (Fort Dodge, Kans)
Heyl, 2d Lt. Charles H. (Fort Hartsuff, Neb)
Higgins, Pvt. Thomas P. (Arizona)
Hill, Sgt. Frank E. (Date Creek, Ariz)
Hill, 1st Sgt. James M. (Turret Mountain, Ariz)
Hillock, Pvt. Marvin C. (Wounded Knee Creek, S Dak)
Himmelsback, Pvt. Michael (Little Blue, Neb)
Hinemann, Sgt. Lehmann (Arizona)
Hobday, Pvt. George (Wounded Knee Creek, S Dak)
Hogan, 1st Sgt. Henry (Cedar Creek, Mont)
  Second award (Bear Paw Mountain, Mont)
Holden, Pvt. Henry (Little Big Horn River, Mont)
Holland, Cpl. David (Cedar Creek, Mont)
*Hooker, Pvt. George (Tonto Creek, Ariz)
Hoover, Bugler Samuel (Santa Maria Mountains, Ariz)

Hornaday, Pvt. Simpson (Sappa Creek, Kans)
Howze, 2d Lt. Robert L. (White River, S Dak)
Hubbard, Pvt. Thomas (Little Blue, Neb)
Huff, Pvt. James W. (Arizona)
Huggins, Capt. Eli L. (O'Fallons Creek, Mont)
Humphrey, 1st Lt. Charles F. (Clearwater, Idaho)
Hunt, Pvt. Fred O. (Cedar Creek, Mont)
Hutchinson, Sgt. Rufus D. (Little Big Horn River, Mont)
Hyde, Sgt. Henry J. (Arizona)
Irwin, Asst. Surgeon Bernard J. D. (Apache Pass, Ariz)
Jackson, Capt. James (Camas Meadows, Idaho)
James, Cpl. John (Upper Wichita, Tex)
Jarvis, Sgt. Frederick (Chiricahua Mountains, Ariz)
Jetter, Sgt. Bernhard (South Dakota)
Jim, Sgt. (Arizona)
Johnson, Sgt. Henry (Milk River, Colo)
Johnston, Cpl. Edward (Cedar Creek, Mont)
Jones, Farrier William H. (Little Muddy Creek, Mont, & Camas Meadows, Idaho)
Jordan, Sgt. George (Fort Tularosa & Carrizo Canyon, N Mex)
Kay, Pvt. John (Arizona)
Keating, Cpl. Daniel (Wichita River, Tex)
Keenan, Trumpeter Bartholomew T. (Chiricahua Mountains, Ariz)
Keenan, Pvt. John (Arizona)
Kelley, Pvt. Charles (Chiricahua Mountains, Ariz)
Kelly, Cpl. John J. H. (Upper Wichita, Tex)
Kelly, Pvt. Thomas (Upper Wichita, Tex)
Kelsay (Arizona)
Kennedy, Pvt. Philip (Cedar Creek, Mont)
Kerr, Capt. John B. (White River, S Dak)
Kerrigan, Sgt. Thomas (Wichita River, Tex)
Kilmartin, Pvt. John (Whetstone Mountains, Ariz)
Kirk, 1st Sgt. John (Wichita River, Tex)
Kirkwood, Sgt. John A. (Slim Buttes, Dak Terr)
Kitchen, Sgt. George K. (Upper Wichita, Tex)
Knaak, Pvt. Albert (Arizona)
Knight, Sgt. Joseph F. (White River, S Dak)
Knox, Sgt. John W. (Upper Wichita, Tex)
Koelpin, Sgt. William (Upper Wichita, Tex)
Kosoha (Arizona)
Kreher, 1st Sgt. Wendelin (Cedar Creek, Mont)
Kyle, Cpl. John (Republican River, Kans)
Larkin, Farrier David (Red River, Tex)
Lawrence, Pvt. James (Arizona)
Lawton, Sgt. John S. (Milk River, Colo)
Lenihan, Pvt. James (Clear Creek, Ariz)
Leonard, Sgt. Patrick (Little Blue, Neb)
Leonard, Cpl. Patrick T. (Fort Hartsuff, Neb)
Leonard, Pvt. William (Muddy Creek, Mont)
Lewis, Sgt. William B. (Bluff Station, Wyo)
Little, Bugler Thomas (Arizona)
Lohnes, Pvt. Francis W. (Gilman's Ranch, Neb)
Long, 2d Lt. Oscar F. (Bear Paw Mountain, Mont)
Lowthers, Pvt. James (Sappa Creek, Kans)
*Loyd, Sgt. George (Wounded Knee Creek, S Dak)
Lytle, Sgt. Leonidas S. (Fort Selden, N Mex)
Lytton, Cpl. Jeptha L. (Fort Hartsuff, Neb)
McBride, Pvt. Bernard (Arizona)
McBryar, Sgt. William (Arizona)
McCabe, Pvt. William (Red River, Tex)

*McCann, Pvt. Bernard (Cedar Creek, Mont)
McCarthy, 1st Sgt. Michael (White Bird Canyon, Idaho)
McClernand, 2d Lt. Edward J. (Bear Paw Mountain, Mont)
McCormick, Pvt. Michael (Cedar Creek, Mont)
McDonald, Pvt. Franklin M. (Fort Griffin, Tex)
McDonald, Cpl. James (Arizona)
McDonald, 1st Lt. Robert (Wolf Mountain, Mont)
McGann, 1st Sgt. Michael A. (Rosebud River, Mont)
McGar, Pvt. Owen (Cedar Creek, Mont)
Machol, Pvt. (Arizona)
McHugh, Pvt. John (Cedar Creek, Mont)
McKinley, Pvt. Daniel (Arizona)
McLennon, Musician John (Big Hole, Mont)
McLoughlin, Sgt. Michael (Cedar Creek, Mont)
*McMasters, Cpl. Henry A. (Red River, Tex)
McMillan, Sgt. Albert W. (Wounded Knee Creek, S Dak)
McNally, 1st Sgt. James (Arizona)
McNamara, 1st Sgt. William (Red River, Tex)
McPhelan, Sgt. Robert (Cedar Creek, Mont)
McVeagh, Pvt. Charles H. (Arizona)
Mahers, Pvt. Herbert (Seneca Mountain, Ariz)
Mahoney, Pvt. Gregory (Red River, Tex)
Martin, Sgt. Patrick (Castle Dome & Santa Maria Mountains, Ariz)
Matthews, Cpl. David A. (Arizona)
Maus, 1st Lt. Marion P. (Sierra Madre Mountains, Mex)
May, Sgt. John (Wichita River, Tex)
Mays, Cpl. Isaiah (Arizona)
Meaher, Cpl. Nicholas (Chiricahua Mountains, Ariz)
Mechlin, Blacksmith Henry W. B. (Little Big Horn, Mont)
Merrill, Sgt. John (Milk River, Colo)
Miller, Pvt. Daniel H. (Whetstone Mountains, Ariz)
Miller, Cpl. George (Cedar Creek, Mont)
Miller, Pvt. George W. (Arizona)
Mitchell, 1st Sgt. John (Upper Washita, Tex)
Mitchell, Cpl. John J. (Hell Canyon, Ariz)
Montrose, Pvt. Charles H. (Cedar Creek, Mont)
Moquin, Cpl. George (Milk River, Colo)
Moran, Pvt. John (Seneca Mountain, Ariz)
Morgan, 2d Lt. George H. (Big Dry Fork, Ariz)
Moriarity, Sgt. John (Arizona)
Morris, 1st Sgt. James L. (Fort Selden, N Mex)
Morris, Cpl. William W. (Upper Washita, Tex)
Mott, Sgt. John (Whetstone Mountains, Ariz)
Moylan, Capt. Myles (Bear Paw Mountain, Mont)
Murphy, Pvt. Edward (Chiricahua Mountains, Ariz)
Murphy, Cpl. Edward F. (Milk River, Colo)
Murphy, Pvt. Jeremiah (Powder River, Mont)
Murphy, Cpl. Philip (Seneca Mountain, Ariz)
Murphy, Cpl. Thomas (Seneca Mountain, Ariz)
Murray, Sgt. Thomas (Little Big Horn, Mont)
Myers, Sgt. Fred (White River, S Dak)
Nannasaddie (Arizona)
Nantaje (Arizona)
Neal, Pvt. Solon D. (Wichita River, Tex)
Neder, Pvt. Adam (South Dakota)
Neilon, Sgt. Frederick S. (Upper Washita, Tex)
Newman, 1st Sgt. Henry (Whetstone Mountains, Ariz)

Nihill, Pvt. John (Whetstone Mountains, Ariz)
Nolan, Farrier Richard J. (White Clay Creek, S Dak)
O'Callaghan, Sgt. John (Arizona)
Oliver, 1st Sgt. Francis (Chiricahua Mountains, Ariz)
O'Neill, Cpl. William (Red River, Tex)
O'Regan, Pvt. Michael (Arizona)
Orr, Pvt. Moses (Arizona)
Osborne, Sgt. William (Arizona)
O'Sullivan, Pvt. John (Staked Plains, Tex)
Paine, Pvt. Adam (Red River, Tex)
Parnell, 1st Lt. William R. (White Bird Canyon, Idaho)
Payne, Trumpeter Isaac (Pecos River, Tex)
Pengally, Pvt. Edward (Chiricahua Mountains, Ariz)
Pennsyl, Sgt. Josiah (Upper Washita, Tex)
Phife, Sgt. Lewis (Arizona)
Philipsen, Blacksmith Wilhelm O. (Milk River, Colo)
Phillips, Pvt. Samuel D. (Muddy Creek, Mont)
Phoenix, Cpl. Edwin (Red River, Tex)
Platten, Sgt. Frederick (Sappa Creek, Kans)
Poppe, Sgt. John A. (Milk River, Colo)
Porter, Farrier Samuel (Wichita River, Tex)
Powers, Cpl. Thomas (Chiricahua Mountains, Ariz)
Pratt, Blacksmith James (Red River, Tex)
Pym, Pvt. James (Little Big Horn River, Mont)
Raerick, Pvt. John (Lyry Creek, Ariz)
Ragnar, 1st Sgt. Theodore (White Clay Creek, S Dak)
Rankin, Pvt. William (Red River, Tex)
Reed, Pvt. James C. (Arizona)
Richman, Pvt. Samuel (Arizona)
Roach, Cpl. Hampton M. (Milk River, Colo)
Robbins, Pvt. Marcus M. (Sappa Creek, Kans)
Robinson, 1st Sgt. Joseph (Rosebud River, Mont)
Roche, 1st Sgt. David (Cedar Creek, Mont)
Rodenburg, Pvt. Henry (Cedar Creek, Mont)
Rogan, Sgt. Patrick (Big Hole, Mont)
Romeyn, 1st Lt. Henry (Bear Paw Mountain, Mont)
Rooney, Pvt. Edward (Cedar Creek, Mont)
Roth, Pvt. Peter (Wichita River, Tex)
Rowalt, Pvt. John F. (Lyry Creek, Ariz)
Rowdy, Sgt. (Arizona)
Roy, Sgt. Stanislaus (Little Big Horn, Mont)
Russell, Pvt. James (Chiricahua Mountains, Ariz)
Ryan, Pvt. David (Cedar Creek, Mont)
Ryan, 1st Sgt. Dennis (Gageby Creek, Indian Terr)
Sale, Pvt. Albert (Santa Maria River, Ariz)
Schnitzer, Wagoner John (Horseshoe Canyon, N Mex)
Schou, Cpl. Julius (Dakota Territory)
Schroeter, Pvt. Charles (Chiricahua Mountains, Ariz)
Scott, Pvt. George D. (Little Big Horn, Mont)
Scott, Pvt. Robert B. (Chiricahua Mountains, Ariz)
Seward, Wagoner Griffin (Chiricahua Mountains, Ariz)
Shaffer, Pvt. William (Arizona)
Sharpless, Cpl. Edward C. (Upper Washita, Tex)
Shaw, Sgt. Thomas (Carrizo Canyon, N Mex)
Sheerin, Blacksmith John (Fort Selden, N Mex)
Sheppard, Pvt. Charles (Cedar Creek, Mont)
Shingle, 1st Sgt. John H. (Rosebud River, Mont)
Skinner, Contract Surgeon John O. (Lava Beds, Ore)
Smith, Sgt. Andrew J. (Chiricahua Mountains, Ariz)
Smith, Cpl. Charles E. (Wichita River, Tex)
Smith, Cpl. Cornelius C. (White River, S Dak)
*Smith, Pvt. George W. (Wichita River, Tex)

Smith, Pvt. Otto (Arizona)
Smith, Pvt. Robert (Slim Buttes, Mont)
Smith, Pvt. Theodore F. (Chiricahua Mountains, Ariz)
Smith, Pvt. Thomas (Chiricahua Mountains, Ariz)
Smith, Pvt. Thomas J. (Chiricahua Mountains, Ariz)
Smith, Pvt. William (Chiricahua Mountains, Ariz)
Smith, Pvt. William H. (Chiricahua Mountains, Ariz)
Snow, Trumpeter Elmer A. (Rosebud Creek, Mont)
Spence, Pvt. Orizoba (Chiricahua Mountains, Ariz)
Springer, Pvt. George (Chiricahua Mountains, Ariz)
Stance, Sgt. Emanuel (Kickapoo Springs, Tex)
Stanley, Pvt. Eben (Turret Mountain, Ariz)
Stanley, Cpl. Edward (Seneca Mountain, Ariz)
Stauffer, 1st Sgt. Rudolph (Camp Hualpai, Ariz)
Steiner, Saddler Christian (Chiricahua Mountains, Ariz)
Stewart, Pvt. Benjamin F. (Big Horn River, Mont)
Stickoffer, Saddler Julius H. (Cienaga Springs, Utah)
Stivers, Pvt. Thomas W. (Little Big Horn, Mont)
Stokes, 1st Sgt. Alonzo (Wichita River, Tex)
Strayer, Pvt. William H. (Platte River, Neb)
Strivson, Pvt. Benoni (Arizona)
Sullivan, Pvt. Thomas (Chiricahua Mountains, Ariz)
Sullivan, Pvt. Thomas (Wounded Knee Creek, S Dak)
Sumner, Pvt. James (Chiricahua Mountains, Ariz)
Sutherland, Cpl. John A. (Arizona)
Taylor, Sgt. Bernard (Sunset Pass, Ariz)
Taylor, 1st Sgt. Charles (Big Dry Wash, Ariz)
Taylor, Cpl. Wilbur N. (Arizona)

Tea, Sgt. Richard L. (Sappa Creek, Kans)
Thomas, Sgt. Charles L. (Dakota Territory)
Thompson, Pvt. George W. (Little Blue, Neb)
Thompson, Sgt. John (Chiricahua Mountains, Ariz)
Thompson, Pvt. Peter (Little Big Horn, Mont)
Tilton, Maj. & Surgeon Henry R. (Bear Paw Mountain, Mont)
Tolan, Pvt. Frank (Little Big Horn, Mont)
Toy, 1st Sgt. Frederick E. (Wounded Knee Creek, S Dak)
Tracy, Pvt. John (Chiricahua Mountains, Ariz)
Trautman, 1st Sgt. Jacob (Wounded Knee Creek, S Dak)
Turpin, 1st Sgt. James H. (Arizona)
Varnum, Capt. Charles A. (White Clay Creek, S Dak)
Veuve, Farrier Ernest (Staked Plains, Tex)
Voit, Saddler Otto (Little Big Horn, Mont)
Vokes, 1st Sgt. Leroy H. (Platte River, Neb)
Von Medem, Sgt. Rudolph (Arizona)
Walker, Pvt. Allen (Texas)
Walker, Pvt. John (Red Creek, Ariz)
Wallace, Sgt. William (Cedar Creek, Mont)
Walley, Pvt. Augustus (Cuchillo Negro Mountains, N Mex)
Ward, Pvt. Charles H. (Chiricahua Mountains, Ariz)
Ward, Sgt. James (Wounded Knee Creek, S Dak)
Ward, Sgt. John (Pecos River, Tex)
Warrington, 1st Lt. Lewis (Muchague Valley, Tex)
Watson, Cpl. James C. (Wichita River, Tex)
Watson, Pvt. Joseph (Picacho Mountain, Ariz)
Weaher, Pvt. Andrew J. (Arizona)

Weinert, Cpl. Paul H. (Wounded Knee Creek, S Dak)
Weiss, Pvt. Enoch R. (Chiricahua Mountains, Ariz)
Welch, Sgt. Charles H. (Little Big Horn, Mont)
Welch, Sgt. Michael (Wichita River, Tex)
West, 1st Lt. Frank (Big Dry Wash, Ariz)
Whitehead, Pvt. Patton G. (Cedar Creek, Mont)
Widmer, 1st Sgt. Jacob (Milk River, Colo)
Wilder, 1st Lt. Wilber E. (Horseshoe Canyon, N Mex)
Wilkens, 1st Sgt. Henry (Little Muddy Creek, Mont)
Williams, 1st Sgt. Moses (Cuchillo Negro Mountains, N Mex)
Wills, Pvt. Henry (Fort Selden, N Mex)
Wilson, Pvt. Benjamin (Wichita River, Tex)
Wilson, Cpl. Charles (Cedar Creek, Mont)
Wilson, Sgt. Milden H. (Big Hole, Mont)
Wilson, Sgt. William (Colorado Valley, Tex) Second award (Red River, Tex)
Wilson, Cpl. William O. (South Dakota)
Windolph, Pvt. Charles (Little Big Horn, Mont)
Windus, Bugler Claron A. (Wichita River, Tex)
Winterbottom, Sgt. William (Wichita River, Tex)
Witcome, Pvt. Joseph (Arizona)
Wood, Asst. Surgeon Leonard (Arizona & Mexico)
Woodall, Sgt. Zachariah (Wichita River, Tex)
Woods, Sgt. Brent (New Mexico)
Wortman, Sgt. George G. (Arizona)
Yount, Pvt. John P. (Whetstone Mountains, Ariz)
Ziegner, Pvt. Hermann (Wounded Knee Creek & White Clay Creek, S Dak)

The Wars of American Expansion   1871–1933

Korea   1871

Number of medals: 15

MARINES: 6
NAVY: 9

NAVY

Andrews, Ord. Sman John (Korea)
Franklin, QM Frederick (Korea)
Grace, Chief QM Patrick H. (Korea)
Hayden, Carpenter Cyrus (Korea)
Lukes, Lman William F. (Korea)
McKenzie, BM Alexander (Korea)
Merton, Lman James F. (Korea)
Rogers, QM Samuel F. (Korea)
Troy, Ord. Sman William (Korea)

MARINES

Brown, Cpl. Charles (Korea)
Coleman, Pvt. John (Korea)
Dougherty, Pvt. James (Korea)
McNamara, Pvt. Michael (Korea)
Owens, Pvt. Michael (Korea)
Purvis, Pvt. Hugh (Korea)

The Spanish–American War   1898

Number of medals: 109

    ARMY: 30
    MARINES: 15
    NAVY: 64

ARMY

Baker, Sgt. Maj. Edward L., Jr. (Santiago, Cuba)
Bell, Pvt. Dennis (Tayabacoa, Cuba)
Berg, Pvt. George (El Caney, Cuba)
Brookin, Pvt. Oscar (El Caney, Cuba)
Buzzard, Cpl. Ulysses G. (El Caney, Cuba)
Cantrell, Pvt. Charles P. (Santiago, Cuba)
Church, Asst. Surgeon James R. (Las Guasimas, Cuba)
Cummins, Sgt. Andrew J. (Santiago, Cuba)
De Swan, Pvt. John F. (Santiago, Cuba)
Doherty, Cpl. Thomas M. (Santiago, Cuba)
Fournia, Pvt. Frank O. (Santiago, Cuba)
Graves, Pvt. Thomas J. (El Caney, Cuba)
Hardaway, 1st Lt. Benjamin F. (El Caney, Cuba)
Heard, 1st Lt. John W. (Manimani River, Cuba)
Keller, Pvt. William (Santiago, Cuba)
Kelly, Pvt. Thomas (Santiago, Cuba)
Lee, Pvt. Fitz (Tayabacoa, Cuba)
Mills, Capt. & Asst. Adj. Gen. Albert L. (Santiago, Cuba)
Nash, Pvt. James J. (Santiago, Cuba)
Nee, Pvt. George H. (Santiago, Cuba)
Pfisterer, Musician Herman (Santiago, Cuba)
Polond, Pvt. Alfred (Santiago, Cuba)
Quinn, Sgt. Alexander M. (Santiago, Cuba)
Ressler, Cpl. Norman W. (El Caney, Cuba)
Roberts, 2d Lt. Charles D. (El Caney, Cuba)
Shepherd, Cpl. Warren J. (El Caney, Cuba)
Thompkins, Pvt. William H. (Tayabacoa, Cuba)
Wanton, Pvt. George H. (Tayabacoa, Cuba)
Welborn, 2d Lt. Ira C. (Santiago, Cuba)
Wende, Pvt. Bruno (El Caney, Cuba)

MARINES

Campbell, Pvt. Daniel (Cienfuegos, Cuba)
Field, Pvt. Oscar W. (Cienfuegos, Cuba)
Fitzgerald, Pvt. John (Cuzco, Cuba)
Franklin, Pvt. Joseph J. (Cienfuegos, Cuba)
Gaughan, Sgt. Philip (Cienfuegos, Cuba)
Hill, Pvt. Frank (Cienfuegos, Cuba)

Kearney, Pvt. Michael (Cienfuegos, Cuba)
Kuchneister, Pvt. Hermann W. (Cienfuegos, Cuba)
MacNeal, Pvt. Harry L. (Santiago, Cuba)
Meredith, Pvt. James (Cienfuegos, Cuba)
Parker, Pvt. Pomeroy (Cienfuegos, Cuba)
Quick, Sgt. John H. (Cuzco, Cuba)
Scott, Pvt. Joseph F. (Cienfuegos, Cuba)
Sullivan, Pvt. Edward (Cienfuegos, Cuba)
West, Pvt. Walter S. (Cienfuegos, Cuba)

NAVY

Baker, Coxswain Benjamin F. (Cienfuegos, Cuba)
Barrow, Sman David D. (Cienfuegos, Cuba)
Bennett, Chief BM James H. (Cienfuegos, Cuba)
Beyer, Coxswain Albert (Cienfuegos, Cuba)
Blume, Sman Robert (Cienfuegos, Cuba)
Brady, Chief GM George F. (Cardenas, Cuba)
Bright, Coal Passer George W. (Cienfuegos, Cuba)
Carter, Blacksmith Joseph E. (Cienfuegos, Cuba)
Chadwick, Apprentice 1st Class Leonard (Cienfuegos, Cuba)
Charette, GM 1st Class George (Santiago, Cuba)
Clausen, Coxswain Claus K. (Santiago, Cuba)
Cooney, Chief Machinist Thomas C. (Cardenas, Cuba)
Crouse, Watertender William A. (Cavite, Philippines)
Davis, GM 3d Class John (Cienfuegos, Cuba)
Deignan, Coxswain Osborn (Santiago, Cuba)
Doran, BM 2d Class John J. (Cienfuegos, Cuba)
Durney, Blacksmith Austin J. (Cienfuegos, Cuba)
Eglit, Sman John (Cienfuegos, Cuba)
Ehle, Fireman 1st Class John W. (Cavite, Philippines)
Erickson, Coxswain Nick (Cienfuegos, Cuba)
Foss, Sman Herbert L. (Cienfuegos, Cuba)
Gibbons, Oiler Michael (Cienfuegos, Cuba)
Gill, GM 1st Class Freeman (Cienfuegos, Cuba)
Hart, Machinist 1st Class William (Cienfuegos, Cuba)
Hendrickson, Sman Henry (Cienfuegos, Cuba)
Hoban, Coxswain Thomas (Cienfuegos, Cuba)
Hobson, Lt. Richmond P. (Santiago, Cuba)
Hull, Fireman 1st Class James L. (Cavite, Philippines)
Itrich, Chief Carpenter's Mate Franz A. (Manila, Philippines)

Johanson, Sman John P. (Cienfuegos, Cuba)
Johansson, Ord. Sman Johan J. (Cienfuegos, Cuba)
Johnsen, Chief Machinist Hans (Cardenas, Cuba)
Johnson, Fireman 1st Class Peter (NOR)
Keefer, Coppersmith Philip B. (Santiago, Cuba)
Kelly, Watertender Francis (Santiago, Cuba)
Kramer, Sman Franz (Cienfuegos, Cuba)
Krause, Coxswain Ernest (Cienfuegos, Cuba)
Levery, Apprentice 1st Class William (Cienfuegos, Cuba)
Mager, Apprentice 1st Class George F. (Cienfuegos, Cuba)
Mahoney, Fireman 1st Class George (NOR)
Maxwell, Fireman 2d Class John (Cienfuegos, Cuba)
Meyer, Carpenter's Mate 3d Class William (Cienfuegos, Cuba)
Miller, Sman Harry H. (Cienfuegos, Cuba)
Miller, Sman Willard (Cienfuegos, Cuba)
Montague, Chief Master-at-Arms Daniel (Santiago, Cuba)
Morin, BM 2d Class William H. (Caimanera, Cuba)
Muller, Mate Frederick (Manzanillo, Cuba)
Murphy, Coxswain John E. (Santiago, Cuba)
Nelson, Sailmaker's Mate Lauritz (Cienfuegos, Cuba)
Oakley, GM 2d Class William (Cienfuegos, Cuba)
Olsen, Ord. Sman Anton (Cienfuegos, Cuba)
Penn, Fireman 1st Class Robert (Santiago, Cuba)
Phillips, Machinist 1st Class George F. (Santiago, Cuba)
Rilley, Lman John P. (Cienfuegos, Cuba)
Russell, Lman Henry P. (Cienfuegos, Cuba)
Spicer, GM 1st Class William (Caimanera, Cuba)
Sundquist, Chief Carpenter's Mate Axel (Caimanera, Cuba)
Sundquist, Ord. Sman Gustave A. (Cienfuegos, Cuba)
Triplett, Ord. Sman Samuel (Caimanera, Cuba)
Vadas, Sman Albert (Cienfuegos, Cuba)
Van Etten, Sman Hudson (Cienfuegos, Cuba)
Volz, Sman Robert (Cienfuegos, Cuba)
Wilke, BM 1st Class Julius A. R. (Cienfuegos, Cuba)
Williams, Sman Frank (Cienfuegos, Cuba)

Philippines/Samoa   1899–1913

Number of medals: 91

    ARMY: 70
    MARINES: 9
    NAVY: 12

ARMY

Anders, Cpl. Frank L. (San Miguel de Mayumo, Luzon)
Batson, 1st Lt. Matthew A. (Calamba, Luzon)
Bell, Capt. Harry (Porac, Luzon)
Bell, Col. J. Franklin (Porac, Luzon)
Bickham, 1st Lt. Charles G. (Bayong, Mindinao)

Biegler, Capt. George W. (Loac, Luzon)
Birkhimer, Capt. William E. (San Miguel de Mayumo, Luzon)
Boehler, Pvt. Otto (San Isidro, Luzon)
Byrne, Capt. Bernard A. (Bobong, Negros)
Carson, Cpl. Anthony J. (Catubig, Samar)
Cawetzka, Pvt. Charles (Sariaya, Luzon)
Cecil, 1st Lt. Josephus S. (Bud-Dajo, Jolo)

Condon, Sgt. Clarence M. (Calulut, Luzon)
Davis, Pvt. Charles P. (San Isidro, Luzon)
Downs, Pvt. Willis H. (San Miguel de Mayumo, Luzon)
Epps, Pvt. Joseph L. (Vigan, Luzon)
Ferguson, 1st Lt. Arthur M. (Porac, Luzon)
Funston, Col. Frederick (Rio Grande de la Pampanga, Luzon)

Galt, Artificer Sterling A. (Bamban, Luzon)
Gaujot, Cpl. Antoine A. (San Mateo)
Gedeon, Pvt. Louis (Mount Amia, Cebu)
Gibson, Sgt. Edward H. (San Mateo)
Gillenwater, Cpl. James R. (Porac, Luzon)
Greer, 2d Lt. Allen J. (Majada, Laguna Province)
Grove, Lt. Col. William R. (Porac, Luzon)
Hayes, Lt. Col. Webb C. (Vigan, Luzon)
Henderson, Sgt. Joseph (Patian Island)
High, Pvt. Frank C. (San Isidro, Luzon)
Huntsman, Sgt. John A. (Bamban, Luzon)
Jensen, Pvt. Gotfred (San Miguel de Mayumo, Luzon)
Johnston, 1st Lt. Gordon (Mount Bud Dajo, Jolo)
Kennedy, 2d Lt. John T. (Patian Island)
Kilbourne, 1st Lt. Charles E. (Paco Bridge)
Kinne, Pvt. John B. (San Isidro, Luzon)
Leahy, Pvt. Cornelius J. (Porac, Luzon)
*Logan, Maj. John A. (San Jacinto)
Longfellow, Pvt. Richard M. (San Isidro, Luzon)
Lyon, Pvt. Edward E. (San Miguel de Mayumo, Luzon)
McConnell, Pvt. James (Vigan, Luzon)
McGrath, Capt. Hugh J. (Calamba, Luzon)
Maclay, Pvt. William P. (Hilongas, Leyte)
Mathews, Asst. Surgeon George W. (Labo, Luzon)
Miller, 1st Lt. Archie (Patian Island)
Moran, Capt. John E. (Mabitac, Luzon)
Mosher, 2d Lt. Louis C. (Gagsak Mountain, Jolo)
Nisperos, Pvt. Jose B. (Lapurap, Basilan)

Nolan, Artificer Joseph A. (Labo, Luzon)
Parker, Lt. Col. James (Vigan, Luzon)
Pierce, Pvt. Charles H. (San Isidro, Luzon)
Quinn, Pvt. Peter H. (San Miguel de Mayumo, Luzon)
Ray, Sgt. Charles W. (San Isidro, Luzon)
Robertson, Pvt. Marcus W. (San Isidro, Luzon)
Ross, Pvt. Frank F. (San Isidro, Luzon)
Sage, Capt. William H. (Zapote River, Luzon)
Schroeder, Sgt. Henry F. (Carig, Leyte)
Shaw, 1st Lt. George C. (Fort Pitacus, Mindinao)
Shelton, Pvt. George M. (La Paz, Leyte)
Shiels, Surgeon George F. (Tuliahan River)
Sletteland, Pvt. Thomas (Paete, Luzon)
Stewart, 2d Lt. George E. (Passi, Panay)
Straub, Surgeon Paul F. (Alos, Luzon)
Trembley, Pvt. William B. (Calumpit, Luzon)
Van Schaick, 1st Lt. Louis J. (Nasugbu, Batangas)
Walker, Pvt. Frank O. (Taal, Luzon)
Wallace, 2d Lt. George W. (Tinuba, Luzon)
Weaver, Sgt. Amos (Calubus-Malalong, Luzon)
Weld, Cpl. Seth L. (La Paz, Leyte)
Wetherby, Pvt. John C. (Imus, Luzon)
White, Pvt. Edward (Calumpit, Luzon)
Wilson, 2d Lt. Arthur H. (Patian Island)

MARINES

Bearss, Col. Hiram I. (Cadacan & Sohoton Rivers, Samar)

Buckley, Pvt. Howard M. (NOR)
Forsterer, Sgt. Bruno A. (Samoa)
Harvey, Sgt. Harry (Benictican)
Hulbert, Pvt. Henry L. (Samoa)
Leonard, Pvt. Joseph M. (NOR)
McNally, Sgt. Michael J. (Samoa)
Porter, Col. David D. (Cadacan & Sohoton Rivers, Samar)
Prendergast, Cpl. Thomas F. (NOR)

NAVY

Catherwood, Ord. Sman John H. (Basilan)
Fisher, GM 1st Class Frederick T. (Samoa)
Fitz, Ord. Sman Joseph (Mount Dajo Jolo)
Forbeck, Sman Andrew P. (Katbalogan, Samar)
Galbraith, GM 3d Class Robert (El Pardo, Cebu)
Harrison, Sman Bolden R. (Basilan)
Henrechon, Machinist's Mate 2d Class George F. (Basilan)
McGuire, Hospital Apprentice Fred H. (Basilan)
Shanahan, Chief BM Patrick (NOR)
Stoltenberg, GM 2d Class Andrew V. (Katbalogan, Samar)
Thordsen, Coxswain William G. (Hilongas)
Volz, Carpenter's Mate 3d Class Jacob (Basilan)

The Boxer Rebellion   1900

Number of medals: 59

	ARMY:	4
	MARINES:	33
	NAVY:	22

ARMY

Brewster, Capt. Andre W. (Tientsin)
Lawton, 1st Lt. Louis B. (Tientsin)
Titus, Musician Calvin P. (Peking)
Von Schlick, Pvt. Robert H. (Tientsin)

MARINES

Adams, Sgt. John M. (Tientsin)
Adriance, Cpl. Harry C. (Tientsin)
Appleton, Cpl. Edwin N. (Tientsin)
Boydston, Pvt. Erwin J. (Peking)
Burnes, Pvt. James (Tientsin)
Campbell, Pvt. Albert R. (Tientsin)
Carr, Pvt. William L. (Peking)
Cooney, Pvt. James (Tientsin)
Dahlgren, Cpl. John O. (Peking)
Daly, Pvt. Daniel J. (Peking)
*Fisher, Pvt. Harry (Peking)
Foley, Sgt. Alexander J. (Tientsin)
Francis, Pvt. Charles R. (Tientsin)
Gaiennie, Pvt. Louis R. (Peking)

Heisch, Pvt. Henry W. (Tientsin)
Horton, Pvt. William C. (Peking)
Hunt, Pvt. Martin (Peking)
Kates, Pvt. Thomas W. (Tientsin)
Mathias, Pvt. Clarence E. (Tientsin)
Moore, Pvt. Albert (Peking)
Murphy, Drummer John A. (Peking)
Murray, Pvt. William H. (Peking)
Orndoff, Pvt. Harry W. (NOR)
Phillips, Cpl. Reuben J. (NOR)
Preston, Pvt. Herbert I. (Peking)
Scannell, Pvt. David J. (Peking)
Silva, Pvt. France (Peking)
Stewart, Gy. Sgt. Peter (NOR)
Sutton, Sgt. Clarence E. (Tientsin)
Upham, Pvt. Oscar J. (Peking)
Walker, Sgt. Edward A. (Peking)
Young, Pvt. Frank A. (Peking)
Zion, Pvt. William (Peking)

NAVY

Allen, BM 1st Class Edward (NOR)

Chatham, GM 2d Class John P. (NOR)
Clancy, Chief BM Joseph (NOR)
Hamberger, Chief Carpenter's Mate William F. (NOR)
Hanford, Machinist 1st Class Burke (NOR)
Hansen Sman Hans A. (NOR)
Holyoke, BM 1st Class William E. (NOR)
Killackey, Lman Joseph (NOR)
McAllister, Ord. Sman Samuel (Tientsin)
McCloy, Coxswain John (China)
Mitchell, GM 1st Class Joseph (Peking)
Petersen, Chief Machinist Carl E. (Peking)
Rose, Sman George (Peking)
Ryan, Coxswain Francis T. (NOR)
Seach, Ord. Sman William (NOR)
Smith, Oiler Frank E. (NOR)
Smith, Lman James (NOR)
Stanley, Hospital Apprentice Robert H. (Peking)
Thomas, Coxswain Karl (NOR)
Torgerson, GM 3d Class Martin T. (NOR)
Westermark, Sman Axel (Peking)
Williams, Coxswain Jay (China)

Veracruz   1914

Number of medals: 55

MARINES: 9
NAVY: 46

MARINES

Berkeley, Maj. Randolph C. (Veracruz)
Butler, Maj. Smedley D. (Veracruz)
Catlin, Maj. Albertus W. (Veracruz)
Dyer, Capt. Jesse F. (Veracruz)
Fryer, Capt. Eli T. (Veracruz)
Hill, Capt. Walter N. (Veracruz)
Hughes, Capt. John A. (Veracruz)
Neville, Lt. Col. Wendell C. (Veracruz)
Reid, Maj. George C. (Veracruz)

NAVY

Anderson, Capt. Edwin A. (Veracruz)
Badger, Ensign Oscar C. (Veracruz)
Beasley, Sman Harry C. (Veracruz)
Bishop, QM 2d Class Charles F. (Veracruz)
Bradley, Chief GM George (Veracruz)
Buchanan, Lt. Cmdr. Allen (Veracruz)
Castle, Lt. Guy W. S. (Veracruz)

Courts, Lt. (j.g.) George M. (Veracruz)
Cregan, Coxswain George (Veracruz)
Decker, BM 2d Class Percy A. (Veracruz)
DeSomer, Lt. Abraham (Veracruz)
Drustrup, Lt. Neils (Veracruz)
Elliott, Surgeon Middleton S. (Veracruz)
Fletcher, Rear Adm. Frank F. (Veracruz)
Fletcher, Lt. Frank J. (Veracruz)
Foster, Ensign Paul F. (Veracruz)
Frazer, Ensign Hugh C. (Veracruz)
Gisburne, Electrician 3d Class Edward A. (Veracruz)
Grady, Lt. John (Veracruz)
Harner, BM 2d Class Joseph G. (Veracruz)
Harrison, Cmdr. William K. (Veracruz)
Hartigan, Lt. Charles C. (Veracruz)
Huse, Capt. Henry M. P. (Veracruz)
Ingram, Lt. (j.g.) Jonas H. (Veracruz)
Jarrett, Sman Berrie H. (Veracruz)
Johnston, Lt. Cmdr. Rufus Z. (Veracruz)
Langhorne, Surgeon Cary D. (Veracruz)
Lannon, Lt. James P. (Veracruz)
Lowry, Ensign George M. (Veracruz)

+ McCloy, Chief Boatswain John (Veracruz)
McDonnell, Ensign Edward O. (Veracruz)
McNair, Lt. Frederick V., Jr. (Veracruz)
Moffett, Cmdr. William A. (Veracruz)
Nickerson, BM 2d Class Henry N. (Veracruz)
Nordsiek, Ord. Sman Charles L. (Veracruz)
Rush, Capt. William R. (Veracruz)
Schnepel, Ord. Sman Fred J. (Veracruz)
Semple, Chief Gunner Robert (Veracruz)
Sinnett, Sman Lawrence C. (Veracruz)
Staton, Lt. Adolphus (Veracruz)
Stickney, Cmdr. Herman O. (Veracruz)
Townsend, Lt. Julius C. (Veracruz)
Wainwright, Lt. Richard, Jr. (Veracruz)
Walsh, Sman James A. (Veracruz)
Wilkinson, Ensign Theodore S., Jr. (Veracruz)
Zuiderveld, Hospital Apprentice 1st Class William (Veracruz)

Haiti   1915

Number of medals: 6

MARINES: 6

+ Butler, Maj. Smedley D. (Fort Rivière)
+ Daly, Gy. Sgt. Daniel J. (Fort Liberté)
  Gross, Pvt. Samuel (Fort Rivière)
  Iams, Sgt. Ross L. (Fort Rivière)
  Ostermann, 1st Lt. Edward A. (Fort Liberté)
  Upshur, Capt. William P. (Fort Liberté)

Dominican Republic 1916

Number of medals: 3

MARINES: 3

Glowin, Cpl. Joseph A. (Guayacanas)
Williams, 1st Lt. Ernest C. (San Francisco de Macoris)
Winans, 1st Sgt. Roswell (Guayacanas)

Haiti   1919–1920

Number of medals: 2

MARINES: 2

Button, Cpl. William R. (Grande Rivière)
Hanneken, Sgt. Herman H. (Grande Rivière)

Nicaragua   1927–1933

Number of medals: 2

MARINES: 2

Schilt, 1st Lt. Christian F. (Quilali)
Truesdell, Cpl. Donald L. (Constancia)

The Medal in Peacetime   1865–1940

1865–1870

Number of medals: 12

NAVY: 12

Bates, Sman Richard (Eastport, Maine)
Brown, Capt. of the Afterguard John (Eastport, Maine)
Burke, Sman Thomas (Eastport, Maine)
Carey, Sman James (NOR)

+ Cooper, QM John (Mobile, Ala)
Du Moulin, Apprentice Frank (New London, Conn)
Halford, Coxswain William (Sandwich Islands)
+ Mullen, BM Patrick (NOR)
Robinson, Capt. of the Hold John (Pensacola Bay, Fla)

Robinson, Capt. of the Afterguard Thomas (New Orleans, La)
Stacy, Sman William B. (Cape Haiten, Haiti)
Taylor, Sman John (New York, NY)

1871–1898

Number of medals: 103

MARINES: 2
NAVY: 101

MARINES

Morris, Cpl. John (Villefranche, France)
Stewart, Cpl. James A. (Villefranche, France)

NAVY

Ahearn, Watertender William (NOR)
Anderson, Coxswain William (NOR)
Atkins, Ship's Cook Daniel (NOR)
Auer, Ord. Sman Apprentice John F. (Marseille, France)
Barrett, 2d Class Fireman Edward (Callao Bay, Peru)
Belpitt, Capt. of the Afterguard W. H. (Foochow, China)
Benson, Sman James (NOR)
Bradley, Lman Alexander (Cowes, England)
Buchanan, Apprentice David M. (New York, NY)
Cavanaugh, Fireman 1st Class Thomas (Cat Island–Nassau)
Chandron, Sman Apprentice August (Alexandria, Egypt)
Connolly, Ord. Sman Michael (Halifax Harbor, Nova Scotia)
Corey, Lman William (New York, NY)
Costello, Ord. Sman John (Philadelphia, Pa)
Courtney, Sman Henry C. (Washington Navy Yard, DC)
Cramen, BM Thomas (Washington Navy Yard, DC)
Creelman, Lman William J. (NOR)
Cutter, Lman George W. (Norfolk, Va)
Davis, Ord. Sman John (Toulon, France)
Davis, Lman Joseph H. (Norfolk, Va)
Dempsey, Sman John (Shanghai, China)
Deneef, Capt. of the Top Michael (Para, Brazil)
Denham, Sman Austin (Greytown, Nicaragua)
Eilers, GM Henry A. (Fort McHenry, Md)
Elmore, Lman Walter (Mediterranean Sea)
Enright, Lman John (Ensenada, Mexico)
Everetts, GM 3d Class John (NOR)

Fasseur, Ord. Sman Isaac L. (Callao, Peru)
Flannagan, BM John (Le Havre, France)
Fowler, QM Christopher (Point Zapotitlan, Mexico)
Gidding, Sman Charles (New York, NY)
Gillick, BM Matthew (Marseilles, France)
Handran, Sman John (Lisbon, Portugal)
Harrington, 1st Class Fireman David (NOR)
Hayden, Apprentice John (New York, NY)
Hill, Chief QG George (Greytown, Nicaragua)
Hill, Capt. of the Top William L. (Newport, RI)
Holt, QG George (Hamburg, Germany)
Horton, Capt. of the Top James (NOR)
Jardine, Fireman 1st Class Alexander (Cat Island–Nassau)
Johnson, Sman John (Greytown, Nicaragua)
Johnson, Cooper William (Mare Island, Calif)
Kersey, Ord. Sman Thomas (New York, NY)
King, Ord. Sman Hugh (Delaware River, NJ)
Kyle, Lman Patrick J. (Port Mahon, Minorca)
Lakin, Sman Thomas (Mare Island, Calif)
Laverty, 1st Class Fireman John (Callao, Peru)
Lejeune, Sman Emile (Port Royal, SC)
Low, Sman George (New Orleans, La)
Lucy, 2d Class Boy John (Castle Garden, NY)
McCarton, Ship's Printer John (Coaster's Harbor Island, RI)
Maddin, Ord. Sman Edward (Lisbon, Portugal)
Magee, 2d Class Fireman John W. (NOR)
Manning, QM Henry J. (Newport, RI)
Matthews, Capt. of the Top Joseph (NOR)
Miller, BM Hugh (Alexandria, Egypt)
Millmore, Ord. Sman John (Monrovia, Liberia)
Mitchell, Lman Thomas (Shanghai, China)
Moore, BM Francis (Washington Navy Yard, DC)
Moore, Sman Philip (Genoa, Italy)
Morse, Sman William (Rio de Janeiro, Brazil)
Noil, Sman Joseph B. (Norfolk, Va)
Norris, Lman J. W. (New York, NY)
O'Conner, Sman James F. (Norfolk, Va)
Ohmsen, Master-at-Arms August (NOR)

O'Neal, BM John (Greytown, Nicaragua)
Osborne, Sman John (Philadelphia, Pa)
Osepins, Sman Christian (Hampton Roads, Va)
Parker, BM Alexander (Mare Island, Calif)
Pile, Ord. Sman Richard (Greytown, Nicaragua)
Regan, Ord. Sman Patrick (Coquimbor, Chile)
Rouning, Ord. Sman Johannes (Hampton Roads, Va)
Russell, Sman John (Genoa, Italy)
Ryan, Ord. Sman Richard (Norfolk, Va)
Sadler, Capt. of the Top William (Coaster's Harbor Island, RI)
Sapp, Sman Isacc (Villefranche, France)
Simpson, 1st Class Fireman Henry (Monrovia, Liberia)
Smith, Sman James (Greytown, Nicaragua)
Smith, Sman John (Rio de Janeiro, Brazil)
Smith, Sman Thomas (Para, Brazil)
Sullivan, BM James F. (Newport, RI)
Sweeney, Ord. Sman Robert (Hampton Roads, Va)
Second award (New York, NY)
Sweeney, Lman William (Norfolk, Va)
Taylor, QM Richard H. (Apia, Samoa)
Thayer, Ship's Cpl. James (Norfolk, Va)
Thompson, Sman Henry (Mare Island, Calif)
Thornton, Sman Michael (Boston, Mass)
Tobin, Lman Paul (Hamburg, Germany)
Trout, 2d Class Fireman James M. (Montevideo, Uruguay)
Troy, Chief BM Jeremiah (Newport, RI)
Turvelin, Sman Alexander H. (Toulon, France)
Weisbogel, Capt. of the Mizzen Top Albert (NOR)
Second award (NOR)
Weissel, Ship's Cook Adam (Newport, RI)
Williams, Sman Antonio (NOR)
Williams, Carpenter's Mate Henry (NOR)
Williams, Capt. of the Hold Louis (Honolulu, Hawaii)
Second award (Callao, Peru)
Willis, Coxswain George (Greenland)
Wilson, Boilermaker August (NOR)

1899–1911

Number of medals: 51

ARMY: 1
MARINES: 2
NAVY: 48

ARMY

Gaujot, Capt. Julien E. (Aqua Prieta, Mex)

MARINES

Helms, Sgt. John H. (Montevideo, Uruguay)
Pfeifer, Pvt. Louis F. (NOR)

NAVY

Behne, Fireman 1st Class Frederick (NOR)
Behnke, Sman 1st Class Heinrich (NOR)
Bjorkman, Ord. Sman Ernest H. (NOR)
Boers, Sman Edward W. (San Diego, Calif)
Bonney, Chief Watertender Robert E. (NOR)
Breeman, Sman George (NOR)
Bresnahan, Watertender Patrick F. (NOR)
Brock, Carpenter's Mate 2d Class George F. (San Diego, Calif)
Cahey, Sman Thomas (NOR)
Clary, Watertender Edward A. (NOR)

Clausey, Chief GM John J. (San Diego, Calif)
Corahorgi, Fireman 1st Class Demetri (NOR)
Cox, Chief GM Robert E. (Pensacola, Fla)
Cronan, BM Willie (San Diego, Calif)
Davis, QM 3d Class Raymond E. (San Diego, Calif)
Fadden, Coxswain Harry D. (NOR)
Floyd, Boilermaker Edward (NOR)
Fredericksen, Watertender Emil (San Diego, Calif)
Girandy, Sman Alphonse (NOR)
Gowan, BM William H. (Coquimbo, Chile)
Grbitch, Sman Rade (San Diego, Calif)
Halling, BM 1st Class Luovi (NOR)
Hill, Ship's Cook 1st Class Frank E. (San Diego, Calif)
Holtz, Chief Watertender August (NOR)
Johannessen, Chief Watertender Johannes J. (NOR)
King, Watertender John (NOR)
    Second award (NOR)
Klein, Chief Carpenter's Mate Robert (NOR)
Lipscomb, Watertender Harry (NOR)
Monssen, Chief GM Mons (NOR)
Mullin, Sman Hugh P. (Hampton Roads, Va)

Nelson, Machinist's Mate 1st Class Oscar F. (San Diego, Calif)
Nordstrom, Chief Boatswain Isidor (NOR)
Peters, BM 1st Class Alexander (NOR)
Quick, Coxswain Joseph (Yokohama, Japan)
Reid, Chief Watertender Patrick (NOR)
Roberts, Machinist's Mate 1st Class Charles C. (NOR)
Schepke, GM 1st Class Charles S. (NOR)
Schmidt, Sman Otto D. (San Diego, Calif)
Shacklette, Hospital Steward William S. (San Diego, Calif)
Snyder, Chief Electrician William E. (Hampton Roads, Va)
Stanton, Chief Machinist's Mate Thomas (NOR)
Stokes, Chief Master-at-Arms John (Jamaica)
Stupka, Fireman 1st Class Loddie (NOR)
Teytand, QM 3d Class August P. (NOR)
Walsh, Chief Machinist Michael (NOR)
Westa, Chief Machinist's Mate Karl (NOR)
Wheeler, Shipfitter 1st Class George H. (Coquimbo, Chile)

1915–1916

Number of medals: 8

NAVY: 8

Cary, Lt. Cmdr. Robert W. (NOR)
Crilley, Chief GM Frank W. (Honolulu, Hawaii)
Jones, Cmdr. Claud A. (Santo Domingo)

*Rud, Chief Machinist's Mate George W. (Santo Domingo)
Smith, Chief Watertender Eugene P. (NOR)

Smith, GM 1st Class Wilhelm (NOR)
Trinidad, Fireman 2d Class Telesforo (NOR)
Willey, Machinist Charles H. (Santo Domingo)

1920–1940

Number of medals: 18

ARMY: 2
MARINES: 1
NAVY: 15

ARMY

Greely, Maj. Gen. Adolphus W. (Various)
Lindbergh, Capt. Charles A. (New York City–Paris, France)

MARINES

Smith, Pvt. Albert J. (Pensacola, Fla)

NAVY

Badders, Chief Machinist's Mate William (Portsmouth, NH)
Bennett, Machinist Floyd (North Pole)
Breault, Torpedoman 2d Class Henry (NOR)
Byrd, Cmdr. Richard E., Jr. (North Pole)
*Cholister, BM 1st Class George R. (Off Virginia coast)
*Corry, Lt. Cmdr. William M., Jr. (Hartford, Conn)
Crandall, Chief BM Orson L. (Portsmouth, NH)
*Drexler, Ensign Henry C. (NOR)

Eadie, Chief GM Thomas (Provincetown, Mass)
Edwards, Lt. Cmdr. Walter A. (Sea of Marmara, Turkey)
Huber, Machinist's Mate William R. (Norfolk, Va)
*Hutchins, Lt. Carlton B. (Off California coast)
McDonald, Chief Metalsmith James H. (Portsmouth, NH)
Mihalowski, Torpedoman 1st Class John (Portsmouth, NH)
Ryan, Ensign Thomas J. (Yokohama, Japan)

World War I 1914–1918

Number of medals: 123

      ARMY: 95**
MARINES: 7
    NAVY: 21

**Includes five marines who also received army medal and one marine who received army medal only.

ARMY

Adkinson, Sgt. Joseph B. (Bellicourt, France)
Allex, Cpl. Jake (Chipilly Ridge, France)
Allworth, Capt. Edward C. (Clery-le-Petit, France)
Anderson, 1st Sgt. Johannes S. (Consenvoye, France)
*Baesel, 2d Lt. Albert E. (Ivoiry, France)
Barger, Pvt. Charles D. (Bois-de-Bantheville, France)
*Barkeley, Pvt. David B. (Pouilly, France)
Barkley, Pfc. John L. (Cunel, France)
Bart, Pvt. Frank J. (Medeah Ferme, France)
*Blackwell, Pvt. Robert L. (St. Soupplets, France)
*Bleckley, 2d Lt. Erwin R. (Binarville, France)
Bronson, 1st Lt. Deming (Eclisfontaine, France)
Call, Cpl. Donald M. (Varennes, France)
*Chiles, Capt. Marcellus H. (Le Champy Bas, France)
*Colyer, Sgt. Wilbur E. (Verdun, France)
*Costin, Pvt. Henry G. (Bois-de-Consenvoye, France)
*Dilboy, Pfc. George (Belleau, France)
Donaldson, Sgt. Michael A. (Sommerance-Landres-et-St. Georges Road, France)
Donovan, Lt. Col. William J. (Landres-et-St. Georges, France)
Dozier, 1st Lt. James C. (Montbrehain, France)
*Dunn, Pvt. Parker F. (Grand-Pre, France)
Edwards, Pfc. Daniel R. (Soissons, France)
Eggers, Sgt. Alan L. (Le Catelet, France)
Ellis, Sgt. Michael B. (Exermont, France)
Forrest, Sgt. Arthur J. (Remonville, France)
Foster, Sgt. Gary E. (Montbrehain, France)
Funk, Pfc. Jesse N. (Bois-de-Bantheville, France)
Furlong, 1st Lt. Harold A. (Bantheville, France)
Gaffney, Pfc. Frank (Ronssoy, France)
*Goettler, 1st Lt. Harold E. (Binarville, France)
Gregory, Sgt. Earl D. (Bois-de-Consenvoye, France)
Gumpertz, 1st Sgt. Sydney G. (Bois-de-Forges, France)
*Hall, Sgt. Thomas L. (Montbrehain, France)
Hatler, Sgt. M. Waldo (Pouilly, France)
Hays, 1st Lt. George P. (Greves Farm, France)
*Heriot, Cpl. James D. (Vaux-Andigny, France)
Hill, Cpl. Ralyn M. (Donnevoux, France)
Hilton, Sgt. Richmond H. (Brancourt, France)
Holderman, Capt. Nelson M. (Binarville, France)
Johnston, Sgt. Harold I. (Pouilly, France)
Karnes, Sgt. James E. (Estres, France)
Katz, Sgt. Phillip C. (Eclisfontaine, France)
Kaufman, 1st Sgt. Benjamin (Argonne Forest, France)
Latham, Sgt. John C. (Le Catelet, France)
*Lemert, 1st Sgt. Milo (Bellicourt, France)
Loman, Pvt. Berger (Consenvoye, France)
*Luke, 2d Lt. Frank, Jr. (Murvaux, France)
Mallon, Capt. George H. (Bois-de-Forges, France)
Manning, Cpl. Sidney E. (Breuvannes, France)
McMurtry, Capt. George G. (Charlevaux, France)
*Mestrovitch, Sgt. James I. (Fismette, France)
Miles, Capt. L. W. (Revillon, France)
*Miller, Maj. Oscar F. (Gesnes, France)
Morelock, Pvt. Sterling (Exermont, France)
Neibaur, Pvt. Thomas C. (Landres-et-St. Georges, France)
O'Neil, Sgt. Richard W. (Ourcq River, France)
*O'Shea, Cpl. Thomas E. (Le Catelet, France)
Parker, 2d Lt. Samuel I. (Soissons, France)
Peck, Pvt. Archie A. (Argonne Forest, France)
*Perkins, Pfc. Michael J. (Belieu Bois, France)
*Pike, Lt. Col. Emory J. (Vandières, France)
Pope, Cpl. Thomas A. (Hamel, France)
Regan, 2d Lt. Patrick (Bois-de-Consenvoye, France)
Rickenbacker, 1st Lt. Edward V. (Billy, France)
Robb, 1st Lt. George S. (Sechault, France)
*Roberts, Cpl. Harold W. (Montrebeau Woods, France)
Sampler, Cpl. Samuel M. (St. Etienne, France)
Sandlin, Sgt. Willie (Bois-de-Forges, France)
*Sawelson, Sgt. William (Grand-Pre, France)
Schaffner, 1st Lt. Dwite H. (Boureuilles, France)
Seibert, Sgt. Lloyd M. (Epinonville, France)
*Skinker, Capt. Alexander R. (Cheppy, France)
Slack, Pvt. Clayton K. (Consenvoye, France)
*Smith, Lt. Col. Fred E. (Binarville, France)
Talley, Sgt. Edward R. (Ponchaux, France)
Thompson, Maj. Joseph H. (Apremont, France)
Turner, Cpl. Harold L. (St. Etienne, France)
*Turner, 1st Lt. William B. (Ronssoy, France)
Valente, Pvt. Michael (Ronssoy, France)
Van Iersel, Sgt. Ludovicus M. (Mouzon, France)
Villepigue, Cpl. John C. (Vaux-Andigny, France)
Waaler, Sgt. Reidar (Ronssoy, France)
Ward, Pvt. Calvin J. (Estress, France)
West, 1st Sgt. Chester H. (Bois-de-Cheppy, France)
Whittlesey, Maj. Charles W. (Argonne Forest, France)
*Wickersham, 2d Lt. J. Hunter (Limey, France)
*Wold, Pvt. Nels (Cheppy, France)
Woodfill, 1st Lt. Samuel (Cunel, France)
York, Cpl. Alvin C. (Chatel-Chehery, France)

MARINES

† Cukela, Sgt. Louis (Villers-Cotterets, France)
† Janson, Gy. Sgt. Ernest A. (Château-Thierry, France)
† Kelly, Pvt. John J. (Blanc Mont Ridge, France)
*† Kocak, Sgt. Matej (Villers-Cotterets, France)
*† Pruitt, Cpl. John H. (Blanc Mont Ridge, France)
Robinson, Gy. Sgt. Robert G. (Pittham, Belgium)
*#Stockham, Gy. Sgt. Fred W. (Bois-de-Belleau, France)
* Talbot, 2d Lt. Ralph (France & Pittham, Belgium)

NAVY

Balch, Pharmacist's Mate 1st Class John H. (Vierzy & Somme-Py, France)
Boone, Lt. Joel T. (Vierzy, France)
Bradley, Cmdr. Willis W., Jr. (NOR)
Cann, Sman Tedford H. (NOR)
Covington, Ship's Cook 3d Class Jesse W. (NOR)
Graves, Sman Ora (NOR)
Hammann, Ensign Charles H. (Pola, Aegean Sea)
Hayden, Hospital Apprentice 1st Class David E. (Thiaucourt, France)
* Ingram, GM 1st Class Osmond K. (NOR)
Izac, Lt. Edouard V. M. (German submarine U-90)
Lyle, Lt. Cmdr. Alexander G. (French Front)
MacKenzie, Chief BM John (NOR)
Madison, Lt. Cmdr. James J. (NOR)
McGunigal, Shipfitter 1st Class Patrick (NOR)
Ormsbee, Chief Machinist's Mate Francis E., Jr. (Pensacola, Fla)
* Osborne, Lt.(j.g.) Weedon E. (Bouresche, France)
Petty, Lt. Orlando H. (Bois-de-Belleau, France)
Schmidt, Chief GM Oscar, Jr. (NOR)
Siegel, BM 2d Class John O. (NOR)
Sullivan, Ensign Daniel A. J. (NOR)
Upton, QM Frank M. (NOR)

† Also received army Medal of Honor for same action.
#Received army medal only.

World War II   1939–1945

Number of medals: 433

ARMY:	294
COAST GUARD:	1
MARINES:	81
NAVY:	57

ARMY

Adams, SSgt. Lucian (St. Die, France)
Anderson, TSgt. Beaufort T. (Okinawa)
*Antolak, Sgt. Sylvester (Cisterna di Littoria, Italy)
Atkins, Pfc. Thomas E. (Villa Verde Trail, Philippines)
*Baker, Lt. Col. Addison E. (Ploesti, Rumania)
*Baker, Pvt. Thomas A. (Saipan, Mariana Islands)
Barfoot, TSgt. Van T. (Carano, Italy)
Barrett, Pvt. Carlton W. (St. Laurent-sur-Mer, France)
*Beaudoin, 1st Lt. Raymond O. (Hamelin, Germany)
Bell, TSgt. Bernard P. (Mittelwihr, France)
Bender, SSgt. Stanley (La Lande, France)
*Benjamin, Pfc. George, Jr. (Leyte, Philippines)
Bennett, Cpl. Edward A. (Heckhuscheid, Germany)
Bertoldo, MSgt. Vito R. (Hatten, France)
Beyer, Cpl. Arthur O. (Arloncourt, Belgium)
*Bianchi, 1st Lt. Willibald C. (Bagac, Philippines)
Biddle, Pfc. Melvin E. (Soy, Belgium)
Bjorklund, 1st Lt. Arnold L. (Altavilla, Italy)
Bloch, 1st Lt. Orville E. (Firenzuola, Italy)
Bolden, SSgt. Paul L. (Petit-Coo, Belgium)
Bolton, 1st Lt. Cecil H. (Mark River, Holland)
Bong, Maj. Richard I. (Borneo & Leyte, Philippines)
*Booker, Pvt. Robert D. (Fondouk, Tunisia)
*Boyce, 2d Lt. George W. G., Jr. (Afua, New Guinea)
Briles, SSgt. Herschel F. (Scherpenseel, Germany)
Britt, Lt. Maurice L. (Mignano, Italy)
*Brostrom, Pfc. Leonard C. (Dagami, Philippines)
Brown, Capt. Bobbie E. (Aachen, Germany)
Burke, 1st Lt. Francis X. (Nuremberg, Germany)
*Burr, 1st Sgt. Elmer J. (Buna, New Guinea)
Burr, SSgt. Herbert H. (Dorrmoschel, Germany)
Burt, Capt. James M. (Wurselen, Germany)
*Butts, 2d Lt. John E. (Normandy, France)
Calugas, Sgt. Jose (Culis, Philippines)
*Carey, SSgt. Alvin P. (Plougastel, France)
*Carey, TSgt. Charles F., Jr. (Rimling, France)
*Carswell, Maj. Horace S., Jr. (South China Sea)
*Castle, Brig. Gen. Frederick W. (Germany)
*Cheli, Maj. Ralph (Wewak, New Guinea)
Childers, 2d Lt. Ernest (Oliveto, Italy)
Choate, SSgt. Clyde L. (Bruyères, France)
*Christensen, 2d Lt. Dale E. (Driniumor River, New Guinea)
*Christian, Pvt. Herbert F. (Valmontone, Italy)
*Cicchetti, Pfc. Joseph J. (South Manila, Philippines)
Clark, TSgt. Francis J. (Kalborn, Luxembourg, & Sevenig, Germany)
Colalillo, Pfc. Mike (Untergriesheim, Germany)
*Cole, Lt. Col. Robert G. (Carentan, France)
Connor, Sgt. James P. (Cape Cavalaire, France)
Cooley, SSgt. Raymond H. (Lumboy, Philippines)
Coolidge, TSgt. Charles H. (Belmont-sur-Buttant, France)
*Cowan, Pfc. Richard E. (Krinkelter Wald, Belgium)
Craft, Pfc. Clarence B. (Okinawa)
*Craig, 2d Lt. Robert (Favoratta, Sicily)
*Crain, TSgt. Morris E. (Haguenau, France)
*Craw, Col. Demas T. (Port Lyautey, French Morocco)
Crawford, Pvt. William J. (Altavilla, Italy)
Crews, SSgt. John R. (Lobenbacherhof, Germany)

Currey, Sgt. Francis S. (Malmedy, Belgium)
Dahlgren, Sgt. Edward C. (Oberhoffen, France)
Dalessondro, TSgt. Peter J. (Kalterherberg, Germany)
Daly, Lt. Michael J. (Nuremberg, Germany)
Davis, Capt. Charles W. (Guadalcanal)
*DeFranzo, SSgt. Arthur F. (Vaubadon, France)
*DeGlopper, Pfc. Charles N. (La Fière, France)
*Deleau, Sgt. Emile, Jr. (Oberhoffen, France)
Dervishian, TSgt. Ernest H. (Cisterna, Italy)
*Diamond, Pfc. James H. (Mintal, Philippines)
*Dietz, SSgt. Robert H. (Kirchain, Germany)
Doolittle, Lt. Col. James H. (Over Japan)
Doss, Pfc. Desmond T. (Okinawa)
Drowley, SSgt. Jesse R. (Bougainville Island)
Dunham, TSgt. Russell E. (Kayserberg, France)
*Dutko, Pfc. John W. (Ponte Rotto, Italy)
Ehlers, SSgt. Walter D. (Goville, France)
*Endl, SSgt. Gerald L. (Anamo, New Guinea)
Erwin, SSgt. Henry E. (Koriyama, Japan)
*Eubanks, Sgt. Ray E. (Noemfoor Island, Dutch New Guinea)
Everhart, TSgt. Forrest E. (Kerling, France)
*Femoyer, 2d Lt. Robert E. (Merseburg, Germany)
Fields, 1st Lt. James H. (Rechicourt, France)
Fisher, 2d Lt. Almond E. (Grammont, France)
*Fournier, Sgt. William G. (Guadalcanal)
*Fowler, 2d Lt. Thomas W. (Carano, Italy)
Fryar, Pvt. Elmer E. (Leyte, Philippines)
Funk, 1st Sgt. Leonard A., Jr. (Holzheim, Belgium)
*Galt, Capt. William W. (Villa Crocetta, Italy)
*Gammon, SSgt. Archer T. (Bastogne, Belgium)
Garcia, SSgt. Marcario (Grosshau, Germany)
Garman, Pvt. Harold A. (Montereau, France)
Gerstung, TSgt. Robert E. (Berg, Germany)
*Gibson, Technician 5th Grade Eric G. (Isola Bella, Italy)
*Gonzales, Pfc. David M. (Villa Verde Trail, Philippines)
*Gott, 1st Lt. Donald J. (Saarbrucken, Germany)
*Grabiarz, Pfc. William J. (Manila, Philippines)
Gregg, TSgt. Stephen R. (Montelimar, France)
*Gruennert, Sgt. Kenneth E. (Buna, New Guinea)
Hall, SSgt. George J. (Anzio, Italy)
*Hall, Technician 5th Grade Lewis (Guadalcanal)
*Hallman, SSgt. Sherwood H. (Brest, France)
Hamilton, Maj. Pierpont M. (Port Lyautey, French Morocco)
*Harmon, Sgt. Roy W. (Casaglia, Italy)
*Harr, Cpl. Harry R. (Maglamin, Philippines)
*Harris, 2d Lt. James L. (Vagney, France)
*Hastings, Pfc. Joe R. (Drabenderhohe, Germany)
Hawk, Sgt. John D. (Chambois, France)
Hawks, Pfc. Lloyd C. (Carano, Italy)
*Hedrick, TSgt. Clinton M. (Lembeck, Germany)
Hendrix, Pvt. James R. (Assenois, Belgium)
*Henry, Pvt. Robert T. (Luchem, Germany)
Herrera, Pfc. Silvestre S. (Mertzwiller, France)
Horner, SSgt. Freeman V. (Wurselen, Germany)
Howard, Lt. Col. James H. (Oschersleben, Germany)
Huff, Cpl. Paul B. (Carano, Italy)
*Hughes, 2d Lt. Lloyd H. (Ploesti, Rumania)
*Jachman, SSgt. Isadore S. (Flamièrge, Belgium)
*Jerstad, Maj. John L. (Ploesti, Rumania)
*Johnson, Pvt. Elden H. (Valmontone, Italy)

Johnson, Col. Leon W. (Ploesti, Rumania)
*Johnson, Sgt. Leroy (Limon, Philippines)
Johnson, Sgt. Oscar G. (Scarperia, Italy)
Johnston, Pfc. William J. (Padiglione, Italy)
*Kandle, 1st Lt. Victor L. (La Forge, France)
Kane, Col. John R. (Ploesti, Rumania)
Karaberis, Sgt. Christos H. (Guignola, Italy)
Kearby, Col. Neel E. (Wewak, New Guinea)
*Keathley, SSgt. George D. (Mt. Altuzzo, Italy)
*Kefurt, SSgt. Gus (Bennwihr, France)
*Kelley, SSgt. Jonah E. (Kesternich, Germany)
*Kelley, Pvt. Ova A. (Leyte, Philippines)
Kelly, Cpl. Charles E. (Altavilla, Italy)
*Kelly, Cpl. John D. (Fort du Roule, France)
Kelly, Cpl. Thomas J. (Alemert, Germany)
Kerstetter, Pfc. Dexter J. (Galiano, Philippines)
*Kessler, Pfc. Patrick L. (Ponte Rotto, Italy)
*Kimbro, Technician 4th Grade Truman (Rocherath, Belgium)
*Kiner, Pvt. Harold G. (Palenberg, Germany)
*Kingsley, 2d Lt. David R. (Ploesti, Rumania)
Kisters, Sgt. Gerry H. (Gagliano, Sicily)
Knappenberger, Pfc. Alton W. (Cisterna di Littoria, Italy)
*Knight, 1st Lt. Jack L. (Loi-Kang, Burma)
*Knight, 1st Lt. Raymond L. (Northern Po Valley, Italy)
*Krotiak, Pfc. Anthony L. (Balete Pass, Philippines)
Lawley, 1st Lt. William R., Jr. (Over Europe)
Laws, SSgt. Robert E. (Pangasinan Province, Philippines)
Lee, 1st Lt. Daniel W. (Montreval, France)
*Leonard, 1st Lt. Turney W. (Kommerscheidt, Germany)
*Lindsey, Capt. Darrell R. (L'Isle Adam Bridge, France)
Lindsey, TSgt. Jake W. (Hamich, Germany)
*Lindstrom, Pfc. Floyd K. (Mignano, Italy)
*Lloyd, 1st Lt. Edgar H. (Pompey, France)
*Lobaugh, Pvt. Donald R. (Afua, New Guinea)
Logan, Sgt. James M. (Salerno, Italy)
Lopez, Sgt. Jose M. (Krinkelt, Belgium)
Mabry, Lt. Col. George L., Jr. (Hurtgen Forest, Germany)
MacArthur, Gen. Douglas (Bataan Peninsula, Philippines)
McCall, SSgt. Thomas E. (San Angelo, Italy)
McCarter, Pvt. Lloyd G. (Corregidor, Philippines)
McGaha, MSgt. Charles L. (Lupao, Philippines)
McGarity, TSgt. Vernon (Krinkelt, Belgium)
*McGee, Pfc. William D. (Mulheim, Germany)
*McGill, Sgt. Troy A. (Los Negros Islands)
MacGillivary, Sgt. Charles A. (Woelfling, France)
*McGraw, Pfc. Francis X. (Schevenhutte, Germany)
*McGuire, Maj. Thomas B., Jr. (Luzon, Philippines)
McKinney, Pvt. John R. (Tayabas Province, Philippines)
*McVeigh, Sgt. John J. (Brest, France)
*McWhorter, Pfc. William A. (Leyte, Philippines)
*Magrath, Pfc. John D. (Castel d'Aiano, Italy)
*Mann, Pfc. Joe E. (Best, Holland)
*Martinez, Pvt. Joe P. (Attu, Aleutian Islands)
*Mathies, Sgt. Archibald (Over Europe)
*Mathis, 1st Lt. Jack W. (Vegesack, Germany)

Maxwell, Technician 5th Grade Robert D. (Besancon, France)
*May, Pfc. Martin O. (Ie Shima, Ryukyu Islands)
Mayfield, Cpl. Melvin (Cordillera Mountains, Philippines)
Meagher, TSgt. John (Ozato, Okinawa)
Merli, Pfc. Gino J. (Sars la Bruyère, Belgium)
*Merrell, Pvt. Joseph F. (Lohe, Germany)
*Messerschmidt, Sgt. Harold O. (Radden, France)
*Metzger, 2d Lt. William E., Jr. (Saarbrucken, Germany)
Michael, 1st Lt. Edward S. (Over Germany)
*Michael, 2d Lt. Harry J. (Neiderzerf, Germany)
*Miller, SSgt. Andrew (Woippy, France–Kerprich Hemmersdorf, Germany)
Mills, Pvt. James H. (Cisterna di Littoria, Italy)
*Minick, SSgt. John W. (Hurtgen, Germany)
*Minue, Pvt. Nicholas (Medjez-el-Bab, Tunisia)
*Monteith, 1st Lt. Jimmie W., Jr. (Collesville-sur-Mer, France)
Montgomery, 1st Lt. Jack C. (Padiglione, Italy)
*Moon, Pvt. Harold H., Jr. (Pawig, Philippines)
Morgan, 2d Lt. John C. (Over Europe)
*Moskala, Pfc. Edward J. (Kakazu Ridge, Okinawa)
*Mower, Sgt. Charles E. (Capoocan, Philippines)
*Muller, Sgt. Joseph E. (Ishimmi, Okinawa)
*Munemori, Pfc. Sadao S. (Seravezza, Italy)
Murphy, 2d Lt. Audie L. (Holtzwihr, France)
*Murphy, Pfc. Frederick C. (Saarlautern, Germany)
Murray, 1st Lt. Charles P., Jr. (Kaysersberg, France)
*Nelson, Sgt. William L. (Djebel Dardys, Tunisia)
Neppel, Sgt. Ralph G. (Birgel, Germany)
Nett, Lt. Robert P. (Cognon, Philippines)
Newman, 1st Lt. Beryl R. (Cisterna, Italy)
*Nininger, 2d Lt. Alexander R., Jr. (Abucay, Philippines)
*O'Brien, Lt. Col. William J. (Saipan, Mariana Islands)
Ogden, 1st Lt. Carlos C. (Fort du Roule, France)
*Olson, Capt. Arlo L. (Volturno River, Italy)
*Olson, Sgt. Truman O. (Cisterna di Littoria, Italy)
Oresko, MSgt. Nicholas (Tettington, Germany)
*Parrish, Technician 4th Grade Laverne (Binalonan, Philippines)
*Pease, Capt. Harl, Jr. (Rabaul, New Britain)
*Peden, Technician 5th Grade Forrest E. (Biesheim, France)
*Pendleton, SSgt. Jack J. (Bardenberg, Germany)
*Peregory, TSgt. Frank D. (Grandcampe, France)
*Perez, Pfc. Manuel, Jr. (Fort William McKinley, Philippines)
*Peters, Pvt. George J. (Fluren, Germany)
*Peterson, SSgt. George (Eisern, Germany)
*Petrarca, Pfc. Frank J. (New Georgia, Solomon Islands)
*Pinder, Technician 5th Grade John J., Jr. (Colleville-sur-Mer, France)
Powers, Pfc. Leo J. (Cassino, Italy)
*Prussman, Pfc. Ernest W. (Les Coates, France)
*Pucket, 1st Lt. Donald D. (Ploesti, Rumania)
*Ray, 1st Lt. Bernard J. (Hurtgen Forest, Germany)
*Reese, Pvt. James W. (Mt. Vassillio, Sicily)
*Reese, Pfc. John N., Jr. (Manila, Philippines)
*Riordan, 2d Lt. Paul F. (Cassino, Italy)

*Robinson, 1st Lt. James E., Jr. (Untergriesheim, Germany)
Rodriguez, Pvt. Cleto (Manila, Philippines)
*Roeder, Capt. Robert E. (Mt. Battaglia, Italy)
*Roosevelt, Brig. Gen. Theodore, Jr. (Normandy, France)
Ross, Pvt. Wilburn K. (St. Jacques, France)
Rudolph, TSgt. Donald E. (Munoz, Philippines)
Ruiz, Pfc. Alejandro R. (Okinawa)
*Sadowski, Sgt. Joseph J. (Valhey, France)
*Sarnoski, 2d Lt. Joseph R. (Buka Area, Solomon Islands)
*Sayers, Pfc. Foster J. (Thionville, France)
Schaefer, SSgt. Joseph E. (Stolberg, Germany)
Schauer, Pfc. Henry (Cisterna di Littoria, Italy)
Scott, Lt. Robert S. (New Georgia, Solomon Islands)
Shea, 2d Lt. Charles W. (Mt. Damiano, Italy)
*Sheridan, Pfc. Carl V. (Weisweiler, Germany)
*Shockley, Pfc. William R. (Villa Verde Trail, Philippines)
Shomo, Maj. William A. (Luzon, Philippines)
*Shoup, SSgt. Curtis F. (Tillet, Belgium)
Silk, 1st Lt. Edward A. (St. Pravel, France)
Siogren, SSgt. John C. (San José Hacienda, Philippines)
Slaton, Cpl. James D. (Oliveto, Italy)
*Smith, Pvt. Furman L. (Lanuvio, Italy)
Smith, Sgt. Maynard H. (Over Europe)
Soderman, Pfc. William A. (Rocherath, Belgium)
*Specker, Sgt. Joe C. (Mt. Porchia, Italy)
Spurrier, SSgt. Junior J. (Achain, France)
*Squires, Pfc. John C. (Padiglione, Italy)
*Stryker, Pfc. Stuart S. (Wesel, Germany)
*Terry, 1st Lt. Seymour W. (Okinawa)
*Thomas, Pfc. William H. (Zambales Mountains, Philippines)
Thompson, Sgt. Max (Haaren, Germany)
*Thorne, Cpl. Horace M. (Grufflingen, Belgium)
*Thorson, Pfc. John F. (Dagami, Philippines)
Tominac, 1st Lt. John J. (Saulx de Vesoul, France)
*Towle, Pvt. John R. (Oosterhout, Holland)
Treadwell, Capt. Jack L. (Nieder–Wurzbach, Germany)
*Truemper, 2d Lt. Walter E. (Over Europe)
*Turner, Sgt. Day G. (Dahl, Luxembourg)
Turner, Pfc. George B. (Philipsbourg, France)
Urban, Capt. Matt (Renouf & St. Lo, France, & Meuse River, Belgium)
*Valdez, Pfc. Jose F. (Rosenkrantz, France)
*Van Noy, Pvt. Junior (Finschafen, New Guinea)
*Vance, Lt. Col. Leon R., Jr. (Wimereaux, France)
*Viale, 2d Lt. Robert M. (Manila, Philippines)
*Villegas, SSgt. Ysmael R. (Villa Verde Trail, Philippines)
Vlug, Pfc. Dirk J. (Limon, Philippines)
Vosler, TSgt. Forrest T. (Bremen, Germany)
Wainwright, Gen. Jonathan M. (Philippines)
*Walker, Brig. Gen. Kenneth N. (Rabaul, New Britain)
*Wallace, Pfc. Herman C. (Prumzurley, Germany)
Ware, Lt. Col. Keith L. (Sigolsheim, France)
*Warner, Cpl. Henry F. (Dom Butgenbach, Belgium)
*Waugh, 1st Lt. Robert T. (Tremensucli, Italy)
Waybur, 1st Lt. David C. (Agrigento, Sicily)

*Weicht, Sgt. Ellis R. (St. Hippolyte, France)
*Wetzel, Pfc. Walter C. (Birken, Germany)
Whiteley, 1st Lt. Eli (Sigolsheim, France)
Whittington, Sgt. Hulon B. (Grimesnil, France)
Wiedorfer, Pvt. Paul J. (Chaumont, Belgium)
*Wigle, 2d Lt. Thomas W. (Monte Frassino, Italy)
Wilbur, Col. William H. (Fedala, French Morocco)
*Wilkin, Cpl. Edward G. (Siegfried line, Germany)
Wilkins, Maj. Raymond H. (Rabaul, New Britain)
*Will, 1st Lt. Walter J. (Eisern, Germany)
*Wilson, Technician 5th Grade Alfred L. (Bezange la Petite, France)
Wise, SSgt. Homer L. (Magliano, Italy)
*Woodford, SSgt. Howard E. (Tabio, Philippines)
*Young, Pvt. Rodger W. (New Georgia, Solomon Islands)
Zeamer, Capt. Jay, Jr. (Buka Area, Solomon Islands)
*Zussman, 2d Lt. Raymond (Noroy le Bourg, France)

COAST GUARD

*Munro, Signalman 1st Class Douglas A. (Point Cruz, Guadalcanal)

MARINES

*Agerholm, Pfc. Harold C. (Saipan, Mariana Islands)
*Anderson, Pfc. Richard B. (Roi Island, Marshall Islands)
*Bailey, Maj. Kenneth D. (Guadalcanal)
Basilone, Sgt. John (Guadalcanal)
*Bauer, Lt. Col. Harold W. (Solomon Islands Area)
*Bausell, Cpl. Lewis K. (Peleliu Island)
*Berry, Cpl. Charles J. (Iwo Jima)
*Bonnyman, 1st Lt. Alexander, Jr. (Tarawa)
*Bordelon, SSgt. William J. (Tarawa)
Boyington, Maj. Gregory (Central Solomons Area)
Bush, Cpl. Richard E. (Okinawa)
*Caddy, Pfc. William R. (Iwo Jima)
*Cannon, 1st Lt. George H. (Sand Island, Midway Islands)
Casamento, Cpl. Anthony (Guadalcanal)
Chambers, Lt. Col. Justice M. (Iwo Jima)
*Cole, Sgt. Darrell S. (Iwo Jima)
Courtney, Maj. Henry A., Jr. (Okinawa Shima)
*Damato, Cpl. Anthony P. (Engebi Island, Marshall Islands)
DeBlanc, Capt. Jefferson J. (Kolombangara Island, Solomon Islands)
Dunlap, Capt. Robert H. (Iwo Jima)
*Dyess, Lt. Col. Aquilla J. (Namur Island, Marshall Islands)
Edson, Col. Merritt A. (Guadalcanal)
*Elrod, Capt. Henry T. (Wake Island)
*Epperson, Pfc. Harold G. (Saipan Island, Mariana Islands)
*Fardy, Cpl. John P. (Okinawa Shima)
*Fleming, Capt. Richard E. (Midway)
Foss, Capt. Joseph J. (Guadalcanal)
*Foster, Pfc. William A. (Okinawa Shima)
Galer, Maj. Robert E. (Solomon Islands Area)
*Gonsalves, Pfc. Harold (Okinawa Shima)
*Gray, Sgt. Ross F. (Iwo Jima)
*Gurke, Pfc. Henry (Bougainville Island)

Above and Beyond

*Hansen, Pvt. Dale M. (Okinawa Shima)
*Hanson, 1st Lt. Robert M. (Bougainville Island & New Britain Island)
Harrell, Sgt. William G. (Iwo Jima)
*Hauge, Cpl. Louis J., Jr. (Okinawa Shima)
*Hawkins, 1st Lt. William D. (Tarawa)
Jackson, Pfc. Arthur J. (Peleliu Island)
Jacobson, Pfc. Douglas T. (Iwo Jima)
*Julian, Sgt. Joseph R. (Iwo Jima)
*Kinser, Sgt. Elbert L. (Okinawa Shima)
*Kraus, Pfc. Richard E. (Peleliu Island)
*La Belle, Pfc. James D. (Iwo Jima)
Leims, 2d Lt. John H. (Iwo Jima)
Lucas, Pfc. Jacklyn H. (Iwo Jima)
*Lummus, 1st Lt. Jack (Iwo Jima)
*McCard, Gy. Sgt. Robert H. (Saipan, Mariana Islands)
McCarthy, Capt. Joseph J. (Iwo Jima)
*McTureous, Pvt. Robert M., Jr. (Okinawa)
*Martin, 1st Lt. Harry L. (Iwo Jima)
*Mason, Pfc. Leonard F. (Guam)
*New, Pfc. John D. (Peleliu Island)
*Owens, Sgt. Robert A. (Cape Torokina, Bougainville Island)
*Ozbourn, Pvt. Joseph W. (Tinian Island, Mariana Islands)
Paige, Sgt. Mitchell (Guadalcanal)
*Phelps, Pvt. Wesley (Peleliu Island)
*Phillips, Pvt. George (Iwo Jima)
Pope, Capt. Everett P. (Peleliu Island)
*Power, 1st Lt. John V. (Namur Island, Marshall Islands)
*Roan, Pfc. Charles H. (Peleliu Island)
Rouh, 1st Lt. Carlton R. (Peleliu Island)
*Ruhl, Pfc. Donald J. (Iwo Jima)
*Schwab, Pfc. Albert E. (Okinawa Shima)
Shoup, Col. David M. (Betio Island, Tarawa)
Sigler, Pvt. Franklin E. (Iwo Jima)
Skaggs, Pfc. Luther, Jr. (Guam)
Smith, Maj. John L. (Solomon Islands Area)
Sorenson, Pvt. Richard K. (Namur Island, Marshall Islands)
*Stein, Cpl. Tony (Iwo Jima)
Swett, 1st Lt. James E. (Solomon Islands Area)
*Thomas, Sgt. Herbert J. (Koromokina River, Bougainville Island)
*Thomason, Sgt. Clyde (Makin Island)
*Timmerman, Sgt. Grant F. (Saipan, Mariana Islands)
Vandegrift, Maj. Gen. Alexander A. (Guadalcanal)
Walsh, 1st Lt. Kenneth A. (Solomon Islands Area)
*Walsh, Gy. Sgt. William G. (Iwo Jima)
Watson, Pvt. Wilson D. (Iwo Jima)
Williams, Cpl. Hershel W. (Iwo Jima)
Wilson, Capt. Louis H., Jr. (Fonte Hill, Guam)
*Wilson, Pfc. Robert L. (Tinian Island, Mariana Islands)
*Witek, Pfc. Frank P. (Guam)

NAVY

Antrim, Lt. Richard N. (Makassar, Netherlands East Indies)
*Bennion, Capt. Mervyn S. (Pearl Harbor, Hawaii)
*Bigelow, Watertender 1st Class Elmer C. (Corregidor Island, Philippines)
Bulkeley, Lt. Cmdr. John D. (Philippines)
Bush, Hospital Apprentice 1st Class Robert E. (Okinawa)
*Callaghan, Rear Adm. Daniel J. (Savo Island, Solomon Islands)
*Cromwell, Capt. John P. (Truk Island)
*David, Lt.(j.g.) Albert L. (French West Africa)
*Davis, Cmdr. George F. (Lingayen Gulf, Philippines)
*Dealey, Cmdr. Samuel D. (Sulu Sea, Borneo)
*Evans, Cmdr. Ernest E. (Samar, Philippines)
Finn, Lt. John W. (Kaneohe Bay, Hawaii)
*Flaherty, Ensign Francis C. (Pearl Harbor, Hawaii)
Fluckey, Cmdr. Eugene B. (Coast of China)
Fuqua, Capt. Samuel G. (Pearl Harbor, Hawaii)
Gary, Lt.(j.g.) Donald A. (Kobe, Japan)
*Gilmore, Cmdr. Howard W. (Southwest Pacific)
Gordon, Lt. Nathan G. (Bismarck Sea)
Hall, Lt.(j.g.) William E. (Coral Sea)
*Halyburton, Pharmacist's Mate 2d Class William D., Jr. (Okinawa Shima)
*Hammerberg, BM 2d Class Owen F. P. (Pearl Harbor, Hawaii)
Herring, Lt. Rufus G. (Iwo Jima)
*Hill, Chief Boatswain Edwin J. (Pearl Harbor, Hawaii)
*Hutchins, Sman 1st Class Johnnie D. (Lae, New Guinea)
*Jones, Ensign Herbert C. (Pearl Harbor, Hawaii)
*Keppler, BM 1st Class Reinhardt J. (Solomon Islands)
*Kidd, Rear Adm. Isaac C. (Pearl Harbor, Hawaii)
*Lester, Hospital Apprentice 1st Class Fred F. (Okinawa Shima)
McCampbell, Cmdr. David (Philippine Sea)
McCandless, Cmdr. Bruce (Savo Island, Solomon Islands)
McCool, Lt. Richard M., Jr. (Okinawa)
O'Callahan, Cmdr. Joseph T. (Kobe, Japan)
O'Hare, Lt. Edward H. (Raboul, New Britain)
O'Kane, Cmdr. Richard H. (Formosa Strait)
*Parle, Ensign John J. (Sicily, Italy)
*Peterson, Chief Watertender Oscar V. (NOR)
Pharris, Lt. Jackson C. (Pearl Harbor, Hawaii)
Pierce, Pharmacist's Mate 1st Class Francis J. (Iwo Jima)
*Powers, Lt. John J. (Coral Sea)
Preston, Lt. Arthur M. (Wasile Bay, Halmahera Island)
Ramage, Cmdr. Lawson P. (Pacific)
*Reeves, Radio Electrician Thomas J. (Pearl Harbor, Hawaii)
*Ricketts, Lt. Milton E. (Coral Sea)
*Rooks, Capt. Albert H. (Java, Indonesia)
Ross, Machinist Donald K. (Pearl Harbor, Hawaii)
Schonland, Lt. Cmdr. Herbert E. (Savo Island, Solomon Islands)
*Scott, Rear Adm. Norman (Savo Island, Solomon Islands)
*Scott, Machinist's Mate 1st Class Robert R. (Pearl Harbor, Hawaii)
Street, Cmdr. George L. III (Quelpart Island, Korea)
*Tomich, Chief Watertender Peter (Pearl Harbor, Hawaii)
*Van Valkenburgh, Capt. Franklin (Pearl Harbor, Hawaii)
*Van Voorhis, Lt. Cmdr. Bruce A. (Greenwich Island, Solomon Islands)
Wahlen, Pharmacist's Mate 2d Class George E. (Iwo Jima)
*Ward, Sman 1st Class James R. (Pearl Harbor, Hawaii)
*Williams, Pharmacist's Mate 3d Class Jack (Iwo Jima)
*Willis, Pharmacist's Mate 1st Class John H. (Iwo Jima)
Young, Cmdr. Cassin (Pearl Harbor, Hawaii)

The Korean War 1950–1953

Number of medals: 131

AIR FORCE:	4
ARMY:	78
MARINES:	42
NAVY:	7

AIR FORCE

*Davis, Maj. George A., Jr. (Sinuiju-Yalu River Area)
*Loring, Maj. Charles J., Jr. (Sniper Ridge, N. Korea)
*Sebille, Maj. Louis J. (Hanchang)
*Walmsley, Capt. John S., Jr. (Yangdok)

ARMY

Adams, Sfc. Stanley T. (Sesim-ni)
*Barker, Pvt. Charles H. (Sokkogae)
*Bennett, Pfc. Emory L. (Sobangsan)
Bleak, Sgt. David B. (Minari-gol)
*Brittin, Sfc. Nelson V. (Yonggong-ni)
*Brown, Pfc. Melvin L. (Kasan)
Burke, 1st Lt. Lloyd L. (Chong-dong)
*Burris, Sfc. Tony K. (Mundung-ni)
*Charlton, Sgt. Cornelius H. (Chipo-ri)
*Collier, Cpl. Gilbert G. (Tutayon)
*Collier, Cpl. John W. (Chindong-ni)
*Coursen, 1st Lt. Samuel S. (Kaesong)
*Craig, Cpl. Gordon M. (Kasan)
Crump, Cpl. Jerry K. (Chorwon)
Dean, Maj. Gen. William F. (Taejon)
*Desiderio, Capt. Reginald B. (Ipsok)
Dodd, 2d Lt. Carl H. (Subuk)
*Duke, Sfc. Ray E. (Mugok)
*Edwards, Sfc. Junior D. (Changbong-ni)
*Essebagger, Cpl. John, Jr. (Popsudong)
Faith, Lt. Col. Don C., Jr. (Hagaru-ri)
*George, Pfc. Charles (Songnae-dong)
*Gilliland, Pfc. Charles L. (Tongmang-ni)
*Goodblood, Cpl. Clair (Popsudong)
*Hammond, Cpl. Lester, Jr. (Kumwha)
*Handrich, MSgt. Melvin O. (Sobuk San Mountain)
*Hanson, Pfc. Jack G. (Pachi-dong)
*Hartell, 1st Lt. Lee R. (Kobangsan-ni)
Harvey, Capt. Raymond (Taemi-Dong)
*Henry, 1st Lt. Frederick F. (Am-Dong)
Hernandez, Cpl. Rodolfo P. (Wontong-ni)
Ingman, Cpl. Einar H., Jr. (Maltari)
*Jecelin, Sgt. William R. (Saga)
*Jordan, Pfc. Mack A. (Kumsong)
*Kanell, Pvt. Billie G. (Pyongyang)
*Kaufman, Sfc. Loren R. (Yongsan)
*Knight, Pfc. Noah O. (Kowang-San)
Kouma, Sfc. Ernest R. (Agok)
*Krzyzowski, Capt. Edward C. (Tondul)
*Kyle, 2d Lt. Darwin K. (Kamil-ni)
Lee, MSgt. Hubert L. (Ip-o-ri)
*Libby, Sgt. George D. (Taejon)
*Long, Sgt. Charles R. (Hoeng-song)
*Lyell, Cpl. William F. (Chup'a-ri)
*McGovern, 1st Lt. Robert M. (Kamyangjan-ni)
*Martinez, Cpl. Benito (Satae-ri)
*Mendonca, Sgt. Leroy A. (Chich-on)
Millett, Capt. Lewis L. (Soam-Ni)
Miyamura, Cpl. Hiroshi H. (Taejon-ni)
Mize, Sgt. Ola L. (Surang-ni)
*Moyer, Sfc. Donald R. (Seoul)
*Ouellette, Pfc. Joseph R. (Yongsan)
Page, Lt. Col. John U. D. (Chosin Reservoir)
*Pendleton, Cpl. Charles F. (Choo Gung-Dong)

*Pililaau, Pfc. Herbert K. (Pia-ri)
Pittman, Sgt. John A. (Kujang-dong)
*Pomeroy, Pfc. Ralph E. (Kumhwa)
*Porter, Sgt. Donn F. (Mundung-ni)
*Red Cloud, Cpl. Mitchell, Jr. (Chonghyon)
Rodriguez, Pfc. Joseph C. (Munye-ri)
Rosser, Cpl. Ronald E. (Ponggilli)
*Schoonover, Cpl. Dan D. (Sokkogae)
Schowalter, 1st Lt. Edward R., Jr. (Kumhwa)
*Shea, 1st Lt. Richard T., Jr. (Sokkogae)
*Sitman, Sfc. William S. (Chipyong-ni)
*Smith, Pfc. David M. (Yongsan)
*Speicher, Cpl. Clifton T. (Minari-gol)
Stone, 1st Lt. James L. (Sokkogae)
*Story, Pfc. Luther H. (Agok)
*Sudut, 2d Lt. Jerome A. (Kumhwa)
*Thompson, Pfc. William (Haman)
*Turner, Sfc. Charles W. (Yongsan)
*Watkins, MSgt. Travis E. (Yongsan)
West, Pfc. Ernest E. (Sataeri)
Wilson, MSgt. Benjamin F. (Hwach'on-Myon)
*Wilson, Pfc. Richard G. (Opari)
*Womack, Pfc. Bryant H. (Sokso-ri)
*Young, Pfc. Robert H. (Kaesong)

MARINES

*Abrell, Cpl. Charles G. (Hangnyong)
Barber, Capt. William E. (Chosin Reservoir)
*Baugh, Pfc. William B. (Koto-ri to Hagaru-ri)
Cafferata, Pvt. Hector A., Jr. (Chosin Reservoir)
*Champagne, Cpl. David B. (Korea)
*Christianson, Pfc. Stanley (Seoul)
Commiskey, 2d Lt. Henry A., Sr. (Yongdungp'o)
*Davenport, Cpl. Jack A. (Songnae-Dong)
Davis, Lt. Col. Raymond G. (Hagaru-ri)
Dewey, Cpl. Duane E. (Panmunjon)
*Garcia, Pfc. Fernando L. (Korea)
*Gomez, Pfc. Edward (Hill 749)
*Guillen, SSgt. Ambrosio (Songuch-on)
*Johnson, Sgt. James E. (Yudam-ni)
*Kelly, Pfc. John D. (Korea)
*Kelso, Pfc. Jack W. (Korea)
Kennemore, SSgt. Robert S. (Yudam-ni)
*Littleton, Pfc. Herbert A. (Chungchon)
*Lopez, 1st Lt. Baldomero (Inchon)
McLaughlin, Pfc. Alford L. (Korea)
*Matthews, Sgt. Daniel P. (Vegas Hill)
*Mausert, Sgt. Frederick W., III (Songnap-yong)
*Mitchell, 1st Lt. Frank N. (Hansan-ni)
*Monegan, Pfc. Walter C., Jr. (Sosa-ri)
*Moreland, Pfc. Whitt L. (Kwagch'i-Dong)
Murphy, 2d Lt. Raymond G. (Korea)
Myers, Maj. Reginald R. (Hagaru-ri)
*Obregon, Pfc. Eugene A. (Seoul)
O'Brien, 2d Lt. George H., Jr. (Korea)
*Phillips, Cpl. Lee H. (Korea)
*Poynter, Sgt. James I. (Sudong)
*Ramer, 2d Lt. George H. (Korea)
*Reem, 2d Lt. Robert D. (Chinhung-ni)
*Shuck, SSgt. William E., Jr. (Korea)
Simanek, Pfc. Robert E. (Korea)
Sitter, Capt. Carl L. (Hagaru-ri)
*Skinner, 2d Lt. Sherrod E., Jr. (Korea)

Van Winkle, SSgt. Archie (Sudong)
*Vittori, Cpl. Joseph (Hill 749)
*Watkins, SSgt. Lewis G. (Korea)
Wilson, TSgt. Harold E. (Korea)
*Windrich, SSgt. William G. (Yudam-ni)

NAVY

*Benford, Hospital Corpsman 3d Class Edward C. (Korea)
Charette, Hospital Corpsman 3d Class William R. (Korea)
*Dewert, Hospital Corpsman Richard D. (Korea)
*Hammond, Hospital Corpsman Francis C. (Korea)
Hudner, Lt.(j.g.) Thomas J., Jr. (Chosin Reservoir)
*Kilmer, Hospital Corpsman John E. (Korea)
*Koelsch, Lt.(j.g.) John K. (North Korea)

337

The Vietnam War   1964–1973

Number of medals: 238

AIR FORCE:	12
ARMY:	155
MARINES:	57
NAVY:	14

AIR FORCE

*Bennett, Capt. Steven L. (Quang Tri)
Day, Maj. George E. (North Vietnam)
Dethlefsen, Capt. Merlyn H. (North Vietnam)
Fisher, Maj. Bernard F. (A Shau)
Fleming, 1st Lt. James P. (Duc Co)
Jackson, Lt. Col. Joe M. (Kham Duc)
*Jones, Lt. Col. William A. III (Dong Hoi, N. Vietnam)
Levitow, Airman 1st Class John L. (Long Binh)
*Sijan, Capt. Lance P. (North Vietnam)
Thorsness, Maj. Leo K. (North Vietnam)
*Wilbanks, Capt. Hilliard A. (Da Lat)
Young, Capt. Gerald O. (Khe Sanh)

ARMY

*Adams, Maj. William E. (Kontum Province)
*Albanese, Pfc. Lewis (Phu Muu-2)
Anderson, SSgt. Webster (Tam Ky)
*Ashley, Sfc. Eugene, Jr. (Lang Vei)
Baca, Sp4c. John P. (Phuoc Long Province)
Bacon, SSgt. Nicky D. (Tam Ky)
Baker, Pfc. John F., Jr. (South Vietnam)
*Barnes, Pfc. John A. III (Dak To)
Beikirch, Sgt. Gary B. (Kontum Province)
*Belcher, Sgt. Ted (Plei Jrang)
*Bellrichard, Pfc. Leslie A. (Kontum Province)
Benavidez, SSgt. Roy P. (Cambodia)
*Bennett, Cpl. Thomas W. (Pleiku Province)
*Blanchfield, Sp4c. Michael R. (Binh Dinh Province)
Bondsteel, SSgt. James L. (An Loc Province)
*Bowen, SSgt. Hammett L., Jr. (Binh Duong Province)
Brady, Maj. Patrick H. (Chu Lai)
*Bryant, Sfc. William M. (Long Khanh Province)
Bucha, Capt. Paul W. (Phuoc Vinh)
*Buker, Sgt. Brian L. (Chau Doc Province)
Cavaiani, SSgt. Jon R. (Quang Tri Province)
*Crescenz, Cpl. Michael J. (Hiep Duc Valley)
*Cutinha, Sp4c. Nicholas J. (Gia Dinh)
*Dahl, Sp4c. Larry G. (An Khe)
Davis, Sgt. Sammy L. (Cai Lay)
*Devore, Sp4c. Edward A., Jr. (Saigon)
Dix, SSgt. Drew D. (Chau Doc Province)
*Doane, 1st Lt. Stephen H. (Hau Nghia Province)
Dolby, Sp4c. David C. (South Vietnam)
Donlon, Capt. Roger H. C. (Nam Dong)
Dunagan, Capt. Kern W. (Quang Tin Province)
*Durham, 2d Lt. Harold B., Jr. (South Vietnam)
*English, SSgt. Glenn H., Jr. (Phu My)
*Evans, Sp4c. Donald W., Jr. (Tri Tam)
*Evans, Sgt. Rodney J. (Tay Ninh Province)
Ferguson, CWO Frederick E. (Hue)
*Fernandez, Sp4c. Daniel (Cu Chi)
Fitzmaurice, Sp4c. Michael J. (Khe Sanh)
*Fleek, Sgt. Charles C. (Binh Duong Province)
Foley, Capt. Robert F. (Quan Dau Tieng)
*Folland, Cpl. Michael F. (Long Khanh)
*Fournet, 1st Lt. Douglas B. (A Shau Valley)
*Fous, Pfc. James W. (Kien Hoa Province)
*Fratellenico, Cpl. Frank R. (Quang Tri Province)

Fritz, Capt. Harold A. (Binh Long Province)
*Gardner, 1st Lt. James A. (My Canh)
*Gertsch, SSgt. John G. (A Shau Valley)
*Grandstaff, Sgt. Bruce A. (Pleiku Province)
*Grant, 1st Lt. Joseph X. (South Vietnam)
*Guenette, Sp4c. Peter M. (Quan Tan Uyen)
Hagemeister, Sp4c. Charles C. (Binh Dinh Province)
*Hagen, 1st Lt. Loren D. (South Vietnam)
*Hartsock, SSgt. Robert W. (Hau Nghia Province)
*Harvey, Sp4c. Carmel B., Jr. (Binh Dinh Province)
Herda, Pfc. Frank A. (Dak To)
*Hibbs, 2d Lt. Robert J. (Don Dien Lo Ke)
*Holcomb, Sgt. John N. (Quan Loi)
Hooper, Sgt. Joe R. (Hue)
*Hosking, MSgt. Charles E., Jr. (Phuoc Long Province)
Howard, Sfc. Robert L. (Laos)
*Ingalls, Sp4c. George A. (Duc Pho)
Jacobs, 1st Lt. Jack H. (Kien Phong Province)
Jenkins, Pfc. Don J. (Kien Phong Province)
Jennings, SSgt. Delbert O. (Kim Song Valley)
Joel, Sp5c. Lawrence (War Zone D)
Johnson, Sp5c. Dwight H. (Dak To)
*Johnston, Sp4c. Donald R. (Tay Ninh Province)
*Karopczyc, 1st Lt. Stephen E. (Kontum Province)
*Kawamura, Cpl. Terry T. (Camp Radcliff)
Kays, Pvt. Kenneth M. (Thua Thien Province)
*Kedenburg, Sp5c. John J. (Laos)
Keller, Sgt. Leonard B. (Ap Bac)
Kinsman, Pfc. Thomas J. (Vinh Long)
Lambers, Sgt. Paul R. (Tay Ninh Province)
Lang, Sp4c. George C. (Kien Hoa Province)
*Langhorn, Pfc. Garfield M. (Pleiku Province)
*LaPointe, Sp4c. Joseph G., Jr. (Quang Tin Province)
*Lauffer, Pfc. Billy L. (Bong Son)
*Law, Sp4c. Robert D. (Tinh Phuoc Thanh)
*Lee, Pfc. Milton A. (Phu Bai)
*Leisy, 2d Lt. Robert R. (Phuoc Long Province)
Lemon, Sp4c. Peter C. (Tay Ninh Province)
*Leonard, Sgt. Matthew (Suoi Da)
Liteky, Capt. Angelo J. (Phuoc Lac)
Littrell, Sfc. Gary L. (Kontum Province)
*Long, Sgt. Donald R. (South Vietnam)
*Lozada, Pfc. Carlos J. (Dak To)
*Lucas, Lt. Col. Andre C. (FSB Ripcord)
Lynch, Sp4c. Allen J. (My An-2)
McCleery, Sgt. Finnis D. (Quang Tin Province)
*McDonald, Pfc. Phill G. (Kontum City)
*McKibben, Sgt. Ray (Song Mao)
*McMahon, Sp4c. Thomas J. (Quang Tin Province)
McNerney, 1st Sgt. David H. (Polei Doc)
*McWethy, Sp5c. Edgar L., Jr. (Binh Dinh Province)
Marm, 2d Lt. Walter J., Jr. (Ia Drang Valley)
*Michael, Sp4c. Don L. (South Vietnam)
Miller, SSgt. Franklin D. (Kontum Province)
*Miller, 1st Lt. Gary L. (Binh Duong Province)
Molnar, SSgt. Frankie Z. (Kontum Province)
*Monroe, Pfc. James H. (Bong Son)
Morris, SSgt. Charles B. (South Vietnam)
*Murray, SSgt. Robert C. (Hiep Duc)
*Nash, Pfc. David P. (Giao Duc)
Novosel, CWO Michael J. (Kien Tuong Province)
*Olive, Pfc. Milton L. III (Phu Cuong)
*Olson, Sp4c. Kenneth L. (South Vietnam)

Patterson, Sgt. Robert M. (La Chu)
Penry, Sgt. Richard A. (Binh Tuy Province)
*Petersen, Sp4c. Danny J. (Tay Ninh Province)
*Pierce, Sgt. Larry South (Ben Cat)
Pitts, Capt. Riley L. (Ap Dong)
*Port, Pfc. William D. (Que Son Valley)
*Poxon, 1st Lt. Robert L. (Tay Ninh Province)
*Pruden, SSgt. Robert J. (Quang Ngai Province)
*Rabel, SSgt. Laszlo (Binh Dinh Province)
Ray, 1st Lt. Ronald E. (Ia Drang Valley)
*Roark, Sgt. Anund C. (Kontum Province)
Roberts, Sp4c. Gordon R. (Thua Thien Province)
*Robinson, Sgt. James W., Jr. (South Vietnam)
Rocco, Sfc. Louis R. (Katum)
Rogers, Lt. Col. Charles C. (Fishhook, Cambodian border)
*Rubio, Capt. Euripides (Tay Ninh Province)
*Santiago-Colon, Sp4c. Hector (Quang Tri Province)
*Sargent, 1st Lt. Ruppert L. (Hau Nghia Province)
Sasser, Pfc. Clarence E. (Dinh Tuong Province)
*Seay, Sgt. William W. (Ap Nhi)
*Shea, Pfc. Daniel J. (Quang Tri Province)
*Sims, SSgt. Clifford C. (Hue)
*Sisler, 1st Lt. George K. (Laos)
*Skidgel, Sgt. Donald South (Song Be)
*Smith, SSgt. Elmelindo R. (South Vietnam)
Sprayberry, 1st Lt. James M. (South Vietnam)
*Steindam, 1st Lt. Russell A. (Tay Ninh Province)
*Stewart, SSgt. Jimmy G. (South Vietnam)
*Stone, Sgt. Lester R., Jr. (LZ Liz)
*Stout, Sgt. Mitchell W. (Khe Gio Bridge)
*Stryker, Sp4c. Robert F. (Loc Ninh)
Stumpf, Sp4c. Kenneth E. (Duc Pho)
Taylor, 1st Lt. James A. (Que Son)
Thacker, 1st Lt. Brian M. (Kontum Province)
*Warren, 1st Lt. John E., Jr. (Tay Ninh Province)
*Watters, Maj. Charles J. (Dak To)
*Wayrynen, Sp4c. Dale E. (Quang Ngai Province)
Wetzel, Pfc. Gary G. (Ap Dong An)
*Wickam, Cpl. Jerry W. (Loc Ninh)
*Willett, Pfc. Louis E. (Kontum Province)
Williams, 2d Lt. Charles Q. (Dong Xoai)
*Winder, Pfc. David F. (South Vietnam)
Wright, Sp4c. Raymond R. (Ap Bac)
*Yabes, 1st Sgt. Maximo (Phu Hoa Dong)
*Yano, Sfc. Rodney J. T. (Bien Hoa)
*Yntema, Sgt. Gordon D. (Thong Binh)
*Young, SSgt. Marvin R. (Ben Cui)
Zabitosky, SSgt. Fred W. (Laos)

MARINES

*Anderson, Pfc. James, Jr. (South Vietnam)
*Anderson, LCpl. Richard A. (Quang Tri Province)
*Austin, Pfc. Oscar P. (Da Nang)
*Barker, LCpl. Jedh C. (Con Thien)
Barnum, Lt. Harvey C., Jr. (Ky Phu)
*Bobo, 2d Lt. John P. (Quang Tri Province)
*Bruce, Pfc. Daniel D. (Quang Nam Province)
*Burke, Pfc. Robert C. (Quang Nam Province)
*Carter, Pfc. Bruce W. (Quang Tri Province)
Clausen, Pfc. Raymond M. (South Vietnam)
*Coker, Pfc. Ronald L. (Quang Tri Province)
*Connor, SSgt. Peter South (Quang Ngai Province)

*Cook, Capt. Donald G. (Phuoc Tuy Province)
*Creek, LCpl. Thomas E. (Cam Lo)
*Davis, Sgt. Rodney M. (Quang Nam Province)
*De La Garza, LCpl. Emilio A., Jr. (Da Nang)
*Dias, Pfc. Ralph E. (Que Son Mountains)
*Dickey, Pfc. Douglas E. (South Vietnam)
*Foster, Sgt. Paul H. (Con Thien)
 Fox, 1st Lt. Wesley L. (Quang Tri Province)
*Gonzalez, Sgt. Alfredo (Hue)
*Graham, Capt. James A. (South Vietnam)
*Graves, 2d Lt. Terrence C. (Quang Tri Province)
 Howard, SSgt. Jimmie E. (Nui Vu)
*Howe, LCpl. James D. (South Vietnam)
*Jenkins, Pfc. Robert H., Jr. (FSB Argonne)
*Jimenez, LCpl. Jose F. (Quang Nam Province)
*Johnson, Pfc. Ralph H. (Quan Duc Valley)
*Keith, LCpl. Miguel (Quang Ngai Province)
 Kellogg, SSgt. Allan J., Jr. (Quang Nam Province)
 Lee, Capt. Howard V. (Cam Lo)
 Livingston, Capt. James E. (Dai Do)
 McGinty, SSgt. John J. III (Song Ngam Valley)
*Martini, Pfc. Gary W. (Binh Son)
*Maxam, Cpl. Larry L. (Cam Lo)
 Modrzejewski, Capt. Robert J. (Song Ngam Valley)
*Morgan, Cpl. William D. (Laos)
*Newlin, Pfc. Melvin E. (Quang Nam Province)
*Noonan, LCpl. Thomas P., Jr. (A Shau Valley)
 O'Malley, Cpl. Robert E. (An Cu'ong-2)
*Paul, LCpl. Joe C. (Chu Lai)
*Perkins, Cpl. William T., Jr. (Quang Tri Province)
*Peters, Sgt. Lawrence D. (Quang Tin Province)
*Phipps, Pfc. Jimmy W. (An Hoa)
 Pittman, LCpl. Richard A. (DMZ)
 Pless, Capt. Stephen W. (Quang Ngai)
*Prom, LCpl. William R. (An Hoa)
*Reasoner, 1st Lt. Frank S. (Da Nang)
*Singleton, Sgt. Walter K. (Gio Linh)
*Smedley, Cpl. Larry E. (Quang Nam Province)
*Taylor, SSgt. Karl G., Sr. (South Vietnam)
 Vargas, Capt. Jay R. (Dai Do)
*Weber, LCpl. Lester W. (Quang Nam Province)
*Wheat, LCpl. Roy M. (Quang Nam Province)
*Williams, Pfc. Dewayne T. (Quang Nam Province)
*Wilson, Pfc. Alfred M. (Quang Tri Province)
*Worley, LCpl. Kenneth L. (Bo Ban)

NAVY

 Ballard, Hospital Corpsman 2d Class Donald E.
    (Quang Tri Province)
*Capodanno, Lt. Vincent R. (Quang Tin Province)
*Caron, Hospital Corpsman 3d Class Wayne M.
    (Quang Nam Province)
*Estocin, Lt. Cmdr. Michael J. (Haiphong, N.
    Vietnam)
 Kelley, Lt. Thomas G. (Kien Hoa Province)
 Kerrey, Lt.(j.g.) Joseph R. (Nha Trang Bay)
 Lassen, Lt.(j.g.) Clyde E. (North Vietnam)
‡McGonagle, Cmdr. William L. (Eastern
    Mediterranean)
 Norris, Lt. Thomas R. (Quang Tri Province)

*Ouellet, Sman David G. (Mekong River)
*Ray, Hospital Corpsman 2d Class David R. (Quang
    Nam Province)
*Shields, Construction Mechanic 3d Class Marvin G.
    (Dong Xoai)
 Stockdale, Capt. James B. (Hanoi, N. Vietnam)
 Thornton, Petty Officer Michael E. (South Vietnam)
 Williams, BM 1st Class James E. (Mekong River)

‡Six Day War, 1967—not included in Vietnam total

Bibliography

I. BOOKS AND ARTICLES

General Works

Belden, Bauman L. *United States War Medals.* The American Numismatic Society, 1916.

Beyer, Walter F., and Oscar F. Keydel. *Deeds of Valor.* 2 vols. Perrien-Keydel Co., 1906.

Dewey, William S. "Epitome of the History of Military Medals." *The Numismatist,* April 1943.

Donovan, Frank. *The Medal.* Dodd, Mead, 1962.

Gleim, Lt. Col. Albert F. *The Certificate of Merit.* 1979.

Jacobs, Bruce. *Heroes of the Army.* Norton, 1956.

Kayser, Hugh. *The Spirit of America.* ETC Publications, 1982.

Kerrigan, Evans E. *American War Medals and Decorations.* Rev. ed. Viking, 1971.

Lee, Irvin. *Negro Medal of Honor Men.* Dodd, Mead, 1967.

McSherry, Richard M. *The National Medals of the United States.* Maryland Historical Society, 1887.

Peterson, Mendel L. "The Navy Medal of Honor." *The Numismatist,* June 1950.

Pullen, John J. *A Shower of Stars.* Lippincott, 1966.

Ross, Donald K., and Helen Ross. *Washington State Men of Valor.* Coffee Break Pr., 1980.

Schott, Joseph L. *Above and Beyond.* G. P. Putnam's Sons, 1963.

U.S. Congress. Senate. Committee on Veterans' Affairs. *Medal of Honor Recipients, 1863-1978.* 1979.

U.S. Congress. Senate. *General Staff Corps and Medals of Honor.* 66th Cong., 1st sess., July 23, 1919, Doc. 58.

U.S. Department of the Army, Public Information Division. *The Medal of Honor of the United States Army.* GPO, 1948.

U.S. Department of the Navy, Bureau of Naval Personnel. *Medal of Honor 1861-1949.* GPO, 1949.

Willey, W. L., and John C. Fitzpatrick. *The Order of Military Merit/The Story of the Purple Heart.* Society of the Cincinnati in the State of New Hampshire, 1925.

The Civil War

The American Heritage Picture History of the Civil War. American Heritage Publishing Co., 1960.

Blassingame, John W. "The Freedom Fighters." *Negro History Bulletin,* February 1965.

Boatner, Mark M. *Civil War Dictionary.* David McKay Co., 1959.

Buel, C. C., and Robert Johnson. *Battles and Leaders of the Civil War.* Century, 1884.

Chesnut, Mary B. *A Diary From Dixie.* Yale Univ. Pr., 1982.

Davis, William C. *Duel Between the First Ironclads.* Doubleday, 1975.

————. *The Battle of New Market.* Doubleday, 1975.

Heitman, Francis B. *Historical Register and Dictionary of the United States Army.* GPO, 1903.

Kurtz, Wilbur G. "The Andrews Railroad Raid." *Civil War Times,* April 1966.

Lockwood, Allison. "Pantsuited Pioneer of Women's Lib, Dr. Mary Walker." *Smithsonian,* March 1977.

Long, E. B. *The Civil War Day by Day.* Doubleday, 1974.

Ott, Lana. "Dr. Mary Walker: Civil War Surgeon." *Soldiers,* November 1979.

Pittenger, William. *In Pursuit of the General.* Sunset Pr., 1965.

Rodenbough, Theophilus F. *The Bravest Five Hundred of '61.* Putnam, 1891.

Southern Historical Society Papers. Vols. 26 (1898), 36 (1908), 45 (1923-25), and 46 (1925).

War of the Rebellion: Official Records of the Union and Confederate Armies. 70 vols. U.S. War Department, 1880-1901.

Warner, Ezra. *Generals in Blue.* Louisiana State Univ. Pr., 1964.

Werlich, Robert. "Mary Walker: From Union Army Surgeon to Sideshow Freak." *Civil War Times,* June 1967.

The Indian Campaigns

The American Heritage Book of Indians. American Heritage Co., 1961.

Annual Report of the Secretary of War. U.S. Department of War, 1846-91.

Brady, Cyrus T. *Indian Fights and Fighters.* Doubleday, Page & Co., 1913.

————. *Northwest Fights and Fighters.* McClure Co., 1907.

Brandes, Ray, ed. *Troopers West.* Frontier Heritage Pr., 1970.

Brown, Dee. *Bury My Heart at Wounded Knee.* Holt, Rinehart & Winston, 1973.

Capps, Benjamin. *The Old West: The Great Chiefs.* Time-Life Bks., 1975.

————. *The Old West: The Indians.* Time-Life Bks., 1973.

Cruse, Thomas. *Apache Days and After.* Caxton Printer, Ltd., 1941.

Dillon, Richard. *Burnt-Out Fires.* Prentice-Hall, 1973.

Dunlay, Thomas. *Wolves for the Blue Soldiers.* Univ. of Nebraska Pr., 1982.

Faulk, Odie B. *Crimson Desert.* Oxford Univ. Pr., 1974.

Hagedorn, Hermann. *Leonard Wood: A Biography.* Harper & Bros., 1931.

Ingersoll, L. D. *A History of the War Department of the United States.* Francis B. Mohun Co., 1879.

Johnson, Virginia W. *The Unregimented General.* Houghton Mifflin, 1962.

Josephy, Alvin M., Jr. *The Nez Perce Indians and the Opening of the Northwest.* Yale Univ. Pr., 1965.

Krause, Herbert, and Gary D. Olson. *Prelude to Glory.* Brevet Pr., 1974.

Lane, Jack C., ed. *Chasing Geronimo.* Univ. of New Mexico Pr., 1970.

Leckie, William H. *The Buffalo Soldiers.* Univ. of Oklahoma Pr., 1967.

Magnussen, Daniel O., ed. *Peter Thompson's Narrative of the Little Bighorn Campaign.* Arthur H. Clark Co., 1974.

Marshall, S. L. A. *Crimson Prairie.* Charles Scribner's Sons, 1972.

Miles, Gen. Nelson A. *Personal Recollections and Observations.* The Werner Co., 1896.

Murray, Keith A. *The Modocs and Their War.* Univ. of Oklahoma Pr., 1959.

Nevin, David. *The Old West: The Soldiers.* Time-Life Bks., 1974.

Rickey, Don, Jr. *Forty Miles a Day on Beans and Hay.* Univ. of Oklahoma Pr., 1963.

Stewart, Edgar I. *Custer's Luck.* Univ. of Oklahoma Pr., 1955.

Tebbel, John. *The Compact History of the Indian Wars.* Tower Bks., 1966.

Thompson, Neil B. *Crazy Horse Called Them Walk-a-Heaps.* North Star Pr., 1979.

Utley, Robert M. *Frontier Regulars.* Macmillan, 1967.

————. *Frontiersmen in Blue.* Macmillan, 1967.

————. *The Indian Frontier of the American West, 1846-1890.* Univ. of New Mexico Pr., 1984.

————. *Indian, Soldier and Settler.* Jefferson National Expansion Historical Assn., 1979.

————. *The Last Days of the Sioux Nation.* Yale Univ. Pr., 1963.

————, and Wilcomb E. Washburn. *The American Heritage History of the Indian Wars.* American Heritage Co., 1977.

Wellman, Paul I. *The Indian Wars of the West.* Doubleday, 1947.

White, Lonnie J. *Hostiles and Horse Soldiers.* Pruett Publishing Co., 1972.

The Wars of American Expansion

Butler, Maj. Gen. Smedley D. "America's Armed Forces, 2. 'In Time of Peace': The Army." *Common Sense,* November 1935.

Craige, John H. *Cannibal Cousins.* Minton, Balch & Co., 1934.

Fleming, Peter. *The Siege at Peking.* Harper & Row, 1959.

Fuller, Stephen M., and Graham Cosmas. *Marines in the Dominican Republic, 1861-1924.* History and Museums Division, USMC, 1975.

Hagan, Kenneth J., ed. *In Peace and War.* Greenwood Pr., 1984.

Heinl, Robert D. *Soldiers of the Sea.* U.S. Naval Institute Pr., 1962.

————, and Nancy G. Heinl. *Written in Blood.* Houghton Mifflin, 1978.

Hobson, Richmond P. *The Sinking of the Merrimac.* The Century Co., 1899.

Jacobs, Bruce. "Heroes of the National Guard." *The National Guardsman,* November 1960.

Johnson, Robert E. *Rear Admiral John Rodgers, 1812-1883.* U.S. Naval Institute Pr., 1967.

Langley, Lester D. *The Banana Wars.* The Univ. Pr. of Kentucky, 1983.

Lodge, Henry Cabot. *Selections From the Correspondence of Theodore Roosevelt and Henry Cabot Lodge, 1884-1918.* Charles Scribner's Sons, 1925.

McAndrews, Eugene V. "Theodore Roosevelt and the Medal of Honor." *Military Review,* September 1967.

Macauley, Neill. *The Sandino Affair.* Quadrangle Bks., 1971.

McCrocklin, James H. *Garde d'Haiti, 1915-1934.* U.S. Naval Institute Pr., 1956.

Millett, Allan R. *Semper Fidelis.* Macmillan, 1980.

Morison, Elting E., and John Blum, eds. *The Letters of Theodore Roosevelt.* 8 vols. Harvard Univ. Pr., 1951-54.

Moskin, J. Robert. *The U.S. Marine Corps Story.* McGraw-Hill, 1977.

Mulholland, St. Clair. *Military Orders, Congressional Medal of Honor Legion of the United States.* Town Printing Co., 1905.

Nalty, Bernard C. *The United States Marines in Nicaragua.* Historical Branch, USMC, 1968.

Roosevelt, Theodore. *Theodore Roosevelt: An Autobiography.* Macmillan, 1913.

Roth, Russell. *Muddy Glory.* Christopher Publishing House, 1981.

Schott, Joseph L. *The Ordeal of Samar.* Bobbs-Merrill, 1964.

Schuon, Karl. *U.S. Marine Corps Autobiographical Dictionary.* Franklin Watts, 1963.

———. *U.S. Navy Biographical Dictionary.* Franklin Watts, 1964.

Simmons, Edwin H. *The United States Marines.* Viking, 1976.

Sweetman, Jack. *American Naval History.* U.S. Naval Institute Pr., 1984.

———. *The Landing at Veracruz: 1914.* U.S. Naval Institute Pr., 1968.

Thomas, Lowell. *Old Gimlet Eye.* Farrar & Rinehart, 1933.

Wise, Frederic M., and Miegs O. Frost. *A Marine Tells It All to You.* J. H. Sears & Co., 1929.

World War I

Asprey, Robert B. *At Belleau Wood.* G. P. Putnam's Sons, 1965.

Bamford, MSgt. Hal. "Mystery of an Airman." *Airman,* November 1958.

Bennet, TSgt. William. "Medal of Honor." *American Aviation Historical Society Quarterly* Fall 1975.

Coffman, Edward M. *The War to End All Wars.* Oxford Univ. Pr., 1968.

"Conscience Plus Red Hair Are Bad for Germans." *The Literary Digest,* June 14, 1919.

Cowan, Sam K. *Sergeant York and His People.* Funk & Wagnalls, 1922.

De Chambrun, Col., and Capt. De Marenches. *The American Army in the European Conflict.* Macmillan, 1919.

Esposito, Col. Vincent H., ed. *The Concise History of World War I.* Praeger, 1964.

Everett, Susanne, and Brig. Gen. Peter Young. *The Two World Wars.* Bison Bks., 1980.

Fredette, Lt. Col. Raymond H. "Luke: Watch for Burning Balloons." *Air Force,* May 9, 1973.

Harbord, James G. *The American Army in France, 1917-19.* Little, Brown, 1936.

Hartney, Lt. Col. Harold. *Wings Over France.* Bailey Bros. & Swinfen, 1971.

Hudson, James H. *Hostile Skies.* Syracuse Univ. Pr., 1968.

Isaacs [Izac], Edouard. *Prisoner of the U-90.* Houghton Mifflin, 1919.

Jablonski, Edward. *The Great War.* Whitman, 1965.

Johnson, Thomas M., and Fletcher Pratt. *The Lost Battalion.* Bobbs-Merrill, 1938.

Marshall, S. L. A. *The American Heritage History of World War I.* Bonanza Bks., 1982.

Rickenbacker, Eddie V. *Fighting the Flying Circus.* Avon Bks., 1965.

Roosevelt, Theodore. *Rank and File.* Charles Scribner's Sons, 1928.

Stallings, Laurence. *The Doughboys.* Harper & Row, 1963.

Toland, John. *No Man's Land.* Doubleday, 1980.

The Medal in Peacetime

Barrows, Nat A. *Blow All Ballast!* Dodd, Mead, 1940.

Botting, Douglas. *The Epic of Flight: The Giant Airships.* Time-Life Bks., 1981.

Bowen, Ezra. *The Epic of Flight: Knights of the Air.* Time-Life Bks., 1981.

Byrd, Richard E. *Skyward.* G. P. Putnam's Sons, 1928.

Davis, Burke. *The Billy Mitchell Affair.* Random, 1967.

Hurley, Alfred F. *Billy Mitchell, Crusader for Air Power.* Indiana Univ. Pr., 1964.

Jackson, Donald D. *The Epic of Flight: The Explorers.* Time-Life Bks., 1983.

Lindbergh, Charles A. *The Spirit of St. Louis.* Charles Scribner's Sons, 1953.

Mosley, Leonard. *Lindbergh: A Biography.* Doubleday, 1976.

Nevin, David. *The Epic of Flight: The Pathfinders.* Time-Life Bks., 1980.

Powell, Theodore. *The Long Rescue.* Doubleday, 1960.

Ross, Walter S. *The Last Hero.* Harper & Row, 1964.

Todd, A. L. *Abandoned.* McGraw-Hill, 1961.

World War II

Allen, Mel. "Only Afraid to Show Fear." *Yankee,* May 1983.

Auden, W. H. *The Collected Poetry of W. H. Auden.* Random, 1945.

Bailey, Ronald H. *World War II: The Air War in Europe.* Time-Life Bks., 1979.

Baudot, Marcel, et al. *The Historical Encyclopedia of World War II.* Greenwich House, 1984.

Blum, John M. *V Was for Victory.* Harcourt Brace Jovanovich, 1976.

Boyington, Gregory. *Baa Baa Black Sheep.* Arno, 1972.

Brereton, Lewis H. *The Brereton Diaries.* Morrow, 1946.

Buchanan, A. Russell. *The U.S. and World War II.* 2 vols. Harper & Row, 1964.

Churchill, Winston. *The Second World War.* 6 vols. Houghton Mifflin, 1949-60.

Congdon, Don, ed. *Combat: European Theater.* Dell, 1958.

———. *Combat: The War With Germany.* Dell, 1963.

Conroy, Robert. *The Battle of Bataan.* Macmillan, 1969.

Craven, Wesley F., and James L. Cate, eds. *The Army Air Forces in World War II.* 7 vols. Univ. of Chicago Pr., 1948-55.

Divine, Robert. *The Reluctant Belligerent.* Wiley, 1967.

Dugan, James, and Carroll Stewart. *Ploesti.* Random, 1962.

Elson, Robert. *World War II: Prelude to War.* Time-Life Bks., 1977.

Esposito, Col. Vincent H. *The West Point Atlas of American Wars.* Vol. 2. Praeger, 1959.

Fuqua, Samuel. Unpublished speeches.

Glines, Carroll V. *Doolittle's Tokyo Raiders.* D. Van Nostrand, 1964.

Haines, C. Grove, and Ross J. S. Hoffman. *The Origins and Background of the Second World War.* Oxford Univ. Pr., 1943.

Henn, Sharon. "Heart of Courage, Body of Steel." Unpublished paper, May 27, 1975.

Hirsch, Phil, ed. *Medal of Honor.* Pyramid, 1967.

The History of the U.S. Marine Corps Operations in World War II. 5 vols. Historical Division, USMC, 1958-1971.

Hoyle, Martha B. *A World in Flames.* Atheneum, 1970.

Hubbel, John G. "The Hero We Nearly Forgot." *Reader's Digest,* December 1981.

Jones, James. *World War II.* Ballantine, 1977.

Kelly, Charles, with Pete Martin. *One Man's War.* Knopf, 1944.

Kenney, Gen. George C. *Dick Bong: Ace of Aces.* Popular Library, 1960.

Lawson, Ted W. *Thirty Seconds Over Tokyo.* Random, 1943.

Liddell-Hart, B. H. *History of the Second World War.* Cassell, 1970.

Lord, Walter. *Incredible Victory.* Harper & Row, 1967.

MacArthur, Gen. Douglas. *Reminiscences.* McGraw-Hill, 1964.

Manchester, William. *American Caesar.* Little, Brown, 1978.

Morella, Joe, et al. *The Films of World War II.* Citadel Pr., 1973.

Morison, Samuel E. *History of U.S. Naval Operations in World War II.* 15 vols. Little, Brown, 1947-62.

———. *The Two-Ocean War.* Atlantic-Little, Brown, 1963.

Murphy, Audie. *To Hell and Back.* Bantam, 1983.

O'Kane, Richard H. *Clear the Bridge!* Rand McNally, 1977.

Parker, William, ed. *Above and Beyond the Call of Duty.* McFadden, 1963.

Prange, Gordon W. *At Dawn We Slept.* McGraw-Hill, 1981.

Pyle, Ernie. *Brave Men.* Holt, 1944.

———. *Last Chapter.* Holt, 1946.

Reck, Franklin M. *Beyond the Call of Duty.* Thomas Crowell Co., 1944.

Reynolds, Clark G. *The Epic of Flight: The Carrier War.* Time-Life Bks., 1982.

Roscoe, Theodore. *U.S. Submarine Operations in World War II.* U.S. Naval Institute Pr., 1965.

Ross, Bill D. *Iwo Jima: Legacy of Valor.* The Vanguard Pr., 1985.

Salisbury, Harrison E. *The 900 Days.* Harper & Row, 1969.

Scott, Jay. *America's War Heroes.* Monarch, 1961.

Sherrod, Robert. *History of Marine Corps Aviation in World War II.* Combat Forces Pr., 1952.

Simpson, Col. Harold B. *Audie Murphy, American Soldier.* Hill Jr. College Press, 1975.

Steiner, George. *In Bluebeard's Castle.* Yale Univ. Pr., 1971.

Suid, Lawrence H. *Guts and Glory.* Addison-Wesley, 1978.

Sulzberger, C. L. *The American Heritage Pictorial History of World War II.* American Heritage Co., 1966.

Taylor, A. J. P. *The Origins of the Second World War.* Atheneum, 1966.

Thomas, Lowell. *These Men Shall Never Die.* John C. Winston Co., 1943.

Toland, John. *But Not in Shame.* Random, 1961.

———. *Infamy.* Berkley, 1982.

The U.S. Army in World War II. 80 vols. GPO, 1947-68.

Wainwright, Jonathan. *General Wainwright's Story.* Greenwood, 1970.

Wheeler, Keith. *World War II: War Under the Pacific.* Time-Life Bks., 1980.

Wolff, Leon. *Low Level Mission.* Doubleday, 1957.

The Korean War

Appleman, Roy E. *South to Naktong, North to Yalu.* GPO, 1961.

Canzona, Capt. N. A., and John C. Hubbell. "The Twelve Incredible Days of Col. John Page." *Reader's Digest,* April 1956.

Cooke, Donald E. *For Conspicuous Gallantry.* C. S. Hammond & Co., 1966.

Dean, William F. *General Dean's Story.* Viking, 1954.

Fehrenbach, T. R. *This Kind of War.* Macmillan, 1963.

Futrell, Frank. *The U.S. Air Force in Korea, 1950-53.* Duell, Sloan & Pearce, 1961.

Goulden, Joseph C. *Korea: The Untold Story of the War.* Times Bks., 1982.

Gugeler, Russell A. *Combat Actions in Korea.* Office of the Chief of Military History, 1970.

Hammel, Eric M. *Chosin.* Vanguard Pr., 1981.

Hermes, Walter G. *Truce Tent and Fighting Front.* GPO, 1966.

Jacobs, Bruce. *Korea's Heroes.* Berkley, 1961.

Kleinman, MSgt. Forrest K. "Truth of Taejon." *Army,* June 1960.

Marshall, S. L. A. *The Military History of the Korean War.* Franklin Watts, 1963.

———. *The River and the Gauntlet.* Morrow, 1953.

Middleton, Harry J. *Compact History of the Korean War.* Hawthorn, 1965.

Miller, Merle. *Plain Speaking.* G. P. Putnam's Sons, 1973.

Ministry of National Defense, Republic of Korea. *History of U.S. Forces in the Korean War.* Vols. 4-5. GPO, ROK, 1975-76.

Montross, Lynn, et al. *U.S. Marine Operations in Korea, 1950-53.* Vols. 1-4. Historical Branch, USMC, 1954-55, 1957, 1962.

Munroe, Lt. Clark C. *The 2nd U.S. Infantry Division in Korea 1950-51.* Toppan Printing Co., n.d.

Neustadt, Richard E. *Presidential Power.* Rev. Ed. Wiley, 1980.

Poats, Rutherford M. *Decision in Korea.* McBride Co., 1954.

Truman, Harry S. *Memoirs.* Vol. 2, *Years of Trial and Hope, 1946-1952.* Doubleday, 1956.

The Vietnam War

Bamford, James. *The Puzzle Palace.* Penguin Bks., 1983.

Barbee, Fred. "Roy Benavidez . . . Sometimes Patience Wears Thin." *El Campo Leader-News,* February 22, 1978.

Binder, L. James. "Dean of the Dustoffers." *Army,* August 1971.

Caputo, Philip. *A Rumor of War.* Ballantine, 1977.

Combat Operations After-Action Report. Battle for Dak To: 173d Airborne Brigade (Separate), November 1-December 1, 1967; Company C, 4th Battalion, 503d Infantry, November 11-12, 1967.

Combat Operations After-Action Report. Operation Dewey Canyon: 2d Battalion, 9th Marines, 3d Marine Division, February 25, 1969.

"Confinement Summary of Captain James Bond Stockdale, USN, Senior US Navy Returnee From Captivity . . . " U.S. Navy, July 1976.

"The Cross and the Flag." Advisory Council of the Military Vicariate, April 1976.

Davis, 1st Lt. Gordon M. "DEWEY CANYON: All Weather Classic." *Marine Corps Gazette,* July 1969.

Donlon, Capt. Roger H. C., and Warren Rogers. *Outpost of Freedom.* McGraw-Hill, 1965.

Dorland, Peter, and James Nanney. *Dustoff.* U.S. Army Center of Military History, 1982.

Dougan, Clark, et al. *The Vietnam Experience.* Vols. 1-12. Boston Publishing Co., 1981-84.

Du Pre, Flint. "Rescue at a Place Called Kham Duc." *Air Force,* March 1969.

Ennes, James M., Jr. *Assault on the Liberty.* Random, 1979.

Fallaci, Oriana. *Nothing and So Be It.* Doubleday, 1972.

"For Leo K. Thorsness, the Medal of Honor." *Air Force,* December 1973.

Gropman, Lt. Col. Alan L. *Airpower and the Airlift Evacuation of Kham Duc.* GPO, 1979.

Guimond, Capt. Gary A. "Hot Flare! Hot Flare!" *Airman,* June 1970.

Herring, George C. *America's Longest War.* Wiley, 1979.

Jackson, Lt. Col. Wilfred A. "Stay Clear of Hue!" *U.S. Army Aviation Digest,* April 1970.

Karnow, Stanley. *Vietnam: A History.* Viking, 1983.

Lowther, William A. "A Medal for Roy Benavidez." *Reader's Digest,* April 1983.

"Medals of Honor to Two Air Force Heroes." *Air Force,* July 1970.

Oberdorfer, Don. *Tet!* Doubleday, 1971.

Pearson, Anthony. *Conspiracy of Silence.* Quartet Bks., 1978.

Ruhl, Robert K. "All Day's Tomorrows." *Airman,* November 1976.

———. "Rendezvous with the Rattlesnake." *Airman,* December 1974.

Schneider, Maj. Donald K. *Air Force Heroes in Vietnam.* Airpower Research Institute/GPO, 1979.

Smith, Richard K. "The Violation of the 'Liberty.' " *U.S. Naval Institute Proceedings,* June 1978.

Smith, William. "Honor Times 29." *U.S. Army Aviation Digest,* January 1974.

Stockdale, Jim, and Sybil Stockdale. *In Love and War.* Harper & Row, 1984.

Sturm, Ted R. "Flight Check to Glory." *Airman,* September 1969.

"Up From the Ranks." *Marine Corps Gazette,* November 1970.

White, Cpl. Larry. "Firefight Rages as Co. Claims Hill." *Sea Tiger,* March 28, 1969.

II. NEWSPAPERS AND PERIODICALS CONSULTED

Boston Globe, Life, Medal of Honor Historical Notes, Medal of Honor Historical Society *Annals, New York Times, Newsweek, Time, Washington Post.*

III. ARCHIVES

The authors consulted documents held in the archives of the Congressional Medal of Honor Society of the United States of America, New York, New York; the Freedoms Foundation at Valley Forge, Valley Forge, Pennsylvania; and the Medal of Honor Historical Society, Lombard, Illinois.

IV. INTERVIEWS AND CORRESPONDENCE WITH MEDAL OF HONOR RECIPIENTS

Nicky D. Bacon; William E. Barber; Roy P. Benavidez; Melvin E. Biddle; Patrick H. Brady; John D. Bulkeley; Richard E. Bush; Robert E. Bush; Jose Calugas; Anthony Casamento; William R. Charette; Michael J. Daly; Charles W. Davis; Raymond G. Davis; George E. Day; Merlyn H. Dethlefsen; Drew D. Dix; Roger H. C. Donlon; James H. Doolittle; Walter D. Ehlers; Henry E. Erwin; Frederick E. Ferguson; Joseph Foss; Wesley L. Fox; Leonard A. Funk, Jr.; Samuel G. Fuqua; Harold A. Furlong; Thomas J. Hudner; Edouard V. Izac; Joe M. Jackson; Leon W. Johnson; Phillip C. Katz; Charles E. Kelly; Gerry H. Kisters; Clyde E. Lassen; William R. Lawley, Jr.; John L. Levitow; David McCampbell; Charles A. MacGillivary; John Mihalowski; Hiroshi H. Miyamura; Reginald R. Myers; Ralph G. Neppel; Michael J. Novosel; Richard H. O'Kane; Nicholas Oresko; Francis J. Pierce; Thomas A. Pope; Lawson P. Ramage; Ronald E. Ray; Donald K. Ross; Donald E. Rudolph; Herbert E. Schonland; William A. Shomo; Carl E. Sitter; John C. Sjogren; Richard K. Sorenson; James B. Stockdale; George L. Street III; Leo K. Thorsness; Donald L. Truesdell; Matt Urban; Louis M. Van Iersel; Jay R. Vargas; Forrest L. Vosler; Gerald O. Young.

Acknowledgments

The editors and authors wish to thank the officers, members, and staff of the Congressional Medal of Honor Society of the United States of America, especially Ronald Ray, Paul Bucha, Nicholas Oresko, John E. Mofield, and Gerard F. White. Thanks also to J. Ashley Alexander; Charlene Alling, Museum of the Confederacy, Richmond, Virginia; Preston Amos; Jeanine Basinger, Wesleyan University; Michael Casey; Raymond L. Collins; Oscar Fitzgerald, Navy Memorial Museum, Washington, D.C.; Edna Fuqua; Richard Glass; CW3 Carl Hansen, Office of the Army Chief of Staff, Washington, D.C.; Office of Public Affairs, Air University, Maxwell AFB, Alabama; Bill D. Ross; Donald & Helen Ross; and Sister Maria Veronica, I.H.M.

Picture Credits

Cover: Ned McCormick, medals courtesy the Institute of Heraldry, U.S. Army
Chapter Two: pp. 6-7, Bucks County Historical Society, photograph by Al Freni, © Time-Life Books, Inc., from the Civil War series. p. 8, Bettmann Archives. p. 9, M. and M. Karolik Collection, Boston Museum of Fine Arts. pp. 10-11, Library of Congress. p. 12, American Heritage Century Collection. p. 14, U.S. Naval Academy. p. 15, Clements Library, University of Michigan. p. 16, top, U.S. Army Military History Institute, Carlisle, PA; bottom, Library of Congress. pp. 16-17, Library of Congress. p. 17, National Archives. p. 18, courtesy *Civil War Times Illustrated.* p. 19, Library of Congress. p. 20, left, courtesy *Civil War Times Illustrated;* right, American Heritage Century Collection. p. 21, top left, Time-Life Books, from the Collector's Library of the Civil War series; all others, courtesy *Civil War Times Illustrated.* p. 22, U.S. Army Military History Institute. p. 23, courtesy Seventh Regiment Fund, Inc., photograph by Al Freni. pp. 24-26, *Deeds of Valor,* Perrien-Keydel Company, Detroit, 1906. pp. 26-27, The Kennedy Gallery, New York. pp. 28-32, *Deeds of Valor.* p. 30, bottom, Library of Congress. pp. 31-32, paintings courtesy Pennsylvania Historical and Museum Commission, photographs by Henry Grosinsky, © Time-Life Books, from the Civil War series. p. 33, Maine State Archives. p. 34, National Archives. p. 35, courtesy Seventh Regiment Fund, Inc., photograph by Al Freni. p. 36, Frank & Marie Wood Print Collection, Alexandria, VA. pp. 36-38, portraits from *Deeds of Valor.* p. 39, Library of Congress. p. 40, top, courtesy Seventh Regiment Fund, Inc., photograph by Al Freni; bottom, U.S. Army Military History Institute. p. 41, Library of Congress. p. 42, top, left to right, National Archives; Lloyd House Library; *Deeds of Valor;* bottom, Lloyd House Library. p. 43, top left, Moorland-Spingarn Research Center, Howard University; bottom, West Point Museum Collections, U.S. Military Academy. p. 44, from the book *History of the 54th Regiment of Massachusetts Volunteer Infantry, 1863-65.* p. 46, left, U.S. Army Military History Institute; right, *Deeds of Valor.* p. 47, top, *Deeds of Valor;* bottom, Frank & Marie Wood Print Collection. p. 48, Union League of

Philadelphia. p. 49, Library of Congress. p. 50, Frank & Marie Wood Print Collection. p. 51, top, Chicago Historical Society; bottom, U.S. Army Military History Institute. p. 52, courtesy National Park Service, Department of the Interior. p. 54, courtesy the Americana Image Gallery, Gettysburg, PA.
Chapter Three: pp. 58-59, State Historical Society of Colorado, photograph by Benschneider, © Time-Life Books, from the Old West series. p. 60, 63, Rare Book Division, New York Public Library. p. 64, top, National Park Service, Fort Davis Historical Site; bottom, National Archives. p. 65, top and bottom right, National Archives; bottom left, Library of Congress. p. 66, National Archives. p. 67, *Illustrated London News* Picture Library. p. 68, Denver Public Library, Western History Division. p. 69, Library of Congress. p. 70, National Archives. p. 71, West Point Museum Collection, U.S. Military Academy. p. 72, courtesy National Park Service, Department of the Interior. pp. 72-73, courtesy Buffalo Bill Historical Center, Cody, WY. p. 74, Smithsonian Institution National Anthropological Archives. p. 75, left, Bancroft Library, University of California, Berkeley; right, collection of Brian Pohanka. p. 76, Library of Congress. p. 77, Bettmann Archive. p. 78, top, U.S. Army Military History Institute; bottom, Library of Congress. p. 79, Library of Congress. p. 80, National Archives. p. 81, Congressional Medal of Honor Society. p. 82, National Archives. p. 83, Denver Public Library, Western History Department. p. 84, Library of Congress. p. 85, Montana Historical Society. p. 86, top and bottom left, Library of Congress. p. 86, bottom right, p. 87, Western History Collection, University of Oklahoma Library.
Chapter Four: pp. 88-89, Franklin D. Roosevelt Library, Hyde Park, NY, photograph by Al Freni. p. 90, Library of Congress. p. 92, New York Historical Society. p. 95, Library of Congress. pp. 96-97, top left, courtesy Donald J. Robinson; all others, Naval Historical Center. pp. 98-99, Naval Historical Center. p. 100, top, Naval Historical Center; bottom, *Deeds of Valor.* p. 101, Naval Historical Center. p. 102, top left, National Archives; all others, *Deeds of Valor.* p. 103, National Archives. p. 104, Library of Congress. pp. 105-7, U.S. Army Military History Institute. pp. 108-9, National Archives. p. 110, top, Congressional Medal of Honor Society; bottom, U.S. Army Military History Institute. pp. 111-13, Naval Historical Center. pp. 114-18, National Archives. p. 119, Naval Historical Center. pp. 120-21, National Archives. pp. 124-25, Ned McCormick; medals p. 124, courtesy of Institute of Heraldry, U.S. Army. p. 125, medals in top row, left to right, courtesy of the Navy Memorial Museum, Washington, D.C.; Richard Glass; and the Freedoms Foundation at Valley Forge, PA. Medals in middle row, left to right, courtesy of Edward F. Murphy; Congressional Medal of Honor Society, New York; and the Navy Memorial Museum. Ribbon and rosette, bottom row, courtesy of Institute of Heraldry, U.S. Army.
Chapter Five: pp. 126-27, Pierre Boulat/Cosmos, Paris. p. 128, UPI/Bettmann Archive. p. 129, Wide World. p. 131, National Archives. pp. 132-33, top left, Herb Orth/Life Picture Service, copyright Time Inc.; all others, National Archives. p. 134, Naval Historical Center. p. 135, U.S. Navy. p. 136, Ullstein Bilderdienst, West Berlin. pp. 137-38, Navy Memorial Museum, Washington, D.C. p. 139, Congressional Medal of Honor Society. p. 140, copyright Musse de l'armee, Paris. pp. 141-42, National Archives. p. 143, U.S. Army. p. 144, National Archives. p. 146, top left, Congressional Medal of Honor Society; top right, National Archives; bottom, Museum of American History, Smithsonian Institution. p. 147, left to right, National Air and Space Museum, Smithsonian Institution; Air Force Museum, Wright-Patterson AFB, Dayton, Ohio; National Archives. p. 148, National Archives. p. 149, Congressional Medal of Honor Society. pp. 150-51, National Archives. p. 152, The *New York Times.* p. 153, National Archives. p. 154, 156, U.S. Air Force. p. 157, National Archives.
Chapter Six: pp. 158-59, William Reynolds. pp. 162-63, top, Wide World; bottom, left to right, UPI/Bettmann Archive; Congressional Medal of Honor Society; Naval Historical Center. pp. 164-69, National Archives. p. 170, National Air and Space Museum, Smithsonian Institution. p. 171, Library of Congress. p. 172, top, Library of Congress; bottom, National Air and Space Museum, Smithsonian Institution. p. 173, top, National Air and Space Museum, Smithsonian Institution;

bottom, National Archives. p. 174, National Air and Space Museum, Smithsonian Institution. p. 176, Bettmann Archive. p. 177, top, Brown Brothers; bottom, Bettmann Archive. p. 178, *New York Daily News;* insert top, Time Inc.; bottom, Missouri Historical Society, photograph by Henry Grosinsky, © Time-Life Books, Inc., from the Epic of Flight series. p. 179, National Air and Space Museum, Smithsonian Institution. p. 180, Library of Congress. p. 181, U.S. Navy. p. 182, Naval Historical Center. p. 183, top, National Archives; bottom, Naval Historical Center; right, U.S. Navy. p. 184, left, Naval Historical Center; right, U.S. Navy. p. 185, left, National Archives; right, Naval Historical Center.
Chapter Seven: pp. 186-87, Robert Capa, Magnum. p. 188, Estate of Margaret Bourke-White, courtesy Life Picture Service. p. 189, Hugo Jaeger, Life Picture Service, copyright Time Inc. p. 192, UPI/Bettmann Archive. p. 193, National Archives, photograph by Henry Beville, © Time-Life Books, Inc., from the World War II series. p. 194, inset, U.S. Navy. pp. 194-195, Wide World. p. 195, top to bottom, U.S. Navy; UPI/Bettmann Archive; National Archives. p. 196, left, courtesy Samuel Fuqua. pp. 196-198, U.S. Navy. p. 199, U.S. Army. p. 200, left, Congressional Medal of Honor Society; right, Wide World. p. 201, National Archives. p. 202, National Air and Space Museum, Smithsonian Institution. p. 203, UPI/Bettmann Archive. p. 204, top, Congressional Medal of Honor Society; bottom, Naval Historical Center. pp. 204-5, U.S. Navy. pp. 206-8, U.S. Navy. p. 210, top, courtesy Forrest Vosler; bottom, National Air and Space Museum, Smithsonian Institution. p. 211, left, U.S. Air Force; right, Congressional Medal of Honor Society. p. 212, National Archives. p. 213-14, courtesy Gerry Kisters. p. 215, UPI/Bettmann Archive. p. 216, courtesy Matt Urban. p. 217, UPI/Bettmann Archive. p. 218, Wide World. p. 220, Congressional Medal of Honor Society. p. 221, left, Bildarchiv Preussischer Kulturbesitz, West Berlin; right, Wide World. p. 222, top to bottom, National Archives; U.S. Army; Congressional Medal of Honor Society. p. 223, courtesy Leonard Funk. p. 224, U.S. Army. p. 225, top, U.S. Army; bottom, courtesy Nicholas Oresko. p. 226, MGM/UA Entertainment. p. 227, top, bottom left, MGM/UA Entertainment; bottom right, Universal/International. p. 228, top, UPI/Bettmann Archive; bottom, courtesy Michael Daly. p. 229, U.S. Navy. p. 230, Fred Freeman, Mystic Maritime Museum, photograph by Henry Grosinsky, © Time-Life Books, Inc., from the World War II series. p. 231, U.S. Navy. p. 232, U.S. Submarine Force Library and Museum, photograph by Henry Grosinsky, © Time-Life Books, Inc., from the World War II series. p. 233, Wide World. p. 234, left, U.S. Marine Corps; right, U.S. Navy. p. 235, Freedoms Foundation at Valley Forge, PA. p. 236, left, Naval Historical Center; right, National Archives. p. 237, left, Congressional Medal of Honor Society; right, courtesy Henry Erwin. p. 238, Freedoms Foundation at Valley Forge. p. 239, courtesy John Sjogren. p. 240, Wide World. p. 241, top, family of Richard Bong; bottom, left to right, U.S. Navy; Wide World; U.S. Navy. p. 242-43, UPI/Bettmann Archive. p. 243, U.S. Army.
Chapter Eight: pp. 244-45, David Douglas Duncan. pp. 246-48, NBC/Walter Daran. p. 250, top left, Wide World; all others, UPI/Bettmann Archive. p, 251, top, U.S. Army; bottom, UPI/Bettmann Archive. p. 252, bottom left, U.S. Army Military History Institute. pp. 252-54, NBC/Walter Daran. p. 255, Wide World. p. 257, U.S. Army. p. 258, UPI/Bettmann Archive. p. 259, top, U.S. Army; bottom, UPI/Bettmann Archive. p. 261, U.S. Marine Corps. p. 262, 263 bottom, David Douglas Duncan. p. 263 top, 264, Congressional Medal of Honor Society. p. 265, Wide World. p. 266, U.S. Air Force. p. 267, Wide World. pp. 268-69, U.S. Air Force. p. 270, John Zimmerman/*TIME* magazine. p. 271, top, John Dominis/*LIFE* magazine, copyright Time Inc.; bottom, courtesy Thomas Hudner. p. 272-73, Naval Historical Center.
Chapter Nine: pp. 276-77, Don Critchfield/U.S. Army. p. 279, Wide World. p. 280, UPI/Bettmann Archive. p. 282, top and middle, Larry Burrows/*LIFE* magazine, copyright Time Inc.; bottom, Mark Jury. p. 283, top, UPI/Bettmann Archive; bottom, Co Rentmeester/*LIFE* magazine, copyright Time Inc. p. 284, U.S. Army. p. 285, courtesy Roger Donlon. pp. 286-87, U.S. Air Force. p. 287, diagram from *Air Force* magazine. pp.

288-89, U.S. Marine Corps. p. 291, courtesy *Retired Officer* magazine. p. 292, UPI/Bettmann Archive. p. 293, top, U.S. Army; bottom, UPI/Bettmann Archive. p. 294, top, courtesy Seton Hall University; bottom, Dirck Halstead/*LIFE* magazine, copyright Time Inc. p. 296, courtesy Fred Ferguson. p. 297, top, U.S. Marine Corps; bottom, UPI/Bettmann Archive. p. 298, U.S. Army. p. 299, courtesy Michael Novosel. p. 300, courtesy Patrick Brady. p. 301, UPI/Bettmann Archive. p. 302, U.S. Air Force. p. 303, courtesy Leo Thorsness. p. 304, Larry Burrows/*LIFE* magazine, copyright Time Inc. p. 305, courtesy John Levitow. p. 306, courtesy Wesley Fox. pp. 307-8, U.S. Marine Corps. p. 310, Congressional Medal of Honor Society. p. 312, top, Gamma/Liaison; bottom, David Hume Kennerly/*TIME* magazine. p. 313, Dirck Halstead/*TIME* magazine.

Map Credits

All maps (except on p. 138) prepared by Diane McCaffery. Sources are as follows: **p. 13**–*Military Heritage of America.* McGraw-Hill, 1956. **p. 29**–Catton, Bruce. *Gettysburg: The Final Fury.* Doubleday, 1974; *Military Heritage of America.* McGraw-Hill, 1956. **p. 62**–Capps, Benjamin. *The Old West: The Indians.* Time-Life Bks., 1973; Nevin, David. *The Old West: The Soldiers.* Time-Life Bks., 1974 . **p. 130**–Marshall, Brig. Gen. S. L. A. *The American Heritage History of World War I.* Bonanza, 1982; Everett, E. Susan and Brig. Peter Young. *The Two World Wars.* Bison Bks., 1982. **p. 138**–diagram reprinted from Isaacs, Edouard. *Prisoner of the U-90.* Houghton Mifflin, 1919.
p. 161–Jackson, Donald D. *The Epic of Flight: The Explorers.* Time-Life Bks., 1983; Todd, Al. *Abandoned.* McGraw-Hill, 1961. **p. 191**–*The American Heritage Pictorial Atlas of U.S. History.* American Heritage Co., 1966; Sulzberger, C. L. *The American Heritage Pictorial History of World War II.* American Heritage Co., 1966. **p. 221**–*The American Heritage Pictorial Atlas of U.S. History.* American Heritage Co., 1966; *Military Heritage of America.* McGraw-Hill, 1956. **p. 249**–*The American Heritage Pictorial Atlas of U.S. History.* American Heritage Co., 1966; *Military Heritage of America.* McGraw-Hill, 1956. U.S. Army; Walker, Bryce. *Fighting Jets.* Time-Life Bks., 1983. **p. 261**–Hammel, Eric. *Chosin.* Vanguard, 1981; Sweetman, Jack. *American Naval History.* Naval Institute Pr., 1984.

Index